National income and related statistics for selected years, 1929–1967*

National income statistics are in billions of current dollars. Details may not add to totals because of rounding.

			1929	1933	1939	1940	1942	1944	1946	1948	1950	1952
THE SUM OF	1	Personal consumption expenditures	77.3	45.8	67.0	71.0	88.6	108.2	143.9	174.9	192.1	219.1
	2	Gross private domestic investment	16.7	1.6	9.5	13.4	10.3	7.7	31.5	47.1	55.1	53.5
	3	Government purchases	8.9	8.3	13.6	14.2	59.9	97.1	29.1	32.6	38.8	75.8
	4	Net exports	0.3	0.1	0.8	1.4	−0.3	−2.2	7.1	5.5	0.7	1.0
EQUALS	5	Gross domestic product	103.2	55.7	90.9	100.1	158.5	210.9	211.6	260.1	286.7	349.4
LESS	6	Consumption of fixed capital	9.9	7.6	9.0	9.4	11.3	12.0	14.2	20.4	23.6	29.2
EQUALS	7	Net domestic product	93.2	48.1	81.9	90.7	147.2	198.9	197.4	239.7	263.1	320.2
PLUS	8	Net American income earned abroad	0.8	0.3	0.4	0.4	0.5	0.5	0.7	1.5	1.5	2.2
LESS	9	Indirect business taxes	9.3	9.0	11.1	11.5	11.5	16.8	17.5	19.7	24.6	30.9
EQUALS	10	National income	84.7	39.4	71.2	79.6	136.2	182.6	180.7	221.5	239.8	291.6
LESS	11	Social security contributions	0.3	0.3	2.2	2.4	3.5	5.2	7.7	6.0	7.4	9.3
	12	Corporate income taxes	1.4	0.5	1.4	2.8	11.4	12.9	9.1	12.4	17.9	19.4
	13	Undistributed corporate profits	2.4	−4.0	0.3	2.0	4.0	6.7	2.5	10.9	8.2	9.6
PLUS	14	Transfer payments	3.7	3.7	4.8	5.2	5.1	6.7	16.2	17.0	21.8	20.5
EQUALS	15	Personal income	84.3	46.3	72.1	77.6	122.4	164.5	177.6	209.2	228.1	273.8
LESS	16	Personal taxes	2.6	1.4	2.4	2.6	5.9	18.9	18.7	21.0	20.6	34.0
EQUALS	17	Disposable income	81.7	44.9	69.7	75.0	116.4	145.6	158.9	188.1	207.5	239.8
	18	Real gross domestic product (in 1987 dollars)	841.0	592.3	852.2	919.1	1,284.4	1,642.9	1,311.9	1,314.7	1,428.2	1,635.7
	19	Percent change in real GDP	—	−2.1	7.9	8.0	18.9	8.2	−19.2	3.9	8.5	4.0
	20	Real disposable income per capita (in 1987 dollars)	4,847.8	3,495.8	4,517.2	4,760.1	6,093.7	6,421.0	6,061.3	5,935.0	6,196.1	6,401.0

RELATED STATISTICS			1929	1933	1939	1940	1942	1944	1946	1948	1950	1952
	21	Consumer price index (1982–84 = 100)	17.0	13.0	13.9	14.0	16.3	17.6	19.5	24.1	24.1	26.5
	22	Rate of inflation (%)	0.0	−5.1	−1.4	0.7	10.9	1.7	8.3	8.1	1.3	1.9
	23	Index of industrial production (1987 = 100)	—	—	—	—	—	—	—	23.6	25.8	29.1
	24	Supply of money, M1 (in billions of dollars)	26.6	19.9	34.2	39.7	55.4	85.3	106.5	112.3	114.1	125.2
	25	Prime interest rate (%)	5.50	1.50	1.50	1.50	1.50	1.50	1.50	1.75	2.07	3.0
	26	Population (in millions)	121.8	125.6	130.8	132.1	134.9	138.4	141.4	146.6	152.3	157.6
	27	Civilian labor force (in millions)	49.2	51.6	55.2	55.6	56.4	54.6	57.5	60.6	62.2	62.1
	28	Unemployment (in millions)	1.6	12.8	9.5	8.1	2.7	0.7	2.3	2.3	3.3	1.9
	29	Unemployment rate as % of civilian labor force	3.2	24.9	17.2	14.6	4.7	1.2	3.9	3.8	5.3	3.0
	30	Index of productivity (1982 = 100)	—	—	—	—	—	—	—	45.7	50.1	53.7
	31	Annual change in productivity (%)	—	—	—	—	—	—	—	—	8.3	3.1
	32	Trade balance on current account (in billions of dollars)	—	—	—	—	—	—	4.9	2.4	−1.8	0.6
	33	Public debt (in billions of dollars)	16.9	22.5	48.2	50.7	79.2	204.1	271.0	252.0	256.9	259.1

*Revised series beginning with 1959. Revised data for GDP and its components for 1929–1958 were not available at the time of publication.

1953	1954	1955	1956	1957	1958	1959	1960	1961	1962	1963	1964	1965	1966	1967
232.6	239.8	257.9	270.6	285.3	294.6	318.1	332.4	343.5	364.4	384.2	412.5	444.6	481.6	509.3
54.9	54.1	69.7	72.7	71.1	63.6	78.8	78.7	77.9	87.9	93.4	101.7	118.0	130.4	128.0
82.8	76.0	75.3	79.7	87.3	95.4	99.0	99.8	107.0	116.8	122.3	128.3	136.3	155.9	175.6
−0.8	0.4	0.4	2.3	3.9	0.4	−1.7	2.4	3.4	2.4	3.3	5.5	3.9	1.9	1.4
369.5	370.3	403.3	425.2	447.7	453.9	494.2	513.4	531.8	571.6	603.1	648.0	702.7	769.8	814.3
30.9	32.5	34.4	38.1	41.1	42.8	44.6	46.3	47.7	49.3	51.3	53.9	57.3	62.1	67.4
338.6	337.8	368.9	387.1	406.6	411.4	449.6	467.1	484.1	522.3	551.8	594.1	645.4	707.7	746.9
2.1	2.2	2.6	3.0	3.4	2.9	2.8	3.2	3.6	4.3	4.5	5.0	5.4	5.2	5.5
34.1	33.7	35.2	33.8	37.1	39.0	42.3	44.6	47.2	52.1	54.8	60.0	63.9	69.2	72.5
306.6	306.3	336.3	356.3	372.8	375.0	410.1	425.7	440.5	474.5	501.5	539.1	586.9	643.7	679.9
9.6	10.6	12.0	13.5	15.5	15.9	18.8	21.9	22.9	25.4	28.5	30.1	31.6	40.6	45.5
20.3	17.6	22.0	22.0	21.4	19.0	23.6	22.7	22.8	24.0	26.2	28.0	30.9	33.7	32.7
8.6	9.9	14.8	12.6	12.4	10.0	15.9	14.5	14.3	14.2	22.6	26.1	31.9	34.0	31.2
22.4	24.8	26.7	29.0	32.8	37.0	39.4	42.6	46.0	42.5	52.2	55.8	60.4	66.3	76.0
290.5	293.0	314.2	337.2	356.3	367.1	391.2	409.2	426.5	453.4	476.4	510.7	552.9	601.7	646.5
35.5	32.5	35.4	39.7	42.4	42.2	44.5	48.7	50.3	54.8	58.0	56.0	61.9	71.0	77.9
255.1	260.5	278.8	297.5	313.9	324.9	346.7	360.5	376.2	398.7	418.4	454.7	491.0	530.7	568.6
1,702.8	1,679.1	1,773.1	1,808.6	1,837.5	1,824.7	1,931.3	1,973.2	2,025.6	2,129.8	2,218.0	2,343.3	2,473.5	2,622.3	2,690.3
4.1	−1.4	5.6	2.0	1.6	−0.7	5.8	2.2	2.7	5.1	4.1	5.6	5.6	6.0	2.6
6,557.3	6,550.9	6,811.1	7,016.0	7,061.3	7,065.9	7,256.0	7,264.0	7,382.0	7,583.0	7,718.0	8,140.0	8,508.0	8,822.0	9,114.0

1953	1954	1955	1956	1957	1958	1959	1960	1961	1962	1963	1964	1965	1966	1967
26.7	26.9	26.8	27.2	28.1	28.9	29.1	29.6	29.9	30.2	30.6	31.0	31.5	32.4	33.4
0.8	0.7	−0.4	1.5	3.3	2.8	0.7	1.7	1.0	1.0	1.3	1.3	1.6	2.9	3.1
31.6	29.9	33.7	35.1	35.6	33.3	37.3	38.1	38.4	41.6	44.0	47.0	51.7	56.3	57.5
128.3	130.3	134.5	136.0	136.8	138.4	140.0	140.7	145.2	147.9	153.4	160.4	167.9	172.1	183.3
3.17	3.05	3.16	3.77	4.20	3.83	4.48	4.82	4.50	4.50	4.50	4.50	4.54	5.63	5.61
160.2	163.0	165.9	168.9	172.0	174.9	177.8	180.7	183.7	186.5	189.2	191.9	194.3	196.6	198.7
63.0	62.3	65.0	66.6	66.9	67.6	68.4	69.6	70.5	70.6	71.8	73.1	74.5	75.8	77.3
1.8	3.5	2.9	2.8	2.9	4.6	3.7	3.9	4.7	3.9	4.1	3.8	3.4	2.9	3.0
2.9	5.5	4.4	4.1	4.3	6.8	5.5	5.5	6.7	5.5	5.7	5.2	4.5	3.8	3.8
55.8	56.7	58.4	59.2	60.7	62.5	64.6	65.6	68.1	70.4	73.3	76.5	78.6	81.0	83.0
3.6	1.6	3.0	1.3	2.6	3.0	3.3	1.6	3.7	3.5	4.1	4.3	2.7	3.0	2.5
−1.3	0.2	0.4	2.7	4.8	0.8	−1.3	2.8	3.8	3.4	4.4	6.8	5.4	3.0	2.6
266.0	270.8	274.4	272.7	272.3	279.7	287.5	290.5	292.6	302.9	310.3	316.1	322.3	328.5	340.4

(Continued)

(Continued)

National income and related statistics for selected years, 1968–1991*

National income statistics are in billions of current dollars. Details may not add to totals because of rounding.

			1968	1969	1970	1971	1972	1973	1974	1975	1976	1977
THE SUM OF	1	Personal consumption expenditures	559.1	603.7	646.5	700.3	767.8	848.1	927.7	1,024.9	1,143.1	1,271.5
	2	Gross private domestic investment	139.9	155.2	150.3	175.5	205.6	243.1	245.8	226.0	286.4	358.3
	3	Government purchases	191.5	201.8	212.7	224.3	241.5	257.7	288.3	321.4	341.3	368.0
	4	Net exports	−1.3	−1.2	1.2	−3.0	−8.0	0.6	−3.1	13.6	−2.3	−23.7
EQUALS	5	Gross domestic product	889.3	959.5	1,010.7	1,097.2	1,207.0	1,349.6	1,458.6	1,585.9	1,768.4	1,974.1
LESS	6	Consumption of fixed capital	73.9	81.5	88.8	97.6	109.9	120.4	140.2	165.2	182.8	205.2
EQUALS	7	Net domestic product	815.4	878.0	921.9	999.6	1,097.1	1,229.2	1,318.4	1,420.7	1,585.6	1,768.9
PLUS	8	Net American income earned abroad	6.2	6.1	6.4	7.7	8.7	12.7	15.7	13.3	17.1	20.5
LESS	9	Indirect business taxes	80.6	85.5	94.8	107.8	112.9	122.4	135.3	148.7	167.2	180.3
EQUALS	10	National income	741.0	798.6	833.5	899.5	992.9	1,119.5	1,198.8	1,285.3	1,435.5	1,609.1
LESS	11	Social security contributions	50.4	57.9	62.2	68.9	79.0	97.6	110.5	118.5	134.5	149.8
	12	Corporate income taxes	39.4	39.7	34.4	37.7	41.9	49.3	51.8	50.9	64.2	73.0
	13	Undistributed corporate profits	28.5	24.6	19.3	28.8	35.6	39.0	22.3	40.8	47.3	61.9
PLUS	14	Transfer payments	87.2	97.3	113.4	129.4	144.1	165.1	191.5	232.2	256.8	276.9
EQUALS	15	Personal income	709.9	773.7	831.0	893.5	980.5	1,098.7	1,205.7	1,307.3	1,446.3	1,601.3
LESS	16	Personal taxes	92.1	109.9	109.0	108.7	132.0	140.6	159.1	156.4	182.3	210.0
EQUALS	17	Disposable income	617.8	663.8	722.0	784.9	848.5	958.1	1046.5	1,150.9	1,264.0	1,391.3
	18	Real gross domestic product (in 1987 dollars)	2,801.0	2,877.1	2,875.8	2,965.1	3,107.1	3,268.6	3,248.1	3,221.7	3,380.8	3,533.2
	19	Percent change in real GDP	4.1	2.7	0.0	3.1	4.8	5.2	−0.6	−0.8	4.9	4.5
	20	Real disposable income per capita (in 1987 dollars)	9,399.0	9,606.0	9,875.0	10,111.0	10,414.0	11,013.0	10,832.0	10,906.0	11,192.0	11,406.0

RELATED STATISTICS			1968	1969	1970	1971	1972	1973	1974	1975	1976	1977
	21	Consumer price index (1982–84 = 100)	34.8	36.7	38.8	40.5	41.8	44.4	49.3	53.8	56.9	60.6
	22	Rate of inflation (%)	4.2	5.5	5.7	4.4	3.2	6.2	11.0	9.1	5.8	6.5
	23	Index of industrial production (1987 = 100)	60.7	63.5	61.4	62.2	68.3	73.8	72.7	66.3	72.4	78.2
	24	Supply of money, M1 (in billions of dollars)	197.5	204.0	214.5	228.4	249.3	262.9	274.4	287.6	306.4	331.3
	25	Prime interest rate (%)	6.30	7.96	7.91	5.72	5.25	8.03	10.81	7.86	6.84	6.83
	26	Population (in millions)	200.7	202.7	205.1	207.7	209.9	211.9	213.9	216.0	218.0	220.2
	27	Civilian labor force (in millions)	78.7	80.7	82.8	84.4	87.0	89.4	91.9	93.8	96.2	99.0
	28	Unemployment (in millions)	2.8	2.8	4.1	5.0	4.9	4.4	5.2	7.9	7.4	7.0
	29	Unemployment rate as % of civilian labor force	3.6	3.5	4.9	5.9	5.6	4.9	5.6	8.5	7.7	7.1
	30	Index of productivity (1982 = 100)	85.4	85.9	87.0	90.2	92.6	95.0	93.3	95.5	98.3	99.8
	31	Annual change in productivity (%)	3.0	0.5	1.3	3.6	2.7	2.6	−1.8	2.3	3.0	1.6
	32	Trade balance on current account (in billions of dollars)	0.6	0.4	2.3	−1.4	−5.8	7.1	2.0	18.1	4.2	−14.5
	33	Public debt (in billions of dollars)	368.7	365.8	380.9	408.2	435.9	466.3	483.9	541.9	629.0	706.4

*Revised series beginning with 1959. Revised data for GDP and its components for 1929–1958 were not available at the time of publication.
**Preliminary data.

1978	1979	1980	1981	1982	1983	1984	1985	1986	1987	1988	1989	1990	1991**
1,421.2	1,583.7	1,748.1	1,926.2	2,059.2	2,257.5	2,460.3	2,667.4	2,850.6	3,052.2	3,296.1	3,517.9	3,742.6	3,886.8
434.0	480.2	467.6	558.0	503.4	546.7	718.9	714.5	717.6	749.3	793.6	837.6	802.6	725.3
403.6	448.5	507.1	561.1	607.6	652.3	700.8	772.3	833.0	881.5	918.7	971.4	1,042.9	1,086.9
−26.1	−23.8	−14.7	−14.7	−20.6	−51.4	−102.7	−115.6	−132.5	−143.1	−108.0	−82.9	−74.4	−27.1
2,232.7	2,488.6	2,708.0	3,030.6	3,149.6	3,405.0	3,777.2	4,038.7	4,268.6	4,539.9	4,900.4	5,244.0	5,513.8	5,671.8
234.8	272.4	311.9	362.4	399.1	418.4	432.2	454.5	478.6	502.2	534.0	574.5	594.8	623.5
1,997.9	2,216.2	2,396.1	2,668.2	2,750.5	2,986.6	3,345.0	3,584.2	3,790.0	4,037.7	4,366.4	4,669.5	4,919.0	5,048.3
21.8	32.2	34.1	33.2	30.2	29.3	24.3	14.9	9.1	4.6	7.9	4.2	10.7	12.0
189.9	209.5	232.0	268.9	258.2	295.1	311.0	330.7	361.2	350.0	371.7	429.0	470.1	521.0
1,829.8	2,038.9	2,198.2	2,432.5	2,522.5	2,720.8	3,058.3	3,268.4	3,437.9	3,692.3	4,002.6	4,244.7	4,459.6	4,540.0
171.7	197.8	216.5	251.2	269.6	290.2	325.0	353.8	379.8	400.7	442.3	473.4	501.7	527.3
83.5	88.0	84.8	81.1	63.1	77.2	94.0	96.5	106.5	127.1	137.0	138.0	135.3	120.0
70.4	62.1	33.9	31.7	18.4	54.2	87.5	91.8	55.4	86.5	112.6	85.9	49.9	47.0
303.7	342.1	402.4	466.2	519.5	563.3	602.8	653.5	694.2	724.0	765.2	832.8	907.1	988.2
1,807.9	2,033.1	2,265.4	2,534.7	2,690.9	2,862.5	3,154.6	3,379.8	3,590.4	3,802.0	4,075.9	4,380.2	4,679.8	4,833.9
240.1	280.2	312.4	360.2	371.4	368.8	395.1	436.8	459.0	512.5	527.7	591.7	621.0	616.0
1,567.8	1,753.0	1,952.9	2,174.5	2,319.6	2,493.7	2,759.5	2,943.0	3,131.5	3,289.5	3,548.2	3,788.6	4,058.8	4,217.8
3,703.5	3,796.8	3,776.3	3,843.1	3,760.3	3,906.6	4,148.5	4,279.8	4,404.5	4,540.0	4,718.6	4,836.9	4,884.9	4,848.4
4.8	2.5	−0.5	1.8	−2.2	3.9	6.2	3.2	2.9	3.1	3.9	2.5	1.0	−0.7
11,851.0	12,039.0	12,005.0	12,156.0	12,146.0	12,349.0	13,029.0	13,258.0	13,552.0	13,545.0	13,890.0	14,030.0	14,154.0	13,987.0

1978	1979	1980	1981	1982	1983	1984	1985	1986	1987	1988	1989	1990	1991**
65.2	72.6	82.4	90.9	96.5	99.6	103.9	107.6	109.6	113.6	118.3	124.0	130.7	136.2
7.6	11.3	13.5	10.3	6.2	3.2	4.3	3.6	1.9	3.6	4.1	4.8	5.4	4.2
82.6	85.7	84.1	85.7	81.9	84.9	92.8	94.4	95.3	100.0	105.4	108.1	109.2	107.1
358.4	382.8	408.8	436.4	474.4	521.2	552.2	619.9	724.3	749.7	786.4	793.6	825.4	896.7
9.06	12.67	15.27	18.87	14.86	10.79	12.04	9.93	8.33	8.21	9.32	10.87	10.01	8.46
222.6	255.1	227.7	230.0	232.3	234.3	236.4	238.5	240.7	242.9	245.1	247.4	250.0	252.7
102.3	105.0	106.9	108.7	110.2	111.6	113.5	115.5	117.8	119.9	121.7	123.9	124.8	125.3
6.2	6.1	7.6	8.3	10.7	10.7	8.5	8.3	8.2	7.4	6.7	6.5	6.9	8.4
6.1	5.8	7.1	7.6	9.7	9.6	7.5	7.2	7.0	6.2	5.5	5.3	5.5	6.7
100.4	99.3	98.6	99.9	100.0	102.2	104.6	106.1	108.3	109.4	110.4	109.5	109.7	11.0
0.6	−1.1	−0.7	1.3	0.1	2.2	2.3	1.4	2.0	1.0	0.9	−0.7	0.2	0.3
−15.4	−1.0	1.2	6.9	−5.9	−40.1	−99.0	−122.3	−145.4	−160.2	−126.2	−106.3	−92.1	___−8.6
776.6	828.9	908.5	994.3	1,136.8	1,371.2	1,564.1	1,817.0	2,120.1	2,345.6	2,600.8	2,867.5	3,206.3	3,599.0

Source: *Survey of Current Business, Federal Reserve Bulletin, Economic Report of the President, Economic Indicators.*

MACRO-ECONOMICS

MACRO-ECONOMICS
Principles, Problems, and Policies

TWELFTH EDITION

Campbell R. McConnell
Professor of Economics, Emeritus
University of Nebraska—Lincoln

Stanley L. Brue
Professor of Economics
Pacific Lutheran University

McGraw-Hill, Inc.

New York   St. Louis   San Francisco   Auckland
Bogotá   Caracas   Lisbon   London   Madrid
Mexico   Milan   Montreal   New Delhi   Paris
San Juan   Singapore   Sydney   Tokyo   Toronto

Macroeconomics: Principles, Problems, and Policies

2 3 4 5 6 7 8 9 0   VNH   VNH   9 0 9 8 7 6 5 4 3

ISBN 0-07-045603-8

This book was set in Century Oldstyle by York Graphic Services, Inc.
The editors were Scott D. Stratford, Michael R. Elia, and Edwin Hanson;
the designer was Joseph A. Piliero;
the production supervisor was Annette Mayeski.
New drawings were done by Vantage Art.
Von Hoffmann Press, Inc., was printer and binder.

Library of Congress Cataloging-in-Publication Data

McConnell, Campbell R.
  Macroeconomics: principles, problems, and policies / Campbell R. McConnell, Stanley L. Brue.—12th ed.
    p.   cm.
  Includes index.
  ISBN 0-07-045603-8
  1. Macroeconomics.   I. Brue, Stanley L., (date).   II. Title.
HB172.5.M3743   1993
339—dc20   92-20050

Campbell R. McConnell earned his Ph.D. from the University of Iowa after receiving degrees from Cornell College and the University of Illinois. He taught at the University of Nebraska–Lincoln from 1953 until his retirement in 1990. He is also coauthor of *Contemporary Labor Economics,* 3d ed. (McGraw-Hill) and has edited readers for the principles and labor economics courses. He is a recipient of both the University of Nebraska Distinguished Teaching Award and the James A. Lake Academic Freedom Award, and is past-president of the Midwest Economics Association. His primary areas of interest are labor economics and economic education. He has an extensive collection of jazz recordings and enjoys reading jazz history.

Stanley L. Brue did his undergraduate work at Augustana College (S.D.) and received his Ph.D. from the University of Nebraska—Lincoln. He teaches at Pacific Lutheran University, where he has been honored as a recipient of the Burlington Northern Faculty Achievement Award for classroom excellence and professional accomplishment. He is national President-elect and member of the International Executive Board of Omicron Delta Epsilon International Honor Society in Economics. Professor Brue is coauthor of *Economic Scenes: Theory in Today's World,* 5th ed. (Prentice-Hall); *The Evolution of Economic Thought,* 4th ed. (Harcourt Brace Jovanovich); and *Contemporary Labor Economics,* 3d ed. (McGraw-Hill). For relaxation, he enjoys boating on Puget Sound and skiing trips with his family.

To Mem
and to Terri and Craig

CONTENTS IN BRIEF

CONTENTS

Note: All chapter sections with substantial global content are indicated in light blue ink.

PREFACE

The publication of the twelfth edition of *Economics* (and its accompanying editions of *Macroeconomics* and *Microeconomics*) follows the most successful edition of this book to date. Naturally, we are pleased that *Economics* continues to be the best selling economics text in the United States. Moreover, we are pleasantly surprised that the Russian translation of *Economics* will soon be the leading economics text in the former Soviet Union; Politizdat Press has taken orders for nearly 500,000 copies. This fact dramatizes how remarkable these times are for teaching and learning economics! The message of our day is clear: People who comprehend economic principles will have a great advantage functioning in, and making sense of, the emerging world. We express our sincere thanks to each of you using *Macroeconomics* for granting us a modest role in your efforts to teach or learn this globally important subject.

THE REVISION

This edition of *Macroeconomics* has been thoroughly revised, polished, and updated. Many of the changes have been motivated by the comments of 36 reviewers and another 13 participants in focus groups. We are especially grateful to these scholars and acknowledge them by name at the end of this preface.

We strive only for an overview of the changes in this edition here; chapter-by-chapter details are provided in the *Instructor's Resource Manual* accompanying this book.

Consolidation of Introductory Chapters

Responding to reviewer suggestions, we have reduced the number of introductory chapters from eight to six, allowing for a quicker start into the macroeconomic theory. The previous edition's Chapters 5 and 7 are consolidated into new Chapter 5 and old Chapters 6 and 8 are combined into new Chapter 6. We have resisted the temptation to compress the introductory material even further, believing that most students inadequately understand the characteristics of capitalism (Chapter 3), the functioning of the market system (Chapter 5), and the extensive role of government in the modern economy (Chapter 6). A strong introduction helps students in their quest to understand and apply macroeconomic theory. We believe we have provided such an introduction, but now in a more expeditious form.

New Topics and Analysis

Much attention has been given to applying economics to the major issues of our day. Also, this edition contains new formal economic analyses. Examples of new discussions and analyses include:

- **The switch to GDP (Gross Domestic Product) accounting.** This edition fully incorporates the United States' recent major switch from GNP to GDP accounting. In particular, Chapter 7 has been carefully revised to present the new accounting. Also, in the macro theory chapters we have designated real output as GDP, rather than NNP and have substituted gross investment, I_g, for net investment, I_n, throughout the discussion and diagrams.
- **Early introduction of comparative advantage theory.** In an optional new section in Chapter 3, we use production possibilities tables to illustrate comparative advantage. By combining this new material with Chapter 4's optional discussion of exchange rates, instructors can effectively introduce international economics early in the course.
- **The crisis in American financial institutions.** A major section in Chapter 13 examines bank and thrift failures, including the role of deposit insurance.
- **Absorption of parts of monetarism and rational expectations theory into the mainstream**

macroeconomics. Although we continue to contrast the various macroeconomic theories, a new section of Chapter 16 emphasizes that mainstream macroeconomics has absorbed important aspects of monetarism and rational expectations theory.

- **Economic growth in Japan.** Chapter 2 now applies production possibilities analysis to relative growth rates in Japan and the United States and stresses the higher saving and investment rates in Japan. Also, Chapter 19 on economic growth now concludes with a Last Word on the Japanese growth miracle.

- **Causes of the productivity slowdown.** Chapter 19 on economic growth contains a completely rewritten section on the causes of the American productivity slowdown.

- **Soviet economy in transition.** A completely rewritten chapter (Chapter 23) presents an up-to-date, thorough analysis of the present crisis and reform efforts in the Soviet Union.

- **Other new discussions.** There are numerous other new discussions in this edition, a few examples being: the Ricardian equivalence theorem; money market deposit accounts and money market mutual funds; the Federal funds market; the social security surplus and the public debt; the Budget Consolidation and Budget Enforcement Acts of 1990; the economic impact of import quotas; strategic trade theory; the proposed North American free-trade zone; Uruguay Round negotiations; and the purchasing power parity theory of exchange rates.

New Last Words

Reviewers indicate that they appreciate the "Last Word" minireadings and their placement toward the conclusion of each chapter. These selections serve several purposes: Some provide current or historical real-world applications of economic concepts; others reveal human-interest aspects of economic problems; and still others present economic concepts or issues in a global context. Eleven Last Words are new and others have been revised and updated.

We have selected Last Word topics which are both highly relevant to the chapter's discussion *and* interesting to the reader. New topics are: fast-food lines viewed from the economic perspective (Chapter 1); the impact of Operation Desert Storm on Iraqi production possibilities (Chapter 2); the increasing use of barter (Chapter 3); the effect of supply interdiction on the price of marijuana (Chapter 4); the mystery of the $96 billion of

paper money unaccounted for by the Federal Reserve (Chapter 13); the bank panics of 1930–1933 (Chapter 14); the Fed as a series of metaphors (Chapter 15); international comparisons of public debt among industrial nations (Chapter 18); the Japanese growth miracle (Chapter 19); the difficulties of "buying American" when many product components are imported (Chapter 22); and an obituary of the Soviet Union (Chapter 23).

Pedagogical Improvements

The principles course has become increasingly demanding for students. Globalization of economies, developments in economic theory, and modern economic problems have added new, sometimes complex material to the course. Concise and understandable explanations are more important than ever before. Accordingly, we have directed much effort toward improving the pedagogy of *Macroeconomics*. We have "gone back to the basics," attempting to bolster what we believe to be this book's comparative advantages: its readability and accessibility. Examples of our pedagogical changes include:

- **Quick Reviews within each chapter.** Two or three new reviews within the body of each chapter allow the student to pause and ponder key points. We believe these Quick Reviews will also help students as they study for exams.

- **Key Graphs.** Students often have a difficult time distinguishing which of the hundreds of graphs in economics are of fundamental importance. To direct students' attention to the essential graphs we have designated 13 figures as Key Graphs. These graphs are specially designed and labeled to make them easily identifiable. Figures 2-1 and 4-5 are representative. A complete listing of the Key Graphs can be found in the Brief Table of Contents on pages ix–x.

- **Motivational introductions.** In many chapters new introductions are added to stimulate reader interest in the chapter's contents. These introductions relate to students' everyday experiences and observations. The opening material for Chapters 2, 6, 8, 14, and 19 is illustrative.

- **Full-color layout.** The full range of colors in the designer's palette makes for a more interesting text and is used functionally to clarify many graphs and diagrams.

- **Functional use of color photos.** Unobtrusive chapter-opening photos are employed as "teasers" for the content of the Last Words, where larger photos are found. The front and back photos visually unite the beginning and ends of the chapters and are designed to spark reader interest in the Last Words.

- **Shorter paragraphs.** In keeping with trends in popular and academic publishing, we have shortened scores of long paragraphs.
- **Tighter sentences.** The two authors and a talented McGraw-Hill editor scrutinized every sentence in the book for unnecessary verbiage. Collectively, we were able to tighten hundreds of sentences without altering the overall style of writing. In economizing on words, we were careful *not* to reduce the thoroughness of our explanations. Where needed, the "extra sentence of explanation" remains a distinguishing characteristic of *Macroeconomics*.
- **Numbered lists and added subheads.** We have substituted numbered and labeled lists for verbal strings of "First," "Second," and "Third." The idea here is to break material into smaller parcels to help students more readily retain the content. Similarly, we have used subheads more liberally so the organizational structure of each chapter and topic will be clearer for readers.
- **Footnote deletion.** We have significantly reduced the number of footnotes. Several lengthy explanatory footnotes have been deleted; a number of shorter footnotes have been integrated into the text. Footnotes suggesting additional reading have been judiciously pruned.
- **Added labeling in graphs.** Taking great care to avoid clutter, in a number of cases we have added labeling in figures to help guide the reader through the analysis. These labels are set in strong type so they are highly readable both within the book and on transparencies.
- **New diagrams.** Some of the added diagrams depict new graphical analyses, such as aggregate demand–aggregate supply analysis of growth (Figure 19-3) and a comparison of the effects of tariffs and quotas (Figure 20-3). Other new diagrams should help students visualize the interrelations of the concepts involved. Examples of these diagrams are Figures 8-4, 10-5, 11-4, and 11-5.
- **Clarified explanations of difficult subject matter.** We have continued to look for ways to explain difficult material more clearly. Even minor improvements in language or labeling of graphs can often help students better understand the material. Improvements of this sort have been made in numerous places throughout the text. Good examples are our revised discussions of efficiency (Chapter 2),

the ratchet effect (Chapter 9), and demand-pull and cost-push inflation in the long run (Chapter 17).

New and Enhanced Ancillaries

The ancillaries in this edition's package are discussed later in this Preface, but three new items are particularly noteworthy.

- **Test Bank III.** New to the *Macroeconomics* package is a test bank allowing an alternative testing approach to the predominantly multiple-choice questions in Test Banks I and II. Written by Professors William Walstad and Joyce Gleason, Test Bank III contains questions that emphasize "constructive response" concepts. Students are more actively involved in creating answers to these questions, which provide a valuable alternative to conventional test questions.
- **Augmented Test Bank I.** We have added approximately 1200 questions to the macroeconomic version of Test Bank I.
- **New macro simulation software.** *Macroeconomics: A Lab Course,* a new macro simulation program, greatly advances the art of economics software. This program is highly interactive and visually spectacular. Also, the successful *Concept Master* software introduced with the previous edition of *Macroeconomics* has been completely updated. Both these software programs are directly tied to the contents of *Macroeconomics*.
- **Enhanced video materials.** The power of videodisks is harnassed in this edition, to provide enhanced classroom presentation of visual material. Also, there are new videotape materials that have been carefully designed for effective classroom use.

We trust that the outcome of this detailed revision effort is a text and package that are clearly superior to their predecessors.

FUNDAMENTAL GOALS

The basic purpose of *Macroeconomics* continues to be to introduce the beginning economics student to those principles essential to an understanding of the fundamental economic problem and the policy alternatives available for dealing with this problem. We hope that the ability to reason accurately and objectively about economic matters and the development of a lasting interest in economics will be two valuable by-products of this basic objective. Our intention remains to present the principles and problems of economics in a straight-forward, logical fashion. To this end, we continue to put great stress on clarity of presentation and on logical organization.

PRODUCT DIFFERENTIATION

This text embraces a number of features which perhaps distinguish it from other books in the field.

- **Comprehensive explanations at an appropriate level.** We have attempted to craft a comprehensive, analytical text which is challenging to better students, yet accessible—with appropriate hard work—to average students. We think the thoroughness and accessibility of *Macroeconomics* enables the instructor to select topics for special classroom emphasis with confidence that students can independently read and comprehend other assigned material in the book.
- **Comprehensive definition of economics.** The principles course sometimes fails to provide students with a comprehensive and meaningful definition of economics. To avoid this shortcoming, all of Chapter 2 is devoted to a careful statement and development of the economizing problem and an exploration of its implications. This foundation should help put the many particular subject areas of economics in proper perspective.
- **Early integration of international economics.** Comparative advantage is discussed in detail in Chapter 3, exchange rates are explained as an application of supply and demand in Chapter 4, and the international trade sector of the American economy is highlighted in Chapter 5. This strong introduction to international economics permits "globalization" of later discussions of macroeconomics, where appropriate.
- **Early treatment of government.** For better or worse, government is an integral component of modern capitalism. Its economic role, therefore, should not be treated piecemeal or as an afterthought. This text introduces the economic functions of government early and accords them systematic treatment in Chapter 6. The controversy about the proper role of government in stabilizing the economy is central to the macroeconomic policy chapters.
- **Emphasis on economic growth.** This volume continues to put considerable emphasis on economic growth. Chapter 2 uses the production possibilities curve to lay bare the basic ingredients of growth. Chapter 19 discusses the rate and causes of American growth, in addition to some of the controversies surrounding growth. Chapter 22 focuses on the less developed countries and the growth obstacles which confront them. A segment of Chapter 23 concerns the stalling of growth in the former Soviet Union.
- **Issue chapters.** As most students see it, Part 4 on macroeconomic issues is where the action is. We have sought to guide the action along logical lines through the application of appropriate analytical tools. Our bias in these parts is in favor of inclusiveness; each instructor can effectively counter this bias by omitting those chapters felt to be less relevant for a particular group of students.

ORGANIZATION AND CONTENT

We believe that the basic prerequisite of an understandable economics text is the logical arrangement and clear exposition of subject matter. This book has been organized so that the exposition of each particular topic and concept is directly related to the level of difficulty which in our experience the average student is likely to encounter. For this reason macro employment theory and money and banking are given comprehensive and careful treatments. Simplicity here is correlated with comprehensiveness, not brevity. Furthermore, our experience suggests that in the treatment of each basic topic—aggregate demand and aggregate supply, aggregate expenditures analysis, money and banking, and international economics—it is highly desirable to couple analysis with policy. A three-step development of basic analytical tools is employed: (1) verbal descriptions and illustrations; (2) numerical examples; and (3) graphical presentation based on these numerical illustrations.

The material in this book is organized into five basic parts. They are: Part 1: An Introduction to Economics and the Economy; Part 2: National Income, Employment, and Fiscal Policy; Part 3: Money. Banking, and Monetary Policy; Part 4: Problems and Controversies in Macroeconomics; and Part 5: International Economics and the World Economy. The Table of Contents lists the specific chapters in each part and details the contents within each chapter.

STUDENT FRIENDLY: STUDY AIDS

Macroeconomics is highly student oriented.

1   Students who are comfortable with graphical analysis and a few related quantitative concepts are in an advantageous position to understand principles of eco-

nomics. To help students in this regard, an appendix to Chapter 1 carefully reviews graphing, line slopes, and linear equations.

2   The introductory paragraphs of each chapter state objectives, present an organizational overview of the chapter, and relate the chapter to what has been covered before and what will follow.

3   Because a significant portion of any introductory course is devoted to terminology, terms are given special emphasis. In particular, each important term is in **boldface** type where it first appears in each chapter. We have tried to make all definitions clear and succinct. At the end of each chapter all new terms are listed in the Terms and Concepts section. Finally, at the end of the book is a comprehensive glossary. This glossary also is contained in the *Study Guide* which accompanies *Macroeconomics.*

4   As we noted earlier, each chapter contains two or three "Quick Reviews" at appropriate places in the chapter to reinforce key points for students and help them study for examinations.

5   Figures worthy of intensive study are given special design treatment and designated as "Key Graphs."

6   The legends accompanying all diagrams are written so that they are self-contained analyses of the relevant concepts. This is a strategic means of reinforcing student comprehension.

7   Much thought has gone into the end-of-chapter questions. Though purposely intermixed, the questions are of three general types. Some are designed to highlight the main points of each chapter. Others are "open-end" discussion, debate, or thought questions. Wherever pertinent, numerical problems which require the student to derive and manipulate key concepts and relationships are employed. Numerical problems are stressed in those chapters which deal with analytical material. Some optional "advanced analysis" questions accompany certain theory chapters. These problems usually involve the stating and manipulation of basic concepts in equation form. Answers to *all* end-of-chapter questions—both quantitative and essay—are provided in the *Instructor's Resource Manual.*

8   Many of the end-of-chapter questions deal with subject matter that is reinforced by the excellent computerized tutorial, *Concept Master II,* that accompanies the text. A floppy disk symbol 💾 appears in conjunction with questions whose content correlates to a lesson in the tutorial program.

9   In addition to its considerable esthetic merit, the multicolor format of *Macroeconomics* stresses the use of color so students will more quickly and easily perceive the ideas expressed in each diagram and chart.

INSTRUCTOR FRIENDLY: THE SUPPLEMENTS

Macroeconomics is accompanied by supplements which we feel equal or surpass competing texts in terms of both quantity and quality.

Study Guide

Professor William Walstad has prepared a new revision of the *Study Guide* to accompany *Macroeconomics* which many students find to be an indispensable aid. It contains for each chapter an introductory statement, a checklist of behavioral objectives, an outline, a list of important terms, fill-in questions, problems and projects, objective questions, and discussion questions. The glossary found at the end of *Macroeconomics* also appears in the *Study Guide.*

In this revision, Professor Walstad has added text page references for every question (true-false, multiple-choice, and discussion); has extensively revised the chapter learning objectives to add more detail; and has added discussion sections to the chapter outlines. He has also increased the number of multiple-choice questions for each chapter, and has increased the number of problems and projects for further study. The *Guide* comprises, in our opinion, a superb "portable tutor" for the principles student.

Economic Concepts

Economic Concepts provides carefully designed programmed materials for all the key analytical areas of the principles course. Revised by Professor W. H. Pope for use with *Macroeconomics,* it can be used as an effective supplement with any mainstream text.

Instructor's Resource Manual

Professor Joyce Gleason of Nebraska Wesleyan University has revised and updated the *Instructor's Resource Manual.* It comprises chapter summaries, listings of "what's new" in each chapter, teaching tips and suggestions, learning objectives, chapter outlines, data and visual aid sources with suggestions for classroom use, and problems. Answers to all the text's end-of-chapter questions are also found in the *Manual.*

The new edition of the *Manual* includes a full, chapter-by-chapter overview of all changes in the revision. Also, the chapter outlines have been consolidated into a separate section of the *Manual,* so they can more readily be used as a resource in classroom lectures. We think instructors will find this *Manual* useful and time-saving.

Available again in this edition is a computerized version of the *Manual,* suitable for use with IBM-PC computers, IBM-PC compatibles, and Macintosh computers. The version for IBM-PCs and compatibles is available in both 5¼-inch and 3½-inch formats. Users of *Macroeconomics* can print out portions of the *Manual's* contents, complete with their own additions or alterations, for use as student handouts or in whatever ways they might wish. This capability includes printing answers to all end-of-chapter questions.

As with the *Study Guide,* a separate edition of the *Instructor's Resource Manual* has been prepared to correspond with the macro paperback edition of *Economics.* Users of *Macroeconomics* will find that the material in the accompanying *Manual* correlates with the chapter sequencing in the text.

Three Test Banks

Macroeconomics is supplemented by two test banks of objective, predominantly multiple-choice, questions and a new test bank of short-answer and essay questions.

Test Bank I now comprises some 2800 questions, all written by the text authors; approximately 2050 are carried over from the previous edition and 750 have been prepared by the authors for the new edition.

Test Bank II, revised by Professor Walstad, contains approximately 2300 questions. For all test items in these two test banks, the nature of each question is identified (e.g., G, graphical; C, complex analysis) as are the pages in the text containing the material which is the basis for each question. Also, each chapter in *Test Banks I* and *II* has an outline or Table of Contents which groups questions by broad topics.

New to this edition, *Test Bank III* will emphasize "constructive response" testing to evaluate student understanding in a manner different from conventional multiple-choice and true-false questions. Prepared by Professors Walstad and Gleason, this unique resource emphasizes short-answer and essay questions designed to enhance critical thinking skills.

Adopters of *Macroeconomics* will be able to use this sizable number of questions, organized into three test banks of equal quality, with maximum flexibility. The fact that the text authors and *Study Guide* authors have prepared all the test items will assure the fullest possible correlation with the content of the text.

As with the *Study Guide* and *Instructor's Resource Manual,* a separate version of the test banks have been prepared to correspond with the individual macro and micro editions of the text.

Computerized testing　Test Banks I, II, and III are available in computerized versions, as well as print. Computerized test generation will be available for IBM-PCs and compatibles, and for MacIntosh computers. All these systems include the capability to produce high-quality graphics from the test bank.

These systems will also feature the ability to generate multiple-tests, with versions "scrambled" to be distinctive, and will have other useful features. They will meet the various needs of the widest spectrum of computer users.

Color transparencies　Full color transparencies for overhead projectors have been prepared especially for *Macroeconomics.* These encompass all the figures which appear in *Macroeconomics* and are available on request to adopters.

Student software　For users of IBM-PCs and compatibles, a student software package, *Concept Master II,* has been prepared by Professor William Gunther, of the University of Alabama, and Irene Gunther. The previous version of this software was widely praised by its users, and it has been improved to provide even more flexibility. It provides the most extensive and varied computer-assisted study material of any software package available.

Over twelve graphics-based tutorial programs provide an opportunity for students to study key topics in the book in an interactive fashion. The tutorial programs are linked to the text. Selected end-of-chapter questions that relate to the content of one of the tutorial programs are highlighted by a floppy disk symbol 💾. The questions themselves are not necessarily contained within the tutorial program, but the tutorial does contain material that relates directly to the concepts underlying the highlighted questions.

In addition to the tutorial programs, students can quiz themselves with a self-testing program accompanying each test chapter. The package also features three macroeconomic simulation games. One simulation involves a global economy in keeping with the globalization of the course and this text. Also included in the package are a list of key terms, a pop-up calculator for computations, and a section that uses the "Key

Graphs" in the text to direct students to the appropriate tutorial lesson.

Professor Norris Peterson of Pacific Lutheran University, working with the talented staff of Intellipro, Inc., has created a new software package, *Macroeconomics: A Lab Course,* to be used in macroeconomics courses. It builds the basic macroeconomic framework in sequential, "building block" laboratory simulations that allow students to grasp the fundamental concepts of macroeconomics in a dynamic and creative manner.

For users of Macintosh computers, there is an exciting tutorial program, *DiscoverEcon.* Developed by Professors Gerald Nelson and Wesley Seitz of the University of Illinois, this innovative package uses Apple's HYPERCARD programming environment to produce an extremely interactive learning experience. Dynamic shifts of curves, screen animation, sound effects, and simple-to-use command keys are features of this program.

Videodisks New to this edition are videodisks designed to harness this exciting new technology for classroom presentation. These videodisks offer an array of graphical illustrations of key economic concepts to further student understanding.

Videos New videotape materials have been assembled for this edition, to illustrate fundamental concepts and economic issues in a manner that will be equally effective in classroom settings or media resource centers. Among these materials is the new "MacNeil/Lehrer Quarterly Report on Economics," an exciting new series of excerpts from the acclaimed PBS news program, "The MacNeil/Lehrer Newshour." Your local McGraw-Hill representative can provide details on all new video ancillaries for the text.

DEBTS

The publication of this edition of *Macroeconomics* will extend the life of *Economics* well into its fourth decade. The acceptance of *Economics,* which was generous from the outset, has expanded with each edition. This gracious reception has no doubt been fostered by the many teachers and students who have been kind enough to provide their suggestions and criticisms.

Our colleagues at the University of Nebraska–Lincoln and Pacific Lutheran University have generously shared knowledge of their specialties with us and have provided encouragement. We are especially indebted to Professors Harish Gupta, Jerry Petr, David Rosenbaum, and Norris Peterson, who have been most helpful in offsetting comparative ignorance in their areas of specialty.

As indicated, this edition has benefited from a number of perceptive reviews. In both quantity and quality, they provided the richest possible source of suggestions for this revision. These contributors are listed at the end of this Preface.

Professors Thomas P. Barbiero and W. H. Pope of Ryerson Polytechnic Institute in their role as coauthors of the Canadian edition of *Economics* have provided innumerable suggestions for improvement. Thanks also go to Professor Lovewell who coded the new *Test Bank* items by type of questions and identified the corresponding text page number for all the items.

We are greatly indebted to the many professionals at McGraw-Hill—and in particular Phil Galea, Annette Mayeski, and Karen Jackson—for their expertise in the production and distribution of the book. Joe Piliero has given the book its unique design. Safra Nimrod and Debra Hershkowitz found suitable photos for the Last Word readings and Cathy Hull provided the creative illustrations for several of them. Margaret Hanson's imaginative editing has been invaluable. Our greatest debts are to Scott Stratford, Edwin Hanson, and Mike Elia for their conscientious supervision of this revision. Their patience and many positive contributions are gratefully acknowledged.

Given this much assistance, we see no compelling reason why the authors should assume full responsibility for errors of omission or commission. But we bow to tradition.

Campbell R. McConnell
Stanley L. Brue

ACKNOWLEDGMENTS

We thank the following instructors for their written reviews and other comments, which greatly helped shape this edition:

Thomas P. Barbiero, *Ryerson Polytechnical Institute*
Arleigh T. Bell, *Loyola College*
Michael S. Blair, *Tarrant County Junior College*
Joseph P. Cairo, *La Salle University*
Robert Campbell, *Indiana University–Bloomington*
Gordon Crocker, *Community College of Allegheny County*
Paul G. Farnham, *Georgia State University*
Walter F. Gall, Jr., *Northeastern Junior College*
John A. Gould, *Garrett Community College*
Paul W. Grimes, *Mississippi State University*
Richard C. Harmstone, *Penn State University*
Gail A. Hawks, *Miami-Dade Community College*
R. Bradley Hoppes, *Southwest Missouri State University*
Matthew Hyle, *Winona State University*
Patrick Joyce, *Michigan Technological University*
James C. Koch, *St. Edwards University*
Fredric Kolb, *University of Wisconsin–Eau Claire*
Patrick Litzinger, *Robert Morris College*
Mark Lovewell, *Ryerson Polytechnical Institute*
George F. Muscat, *Camden County Community College*
Asghar Nazemzadeh, *University of Houston–Downtown*
Margaret O'Donnell, *University of Southwest Louisiana*
Ronald W. Olive, *New Hampshire College*
Diana Petersdorf, *University of Wisconsin–Stout*

David Priddy, *Piedmont Community College*
John J. Rapczak, *Community College of Rhode Island*
Theresa Riley, *Youngstown State University*
Peter Rupert, *SUNY–Buffalo*
Doris Sheets, *Southwest Missouri State University*
Steven P. Skinner, *Western Connecticut State University*
Robert Stuart, *Rutgers University*
Percy O. Vera, *Sinclair Community College*
Howard J. Wall, *West Virginia University*
Paul R. Watro, *Jefferson Community College*
Peter J. Watry, Jr., *Southwestern College*
Dieter Zschock, *SUNY–Stony Brook*

In addition, we thank the following instructors for participating in focus group sessions, which served as very useful complements to the reviewing process:

Barbara Brogan, *Northern Virginia Community College*
Robert F. Brooker, *Gannon University*
Christopher B. Colburn, *Old Dominion University*
Jacob Deutch, *University of Maryland–Baltimore County*
James Halteman, *Wheaton College*
Charles Jewell, *Charles County Community College*
George Kosicki, *College of the Holy Cross*
Patrick Litzinger, *Robert Morris College*
Craig MacPhee, *University of Nebraska–Lincoln*
Norris A. Peterson, *Pacific Lutheran University*
Donald Schilling, *University of Missouri–Columbia*
Robert Tansky, *St. Clair Community College*
Irvin Weintraub, *Towson State University*

MACRO-ECONOMICS

PART

1

An Introduction to Economics and the Economy

The Nature and Method of Economics

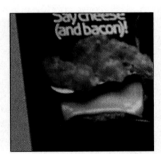

Human beings, unfortunate creatures, are plagued with wants. We want, among other things, love, social recognition, and the material necessities and comforts of life. Our striving to improve our material well-being, to "make a living," is the concern of economics. Specifically, economics is the study of our behavior in producing, distributing, and consuming material goods and services in a world of scarce resources.

But we need a more sophisticated definition of economics. We are, indeed, characterized by both biologically and socially determined wants. We seek food, clothing, shelter, and many goods and services associated with a comfortable or affluent standard of living. We are also blessed with aptitudes and surrounded by quantities of property resources—both natural and manufactured. We use available human and property resources—labor and managerial talents, tools and machinery, land and mineral deposits—to produce goods and services which satisfy these material wants. This is done through the organizational mechanism we call the *economic system.*

Quantitative considerations, however, rule out an ideal solution. The blunt fact is that the total of all our material wants is beyond the productive capacity of all available resources. Hence, absolute material abundance is not a possible outcome. This unyielding fact is the basis for our definition of economics: *Economics is concerned with the efficient use or management of limited productive resources to achieve maximum satisfaction of human material wants.* Though it may not be self-evident, all the headline-grabbing issues of the day—inflation, unemployment, the collapse of communism, government and international trade deficits, free-trade agreements among nations, poverty and inequality, pollution, and government regulation of business—are rooted in the issue of using limited resources efficiently.

In this first chapter, however, we will not plunge into problems and issues. Our immediate concern is with some basic preliminary questions: (1) Of what importance or consequence is the study of economics? (2) How should we study

1

economics—what are the proper procedures? What is the character of the methodology of economics? (3) What specific problems, limitations, and pitfalls might we encounter in studying economics?

THE AGE OF THE ECONOMIST

Is economics a discipline of consequence? Is the study of economics worth your time and effort? Half a century ago John Maynard Keynes (1883–1946)—clearly the most influential economist of this century—offered a telling response:

> The ideas of economists and political philosophers, both when they are right and when they are wrong, are more powerful than is commonly understood. Indeed the world is ruled by little else. Practical men, who believe themselves to be quite exempt from any intellectual influences, are usually the slaves of some defunct economist.

Most of the ideologies of the modern world which compete for our minds have been shaped by the great economists of the past—Adam Smith, David Ricardo, John Stuart Mill, Karl Marx, and John Maynard Keynes.[1] And it is currently commonplace for world leaders to receive and invoke the advice and policy prescriptions of economists.

For example: The President of the United States benefits from the ongoing counsel of his Council of Economic Advisers. The broad spectrum of economic issues facing political leaders is suggested by the contents of the annual *Economic Report of the President.* Areas covered include unemployment and inflation, economic growth and productivity, taxation and public expenditures, poverty and income maintenance, the balance of payments and the international monetary system, labor-management relations, pollution, discrimination, immigration, and competition and antitrust, among others.

Economics for Citizenship

A basic understanding of economics is essential if we are to be well-informed citizens. Most of the specific problems of the day have important economic aspects, and as voters we can influence the decisions of our political leaders in coping with these problems. What are the causes and consequences of the "twin deficits"—the Federal budget deficit and the international trade deficit—that are constantly reported by the news media? What of the depressing stories of homeless street people? Is it desirable that corporate raiders be allowed to achieve hostile takeovers of corporations? Why is inflation undesirable? What can be done to reduce unemployment? Are existing welfare programs effective and justifiable? Should we continue to subsidize farmers? Do we need further reform of our tax system? Does America need to "reindustrialize" to reassert its dominant position in world trade and finance? Has the deregulation of the airlines, trucking, and banking industries been a boon or a bane to society? Since responses to such questions are determined largely by our elected officials, intelligence at the polls requires that we have a basic working knowledge of economics. Needless to say, a sound grasp of economics is more than helpful to politicians themselves!

Personal Applications

Economics is also a vital discipline for more mundane, immediate reasons. It is of practical value in business. An understanding of the overall operation of the economic system enables the business executive to better formulate policies. The executive who understands the causes and consequences of inflation can make more intelligent business decisions during inflationary periods than otherwise. Indeed, more and more economists are appearing on the payrolls of large corporations. Their job is to gather and interpret economic information on which rational business decisions can be made. Economics also gives the individual as a consumer and worker insights on how to make wiser buying and employment decisions. What should one buy and how much? How can one "hedge" against the reduction in the dollar's purchasing power which accompanies inflation? Which occupations pay well; which are most immune to unemployment? Similarly, someone who understands the relationship between budget and trade deficits, on the one hand, and security (stock

---

[1]Any of the following three volumes—Robert Heilbroner, *The Worldly Philosophers,* 6th ed. (New York: Simon and Schuster, Inc., 1986); Daniel R. Fusfeld, *The Age of the Economist,* 6th ed. (Chicago: Scott, Foresman and Company, 1990); or E. Ray Canterbery, *The Making of Economics,* 3d ed. (Belmont, Calif.: Wadsworth Publishing Company, 1987)—will provide the reader with a fascinating introduction to the historical development of economic ideas.

and bond) values, on the other, can make more enlightened personal investment decisions.

In spite of its practical benefits, however, you must be forewarned that economics is mainly an academic, not a vocational, subject. Unlike accounting, advertising, corporation finance, and marketing, economics is not primarily a how-to-make-money area of study. A knowledge of economics will help you run a business or manage personal finances, but this is not its primary objective. In economics, problems are usually examined from the *social,* rather than the *personal,* point of view. The production, exchange, and consumption of goods and services are discussed from the viewpoint of society as a whole, rather than from the standpoint of one's own bankbook.

METHODOLOGY

What do economists do? What are their goals? What procedures do they employ? The title of this volume— *Macroeconomics: Principles, Problems, and Policies*— contains a thumbnail answer to the first two questions. Economists formulate economic *principles* which are useful in the establishment of *policies* designed to solve economic *problems.* The procedures employed by the economist are summarized in Figure 1-1. The economist ascertains and gathers facts relevant to a specific economic problem. This task is sometimes called **descriptive** or **empirical economics** (box 1). The economist also states economic principles, that is, generalizes about the way individuals and institutions actually behave. Deriving principles is called **economic theory** or "economic analysis" (box 2).

As we see in Figure 1-1, economists are as likely to move from theory to facts in studying economic behavior as they are to move from facts to theory. Stated more formally, economists use both deductive and inductive methods. **Induction** distills or creates principles from facts. Here an accumulation of facts is arranged systematically and analyzed to permit the derivation of a generalization or principle. Induction moves from facts to theory, from the particular to the general. The inductive method is suggested by the left upward arrow from box 1 to box 2 in the figure.

Similarly, economists can begin with theory and proceed to the verification or rejection of this theory by an appeal to the facts. This is **deduction** or the hypothetical method. Economists may draw upon casual observation, insight, logic, or intuition to frame a tentative, untested principle called an **hypothesis.** For ex-

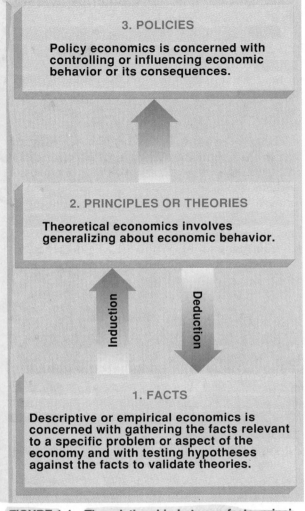

FIGURE 1-1   The relationship between principles, and policies in economics

In analyzing problems or aspects of the economy, economists may use the inductive method whereby they gather, systematically arrange, and generalize on facts. Alternatively, the deductive method entails the development of hypotheses which are then tested against facts. Generalizations derived from either method of inquiry are useful not only in explaining economic behavior, but also as a basis for formulating economic policies.

ample, they may conjecture, on the basis of "armchair logic," that it is rational for consumers to buy more of a product when its price is low than when its price is high. The validity of this hypothesis must then be tested by the systematic and repeated examination of relevant facts. The deductive method goes from the general to the particular, from theory to facts. This method is implicit in the right downward arrow from box 2 to box 1 in Figure 1-1.

Deduction and induction are complementary, rather than opposing, techniques of investigation. Hypotheses formulated by deduction provide guidelines for the economist in gathering and systematizing empirical data. Conversely, some understanding of factual evidence—of the "real world"—is prerequisite to formulation of meaningful hypotheses.

Finally, the general knowledge of economic behavior which economic principles provides can then be used in formulating policies, that is, remedies or solutions, for correcting or avoiding the problem under scrutiny. This final aspect of the field is sometimes called "applied economics" or **policy economics** (box 3).

Continuing to use Figure 1-1 as a reference, we now examine the economist's methodology in more detail.

Descriptive Economics

All sciences are empirical; they are based on facts, that is, on observable and verifiable behavior of certain data or subject matter. In the physical sciences the factual data are inorganic. As a social science, economics examines the behavior of individuals and institutions engaged in the production, exchange, and consumption of goods and services.

Fact-gathering can be an infinitely complex task. Because the world of reality is cluttered with innumerable interrelated facts, the economist must use discretion in gathering them. One must distinguish economic from noneconomic facts and then determine which economic facts are relevant and which irrelevant for the problem under consideration. But even when this sorting process is complete, the relevant economic facts may appear diverse and unrelated.

Economic Theory

The task of economic theory or analysis is to systematically arrange, interpret, and generalize upon facts. Principles and theories—the end result of economic analysis—bring order and meaning to facts by tying them together, putting them in correct relationship to one another, and generalizing upon them. "Theories without facts may be barren, but facts without theories are meaningless."[2]

[2]Kenneth E. Boulding, *Economic Analysis: Microeconomics,* 4th ed. (New York: Harper & Row, Publishers, Incorporated, 1966), p. 5.

Principles and theories are meaningful statements drawn from facts, but facts, in turn, serve as a constant check on the validity of principles already established. Facts—how individuals and institutions actually behave in producing, exchanging, and consuming goods and services—may change with time. This makes it essential that economists continually check existing principles and theories against the changing economic environment.

Terminology   Economists talk about "laws," "principles," "theories," and "models." These terms all mean essentially the same thing: generalizations, or statements of regularity, concerning the economic behavior of individuals and institutions. The term "economic law" is a bit misleading because it implies a high degree of exactness, universal application, and even moral rightness. So, to a lesser degree, does the term **principle.** And some people incorrectly associate the term "theory" with ivory-tower dreams, divorced from the facts and realities of the world. The term "model" has much to commend it. A model is a simplified picture of reality, an abstract generalization of how relevant data actually behave. In this book these four terms will be used synonymously. The choice of terms in labeling any particular generalization will be governed by custom or convenience. Thus, the relationship between the price of a product and the quantity consumers purchase will be called the "law" of demand, rather than the theory or principle of demand, because this is the customary designation.

Several other points regarding the character and derivation of economic principles are in order.

Generalizations   Economic principles are **generalizations** and, as the term implies, characterized by somewhat imprecise quantitative statement. Economic facts are usually diverse; some individuals and institutions act one way and some another way. Economic principles are therefore frequently stated in terms of averages or statistical probabilities. For example, when economists say that the average household earned an income of about $35,000 in 1990, they are generalizing. It is recognized that some households earned much more and a good many others much less. Yet this generalization, properly handled and interpreted, can be very meaningful and useful.

Similarly, economic generalizations are often stated in terms of probabilities. A researcher may tell us there is a 95 percent probability that every $1.00 reduction in personal income taxes will result in a $.92 increase in consumer spending.

"Other Things Equal" Assumption Like other scientists, economists use the ***ceteris paribus*** or **other things being equal assumption** to construct their generalizations. That is, they assume all other variables except those under immediate consideration are held constant. This technique simplifies the reasoning process by isolating the relationship under consideration. For example, in considering the relationship between the price of Pepsi and the amount purchased, it helps to assume that, of all the factors which might influence the amount of Pepsi purchased (for example, the price of Pepsi, the prices of other goods such as Coke, consumer incomes and tastes), only the price of Pepsi varies. The economist can then focus on the "price of Pepsi–purchases of Pepsi" relationship without reasoning being blurred or confused by intrusion of other variables.

In the natural sciences controlled experiments usually can be performed where "all other things" are in fact held constant or virtually so. Thus, scientists can test the assumed relationship between two variables with great precision. But economics is not a laboratory science. The economist's process of empirical verification is based on "real-world" data generated by the actual operation of the economy. In this rather bewildering environment "other things" *do* change. Despite the development of complex statistical techniques designed to hold other things equal, such controls are less than perfect. As a result, economic principles are less certain and less precise in application than those of laboratory sciences.

Abstractions Economic principles, or theories, are necessarily abstractions. They do not mirror the full complexity of reality. The very process of sorting out noneconomic and irrelevant facts in the fact-gathering process involves abstracting from reality. Unfortunately, the abstractness of economic theory prompts the uninformed to identify theory as impractical and unrealistic. This is nonsense! Economic theories are practical simply because they are abstractions. The level of reality is too complex and bewildering to be very meaningful. Economists theorize to give meaning to a maze of facts which would otherwise be confusing and useless, and to put facts into a more usable, practical form. Thus, to generalize is to abstract or purposely simplify; generalization for this purpose is practical, and therefore so is abstraction.

An economic theory is a model—a simplified picture or map—of some segment of the economy. This model helps us understand reality better *because* it avoids the confusing details of reality. Theories—*good*

theories—are grounded on facts and therefore are realistic. Theories which do not fit the facts are simply not good theories.

Macro and Micro There are two different levels of analysis at which the economist may derive laws concerning economic behavior. The level of **macroeconomics** deals either with the economy as a whole or with the basic subdivisions or aggregates—such as the government, household, and business sectors—which make up the economy. An aggregate is a collection of specific economic units which are treated *as if* they were one unit. Thus, we might find it convenient to lump together the over eighteen million businesses in our economy and treat them as if they were one huge unit. In dealing with aggregates, macroeconomics is concerned with obtaining an overview, or general outline, of the structure of the economy and the relationships among the major aggregates which constitute the economy. No attention is given to specific units making up the various aggregates. Macroeconomics speaks of such magnitudes as *total* output, *total* level of employment, *total* income, *aggregate* expenditures, the *general* level of prices, and so forth, in analyzing various economic problems. In short, macroeconomics examines the forest, not the trees. It gives us a bird's-eye view of the economy.

On the other hand, **microeconomics** deals with *specific* economic units and a *detailed* consideration of these individual units. At this level of analysis, the economist figuratively puts an economic unit, or very small segment of the economy, under the microscope to observe details of its operation. Here we talk in terms of an individual industry, firm, or household, and concentrate upon such magnitudes as the output or price of a specific product, the number of workers employed by a single firm, the revenue or income of a particular firm or household, or the expenditures of a given firm or family. In microeconomics we examine the trees, not the forest. Microeconomics is useful in achieving a worm's-eye view of some very specific component of our economic system.

The macro–micro distinction does not mean that the subject matter of economics is so highly compartmentalized that each topic can be readily labeled as "macro" or "micro"; many topics and subdivisions of economics are rooted in both. Indeed, there has been a convergence of macro- and microeconomics in important areas in recent years. While the problem of unemployment was treated primarily as a macroeconomic topic some twenty or twenty-five years ago ("unemployment depends on *aggregate* spending"), economists now recognize that decisions made by *individual* workers in searching for jobs and the manner in which specific product and labor markets function are also critical in determining the unemployment rate.

Graphical Expression Many of the economic models or principles presented in this book will be expressed graphically. The most important of these models are labeled "Key Graphs." You are strongly urged to read the appendix to this chapter to review graphing and other relevant quantitative relationships.

QUICK REVIEW 1-1

♦ **Economics is concerned with the efficient management of scarce resources.**

♦ **Induction involves observing regularities in factual data and drawing generalizations from them; deduction entails the creation of hypotheses which are then tested with factual data.**

♦ **Economic theories ("laws," "principles," or "models") are generalizations, based on facts, concerning the economic behavior of individuals and institutions.**

♦ **Macroeconomics deals with the economy as a whole; microeconomics focuses on specific units which comprise the economy.**

Policy Economics: Positive and Normative

As we move from the fact and principles levels (boxes 1 and 2) of Figure 1-1 to the policy level (box 3) we make a critical leap from positive to normative economics.

Positive economics deals with facts (once removed at the level of theory) and avoids value judgments. Positive economics attempts to set forth scientific statements about economic behavior. **Normative economics,** in contrast, involves someone's value judgments about what the economy should be like or what particular policy action should be recommended based on a given economic generalization or relationship.

Positive economics concerns *what is,* while normative economics embodies subjective feelings about *what ought to be.* Positive economics deals with what the economy is actually like; normative economics examines whether certain conditions or aspects of the economy are desirable or not.

Consider this example: Positive statement: "Unemployment is 7 percent of the labor force." Normative statement: "Unemployment ought to be reduced." Second positive statement: "Other things being the same, if tuition is increased, enrollment at Gigantic State University will fall." Normative statement: "Tuition should be lowered at GSU so that more students can obtain an education." Whenever words such as "ought" or "should" appear in a sentence, there is a strong chance you are dealing with a normative statement.

Most of the apparent disagreement among economists involves normative, value-based policy questions. To be sure, various economists present and support different theories or models of the economy and its component parts. But by far most economic controversy reflects differing opinions or value judgments as to what our society should be like. For example, there is greater agreement about the actual distribution of income in our society than how income should be distributed. The point we reemphasize is that value judgments or normative statements come into play at the level of policy economics.

As noted earlier, successful policy economics draws heavily on economic principles. For example, one almost universally accepted economic principle indicates that, within certain limits, there is a direct relationship between total spending and the level of employment in the economy. "If total spending increases, the volume of employment will rise. Conversely, if total spending decreases, the volume of employment will fall." This principle can be invaluable to government in determining its economic policies. If government economists note that available statistics indicate an actual slackening of total expenditures, the principle will permit them to predict the undesirable consequence of unemployment. Aware of this anticipated result, public officials can set in motion government policies designed to bolster total spending and head off or reduce expected unemployment. In short, we must be able to predict in order to effectively control. Economic principles help make prediction possible and are the basis for sound economic policy.

Economic Goals A number of **economic goals** or value judgments are widely, though not universally, accepted in our own society and in many others. These goals may be briefly listed as follows:

1 Economic Growth The production of more and better goods and services, or, more simply stated, a higher standard of living, is desired.

2 Full Employment Suitable jobs should be available for all willing and able to work.

3 Economic Efficiency We want maximum benefits at minimum cost from the limited productive resources available.

4 Price Level Stability Sizable upswings or downswings in the general price level, that is, inflation and deflation, should be avoided.

5 Economic Freedom Business executives, workers, and consumers should enjoy a high degree of freedom in their economic activities.

6 An Equitable Distribution of Income No group of citizens should face stark poverty while others enjoy extreme luxury.

7 Economic Security Provision should be made for those who are chronically ill, disabled, handicapped, laid off, aged, or otherwise unable to earn minimal levels of income.

8 Balance of Trade We seek a reasonable balance in our international trade and financial transactions.

This list of widely accepted goals[3] is the basis for several significant points.

1 Interpretation Note that this or any other statement of basic economic goals inevitably involves problems of interpretation. What are "sizable" changes in the price level? What is a "high degree" of economic freedom? What is an "equitable" distribution of income? Although most of us might accept the above goals as generally stated, we might also disagree substantially on their specific meanings and hence the types of policies needed to attain these goals. Although goals 1 to 4 and 8 are subject to reasonably accurate measurements, the inability to quantify goals 5 to 7 undoubtedly contributes to controversy over their precise meaning.

2 Complementary Certain of these goals are complementary in that when one goal is achieved, some other goal or goals will also be realized. For example, the achieving of full employment (goal 2) means elimi-

nation of unemployment, a basic cause of low incomes (goal 6) and economic insecurity (goal 7). Furthermore, the sociopolitical tensions which may accompany a highly unequal distribution of income (goal 6) are tempered somewhat when most incomes rise absolutely as a result of economic growth (goal 1).

3 Conflicting Some goals may be conflicting or mutually exclusive. For example, goals 1 and 6 may be in conflict. Some economists point out that efforts to achieve greater equality in the distribution of income may weaken incentives to work, invest, innovate, and take business risks, all of which promote rapid economic growth. They argue that government tends to equalize the distribution of income by taxing high-income people heavily and transferring those tax revenues to low-income people. The incentives of a high-income individual will be diminished because taxation reduces one's income rewards. Similarly, a low-income person will be less motivated to work and engage in other productive activities when government stands ready to subsidize that individual.

International example: Before recent events in the Soviet Union, central planning virtually eliminated unemployment with the result that this source of worker insecurity almost disappeared. However, with little fear of losing one's job, Soviet workers were quite cavalier regarding work effort and therefore productivity and efficiency in the Soviet Union were quite low. Here we have a conflict between goal 7, economic security, and goal 1, the growth of worker productivity.

4 Priorities When basic goals do conflict, society is forced to develop a system of priorities for the objectives it seeks. If full employment and price stability are to some extent mutually exclusive, that is, if full employment is accompanied by some inflation *and* price stability entails some unemployment, society must decide upon the relative importance of these two goals. There is clearly ample room for disagreement here.

Formulating Economic Policy The creation of specific policies designed to achieve the broad economic goals of our society is no simple matter. A brief examination of the basic steps in policy formulation is in order.

1 Stating Goals The first step is to make a clear statement of goals. If we say that we want "full employment," do we mean that everyone between, say, 16 and 65 years of age should have a job? Or do we mean that

[3]There are other goals which might be added. For example, improving the physical environment is a widely held goal.

everyone who wants to work should have a job? Should we allow for some "normal" unemployment caused by workers' voluntarily changing jobs?

2 Policy Options Next, we must state and recognize the possible effects of alternative policies designed to achieve the goal. This requires a clear-cut understanding of the economic impact, benefits, costs, and political feasibility of alternative programs. Thus, for example, economists currently debate the relative merits and demerits of fiscal policy (which involves changing government spending and taxes) and monetary policy (which entails altering the supply of money) as alternative means of achieving and maintaining full employment.

3 Evaluation We are obligated to both ourselves and future generations to review our experiences with chosen policies and evaluate their effectiveness; it is only through this type of evaluation that we can hope to improve policy applications. Did a given change in taxes or the supply of money alter the level of employment to the extent originally predicted? Did deregulation of a particular industry (for example, the airlines) yield the predicted beneficial results? If not, why not?

QUICK REVIEW 1-2

∮   *Positive economics deals with factual statements ("what is"), while normative economics concerns value judgments ("what ought to be").*

∮   *Some of society's economic goals are complementary while others are conflicting.*

PITFALLS TO OBJECTIVE THINKING

Our discussion of the economist's procedure has, up to this point, skirted some specific problems and pitfalls which frequently hinder our thinking objectively about economic problems. Consider the following impediments to valid economic reasoning.

Bias

In contrast to a neophyte physicist or chemist, the budding economist ordinarily brings into economics a bundle of biases and preconceptions about the field. For example, one might be suspicious of business profits or feel that deficit spending is invariably evil. Needless to

say, biases may cloud our thinking and interfere with objective analysis. The beginning economics student must be willing to shed biases and preconceptions which are simply not warranted by facts.

Loaded Terminology

The economic terminology to which we are exposed in newspapers and popular magazines is sometimes emotionally loaded. The writer—or more frequently the particular interest group he or she represents—may have a cause to further or an ax to grind, and terms will be slanted to solicit the support of the reader. A governmental flood-control project in the Great Plains region may be called "creeping socialism" by its opponents and "intelligent democratic planning" by its proponents. We must be prepared to discount such terminology to objectively understand important economic issues.

Definitions

No scientist is obligated to use popularized or immediately understandable definitions of his or her terms. The economist may find it convenient and essential to define terms in such a way that they are clearly at odds with the definitions held by most people in everyday speech. So long as the economist is explicit and consistent in these definitions, he or she is on safe ground. For example, the term "investment" to the average citizen is associated with the buying of bonds and stocks in the securities market. How often have we heard someone talk of "investing" in General Motors stock or government bonds? But to the economist, "investment" means the purchase of real capital assets such as machinery and equipment, or the construction of a new factory building, not the purely financial transaction of swapping cash or part of a bank balance for a neatly engraved piece of paper.

Fallacy of Composition

Another pitfall in economic thinking is assuming that "what is true for the individual or part of a group is necessarily also true for the group or whole." This is a logical **fallacy of composition;** it is *not* correct. The validity of a particular generalization for an individual or part does *not* necessarily ensure its accuracy for the group or whole.

A noneconomic example may help: You are watching a football game and the home team executes an outstanding play. In the excitement, you leap to your feet to get a better view. Generalization: "If you, *an individual,* stand, then your view of the game is improved." But does this also hold true for the group—for everyone watching the game? Certainly not! If everyone stands to watch the play, everyone—including you—will probably have the same or even a worse view than when seated.

Consider two examples from economics: A wage increase for Smith is desirable because, given constant product prices, it increases Smith's purchasing power and standard of living. But if everyone realizes a wage increase, product prices may rise, that is, inflation might occur. Therefore, Smith's standard of living may be unchanged as higher prices offset her larger salary.

Second illustration: An *individual* farmer fortunate enough to reap a bumper crop is likely to realize a sharp gain in income. But this generalization does not apply to farmers as a *group*. For the individual farmer, crop prices will not be influenced (reduced) by this bumper crop, because each farmer produces a negligible fraction of the total farm output. But to farmers as a group, prices vary inversely with total output.[4] Thus, as *all* farmers realize bumper crops, the total output of farm products rises, thereby depressing crop prices. If price declines are relatively greater than the increased output, farm incomes will *fall*.

Recalling our earlier distinction between macroeconomics and microeconomics, the fallacy of composition reminds us that *generalizations which are valid at one of these levels of analysis may or may not be valid at the other.*

Cause and Effect: Post Hoc Fallacy

Still another hazard in economic thinking is to assume that simply because one event precedes another, the first is necessarily the cause of the second. This kind of faulty reasoning is known as the **post hoc, ergo propter hoc,** or **after this, therefore because of this, fallacy.**

A classic example clearly indicates the fallacy inherent in such reasoning. Suppose that early each spring the medicine man of a tribe performs his ritual by cavorting around the village in a green costume. A week or so later the trees and grass turn green. Can we safely conclude that event A, the medicine man's gyrations, has caused event B, the landscape's turning

green? Obviously not. The rooster crows before dawn, but this doesn't mean the rooster is responsible for the sunrise!

It is especially important in analyzing various sets of empirical data *not* to confuse **correlation** with **causation.** *Correlation* is a technical term which indicates that two sets of data are associated in some systematic and dependable way. For example, we may find that when X increases, Y also increases. But this does not necessarily mean that X is the cause of Y. The relationship could be purely coincidental or determined by some other factor, Z, not included in the analysis.

Example: Economists have found a positive correlation between education and income. In general, people with more education earn higher incomes than do people with less education. Common sense prompts us to label education as the cause and higher incomes as the effect; more education suggest a more productive worker and such workers receive larger monetary rewards.

But, on second thought, might not causation run the other way? That is, do people with higher incomes buy more education, just as they buy more automobiles and steaks? Or is the relationship explainable in terms of still other factors? Are education and income positively correlated because the bundle of characteristics—ability, motivation, personal habits—required to succeed in education are the same characteristics required to be a productive and highly paid worker? Upon reflection, seemingly simple cause-effect relationships—"more education means more income"—may prove to be suspect or perhaps flatly incorrect.

In short, cause-and-effect relationships are typically not self-evident in economics; the economist must look carefully before concluding that event A caused event B. The fact that A preceded B is not sufficient to warrant any such conclusion.

THE ECONOMIC PERSPECTIVE

The methodology used by economists is common to all the natural and social sciences. Similarly, all scholars try to avoid the reasoning errors just discussed. Hence, economists do *not* think in a special way. But they *do* think about things from a special perspective. Economists have developed a keen alertness to certain aspects of everyday conduct and situations. Specifically, they look for *rationality* or *purposefulness* in human actions and economic institutions. This purposefulness

---

[4]This assumes there are no government programs which fix farm prices.

LAST WORD

FAST-FOOD LINES: AN ECONOMIC PERSPECTIVE

How might the economic perspective help us understand the behavior of fast-food consumers?

When you enter a fast-food restaurant, which line do you select? What do you do when you are in a long line in the restaurant and a new station opens? Have you ever gone to a fast-food restaurant, only to see long lines, and then leave? Have you ever had someone in front of you in a fast-food line place an order which takes a long time to fill?

The economic perspective is useful in analyzing the behavior of fast-food customers. These customers are at the restaurant because they expect the benefit or satisfaction from the food they buy to match or exceed its cost. When customers enter the restaurant they scurry to the *shortest* line, believing that the shortest line will reduce their time cost of obtaining their food. They are acting purposefully; time is limited and most people would prefer using it in some way other than standing in line.

All lines in the fast-food establishment normally are of roughly equal lengths. If one line is temporarily shorter than other lines, some people will move toward that line. These movers apparently view the time saving associated with the shorter line to exceed the cost of moving from their present line. Line changing normally results in an equilibrium line length. No further movement of customers between lines will occur once all lines are of equal length.

Fast-food customers face another cost-benefit decision when a clerk opens a new station at the counter. Should customers move to the new station or stay put? Those who do shift to the new line decide that the benefit of the time savings from the move exceeds the extra cost of physically moving. In so deciding, customers must also consider just how quickly they can get to the new station compared to others who may be contemplating the same move. (Those who hesitate in this situation are lost!)

Customers at the fast-food establishment select lines without having perfect information. For example, they do not first survey those in the lines to determine what they are ordering before deciding on which line to enter. There are two reasons for this. First, most customers would tell them "It is none of your business,"

and therefore no information would be forthcoming. Second, even if they could obtain the information, the amount of time necessary to get it (cost) would most likely exceed any time saving associated with finding the best line (benefit). Because information is costly to obtain, fast-food patrons select lines on the basis of imperfect information. Thus, not all decisions turn out to be as expected. For example, some people may enter a line in which the person in front of them is ordering hamburgers and fries for the forty people in the Greyhound bus parked out back! Nevertheless, at the time the customer made the decision, he or she thought that it was optimal.

Imperfect information also explains why some people who arrive at a fast-food restaurant and observe long lines decide to leave. These people conclude that the total cost (monetary plus time costs) of obtaining the fast food is too large relative to the benefit. They would not have come to the restaurant in the first place had they known the lines were so long. But, getting that information by, say, employing an advance scout with a cellular phone would cost more than the perceived benefit.

Finally, customers must decide what to order when they arrive at the counter. In making these choices they again compare costs and benefits in attempting to obtain the greatest personal well-being.

Economists believe that what is true for the behavior of customers at fast-food restaurants is true for economic behavior in general. Faced with an array of choices, consumers, workers, and businesses rationally compare costs and benefits in making decisions.

implies that people, individually and collectively, make choices by comparing costs and benefits. It therefore might be said that the **economic perspective** is a *cost-benefit perspective.*

Because people make economic choices from a wide array of alternatives, all choices entail sacrifices or costs. To buy a new VCR may mean not being able to afford a new personal computer. Taking a course in economics may preclude taking a course in accounting, political science, or computer science. A decision by government to provide improved health care for the elderly may mean deteriorating health care for children in poverty. Alas, costs are everywhere! Naturally, people are most aware of personal monetary costs—expenses incurred when paying tuition, buying hamburgers, hiring babysitters, renting apartments, or attending concerts. But in Chapter 2 we will see that costs occur in *all* situations in which incomes or resources are scarce relative to wants.

Economic actions of workers, producers, and consumers, of course, also produce personal economic benefits. Workers receive wages, producers garner profits, and consumers obtain satisfaction. People *compare* these benefits with costs in deciding how to spend their time, which products to buy, whether or not to work, or which goods to produce and sell. If the added benefits associated with a given course of action exceed the added costs, then it is rational to take that action. But if added costs are greater than added benefits, that action is not rational and should not be undertaken. Furthermore, when costs or benefits *change,* people *alter* their behavior accordingly.

Economists look carefully at costs and benefits to understand the everyday activities of people and institutions in the economy. This economic perspective will become increasingly evident as you advance through this book. The accompanying Last Word provides an everyday application of the economic perspective.

QUICK REVIEW 1-3

✦ *Beware of logical errors such as the fallacy of composition and the post hoc fallacy when engaging in economic reasoning.*

✦ *The economic perspective is a cost-benefit perspective; it helps us analyze the everyday behavior of individuals and institutions.*

CHAPTER SUMMARY

1 Economics deals with the efficient use of scarce resources in the production of goods and services to satisfy material wants.

2 Economics is studied for several reasons: **a** It provides valuable knowledge about our social environment and behavior; **b** it equips a democratic citizenry to render fundamental decisions intelligently; **c** although not chiefly a vocational discipline, economics may provide the business executive or consumer with valuable information.

3 The tasks of descriptive or empirical economics are **a** gathering those economic facts relevant to a particular problem or specific segment of the economy, and **b** testing hypotheses against facts to validate theories.

4 Generalizations stated by economists are called "principles," "theories," "laws," or "models." The derivation of these principles is the task of economic theory.

5 Induction distills theories from facts; deduction states a hypothesis and then gathers facts to determine whether the hypothesis is valid.

6 Some economic principles deal with macroeconomics (the economy as a whole or major aggregates), while others pertain to microeconomics (specific economic units or institutions).

7 Economic principles are particularly valuable as predictive devices; they are the bases for the formulation of economic policy designed to solve problems and control undesirable events.

8 Positive statements deal with facts ("what is"), while normative statements encompass value judgments ("what ought to be").

9 Economic growth, full employment, economic efficiency, price level stability, economic freedom, equity in the distribution of income, economic security, and reasonable balance in our international trade and finance are all widely accepted economic goals in our society. Some of these goals are complementary; others are mutually exclusive.

10 In studying economics the beginner may encounter numerous pitfalls. Some of the more important are **a** biases and preconceptions, **b** terminological difficulties, **c** the fallacy of composition, and **d** the difficulty of establishing clear cause-effect relationships.

11 The economic perspective envisions individuals and institutions making rational decisions based on costs and benefits.

TERMS AND CONCEPTS

economics	economic theory	hypothesis	*ceteris paribus* or
descriptive or empirical	induction and	principles or	"other things being
economics	deduction	generalizations	equal" assumption

policy economics
macroeconomics and
microeconomics
economic goals

positive and normative
economics
correlation and
causation

post hoc, ergo propter
hoc or "after this,
therefore because of
this" fallacy

fallacy of composition
economic perspective

QUESTIONS AND STUDY SUGGESTIONS

1 Explain in detail the interrelationships between economic facts, theory, and policy. Critically evaluate: "The trouble with economics is that it is not practical. It has too much to say about theory and not enough to say about facts."

2 Analyze and explain the following quotation.[5]

Facts are seldom simple and usually complicated; theoretical analysis is needed to unravel the complications and interpret the facts before we can understand them . . . the opposition of facts and theory is a false one; the true relationship is complementary. We cannot in practice consider a fact without relating it to other facts, and the relation is a theory. Facts by themselves are dumb; before they will tell us anything we have to arrange them, and the arrangement is a theory. Theory is simply the unavoidable arrangement and interpretation of facts, which gives us generalizations on which we can argue and act, in the place of a mass of disjointed particulars.

3 Of what significance is the fact that economics is not a laboratory science? What problems may be involved in deriving and applying economic principles?

4 Explain each of the following statements:
   a "Like all scientific laws, economic laws are established in order to make successful prediction of the outcome of human actions."[6]
   b "Abstraction . . . is the inevitable price of generality . . . indeed abstraction and generality are virtually synonyms."[7]
   c "Numbers serve to discipline rhetoric."[8]

5 Indicate whether each of the following statements pertains to microeconomics or macroeconomics:
   a The unemployment rate in the United States was 6.8 percent in August of 1991.
   b The Alpo dogfood plant in Bowser, Iowa, laid off 15 workers last month.
   c An unexpected freeze in central Florida reduced the citrus crop and caused the price of oranges to rise.

   d Our national output, adjusted for inflation, grew by about 1 percent in 1990.
   e Last week Manhattan Chemical Bank lowered its interest rate on business loans by one-half of 1 percentage point.
   f The consumer price index rose by more than 6 percent in 1990.

6 Identify each of the following as either a positive or a normative statement:
   a The high temperature today was 89 degrees.
   b It was too hot today.
   c The general price level rose by 4.4 percent last year.
   d Inflation eroded living standards last year and should be reduced by government policies.

7 To what extent would you accept the eight economic goals stated and described in this chapter? What priorities would you assign to them? It has been said that we seek simply four goals: progress, stability, justice, and freedom. Is this list of goals compatible with that given in the chapter?

8 Analyze each of the following specific goals in terms of the eight general goals stated on pages 6 and 7, and note points of conflict and compatibility: a the lessening of environmental pollution; b increasing leisure; and c protection of American producers from foreign competition. Indicate which of these specific goals you favor and justify your position.

9 Explain and give an illustration of a the fallacy of composition, and b the "after this, therefore because of this" fallacy. Why are cause-and-effect relationships difficult to isolate in the social sciences?

10 "Economists should never be popular; men who afflict the comfortable serve equally those who comfort the afflicted and one cannot suppose that American capitalism would long prosper without the critics its leaders find such a profound source of annoyance."[9] Interpret and evaluate.

11 Use the economic perspective to explain why someone who normally is a light eater at a standard restaurant may become somewhat of a glutton at a buffet-style restaurant which charges a single price for all you can eat.

[5]Henry Clay, *Economics for the General Reader* (New York: The Macmillan Company, 1925), pp. 10–11.

[6]Oskar Lange, "The Scope and Method of Economics," *Review of Economic Studies,* vol. 13, 1945–1946, p. 20.

[7]George J. Stigler, *The Theory of Price* (New York: The Macmillan Company, 1947), p. 10.

[8]Victor R. Fuchs, *How We Live* (Cambridge, Mass.: Harvard University Press, 1983), p. 5.

[9]John Kenneth Galbraith, *American Capitalism,* rev. ed. (Boston: Houghton Mifflin Company, 1956), p. 49.

Graphs and Their Meaning

If you glance quickly through this text, you will find graphs. Some will appear to be relatively simple, while others seem more formidable. Contrary to student folklore, graphs are *not* designed by economists to confuse students! On the contrary, graphs are employed to help students visualize and understand important economic relationships. Economists express their theories or models with graphs. The physicist and chemist sometimes illustrate their theories by building Tinker-Toy arrangements of multicolored wooden balls representing protons, neutrons, and so forth, held in proper relation to one another by wires or sticks. Economists often use graphs to illustrate their models, and by understanding these "pictures" students can more readily comprehend what economists are saying.

Most of our principles or models will explain the relationship between just two sets of economic facts; therefore, two-dimensional graphs are a convenient way of visualizing and manipulating these relationships.

Constructing a Graph

A graph is a visual representation of the relationship between two variables. Table 1 is a hypothetical illustration showing the relationship between income and con-

sumption. Without ever having studied economics, one would expect intuitively that high-income people would consume more than low-income people. Thus we are not surprised to find in Table 1 that consumption increases as income increases.

How can the information in Table 1 be expressed graphically? Glance at the graph shown in Figure 1. Now look back at the information in Table 1 and we will explain how to represent that information in a meaningful way by constructing the graph you just examined.

What we want to show visually, or graphically, is how consumption changes as income changes. Since income is the determining factor, we represent it on the horizontal axis of the graph, as is customary. And, because consumption depends on income, we represent it on the vertical axis of the graph, as is also customary. Actually, what we are doing is representing the inde-

TABLE 1   The relationship between income and consumption

Income (per week)	Consumption (per week)	Point
$ 0	$ 50	a
100	100	b
200	150	c
300	200	d
400	250	e

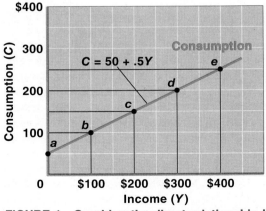

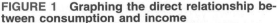

FIGURE 1   Graphing the direct relationship between consumption and income

Two sets of data which are positively or directly related, such as consumption and income, graph as an upsloping line. In this case the vertical intercept is 50 and the slope of the line is $+\frac{1}{2}$.

pendent variable on the horizontal axis and the dependent variable on the vertical axis.

Now we must arrange the vertical and horizontal scales of the graph to reflect the range of values of consumption and income, as well as mark the steps in convenient graphic increments. As you can see, the ranges in the graph cover the ranges of values in Table 1. Similarly, as so happens in this example, the increments on both scales are $100 for approximately each half-inch.

Next, we must locate for each consumption value and the income value that it depends upon a single point which reflects the same information graphically. Our five income–consumption combinations are plotted by drawing perpendiculars from the appropriate points on the **vertical** and **horizontal axes.** For example, in plotting point *c*—the $200 income–$150 consumption point—perpendiculars must be drawn up from the horizontal (income) axis at $200 and across from the vertical (consumption) axis at $150. These perpendiculars intersect at point *c,* which locates this particular income–consumption combination. You should verify that the other income–consumption combinations shown in Table 1 are properly located in Figure 1. By assuming that the same general relationship between income and consumption prevails at all other points between the five points graphed, a line or curve can be drawn to connect these points.

Using Figure 1 as a benchmark, we can now make several additional important comments.

Direct and Inverse Relationships

Our upsloping line depicts a direct relationship between income and consumption. By a positive or **direct relationship** we mean that the two variables—in this case consumption and income—change in the *same* direction. An increase in consumption is associated with an increase in income; conversely, a decrease in consumption accompanies a decrease in income. When two sets of data are positively or directly related, they will always graph as an *upsloping* line as in Figure 1.

In contrast, two sets of data may be inversely related. Consider Table 2, which shows the relationship between the price of basketball tickets and game attendance at Gigantic State University. We observe a negative or **inverse relationship** between ticket prices and attendance; these two variables change in *opposite* directions. When ticket prices decrease, attendance increases. Conversely, when ticket prices increase, atten-

TABLE 2 The relationship between ticket prices and attendance

Ticket price	Attendance (thousands)	Point
$25	0	a
20	4	b
15	8	c
10	12	d
5	16	e
0	20	f

dance decreases. In Figure 2 the six data points of Table 2 are plotted following the same procedure outlined above. Observe that an inverse relationship will always graph as a *downsloping* line.

Dependent and Independent Variables

Although the task is sometimes formidable, economists seek to determine which variable is "cause" and which "effect." Or, more formally, we want to ascertain the independent and the dependent variable. By definition, the **dependent variable** is the "effect" or out-

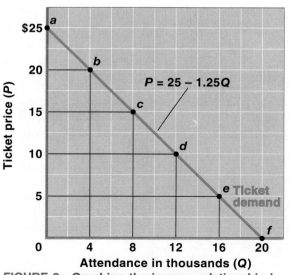

FIGURE 2 Graphing the inverse relationship between ticket prices and game attendance

Two sets of data which are negatively or inversely related, such as ticket price and the attendance at basketball games, graph as a downsloping line. The slope of this line is −1¼.

come; it is the variable which changes because of a change in another (independent) variable.

Similarly, the **independent variable** is the "cause"; it is the variable which causes the change in the dependent variable. As noted earlier in our income–consumption example, generally, income is the independent variable and consumption the dependent variable. Income causes consumption to be what it is rather than the other way around. Similarly, ticket prices determine attendance at GSU basketball games; attendance does not determine ticket prices. Ticket price is the independent variable and the quantity purchased is the dependent variable.

You may recall from your high school courses that mathematicians always put the independent variable (cause) on the horizontal axis and the dependent variable (effect) on the vertical axis. Economists are less tidy; their graphing of independent and dependent variables is more arbitrary. Thus, their conventional graphing of the income–consumption relationship is consistent with mathematical presentation. But economists put price and cost data on the vertical axis. Hence, the economist's graphing of GSU's ticket price–attendance data conflicts with normal mathematical procedure.

Other Variables Held Constant

Our simple two-variable graphs ignore many other factors which might affect the amount of consumption which occurs at each income level or the number of people who attend GSU basketball games at each possible ticket price. When economists plot the relationship between any two variables, they invoke the *ceteris paribus* or "other things being equal" assumption discussed previously. Thus, in Figure 1 all other factors (that is, all factors other than income) which might affect the amount of consumption are presumed to be constant or unchanged. Similarly, in Figure 2 all factors other than ticket price which might influence attendance at GSU basketball games are assumed constant. In reality, we know that "other things" often change, and when they do, the specific relationships presented in our two tables and graphs will change. Specifically, we would expect the lines we have plotted to shift to new locations.

For example, what might happen to the income–consumption relationship if a stock market "crash" such at that of October 1987 occurred? The expected impact of this dramatic fall in the value of stocks would be to make people feel less wealthy and therefore less willing to consume at each income level. In short, we

would anticipate a downward shift of the consumption line in Figure 1. You should plot a new consumption line, assuming that consumption is, say, $20 less at each income level. Note that the relationship remains direct, but the line has merely shifted to reflect less consumer spending at each level of income.

Similarly, factors other than ticket prices might affect GSU game attendance. If the government abandoned its program of student loans, GSU enrollment and hence attendance at games might be less at each ticket price. You should redraw Figure 2, assuming that 2000 fewer students attend GSU games at each ticket price. Question 2 at the end of this appendix introduces other variables which might cause the relationship shown in Figure 2 to shift to another position.

Slope of a Line

Lines can be described in terms of their slopes. The **slope of a straight line** between any two points is defined as the ratio of the vertical change (the rise or fall) to the horizontal change (the run) involved in moving between those points. In moving from point b to point c in Figure 1 the rise or vertical change (the change in consumption) is +$50 and the run or horizontal change (the change in income) is +$100. Therefore:

$$\text{Slope} = \frac{\text{vertical change}}{\text{horizontal change}} = \frac{+50}{+100} = +\frac{1}{2}$$

Note that our slope of $\frac{1}{2}$ is positive because consumption and income change in the same direction, that is, consumption and income are directly or positively related.

This slope of $+\frac{1}{2}$ tells us that there will be a $1 increase in consumption for every $2 increase in income. Similarly, it indicates that for every $2 decrease in income there will be a $1 decrease in consumption.

For our ticket price–attendance data the relationship is negative or inverse with the result that the slope of Figure 2's line is negative. In particular, the vertical change or fall is 5 and the horizontal change or run is 4. Therefore:

$$\text{Slope} = \frac{\text{vertical change}}{\text{horizontal change}} = \frac{-5}{+4} = -1\frac{1}{4}$$

This slope of $-5/+4$ or $-1\frac{1}{4}$ means that lowering the price of a ticket by $5 will increase attendance by 4000 people. Or, alternatively stated, it implies that a $1 price reduction will increase attendance by 800 persons.

In addition to its slope, the only other information needed in locating a line is the vertical intercept. By definition, the **vertical intercept** is the point at which the line meets the vertical axis. For Figure 1 the intercept is $50. This means that, if current income was somehow zero, consumers would still spend $50. How might they manage to consume when they have no current income? Answer: By borrowing or by selling off some of their assets. Similarly, the vertical intercept in Figure 2 shows us that at a $25 ticket price GSU's basketball team would be playing in an empty auditorium.

Given the intercept and the slope, our consumption line can be succinctly described in equation form. In general, a linear equation is written as $y = a + bx$, where y is the dependent variable, a is the vertical intercept, b is the slope of the line, and x is the independent variable. For our income–consumption example, if C represents consumption (the dependent variable) and Y represents income (the independent variable), we can write $C = a + bY$. By substituting the values of the intercept and the slope for our specific data, we have $C = 50 + .5Y$. This equation allows us to determine consumption at *any* level of income. At the $300 income level (point d in Figure 1), our equation predicts that consumption will be $200 [$=$50 + (.5 \times $300)]$. You should confirm that at the $250 income level consumption will be $175.

When economists reverse mathematical convention by putting the independent variable on the vertical axis and the dependent variable on the horizontal axis, the standard linear equation solves for the independent, rather than the dependent, variable. We noted earlier that this case is relevant for our GSU ticket price–attendance data. If P represents the ticket price and Q represents attendance, our relevant equation is $P = 25 - 1.25Q$, where the vertical intercept is 25 and the negative slope is $-1\frac{1}{4}$ or -1.25. But knowing the value for P lets us solve for Q, which is actually our dependent variable. For example, if $P = 15$, then the values in our equation become: $15 = 25 - 1.25(Q)$, or $1.25Q = 10$, or $Q = 8$. You should check this answer against Figure 2 and also use this equation to predict GSU ticket sales when price is $7.50.

Slope of a Nonlinear Curve

We now move from the simple world of linear relationships (straight lines) to the slightly more complex world of nonlinear relationships (curves). By definition, the slope of a straight line is constant throughout. In contrast, the slope of a curve changes as we move from one point to another on the curve. For example, consider the upsloping curve AA in Figure 3a. Although its slope is positive throughout, it diminishes or flattens as we move northeast along the curve. Given

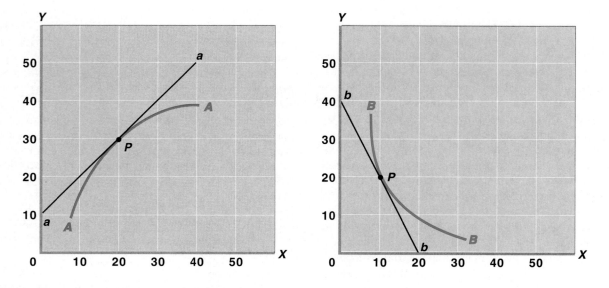

FIGURE 3 Determining the slopes of curves

The slope of a nonlinear curve changes as one moves from point to point on the curve. The slope at any point can be determined by drawing a straight line tangent to that point and calculating the slope of that straight line.

that the slope is constantly changing, we can only measure the slope at some particular point on the curve.

We begin by drawing a straight line which is tangent to the curve at that point where we want to measure its slope. By definition, a line is **tangent** at that point where it touches, but does not intersect, the curve. Thus, line *aa* is tangent to curve *AA* at point *P* in Figure 3a. Having done this, we can measure the slope of *AA* at point *P* by measuring the slope of the straight tangent line *aa*. Specifically, in Figure 3a, when the vertical change (rise) in *aa* is +10, the horizontal

change (run) is also +10. Thus, the slope of the tangent *aa* line is 10/10 or +1 and therefore the slope of *AA* at *P* is also +1.

Now consider the downsloping curve *BB* in Figure 3b. In this case the slope of *BB* is negative and it diminishes as we move southeast along the curve. What is the slope at point *P*? Again, we draw line *bb* which is tangent to curve *BB* at *P*. Here, when the vertical change (fall) in *bb* is −10, the horizontal change is only +5. Thus, the slope of *BB* at point *P* is −10/+5 or −2. Question 6 at the end of this appendix is relevant.

APPENDIX SUMMARY

1 Graphs are a convenient and revealing means of presenting economic relationships or principles.

2 Two variables are positively or directly related when their values change in the same direction. Two variables which are directly related will plot as an upsloping line on a graph.

3 Two variables are negatively or inversely related when their values change in opposite directions. Two variables which are inversely related will graph as a downsloping line.

4 The value of the dependent variable ("effect") is determined by the value of the independent variable ("cause").

5 When "other factors" which might affect a two-variable

relationship are allowed to change, the plotted relationship will likely shift to a new location.

6 The slope of a straight line is the ratio of the vertical change to the horizontal change in moving between any two points. The slope of an upsloping line is positive, while that of a downsloping line is negative.

7 The vertical (or horizontal) intercept and the slope of a line establish its location and are used in expressing the relationship between two variables as an equation.

8 The slope of a curve at any point is determined by calculating the slope of a straight line drawn tangent to that point.

APPENDIX TERMS AND CONCEPTS

vertical and horizontal
  axes
slope of a straight line

dependent and
  independent
  variables

vertical intercept
tangent

direct and inverse
  relationships

APPENDIX QUESTIONS AND STUDY SUGGESTIONS

🖫 *1 Briefly explain the use of graphs as a means of presenting economic principles. What is an inverse relationship? How does it graph? What is a direct relationship? How does it graph? Graph and explain the relationships one would expect to find between a the number of inches of rainfall per month and the sale of umbrellas, b the amount of tuition and the

level of enrollment at a university, and c the size of a university's athletic scholarships and the number of games won by its football team.

In each case cite and explain how considerations other than those specifically mentioned might upset the expected relationship. Is your second generalization consistent with the fact that, historically, enrollments and tuition have both increased? If not, explain any difference.

🖫 2 Indicate how each of the following might affect the data shown in Table 2 and Figure 2 of this appendix:

  a GSU's athletic director schedules higher-quality opponents.

  b GSU's Fighting Aardvarks experience three losing seasons.

  c GSU contracts to have all its home games televised.

*Note to the reader: A floppy disk symbol 🖫 precedes each of the questions in this appendix. This icon is used throughout the text to indicate that a particular question relates to the content of one of the tutorial programs in the student software which accompanies this book. Please refer to the Preface for more detail about this software.

3 The following table contains data on the relationship between saving and income. Rearrange these data as required and graph the data on the accompanying grid. What is the slope of the line? The vertical intercept? Interpret the meaning of both the slope and the intercept. Write the equation which represents this line. What would you predict saving to be at the $12,500 level of income?

Income (per year)	Saving (per year)
$15,000	$1,000
0	−500
10,000	500
5,000	0
20,000	1,500

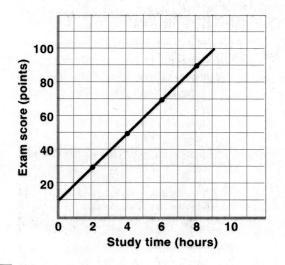

4 Construct a table from the data shown on the accompanying graph. Which is the dependent and which the independent variable? Summarize the data in equation form.

5 Suppose that when the interest rate which must be paid to borrow funds is 16 percent, businesses find it unprofitable to invest in machinery and equipment. However, when the interest rate is 14 percent, $5 billion worth of investment is profitable. At 12 percent, a total of $10 billion of investment is profitable. Similarly, total investment increases by $5 billion for each successive 2 percentage point decline in the interest rate. Indicate the relevant relationship between the interest rate and investment verbally, tabularly, graphically, and as an equation. Put the interest rate on the vertical axis and investment on the horizontal axis. In your equation use the form $i = a - bI$, where i is the interest rate, a is the vertical intercept, b is the slope of the line, and I is the level of investment. Comment on advantages and disadvantages of verbal, tabular, graphical, and equation forms of presentation.

6 The accompanying diagram shows curve XX and three tangents at points A, B, and C. Calculate the slope of the curve at these three points.

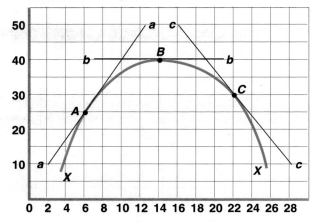

7 In the accompanying diagram, is the slope of curve AA' positive or negative? Does the slope increase or decrease as we move from A to A'? Answer the same two questions for curve BB'.

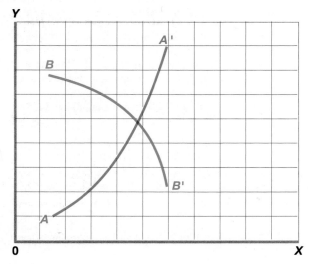

CHAPTER 2

The Economizing Problem

You make decisions every day which capture the essence of economics. Suppose you have $20 and are deciding how to spend it. Should you buy a new pair of blue jeans? A couple of compact discs? A ticket for a rock concert? Similarly, what to do with the time between three and six o'clock on, say, a Thursday afternoon? Should you work extra hours on your part-time job? Do research on a term project? Prepare for an economics quiz? Watch TV? Take a nap? Money and time are both scarce and making decisions in the context of scarcity implies costs. If you choose the jeans, the cost is the forgone CDs or concert. If you nap or watch TV, the cost might be a low grade on your quiz. Scarcity, choices, and costs—these are the building blocks of the present chapter.

This chapter introduces and explores certain fundamental considerations which constitute the foundation of economic science. Basically, we expand on the definition of economics introduced in Chapter 1 and explore the essence of the economizing problem. To this end, we will illustrate, extend, and modify our definition of economics by using so-called production possibilities tables and curves. Finally, we will survey briefly different ways in which institutionally and ideologically diverse economies "solve" or respond to the economizing problem.

THE FOUNDATION OF ECONOMICS

Two fundamental facts which constitute the **economizing problem** provide a foundation for the field of economics. We must carefully state and fully understand these two facts, because everything that follows in our study of economics depends directly or indirectly upon them.

1 *Society's material wants, that is, the material wants of its citizens and institutions, are virtually unlimited or insatiable.*
2 *Economic resources—the means of producing goods and services—are limited or scarce.*

Unlimited Wants

In the first statement, precisely what is meant by "material wants"? We mean, first, the desires of consumers to

19

obtain and use various *goods* and *services* which provide **utility,** the economist's term for pleasure or satisfaction.[1] An amazingly wide range of products fills the bill in this respect: houses, automobiles, toothpaste, compact-disc players, pizzas, sweaters, and the like. In short, innumerable products which we sometimes classify as *necessities* (food, shelter, clothing) and *luxuries* (perfumes, yachts, mink coats) all can satisfy human wants. Needless to say, what is a luxury to Smith may be a necessity to Jones, and what is a commonplace necessity today may have been a luxury a few years ago.

But services satisfy our wants as much as tangible products. A repair job on our car, the removal of our appendix, a haircut, and legal advice have in common with goods the fact that they satisfy human wants. On reflection, we realize that we indeed buy many goods, for example, automobiles and washing machines, for the services they render. The differences between goods and services are often less than they seem to be at first.

Material wants also include those which businesses and units of government seek to satisfy. Businesses want factory buildings, machinery, trucks, warehouses, communications systems, and other things that help them realize their production goals. Government, reflecting the collective wants of its citizenry or goals of its own, seeks highways, schools, hospitals, and military hardware.

As a group, these material wants are, for practical purposes, *insatiable,* or *unlimited,* meaning that material wants for goods and services cannot be completely satisfied. Our wants for a *particular* good or service can be satisfied; that is, over a short period of time we can get enough toothpaste or beer. Certainly one appendicitis operation is par for the course. But goods *in general* are another story. Here we do not, and presumably cannot, get enough. A simple experiment will help verify this point: Suppose we are asked to list those goods and services we want but do not now possess. If we ponder our unfilled material wants, chances are our list will be impressive.

Furthermore, over a period of time, wants multiply so that, as we fill some of the wants on the list, we add new ones. Material wants, like rabbits, have a high reproduction rate. The rapid introduction of new products whets our appetites, and extensive advertising

tries to persuade us that we need items we might not otherwise consider buying. Not long ago, the desire for personal computers, light beer, video recorders, fax machines, and compact discs was nonexistent. Furthermore, we often cannot stop with simple satisfaction: The acquisition of an Escort or Geo has been known to whet the appetite for a Porsche or Mercedes.

At any given time the individuals and institutions which constitute society have innumerable unfulfilled material wants. Some—food, clothing, shelter—have biological roots. But some are also influenced by the conventions and customs of society: The specific kinds of food, clothing, and shelter we seek are frequently determined by the general social and cultural environment in which we live. Over time, wants change and multiply, fueled by development of new products and extensive advertising and sales promotion.

Again, let us stress that the overall objective of all economic activity is the attempt to satisfy these diverse material wants.

Scarce Resources

In considering the second fundamental fact, *economic resources are limited or scarce,* what do we mean by "economic resources"? In general, we mean all natural, human, and manufactured resources that go into the production of goods and services. This covers a lot of ground: factory and farm buildings and all equipment, tools, and machinery used to produce manufactured goods and agricultural products; a variety of transportation and communication facilities; innumerable types of labor; and land and mineral resources of all kinds. Economists broadly classify such resources as either (1) *property* resources—land or raw materials and capital; or (2) *human* resources—labor and entrepreneurial ability.

Resource Categories   Let's examine these various resource categories.

Land   By **land** the economist means much more than do most people. Land is all natural resources—all "gifts of nature"—usable in the productive process. Such resources as arable land, forests, mineral and oil deposits, and water resources come under this classification.

Capital   **Capital,** or investment goods, is all manufactured aids to production, that is, all tools, machinery,

---

[1]This definition leaves a variety of wants—recognition, status, love, and so forth—for the other social sciences to worry about.

equipment, and factory, storage, transportation, and distribution facilities used in producing goods and services and getting them to the ultimate consumer. The process of producing and purchasing capital goods is known as **investment.**

Two other points are pertinent. First, *capital goods* ("tools") differ from *consumer goods* in that the latter satisfy wants directly, whereas the former do so indirectly by facilitating production of consumable goods. Second, the term "capital" as here defined does *not* refer to money. True, business executives and economists often talk of "money capital," meaning money available to purchase machinery, equipment, and other productive facilities. But money, as such, produces nothing; hence, it is not considered an economic resource. *Real capital*—tools, machinery, and other productive equipment—is an economic resource; *money* or *financial capital* is not.

Labor   **Labor** is a broad term the economist uses for all the physical and mental talents of men and women which are available and usable in producing goods and services. (This excludes a special set of human talents—entrepreneurial ability—which, because of their special significance in a capitalistic economy, we will consider separately.) Thus the services of a logger, retail clerk, machinist, teacher, professional football player, and nuclear physicist all fall under the general heading of labor.

Entrepreneurial Ability   Finally, there is the special human resource which we label **entrepreneurial ability,** or, more simply, *enterprise.* We can assign four related functions to the entrepreneur.

1   The entrepreneur takes the initiative in combining the resources of land, capital, and labor to produce a good or service. Both a sparkplug and a catalyst, the entrepreneur is at once the driving force behind production and the agent who combines the other resources in what is hoped will be a profitable venture.

2   The entrepreneur makes basic business-policy decisions, that is, those nonroutine decisions which set the course of a business enterprise.

3   The entrepreneur is an innovator—the one who attempts to introduce on a commercial basis new products, new productive techniques, or even new forms of business organization.

4   The entrepreneur is a risk bearer. This is apparent from a close examination of the other three entrepreneurial functions. The entrepreneur in a capitalistic system has no guarantee of profit. The reward for his or her time, efforts, and abilities may be attractive profits *or* losses and eventual bankruptcy. In short, the entrepreneur risks not only time, effort, and business reputation, but his or her invested funds and those of associates or stockholders.

Resource Payments   We will see shortly how these resources are provided to business institutions in exchange for money income. The income received from supplying property resources—raw materials and capital equipment—is called *rental* and *interest income,* respectively. The income accruing to those who supply labor is called *wages* and includes salaries and various wage and salary supplements in the form of bonuses, commissions, royalties, and so forth. Entrepreneurial income is called *profits,* which, of course, may be a negative figure—that is, losses.

These four broad categories of economic resources, or *factors of production* or *inputs* as they are often called, leave room for debate when it comes to classifying specific resources. For example, suppose you receive a dividend on some newly issued Exxon stock which you own. Is this an interest return for the capital equipment the company bought with the money you provided in buying Exxon stock? Or is this return a profit which compensates you for the risks involved in purchasing corporate stock? What about the earnings of a one-person general store where the owner is both entrepreneur and labor force? Are the owner's earnings considered wages or profit income? The answer to both queries is "some of each." The point is that while we might quibble about classifying a given flow of income as wages, rent, interest, or profits, all income can be fitted under one of these general headings.

Relative Scarcity   Economic resources, or factors of production, have one fundamental characteristic in common: *They are scarce or limited in supply.* Our "spaceship earth" contains only limited amounts of resources to use in producing goods and services. Quantities of arable land, mineral deposits, capital equipment, and labor (time) are all limited; that is, they are available only in finite amounts. Because of the scarcity of productive resources and the constraint this scarcity puts on productive activity, output will necessarily be limited. Society will *not* be able to produce and consume all the goods and services it might want. Thus, in the United States—one of the most affluent nations— output per person was limited to $22,419 in 1991. In the poorest nations annual output per person is as low as $200 or $300!

ECONOMICS AND EFFICIENCY

We have arrived once again at the basic definition of economics first stated at the beginning of Chapter 1. *Economics is the social science concerned with the problem of using or administering scarce resources (the means of producing) to attain the greatest or maximum fulfillment of society's unlimited wants (the goal of producing).* Economics is concerned with "doing the best with what we have." If our wants are virtually unlimited and our resources scarce, we cannot satisfy all of society's material wants. The next best thing is to achieve the greatest possible satisfaction of these wants.

Full Employment and Full Production

Economics is a science of efficiency—efficiency in the use of scarce resources. Society wants to use its limited resources efficiently; that is, it wants to get the maximum amount of useful goods and services produced with its available resources. To achieve this it must realize both full employment and full production.

Full Employment　By **full employment** we mean that all available resources should be employed. No workers should be involuntarily out of work; the economy should provide employment for all who are willing and able to work. Nor should capital equipment or arable land sit idle. Note we say all *available* resources should be employed. Each society has certain customs and practices which determine what particular resources are available for employment. For example, legislation and custom provide that children and the very aged should not be employed. Similarly, it is desirable for productivity to allow farmland to lie fallow periodically.

Full Production　But the employment of all available resources is insufficient to achieve efficiency. Full production must also be realized. By **full production** we mean that all employed resources should be used to make the most valued contributions to the domestic output. If we fail to realize full production, economists say that our resources are *underemployed*.

Full production implies that two kinds of efficiency—allocative and productive efficiency—are achieved.

Allocative efficiency means that resources are devoted to goods most wanted by society; for example, compact discs and cassettes, rather than 45 rpm or long-play records. Society wants resources apportioned to word processors, not mechanical typewriters, and to xerox, not mimeograph, machines. Nor do we want Iowa's farmland planted to cotton and Alabama's to corn when the opposite assignment would provide the nation with substantially more of both products from the same amount of land.

Productive efficiency means that the least costly production techniques are used to produce wanted goods and services. Efficiency requires that Tauruses and Grand Ams be produced with computerized and roboticized assembly techniques rather than with the primitive assembly lines of the 1920s. Nor do we want our farmers harvesting wheat with scythes or picking corn by hand when elaborate harvesting equipment will do the job at a much lower cost per bushel.

In summary, allocative efficiency means that resources are apportioned among firms and industries to obtain the particular mix of products society wants the most. Productive efficiency means that each good or service in this optimal product mix is produced in the least costly fashion. Full production means producing the "right" goods (allocative efficiency) in the "right" way (productive efficiency).

QUICK REVIEW 2-1

◆　*Human material wants are virtually unlimited.*

◆　*Economic resources—land, capital, labor, and entrepreneurial ability—are scarce or limited.*

◆　*Economics is concerned with the efficient management of these scarce resources to achieve the maximum fulfillment of our material wants.*

◆　*Economic efficiency entails full employment and full production.*

Production Possibilities Table

The nature of the economizing problem can be clarified by the use of a production possibilities table. This device reveals the core of the economizing problem: *Because resources are scarce, a full-employment, full-production economy cannot have an unlimited output of goods and services. As a result, choices must be made on which goods and services to produce and which to forgo.*

Assumptions　Several specific assumptions will set the stage for our illustration.

1 Efficiency The economy is operating at full employment and achieving full production.

2 Fixed Resources The available supplies of the factors of production are fixed in both quantity and quality. But, of course, they can be shifted or reallocated, within limits, among different uses; for example, a relatively unskilled laborer can work on a farm, at a fast-food restaurant, or in a gas station.

3 Fixed Technology The state of the technological arts is constant; that is, technology does not change during the course of our analysis. The second and third assumptions are another way of saying that we are looking at our economy at a specific point in time, or over a very short period of time. Over a relatively long period it would be unrealistic to rule out technological advances and the possibility that resource supplies might vary.

4 Two Products To simplify our illustration further, suppose our economy is producing just two products—industrial robots and pizza—instead of the innumerable goods and services actually produced. Pizza is symbolic of **consumer goods,** those goods which directly satisfy our wants; industrial robots are symbolic of **capital goods,** those goods which satisfy our wants *indirectly* by permitting more efficient production of consumer goods.

Necessity of Choice It is evident from our assumptions that a choice must be made among alternatives. Available resources are limited. Consequently, the total amounts of robots and pizza that our economy can produce are limited. *Limited resources mean a limited output.* Since resources are limited in supply and fully employed, any increase in the production of robots will mean shifting resources away from the production of pizza. And the reverse holds true: If we step up the production of pizza, needed resources must come at the expense of robot production. *Society cannot have its cake and eat it, too.* Facetiously put, there's no such thing as a "free lunch." This is the essence of the economizing problem.

Let's generalize by noting in Table 2-1 alternative combinations of robots and pizza which our economy might choose. Though the data in this and the following **production possibilities tables** are hypothetical, the points illustrated have tremendous practical significance. At alternative A, our economy would be devoting all its resources to the production of robots (capital

TABLE 2-1 **Production possibilities of pizza and robots with full employment, 1993** *(hypothetical data)*

Type of product	Production alternatives				
	A	B	C	D	E
Pizza (in hundred thousands)	0	1	2	3	4
Robots (in thousands)	10	9	7	4	0

goods). At alternative E, all available resources would go to pizza production (consumer goods). Both these alternatives are clearly unrealistic extremes; any economy typically strikes a balance in dividing its total output between capital and consumer goods. As we move from alternative A to E, we step up the production of consumer goods (pizza), by shifting resources away from capital goods (robot) production.

Remembering that consumer goods directly satisfy our wants, any movement toward alternative E looks tempting. In making this move, society increases the current satisfaction of its wants; but there is a cost involved. This shift of resources catches up with society over time as its stock of capital goods dwindles—or at least ceases to expand at the current rate—with the result that the potential for greater future production is impaired. In short, in moving from alternative A toward E, society chooses "more now" at the expense of "much more later."

In moving from E toward A, society chooses to forgo current consumption. This sacrifice of current consumption frees resources which can now be used to increase production of capital goods. By building up its stock of capital in this way, society can anticipate greater production and, therefore, greater consumption in the future.

At any point in time, a full-employment, full-production economy must sacrifice some of product X to obtain more of product Y. The basic fact that economic resources are scarce prohibits such an economy from having more of both X and Y.

Production Possibilities Curve

To ensure our understanding of the production possibilities table, let's view these data graphically. We employ a simple two-dimensional graph, arbitrarily putting the output of robots (capital goods) on the vertical

KEY GRAPH

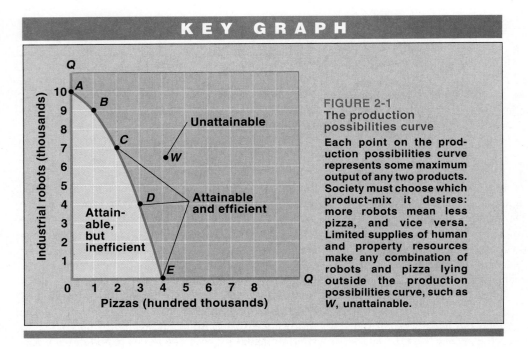

FIGURE 2-1
The production possibilities curve

Each point on the production possibilities curve represents some maximum output of any two products. Society must choose which product-mix it desires: more robots mean less pizza, and vice versa. Limited supplies of human and property resources make any combination of robots and pizza lying outside the production possibilities curve, such as *W*, unattainable.

axis and the output of pizza (consumer goods) on the horizontal axis, as in Figure 2-1 (Key Graph). Following the plotting procedure discussed in the appendix to Chapter 1, we can locate the "production possibilities" curve, as shown in Figure 2-1.

Each point on the production possibilities curve represents some maximum output of the two products. Thus the curve is, in effect, a frontier. To realize the various combinations of pizza and robots which fall on the production possibilities curve, society must achieve full employment and full production. All combinations of pizza and robots *on* the curve represent maximum quantities attainable only as the result of the most efficient use of all available resources. Points lying *inside* the curve are also attainable, but are not as desirable as points on the curve. These points imply a failure to achieve full employment and full production. Points lying *outside* the production possibilities curve, like point *W*, would be superior to any point on the curve; but such points are unattainable, given the current supplies of resources and technology. The production barrier of limited resources prohibits production of any combination of capital and consumer goods lying outside the production possibilities curve.

Optimal Product-Mix

If all outputs on the production possibilities curve reflect full employment and full production, which combination will society prefer? Consider, for example, points *C* and *D* in Figure 2-1. Which output-mix is superior or "best"? This is a nonscientific or normative matter; it reflects the values of society as expressed by its control group—the dictatorship, the party, the electorate, the citizenry, the individual institutions, or some combination thereof. What the economist can say is this: If a society's production possibilities are as in Table 2-1 *and* if that society seeks the product-mix indicated by, say, alternative *C*, it is *not* using its resources efficiently if it realizes a total output composed only of 6 units of robots and 1 unit of pizza. And the economist can also say that the society cannot hope to achieve a domestic output of 8 units of robots and 3 units of pizza with its available resources. These are quantitative, objective, positive statements. But, although the economist may have opinions as an individual, as a social scientist he or she cannot say that combination *C* is "better" or "worse" than combination *D*. This is a qualitative or normative matter.

Law of Increasing Opportunity Costs

We have stressed that resources are scarce relative to the virtually unlimited wants which these resources can be used to satisfy. As a result, choices among alternatives must be made. Specifically, more of X (pizza) means less of Y (robots). *The amount of other products which must be forgone or sacrificed to obtain some amount of any given product is called the opportunity cost of that good.* In our case the amount of Y (robots) which must be forgone or given up to get another unit of X (pizza) is the *opportunity cost,* or simply the *cost,* of that unit of X.

In moving from possibility A to B in Table 2-1, we find that the cost of 1 unit of pizza is 1 unit of robots. But, as we now pursue the concept of cost through the additional production possibilities—B to C, C to D, and so forth—an important economic principle is revealed. In shifting from alternative A to alternative E, the sacrifice or cost of robots involved in getting each additional unit of pizza *increases.* In moving from A to B, just 1 unit of robots is sacrificed for 1 more unit of pizza; but going from B to C sacrifices 2 units of robots for 1 more unit of pizza; then 3 of robots for 1 of pizza; and finally 4 for 1. Conversely, you should confirm that in moving from E to A the cost of an additional robot is $\frac{1}{4}, \frac{1}{3}, \frac{1}{2}$, and 1 unit of pizza respectively for each of the four shifts.

Note that this discussion of opportunity cost is couched in terms of an *added* or *marginal* unit of a good rather than *total,* or cumulative, opportunity cost. For example, the opportunity cost of the third unit of pizza in Table 2-1 is 3 units of robots ($=7-4$). But the total opportunity cost of 3 units of pizza is 6 units of robots ($=10-4$ or $1+2+3$).

Concavity Graphically, the **law of increasing opportunity costs** is reflected in the shape of the production possibilities curve. Specifically, the curve is *concave* or bowed out from the origin. As verified by the white lines in Figure 2-1, when the economy moves from *A* toward *E*, it must give up successively larger amounts of robots (1, 2, 3, 4) as shown on the vertical axis to acquire equal increments of pizza (1, 1, 1, 1) as shown on the horizontal axis. This means that the slope of the production possibilities curve becomes steeper as we move from *A* to *E* and such a curve, by definition, is concave as viewed from the origin.

Rationale What is the economic rationale for the law of increasing opportunity costs? *Why* does the sacrifice of robots increase as we get more pizza? The answer is rather complex, but, simply stated, it amounts to this: *Economic resources are not completely adaptable to alternative uses.* As we step up pizza production, resources which are less and less adaptable to this use must be induced, or "pushed," into this line of production. If we start at *A* and move to *B*, we can first pick resources whose productivity of pizza is greatest in relation to their productivity of robots. But as we move from *B* to *C*, *C* to *D*, and so on, resources highly productive of pizza become increasingly scarce. To get more pizza, resources whose productivity in robots is great in relation to their productivity in pizza will be needed. It will take more and more of such resources—and hence a greater sacrifice of robots—to achieve a given increase of 1 unit in the production of pizza. This lack of perfect flexibility, or interchangeability, on the part of resources and the resulting increase in the sacrifice of one good that must be made in acquiring of more and more units of another good is the rationale for the law of increasing opportunity costs. In this case, these costs are stated as sacrifices of goods and not in terms of dollars and cents.

QUICK REVIEW 2-2

The production possibilities curve illustrates four basic concepts:

✦ *The* scarcity *of resources is implicit in that all combinations of output lying outside the production possibilities curve are unattainable.*

✦ *Choice is reflected in the need for society to select among the various attainable combinations of goods lying on the curve.*

✦ *The downward slope of the curve implies the notion of opportunity cost.*

✦ *The concavity of the curve reveals increasing opportunity costs.*

UNEMPLOYMENT, GROWTH, AND THE FUTURE

It is important to understand what happens when the first three assumptions underlying the production possibilities curve are released.

Unemployment and Underemployment

The first assumption was that our economy is characterized by full employment and full production. How would our analysis and conclusions be altered if idle resources were available (unemployment) or if employed resources were used inefficiently (underemployment)? With full employment and full production, our five alternatives represent a series of maximum outputs; they illustrate combinations of robots and pizzas which might be produced when the economy is operating at full capacity. With *un*employment or *under*employment, the economy would produce less than each alternative shown in Table 2-1.

Graphically, a situation of unemployment or underemployment can be illustrated by a point *inside* the original production possibilities curve, which has been reproduced in Figure 2-2. Point *U* is such a point. Here the economy is falling short of the various maximum combinations of pizza and robots reflected by all the points *on* the production possibilities curve. The arrows in Figure 2-2 indicate three of the possible paths back to full employment and full production. A move

toward full employment and full production will entail a greater output of one or both products.

A Growing Economy

When we drop the remaining assumptions that the quantity and quality of resources and technology are fixed, the production possibilities curve will shift position; that is, the potential total output of the economy will change.

Expanding Resource Supplies Let's now abandon the simplifying assumption that our total supplies of land, labor, capital, and entrepreneurial ability are fixed in both quantity and quality. Common sense tells us that over time a nation's growing population will bring about increases in supplies of labor and entrepreneurial ability.[2] Also, labor quality usually improves over time. For example, the percentage of the labor force with a high school education rose from 30 percent in 1960 to 40 percent in 1989. Historically, our stock of capital has increased at a significant, though unsteady, rate. And although we are depleting some of our energy and mineral resources, new sources are being discovered. The drainage of swamps and the development of irrigation programs add to our supply of arable land.

Assuming continuous full employment and full production, the net result of these increased supplies of the factors of production will be the ability to produce more of both robots and pizza. Thus, in the year 2013, the production possibilities of Table 2-1 for 1993 may be obsolete, having given way to those shown in Table 2-2. Observe that the greater abundance of resources results in a greater potential output of one or both products at each alternative; economic growth, in the sense of an expanded potential output, has occurred.

But note that such a favorable shift in the production possibilities curve does not guarantee that the economy will actually operate at a point on that new curve. The economy might fail to realize fully its new potentialities. Some 125 million jobs will give us full employment now, but ten or twenty years from now our labor force, because of a growing population, will be larger, and 125 million jobs will not be sufficient for

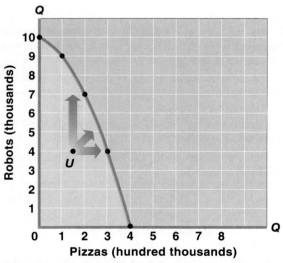

FIGURE 2-2 Unemployment and the production possibilities curve

Any point inside the production possibilities curve, such as *U*, indicates unemployment or underemployment. By moving toward full employment and full production, the economy can produce more of either or both of the two products, as the arrows indicate.

[2]This does not mean that population growth as such is always desirable. In Chapter 22 we will discover that overpopulation can be a constant drag on the living standards of many less developed countries. In advanced countries overpopulation can have adverse effects on the environment and the quality of life.

TABLE 2-2 **Production possibilities of pizza and robots with full employment, 2013** *(hypothetical data)*

Type of product	Production alternatives				
	A'	B'	C'	D'	E'
Pizza (in hundred thousands)	0	2	4	6	8
Robots (in thousands)	14	12	9	5	0

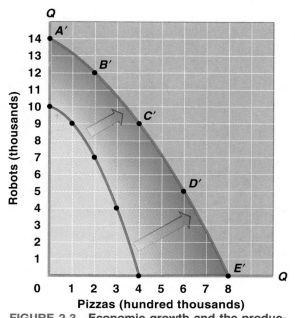

FIGURE 2-3 Economic growth and the production possibilities curve

The expanding resource supplies, improved resource quality, and technological advances which characterize a growing economy move the production possibilities curve outward and to the right. This permits the economy to enjoy larger quantities of both types of goods.

full employment. In short, the production possibilities curve may shift, but the economy may fail to produce at a point on that new curve.

Technological Advance Our other simplifying assumption is a constant or unchanging technology. We know that technology has progressed remarkably over a long period. An advancing technology entails new and better goods *and* improved ways of producing these goods. For now, let's think of technological advance as comprising merely improvements in capital facilities—more efficient machinery and equipment. Such technological advance alters our earlier discussion of the economizing problem by improving productive efficiency, thus allowing society to produce more goods with fixed resources. As with increases in resource supplies, technological advance permits the production of more robots *and* more pizza.

When the supplies of resources increase or an improvement in technology occurs, the production possibilities curve of Figure 2-2 shifts outward and to the right, as illustrated by the *A'B'C'D'E'* curve in Figure 2-3. **Economic growth**—*the ability to produce a larger total output—is reflected in a rightward shift of the production possibilities curve; it is the result of increases in resource supplies, improvements in resource quality, and technological progress.* The consequence of growth is that our full-employment economy can enjoy a greater output of *both* robots and pizza. While a static, no-growth economy must sacrifice some of X to get more Y, a dynamic, growing economy can have larger quantities of both X and Y.

Economic growth does *not* typically mean proportionate increases in a nation's capacity to produce various products. Note in Figure 2-3 that, while the economy can produce twice as much pizza, the increase in robot production is only 40 percent. On Figure 2-3 you should pencil in two new production possibilities curves: one to show the situation where a better tech-

nique for producing robots has been developed, the technology for producing pizza being unchanged, and the other to illustrate an improved technology for pizza, the technology for producing robots being constant.

Present Choices and Future Possibilities An economy's current choice of position on its production possibilities curve is a basic determinant of the future location of that curve. Let's designate the two axes of the production possibilities curve as "goods for the future" and "goods for the present," as in Figures 2-4a and b. "Goods for the future" are such things as capital goods, research and education, and preventive medicine, which increase the quantity and quality of property resources, enlarge the stock of technological information, and improve the quality of human resources. As we have already seen, "goods for the future" are the ingredients of economic growth. "Goods for the present" are pure consumer goods such as foodstuffs, clothing, "boom boxes," and automobiles.

Now suppose there are two economies, Alphania and Betania, which are identical in every respect ex-

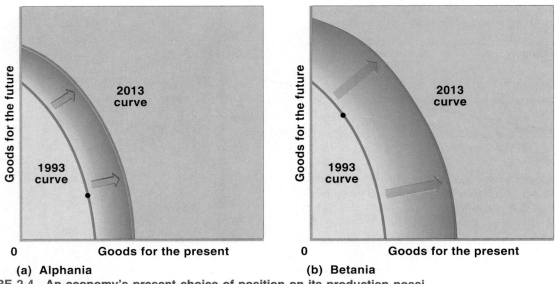

FIGURE 2-4 An economy's present choice of position on its production possibilities curve helps determine the curve's future location

A current choice favoring "present goods," as rendered by Alphania in (a), will cause a modest rightward shift of the curve. A current choice favoring "future goods," as rendered by Betania in (b), will result in a greater rightward shift of the curve.

cept that Alphania's current (1993) choice of position on its production possibilities curve strongly favors "present goods" as opposed to "future goods." The dot in Figure 2-4a indicates this choice. Betania, on the other hand, makes a current (1993) choice which stresses large amounts of "future goods" and lesser amounts of "present goods" (Figure 2-4b).

Now, all other things being the same, we can expect the future (2013) production possibilities curve of Betania to be farther to the right than that of Alphania. That is, by currently choosing an output more conducive to technological advance and to increases in the quantity and quality of property and human resources, Betania will tend to achieve greater economic growth than Alphania, whose current choice of output places less emphasis on those goods and services which cause the production possibilities curve to shift rightward. In terms of capital goods, Betania is choosing to make larger current additions to its "national factory"— that is, to invest more of its current output—than Alphania. The payoff or benefit from this choice is more rapid growth—greater future productive capacity—for Betania. The opportunity cost is fewer consumer goods in the present.

Real-World Applications

There are many possible applications of the production possibilities curve.

1 Microeconomic Budgeting   While our discussion is in macroeconomic terms—that is, in terms of the output of the entire economy—the concepts of scarcity, choice, and opportunity cost also apply at the microeconomic level. You should reread the first paragraph of this chapter at this point.

2 Going to War In beginning to produce war goods for World War II (1939–1945), the United States found itself with considerable unemployment. Our economy was able to produce an almost unbelievably large quantity of war goods and at the same time increase the output of consumer goods (Figure 2-2). The Soviet Union, on the other hand, entered World War II at almost capacity production; that is, the Soviet economy was operating close to full employment. Its military preparations entailed considerable shifting of resources from production of civilian goods with a drop in the standard of living.

Curiously, the United States' position during the Vietnam War was similar to that of the Soviet Union during World War II. Our economy was at full employment in the mid-1960s and the Johnson administration accelerated military spending for Vietnam while simultaneously increasing expenditures on domestic "war on poverty" programs. This attempt to achieve simultaneously more pizza and more robots—or, more accurately, more guns and more butter—in a full-employment economy was doomed to failure. The attempt to spend beyond our capacity to produce—to realize a point like W in Figure 2-1—contributed significantly to the double-digit inflation of the 1970s.

3 Discrimination Discrimination based on race, gender, age, or ethnic background impedes the efficient allocation or employment of human resources, keeping the economy operating at some point inside its production possibilities curve. Discrimination prevents blacks, women, and others from obtaining jobs in which society can use efficiently their skills and talents. Elimination of discrimination would help move the economy from some point inside the production possibilities curve toward a point on the curve.

4 Productivity Slowdown Since the mid-1960s the United States has experienced a rather alarming decline in the rate of growth of labor productivity; that is, the growth of output per worker-hour has diminished. Some economists feel a major cause of this decline is that the rate of increase in the mechanization of labor has slowed because of insufficient investment. One proposed remedy is to increase investment as compared to consumption. That is, a D to C type of shift in Figure 2-1 is recommended. Special tax incentives to

make business investment more profitable are an appropriate policy to facilitate this shift. The expectation is that the restoration of a more rapid rate of productivity growth will accelerate the growth of the economy (that is, the rightward shift of the production possibilities curve) through time.

5 Growth: Japan versus United States The growth impact of a nation's decision on how much of its domestic output will be devoted to investment and how much to consumption is illustrated vividly in comparing Japan and the United States. Recently, Japan has been investing over 25 percent of its domestic output in productive machinery and equipment compared to only about 10 percent for the United States. The consequences are in accord with our earlier discussion. Over the 1960–1990 period Japan's domestic output expanded at about 6.4 percent per year compared to only 3.2 percent for the United States. In other words, Japan's production possibilities curve shifted outward more rapidly than the United States' curve. This is reflected in living standards. In 1980 the per capita output of Japan was $16,711 as compared to $17,643 for the United States. By 1989 these figures had changed to $22,884 and $21,404 respectively.

6 International Trade Aspects The message of the production possibilities curve is that a nation cannot live beyond its means or production potential. When the possibility of international trade is taken into account, this statement must be modified in two ways.

Trade and Growth We will discover in later chapters that a nation can circumvent the output constraint imposed by its domestic production possibilities curve through international specialization and trade. International specialization and trade have the same impact as having more and better resources or discovering improved production techniques. Both have the effect of increasing the quantities of both capital and consumer goods available to society. International specialization and trade are the equivalent of economic growth.

Trade Deficits Within the context of international trade, a nation can achieve a combination of goods outside its domestic production possibilities curve (such as point W in Figure 2-1) by incurring a *trade deficit*. A nation may buy and receive an amount of imported goods from other nations which exceeds the amount of goods it exports. The United States has been doing just that recently. In 1990 the United States had a trade deficit of approximately $108 billion. In other words, we imported $108 billion more worth of goods than we exported. The net result was that in 1990 the United States enjoyed some $108 billion of output over what it produced domestically.

This looks like a very favorable state of affairs. Unfortunately, there is a catch. To finance its deficit—to pay for its excess of imports over exports—the United States must go into debt to its international trading partners *or* it must give up ownership of some of its assets to those other nations. Analogy: How can you live beyond your current income? Answer: Borrow from your parents, the sellers of goods, or a financial institution. Or, alternatively, sell some of your real assets (your car or stereo) or financial assets (stocks or bonds) which you own. This is what the United States has been doing.

A major consequence of our large and persistent trade deficits is that foreign nationals hold larger portions of American private and public debt and own larger amounts of our business corporations, agricultural land, and real estate. To pay our debts and repurchase those assets we must in the future live well *within* our means. We must settle for some combination of goods within our production possibilities curve so that we can export more than we import—that is, incur a *trade surplus*—to pay off our world debts and reacquire ownership of those assets. On the other hand, to the extent that some of our imports are capital goods, our future production possibilities curve will be farther rightward than it might otherwise be.

7 Famine in Africa Modern industrial societies take economic growth—more-or-less continuous rightward shifts of the production possibilities curve—for granted. But, as the recent catastrophic famine in Ethiopia, Chad, the Sudan, and other African nations indicates, in some circumstances the production possibilities curve may shift leftward. In addition to drought, an important cause of the African famine is ecological degradation or, more simply, poor land-use practices. Land has been deforested, overfarmed, and overgrazed, causing the production possibilities of these highly agriculturally oriented countries to diminish. In fact the per capita national outputs of most of these nations declined in the 1980s.

8 Operation Desert Storm This chapter's Last Word chronicles how the Gulf War devastated Iraq's property

and human resources and had the effect of shifting its production possibilities curve inward.

THE "ISMS"

A society can use many different institutional arrangements and coordinating mechanisms to respond to the economizing problem. Historically, the industrially advanced economies of the world have differed essentially on two grounds: (1) the ownership of the means of production, and (2) the method by which economic activity is coordinated and directed. Let's briefly examine the main characteristics of two "polar" types of economic systems.

Pure Capitalism

Pure, or **laissez faire, capitalism** is characterized by the private ownership of resources and the use of a system of markets and prices to coordinate and direct economic activity. In such a system each participant is motivated by his or her own self-interests; each economic unit seeks to maximize its income through individual decision making. The market system functions as a mechanism through which individual decisions and preferences are communicated and coordinated. The fact that goods and services are produced and resources are supplied under competitive conditions means there are many independently acting buyers and sellers of each product and resource. As a result, economic power is widely dispersed. Advocates of pure capitalism argue that such an economy is conducive to efficiency in the use of resources, output and employment stability, and rapid economic growth. Hence, there is little or no need for government planning, control, or intervention. Indeed, the term *laissez faire* roughly translates as "let it be," that is, keep government from interfering with the economy, because such interference will disturb the efficiency with which the market system functions. Government's role is therefore limited to protecting private property and establishing an appropriate legal framework in which free markets function.

The Command Economy

The polar alternative to pure capitalism is the **command economy** or **communism,** characterized by public ownership of virtually all property resources and the rendering of economic decisions through central economic planning. All major decisions concerning the level of resource use, the composition and distribution of output, and the organization of production are determined by a central planning board. Business firms are governmentally owned and produce according to state directives. Production targets are determined by the planning board for each enterprise and the plan specifies the amounts of resources to be allocated to each enterprise so that it might realize its production goals. The division of output between capital and consumer goods is centrally decided and capital goods are allocated among industries in terms of the central planning board's long-term priorities.

Mixed Systems

Real-world economies are arrayed between the extremes of pure capitalism and the command economy. The United States economy leans toward pure capitalism, but with important differences. Government plays an active role in our economy in promoting economic stability and growth, in providing certain goods and services which would be underproduced or not produced at all by the market system, and in modifying the distribution of income. In contrast to the wide dispersion of economic power among many small units which characterizes pure capitalism, American capitalism has spawned powerful economic organizations in the form of large corporations and strong labor unions. The ability of these power blocs to manipulate and distort the functioning of the market system to their advantage is a further reason for governmental involvement in the economy. While the former Soviet Union historically approximated the command economy, it relied to some extent upon market-determined prices and had some vestiges of private ownership. Recent reforms in the former Soviet Union, China, and most of the eastern European nations are designed to move these command economies toward more capitalistic, market-oriented systems.

But note that private ownership and reliance on the market system do not always go together, nor do public ownership and central planning. For example, the *fascism* of Hitler's Nazi Germany has been dubbed **authoritarian capitalism** because the economy was subject to a high degree of governmental control and direction, but property was privately owned. In contrast, the Yugoslavian economy was **market socialism,** characterized by public ownership of resources

coupled with increasing reliance on free markets to organize and coordinate economic activity. The Swedish economy is also a hybrid system. Although over 90 percent of business activity is in private hands, government is deeply involved in achieving economic stability and in redistributing income. Similarly, the capitalistic Japanese economy entails a great deal of planning and "coordination" between government and the business sector. Table 2-3 summarizes the various ways economic systems can be categorized based on the two criteria we are using. Keep in mind that the real-world examples in this framework are only rough approximations.

The Traditional Economy

Table 2-3 is couched in terms of industrially advanced or at least semideveloped economies. Many less developed countries have **traditional** or **customary economies.** Production methods, exchange, and distribution of income are all sanctioned by custom. Heredity and caste circumscribe economic roles of individuals and socioeconomic immobility is pronounced. Technological change and innovation may be closely constrained because they clash with tradition and threaten the social fabric. Economic activity is often secondary to religious and cultural values and society's desire to perpetuate the status quo. In deciding to pursue economic development, traditional economies must face the question as to which model in Table 2-3 will result in growth and simultaneously be the most compatible with other economic and noneconomic goals valued by that society.

The point is that there is no unique or universally accepted way to respond to the economizing problem. Various societies, having different cultural and historical backgrounds, different mores and customs, and

TABLE 2-3 Comparative economic systems

| | | Coordinating mechanism | |
		Market system	Central planning
Ownership of resources	Private	United States	Nazi Germany
	Public	Yugoslavia	Soviet Union

LAST WORD

OPERATION DESERT STORM AND IRAQ'S PRODUCTION POSSIBILITIES

War can seriously diminish a nation's production possibilities.

The quick and decisive military victory of the United States and its allies in Operation Desert Storm has had a devastating economic impact on Iraq. Forty-three days of intensive Allied bombing inflicted great physical damage to Iraq's productive facilities and infrastructure. Civilian factories, roads, bridges, railroads, power plants, water purification plants, and communication facilities were all severely impaired. Commerce and communications have been greatly disrupted. Furthermore, despite Iraq's greatly diminished productive potential, the United Nations has ordered it to pay up to 30 percent of its future oil revenues as war reparations to Kuwait and others harmed by the war. This means that a significant portion of Iraq's future domestic output will be unavailable for its consumers or to rebuild its productive facilities.

Devastation to Iraq's human resources was also severe. One estimate suggests that as many as 100,000 to 120,000 Iraqi troops plus 5,000 to 20,000 civilians were killed in the war. Another 20,000 lost their lives in the postwar rebellion against Saddam Hussein. Finally, an estimated 15,000 to 30,000 Kurds and other displaced people have died in camps and on the road. A Harvard medical team has predicted that 170,000 Iraqi children will die because of delayed effects of the Persian Gulf war. In particular,

typhoid, cholera, diarrhea, malnutrition and other health problems will cause the death rate of children under age 5 to be two or three times higher than before the war. Without electric power water treatment plants are silent; sewage cannot be pumped or treated. Backed-up pipes now drain into rivers and canals from which people have no choice but to bathe and drink. Further, there is no power to run irrigation pumps and little gasoline is available for harvesting machines. Food harvests are in doubt and refrigeration is no longer available to store existing food supplies.

In short, Iraq invaded Kuwait to bring Kuwait's oil resources under its control and by so doing increase Iraq's production possibilities. Instead, Iraq's physical and human resources—and hence its production possibilities—have been seriously diminished by Operation Desert Storm.

contrasting ideological frameworks—not to mention resources which differ both quantitatively and qualitatively—use different institutions in dealing with the reality of relative scarcity. The former Soviet Union, the United States, and Great Britain, for example, are all—in terms of their accepted goals, ideology, technolo-

gies, resources, and culture—attempting to achieve efficiency in the use of their respective resources. The best method for responding to the unlimited wants–scarce resources dilemma in one economy may be inappropriate for another economic system.

CHAPTER SUMMARY

1 Economics centers on two basic facts: first, human material wants are virtually unlimited; second, economic resources are scarce.

2 Economic resources may be classified as property resources—raw materials and capital—or as human resources—labor and entrepreneurial ability.

3 Economics is concerned with the problem of administering scarce resources in the production of goods and services to fulfill the material wants of society. Both full employment and full production of available resources are essential if this administration is to be efficient.

4 At any time a full-employment, full-production economy

must sacrifice the output of some types of goods and services to achieve increased production of others. Because resources are not equally productive in all possible uses, shifting resources from one use to another gives rise to the law of increasing opportunity costs; that is, the production of additional units of product X entails the sacrifice of increasing amounts of product Y.

5 Over time, technological advance and increases in the quantity and quality of human and property resources permit the economy to produce more of all goods and services.

Society's choice as to the composition of current output is a determinant of the future location of the production possibilities curve.

6 The various economic systems of the world differ in their ideologies and also in their responses to the economizing problem. Critical differences center on **a** private versus public ownership of resources, and **b** the use of the market system versus central planning as a coordinating mechanism.

TERMS AND CONCEPTS

economizing problem
utility
land, capital, labor,
 and entrepreneurial
 ability
investment
full employment

full production
allocative efficiency
productive efficiency
consumer goods
capital goods
production possibilities
 table (curve)

law of increasing
 opportunity costs
economic growth
pure or laissez faire
 capitalism
command economy or
 communism

authoritarian
 capitalism
market socialism
traditional or
 customary
 economies

QUESTIONS AND STUDY SUGGESTIONS

1 "Economics is the study of the principles governing the allocation of scarce means among competing ends when the objective of the allocation is to maximize the attainment of the ends."[3] Explain. Why is the problem of unemployment a part of the subject matter of economics?

2 Critically analyze: "Wants aren't insatiable. I can prove it. I get all the coffee I want to drink every morning at breakfast." Explain: "Goods and services are scarce because resources are scarce." Analyze: "It is the nature of all economic problems that absolute solutions are denied us."

3 What are economic resources? What are the major functions of the entrepreneur? "Economics is . . . neither capitalist nor socialist: it applies to every society. Economics would disappear only in a world so rich that no wants were unfulfilled for lack of resources. Such a world is not imminent and may be impossible, for time is always limited."[4] Carefully evaluate and explain these statements. Do you agree that time is an economic resource?

4 Distinguish between allocative efficiency and productive efficiency. Give an illustration of **a** achieving allocative, but not productive, efficiency; and **b** achieving productive, but not allocative, efficiency.

5 Comment on the following statement from a newspaper article: "Our junior high school serves a splendid hot meal for $1 without costing the taxpayers anything, thanks in part to a government subsidy."

6 The following is a production possibilities table for war goods and civilian goods:

Type of production	Production alternatives				
	A	B	C	D	E
Automobiles (in millions)	0	2	4	6	8
Guided missiles (in thousands)	30	27	21	12	0

a Show these production possibilities data graphically. What do the points on the curve indicate? How does the curve reflect the law of increasing opportunity costs? Explain. If the economy is currently at point *C*, what is the cost of 1 million more automobiles in terms of guided missiles? Of 1000 more guided missiles in terms of automobiles?

b Label point *G* inside the curve. What does it indicate? Label point *H* outside the curve. What does this point indicate? What must occur before the economy can attain the level of production indicated by point *H*?

c Upon what specific assumptions is the production possibilities curve based? What happens when each of these assumptions is released?

d Suppose improvement occurs in the technology of producing guided missiles but not in the production of

[3]George J. Stigler, *The Theory of Price* (New York: The Macmillan Company, 1947), p. 12.

[4]Joseph P. McKenna, *Intermediate Economic Theory* (New York: Holt, Rinehart and Winston, Inc., 1958), p. 2.

automobiles. Draw the new production possibilities curve. Now assume that a technological advance occurs in producing automobiles but not in producing guided missiles. Draw the new production possibilities curve. Finally, draw a production possibilities curve which reflects technological improvement in the production of both products.

7 What is the opportunity cost of attending college?

8 Suppose you arrive at a store expecting to pay $100 for an item, but learn that a store two miles away is charging $50 for it. Would you drive there and buy it? How does your decision benefit you? What is the opportunity cost of your decision? Now suppose that you arrive at a store expecting to pay $6000 for an item, but learn that it costs $5950 at the other store. Do you make the same decision as before? Perhaps surprisingly, you should! Explain why.

9 "The present choice of position on the production possibilities curve is a major factor in economic growth." Explain.

10 Contrast the means by which pure capitalism, market socialism, and a command economy attempt to cope with economic scarcity.

11 Explain how an international trade deficit may permit an economy to acquire a combination of goods in excess of its domestic production potential. Explain why nations try to avoid having trade deficits.

CHAPTER 3

Pure Capitalism and the Circular Flow

Fact: In the past few years the media have inundated us with stories of how the centrally planned economies are trying to alter their systems in the direction of capitalism. Question: Precisely what are the features and institutions of capitalism which these nations are trying to emulate?

Fact: You have virtually nothing whatsoever to do with the production of the vast majority of goods and services you consume. Question: Why is it that production is so specialized in modern economies?

Fact: Nearly every day you exchange paper dollars—whose intrinsic value is virtually nil—for a wide variety of products of considerable value. Question: Why do such seemingly irrational monetary transactions occur?

The foregoing questions are just some addressed in the pages that follow. Our initial task is to describe the capitalist ideology and to explain how pure, or laissez faire, capitalism would function.

Strictly speaking, pure capitalism has never existed and probably never will. Why, then, do we bother to consider the operation of such an economy? Because it provides us with a useful first approximation of how the economies of the United States and many other industrially advanced nations function. And approximations or models, when properly handled, can be very useful. In other words, pure capitalism constitutes a simplified model which we will then modify and adjust in later chapters to correspond more closely to the reality of these modern economies.

In explaining the operation of pure capitalism, we will discuss: (1) the institutional framework and basic assumptions which make up the capitalist ideology; (2) certain institutions and practices common to all modern economies; (3) capitalism and the circular flow of income; (4) how product and resource prices are determined; and (5) the market system and the allocating of economic resources. The first three topics are explored in the present chapter; the latter two will be discussed in Chapters 4 and 5.

CAPITALIST IDEOLOGY

Unfortunately, there is no neat, universally accepted definition of capitalism. We therefore must examine in some detail the basic tenets of pure capitalism to clearly understand what it entails. In short, the framework of capitalism embraces the following institutions and assumptions: (1) private property, (2) freedom of enterprise and choice, (3) self-interest as the dominant motive, (4) competition, (5) reliance on the price or market system, and (6) a limited role for government.

Private Property

Under a capitalistic system, property resources are owned by private individuals and private institutions rather than by government. **Private property,** coupled with the freedom to negotiate binding legal contracts, permits private persons or businesses to obtain, control, employ, and dispose of property resources as they see fit. The institution of private property is sustained over time by the *right to bequeath,* that is, by the right of a property owner to designate the recipient of this property at the time of death.

Needless to say, there are broad legal limits to this right of private ownership. For example, the use of one's resources for the production of illicit drugs is prohibited. Nor is public ownership nonexistent. Even in pure capitalism, public ownership of certain "natural monopolies" may be essential to the achievement of efficiency in the use of resources.

Freedom of Enterprise and Choice

Closely related to private ownership of property is freedom of enterprise and choice. Capitalism charges its component economic units with the responsibility of making certain choices, which are registered and made effective through the free markets of the economy.

Freedom of enterprise means that under pure capitalism, private business enterprises are free to obtain economic resources, to organize these resources in the production of a good or service of the firm's own choosing, and to sell it in the markets of their choice. No artificial obstacles or restrictions imposed by government or other producers block an entrepreneur's choice to enter or leave a particular industry.

Freedom of choice means that owners of property resources and money capital can employ or dispose of these resources as they see fit. It also means

that laborers are free to enter any lines of work for which they are qualified. Finally, it means that consumers are at liberty, within the limits of their money incomes, to buy that collection of goods and services they feel is most appropriate in satisfying their wants.

Freedom of *consumer* choice may well be the most profound of these freedoms. The consumer is in a particularly strategic position in a capitalistic economy; in a sense, the consumer is sovereign. The range of free choices for suppliers of human and property resources is circumscribed by the choices of consumers. The consumer ultimately decides what the capitalistic economy should produce, and resource suppliers must make their free choices within these constraints. Resource suppliers and businesses are not really "free" to produce goods and services consumers do not desire.

Again, broad legal limitations prevail in the expression of all these free choices.

Role of Self-Interest

The primary driving force of capitalism is the promotion of one's **self-interest;** each economic unit attempts to do what is best for itself. Hence, entrepreneurs aim to maximize their firm's profits or, as the case might be, minimize losses. And, other things being equal, owners of property resources attempt to achieve the highest price obtainable from the rent or sale of these resources. Given the amount and irksomeness of the effort involved, those who supply human resources will also try to obtain the highest possible incomes from their employment. Consumers, in purchasing a given product, will seek to obtain it at the lowest price. Consumers also apportion their expenditures to maximize their utility or satisfaction. In short, capitalism presumes self-interest as the fundamental *modus operandi* for the various economic units as they express their free choices. The motive of self-interest gives direction and consistency to what might otherwise be an extremely chaotic economy.

Note that pursuit of economic self-interest should not be confused with selfishness. The stockholder who receives corporate dividends may contribute a portion to the United Way or leave bequests to grandchildren. Similarly, a local church official may compare price and quality among various brands in buying new pews for the church.

Competition

Freedom of choice exercised in terms of promoting one's own monetary returns is the basis for **competi-**

tion, or economic rivalry, as a fundamental feature of capitalism. Competition, as economists see it, entails:

1 The presence of large numbers of independently acting buyers and sellers operating in the market for any particular product or resource.

2 The freedom of buyers and sellers to enter or leave particular markets.

Large Numbers The essence of competition is the widespread diffusion of economic power within the two major aggregates—businesses and households—which comprise the economy. When many buyers and sellers are present in a particular market, no one buyer or seller will be able to demand or offer a quantity of the product sufficiently large to noticeably influence its price. Let's examine this statement in terms of the selling or supply side of the product market.

We know that when a product becomes unusually scarce, its price will rise. An unseasonable frost in Florida may seriously curtail the output of citrus crops and sharply increase the price of oranges. Similarly, *if* a single producer, or a small group of producers acting together, can somehow control or restrict the total supply of a product, then price can be raised to the seller's advantage. By controlling supply, the producer can "rig the market" on his or her own behalf. Now the essence of competition is that there are so many independently acting sellers that each, *because he or she is contributing an almost negligible fraction of the total supply,* has virtually no influence over the supply or, therefore, over product price.

For example, suppose there are 10,000 farmers, each of whom is supplying 100 bushels of corn in the Kansas City grain market when the price of corn is $4 per bushel. Could a single farmer who feels dissatisfied with the existing price cause an artificial scarcity of corn and thereby boost the price above $4? The answer clearly is "No." Farmer Jones, by restricting output from 100 to 75 bushels, exerts virtually no effect on the total supply of corn. In fact, the total amount supplied is reduced only from 1,000,000 to 999,975 bushels. This obviously is not much of a shortage! Supply is virtually unchanged, and, therefore, the $4 price persists. In brief, competition means that each seller is providing a drop in the bucket of total supply. Individual sellers can make no noticeable dent in total supply; hence, a seller cannot *as an individual producer* manipulate product price. This is what is meant when it is said that an individual competitive seller is "at the mercy of the market." The same rationale applies to the demand side of the market. Buyers are plentiful and act inde-

pendently. Thus single buyers cannot manipulate the market to their advantage.

The widespread diffusion of economic power underlying competition controls the use and limits the potential abuse of that power. Economic rivalry prevents economic units from wreaking havoc on one another as they attempt to further their self-interests. Competition imposes limits on expressions of self-interest by buyers and sellers. Competition is a basic regulatory force in capitalism.

Entry and Exit Competition also assumes that it is simple for producers to enter or leave a particular industry; there are no artificial legal or institutional obstacles to prohibit expansion or contraction of specific industries. This aspect of competition is prerequisite to the flexibility which is essential if an economy is to remain efficient over time. Freedom of entry is necessary for the economy to adjust appropriately to changes in consumer tastes, technology, or resource supplies. (This is further explored in Chapter 5.)

Markets and Prices

The basic coordinating mechanism of a capitalist economy is the market or price system. *Capitalism is a market economy.* Decisions rendered by buyers and sellers of products and resources are made effective through a system of markets. Indeed, by definition, a **market** is simply a mechanism or arrangement which brings buyers or "demanders" and sellers or "suppliers" of a good or service into contact with one another. A McDonald's, a gas station, a grocery supermarket, a Sotheby's art auction, the New York Stock Exchange, and worldwide foreign exchange markets are but a few illustrations. The preferences of sellers and buyers are registered on the supply and demand sides of various markets, and the outcome of these choices is a system of product and resource prices. These prices are guideposts on which resource owners, entrepreneurs, and consumers make and revise their free choices in furthering their self-interests.

Just as competition is the controlling mechanism, so a system of markets and prices is a basic organizing force. The market system is an elaborate communication system through which innumerable individual free choices are recorded, summarized, and balanced against one another. Those who obey the dictates of the market system are rewarded; those who ignore them are penalized by the system. Through this communication system, society decides what the economy should produce, how production can be efficiently organized, and how the fruits of productive endeavor are distributed among the individual economic units which make up capitalism.

Not only is the market system the mechanism through which society decides how it allocates its resources and distributes the resulting output, but it is through the market system that these decisions are carried out.

Economic systems based on the ideologies of socialism and communism also depend on market systems, but not to the same degree or in the same way as pure capitalism. Socialistic and communistic societies use markets and prices primarily to implement decisions made wholly or in part by a central planning authority. In capitalism, the market system functions both as a device for registering innumerable choices of free individuals and businesses *and* as a mechanism for carrying out these decisions.

In Chapters 4 and 5 we will analyze the mechanics and operation of the market system.

Limited Government

A competitive capitalist economy promotes a high degree of efficiency in the use or allocation of its resources. There is allegedly little real need for governmental intervention in the operation of such an economy beyond its role of imposing broad legal limits on the exercise of individual choices and the use of private property. The concept of pure capitalism as a self-regulating and self-adjusting economy precludes any significant economic role for government. However, as we will find in Chapter 6, a number of limitations and potentially undesirable outcomes associated with capitalism and the market system have resulted in an active economic role for government.

QUICK REVIEW 3-1

◆ *Pure capitalism rests on the private ownership of property and freedom of enterprise and choice.*

◆ *Economic entities—businesses, resource suppliers, and consumers—seek to further their own self-interests.*

◆ *The coordinating mechanism of capitalism is a competitive system of prices or markets.*

◆ *The efficient functioning of the market system under capitalism allegedly precludes significant government intervention.*

OTHER CHARACTERISTICS

Private property, freedom of enterprise and choice, self-interest as a motivating force, competition, and reliance on a market system are all institutions and assumptions more or less exclusively associated with pure capitalism. In addition, there are certain institutions and practices which are characteristic of all modern economies: (1) the use of advanced technology and large amounts of capital goods, (2) specialization, and (3) the use of money. Specialization and an advanced technology are prerequisites to efficient employment of any economy's resources. The use of money is a mechanism which allows society more easily to practice and reap the benefits of specialization and advanced productive techniques.

Extensive Use of Capital Goods

All modern economies—whether they approximate the capitalist, socialist, or communist ideology—are based on advanced technology and the extensive use of capital goods. Under pure capitalism it is competition, coupled with freedom of choice and the desire to further one's self-interest, which provides the means for achieving technological advance. The capitalistic framework is felt to be highly effective in harnessing incentives to develop new products and improved techniques of production, because monetary rewards accrue directly to the innovator. Pure capitalism therefore presupposes extensive use and relatively rapid development of complex capital goods: tools, machinery, large-scale factories, and facilities for storage, transportation, and marketing.

Why are the existence of an advanced technology and the extensive use of capital goods important? Because the most direct method of producing a product is usually the least efficient.[1] Even Robinson Crusoe avoided the inefficiencies of direct production in favor of **roundabout production.** It would be ridiculous for a farmer—even a backyard farmer—to go at production with bare hands. It pays huge dividends in terms of more efficient production and, therefore, a more abundant output, to fashion tools of production, that is, capital equipment, to aid in the productive process. There is a better way of getting water out of a well than to dive in after it!

---

[1]Remember that consumer goods satisfy wants directly, while capital goods do so indirectly through the more efficient future production of consumer goods.

But there is a catch involved. Recall our discussion of the production possibilities curve and the basic nature of the economizing problem. With full employment and full production, resources must be diverted from the production of consumer goods to be used in the production of capital goods. We must currently tighten our belts as consumers to free resources for the production of capital goods which will increase productive efficiency and give us a greater output of consumer goods in the future.

Specialization and Efficiency

The extent to which society relies on **specialization** is astounding. The vast majority of consumers produce virtually none of the goods and services they consume and, conversely, consume little or nothing of what they produce. The hammer-shop laborer who spends a lifetime stamping out parts for jet engines may never "consume" an airplane trip. The assembly-line worker who devotes 8 hours a day to installing windows in Corsicas may own a Honda. Few households seriously consider any extensive production of their own food, shelter, and clothing. Many farmers sell their milk to the local dairy and then buy margarine at the Podunk general store. Society learned long ago that self-sufficiency breeds inefficiency. The jack-of-all-trades may be a very colorful individual, but is certainly not efficient.

Division of Labor

In what specific ways might human specialization— the **division of labor**—enhance productive efficiency?
1   Specialization permits individuals to take advantage of existing differences in their abilities and skills. If caveman A is strong, swift, and accurate with a spear, and caveman B is weak and slow, but patient, this distribution of talents can be most efficiently used by making A a hunter and B a fisherman.
2   Even if the abilities of A and B are identical, specialization may be advantageous. By devoting all one's time to a single task, the doer is more likely to develop the appropriate skills and to discover improved techniques than when apportioning time among a number of diverse tasks. One learns to be a good hunter by hunting!
3   Finally, specialization—devoting all one's time to, say, a single task—avoids the loss of time involved in shifting from one job to another.

For all these reasons the division of labor results in greater productive efficiency in the use of human resources.

Geographic Specialization

Specialization also is desirable on a regional and international basis. Oranges could be grown in Nebraska, but because of the unsuitability of the land, rainfall, and temperature, the costs involved would be exceedingly high. Florida could achieve some success in the production of wheat, but for similar reasons such production would be relatively costly. As a result, Nebraskans produce those products—wheat in particular—for which their resources are best adapted, and Floridians do the same, producing oranges and other citrus fruits. In so doing, both produce surpluses of their specialties. Then, very sensibly, Nebraskans and Floridians swap some of their surpluses. Specialization permits each area to turn out those goods which its resources can most efficiently produce. In this way both Nebraska and Florida can enjoy a larger amount of both wheat and oranges than would otherwise be the case.

Similarly, on an international basis the United States specializes in such items as commercial aircraft and computers which it sells abroad in exchange for video recorders from Japan, bananas from Honduras, shoes from Italy, and woven baskets from Thailand. In short, human and geographical specialization are both essential in achieving efficiency in the use of resources.

Specialization and Comparative Advantage[2]

These simple illustrations clearly show that specialization is economically desirable because it results in more efficient production. Indeed, the point is almost self-explanatory. But, because the concept of specialization is so vital to understanding the production and exchange processes of modern economies, let's tackle a more exacting illustration of the gains which accrue from specialization.

Comparative Costs   Let's pursue our Nebraska–Florida example of specialization at a more advanced level, relying on an already familiar concept—the production possibilities table—as a basic analytical device. Suppose production possibilities data for the Nebraska and Florida economies are as in Tables 3-1 and 3-2, respectively.

These production possibilities tables are "different" from those of Chapter 2 in that we here assume

---

[2]This section may be skipped by instructors who wish to defer detailed treatment of comparative advantage to Part 5 on the world economy.

TABLE 3-1 Nebraska's production possibilities table (hypothetical data; in tons)

Product	Production alternatives			
	A	B	C	D
Wheat	0	20	40	60
Oranges	15	10	5	0

constant costs rather than increasing costs. Each state must give up a constant, rather than an increasing, amount of one product in securing constant increments of the other product. This will simplify our discussion without impairing the validity of our conclusions.

Specialization and trade are mutually beneficial or "profitable" to the two states (individuals, regions, nations) if the comparative costs of the two products within the two states differ.

What's the comparative cost of oranges and wheat in Nebraska? Table 3-1 shows that 5 tons of oranges must be forgone or sacrificed to produce 20 tons of wheat. Or more simply, it costs 1 ton of oranges to get 4 tons of wheat in Nebraska ($1O = 4W$). Because of our constant-cost assumption, this comparative-cost relationship will not change as we expand the output of either product. Similarly, in Table 3-2 at a cost of 10 tons of oranges, Floridians can obtain 30 tons of wheat, that is, in Florida the comparative-cost ratio for the two products is: $1O$ equals $3W$.

The comparative cost of the two products within the two states is clearly different. Economists describe this situation by saying that Florida has a comparative-cost advantage, or more simply, **comparative advantage,** in oranges; that is, Florida must forgo less wheat (3 tons) to get 1 ton of oranges than is the case in Nebraska where 1 ton of oranges costs 4 tons of wheat. Comparatively speaking, oranges are cheap in Florida. *A state or nation has a comparative advantage in some product when it can produce it at a lower opportunity cost than can any other state or nation.* Nebraska, on the other hand, has a comparative (cost) advantage in wheat. While its costs $\frac{1}{3}$ ton of oranges to get 1 ton of

wheat in Florida, by comparison 1 ton of wheat only costs $\frac{1}{4}$ ton of oranges in Nebraska. Comparatively speaking wheat is cheap in Nebraska.

Given these comparative-cost differences, we can demonstrate that if both states specialize according to their comparative advantage, they can achieve a larger total output of oranges and wheat than otherwise. That is, they can get a larger total output with the same total input of resources through specialization and thus will be using their scarce resources more efficiently.

Terms of Trade Given Florida's cost ratio of $1O$ equals $3W$, it stands to reason that Floridians would be pleased to specialize in oranges, if they could obtain *more than* 3 tons of wheat for a ton of oranges through trade with Nebraska. Similarly, recalling Nebraska's $1O$ equals $4W$ cost ratio, it will be advantageous to Nebraskans to specialize in wheat, provided they can get 1 ton of oranges for *less than* 4 tons of wheat.

Suppose through negotiation the two states agree on an exchange rate of 1 ton of oranges for $3\frac{1}{2}$ tons of wheat.[3] Note that these **terms of trade** will be mutually beneficial in that both states can "do better" through trade than they can at home. Floridians get $3\frac{1}{2}$ tons of wheat by sending 1 ton of oranges to Nebraska, whereas they can get only 3 tons of wheat by reallocating resources from oranges to wheat production at home. It would cost Nebraskans 4 tons of wheat to obtain 1 ton of oranges by reallocating their domestic resources, whereas 1 ton of oranges can be obtained through trade with Florida at the smaller cost of only $3\frac{1}{2}$ tons of wheat.

Gains from Specialization and Trade Table 3-3 helps us pinpoint the size of the gains in total output from specialization and trade. Suppose that before specialization and trade, production alternative B was the optimum product-mix for each state (as shown in column 1). That is, Nebraskans preferred 20 tons of wheat and 10 tons of oranges (Table 3-1) and Floridians preferred 30 tons of wheat and 20 tons of oranges (Table 3-2) to all other alternatives available within the respective state economies. Both states now specialize according to comparative advantage, Nebraska producing 60 tons of wheat and no oranges (alternative D) and Florida producing no wheat and 30 tons of oranges (alternative A) as reflected in column 2 of Table 3-3. Using our $1O$ equals $3\frac{1}{2}W$ terms of trade, assume that

TABLE 3-2 Florida's production possibilities table (hypothetical data; in tons)

Product	Production alternatives			
	A	B	C	D
Wheat	0	30	60	90
Oranges	30	20	10	0

[3]In Chapter 20 we will find that market forces—supply and demand— will determine the rate at which the two products are exchanged.

TABLE 3-3 **Regional specialization according to comparative advantage and the gains from trade** *(hypothetical data; in tons)*

State	(1) Outputs before specialization	(2) Outputs after specialization	(3) Amounts	(4) Outputs available after trade	(5) = (4) − (1) Gains from special-ization and trade
Nebraska	20 wheat 10 oranges	60 wheat 0 oranges	−35 wheat +10 oranges	25 wheat 10 oranges	5 wheat 0 oranges
Florida	30 wheat 20 oranges	0 wheat 30 oranges	+35 wheat −10 oranges	35 wheat 20 oranges	5 wheat 0 oranges

Nebraska exchanges 35 tons of its wheat for 10 tons of Florida oranges. Nebraskans will now have 25 tons of wheat and 10 tons of oranges, while Floridians will thus obtain 35 tons of wheat and 20 tons of oranges. Column 3 of Table 3-3 summarizes this trade. Compared with their optimum product-mixes prior to specialization and trade, *both* states now enjoy the same amount of oranges and 5 additional tons of wheat! These extra 10 tons of wheat, equally divided between the two state economies in this instance, represent the *gains from specialization and trade.* You can confirm these figures in column 5 of Table 3-3 where we have subtracted the *before*-specialization outputs of column 1 from the outputs realized *after* specialization in column 4.

The point is that *resource allocation has been improved through specialization according to comparative advantage.* The same total inputs of resources have resulted in a larger total output. By having Nebraska and Florida allocate all their resources to wheat and oranges respectively, the same total inputs of resources have given rise to more output, indicating that resources are being more efficiently used or allocated.

You may recall that we asserted in Chapter 2 that specialization and trade permit a nation or state to overcome the production constraints imposed by its production possibilities curve. In other words, specialization and trade have the same effect as economic growth. Although the domestic production possibilities frontiers of the two states have not been pushed to the right, specialization and trade have circumvented the constraints of the production possibilities curve. *The economic effects of specialization and trade between states (regions, nations) are tantamount to having more or better resources or to achieving technological progress.*

Disadvantages Despite these efficiency advantages, specialization does have certain drawbacks.
1 The potential monotony and drudgery of specialized work are well known. Imagine the boredom of our assembly-line worker who is still putting windows in Corsicas.

2 Specialization and mutual interdependence vary directly with one another. The less one produces for oneself, the more one depends on the output of others.
3 A third problem centers on the exchanging of the surpluses which specialization entails. An examination of this problem leads us into a discussion of the use of money in the domestic and world economies.

Use of Money

Virtually all economies, advanced or primitive, are money-using. Money performs many functions, but first and foremost it is a **medium of exchange.**

In our Nebraska–Florida example, Nebraskans must trade or exchange wheat for Florida's oranges if both states are to share in the benefits of specialization. If trade was highly inconvenient or prohibited for some reason, gains from specializing would be lost to society. Consumers want a wide variety of products and, in the absence of trade, would tend to devote their human and material resources to many diverse types of production. If exchange could not occur or was very inconvenient to transact, Nebraska and Florida would be forced to be more self-sufficient, and the advantages of specialization would not occur. *In short, a convenient means of exchanging goods is a prerequisite of specialization.*

Now exchange can, and sometimes does, occur on the basis of **bartering,** that is, swapping goods for goods. But bartering as a means of exchange can pose serious problems for the economy. Specifically, exchange by barter requires a *coincidence of wants* between the two transactors. In our example, we assumed that Nebraskans had excess wheat to trade and that they wanted oranges. And we assumed Floridians had excess oranges to swap and that they wanted wheat. So exchange occurred. But if this coincidence of wants did not exist, trade would be stymied.

Suppose Nebraska does not want any of Florida's oranges but is interested in buying potatoes from

Idaho. Ironically, Idaho wants Florida's oranges but not Nebraska's wheat. And, to complicate matters, suppose that Florida wants some of Nebraska's wheat but none of Idaho's potatoes. The situation is summarized in Figure 3-1.

In no case do we find a coincidence of wants. Trade by barter clearly would be difficult. To overcome such a stalemate, modern economies use *money,* which is simply a convenient social invention to facilitate exchange of goods and services. Historically, cattle, cigarettes, shells, stones, pieces of metal, and many other diverse commodities have been used, with varying degrees of success, as a medium for facilitating exchange. But to be money, an item needs to pass only one test: *It must be generally acceptable by buyers and sellers in exchange.* Money is socially defined; whatever society accepts as a medium of exchange *is* money. Most modern economies use pieces of paper as money. We shall assume that this is the case with the Nebraska–Florida–Idaho

economy; they use pieces of paper which they call "dollars" as money. Can the use of paper dollars as a medium of exchange overcome our stalemate?

Indeed it can, with trade occurring as shown in Figure 3-1:

1   Floridians can exchange money for some of Nebraska's wheat.

2   Nebraskans can take the money realized from the sale of wheat and exchange it for some of Idaho's potatoes.

3   Idahoans can then exchange the money received from the sale of potatoes for some of Florida's surplus oranges.

The willingness to accept paper money (or any other kind of money, for that matter) as a medium of exchange has permitted a three-way trade which allows each state to specialize in one product and obtain the other product(s) its residents desire, despite the absence of a coincidence of wants between any two of the parties. Barter, resting as it does on a coincidence of wants, would have impeded this exchange and in so doing would have induced the three states not to specialize. Of course, the efficiencies of specialization would then have been lost to those states. Strange as it may first seem, two exchanges—surplus product for money and then money for a wanted product—are simpler than the single product-for-product exchange which bartering entails. Indeed, in this example, product-for-product exchange would not be likely to occur at all.

On a global basis the fact that different nations have different currencies complicates international specialization and exchange. However, the existence of foreign exchange markets permits Americans, Japanese, Germans, Britons, and Mexicans to exchange dollars, yen, marks, pounds, and pesos for one another to complete the desired international exchanges of goods and services.

A final example: Imagine a Detroit laborer producing crankshafts for Oldsmobiles. At the end of the week, instead of receiving a piece of paper endorsed by the company comptroller, or a few pieces of paper engraved in green and black, the laborer receives from the company paymaster four Oldsmobile crankshafts. Inconvenient as this is, and with no desire to hoard crankshafts, the laborer ventures into the Detroit business district, to spend this hard-earned income on a bag of groceries, a pair of jeans, and a movie. Obviously, the worker is faced with some inconvenient and time-consuming trading, and may not be able to negoti-

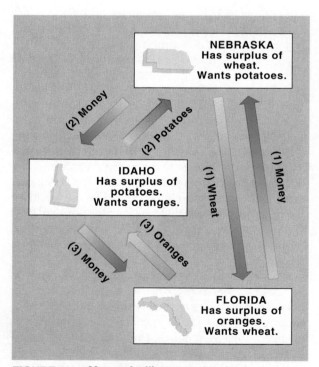

FIGURE 3-1   Money facilitates trade where wants do not coincide

By the use of money as a medium of exchange, trade can be accomplished, as indicated by the arrows, despite a noncoincidence of wants. By facilitating exchange, the use of money permits an economy to realize the efficiencies of specialization.

KEY GRAPH

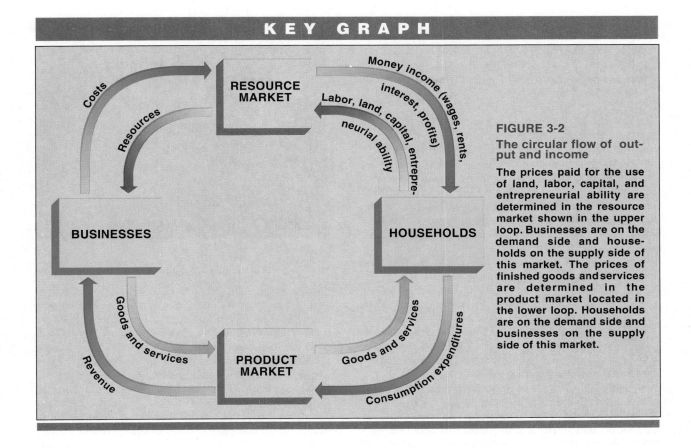

FIGURE 3-2
The circular flow of output and income

The prices paid for the use of land, labor, capital, and entrepreneurial ability are determined in the resource market shown in the upper loop. Businesses are on the demand side and households on the supply side of this market. The prices of finished goods and services are determined in the product market located in the lower loop. Households are on the demand side and businesses on the supply side of this market.

ate any exchanges at all. Finding a clothier with jeans who happens to be in the market for an Oldsmobile crankshaft can be a formidable task. And, if the jeans do not trade evenly for crankshafts, how do the transactors "make change"? Examples such as this demonstrate that money is one of the great social inventions of civilization.

QUICK REVIEW 3-2

*   *Advanced economies achieve greater efficiency in production through the use of large quantities of capital goods.*
*   *Specialization enhances efficiency; by specializing in accordance with comparative advantage a nation or region can realize an output greater than those on its production possibilities curve.*
*   *The use of money facilitates the exchange of goods which specialization entails.*

THE CIRCULAR FLOW MODEL

Our discussion of specialization and the related need for a monetary system to facilitate exchange brings us back to the role of markets and prices in a capitalistic economy. The remainder of this chapter is devoted to the market system, and examines the two basic types of markets of pure capitalism and the transactions occurring within them.

Resource and Product Markets

Figure 3-2 (Key Graph) shows two groups of *decision makers*—households and businesses. (Government will be added as a third decision maker in Chapter 6.) The *coordinating mechanism* which brings the decisions of households and businesses into alignment with one another is the market system, in particular resource and product markets.

LAST WORD

BACK TO BARTER

Despite the advantages of using money, there is evidence that bartering is a "growth industry."

Because money facilitates exchange, it may seem odd that a considerable and growing volume of both domestic and international trade occurs through barter.

Suppose you own a small firm selling equipment to television stations. The economy is in recession; business is slow; your cash flow is down; and your inventories are much higher than desired. What do you do? You approach a local TV station which needs new equipment. But it, too, is feeling the effects of recession. Its advertising revenues are down and it also faces a cash-flow crunch. So a deal is struck. You provide $50,000 worth of equipment in exchange for $50,000 worth of "free" advertising. Advantage to seller: You move unwanted inventory, eliminating warehousing and insurance costs. You also receive valuable advertising time. The TV station gets needed equipment and pays for it with advertising time slots which would otherwise be unfilled. Both parties gain and no money changes hands.

Internationally, a firm might encounter an obstacle in selling its goods to a nation which does not have "hard" (exchangeable) currencies such as dollars, marks, or yen. Barter circumvents this problem. Ex-

ample: Arcon Manufacturing of North Carolina sold its grain silos to a Nicaraguan firm, knowing that the buyer had no hard currency for making payment. Arcon took payment in sesame seeds, which it delivered to a Middle Eastern food manufacturer which was able to pay Arcon in hard currency. PepsiCo swaps cola syrup for Russian vodka. Coca-Cola has traded its syrup for Egyptian oranges, Turkish tomato paste, Polish beer, and Hungarian soft-drink bottles. Recently, large American oil companies such as Chevron and Amoco

---

The upper half of the diagram portrays the **resource market.** Here, households, which directly or indirectly (through their ownership of business corporations) own all economic resources, *supply* these resources to businesses.[4] Businesses, of course, will *demand* resources because they are the means by which firms produce goods and services. The interaction of demand and supply for the immense variety of human and property resources establishes the price of each. The payments which businesses make in obtaining resources are costs to businesses, but simultaneously constitute flows of wage, rent, interest, and profit income to the households supplying these resources.

Now consider the **product market** shown in the bottom half of the diagram. The money income received by households from the sale of resources does not, as such, have real value. Consumers cannot eat or

wear coins and paper money. Hence, through the expenditure of money income, households express their *demand* for a vast array of goods and services. Simultaneously, businesses combine the resources they have obtained to produce and *supply* goods and services in these same markets. The interaction of these demand and supply decisions determines product prices (Chapter 4). Note, too, that the flow of consumer expenditures for goods and services constitutes sales revenues or receipts from the viewpoint of businesses.

The **circular flow model** implies a complex, interrelated web of decision making and economic activity. Note that households and businesses participate in both basic markets, but on different sides of each. Businesses are on the buying or demand side of resource markets, and households, as resource owners and suppliers, are on the selling or supply side. In the product market, these positions are reversed; households, as consumers, are on the buying or demand side, and businesses are on the selling or supply side. Each group of economic units both buys and sells.

---

[4]For present purposes think of businesses simply as organizational charts, that is, institutions on paper apart from the capital, raw materials, labor, and entrepreneurial ability which breathe life into them and make them "going concerns."

have negotiated "joint ventures" with the former Soviet Union based on barter. The Soviets get updated capital equipment, new technologies, and increased oil production; American oil companies take their earnings in oil rather than currency.

Estimates differ on the volume of barter transactions within the United States. One estimate is that 175,000 businesses engaged in barter transactions of almost $1 billion in 1990, a fivefold increase in dollar volume since 1980. A higher estimate indicates that in 1990 some 220,000 firms conducted $5.3 billion worth of barter transactions.

The increasing popularity of barter has partly resulted from the development of "exchange companies" which coordinate barter transactions. The exchange company provides trade credits to members who make goods or services available; these accounts are debited when members make purchases. For its services the exchange company charges a membership fee and receives a percentage of the value of each transaction. At present there are over 400 barter exchanges in America.

Barter does involve time-consuming negotiation and it could undermine and distort the flow of open multilateral trade (Figure 3-1). Yet, as our illustrations make clear, barter is a means of bringing about mutually advantageous transactions which otherwise would not have occurred.

Furthermore, the specter of scarcity haunts these transactions. Because households have only limited amounts of resources to supply to businesses, the money incomes of consumers will be limited. This means that each consumer's income will go only so far. A limited number of dollars clearly will not permit the purchase of all the goods and services the consumer might like to buy. Similarly, because resources are scarce, the output of finished goods and services is also necessarily limited. Scarcity and choice permeate our entire discussion.

To summarize: In a monetary economy, households, as resource owners, sell their resources to businesses and, as consumers, spend the money income received buying goods and services. Businesses must buy resources to produce goods and services; their finished products are then sold to households in exchange for consumption expenditures or, as businesses view it, revenues. The net result is a counterclockwise *real* flow of economic resources and finished goods and services, and a clockwise *money* flow of income and consumption expenditures. These flows are simultaneous and repetitive.

Limitations

Our model simplifies in many ways. Intrahousehold and intrabusiness transactions are concealed. Government and the "rest of the world" are ignored as decision makers. The model subtly implies constant flows of output and income, while in fact these flows are unstable over time. Nor is the circular flow a perpetual motion machine; production exhausts human energies and absorbs physical resources, the latter giving rise to problems of environmental pollution. Finally, our model does not explain how product and resource prices are actually determined, which is examined in Chapter 4.

CHAPTER SUMMARY

1   The capitalistic system is characterized by private ownership of resources and the freedom of individuals to engage in economic activities of their choice to advance their material well-being. Self-interest is the driving force of such an economy, and competition functions as a regulatory or control mechanism.

2   Capitalistic production is not organized in terms of a government plan, but rather features the market system as a means of organizing and making effective the myriad individual decisions which determine what is produced, the methods of production, and the sharing of output. The capitalist ideology envisions government playing a minor and relatively passive economic role.

3   Specialization according to comparative advantage and an advanced technology based on the extensive use of capital goods are features common to all modern economies.

4   Functioning as a medium of exchange, money circumvents problems of bartering and thereby permits greater specialization both domestically and internationally.

5   An overview of the operation of the capitalistic system can be gained through the circular flow of income. This simplified model locates the product and resource markets and presents the major income-expenditure flows and resources-output flows which constitute the lifeblood of the capitalistic economy.

TERMS AND CONCEPTS

private property	competition	specialization and	bartering
freedom of enterprise	market	division of labor	resource and product
freedom of choice	roundabout production	terms of trade	markets
self-interest	comparative advantage	medium of exchange	circular flow model

QUESTIONS AND STUDY SUGGESTIONS

1 "Capitalism may be characterized as an automatic self-regulating system motivated by the self-interest of individuals and regulated by competition."[5] Explain and evaluate.

2 Explain how the market system is a means of communicating and implementing decisions concerning allocation of the economy's resources.

3 What advantages result from "roundabout" production? What problem is involved in increasing a full-employment, full-production economy's stock of capital goods? Illustrate this problem in terms of the production possibilities curve. Does an economy with unemployed resources face the same problem?

4 What are the advantages of specialization in the use of human and material resources? The disadvantages? Explain: "Exchange is the necessary consequence of specialization."

5 Answer question 7 at the end of Chapter 20.

6 What problems does barter entail? Indicate the economic significance of money as a medium of exchange. "Money is the only commodity that is good for nothing but to be gotten rid of. It will not feed you, clothe you, shelter you, or amuse you unless you spend or invest it. It imparts value only in parting."[6] Explain this statement.

7 Describe the operation of pure capitalism as portrayed by the circular flow model. Locate resource and product markets and emphasize the fact of scarcity throughout your discussion. Specify the limitations of the circular flow model.

---

[5]Howard R. Bowen, *Toward Social Economy* (New York: Holt, Rinehart and Winston, Inc., 1948), p. 249.

[6]Federal Reserve Bank of Philadelphia, "Creeping Inflation," *Business Review,* August 1957, p. 3.

Understanding Individual Markets: Demand and Supply

Teach a parrot to say, "Demand and supply," and you have an economist! There is a strong element of truth in this quip. The simple tools of demand and supply can take us far in understanding not only specific economic issues, but also the operation of the entire economic system.

In this chapter we will examine the nature of markets and how prices and outputs are determined. Our circular flow model in Chapter 3 identified the participants in both product and resource markets. But we assumed there that product and resource prices were "given"; no attempt was made to explain how prices are "set" or determined. We now build on the circular flow model by discussing the concept of a market more fully.

MARKETS DEFINED

A **market** is *an institution or mechanism which brings together buyers ("demanders") and sellers ("suppliers") of particular goods and services.* Markets exist in many forms. The corner gas station, the fast-food outlet, the local music store, a farmer's roadside stand—all are familiar markets. The New York Stock Exchange and the Chicago Board of Trade are highly organized markets where buyers and sellers of stocks and bonds and farm commodities, respectively, from all over the world are brought into contact with one another. Similarly, auctioneers bring together potential buyers and sellers of art, livestock, used farm equipment, and sometimes real estate. The all-American quarterback and his agent bargain with the owner of an NFL team. A graduating finance major interviews with Citicorp or Chase Manhattan at the university placement office. All these situations which link potential buyers with potential sellers constitute markets. As our examples imply, some markets are local while others are national or international in scope. Some are highly personal, involving face-to-face contact between demander and supplier; others are impersonal in that buyer and seller never see or know one another.

This chapter concerns the functioning of *purely competitive markets*. Such markets presume large numbers of independently acting buyers and sellers interested in exchanging a standardized product. These markets are not the music store or corner gas station where products have price tags, but competitive markets such as a central grain exchange, a stock market, or a market for foreign currencies where the equilibrium price is "discovered" by the interacting decisions of buyers and sellers. Similarly, we see how prices are established in resource markets by demand decisions of competing businesses and supply decisions of competing households (Figure 3-2). We shall concentrate on the *product market,* then later in the chapter examine the *resource market.* Our goal is to explain the mechanics of prices.

DEMAND

Demand is *a schedule which shows the various amounts of a product consumers are willing and able to purchase at each price in a series of possible prices during a specified period of time.*[1] Demand portrays a series of alternative possibilities which can be set down in tabular form. It shows the quantities of a product which will be demanded at various possible prices, *all other things being equal.*

We usually view demand from the vantage point of price; that is, we read demand as showing the amounts consumers will buy at various possible prices. It is equally correct and sometimes more useful to view demand from the reference point of quantity. Instead of asking what quantities can be sold at various prices, we ask what prices can be gotten from consumers for various quantities of a good. Table 4-1 is a hypothetical **demand schedule** for a single consumer purchasing bushels of corn.

This tabular portrayal of demand reflects the relationship between the price of corn and the quantity the consumer would be willing and able to purchase at each of these prices. Note that we say willing and *able,* because willingness alone is not effective in the market. I may be willing to buy a Porsche, but if this willingness is not backed by the necessary dollars, it will not be effective and, therefore, not reflected in the market. In Table 4-1, if the price of corn were $5 per bushel, our consumer would be willing and able to buy 10 bushels per week; if it were $4, the consumer would be willing and able to buy 20 bushels per week; and so forth.

The demand schedule does not tell us which of the five possible prices will actually exist in the corn market. This depends on demand *and supply.* Demand is simply a tabular statement of a buyer's plans, or intentions, with respect to the purchase of a product.

To be meaningful the quantities demanded at each price must relate to a specific period—a day, a week, a month. To say "a consumer will buy 10 bushels of corn at $5 per bushel" is meaningless. To say "a consumer

[1]In adjusting this definition to the resource market, substitute the word "resources" for "product" and "businesses" for "consumers."

TABLE 4-1 **An individual buyer's demand for corn (hypothetical data)**

Price per bushel	Quantity demanded per week
$5	10
4	20
3	35
2	55
1	80

will buy 10 bushels of corn *per week* at $5 per bushel" is clear and meaningful. Without a specific time period we would not know whether demand for a product was large or small.

Law of Demand

A fundamental characteristic of demand is this: All else being constant, as price falls, the quantity demanded rises. Or, other things being equal, as price increases, the corresponding quantity demanded falls. In short, there is a negative or *inverse* relationship between price and quantity demanded. Economists call this inverse relationship the **law of demand.**

The "other things being constant" assumption is critical here. Many factors other than the price of the product under consideration affect the amount purchased. For example, the quantity of Nikes purchased will depend not only on the price of Nikes, but also on the prices of such substitute shoes as Reeboks, Adidas, and L.A. Gear. The law of demand in this case says that fewer pairs of Nikes will be purchased if the price of Nikes rises *and the prices of Reeboks, Adidas, and L.A. Gear all remain constant.* In short, if the *relative price* of Nikes increases, fewer Nikes will be bought. If the prices of Nikes and all other competing shoes increase by some amount—say $5—consumers might buy more, less, or the same amount of Nikes.

On what foundation does the law of demand rest? There are several levels of analysis on which to argue the case.

1 Common sense and simple observation are consistent with the law of demand. People ordinarily *do* buy more of a given product at a low price than they do at a high price. Price is an obstacle which deters consumers from buying. The higher this obstacle, the less of a product they will buy; the lower the price obstacle, the more they will buy. A high price discourages consumers from buying, and a low price encourages them to buy. The fact that businesses have "sales" is concrete evidence of their belief in the law of demand. "Bargain days" are based on the law of demand. Businesses reduce their inventories by lowering prices, not by raising them.

2 In any given time period each buyer of a product will derive less satisfaction or benefit or utility from each successive unit of a product. The second "Big Mac" will yield less satisfaction to the consumer than the first; and the third still less added benefit or utility than the second. Because consumption is subject to **diminishing marginal utility**—consuming successive units of a particular product yields less and less extra satisfaction—consumers will only buy additional units if price is reduced.

3 The law of demand also can be explained in terms of income and substitution effects. The **income effect** indicates that, at a lower price, you can afford more of the good without giving up other goods. In other words, a decline in the price of a product will increase the purchasing power of your money income, enabling you to buy more of the product than before. A higher price will have the opposite effect.

The **substitution effect** suggests that, at a lower price, you have the incentive to substitute the cheaper good for similar goods which are now relatively more expensive. Consumers tend to substitute cheap products for dear products.

For example, a decline in the price of beef will increase the purchasing power of consumer incomes, enabling them to buy more beef (the income effect). At a lower price, beef is relatively more attractive and is substituted for pork, mutton, chicken, and fish (the substitution effect). The income and substitution effects combine to make consumers able and willing to buy more of a product at a low price than at a high price.

The Demand Curve

This inverse relationship between product price and quantity demanded can be represented on a simple graph wherein, by convention, we measure quantity demanded on the horizontal axis and price on the vertical axis. We locate on the graph those five price–quantity possibilities shown in Table 4-1 by drawing perpendiculars from the appropriate points on the two axes. Thus, in plotting the "$5-price–10-quantity-demanded" possibility, we draw a perpendicular from the horizontal (quantity) axis at 10 to meet a perpendicular drawn from the vertical (price) axis at $5. If this is done for all five possibilities, the result is a series of points as shown in Figure 4-1. Each point represents a specific price and the corresponding quantity the consumer will purchase at that price.

Now, assuming the same inverse relationship between price and quantity demanded at all points between the ones graphed, we can generalize on the inverse relationship between price and quantity demanded by drawing a curve to represent *all* price–quantity-demanded possibilities within the limits shown on the graph. The resulting curve is called a **demand curve,** labeled *DD* in Figure 4-1. It slopes

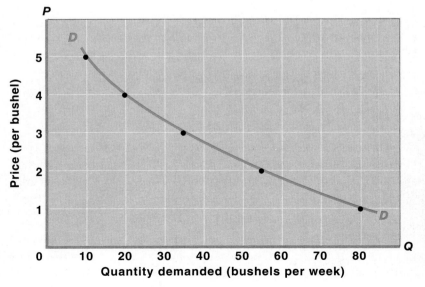

FIGURE 4-1　An individual buyer's demand curve for corn

An individual's demand schedule graphs as a downsloping curve such as *DD*, because price and quantity demanded are inversely related. Specifically, the law of demand generalizes that consumers will buy more of a product as its price declines.

downward and to the right because the relationship it portrays between price and quantity demanded is negative or inverse. The law of demand—people buy more at a low price than at a high price—is reflected in the downward slope of the demand curve.

What is the advantage of graphing our demand schedule? After all, Table 4-1 and Figure 4-1 contain exactly the same data and reflect the same relationship between price and quantity demanded. The advantage of graphing is that we can represent clearly a given relationship—in this case the law of demand—more simply than if we relied on verbal and tabular presentation. A single curve on a graph, if understood, is simpler to state *and manipulate* than tables and lengthy verbal descriptions. Graphs are invaluable tools in economic analysis. They permit clear expression and handling of sometimes complex relationships.

Individual and Market Demand

Until now we have assumed just one consumer. Competition assumes many buyers are in the market. The transition from an *individual* to a *market* demand schedule can be accomplished easily by summing the quantities demanded by each consumer at the various possible prices. If there were just three buyers in the market, as is shown in Table 4-2, it would be easy to determine the total quantities demanded at each price. Figure 4-2 shows the same summing procedure graphically, using only the $3 price to illustrate the adding-up process. Note that we are simply summing the three individual demand curves *horizontally* to derive the total demand curve.

TABLE 4-2 Market demand for corn, three buyers (hypothetical data)

Price per bushel	Quantity demanded						Total quantity demanded per week
	First buyer		Second buyer		Third buyer		
$5	10	+	12	+	8	=	30
4	20	+	23	+	17	=	60
3	35	+	39	+	26	=	100
2	55	+	60	+	39	=	154
1	80	+	87	+	54	=	221

Competition, of course, entails many more than three buyers of a product. So—to avoid a lengthy addition process—suppose there are 200 buyers of corn in the market, each of whom chooses to buy the same amount at each of the various prices as our original consumer does. Thus, we can determine total or market demand by multiplying the quantity-demanded data of Table 4-1 by 200, as in Table 4-3. Curve D_1 in Figure 4-3 indicates this market demand curve for the 200 buyers.

Determinants of Demand

An economist constructing a demand curve such as D_1 in Figure 4-3 assumes that price is the most important influence on the amount of any product purchased. But the economist knows that other factors can and do affect purchases. Thus, in locating a given demand curve such as D_1, it must also be assumed that "other things are equal"; that is, certain *determinants* of the amount demanded are assumed to be constant. When any of

FIGURE 4-2 The market demand curve is the sum of the individual demand curves

Graphically the market demand curve (*D* total) is found by summing horizontally the individual demand curves (*D₁*, *D₂*, and *D₃*) of all consumers in the market.

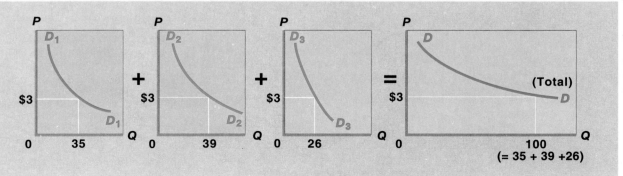

TABLE 4-3 Market demand for corn, 200 buyers (hypothetical data)

(1) Price per bushel	(2) Quantity demanded per week, single buyer		(3) Number of buyers in the market		(4) Total quantity demanded per week
$5	10	×	200	=	2,000
4	20	×	200	=	4,000
3	35	×	200	=	7,000
2	55	×	200	=	11,000
1	80	×	200	=	16,000

these determinants do change, the location of the demand curve will shift to the right or left of D_1. For this reason determinants of demand are referred to as *demand shifters*.

The basic determinants of market demand are: (1) the tastes or preferences of consumers, (2) the number of consumers in the market, (3) the money incomes of consumers, (4) prices of related goods, and (5) consumer expectations about future prices and incomes.

Changes in Demand

A change in one or more of the determinants of demand will change the demand schedule data in Table 4-3 and therefore the location of the demand curve in Figure 4-3. A change in the demand schedule data, or, graphically, a shift in the location of the demand curve, is called a *change in demand*.

If consumers become willing and able to buy more of this particular good at each possible price than is reflected in column 4 of Table 4-3, the result will be an *increase in demand*. In Figure 4-3, this increase in demand is reflected in a shift of the demand curve to the *right,* from D_1 to D_2. Conversely, a *decrease in demand* occurs when, because of a change in one or more of the determinants, consumers buy less of the product at each possible price than indicated in column 4 of Table 4-3. Graphically, a decrease in demand is shown as a shift of the demand curve to the *left,* for example, from D_1 to D_3 in Figure 4-3.

Let's now examine how changes in each determinant affect demand.

1 Tastes A change in consumer tastes or preferences favorable to a product—possibly prompted by

FIGURE 4-3 Changes in the demand for corn

A change in one or more of the determinants of demand—consumer tastes, the number of buyers in the market, money incomes, the prices of other goods, or consumer expectations—will cause a change in demand. An increase in demand shifts the demand curve to the right, as from D_1 to D_2. A decrease in demand shifts the demand curve to the left, as from D_1 to D_3. A change in the quantity demanded is caused by a change in the price of the product, and is shown by a movement from one point to another—as from *a* to *b*—on a fixed demand curve.

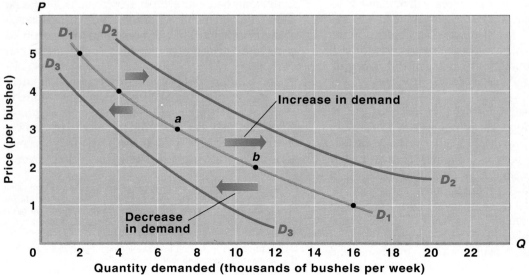

advertising or fashion changes—will mean that more will be demanded at each price; that is, demand will increase. An unfavorable change in consumer preferences will cause demand to decrease, shifting the curve to the left. Technological change in the form of a new product may prompt a revision of consumer tastes. For example, the introduction of compact discs has decreased the demand for long-playing records. Demand for oat bran has increased greatly because of health studies linking it to lower cholesterol levels.

2 Number of Buyers   An increase in the number of consumers in a market will increase demand. Fewer consumers will be reflected by a decrease in demand. For example, dramatic improvements in communications have made financial markets international in scope, increasing demand for stocks, bonds, and other financial instruments. And the "baby boom" after World War II increased demand for diapers, baby lotion, and services of obstetricians. When the "baby boom" generation reached their twenties in the 1970s, the demand for housing increased dramatically. Conversely, the aging of the baby boomers in the 1980s and 1990s has been an important factor in the recent "slump" in housing demand. Also, increasing life expectancy has increased demands for medical care, retirement communities, and nursing homes. Note, too, that American trade negotiators are trying to reduce foreign trade barriers to American farm products to increase demands for those products.

3 Income   The impact of changes in money income on demand is more complex. For most commodities, a rise in income will cause an increase in demand. Consumers typically buy more steaks, sunscreen, and stereos as their incomes increase. Conversely, the demand for such products will decline in response to a fall in incomes. Commodities whose demand varies *directly* with money income are called **superior, or normal, goods.**

Although most products are normal goods, there are a few exceptions. As incomes increase beyond some point, the amounts of bread or lard or cabbages purchased at each price may diminish because higher incomes allow consumers to buy more high-protein foods, such as dairy products and meat. Rising incomes may also decrease demands for used clothing and third-hand automobiles. Similarly, rising incomes may cause demands for hamburger and margarine to decline as wealthier consumers switch to T-bones and butter. Goods whose demand varies *inversely* with a change in money income are called **inferior goods.**

4 Prices of Related Goods   Whether a given change in the price of a related good will increase or decrease the demand for a product will depend on whether the related good is a substitute for it or a complement to it. A substitute is a good which can be used in place of another good. A complement is a good used in conjunction with another good.

Substitutes   For example, butter and margarine are **substitute goods.** When the price of butter rises, consumers will buy less butter, and this will increase the demand for margarine.[2] Conversely, as the price of butter falls, consumers will buy more butter, causing the demand for margarine to decrease. *When two products are substitutes, the price of one good and the demand for the other are directly related.* So it is with Millers and Budweiser, sugar and Nutrasweet, Toyotas and Hondas, and Coke and Pepsi.

Complements   Other pairs of products are **complementary goods;** they "go together" in that they are jointly demanded. If the price of gasoline falls and, as a result, you drive your car more, this extra driving will increase your demand for motor oil. Conversely, an increase in the price of gasoline will diminish the demand for motor oil.[3] Thus gas and oil are jointly demanded; they are complements. So it is with ham and eggs, tuition and textbooks, VCRs and video cassettes, golf clubs and golf balls, cameras and rolls of film. *When two commodities are complements, the price of one good and the demand for the other are inversely related.*

Many pairs of goods, of course, are not related at all—they are *independent* goods. For such pairs of commodities as, for example, butter and golf balls, potatoes and automobiles, bananas and wristwatches, a change in the price of one would have little or no impact on the demand for the other.

5 Expectations   Consumer expectations about future product prices, product availability, and future income can shift demand. Consumer expectations of higher future prices may prompt them to buy now to "beat" anticipated price rises; similarly, the expectation of rising incomes may induce consumers to be freer in

---

[2]Note that the consumer is moving up a stable demand curve for butter. But the demand curve for margarine shifts to the right (increases). Given the supply of margarine, this rightward shift in demand means more margarine will be purchased and that its price will also rise.

[3]While the buyer is moving up a stable demand curve for gasoline, the demand for motor oil shifts to the left (decreases). Given the supply of motor oil, this decline in the demand for motor oil will reduce both the amount purchased and its price.

current spending. Conversely, expectations of falling prices and income will decrease current demand for products. First example: If freezing weather destroys much of Florida's citrus crop, consumers may reason that forthcoming shortages of frozen orange juice will escalate its price. They may stock up on orange juice by purchasing extraordinarily large quantities now. Second example: Several years ago Johnny Carson jokingly predicted a toilet paper shortage. Many of his TV fans took this seriously and within a few days toilet paper was not to be found on the shelves of many supermarkets. Third example: A first-round NFL draft choice might splurge for a new Mercedes in anticipation of a lucrative professional football contract. Final example: Additional Federal excise taxes imposed on beer, wine, and distilled liquor on January 1, 1991, sharply increased demand in December of 1990 as consumers "bought early" to beat anticipated price increases.

In summary, an *increase* in demand—the decision by consumers to buy larger quantities of a product at each possible price—can be caused by:
1   A favorable change in consumer tastes
2   An increase in the number of buyers
3   Rising incomes if the product is a normal good
4   Falling incomes if the product is an inferior good
5   An increase in the price of a substitute good
6   A decrease in the price of a complementary good
7   Consumer expectations of higher future prices and incomes
Be sure you can "reverse" these generalizations to explain a *decrease* in demand. Table 4-4 provides additional illustrations to reinforce your understanding of the determinants of demand.

Changes in Quantity Demanded

A "change in demand" must not be confused with a "change in quantity demanded." A **change in demand** is a shift in the entire demand curve either to the right (an increase in demand) or to the left (a decrease in demand). The consumer's state of mind concerning purchases of this product has been altered. The cause: a change in one or more of the determinants of demand. The term "demand" refers to a schedule or curve; therefore, a "change in demand" means that the entire schedule has changed and that graphically the curve has shifted its position.

In contrast, a **change in the quantity demanded** designates the movement from one point to another point—from one price-quantity combination to an-

TABLE 4-4   Determinants of demand: factors that shift the demand curve

1   **Change in buyer tastes   Example: Physical fitness increases in popularity, increasing the demand for jogging shoes and bicycles**

2   **Change in number of buyers   Examples: Japanese reduce import quotas on American telecommunications equipment, thereby increasing the demand for such equipment; a decline in the birthrate reduces the demand for education**

3   **Change in income   Examples: An increase in incomes increases the demand for such normal goods as butter, lobster, and filet mignon, while reducing the demand for such inferior goods as cabbage, turnips, retreaded tires, and used clothing**

4   **Change in the prices of related goods   Examples: A reduction in air fares reduces the demand for bus transportation (substitute goods); a decline in the price of compact disc players increases the demand for compact discs (complementary goods)**

5   **Change in expectations   Example: Inclement weather in South America causes the expectation of higher future coffee prices, thereby increasing the current demand for coffee**

other—on a fixed demand curve. The cause of a change in quantity demanded is a change in the price of the product under consideration. In Table 4-3 a decline in the price from $5 to $4 will increase the quantity of corn demanded from 2000 to 4000 bushels.

The distinction between a change in demand and a change in the quantity demanded can be seen in Figure 4-3. The shift of the demand curve D_1 to either D_2 or D_3 is a "change in demand." But the movement from point a to point b on curve D_1 is a "change in the quantity demanded."

You should decide whether a change in demand or a change in quantity demanded is involved in each of the following illustrations:
1   Consumer incomes rise, with the result that more jewelry is purchased.
2   A barber raises the price of haircuts and experiences a decline in volume of business.
3   The price of Toyotas goes up, and, as a consequence, the sales of Chevrolets increase.

QUICK REVIEW 4-1

✦   *A market is any arrangement which facilitates purchase and sale of goods, services, or resources.*

✦   *The law of demand indicates that, other things being constant, the quantity of a good purchased will vary inversely with its price.*

♦ *The demand curve will shift because of changes in a consumer tastes, b the number of buyers in the market, c incomes, d the prices of substitute or complementary goods, and e expectations.*

♦ *A "change in quantity demanded" refers to a movement from one point to another on a stable demand curve; a "change in demand" designates a shift in the entire demand curve.*

SUPPLY

Supply *is a schedule which shows the amounts of a product a producer is willing and able to produce and make available for sale at each price in a series of possible prices during a specified period.*[4] This **supply schedule** portrays a series of alternative possibilities, such as shown in Table 4-5, for a single producer of corn. Supply tells us the quantities of a product which will be supplied at various prices, all other factors held constant.

Our definition of supply indicates that supply is usually viewed from the vantage point of price. That is, we read supply as showing the amounts producers will offer at various prices. It is equally correct and more useful in some instances to view supply from the reference point of quantity. Instead of asking what quantities will be offered at various prices, we can ask what prices will be required to induce producers to offer various quantities of a good.

Law of Supply

Table 4-5 shows a positive or *direct* relationship between price and quantity supplied. As price rises, the corresponding quantity supplied rises; as price falls, the quantity supplied also falls. This particular relationship is called the **law of supply.** Producers will produce and offer for sale more of their product at a high price than at a low price. This again is basically a commonsense matter.

Price is a deterrent from the consumer's standpoint. The obstacle of a high price means that the consumer, being on the paying end of this price, will buy a relatively small amount of the product; the lower the price obstacle, the more the consumer will buy. The supplier is on the receiving end of the product's price.

[4]In talking of the resource market, our definition of supply reads: a schedule which shows the various amounts of a resource which its owners are willing to supply in the market at each possible price in a series of prices during a specified time.

TABLE 4-5 An individual producer's supply of corn (hypothetical data)

Price per bushel	Quantity supplied per week
$5	60
4	50
3	35
2	20
1	5

To a supplier, price is revenue per unit and therefore an inducement or incentive to produce and sell a product. Given production costs, a higher product price means greater profits for the supplier and thus an incentive to increase the quantity supplied.

Consider a farmer who can shift resources within limits among alternative products. As price moves up in Table 4-5, the farmer will find it profitable to take land out of wheat, oats, and soybean production and put it into corn. Furthermore, higher corn prices will make it possible for the farmer to cover the costs associated with more intensive cultivation and the use of larger quantities of fertilizers and pesticides. All these efforts result in more output of corn.

Now consider a manufacturing concern. Beyond some point manufacturers usually encounter increasing production costs per added unit of output. Therefore, a higher product price is necessary to cover these rising costs. Costs rise because certain productive resources—in particular, the firm's plant and machinery—cannot be expanded quickly. As the firm increases the amounts of more readily variable resources such as labor, materials, and component parts, the fixed plant will at some point become crowded or congested. Productive efficiency will decline and the cost of successive units of output will increase. Producers must receive a higher price to produce these more costly units. Price and quantity supplied are directly related.

The Supply Curve

As with demand, it is convenient to represent graphically the concept of supply. Our axes in Figure 4-4 are the same as those in Figure 4-3, except for the change of "quantity demanded" to "quantity supplied" on the horizontal axis. The graphing procedure is the same, but the quantity data and relationship involved are different. The market supply data graphed in Figure 4-4 as S_1 are shown in Table 4-6, which assumes there are 200 suppliers in the market having the same supply

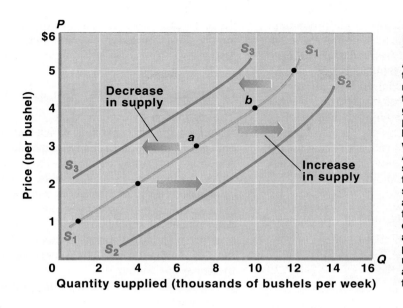

FIGURE 4-4 Changes in the supply of corn

A change in one or more of the determinants of supply—resource prices, productive techniques, the prices of other goods, taxes and subsidies, price expectations, or the number of sellers in the market—will cause a change in supply. An increase in supply shifts the supply curve to the right, as from S_1 to S_2. A decrease in supply is shown graphically as a shift of the curve to the left, as from S_1 to S_3. A change in the quantity supplied is caused by a change in the price of the product and is shown by a movement from one point to another—as from *a* to *b*—on a fixed supply curve.

schedules as the producer previously portrayed in Table 4-5.

Determinants of Supply

In constructing a supply curve, the economist assumes that price is the most significant influence on the quantity supplied of any product. But, as with the demand curve, the supply curve is anchored on the "other things are equal" assumption. The supply curve is drawn assuming that certain determinants of the amount supplied are given and do not change. If any of these determinants of supply do change, the supply curve will shift.

The basic determinants of supply are (1) resource prices, (2) the technique of production, (3) taxes and subsidies, (4) prices of other goods, (5) price expectations, and (6) the number of sellers in the market. A change in any one or more of these determinants or *supply shifters* will cause the supply curve for a product to shift either to the right or the left. A shift to the *right,* from S_1 to S_2 in Figure 4-4, designates an *increase in supply:* Producers are now supplying larger quantities of the product at each possible price. A shift to the *left,* S_1 to S_3 in Figure 4-4, indicates a *decrease in supply:* Suppliers are offering less at each price.

Changes in Supply

Let's consider how changes in each of these determinants affect supply.

1 Resource Prices As indicated in our explanation of the law of supply, the relationship between production costs and supply is an intimate one. A firm's supply curve is based on production costs; a firm must receive higher prices for additional units of output because those extra units cost more to produce. It follows that a decrease in resource prices will lower production costs and increase supply, that is, shift the supply curve to the right. If prices of seed and fertilizer decrease, we can expect the supply of corn to increase. Conversely, an increase in resource prices will raise production costs and reduce supply, that is, shift the supply curve to the left. Increases in the prices of iron ore and coke will increase the cost of producing steel and reduce its supply.

TABLE 4-6 Market supply of corn, 200 producers (hypothetical data)

(1) Price per bushel	(2) Quantity supplied per week, single producer		(3) Number of sellers in the market		(4) Total quantity supplied per week
$5	60	×	200	=	12,000
4	50	×	200	=	10,000
3	35	×	200	=	7,000
2	20	×	200	=	4,000
1	5	×	200	=	1,000

2 Technology A technological improvement means new knowledge permits us to produce a unit of output with fewer resources. Given the prices of these resources, this will lower production costs and increase supply. Recent breakthroughs in superconductivity portend the possibility of transporting electric power with little or no loss. Currently, about 30 percent of electric power transmitted by copper cable is lost. Consequence? Significant cost reductions and supply increases might occur in a wide range of products where energy is an important input.

3 Taxes and Subsidies Businesses treat most taxes as costs. Therefore, an increase in sales or property taxes will increase costs and reduce supply. Conversely, subsidies are "taxes in reverse." If government subsidizes the production of a good, it in effect lowers costs and increases supply.

4 Prices of Other Goods Changes in the prices of other goods can also shift the supply curve for a product. A decline in the price of wheat may cause a farmer to produce and offer more oats at each possible price. Conversely, a rise in the price of wheat may make farmers less willing to produce and offer oats in the market. A firm manufacturing athletic equipment might reduce its supply of basketballs in response to a rise in the price of soccer balls.

5 Expectations Expectations concerning the future price of a product can affect a producer's current willingness to supply that product. It is difficult, however, to generalize how the expectation of higher prices will affect the present supply of a product. Farmers might withhold some of their current corn harvest from the market, anticipating a higher corn price in the future. This will cause a decrease in the current supply of corn. Similarly, if the price of IBM stock is expected to rise significantly in the near future, the supply offered today for sale might decrease. On the other hand, in many types of manufacturing, expected price increases may induce firms to add another shift of workers or expand their production facilities, causing supply to increase.

6 Number of Sellers Given the scale of operations of each firm, the larger the number of suppliers, the greater the market supply. As more firms enter an industry, the supply curve will shift to the right. The smaller the number of firms in an industry, the less the market supply will be. This means that as firms leave an industry, the supply curve will shift to the left.

Table 4-7 provides a checklist of the determinants of supply; the accompanying illustrations deserve careful study.

Changes in Quantity Supplied

The distinction between a "change in supply" and a "change in quantity supplied" parallels that between a change in demand and a change in quantity demanded. A **change in supply** means the entire supply curve shifts. An increase in supply shifts the curve to the right; a decrease in supply shifts it to the left. The cause of a change in supply is a change in one or more of the determinants of supply. The term "supply" refers to a schedule or curve. A "change in supply" therefore must mean that the entire schedule has changed and that the curve has shifted.

A **change in the quantity supplied** refers to the movement from one point to another on a stable supply curve. The cause of such a movement is a change in the price of the specific product under consideration. In Table 4-6 a decline in the price of corn from $5 to $4 decreases the quantity of corn supplied from 12,000 to 10,000 bushels.

Shifting the supply curve from S_1 to S_2 or S_3 in Figure 4-4 entails "changes in supply." The movement

TABLE 4-7 **Determinants of supply: factors that shift the supply curve**

1 **Change in resource prices** **Examples: A decline in the price of fertilizer increases the supply of wheat; an increase in the price of irrigation equipment reduces the supply of corn**

2 **Change in technology** **Example: The development of a more effective insecticide for corn rootworm increases the supply of corn**

3 **Changes in taxes and subsidies** **Examples: An increase in the excise tax on cigarettes reduces the supply of cigarettes; a decline in subsidies to state universities reduces the supply of higher education**

4 **Change in prices of other goods** **Example: A decline in the prices of mutton and pork increases the supply of beef**

5 **Change in expectations** **Example: Expectations of substantial declines in future oil prices cause oil companies to increase current supply**

6 **Change in number of suppliers** **Examples: An increase in the number of firms producing personal computers increases the supply of personal computers; formation of a new professional football league increases the supply of professional football games**

from point *a* to point *b* on S_1, however, is a "change in quantity supplied."

You should determine which of the following involves a change in supply and which a change in quantity supplied:

1 Because production costs decline, producers sell more automobiles.

2 The price of wheat declines, causing the number of bushels of corn sold per month to increase.

3 Fewer oranges are offered for sale because their price has decreased in retail markets.

4 The Federal government doubles its excise tax on liquor.

QUICK REVIEW 4-2

♪ *The law of supply states that, other things being unchanged, the quantity of a good supplied varies directly with its price.*

♪ *The supply curve will shift because of changes in* **a** *resource prices,* **b** *technology,* **c** *taxes or subsidies,* **d** *prices of other goods,* **e** *expectations regarding future product prices, and* **f** *the number of suppliers.*

♪ *A "change in supply" means a shift in the supply curve; a "change in quantity supplied" designates the movement from one point to another on a given supply curve.*

SUPPLY AND DEMAND: MARKET EQUILIBRIUM

We may now bring the concepts of supply and demand together to see how interaction of the buying decisions of households and the selling decisions of producers will determine the price of a product and the quantity actually bought and sold in the market. In Table 4-8,

TABLE 4-8 Market supply and demand for corn (hypothetical data)

(1) Total quantity supplied per week	(2) Price per bushel	(3) Total quantity demanded per week	(4) Surplus (+) or shortage (−) (arrows indicate effect on price)
12,000	$5	2,000	+10,000 ↓
10,000	4	4,000	+ 6,000 ↓
7,000	3	7,000	0
4,000	2	11,000	− 7,000 ↑
1,000	1	16,000	−15,000 ↑

columns 1 and 2 reproduce the market supply schedule for corn (from Table 4-6), and columns 2 and 3, the market demand schedule for corn (from Table 4-3). Note that in column 2 we are using a common set of prices. We assume competition—a large number of buyers and sellers.

Surpluses

Of the five[5] possible prices at which corn might sell in this market, which will actually prevail as the market price for corn? Let us derive our answer through the simple process of trial and error. For no particular reason, we start with $5. Could this be the prevailing market price for corn? The answer is "No," because producers are willing to produce and offer in the market some 12,000 bushels of corn at this price while buyers are willing to buy only 2000 bushels at this price. The relatively high price of $5 encourages farmers to produce a great deal of corn, but discourages most consumers from buying it. Other products appear as "better buys" when corn is high-priced. The result here is a 10,000-bushel **surplus** or *excess supply* of corn in the market. This surplus, shown in column 4, is the excess of quantity supplied over quantity demanded at the price of $5. Corn farmers find themselves with unwanted inventories of output.

A price of $5—even if it existed temporarily in the corn market—could not persist over a period of time. The very large surplus of corn would prompt competing sellers to bid down the price to encourage buyers to take this surplus off their hands.

Suppose price goes down to $4. Now the situation has changed considerably. The lower price has encouraged buyers to take more of this product off the market and, at the same time, has induced farmers to use a smaller amount of resources in producing corn. The surplus has diminished to 6000 bushels. However, a surplus or excess supply still exists and competition among sellers will once again bid down the price of corn. We can conclude, then, that prices of $5 and $4 will be unstable because they are "too high." The market price for corn must be something less than $4.

Shortages

Let's now jump to the other end of our price column and examine $1 as the possible market price for corn.

---

[5]Of course, there are many possible prices; our example shows only five of them.

Observe in column 4 that at this price, quantity demanded is in excess of quantity supplied by 15,000 units. This relatively low price discourages farmers from devoting their resources to corn production and encourages consumers to attempt to buy more than is available. The result is a 15,000-bushel **shortage** of, or *excess demand* for, corn. This price of $1 cannot persist as the market price. Competition among buyers will bid up the price to something greater than $1. At a price of $1, many consumers who are willing and able to buy at this price will be left out in the cold. Many potential consumers will express a willingness to pay a price above $1 to ensure getting some of the available corn.

Suppose this competitive bidding up of price by buyers boosts the price of corn to $2. This higher price has reduced, but not eliminated, the shortage of corn. For $2, farmers are willing to devote more resources to corn production, and some buyers who were willing to pay $1 for a bushel of corn will choose not to buy at $2. But a shortage of 7000 bushels still exists at $2. We can conclude that competitive bidding among buyers will push market price above $2.

Equilibrium

By trial and error we have eliminated every price but $3. At a price of $3, *and only at this price,* the quantity which farmers are willing to produce and supply in the market is identical with the amount consumers are willing and able to buy. As a result, there is neither a shortage nor a surplus of corn at this price. A surplus causes price to decline and a shortage causes price to rise.

With neither a shortage nor a surplus at $3, there is no reason for the actual price of corn to move away from this price. The economist calls this price the *market-clearing* or **equilibrium price,** equilibrium meaning "in balance" or "at rest." At $3, quantity supplied and quantity demanded are in balance; that is, **equilibrium quantity** is 7000 bushels. Hence $3 is the only stable price of corn under the supply and demand conditions shown in Table 4-8. Or, stated differently, the price of corn will be established where the supply decisions of producers and the demand decisions of buyers are mutually consistent. Such decisions are consistent with one another only at a price of $3. At any higher price, suppliers want to sell more than consumers want to buy and a surplus will result; at any lower price, consumers want to buy more than producers are willing to offer for sale, as shown by the consequent

shortage. Discrepancies between supply and demand intentions of sellers and buyers will prompt price changes which will bring these two sets of plans into accord with one another.

A graphical analysis of supply and demand should yield the same conclusions. Figure 4-5 (Key Graph) puts the market supply and market demand curves for corn on the same graph, the horizontal axis now measuring both quantity demanded and quantity supplied. At any price above the equilibrium price of $3, quantity supplied will exceed quantity demanded. This surplus will cause a competitive bidding down of price by sellers eager to rid themselves of their surplus. The falling price will cause less corn to be offered and will simultaneously encourage consumers to buy more.

Any price below the equilibrium price will entail a shortage; quantity demanded will exceed quantity supplied. Competitive bidding by buyers will push the price up toward the equilibrium level. And this rising price will simultaneously cause producers to increase the quantity supplied and ration buyers out of the market, thereby eliminating the shortage. *Graphically, the intersection of the supply curve and the demand curve for the product will indicate the equilibrium point.* In this case equilibrium price and quantity are $3 per bushel and 7000 bushels.

Rationing Function of Prices

The ability of the competitive forces of supply and demand to establish a price where selling and buying decisions are synchronized or coordinated is called the **rationing function of prices.** In this case, the equilibrium price of $3 clears the market, leaving no burdensome surplus for sellers and no inconvenient shortage for potential buyers. The composite of freely made individual buying and selling decisions sets this price which clears the market. In effect, the market mechanism of supply and demand says that any buyer willing and able to pay $3 for a bushel of corn will be able to acquire one; those who are not, will not. Similarly, any seller willing and able to produce bushels of corn and offer them for sale at $3 will be able to do so; those who are not, will not.

Changes in Supply and Demand

We know that demand might change because of fluctuations in consumer tastes or incomes, changes in consumer expectations, or variations in the prices of related goods. Supply might vary in response to changes

KEY GRAPH

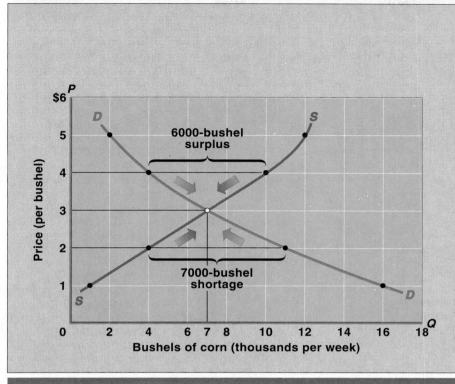

FIGURE 4-5

The equilibrium price and quantity for corn as determined by market demand and supply

The intersection of the down-sloping demand curve *D* and the upsloping supply curve *S* indicates the equilibrium price and quantity, $3 and 7000 bushels in this instance. The shortages of corn which would exist at below-equilibrium prices, for example, 7000 bushels at $2, drive price up, and in so doing, increase the quantity supplied and reduce the quantity demanded until equilibrium is achieved. The surpluses which above-equilibrium prices would entail, for example, 6000 bushels at $4, push price down and thereby increase the quantity demanded and reduce the quantity supplied until equilibrium is achieved.

---

in technology, resource prices, or taxes. Our analysis would be incomplete if we did not consider the effect of changes in supply and demand on equilibrium price.

Changing Demand　First, we analyze the effects of a change in demand, assuming supply is constant. Suppose demand increases, as shown in Figure 4-6a. What is the effect on price? Since the new intersection of the supply and demand curves is at a higher point on both the price and quantity axes, an increase in demand, other things (supply) being equal, will have a *price-increasing effect* and a *quantity-increasing effect*. (The value of graphical analysis is now apparent; we need not fumble with columns of figures in determining the effect on price and quantity but only compare the new with the old point of intersection on the graph.)

A decrease in demand, shown in Figure 4-6b, reveals both *price-decreasing* and *quantity-decreasing effects*. Price falls, and quantity also declines. *In brief, we*

find a direct relationship between a change in demand and resulting changes in both equilibrium price and quantity.

Changing Supply　Let's now analyze the effect of a change in supply on price, assuming that demand is constant. If supply increases, as in Figure 4-6c, the new intersection of supply and demand is located at a lower equilibrium price. Equilibrium quantity, however, increases. If supply decreases, product price will rise. Figure 4-6d illustrates this situation. Here, price increases but quantity declines.

In short, an increase in supply has a *price-decreasing* and a *quantity-increasing effect*. A decrease in supply has a *price-increasing* and a *quantity-decreasing effect*. *There is an inverse relationship between a change in supply and the resulting change in equilibrium price, but the relationship between a change in supply and the resulting change in equilibrium quantity is direct.*

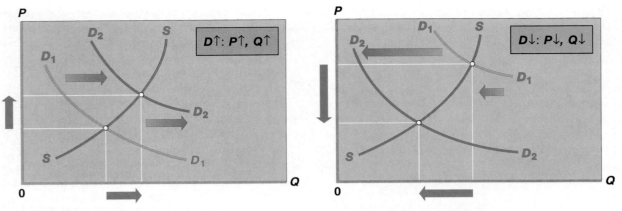

(a) Increase in demand (b) Decrease in demand

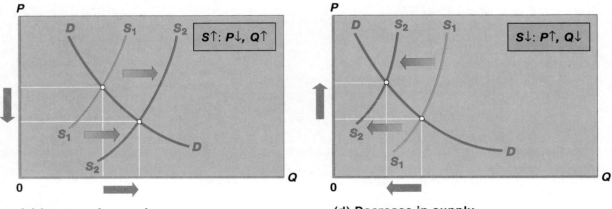

(c) Increase in supply (d) Decrease in supply

FIGURE 4-6 Changes in demand and supply and the effects on price and quantity

The increase in demand of (a) and the decrease in demand of (b) indicate a direct relationship between a change in demand and the resulting changes in equilibrium price and quantity. The increase in supply of (c) and the decrease in supply of (d) show an inverse relationship between a change in supply and the resulting change in equilibrium price, but a direct relationship between a change in supply and the accompanying change in equilibrium quantity.

Complex Cases A host of more complex cases might arise, involving changes in both supply and demand.

1 Supply Increase; Demand Decrease Assume first that supply increases and demand decreases. What effect does this have on equilibrium price? This example couples two price-decreasing effects, and the net result will be a price fall greater than what would result from either change alone. How about equilib-

rium quantity? Here the effects of the changes in supply and demand are opposed: The increase in supply increases equilibrium quantity, but the decrease in demand reduces the equilibrium quantity. The direction of the change in quantity depends on the relative sizes of the changes in supply and demand.

2 Supply Decrease; Demand Increase Another possibility is for supply to decrease and demand to increase. Two price-increasing effects are involved here.

We can predict an increase in equilibrium price greater than that caused by either change separately. The effect on equilibrium quantity is again indeterminate, depending on the relative size of the changes in supply and demand. If the decrease in supply is relatively larger than the increase in demand, the equilibrium quantity will be less than initially. But if the decrease in supply is relatively smaller than the increase in demand, the equilibrium quantity will increase as a result of these changes. You should trace through these two cases graphically to verify these conclusions.

3 Supply Increase; Demand Increase What if supply and demand both increase? What is the effect on equilibrium price? It depends. Here we must compare two conflicting effects on price—the price-decreasing effect of the increase in supply and the price-increasing effect of the increase in demand. If the increase in supply is greater than the increase in demand, the equilibrium price will decrease. If the opposite holds, equilibrium price will increase.

The effect on equilibrium quantity is certain: Increases in supply and in demand both have quantity-increasing effects. This means that equilibrium quantity will increase by an amount greater than either change alone.

4 Supply Decrease; Demand Decrease A decrease in both supply and demand can be similarly analyzed. If the decrease in supply is greater than the decrease in demand, equilibrium price will rise. If the reverse holds true, equilibrium price will fall. Because decreases in supply and demand both have quantity-decreasing effects, it can be predicted with certainty that equilibrium quantity will be less than that which prevailed initially.

Special cases might arise where a decrease in demand and a decrease in supply, on the one hand, and an increase in demand and an increase in supply, on the other, exactly cancel out. In both these cases, the net effect on equilibrium price will be zero; price will not change. You should also work out these more complex cases in terms of supply and demand curves to verify all these results.

The Resource Market

As in the product market, resource supply curves are typically upsloping, and resource demand curves are downsloping.

Resource supply curves reflect a *direct* relationship between resource price and quantity supplied, because it is in the interest of resource owners to supply more of a particular resource at a high price than at a low price. High income payments in a particular occupation or industry encourage households to supply more human and property resources. Low-income payments discourage resource owners from supplying resources in this particular occupation or industry and encourage them to supply their resources elsewhere. There is strong evidence, incidentally, that most college students choose their major (their occupation) on the basis of prospective financial rewards.

On the demand side, businesses buy less of a given resource as its price rises, and they substitute other relatively low-priced resources for it. Entrepreneurs will find it profitable to substitute low- for high-priced resources as they try to minimize costs. More of a particular resource will be demanded at a low price than at a high price. The result? A downsloping demand curve for the various resources.

Just as supply decisions of businesses and the demand decisions of consumers determine prices in the product market, so the supply decisions of households and demand decisions of businesses set prices in the resource market.

"Other Things Equal" Revisited

Recall from Chapter 1 that as a substitute for their inability to conduct controlled experiments, economists invoke the "other things being equal" assumption in their analyses. We have seen in the present chapter that a number of forces bear on both supply and demand. Hence, in locating specific supply and demand curves, such as D_1 and S in Figure 4-6a, economists isolate the impact of what they judge to be the most important influence on the amounts supplied and demanded—the price of the specific product under consideration. In thus representing the laws of demand and supply by downsloping and upsloping curves respectively, the economist assumes that the determinants of demand (incomes, tastes, and so forth) and supply (resource prices, technology, and other factors) are constant or unchanging. That is, price and quantity demanded are inversely related, *other things being equal.* And price and quantity supplied are directly related, *other things being equal.*

If you forget the "other things equal" assumption, you can encounter situations which *seem* to be in conflict with the laws of demand and supply. For example, suppose Ford sells 200,000 Escorts in 1990 at $8000; 300,000 at $8500 in 1991; and 400,000 in 1992 at $9000. Price and the number purchased vary *directly,* and these real-world data seem to be at odds with the law of demand. But there is really not a conflict here; these data do *not* refute the law of demand. The catch is that the law of demand's "other things equal" assumption has been violated over the three years in the example. Specifically, because of, for example, growing incomes, population growth, and relatively high gasoline prices which increase the attractiveness of compact cars, the demand curve for Escorts has increased over the years—shifted to the right as from D_1 to D_2 in Figure 4-6a—causing price to rise and, simultaneously, a larger quantity to be purchased.

Conversely, consider Figure 4-6d. Comparing the original S_1D and the new S_2D equilibrium positions, *less* of the product is being sold or supplied at a higher price; that is, price and quantity supplied seem to be *inversely* related, rather than *directly* related as the law of supply indicates. The catch again is that the "other things equal" assumption underlying the upsloping supply curve has been violated. Perhaps production costs have gone up or a specific tax has been levied on this product, shifting the supply curve from S_1 to S_2. These examples also emphasize the importance of our earlier distinction between a "change in quantity demanded (or supplied)" and a "change in demand (supply)."

QUICK REVIEW 4-3

♦   *In competitive markets price adjusts to the equilibrium level at which quantity demanded equals quantity supplied.*

♦   *A change in demand alters both equilibrium price and equilibrium quantity in the same direction as the change in demand.*

♦   *A change in supply causes equilibrium price to change in the opposite direction, but equilibrium quantity to change in the same direction, as the change in supply.*

♦   *Over time equilibrium price and quantity may change in directions which seem at odds with the laws of demand and supply because the "other things equal" assumption is violated.*

APPLICATION: THE FOREIGN EXCHANGE MARKET[6]

We close this chapter by applying our understanding of demand and supply to the **foreign exchange market,** the market where various national currencies are exchanged for one another. At the outset two points merit emphasis.

1   Real-world foreign exchange markets conform closely to the kinds of markets studied in this chapter. These are competitive markets characterized by large numbers of buyers and sellers dealing in a standardized "product" such as the American dollar, the German mark, the British pound, or the Japanese yen.

2   The price or exchange value of a nation's currency is an unusual price in that it links *all* domestic (United States) prices with *all* foreign (say, Japanese or German) prices. Exchange rates enable consumers in one country to translate prices of foreign goods into units of their own currency by multiplying the foreign product price by the exchange rate. For example, if the dollar-yen exchange rate is 1 cent per yen, a Sony cassette player priced at 20,000 yen will cost an American $200 (=20,000 × 1¢). But if the exchange rate is 2 cents per yen, the Sony will cost an American $400 (=20,000 × 2¢). Similarly, all other Japanese products will double in price to American buyers. As we shall see, a change in exchange rates has important implications for a nation's levels of domestic production and employment.

The Dollar-Yen Market

Skirting technical details, we now examine how the foreign exchange market for dollars and yen might work. When nations trade they need to exchange their currencies. American exporters who sell to Japan want to be paid in dollars, not yen; but Japanese importers of American goods possess yen, not dollars. This problem is resolved by Japanese offering or supplying yen in exchange for dollars. Conversely, American importers need to pay Japanese exporters with yen, not dollars. To do so they go to the foreign exchange market as demanders of yen. We can think of Japanese importers as suppliers of yen and American importers as demanders of yen. The interaction of the demand for yen and the supply of yen will establish the dollar price of yen. Suppose the equilibrium dollar price of yen—the dollar-yen exchange rate—is $1 = ¥100. That is, a

---

[6]Some instructors may choose to skip this section.

LAST WORD

THE HIGH PRICE OF MARIJUANA

In late 1990 and early 1991 the Drug Enforcement Agency reported that the price of marijuana reached historic highs.

At the start of this decade the price of a "lid" (an ounce) of marijuana ranged from $200 to $400 in the United States. In comparison an ounce of gold was selling for $370.

Simple supply and demand explains this "reefer madness." On the demand side marijuana is by far the nation's most commonly used illegal drug. It is estimated that about one-third of all American adults— some 66 million people—have used pot at least once during their lives. However, the demand for marijuana is declining. In 1979 over 35 percent of all young adults (aged 18–25) used pot at least once a month. By 1990 this figure had declined to less than 13 percent. Stated differently, over 22 million people smoked marijuana in 1979 compared to slightly over 10 million in 1990. Other things the same, a declining demand should mean lower, not higher, pot prices.

But other things have not been the same. For a variety of reasons substantial reductions in marijuana supply have occurred. First, law enforcement in Mexico—a major exporter of pot to the United States— has improved. Second, many pot producers have shifted their resources to alternative drugs. In particu-

lar, Colombia's incredibly profitable cocaine industry has expanded and attracted resources from marijuana. It is also cheaper and easier to smuggle small quantities of cocaine compared to bulky truck- and plane-loads of marijuana. Third, the interdiction of pot smugglers has improved; less marijuana is coming over our borders. Finally, within the United States efforts to apprehend marijuana growers and destroy their crops have been increasingly effective.

How to explain the high price of pot? Quite simply: Supply has fallen much more dramatically than has demand.

dollar will buy 100 yen (the "dollar price" of 1 yen is 1 cent) and therefore 100 yen worth of Japanese goods. Conversely, 100 yen will buy $1 worth of American goods.

Changing Rates: Depreciation and Appreciation

What might cause this exchange rate to change? The determinants of the demand for and the supply of yen are similar to those we have already discussed. From the vantage point of the United States, several things might take place to increase the demand for —and therefore the dollar price of—yen. Incomes might rise in the United States, causing Americans to buy not only more domestic goods, but also more Sony televisions, Nikon cameras, and Nissan automobiles from Japan. To do this Americans need more yen, so

the demand for yen increases. Or there may be a change in American tastes which enhances our preferences for Japanese goods. For instance, when gasoline prices soared in the 1970s, many American auto buyers shifted their demands from large, gas-guzzling domestic cars to gas-efficient Japanese compact cars. In so doing the demand for yen increased.

The point is that an increase in the American demand for Japanese goods will increase the demand for yen and raise the dollar price of yen. Let's suppose the dollar price of yen rises from $1 = ¥100 (or 1¢ = ¥1) to $2 = ¥100 (or 2¢ = ¥1). When the dollar price of yen *increases,* a **depreciation** of the dollar relative to the yen has occurred. Dollar depreciation means that it takes more dollars (pennies in this case) to buy a single unit of a foreign currency (the yen). A dollar is worth less because it will buy fewer yen and therefore fewer Japanese goods.

If events opposite to those we have presumed had occurred—that is, if incomes rose in Japan and Japanese preferences for American goods strengthened—then the *supply* of yen in foreign exchange markets would increase. This increase in the supply of yen relative to demand would *decrease* the equilibrium dollar price of yen. For example, supply might increase to the extent that the dollar price of yen declines from the original $1 = ¥100, or 1¢ = ¥1, to $.50 = ¥100 or ½¢ = ¥1.

This *decrease* in the dollar price of yen means there has been an **appreciation** of the dollar relative to the yen. Appreciation means it takes fewer dollars (pennies) to buy a single yen than previously. The dollar is worth more because it can purchase more yen and therefore more Japanese goods.

Economic Consequences

The profound consequences of changes in exchange rates are easily perceived. Suppose America is operating at a point inside its production possibilities curve and the dollar depreciates, that is, the dollar price of yen rises from 1¢ = ¥1 to 2¢ = ¥1. This means that the yen and therefore *all* Japanese goods are now more expensive to Americans. Therefore, American consumers shift their expenditures from Japanese to American goods. The Chevy Corsica is now relatively more attractive than the Honda Accord to American consumers. American industries are stimulated by this shift in expenditures and their production and employment both rise. Conversely, Japanese export industries find the sales of their products diminishing, so output and employment both tend to decline. The depreciation of the dollar has caused America to become more prosperous and Japan less so.

You are urged to confirm that an appreciation of the dollar's value relative to the yen will tend to depress the American economy and stimulate the Japanese economy.

With the economic stakes so high, it is easy to understand why governments often interfere with otherwise "free" foreign exchange markets. Thus, the United States government might attempt to depreciate the dollar when our economy is at less than full employment. The problem, however, is that the consequent shift in American expenditures from foreign goods to domestic goods will lower Japanese exports and tend to depress *their* economy. The Japanese government may well be interested in offsetting the depreciation of the dollar which the Americans desire. Both the economic and political implications of exchange rates are great, and they will be considered in later chapters.

CHAPTER SUMMARY

1 A market is any institution or arrangement which brings buyers and sellers of some product or service together.

2 Demand refers to a schedule which summarizes the willingness of buyers to purchase a given product during a specific time period at each of the various prices at which it might be sold. According to the law of demand, consumers will ordinarily buy more of a product at a low price than they will at a high price. Therefore, other things being equal, the relationship between price and quantity demanded is negative or inverse and demand graphs as a downsloping curve.

3 Changes in one or more of the basic determinants of demand—consumer tastes, the number of buyers in the market, the money incomes of consumers, the prices of related goods, and consumer expectations—will cause the market demand curve to shift. A shift to the right is an increase in demand; a shift to the left, a decrease in demand. A "change in demand" is distinguished from a "change in the quantity demanded," the latter involving movement from one point to another point on a fixed demand curve because of a change in the price of the product under consideration.

4 Supply is a schedule showing the amounts of a product which producers would be willing to offer in the market during a given period at each possible price. The law of supply says that, other things equal, producers will offer more of a product at a high price than they will at a low price. As a result, the relationship between price and quantity supplied is a direct one, and the supply curve is upsloping.

5 A change in resource prices, production techniques, taxes or subsidies, the prices of other goods, price expectations, or the number of sellers in the market will cause the supply curve of a product to shift. A shift to the right is an increase in supply; a shift to the left, a decrease in supply. In contrast, a change in the price of the product under consideration will result in a change in the quantity supplied, that is, a movement from one point to another on a given supply curve.

6 Under competition, the interaction of market demand and market supply will adjust price to that point where quantity demanded and quantity supplied are equal. This is the equilibrium price. The corresponding quantity is the equilibrium quantity.

7 The ability of market forces to synchronize selling and buying decisions to eliminate potential surpluses or shortages is termed the "rationing function" of prices.

8 A change in either demand or supply will cause equilibrium price and quantity to change. There is a positive or direct relationship between a change in demand and the resulting changes in equilibrium price and quantity. Though the relationship between a change in supply and resulting change in equilibrium price is inverse, the relationship between a change in supply and equilibrium quantity is direct.

9 The concepts of supply and demand also apply to the resource market.

10 The foreign exchange market is an important application of demand and supply analysis. Foreign importers are suppliers of their currencies and American importers are demanders of foreign currencies. The resulting equilibrium exchange rates link the price levels of all nations.

11 Depreciation of the dollar reduces our imports and stimulates our domestic economy; dollar appreciation increases our imports and depresses our domestic economy.

TERMS AND CONCEPTS

market
demand
demand schedule
    (curve)
law of demand
diminishing marginal
    utility
income and
    substitution effects

normal (superior) good
inferior good
substitute goods
complementary goods
change in demand
    (supply) versus
    change in the
    quantity demanded
    (supplied)

supply
supply schedule
    (curve)
law of supply
surplus
shortage
equilibrium price and
    quantity

rationing function of
    prices
foreign exchange
    market
depreciation and
    appreciation of the
    dollar

QUESTIONS AND STUDY SUGGESTIONS

1 Explain the law of demand. Why does a demand curve slope downward? What are the determinants of demand? What happens to the demand curve when each of these determinants changes? Distinguish between a change in demand and a change in the quantity demanded, noting the cause(s) of each.

2 Critically evaluate: "In comparing the two equilibrium positions in Figure 4-6a, I note that a larger amount is actually purchased at a higher price. This refutes the law of demand."

3 Explain the law of supply. Why does the supply curve slope upward? What are the determinants of supply? What happens to the supply curve when each of these determinants changes? Distinguish between a change in supply and a change in the quantity supplied, noting the cause(s) of each.

4 Explain the following news dispatch from Hull, England: "The fish market here slumped today to what local commentators called 'a disastrous level'—all because of a shortage of potatoes. The potatoes are one of the main ingredients in a dish that figures on almost every café-menu—fish and chips."

5 Suppose the total demand for wheat and the total supply of wheat per month in the Kansas City grain market are as follows:

Thousands of bushels demanded	Price per bushel	Thousands of bushels supplied	Surplus (+) or shortage (−)
85	$3.40	72	_____
80	3.70	73	_____
75	4.00	75	_____
70	4.30	77	_____
65	4.60	79	_____
60	4.90	81	_____

a What will be the market or equilibrium price? What is the equilibrium quantity? Using the surplus-shortage column, explain why your answers are correct.

b Using the above data, graph the demand for wheat and the supply of wheat. Be sure to label the axes of your graph correctly. Label equilibrium price "P" and equilibrium quantity "Q."

c Why will $3.40 not be the equilibrium price in this market? Why not $4.90? "Surpluses drive prices up; shortages drive them down." Do you agree?

d Now suppose that the government establishes a ceiling price of, say, $3.70 for wheat. Explain carefully the effects of this ceiling price. Demonstrate your answer graphically. What might prompt government to establish a ceiling price?

e   Assume now that the government establishes a price floor of, say, $4.60 for wheat. Explain carefully the effects of this supported price. Demonstrate your answer graphically. What might prompt the government to establish this price support?

f   "Legally fixed prices strip the price mechanism of its rationing function." Explain this statement in terms of your answers to 5d and 5e.

6 Given supply, what effect will each of the following have on the demand for, and the equilibrium price and quantity of, product B?

a   Product B becomes more fashionable.

b   The price of product C, a good substitute for B, goes down.

c   Consumers anticipate declining prices and falling incomes.

d   There is a rapid upsurge in population growth.

7 Given demand, what effect will each of the following have on the supply and equilibrium price and quantity of product B?

a   A technological advance in the methods of producing B.

b   A decline in the number of firms in industry B.

c   An increase in the prices of resources required in the production of B.

d   The expectation that the equilibrium price of B will be lower in the future than it is currently.

e   A decline in the price of product A, a good whose production requires substantially the same techniques and resources as does the production of B.

f   The levying of a specific sales tax on B.

g   The granting of a 50-cent per unit subsidy for each unit of B produced.

8 Explain and illustrate graphically the effect of:

a   An increase in income on the demand curve of an inferior good.

b   A drop in the price of product S on the demand for substitute product T.

c   A decline in income on the demand curve of a normal good.

d   An increase in the price of product J on the demand for complementary good K.

9 "In the corn market, demand often exceeds supply and supply sometimes exceeds demand." "The price of corn rises and falls in response to changes in supply and demand." In which of these two statements are the terms "supply" and "demand" used correctly? Explain.

10 How will each of the following changes in demand and/or supply affect equilibrium price and equilibrium quantity in a competitive market; that is, do price and quantity *rise, fall, remain unchanged,* or are the answers *indeterminate,* depending on the magnitudes of the shifts in supply and demand? You should rely on a supply and demand diagram to verify answers.

a   Supply decreases and demand remains constant.

b   Demand decreases and supply remains constant.

c   Supply increases and demand is constant.

d   Demand increases and supply increases.

e   Demand increases and supply is constant.

f   Supply increases and demand decreases.

g   Demand increases and supply decreases.

h   Demand decreases and supply decreases.

11 "Prices are the automatic regulator that tends to keep production and consumption in line with each other." Explain.

12 Explain: "Even though parking meters may yield little or no net revenue, they should nevertheless be retained because of the rationing function they perform."

13 Use two market diagrams to explain how an increase in state subsidies to public colleges might affect tuition and enrollments in both public and private colleges.

14 What effects would United States import quotas on Japanese automobiles have on the American price of Japanese cars *and* on the demand for, and price of, American-made cars?

15 Many states have had usury laws stipulating the maximum interest rate which lenders (commercial banks, savings and loan associations, etc.) can charge borrowers. Indicate in some detail what would happen in the loan market during periods when the equilibrium interest rate exceeds the stipulated maximum. On the basis of your analysis, do you favor usury laws?

16 Explain why labor unions—whose members are paid wage rates far above the legal minimum—strongly and actively support increases in the minimum wage.

17 "Our imports create a demand for foreign monies; foreign imports of our goods generate supplies of foreign monies." Do you agree? Other things being equal, would a decline in American incomes or a weakening of American preferences for foreign products cause the dollar to depreciate or appreciate? What would be the effects of that depreciation or appreciation on production and employment domestically and abroad?

18 **Advanced analysis:** Assume that demand for a commodity is represented by the equation $P = 10 - .2Q_d$ and supply by the equation $P = 2 + .2Q_s$, where Q_d and Q_s are quantity demanded and quantity supplied, respectively, and P is price. Using the equilibrium condition $Q_s = Q_d$, solve the equations to determine equilibrium price. Now determine equilibrium quantity. Graph the two equations to substantiate your answers.

The Private Sectors and the Market System

hapters 5 and 6 will put meat on the bare-bones model of capitalism developed thus far. In this chapter we consider the private sectors—households, businesses, and the foreign sector. Chapter 6 is devoted to the public or governmental sector.

Our main goals in this chapter are twofold:

1 Households and businesses are the primary *decision makers* in our economy and we need to know more about them. We flesh out our discussion of a market economy by exploring the characteristics of the household, business, and foreign components of the private economy.

2 A system of markets and prices is the basic *coordinating mechanism* of a capitalistic system. We will examine how the market system synchronizes the innumerable decisions of the consumers, businesses, and resource suppliers which comprise the private sector.

HOUSEHOLDS AS INCOME RECEIVERS

The household sector of American capitalism is currently composed of some 94 million households. These households are the ultimate suppliers of all economic resources and simultaneously the major spending group in the economy. We will consider households first as income receivers and second as spenders.

There are two related approaches to studying the facts of income distribution.

1 The **functional distribution** of income indicates how society's money income is divided among wages, rents, interest, and profits. Here total income is distributed according to the function performed by the income receiver. Wages are paid to labor, rents and interest compensate property resources, and profits flow to the owners of corporations and unincorporated businesses.

2 The **personal distribution** of income shows the way total money income of society is apportioned among individual households.

The Functional Distribution of Income

The functional distribution of the nation's total earned income for 1991 is shown in Figure 5-1. Clearly the largest source of income for households is the wages and salaries paid to workers by the businesses and governmental units hiring them. In our capitalist system the bulk of total income goes to labor and not to

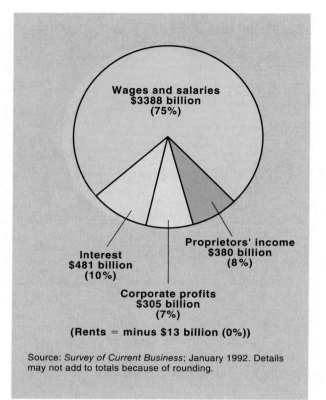

Source: *Survey of Current Business*; January 1992. Details may not add to totals because of rounding.

	Billions of dollars	*Percent of total*
Wages and salaries..........	$3388	75
Proprietors' income	380	8
Corporate profits	305	7
Interest	481	10
Rents	−13	0
Total earnings	$4541	100

FIGURE 5-1 The functional distribution of income, 1991

Almost three-fourths of national income is received as wages and salaries. Capitalist income—corporate profits, interest, and rents—only account for less than one-fifth of total income. (The "rents" figure is negative because depreciation exceeded rental income.)

"capital." Proprietors' income—that is, the incomes of doctors, lawyers, small business owners, farmers, and other unincorporated enterprises—is in fact a combination of wage, profit, rent, and interest incomes. The other three sources of earnings are virtually self-defining. Some households own corporate stock and receive dividend income on their holdings. Many households also own bonds and savings accounts which yield interest income. Rental income results from households providing buildings, land, and other natural resources to businesses.

Personal Distribution of Income

Figure 5-2 is an overall view of how total income is distributed among households. Here we divide families into five numerically equal groups or *quintiles* and show the percentage of total income received by each group. In 1990 the poorest 20 percent of all families received less than 5 percent of total personal income in contrast to the 20 percent they would have received if income were equally distributed. In comparison the richest 20 percent of all families received over 44 per-

cent of personal income. Thus the richest fifth of the population received almost ten times as much income as the poorest fifth. Given these data, most economists agree there is considerable inequality in the distribution of income.

HOUSEHOLDS AS SPENDERS

How do households dispose of the income they earn? Part flows to government in the form of personal taxes, and the rest is divided between personal consumption expenditures and personal saving. Specifically, households disposed of their total personal income in 1991 as shown in Figure 5-3.[1]

Personal Taxes

Personal taxes, of which the Federal personal income tax is the major component, have risen sharply in both

[1]The income concepts used in Figures 5-1 and 5-3 are different, accounting for the quantitative discrepancy between "total income" in the two figures.

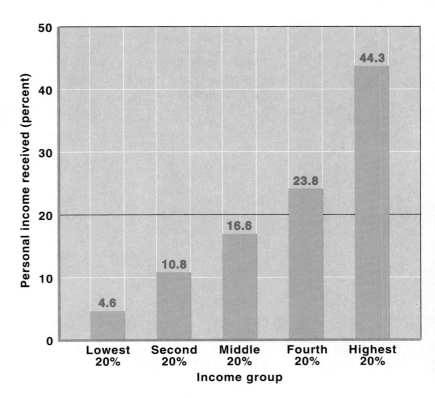

FIGURE 5-2 The distribution of income among families, 1990

Personal income is quite unequally distributed in the United States. An equal distribution would mean that all vertical bars would be equal to the horizontal line drawn at 20 percent; each 20 percent of the families would get 20 percent of total personal income. In fact, the richest fifth of the families gets almost ten times as much income as does the poorest fifth.

absolute and relative terms since World War II. In 1941, households paid $3.3 billion, or about 3 percent of their $95.3 billion total income, in personal taxes, compared to $616 billion, or about 13 percent of that year's $4724 billion total income in 1991.

Personal Saving

Economists define saving as "that part of after-tax income which is *not* consumed"; hence, households have just two choices with their incomes after taxes—to consume or to save.

Saving is defined as that portion of current (this year's) income not paid out in taxes or in the purchase of consumer goods, but which flows into bank accounts, insurance policies, bonds and stocks, and other financial assets.

Reasons for saving are many and diverse, but they center around *security* and *speculation*. Households save to provide a nest egg for unforeseen contingencies—sickness, accident, unemployment—for retirement from the work force, to finance the education of children, or simply for the overall financial security of one's family. On the other hand, saving might well occur for speculation. One might channel part of one's income to the purchase of securities, speculating as to increases in their monetary values.

The desire or willingness to save, however, is not enough. This willingness must be accompanied by the *ability* to save, which depends basically on the size of one's income. If income is very low, households may *dissave;* that is, they may consume in excess of their after-tax incomes. They do this by borrowing and by digging into savings they may have accumulated in years when their incomes were higher. However, both saving and consumption vary directly with income; as households get more income, they divide it between saving and consumption. In fact, the top 10 percent of income receivers account for most of the personal saving in our society.

Personal Consumption Expenditures

Figure 5-3 shows that the bulk of total income flows from income receivers back into the business sector of the economy as personal consumption expenditures.

The size and composition of the economy's total output depend to a great extent on the size and composition of the flow of consumer spending. It is thus imperative that we examine how households divide their

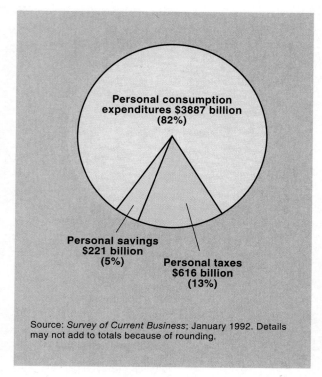

Personal consumption
expenditures $3887 billion
(82%)

Personal savings
$221 billion
(5%)

Personal taxes
$616 billion
(13%)

Source: *Survey of Current Business*; January 1992. Details
may not add to totals because of rounding.

	Billions of dollars	Percent of total
Personal taxes	$ 616	13
Personal saving	221	5
Personal consumption expenditures	3887	82
Total income	$4724	100

FIGURE 5-3 **The disposition of household income, 1991**

Household income is apportioned between taxes, saving, and consumption, with consumption being the dominant use of income.

expenditures among the various goods and services competing for their dollars. The U.S. Department of Commerce classifies consumer spending as (1) expenditures on durables, (2) expenditures on nondurables, and (3) expenditures on services. If a product generally has an expected life of one year or more, it is called a **durable good;** if its life is less than one year, it is labeled **nondurable.** Automobiles, video recorders, washing machines, personal computers, and most furniture are good examples of consumer durables. Most food and clothing items are representative of nondurables. **Services** refer to the services which lawyers, barbers, doctors, mechanics, and others provide to consumers. Note in Table 5-1 that *ours is a service-oriented economy in that over one-half of consumer outlays are for services.*

This threefold breakdown, detailed in Table 5-1, implies that many consumer outlays are discretionary or postponable. During prosperity, durable, or "hard," goods are typically traded in or scrapped before they become utterly useless. This is ordinarily the case with automobiles and most major household appliances. But if a recession materializes, consumers tend to forgo expenditures on durables, having little choice but to put up with an old model car and outdated house-

hold appliances. The desire to conserve dollars for the nondurable necessities of food and clothing may cause a radical shrinkage of expenditures on durables. Much the same is true of many services. True, one cannot postpone an operation for acute appendicitis. But education, dental work, and a wide variety of less pressing services can be deferred or, if necessary, forgone entirely. In brief, the durable goods and services segments of personal consumption expenditures are subject to much more variation over time than are expenditures on nondurables.

QUICK REVIEW 5-1

◢   The functional distribution of income indicates how income is divided among wages, rents, interest, and profits; the personal distribution of income shows how income is apportioned among households.

◢   Wages and salaries are the major component of the functional distribution of income. The personal distribution reveals considerable inequality.

◢   Over 80 percent of household income is consumed, the remainder being saved or paid in taxes.

◢   Over half of consumer spending is for services.

TABLE 5-1 **The composition of personal consumption expenditures, 1991***

Types of consumption	Amount (billions of dollars)	Percent of total
Durable goods	**$ 445**	**11**
Motor vehicles and parts	$184	5
Furniture and household equipment	172	4
All others	90	2
Nondurable goods	**1251**	**32**
Food	619	16
Clothing and shoes	211	5
Gasoline and oil	103	3
Fuel oil and coal	12	1
All others	307	8
Services	**2191**	**56**
Housing	575	15
Household operations	225	6
Medical care	577	15
Transportation	156	4
Personal services, recreation, and others	658	17
Personal consumption expenditures	**$3887**	**100**

*Excludes interest paid to businesses.

Sources: Survey of Current Business, January 1992. Details may not add to totals because of rounding.

THE BUSINESS POPULATION

Businesses constitute the second major aggregate of the private sector. To avoid confusion, we preface our discussion with some comments on terminology. In particular, we must distinguish among a plant, a firm, and an industry.

1 A **plant** is a physical establishment in the form of a factory, farm, mine, retail or wholesale store, or warehouse which performs one or more specific functions in the fabrication and distribution of goods and services.

2 A business **firm,** on the other hand, is the business organization which owns and operates these plants. Although most firms operate only one plant, many own and operate a number of plants. Multiplant firms may be "horizontal," "vertical," or "conglomerate" combinations. For example, without exception all the large steel firms of our economy—USX Corporation (United States Steel), Bethlehem Steel, Republic Steel, and the others—are **vertical combinations** of plants; that is, each company owns plants at various stages of the production process. Each steelmaker owns ore and coal mines, limestone quarries, coke ovens, blast furnaces, rolling mills, forge shops, foundries, and, in some cases, fabricating shops.

The large chain stores in the retail field— A&P, Kroger, Safeway, J.C. Penney—are **horizontal combinations** in that each plant is at the same stage of production. Other firms are **conglomerates;** they comprise plants which operate across many different markets and industries. For example, International Telephone and Telegraph, apart from operations implied by its name, is involved through affiliated plants on a large-scale basis in such diverse fields as hotels, baking products, educational materials, and insurance.

3 An **industry** is a group of firms producing the same, or at least similar, products. Though an apparently uncomplicated concept, industries are usually difficult to identify in practice. For example, how do we identify the automobile industry? The simplest answer is, "All firms producing automobiles." But automobiles are heterogeneous products. While Cadillacs and Buicks are similar products, and Buicks and Fords are similar, and Fords and Geos are similar, it is clear that Geos and Cadillacs are very dissimilar. At least most buyers think so. And what about trucks? Certainly, small pickup trucks are similar in some respects to station wagons. Is it better to speak of the "motor vehicle industry" rather than of the "automobile industry"?

This matter of delineating an industry becomes even more complex because most enterprises are multiproduct firms. American automobile manufacturers are also responsible for such diverse products as diesel locomotives, buses, refrigerators, guided missiles, and air conditioners. As you can see, industry classifications are usually somewhat arbitrary.

LEGAL FORMS OF BUSINESS ENTERPRISES

The business population is extremely diverse, ranging from giant corporations like General Motors with 1990 sales of $126 billion and 761,000 employees to neighborhood speciality shops and "mom and pop" groceries with one or two employees and sales of only $100 or $150 per day. This diversity makes it necessary to classify business firms by some criterion such as legal structure, industry or product, or size. Figure 5-4 shows how the business population is distributed among the three major legal forms: (1) the sole proprietorship, (2) the partnership, and (3) the corporation.

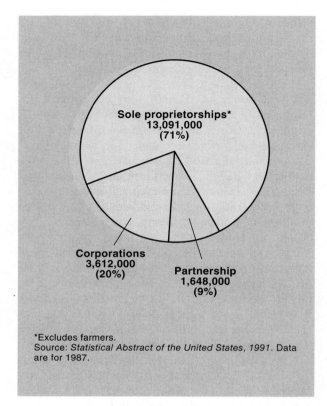

*Excludes farmers.
Source: *Statistical Abstract of the United States, 1991.* Data are for 1987.

The business population by form of legal organization and volume of sales

Form	Number of firms	Percent of total	Volume of sales (billions)	Percent of total
Sole proprietorships*	13,091,000	71	$ 611	6
Partnerships	1,648,000	9	411	4
Corporations	3,612,000	20	9,185	90
Total	18,351,000	100	$10,207	100

*Excludes farmers.

FIGURE 5-4 The business population by form of legal organization

Although sole proprietorships dominate the business population numerically, corporations account for 90 percent of total sales.

Sole Proprietorship

A **sole proprietorship** is literally an individual in business for himself or herself. The proprietor owns or obtains the materials and capital equipment needed by the business and personally supervises its operation.

Advantages This simple type of business organization has certain distinct advantages:
1 A sole proprietorship is very easy to organize—there is virtually no legal red tape or expense.
2 The proprietor is his or her own boss and has substantial freedom of action. Since the proprietor's profit income depends on the enterprise's success, there is a strong and immediate incentive to manage the affairs of the business efficiently.

Disadvantages But the disadvantages of this form of business organization are great. They include financial restrictions on firm growth, the inability to specialize in management, and the fact that all of a proprietor's assets are potentially available to creditors.

1 With rare exceptions, the financial resources of a sole proprietorship are insufficient to permit the firm to grow into a large-scale enterprise. Finances are usually limited to what the proprietor has in his or her bank account and to what he or she can borrow. Since proprietorships often fail, commercial banks are not eager to extend much credit to them.
2 Being in complete control of an enterprise forces the proprietor to carry out all basic management functions. A proprietor must make all basic decisions concerning buying, selling, and the hiring and training of personnel, not to mention the technical aspects involved in producing, advertising, and distributing the product. In short, the potential benefits of specialization in business management are usually inaccessible to the typical small-scale proprietorship.
3 Most important of all, the proprietor is subject to *unlimited liability.* Individuals in business for themselves risk not only the assets of the firm but also their personal assets. If assets of an unsuccessful proprietorship are insufficient to satisfy the claims of creditors, those creditors can file claims against the proprietor's personal property.

Partnership

The **partnership** form of business organization is more or less a natural outgrowth of the sole proprietorship. Partnerships were developed to overcome some of the major shortcomings of proprietorships. In a partnership, two or more individuals agree to own and operate a business. Usually they pool their financial resources and business skills. Similarly, they share the risks and the profits or losses.

Advantages   What are the advantages of a partnership arrangement?
1   Like the sole proprietorship, it is easy to organize. Although a written agreement is almost invariably involved, legal red tape is not great.
2   Greater specialization in management is possible because there are more participants.
3   Again, because there are several participants, the odds are that the financial resources of a partnership will be greater than those of a sole proprietorship. Partners can pool their money capital and are usually somewhat better risks in the eyes of lending institutions.

Disadvantages   The partnership often does less to overcome the shortcomings of the proprietorship than first appears, and raises some new potential problems which the sole proprietorship does not have.
1   Whenever several people participate in management, this division of authority can lead to inconsistent, divided policies or to inaction when action is required. Worse yet, partners may flatly disagree on basic policy. For all these reasons, management in a partnership may be unwieldy and cumbersome.
2   The finances of partnerships are still limited, although generally superior to those of a sole proprietorship. But the financial resources of three or four partners may still not be enough for the growth of a successful enterprise.
3   The continuity of a partnership is very precarious. The withdrawal or death of a partner generally means dissolution and complete reorganization of the firm, disrupting its operations.
4   Finally, unlimited liability plagues a partnership, just as it does a proprietorship. In fact, each partner is liable for all business debts incurred, not only as a result of each partner's own management decisions, but also as a consequence of the actions of any other partner. A wealthy partner risks money on the prudence of less affluent partners.

Corporation

Corporations are legal entities, distinct and separate from the individuals who own them. As such, these governmentally designated "legal persons" can acquire resources, own assets, produce and sell products, incur debts, extend credit, sue and be sued, and carry on all those functions which any other type of enterprise performs.

Advantages   The advantages of the corporate form of business enterprise have catapulted it into a dominant position in modern American capitalism. Although corporations are relatively small in number (Table 5-2), they are frequently large in size and scale of operations. Although only 20 percent of all businesses are corporations, they account for roughly 90 percent of all business sales.
1   The corporation is by far the most effective form of business organization for raising money capital. As this chapter's Last Word reveals, the corporation features unique methods of finance—the selling of stocks and bonds—which allow the firm to tap the savings of untold thousands of households. Through the securities market, corporations can pool the financial resources of extremely large numbers of people.
    Financing by the sale of securities also has advantages from the viewpoint of the purchasers of these securities. First, households can now participate in enterprise and share the expected monetary reward therefrom without assuming an active part in management. In addition, an individual can spread any risks by buying the securities of several corporations. Finally, it is usually easy for the holder of corporate securities to dispose of these holdings. Organized stock exchanges facilitate transfer of securities among buyers and sellers, which increases the willingness of savers to buy corporate securities.
    Corporations have easier access to bank credit than other types of business organizations. Corporations are better risks and are more likely to provide banks with profitable accounts.
2   Corporations have the distinct advantage of **limited liability.** The owners (stockholders) of a corporation risk *only* what they paid for the stock purchased. Their personal assets are not at stake if the corporation founders on the rocks of bankruptcy. Creditors can sue the corporation as a legal person, but not the owners of the corporation as individuals. Limited liability clearly eases the corporation's task in acquiring money capital.

3 Because of their advantage in attracting money capital, successful corporations find it easier to expand the size and scope of their operations and to realize associated advantages. In particular, corporations can take advantage of mass-production technologies. Similarly, size permits greater specialization in the use of human resources. While the manager of a sole proprietorship may be forced to share her time between production, accounting, and marketing functions, a corporation can hire specialized personnel in these areas and achieve greater efficiency.

4 As a legal entity, the corporation has a life independent of its owners and, for that matter, of its individual officers. Proprietorships are subject to sudden and unpredictable demise, but, legally at least, corporations are immortal. The transfer of corporate ownership through the sale of stock will not disrupt the continuity of the corporation. Corporations have a certain permanence, lacking in other forms of business organization, which is conducive to long-range planning and growth.

Disadvantages The corporation's advantages are of tremendous significance and typically override any accompanying disadvantages. Yet the following drawbacks of the corporate form of organization merit mentioning:

1 There are some red tape and legal expense in obtaining a corporate charter.

2 From the social point of view, the corporate form of enterprise lends itself to certain abuses. Because the corporation is a legal entity, unscrupulous business owners sometimes can avoid personal responsibility for questionable business activities by adopting the corporate form of enterprise. And, despite legislation to the contrary, the corporate form of organization has been a cornerstone for the issue and sale of worthless securities. Note, however, that these are potential abuses of the corporate form, not inherent defects.

3 A further disadvantage of corporations is the **double taxation** of corporate income. That part of corporate income paid out as dividends to stockholders is taxed twice—once as part of corporate profits and again as part of stockholders' personal incomes.

4 In the sole proprietorship and partnership forms, those owning the real and financial assets of the firm also directly manage or control those assets. But, in larger corporations where ownership of common stock is widely diffused over tens or hundreds of thousands of stockholders, a fundamental **separation of ownership and control** will arise. The roots of this cleavage lie in the lethargy of the typical stockholder. Most stockholders do not exercise their voting rights, or, if they do, merely sign these rights over by proxy to the corporation's present officers. And why not? Average stockholders know little or nothing about the efficiency with which "their" corporation is being managed. Because the typical stockholder may own only 1000 of 15,000,000 shares of common stock outstanding, one vote "really doesn't make a bit of difference." Not voting, or the automatic signing over of one's proxy to current corporate officials, makes those officials self-perpetuating.

The separation of ownership and control is of no fundamental consequence so long as the actions of the control (management) group and the wishes of the ownership (stockholder) group are in accord. In fact, the interests of the two groups are not always identical. Management, seeking the power and prestige which accompany control over a *large* enterprise, may favor unprofitable expansion of the firm's operations. Or a conflict of interest can develop on current dividend policies. What portion of corporate earnings after taxes should be paid out as dividends, and what amount should be retained by the firm as undistributed profits? And corporation officials may vote themselves large salaries, pensions, bonuses, and so forth, out of corporate earnings which might otherwise be used for increased dividend payments. In short, the separation of ownership and control raises important and intriguing questions about the distribution of power and authority, the accountability of corporate managers, and the possibility of intramural conflicts between managers and shareholders.

Incorporate or Not?

The need for money capital is a critical determinant of whether or not a firm incorporates. The money capital required to establish and operate a barbershop, a shoeshine stand, or a small gift shop is modest, making incorporation unnecessary. In contrast, modern technology and a much larger dollar volume of business make incorporation imperative in many lines of production. In most branches of manufacturing—automobiles, steel, fabricated metal products, electrical equipment, and household appliances—substantial money requirements for investment in fixed assets and for working capital are involved. Given these circumstances, there is no choice but to incorporate.

INDUSTRIAL DISTRIBUTION AND BIGNESS

What do the 18.4 million firms which compose the business sector of our economy produce?

Types of Industries

Table 5-2 measures the significance of the various industry classifications in several different ways. Column 2 indicates the numerical and percentage distribution of the business population among various industries. Column 3 shows in both absolute and relative terms the portion of the domestic output originating in various industries. Column 4 indicates the absolute and relative amounts of employment provided by each industry. Several points in Table 5-2 are noteworthy:

1 Many firms are engaged in agriculture, but agriculture is relatively insignificant as a provider of incomes and jobs. This implies that agriculture comprises a large number of small, competitive producers.

2 The wholesale and retail industries and the service industries (hotels, motels, and personal services) are heavily populated with firms and are simultaneously important sources of employment and incomes in the economy.

3 Table 5-2 reminds us that not all the economy's income and employment originate in private domestic enterprises. Government and foreign enterprises account for about 13 percent of the economy's domestic output and employ about 16 percent of the labor force.

4 The relatively small number of firms in manufacturing account for almost one-fifth of domestic output and total employment. These figures correctly suggest that our economy is highly industrialized, characterized by gigantic business corporations in its manufacturing industries. This point merits brief elaboration.

Big Business

To what degree does big business prevail in our economy? Casual evidence suggests that many of our major industries are dominated by corporate giants which enjoy assets and annual sales revenues of billions of dollars, employ hundreds of thousands of workers, have a hundred thousand or more stockholders, and earn annual profits after taxes running into hundreds of millions of dollars. We have already cited the vital statistics of General Motors, America's largest corporation, for 1990: sales, about $126 *billion;* assets, about $180 *billion;* employees, about 761,000. Remarkably, there are only 20 or so nations in the world whose

TABLE 5-2   Industry classes: number of firms, domestic output originating, and employment provided*

(1) Industry	(2) Number of private businesses		(3) Contribution to domestic output		(4) Workers employed	
	Thousands	Percent	Billions	Percent	Thousands	Percent
Agriculture, forestry, and fisheries	2,088	11	$ 114	2	2,863	3
Mining	258	1	80	2	735	1
Construction	2,067	11	248	5	5,204	5
Manufacturing	686	4	966	18	19,063	17
Wholesale and retail trade	3,521	18	826	16	26,150	23
Finance, insurance, and real estate	2,571	13	897	17	6,832	6
Transportation, communications, and public utilities	824	4	461	9	5,839	5
Services	7,384	38	971	19	28,208	25
Government			619	12	18,291	16
Rest of world			38	1		
Total	19,399	100	$5,220	100	113,185	100

*Column 2 is for 1987; 3 for 1989; and 4 for 1990. Includes farms.

Source: Statistical Abstract of the United States, 1991, p. 526; and *Survey of Current Business.* Details may not add to totals because of rounding.

annual domestic outputs are more than GM's annual sales!

In 1990 some 123 industrial corporations enjoyed annual sales of over $4 billion; 213 industrial firms realized sales over $2 billion. Generally, the fact that corporations, constituting only 20 percent of the business population, produce about nine-tenths of total business output, hints at the dominant role of large corporations in our economy.

But the influential position of giant corporations varies significantly from industry to industry. Big business dominates manufacturing and is pronounced in the transportation, communications, power utilities, and banking and financial industries. At the other extreme are some 2 million farmers whose total sales in 1990 were less than the economy's two largest industrial corporations! In between are a wide variety of retail and service industries characterized by relatively small firms. Despite great diversity by industry, it is reasonably accurate to say that large corporations dominate the American business landscape and grounds exist for labeling the United States a "big business" economy.

THE FOREIGN SECTOR

Our economy is deeply enmeshed in a complex web of economic relationships with the rest of the world. Evidence of the growing importance of international trade and finance is all around us. You may be wearing a T-shirt made in Thailand and a wristwatch from Japan; your stereo or television may be from Korea; your bicycle may have been manufactured in England or West Germany. Newspapers feature stories about our seemingly chronic trade deficits, the changing international value of the dollar, trade negotiations with Japan, and the indebtedness of the less developed countries to American banks. It is clear that the "rest of the world" sector has manifold effects on our domestic economy.

In this section we explore the quantitative importance of the international sector *and* will see how international trade and finance affects the American economy.

Volume, Pattern, and Linkages

The volume of United States merchandise trade with the rest of the world has increased both absolutely and relatively. In 1960 American merchandise exports and imports were each in the $25 to $30 billion range and constituted about 5 percent of our domestic output. By 1990 these figures had grown to $390 and $498 billion and 7 to 9 percent of domestic output.

Table 5-3 identifies our major trading partners. The most apparent generalization is that most of our trade is with other industrially advanced nations. Note that Canada, not Japan, is our major trade partner.

Table 5-3 also implies a complex set of financial linkages which exist between nations. Note that the

TABLE 5-3 U.S. merchandise exports and imports by area, 1990

Exports to	Value (in billions) of dollars)	Percentage of total	Imports from	Value (in billions) of dollars)	Percentage of total
Industrial countries	$251	64	**Industrial countries**	$296	59
Canada	84	22	Canada	93	19
Japan	48	12	Japan	90	18
Western Europe	111	28	Western Europe	109	22
Australia	8	2	Australia	4	1
Developing countries	135	35	**Developing countries**	199	40
OPEC	13	3	OPEC	38	8
Other	122	31	Other	161	32
Eastern Europe	4	1	**Eastern Europe**	2	1
Total	$390	100	Total	$498	100

Source: Survey of Current Business, December 1991.

Note: Data are on international transactions basis and exclude military shipments. Data will not add to totals because of rounding.

United States incurred a $108 billion *trade deficit* in 1990; that is, we imported $108 billion more merchandise than we exported in that year. Indeed, we have had large trade deficits for the last decade or so.

How are such deficits financed? How does a nation—or an individual—obtain more goods from others than is provided to them? The answer is by borrowing from them or by giving up ownership of some of your assets or wealth. This is precisely what has been happening to the United States. We have financed our trade deficits by borrowing from (selling securities to) other nations. The United States is now the world's largest debtor nation. Similarly, nations with which we have large trade deficits such as Japan (Table 5-3) are acquiring assets in America. For example, Doubleday Publishing and RCA are owned by German firms; Standard Oil is in British hands; and CBS Records and Firestone Tire are Japanese.

Economic Implications

The impacts of global trade and finance on the United States economy are numerous and important.

1 Specialization and Living Standards We emphasized in Chapter 3 that individuals and regions within a given nation specialize according to comparative advantage because productive efficiency is enhanced and living standards increased. Our illustration indicated that Nebraska grows wheat to which its resources are suited, and Florida grows oranges. By trading part of their outputs, people in both states can enjoy larger aggregate amounts of wheat and oranges than otherwise. The same reasoning applies across international boundaries. International specialization allows each nation to concentrate its resources on goods it can produce most efficiently, and to obtain through trade with other nations products it cannot produce efficiently. Such international specialization contributes to a higher "world income."

2 Competition A large and growing volume of trade usually means more competition. Not many years ago our domestic automobile industry was dominated by three large domestic producers. Imported autos were an oddity which accounted for only a miniscule portion of the market. But now about one-third of all autos sold in the United States are imports. General Motors, Ford,

and Chrysler now face a much more competitive environment as they struggle for market shares with Nissan, Honda, Toyota, Hyundai, Volkswagen, Mercedes, and so on.

Is greater competition a good thing? Although domestic auto producers may not be thrilled by it, competition is good for consumers. Foreign competition provides consumers with a greater variety of goods and forces domestic producers to be more efficient.

3 Finance and Banking Dramatic improvements in communications have globalized financial markets and banking industries. Developments in the New York Stock Exchange affect stock markets in London and Tokyo and vice versa. The United States has become the world's largest debtor nation as a result of large and persistent trade deficits. Furthermore, major American banks have made billions of dollars worth of loans to less developed nations; potential default on these loans is a threat to individual American banks and a source of apprehension for our entire banking system.

4 Instability and Policy Two related points are relevant with respect to macroeconomic instability and policy. First, a nation engaged in world trade faces potential sources of instability which would not affect a nation "closed" to the world economy. Second, these new sources of instability complicate domestic stabilization policy and *may* make it less effective. For example, recessions and inflations can be highly contagious among nations. Suppose the nations of western Europe experienced a rather severe recession. As their incomes declined, they would curtail purchases of American goods. As a result, inventories of unsold American goods would rise and American firms would respond by reducing their production and employment. In short, recession in Europe might contribute to a recession in the United States.

Another example: Recall from Chapter 4 that changes in exchange rates can affect a nation's exports and imports and therefore domestic output. If the dollar were to *appreciate* vis-a-vis other currencies—that is, if it now took fewer dollars to buy units of foreign monies—domestic output and employment would tend to be depressed. If foreign currencies become relatively cheaper to Americans so do all foreign goods and Americans will respond by shifting their expenditures from domestic to foreign goods. In both instances policy makers would have to take these developments into account in formulating and applying domestic stabilization policies.

QUICK REVIEW 5-2

♦ *Business firms are either sole proprietorships, partnerships, or corporations.*

♦ *Although relatively small in number, corporations dominate our economy because of their limited liability and superior ability to raise money capital.*

♦ *Our international trade, which is primarily with other industrially advanced nations, has increased absolutely and relative to our domestic output.*

♦ *The main advantages of international trade are* *a* *it permits greater worldwide specialization, and* *b* *it enhances competition.*

THE COMPETITIVE MARKET SYSTEM

Now that we have some understanding of the economy's private decision makers, let's consider an intriguing problem. We stressed in Chapter 3 that a capitalistic system is characterized by freedom of enterprise and choice. Consumers are free to buy what they choose; businesses, to produce and sell what they choose; and resource suppliers, to make their property and human resources available in whatever occupations they choose. We may well wonder why such an economy does not collapse in chaos. If consumers want breakfast cereal, businesses choose to produce aerobic shoes, and resource suppliers want to offer their services in manufacturing computer software, production would seem to be deadlocked because of the apparent inconsistency of these free choices.

In reality, the millions of decisions made by households and businesses are highly consistent with one another. Firms do produce those particular goods and services consumers want. Households provide the kinds of labor businesses want to hire. Here we will see how a competitive market system constitutes a coordinating mechanism which overcomes the potential chaos suggested by freedom of enterprise and choice. The competitive market system is a mechanism both for communicating decisions of consumers, producers, and resource suppliers to one another and for synchronizing those decisions toward consistent production objectives.

THE FIVE FUNDAMENTAL QUESTIONS

To understand the operation of a market economy we must first recognize that there are **Five Fundamental Questions** to which *every* economy must respond:
1   *How much* is to be produced? At what level—to what degree—should available resources be employed or used in the production process?
2   *What* is to be produced? What collection of goods and services will best satisfy society's material wants?
3   *How* is that output to be produced? How should production be organized? What firms should do the producing and what productive techniques should they use?
4   *Who* is to receive the output? In particular, how should the output of the economy be shared by consumers?
5   Can the system *adapt* to change? Can the system negotiate appropriate adjustments when changes occur in consumer wants, resource supplies, and technology?

Two points are relevant. First, we will defer the "how much" question for now. Macroeconomics deals in detail with the complex question of the level of resource employment.

Second, the Five Fundamental Questions are merely an elaboration of the choices underlying Chapter 2's production possibilities curve. These questions would be irrelevant were it not for the economizing problem.

THE MARKET SYSTEM AT WORK

Chapter 3's circular flow diagram (Figure 3-2) provides the setting for our discussion. In examining how the market system answers the Fundamental Questions, we must add demand and supply diagrams as developed in Chapter 4 to represent the various product and resource markets embodied in the circular flow model.

Determining What Is to Be Produced

Given the product and resource prices established by competing buyers and sellers in both the product and resource markets, how would a purely capitalistic economy decide the types and quantities of goods to be produced? Remembering that businesses seek profits and want to avoid losses, we can generalize that those goods and services which can be produced at a profit will be produced and those whose production entails a loss will not. Two things determine profits or losses.

1 The total revenue a firm receives when it sells a product.

2 The total costs of producing the product.

Both total revenue and total costs are price-times-quantity figures. Total revenue is found by multiplying product price by the quantity of the product sold. Total costs are found by multiplying the price of each resource used by the amount employed and summing the costs of each.

Economic Costs and Profits

To say that those products which can be produced profitably will be produced and those which cannot will not is only an accurate generalization if the meaning of **economic costs** is clearly understood.

Let's again think of businesses as simply organizational charts, that is, businesses "on paper," distinct from the capital, raw materials, labor, and entrepreneurial ability which make them going concerns. To become actual producing firms, these "on paper" businesses must secure all four types of resources. *Economic costs are the payments which must be made to secure and retain the needed amounts of these resources.* The per unit size of these costs—that is, resource prices—will be determined by supply and demand in the resource market. Like land, labor, and capital, entrepreneurial ability is a scarce resource and has a price tag on it. Costs therefore must include not only wage and salary payments to labor and interest and rental payments for capital and land, but also payments to the entrepreneur for the functions he or she performs in organizing and combining the other resources in the production of a commodity. The cost payment for these contributions by the entrepreneur is called a **normal profit.**

A product will be produced only when total revenue is large enough to pay wage, interest, rental, *and* normal profit costs. Now if total revenues from the sale of a product exceed all production costs, including a normal profit, the remainder will go to the entrepreneur as the risk taker and organizing force. This return above all costs is called a **pure,** or **economic, profit.** It is *not* an economic cost, because it need not be realized for the business to acquire and retain entrepreneurial ability.

Profits and Expanding Industries

A few hypothetical examples will explain how the market system determines what is to be produced. Suppose the most favor-able relationship between total revenue and total cost in producing product X occurs when the firm's output is 15 units. Assume, too, that the least-cost combination of resources to use in producing 15 units of X is 2 units of labor, 3 units of land, 1 of capital, and 1 of entrepreneurial ability, selling at prices of $2, $1, $3, and $3, respectively. Finally, suppose that the 15 units of X which these resources produce can be sold for $1 per unit. Will firms enter into the production of product X? Yes, because the firm will be able to pay wage, rent, interest, and normal profit costs of $13 [= $(2 \times \$2) + (3 \times \$1) + (1 \times \$3) + (1 \times \$3)$]. The difference between total revenue of $15 and total costs of $13 will be an economic profit of $2.

This economic profit is evidence that industry X is a prosperous one. Such an industry will become an **expanding industry** as new firms, attracted by these above-normal profits, are created or shift from less profitable industries.

But the entry of new firms will be a self-limiting process. As new firms enter industry X, the market supply of X will increase relative to the market demand. This will lower the market price of X (Figure 4-6c) and economic profits will in time be competed away. The market supply and demand situation prevailing when economic profits become zero will determine the total amount of X produced. At this point the industry will have achieved its "equilibrium size," at least until a further change in market demand or supply upsets that equilibrium.

Losses and Declining Industries

But what if the initial market situation for product X were less favorable? Suppose conditions in the product market were such that the firm could sell the 15 units of X at a price of just 75 cents per unit. Total revenue would be $11.25 (= 15 × 75 cents). After paying wage, rental, and interest costs of $10, the firm would obtain a below-normal profit of $1.25. In other words, *losses* of $1.75 (= $11.25 − $13) would be incurred.

Certainly, firms would not be attracted to this unprosperous **declining industry.** On the contrary, if these losses persisted, entrepreneurs would seek the normal profits or possibly even the economic profits offered by more prosperous industries. In time existing firms in industry X would go out of business entirely or migrate to other industries where normal or better profits prevail. However, as this happens, the market supply of X will fall relative to the market demand. Product price will rise (Figure 4-6d) and losses will eventually disappear. Industry X will then stabilize itself in size. The market supply and demand situation that prevails at that point where economic profits are zero will determine the total output of product X. Again, the industry for the moment will have reached its equilibrium size.

"Dollar Votes"   Consumer demand plays a crucial role in determining the types and quantities of goods produced. Consumers, unrestrained by government and with money incomes from the sale of resources, spend their dollars on those goods they are most willing and able to buy. These expenditures are **dollar votes** by which consumers register their wants through the demand side of the product market. If these votes are great enough to provide a normal profit, businesses will produce that product. An increase in consumer demand, that is, an increase in the dollar votes cast for a product, will mean economic profits for the industry producing it. These profits will signal expansion of that industry and increases in the output of the product.

Conversely, a decrease in consumer demand, that is, fewer votes cast for the product, will result in losses and, in time, contraction of the industry. As firms leave the industry, the output of the product declines. Indeed, the industry may cease to exist. The dollar votes of consumers play a key role in determining what products profit-seeking businesses will produce. As noted in Chapter 3, the capitalistic system is characterized by **consumer sovereignty** because of the strategic role consumers have in determining the types and quantities of goods produced.

A much-publicized illustration of consumer sovereignty occurred a few years ago when a substantial number of consumers rejected the "new" Coca-Cola. Despite elaborate market surveys and extensive advertising, many Coke drinkers judged the new product inferior and engaged in organized protests until the manufacturer responded by again making original "classic" Coke available.

Market Restraints on Freedom   From the viewpoint of businesses, we now see that firms are not really "free" to produce what they wish. The demand decisions of consumers, by making production of some products profitable and others not, restrict the choice of businesses in deciding what to produce. Businesses must match their production choices with consumer choices or face losses and eventual bankruptcy.

Much the same holds true for resource suppliers. The demand for resources is a **derived demand**—derived, that is, from the demand for the goods and services which the resources help produce. There is a demand for autoworkers only because there is a demand for automobiles. Generally, in seeking to maximize returns from the sale of their human and property resources, resource suppliers are prompted by the market system to make their choices in accord with consumer demands. If only those firms which produce goods wanted by consumers can operate profitably, only those firms will demand resources. Resource suppliers will not be "free" to allocate their resources to the production of goods which consumers do not value highly. There will be no firms producing such products, because consumer demand is not sufficient to make it profitable.

In brief, consumers register their preferences on the demand side of the product market, and producers and resource suppliers respond appropriately in seeking to further their own self-interests. The market system communicates the wants of consumers to businesses and resource suppliers and elicits appropriate responses.

Organizing Production

How is production to be organized in a market economy? This Fundamental Question is composed of three subquestions:

1   How should resources be allocated among specific industries?
2   What specific firm should do the producing in each industry?
3   What combinations of resources—what technology—should each firm employ?

Production and Profits   The preceding section has answered the first subquestion. The market system steers resources to those industries whose products consumers want badly enough to make their production profitable. It simultaneously deprives unprofitable industries of scarce resources. If all firms had sufficient time to enter prosperous industries and to leave unprosperous industries, the output of each industry would be large enough for the firms to make just normal profits. If total industry output at this point happens to be 1500 units and the most profitable output for each firm is 15 units, as in our previous example, the industry will be made up of 100 competing firms.

The second and third subquestions are closely intertwined. In a competitive market economy, the firms which do the producing are those which are willing and able to employ the economically most efficient technique of production. And what determines the most efficient technique? Economic efficiency depends on:

1 Available technology, that is, the alternative combinations of resources or inputs which will produce the desired output.

2 The prices at which needed resources can be obtained.

Least-Cost Production The combination of resources which is most efficient economically depends not only on the physical or engineering data provided by available technology but also on the relative worth of the required resources as measured by their market prices. Thus, a technique which requires just a few physical inputs of resources to produce a given output may be highly *in*efficient economically *if* the required resources are valued very highly in the market. *Economic efficiency entails getting a given output of product with the smallest input of scarce resources, when both output and resource inputs are measured in dollars-and-cents terms.* That combination of resources which will produce, say, $15 worth of product X at the lowest possible money cost is the most efficient.

An example will help. Suppose there are three techniques by which the desired $15 worth of product X can be produced. The quantity of each resource required by each production technology and the prices of the required resources are shown in Table 5-4. By multiplying the quantities of the various resources required by the resource prices in each of the three techniques, the total cost of producing $15 worth of X by each technique can be determined.

Technique No. 2 is economically the most efficient of the three techniques because it is the least costly. Technique No. 2 permits society to obtain $15 worth of output by using a smaller amount of resources—$13 worth in this instance—than the $15 worth which would be used by the two alternative techniques.

But what guarantee is there that firms will actually use technique No. 2? The answer is that firms will want to use the most efficient technique because it yields the greatest profit.

A change in *either* technology *or* resource prices may cause the firm to shift from the technology now employed. If the price of labor falls to 50 cents, technique No. 1 will now be superior to technique No. 2. Businesses will find they can lower their costs by shifting to a technology which uses more of that resource whose price has fallen. You should verify that a new technique involving 1 unit of labor, 4 of land, 1 of capital, and 1 of entrepreneurial ability will be preferable to all three techniques listed in Table 5-4, assuming the resource prices given there.

Distributing Total Output

The market system enters the picture in two ways in solving the problem of distributing total output. Generally, any given product will be distributed to consumers on the basis of their ability and willingness to pay the existing market price for it. If the price of X is $1 per unit, those buyers who are able and willing to pay that price will get a unit of this product; those who are not, will not. This is the rationing function of equilibrium prices.

The size of one's money income determines a consumer's ability to pay the equilibrium price for X and other available products. And money income depends on the quantities of the various property and human resources which the income receiver supplies and the prices which they command in the resource market. Thus, resource prices play a key role in determining the size of each household's income claim against the total output of society. Within the limits of a consumer's money income, his or her willingness to pay the equilibrium price for X determines whether or not some of this product is distributed to that person. And this will-

TABLE 5-4 Techniques for producing $15 worth of product X (*hypothetical data*)

Resource	Price per unit of resource	Units of resource		
		Technique no. 1	Technique no. 2	Technique no. 3
Labor	$2	4	2	1
Land	1	1	3	4
Capital	3	1	1	2
Entrepreneurial ability	3	1	1	1
Total cost of $15 worth of X		$15	$13	$15

ingness to buy X will depend on one's preference for X compared to available close substitutes for X and their relative prices. Thus, product prices play a key role in determining spending patterns of consumers.

There is nothing particularly ethical about the market system as a mechanism for distributing output. Households which accumulate large amounts of property resources by inheritance, through hard work and frugality, through business acumen, or by crook will receive large incomes and thus command large shares of the economy's total output. Others, offering unskilled and relatively unproductive labor resources which elicit low wages, will receive meager money incomes and small portions of total output.

Accommodating Change

Industrial societies are dynamic: Consumer preferences, technology, and resource supplies all change. This means that the particular allocation of resources which is *now* the most efficient for a *given* pattern of consumer tastes, for a *given* range of technological alternatives, and for *given* supplies of resources will become obsolete and inefficient as consumer preferences change, new techniques of production are discovered, and resource supplies alter over time. Can the market economy negotiate adjustments to these changes so that resources are still used efficiently?

Guiding Function of Prices Suppose consumer tastes change. Specifically, assume that, because of greater health consciousness, consumers decide they want more exercise bikes and fewer cigarettes than the economy currently provides. This change in consumers' taste will be communicated to producers through an increase in demand for bikes and a decline in demand for cigarettes. Bike prices will rise and cigarette prices will fall. Now, assuming firms in both industries were enjoying precisely normal profits before these changes in consumer demand, higher exercise bike prices mean economic profits for the bike industry, and lower cigarette prices mean losses for the cigarette industry. Self-interest induces new competitors to enter the prosperous bike industry. Losses will in time force firms to leave the depressed cigarette industry.

But these adjustments are both self-limiting. The expansion of the bike industry will continue only until the resulting increase in the market supply of bikes brings bike prices back down to a level where normal profits again prevail. Similarly, contraction in the cigarette industry will persist until the accompanying decline in the market supply of cigarettes brings cigarette prices up to a level where remaining firms can receive a normal profit. Or, in the extreme, the cigarette industry may cease to exist.

The point is that these adjustments in the business sector are completely appropriate to changes in consumer tastes. Society—meaning consumers—wants more exercise bikes and fewer cigarettes, and that is precisely what it is getting as the bike industry expands and the cigarette industry contracts. These adjustments, incidentally, portray the concept of consumer sovereignty at work.

This analysis assumes that resource suppliers are agreeable to these adjustments. Will the market system prompt resource suppliers to reallocate their human and property resources from the cigarette to the bike industry, thereby permitting the output of bikes to expand at the expense of cigarette production? The answer is "Yes."

The economic profits which initially follow the increase in demand for bikes will not only provide that industry with the inducement to expand but will also give it the revenue needed to obtain the resources essential to its growth. Higher bike prices will permit firms in that industry to pay higher prices for resources, thereby drawing resources from what are now less urgent alternative employments. Willingness and ability to employ more resources in the exercise bike industry will be communicated back into the resource market through an increase in the demand for resources.

The reverse occurs in the adversely affected cigarette industry. The losses which the decline in consumer demand initially entails will cause a decline in the demand for resources in that industry. Workers and other resources released from the contracting cigarette industry can now find employment in the expanding bike industry. Furthermore, the increased demand for resources in the bike industry will mean higher resource prices in that industry than those being paid in the cigarette industry, where declines in resource demand have lowered resource prices. The resulting differential in resource prices will provide the incentive for resource owners to further their self-interests by reallocating their resources from the cigarette to the bike industry. And this is the precise shift needed to permit the bike industry to expand and the cigarette industry to contract.

The ability of the market system to communicate changes in such basic data as consumer tastes and to elicit appropriate responses from both businesses and resource suppliers is called the **directing** or **guiding function of prices.** By affecting product prices and profits, changes in consumer tastes direct the expansion of some industries and the contraction of others. These adjustments carry through to the resource market as expanding industries demand more resources and contracting industries demand fewer. The resulting changes in resource prices guide resources from the contracting to the expanding industries. Without a market system, some administrative agency, presumably a governmental planning board, would have to direct business institutions and resources into specific lines of production.

Similar analysis would indicate that the market system would adjust to similar fundamental changes—for example, to changes in technology and in the relative supplies of various resources.

Initiating Progress Adjusting to changes is one thing; initiating changes, particularly desirable changes, is something else again. Is the competitive market system congenial to technological improvements and capital accumulation—the interrelated changes which lead to greater productivity and a higher level of material well-being for society? This question is not easy to answer. Our answer at this point will not consider qualifications and modifications.

Technological Advance The competitive market system contains the incentive for technological advance. New cost-cutting techniques give the innovating firm a temporary advantage over its rivals. Lower production costs mean economic profits for the pioneering firm. By passing part of its cost reduction to the consumer through a lower product price, the firm can increase sales and obtain economic profits at the expense of rival firms. Furthermore, the competitive market system provides an environment favorable to the rapid spread of a technological advance. Rivals *must* follow the lead of the most progressive firm or suffer immediate losses and eventual bankruptcy.

The lower product price which technological advance permits will cause the innovating industry to expand. This expansion may be the result of existing firms' expanding their rates of output or of new firms entering the industry lured by the economic profits initially created by technological advance. This expansion, that is, the diversion of resources from less progressive to more progressive industries, is as it should be. Sustained efficiency in the use of scarce resources demands that resources be continually reallocated from industries whose productive techniques are relatively less efficient to those whose techniques are relatively more efficient.

Capital Accumulation But technological advance typically requires increased amounts of capital goods. The entrepreneur as an innovator can command through the market system the resources necessary to produce the machinery and equipment upon which technological advance depends.

If society registers dollar votes for capital goods, the product market and the resource market will adjust to these votes by producing capital goods. The market system acknowledges dollar voting for both consumer and capital goods.

But who, specifically, will register votes for capital goods? First, the entrepreneur as a receiver of profit income can be expected to apportion part of that income to accumulation of capital goods. By doing so, an even greater profit income can be achieved in the future if innovation is successful. Furthermore, by paying interest, entrepreneurs can borrow portions of the incomes of households and use these borrowed funds in casting dollar votes for the production of more capital goods.

Competition and Control: The "Invisible Hand"

Though the market system is the organizing mechanism of pure capitalism, competition is the mechanism of control. The market mechanism of supply and demand communicates the wants of consumers (society) to businesses and through businesses to resource suppliers. It is competition, however, which forces businesses and resource suppliers to make appropriate responses.

To illustrate: We have seen that an increase in consumer demand for some product will raise that good's price above the wage, rent, interest, and normal profit costs of production. The resulting economic profits are a signal to producers that society wants more of the product. It is competition—new firms entering the industry—that simultaneously brings an expansion of output and a lowering of price back to a level just consistent with production costs. However, if the industry was dominated by, say, one huge firm (a monopolist) which was able to prohibit entry of potential competitors, that firm could continue to enjoy economic profits by preventing expansion of the industry.

But competition does more than guarantee responses appropriate to the wishes of society. It also forces firms to adopt the most efficient productive techniques. In a competitive market, the failure of some

THE FINANCING OF CORPORATE ACTIVITY

One of the main advantages of corporations is their ability to finance their operations through the sale of stocks and bonds. It is informative to examine the nature of corporate finance in more detail.

Generally speaking, corporations finance their activities in three different ways. First, a very large portion of a corporation's activity is financed internally out of undistributed corporate profits. Second, like individuals or unincorporated businesses, corporations may borrow from financial institutions. For example, a small corporation which wants to build a new plant or warehouse may obtain the funds from a commercial bank, a savings and loan association, or an insurance company. Third, unique to corporations, common stocks and bonds can be issued.

A common stock is an ownership share. The purchaser of a stock certificate has the right to vote in the selection of corporate officers and to share in any declared dividends. If you own 1000 of the 100,000 shares issued by Specific Motors, Inc. (hereafter SM), then you own 1 percent of the company, are entitled to 1 percent of any dividends declared by the board of directors, and control 1 percent of the votes in the annual election of corporate officials. In contrast, a bond is not an ownership share. A bond purchaser is simply lending money to a corporation. A bond is merely an IOU, in acknowledgment of a loan, whereby the corporation promises to pay the holder a fixed amount at some specified future date and other fixed amounts (interest payments) every year up to the bond's matu-

rity date. For example, one might purchase a ten-year SM bond with a face value of $1000 with a 10 percent stated rate of interest. This means that in exchange for your $1000 SM guarantees you a $100 interest payment for each of the next ten years and then to repay your $1000 principal at the end of that period.

There are clearly important differences between stocks and bonds. First, as noted, the bondholder is not an owner of the company, but is only a lender. Second, bonds are considered to be less risky than stocks for two reasons. On the one hand, bondholders have a "legally prior claim" upon a corporation's earnings. Dividends cannot be paid to stockholders until all interest payments due to bondholders have been paid. On the other hand, holders of SM stock do not know how much their dividends will be or how much they might obtain for their stock if they decide to sell. If Specific Motors falls on hard times, stockholders may receive no dividends at all and the value of their stock

---

firms to use the least costly production technique means their eventual elimination by more efficient firms. Finally, we have seen that competition provides an environment conducive to technological advance.

The operation and adjustments of a competitive market system create a curious and important identity —the identity of private and social interests. Firms and resource suppliers, seeking to further their own self-interest and operating within the framework of a highly competitive market system, will simultaneously, as though guided by an **"invisible hand,"**[2] promote the public or social interest. For example, we have seen

that given a competitive environment, business firms use the least costly combination of resources in producing a given output because it is in their private self-interest to do so. To act otherwise would be to forgo profits or even to risk bankruptcy. But, at the same time, it is clearly also in the social interest to use scarce resources in the least costly, that is, most efficient, manner. Not to do so would be to produce a given output at a greater cost or sacrifice of alternative goods than is necessary.

In our more-bikes–fewer-cigarettes illustration, it is self-interest, awakened and guided by the competitive market system, which induces responses appropriate to the assumed change in society's wants. Businesses seeking to make higher profits and to avoid

[2]Adam Smith, *The Wealth of Nations* (New York: Modern Library, Inc., originally published in 1776), p. 423.

may plummet. Provided the corporation does not go bankrupt, the holder of an SM bond is guaranteed a $100 interest payment each year and the return of his or her $1000 at the end of ten years.

But this is not to imply that the purchase of corporate bonds is riskless. The market value of your SM bond may vary over time in accordance with the financial health of the corporation. If SM encounters economic misfortunes which raise questions about its financial integrity, the market value of your bond may fall. Should you sell the bond prior to maturity you may receive only $600 or $700 for it (rather than $1000) and thereby incur a capital loss.

Changes in interest rates also affect the market prices of bonds. Specifically, increases in interest rates cause bond prices to fall and vice versa. Assume you purchase a $1000 ten-year SM bond this year (1993) when the going interest rate is 10 percent. This obviously means that your bond provides a $100 fixed interest payment each year. But now suppose that by next year the interest rate has jumped to 15 percent and SM must now guarantee a $150 fixed annual payment on its new 1994 $1000 ten-year bonds. Clearly, no sensible person will pay you $1000 for your bond which pays only $100 of interest income per year when new bonds can be purchased for $1000 which pay the holder $150 per year. Hence, if you sell your 1993 bond before maturity, you will suffer a capital loss.

Bondholders face another element of risk due to inflation. If substantial inflation occurs over the ten-year period you hold a SM bond, the $1000 principal repaid to you at the end of that period will represent substantially less purchasing power than the $1000 you loaned to SM ten years earlier. You will have lent "dear" dollars, but will be repaid in "cheap" dollars.

losses, on the one hand, and resource suppliers pursuing greater monetary rewards, on the other, negotiate the changes in the allocation of resources and therefore the composition of output which society demands. The force of competition controls or guides the self-interest motive in such a way that it automatically, and quite unintentionally, furthers the best interests of society. The "invisible hand" tells us that when firms maximize their profits, society's domestic output is also maximized.

The Case for the Market System

The virtues of the market system are implicit in our discussion of its operation. Two merit emphasis.

Allocative Efficiency   The basic economic argument for the market system is that it promotes an efficient allocation of resources. The competitive market system guides resources into production of those goods and services most wanted by society. It forces use of the most efficient techniques in organizing resources for production, and is conducive to the development and adoption of new and more efficient production techniques. The "invisible hand" will in effect harness self-interest so as to provide society with the greatest output of wanted goods from its available resources. This, then, suggests the maximum economic efficiency. This presumption of allocative efficiency makes most economists hesitant to advocate governmental interference with, or regulation of, free markets unless reasons for such interference are clear and compelling.

Freedom   The major noneconomic argument for the market system is its great emphasis on personal freedom. One of the fundamental problems of social organization is how to coordinate the economic activities of large numbers of individuals and businesses. We recall from Chapter 2 that there are two contrasting ways of providing this coordination: one is central direction and the use of coercion; the other is voluntary cooperation through the market system. Only the market system can coordinate economic activity without coercion. The market system permits—indeed, it thrives on—freedom of enterprise and choice. Entrepreneurs and workers are not herded from industry to industry by government directives to meet production targets established by some omnipotent governmental agency. On the contrary, they are free to further their own self-interests, subject, of course, to the rewards and penalties imposed by the market system itself.

QUICK REVIEW 5-3

♪   **The output mix of the competitive market system is determined by profits. Profits cause industries to expand; losses cause them to contract.**

♪   **Competition forces firms to use the least costly (most efficient) production methods.**

♪   **The distribution of output in a market economy is determined by consumer incomes and product prices.**

♪   **Competitive markets reallocate resources in response to changes in consumer tastes, technological progress, and changes in resource supplies.**

CHAPTER SUMMARY

1 The functional distribution of income shows how society's total income is divided among wages, rents, interest, and profits; the personal distribution of income shows how total income is divided among individual households.

2 Households divide their total incomes among personal taxes, saving, and consumer goods. Consumer expenditures on durables and some services are discretionary and therefore postponable.

3 Sole proprietorships, partnerships, and corporations are the major legal forms of business enterprises. Corporations dominate the business sector because they **a** have limited liability, and **b** are in a superior position to acquire money capital for expansion.

4 Ours is a "big business" economy in that many industries are dominated by a small number of large corporations.

5 United States world trade has grown both absolutely and as a proportion of domestic output. The other industrially advanced nations are our major trading partners.

6 International trade yields significant economic benefits in the form of **a** more efficient use of world resources, and **b** enhanced competition. A potential disadvantage is that a nation's international economic interrelationships may create new sources of macroeconomic instability which complicate policy making.

7 Every economy is confronted with Five Fundamental Questions: **a** At what level should available resources be employed? **b** What goods and services are to be produced? **c** How is that output to be produced? **d** To whom should the output be distributed? **e** Can the system adapt to changes in consumer tastes, resource supplies, and technology?

8 Those products whose production and sale yield total revenue sufficient to cover all costs, including a normal profit, will be produced. Those whose production will not yield a normal profit will not be produced.

9 Economic profits designate an industry as prosperous and signal its expansion. Losses mean an industry is unprosperous and result in contraction of that industry.

10 Consumer sovereignty means that both businesses and resource suppliers channel their efforts in accordance with the wants of consumers.

11 Competition forces firms to use the least costly, and therefore the most economically efficient, productive techniques.

12 The prices commanded by the quantities and types of resources supplied by each household will determine the number of dollar claims against the economy's output which each household receives. Within the limits of each household's money income, consumer preferences and the relative prices of products determine the distribution of total output.

13 The competitive market system can communicate changes in consumer tastes to resource suppliers and entrepreneurs, thereby prompting appropriate adjustments in the allocation of the economy's resources. The competitive market system also provides an environment conducive to technological advance and capital accumulation.

14 Competition, the primary mechanism of control in the market economy, will foster an identity of private and social interests; as though directed by an "invisible hand," competition harnesses the self-interest motives of businesses and resource suppliers to simultaneously further the social interest in using scarce resources efficiently.

TERMS AND CONCEPTS

functional and personal distribution of income	firm	separation of ownership and control	expanding industry versus declining industry
durable and nondurable goods	conglomerates	Five Fundamental Questions	consumer sovereignty
services	industry	normal versus economic profits	derived demand
plant	sole proprietorship	dollar votes	directing (guiding) function of prices
horizontal and vertical combinations	partnership		"invisible hand"
	corporation		
	limited liability		
	double taxation		
	economic costs		

QUESTIONS AND STUDY SUGGESTIONS

1 Distinguish between functional and personal distributions of income. What effects do you think a change in the personal distribution of income from that shown in Figure 5-2 to one of complete equality would have on the composition of output and the allocation of resources?

2 What is the demand for consumer durable goods less stable than that for nondurables?

3 Distinguish clearly between a plant, a firm, and an industry. Why is an "industry" often difficult to define in practice?

4 What are the major legal forms of business organization? Briefly state the advantages and disadvantages of each. How do you account for the dominant role of corporations in our economy? Explain and evaluate the separation of ownership and control which characterizes the corporate form of business enterprise.

5 What are the major industries in American capitalism in terms of **a** the number of firms in operation, and **b** the amount of income and employment provided?

6 Explain and evaluate the following statements:

a   "It is the consumer, and the consumer alone, who casts the vote that determines how big any company should be."

b   "The very nature of modern industrial society requires labor, government, and businesses to be 'big' and their bigness renders impossible the functioning of the older, small-scale, simpler, and more flexible capitalist system."

c   "The legal form which an enterprise assumes is dictated primarily by the financial requirements of its particular line of production."

d   "If we want capitalism, we must also accept inequality of income distribution."

7 What is the quantitative importance of world trade to the United States? Explain: "Nations engage in international trade because it allows them to realize the benefits of specialization."

8 How have persistent United States trade deficits been financed? "Trade deficits mean we get more merchandise from the rest of the world than we provide in return. Therefore, trade deficits are economically desirable." Do you agree?

9 Suppose excessive aggregate expenditures in the United States are causing inflation. Explain the effect of **a** appreciation, and **b** depreciation of the dollar on domestic inflation.

10 Describe in detail how the market system answers the Fundamental Questions. Why must economic choices be made? Explain: "The capitalistic system is a profit and loss economy."

11 Evaluate and explain the following statements:

a   "The most important feature of capitalism is the absence of a central economic plan."

b   "Competition is the indispensable disciplinarian of the market economy."

c   "Production methods which are inferior in the engineering sense may be the most efficient methods in the economic sense."

12 Explain fully the meaning and implications of the following quotation.

The beautiful consequence of the market is that it is its own guardian. If output prices or certain kinds of remuneration stray away from their socially ordained levels, forces are set into motion to bring them back to the fold. It is a curious paradox which thus ensues: the market, which is the acme of individual economic freedom, is the strictest taskmaster of all. One may appeal the ruling of a planning board or win the dispensation of a minister; but there is no appeal, no dispensation, from the anonymous pressures of the market mechanism. Economic freedom is thus more illusory than at first appears. One can do as one pleases in the market. But if one pleases to do what the market disapproves, the price of individual freedom is economic ruination.[3]

13 Assume that a business firm finds that its profits will be at maximum when it produces $40 worth of product A. Suppose also that each of the three techniques shown in the following table will produce the desired output.

Resource	Price per unit of resource	Technique no. 1	Technique no. 2	Technique no. 3
Labor	$3	5	2	3
Land	4	2	4	2
Capital	2	2	4	5
Entrepreneurial ability	2	4	2	4

a   Given the resource prices shown, which technique will the firm choose? Why? Will production entail profits or losses? Will the industry expand or contract? When is a new equilibrium output achieved?

b   Assume now that a new technique, technique No. 4, is developed. It entails the use of 2 units of labor, 2 of land, 6 of capital, and 3 of entrepreneurial ability. Given the resource prices in the table, will the firm adopt the new technique? Explain your answer.

c   Suppose now that an increase in labor supply causes the price of labor to fall to $1.50 per unit, all other resource prices being unchanged. Which technique will the producer now choose? Explain.

d   "The market system causes the economy to conserve most in the use of those resources which are particularly scarce in supply. Resources which are scarcest relative to the demand for them have the highest prices. As a result, producers use these resources as sparingly as is possible." Evaluate this statement. Does your answer to question 13c bear out this contention? Explain.

14 Foreigners frequently point out that, comparatively speaking, Americans are very wasteful of food and material goods and very conscious, and overly economical, in their use of time. Can you provide an explanation for this observation?

[3]Robert L. Heilbroner, *The Worldly Philosophers,* 3d ed. (New York: Simon & Schuster, Inc., 1967), p. 42.

CHAPTER 6

The Public Sector

The economic activities of government affect your well-being every day of your life. If you attend a public college or university, taxpayers heavily subsidize your education. When you receive a check from your part-time or summer job, you see significant deductions for income and social security taxes. The ground beef in your Big Mac has been examined by government inspectors to prevent contamination and to ensure quality. Laws requiring seat belts and motorcycle helmets—not to mention the sprinkler system government mandates in your dormitory—are all intended to enhance your safety. If you are a woman or a member of a minority group, an array of legislation is designed to enhance your education, housing, and employment opportunities.

All real-life economies are "mixed"; government and the market system share the responsibility of responding to the Five Fundamental Questions. Our economy is predominantly a market economy, yet the economic activities of government are of great significance. In this chapter we will (1) state and illustrate the major economic functions of the public sector; (2) add government to the circular flow model; and (3) examine the major expenditures and sources of tax revenue for Federal, state, and local governments.

ECONOMIC FUNCTIONS OF GOVERNMENT

The economic functions of government are many and varied. The economic role of government is so broad that it is virtually impossible to establish an all-inclusive list of its economic functions. The following breakdown of government's economic activities will serve as a pattern for our discussion, although some overlapping is unavoidable.

First, some economic functions of government strengthen and facilitate the operation of the market system. The two major activities of government in this area are:

1 Providing the legal foundation and a social environment conducive to the effective operation of the market system.

2 Maintaining competition.

Through a second group of functions, government supplements and modifies the operation of the market system. The three major functions of government here involve:

3 Redistributing income and wealth.

4 Adjusting the allocation of resources to alter the composition of the domestic output.

5 Stabilizing the economy, that is, controlling unemployment and inflation caused by business fluctuations, and promoting economic growth.

In reality most government activities and policies have *some* impact in all these areas. For example, a program to redistribute income to the poor affects the allocation of resources in that the poor buy somewhat different goods and services than the wealthy. A decline in, say, government military spending to lessen inflationary pressures also reallocates resources from public to private uses.

LEGAL AND SOCIAL FRAMEWORK

Government provides the legal framework and certain basic services prerequisite to the effective operation of a market economy. The necessary legal framework includes providing for the legal status of business enterprises, defining the rights of private ownership, and providing for enforcement of contracts. Government also establishes legal "rules of the game" governing the relationships of businesses, resource suppliers, and consumers with one another. Through legislation, government can referee economic relationships, detect foul play, and exercise authority in imposing appropriate penalties.

Basic services provided by government include police powers to maintain internal order, a system of standards for measuring the weight and quality of products, and a monetary system to facilitate exchange of goods and services.

The Pure Food and Drug Act of 1906 and its various amendments are an excellent example of how government has strengthened the operation of the market system. This act sets rules of conduct governing producers in their relationships with consumers. It prohibits the sale of adulterated and misbranded foods and drugs, requires net weights and ingredients of products to be specified on their containers, establishes quality standards which must be stated on labels of canned foods, and prohibits deceptive claims on patent-medicine labels. All these measures are designed to prevent fraudulent activities on the part of producers and, simultaneously, to increase the public's confidence in the integrity of the market system. Similar legislation pertains to labor-management relations and relations of business firms to one another.

The presumption is that this type of government activity will improve resource allocation. Supplying a medium of exchange, ensuring product quality, defining ownership rights, and enforcing contracts tend to increase the volume of exchange. This widens markets and permits greater specialization in the use of both property and human resources. Such specialization means a more efficient allocation of resources. However, some argue that government has overregulated interactions of businesses, consumers, and workers, stifling economic incentives and impairing productive efficiency.

MAINTAINING COMPETITION

Competition is the basic regulatory mechanism in a capitalistic economy. It is the force which subjects producers and resource suppliers to the dictates of consumer sovereignty. With competition, the supply and demand decisions of *many* sellers and buyers determine market prices. Individual producers and resource suppliers can only adjust to the wishes of buyers as tabulated and communicated by the market system. Profits and survival await the competitive producers who obey the market system; losses and eventual bankruptcy are the lot of those who deviate from it. With competition, buyers are the boss, the market is their agent, and businesses are their servants.

The growth of **monopoly** drastically alters this situation. *Monopoly exists when the number of sellers becomes small enough for each seller to influence total supply and therefore the price of the commodity being sold.*

When monopoly supplants competition, sellers can influence, or "rig," the market in their own self-interests, to the detriment of society as a whole. Through their ability to influence total supply, monopolists can artificially restrict the output of products and enjoy higher prices and, frequently, persistent economic profits. These above-competitive prices and profits directly conflict with the interests of consumers. Monopolists are not regulated by the will of society as are competitive sellers. Producer sovereignty supplants consumer sovereignty to the degree that monopoly supplants competition. Resources are then allocated in terms of the profit-seeking interests of monopolistic sellers rather than in terms of the wants of society as a whole. Monopoly causes a misallocation of economic resources.

In the United States, government has attempted to control monopoly primarily in two ways.

1 In the case of "natural monopolies"—industries in

which technological and economic realities rule out competitive markets—government has created public commissions regulating prices and service standards. Transportation, communications, and electric and other utilities are industries which are regulated in varying degrees. At local levels of government, public ownership of electric and water utilities is common.

2 In the vast majority of markets, efficient production can be attained with a high degree of competition. The Federal government has therefore enacted a series of antimonopoly or antitrust laws, beginning with the Sherman Act of 1890, to maintain and strengthen competition as an effective regulator of business behavior.

Even if the legal foundation of capitalistic institutions is assured and competition is maintained, there is still a need for certain additional economic functions on the part of government. *The market economy has certain biases and shortcomings which compel government to supplement and modify its operation.*

REDISTRIBUTION OF INCOME

The market system is an impersonal mechanism, and the distribution of income to which it gives rise may entail more inequality than society desires. The market system yields very large incomes to those whose labor, by virtue of inherent ability and acquired education and skills, commands high wages. Similarly, those who possess—through hard work or easy inheritance— valuable capital and land receive large property incomes.

But others in our society have less ability and have received modest amounts of education and training. These same people typically have accumulated or inherited no property resources. Hence, their incomes are very low. Furthermore, many of the aged, the physically and mentally handicapped, and husbandless women with dependent children earn only very small incomes or, like the unemployed, no incomes at all through the market system. In short, the market system involves considerable inequality in the distribution of money income (recall Figure 5-2) and therefore in the distribution of total output among individual households. Poverty amidst overall plenty in our economy persists as a major economic and political issue.

Government responsibility for ameliorating income inequality is reflected in a variety of policies and programs.

1 *Transfer payments* provide relief to the destitute, aid to the dependent and handicapped, and unemploy-

ment compensation to the unemployed. Similarly, our social security and Medicare programs provide financial support for the retired and aged sick. All these programs transfer income from government to households which would otherwise have little or none.

2 Government also alters the distribution of income by *market intervention,* that is, by modifying the prices established by market forces. Price supports for farmers and minimum-wage legislation are illustrations of government price fixing designed to raise incomes of specific groups.

3 Finally, the personal income tax has been used historically to take a larger proportion of the incomes of the rich than the poor. However, recent revisions of the personal income tax have significantly reduced its redistributive impact.

REALLOCATION OF RESOURCES

Economists recognize two major cases of *market failure,* that is, situations in which the competitive market system would either (1) produce the "wrong" amounts of certain goods and services, or (2) fail to allocate any resources whatsoever to the production of certain goods and services whose output is economically justified. The first case involves "spillovers" or "externalities" and the second "public" or "social" goods.

Spillovers or Externalities

One of the virtues of a competitive market system is that it would result in an efficient allocation of resources. The "right" or optimal amount of resources would be allocated to each of the various goods and services produced. Hence, the equilibrium output in a competitive market is also identified as the optimal output.

But the conclusion that competitive markets automatically bring about allocative efficiency rests on the hidden assumption that *all* the benefits and costs of production and consumption of each product are fully reflected in the market demand and supply curves respectively. It is assumed that there are no *spillovers* or *externalities* associated with the production or consumption of any good or service.

A *spillover*[1] occurs when some of the benefits or costs of production or consumption of a good "spill over" onto third parties, that is, to parties other than the

---

[1]Spillovers may go by other names—for example, external economies and diseconomies, neighborhood effects, and social benefits and costs.

immediate buyer or seller. Spillovers are also termed *externalities* because they are benefits and costs accruing to some individual or group external to the market transaction.

Spillover Costs   When production or consumption of a commodity inflicts costs on a third party without compensation, there exists a **spillover cost.** Obvious examples of spillover costs involve environmental pollution. When a chemical manufacturer or meat-packing plant dumps its wastes into a lake or river, swimmers, fishermen, and boaters—not to mention communities' water supplies—suffer spillover costs. When a petroleum refinery pollutes the air with smoke or a paint factory creates distressing odors, the community bears spillover costs for which it is not compensated.

Figure 6-1a illustrates how spillover or external costs affect the allocation of resources. When spillover costs occur—when producers shift some of their costs onto the community—their production costs are lower than otherwise. The supply curve does not include or "capture" all the costs which can be legitimately associated with production of the good. Hence, the producer's supply curve, S, understates total costs of production and therefore lies to the right of the supply curve which would include all costs, S_t. By polluting, that is, by creating spillover costs, the firm enjoys lower production costs and the supply curve S. The result,

shown in Figure 6-1a, is that equilibrium output Q_e is larger than optimal output Q_o. This means resources are *overallocated* to the production of this commodity.

Correcting for Spillover Costs   Government can take several actions to correct the overallocation of resources associated with spillover costs and "internalize" the external costs. Two basic types of corrective action are common: legislative action and specific taxes.

1   Legislation   In our examples of air and water pollution, we find that the most direct action is to pass *legislation* prohibiting or limiting pollution. Such legislation forces potential polluters to bear costs of properly disposing of industrial wastes. Firms must buy and install smoke-abatement equipment or facilities to purify water contaminated by manufacturing processes. Such action forces potential offenders, under the threat of legal action, to bear *all* costs associated with their production. In short, legislation can shift the supply curve S toward S_t in Figure 6-1b, bringing equilibrium and optimal outputs into equality.

2   Specific Taxes   A second, less direct action is based upon the fact that taxes are a cost and therefore a determinant of a firm's supply curve (Chapter 4). Government might levy a *specific tax* which equals or ap-

FIGURE 6-1   Spillover costs and the overallocation of resources
With spillover costs in (a) we find that the lower costs borne by businesses, as reflected in *S,* fail to reflect all costs, as embodied in S_t. Consequently, the equilibrium output Q_e is greater than the efficient or optimal output Q_o. This overallocation of resources can be corrected by legislation or, as shown in (b), by imposing a specific tax, *T,* which raises the firm's costs and shifts its supply curve from S to S_t.

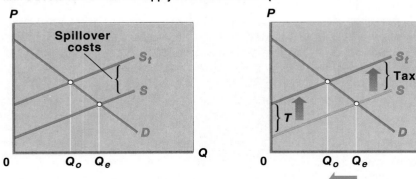

proximates the spillover costs per unit of output. Through this tax, government attempts to shove back onto the offending firm those external or spillover costs which private industry would otherwise avoid. A specific tax equal to T per unit in Figure 6-1b will increase the firm's costs, shifting the supply curve from S to S_t. The result is that the equilibrium output Q_e will decline so that it corresponds with the optimal output Q_o and the overallocation of resources will be eliminated.

Spillover Benefits But spillovers may also take the form of benefits. Production or consumption of certain goods and services may confer spillover or external benefits on third parties or the community at large for which payment or compensation is not required. For example, measles and polio immunization shots result in direct benefits to the immediate consumer. But immunization against these contagious diseases yields widespread and substantial spillover benefits to the entire community.

Education is another example of **spillover benefits.** Education benefits individual consumers: "More educated" people generally achieve higher incomes than "less educated" people. But education also confers sizable benefits upon society. The economy as a whole benefits from a more versatile and more productive labor force, on the one hand, and smaller outlays in crime prevention, law enforcement, and welfare programs, on the other. Significant, too, is the fact that political participation correlates positively with the level of education in that the percentage of persons who vote increases with educational attainment.

Figure 6-2a shows the impact of spillover benefits on resource allocation. The existence of spillover benefits means that the market demand curve, which reflects only private benefits, understates total benefits. The market demand curve fails to capture all the benefits associated with the provision and consumption of goods and services which entail spillover benefits. Thus D in Figure 6-2a indicates the benefits which private individuals derive from education; D_t is drawn to include these private benefits *plus* the additional spillover benefits accruing to society at large. While market demand D and supply S_t would yield an equilibrium output of Q_e, this output would be less than the optimal output Q_o. The market system would not produce enough education; resources would be *underallocated* to education.

Correcting for Spillover Benefits How might the underallocation of resources associated with the presence of spillover benefits be corrected?

1 Increase Demand One approach is to increase demand by providing consumers with purchasing power which can be used *only* to obtain the particular good or service producing spillover benefits. Example: Our food stamp program is designed to improve the diets of low-income families. The food stamps which government provides to such families can be spent

---

FIGURE 6-2 Spillover benefits and the underallocation of resources

Spillover benefits in (a) cause society's total benefits from a product, as shown by D_t, to be understated by the market demand curve, D. As a result, the equilibrium output Q_e is less than the optimal output Q_o. This can be corrected by a subsidy to consumers, as shown in (b), which increases market demand from D to D_t. Alternatively, the underallocation can be eliminated by providing producers with a subsidy of U, which increases their supply curve from S_t to S_t'.

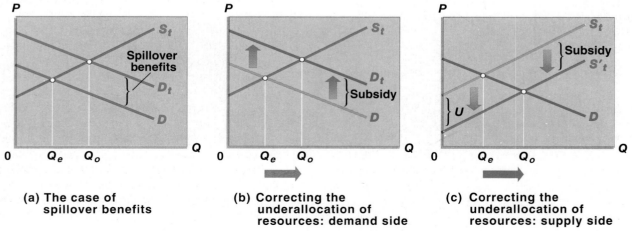

(a) The case of spillover benefits

(b) Correcting the underallocation of resources: demand side

(c) Correcting the underallocation of resources: supply side

only on food. Stores accepting food stamps are reimbursed with money by the government. Part of the rationale for this program is that improved nutrition will help disadvantaged children perform better in school and disadvantaged adults to be better employees. In brief, the program is designed to help disadvantaged people become productive participants in the economy, an outcome benefiting society as a whole. In terms of Figure 6-2b the program increases the demand for food from from D to D_t, thereby alleviating or eliminating the underallocation of resources.

2 Increase Supply An alternative approach works through the supply side of the market. Instead of subsidizing consumers of a particular good, government may find it more convenient and administratively simpler to subsidize producers. A *subsidy* is a specific tax in reverse; taxes impose an extra cost on producers, whereas subsidies reduce their costs. In Figure 6-2c a subsidy of U per unit to producers will reduce costs and shift the supply curve downward from S_t to S_t', and output will increase from Q_e to the optimal level Q_o. Hence, the underallocation of resources will be corrected. Public subsidization of higher education, mass immunization programs, and public hospitals and health clinics are cases in point.

3 Government Provision A third policy option arises if spillover benefits are extremely large: Government may simply choose to finance or, in the extreme, to own and operate such industries. This option leads us into a discussion of public goods and services.

Public Goods and Services

Private goods, which are produced through the market system, are *divisible* in that they come in units small enough to be afforded by individual buyers. Furthermore, private goods are subject to the **exclusion principle,** the idea that those willing and able to pay the equilibrium price get the product, but those unable or unwilling to pay are excluded from the benefits provided by that product.

Certain goods and services—**public** or **social goods**—would not be produced at all by the market system because their characteristics are essentially opposite those of private goods. Public goods are *indivisible,* involving such large units that they cannot be sold to individual buyers. Individuals can buy hamburgers, computers, and automobiles through the market, but not Patriot missiles, highways, and air-traffic control.

More importantly, the exclusion principle does *not* apply; there is no effective way of excluding individuals from the benefits of public goods once those goods come into existence. Obtaining the benefits of private goods is predicated upon *purchase;* benefits from public goods accrue to society from the *production* of such goods.

Illustrations The classic public goods example is a lighthouse on a treacherous coast or harbor. The construction of a lighthouse would be economically justified if benefits (fewer shipwrecks) exceeded production costs. But the benefit accruing to each individual user would not justify the purchase of such a large and indivisible product. In any event, once in operation, its warning light is a guide to *all* ships. There is no practical way to exclude certain ships from its benefits. Therefore, why should any ship owner voluntarily pay for the benefits received from the light? The light is there for all to see, and a ship captain cannot be excluded from seeing it if the ship owner chooses not to pay. Economists call this the **free-rider problem;** *people can receive benefits from a good without contributing to its costs.*

Given the inapplicability of the exclusion principle, there is no economic incentive for private enterprises to supply lighthouses. If the services of the lighthouse cannot be priced and sold, it will be unprofitable for private firms to devote resources to lighthouses. Here is a service which yields substantial benefits but for which the market would allocate no resources. National defense, flood-control, public health, and insect-abatement programs are other public goods. If society is to enjoy such goods and services, they must be provided by the public sector and financed by compulsory charges in the form of taxes.

Large Spillover Benefits While the inapplicability of the exclusion principle sets off public from private goods, many other goods and services are provided by government even though the exclusion principle *could* be applied. Such goods and services as education, streets and highways, police and fire protection, libraries and museums, preventive medicine, and sewage disposal could be subject to the exclusion principle, that is, they could be priced and provided by private producers through the market system. But, as noted earlier, these are all services with substantial spillover benefits and would be underproduced by the market system. Therefore, government undertakes or sponsors their provision to avoid the underallocation of resources which would otherwise occur. Such goods and services are sometimes called *quasi-public goods.* One can understand the long-standing controversies surrounding the status of medical care and housing. Are these private goods to be provided through the market system, or are they quasi-public goods to be provided by government?

Allocating Resources to Public Goods

Given that the price system would fail to allocate resources for public goods and would underallocate resources for quasi-public goods, what is the mechanism by which such goods get produced?

Public goods are purchased through the government on the basis of group, or collective, choices, in contrast to private goods, which are purchased from private enterprises on the basis of individual choices. The types and quantities of the various public goods produced are determined in a democracy by political means, that is, by voting. The quantities of the various public goods consumed are a matter of public policy.[2] These group decisions, made in the political arena, supplement the choices of households and businesses in answering the Five Fundamental Questions.

Given these group decisions, precisely how are resources reallocated from production of private goods to production of public goods? In a full-employment economy, government must free resources from private employment to make them available for production of public goods. The apparent means of releasing resources from private uses is to reduce private demand for them. This is accomplished by levying taxes on businesses and households, diverting some of their incomes—some of their potential purchasing power—out of the income-expenditure streams. With lower incomes, businesses and households must curtail their investment and consumption spending. *Taxes diminish private demand for goods and services, and this decrease in turn prompts a drop in the private demand for resources.* By diverting purchasing power from private spenders to government, taxes free resources from private uses.

Government expenditure of the tax proceeds can then reabsorb these resources in the provision of public goods and services. Corporation and personal income taxes

release resources from production of investment goods—printing presses, boxcars, warehouses—and consumer goods—food, clothing, and television sets. Government expenditures can reabsorb these resources in production of guided missiles, military aircraft, and new schools and highways. Government purposely reallocates resources to bring about significant changes in the composition of the economy's total output.

Stabilization

Historically, the most recent function of government is that of stabilizing the economy—assisting the private economy to achieve both the full employment of resources and a stable price level. At this point we will only outline (rather than fully explain) the stabilization function of government.

The level of output depends directly on total or aggregate expenditures. A high level of total spending means it will be profitable for industries to produce large outputs. This condition, in turn, will necessitate that both property and human resources be employed at high levels. But aggregate spending may either fall short of, or exceed, that particular level which will provide for full employment and price stability. Two possibilities, unemployment or inflation, may then occur.

1 Unemployment The level of total spending in the private sector may be too low for full employment. Thus, the government may choose to augment private spending so that total spending—private *and* public—will be sufficient to generate full employment. Government can do this by using the same techniques—government spending and taxes—as it uses to reallocate resources to production of public goods. Specifically, government might increase its own spending on public goods and services on the one hand, and reduce taxes to stimulate private spending on the other.[3]

2 Inflation The second possibility is that the economy may attempt to spend in excess of its productive capacity. If aggregate spending exceeds the full-employment output, the excess spending will pull up the price level. Excessive aggregate spending is inflationary. Government's obligation here is to eliminate the excess spending. It can do this primarily by cutting its own expenditures and by raising taxes to curtail private spending.

---

[2]There are differences between *dollar voting,* which dictates ouput in the private sector of the economy, and *political voting,* which determines ouput in the public sector. The rich person has many more votes to cast in the private sector than does the poor person. In the public sector, each—at least in theory—has an equal say. Furthermore, the children who cast their votes for bubble gum and comic books in the private sector are banned by virtue of their age from the registering of social choices.

[3]In macroeconomics we learn that government can also use monetary policy—changes in the nation's money supply and interest rates—to help achieve economic stability.

THE CIRCULAR FLOW REVISITED

Government is thoroughly integrated into the real and monetary flows which comprise our economy. It is informative to reexamine the redistributional, allocative, and stabilization functions of government in terms of Chapter 3's circular flow model. In Figure 6-3 flows (1) through (4) restate Figure 3-2. Flows (1) and (2) show business expenditures for the resources provided by households. These expenditures are costs to businesses, but represent wage, rent, interest, and profit income to households. Flows (3) and (4) portray households making consumer expenditures for the goods and services produced by businesses.

Now consider the numerous modifications which stem from the addition of government. Flows (5)

FIGURE 6-3 The circular flow and the public sector

Government expenditures, taxes, and transfer payments affect the distribution of income, the allocation of resources, and the level of economic activity.

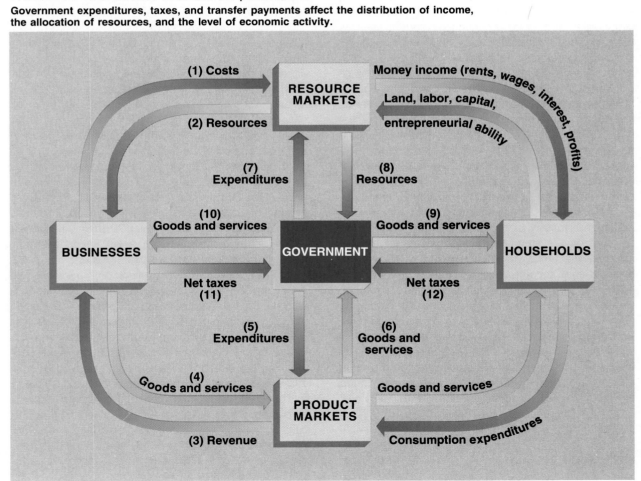

through (8) tell us that government makes purchases in both product and resource markets. Specifically, flows (5) and (6) represent government purchasing such things as paper clips, computers, and military hardware from private businesses. Flows (7) and (8) reflect government purchases of resources. The Federal government employs and pays salaries to members of Congress, the armed forces, Justice Department lawyers, various bureaucrats, and so on. State and local governments hire teachers, bus drivers, police, and firefighters. The Federal government might lease or purchase land to expand a military base; a city may buy land to build a new elementary school.

Government then provides public goods and services to both households and businesses as shown by flows (9) and (10). The financing of public goods and services requires tax payments by businesses and households as reflected in flows (11) and (12). We have labeled these flows as *net* taxes to acknowledge that they also include "taxes in reverse" in the form of transfer payments to households and subsidies to businesses. Thus, flow (11) entails not merely corporate income, sales, and excise taxes flowing from businesses to government, but also various subsidies to farmers, shipbuilders, and some airlines.[4] Similarly, government also collects taxes (personal income taxes, payroll taxes) directly from households and makes available transfer payments, for example, welfare payments and social security benefits as shown by flow (12).

Our expanded circular flow model clearly shows us how government can alter the distribution of income, reallocate resources, and change the level of economic activity. The structure of taxes and transfer payments can have a significant impact on income distribution. In flow (12) a tax structure which draws tax revenues primarily from well-to-do households combined with a system of transfer payments to low-income households will result in greater equality in the distribution of income.

Flows (6) and (8) imply an allocation of resources which differs from that of a purely private economy. Government buys goods and labor services which differ from those purchased by households.

Finally, all governmental flows suggest means by which government might attempt to stabilize the economy. If the economy was experiencing unemployment, an increase in government spending with taxes and

transfers held constant would increase aggregate spending, output, and employment. Similarly, given the level of government expenditures, a decline in taxes or an increase in transfer payments would increase spendable incomes and boost private spending. Conversely, with inflation the opposite government policies would be in order: reduced government spending, increased taxes, and reduced transfers.

GOVERNMENT FINANCE

How large is the public sector? What are the main economic programs of Federal, state, and local governments? How are these programs financed?

Government Growth: Purchases and Transfers

We can get a general impression of the size and growth of government's economic role by examining government purchases of goods and services and government transfer payments. The distinction between these two kinds of outlays is significant.

1 **Government purchases** are "exhaustive" in that they directly absorb or employ resources and the resulting production is part of the domestic output. For example, the purchase of a missile absorbs the labor of physicists and engineers along with steel, explosives, and a host of other inputs.

2 **Transfer payments** are "nonexhaustive" in that they do not directly absorb resources or account for production. Social security benefits, welfare payments, veterans' benefits, and unemployment compensation are examples of transfer payments. Their key characteristic is that recipients make no current contribution to output in return for these payments.

Figure 6-4 compares *government purchases* of goods and services with the domestic output, that is, with the total amount of goods and services produced in the economy for the 1929–1991 period. Total government purchases rose significantly relative to domestic output over the 1929–1940 period, but then skyrocketed during World War II. However, since the early 1950s government spending for goods and services has hovered around 20 percent of the domestic output. Of course, the domestic output has expanded dramatically over the 1929–1991 period so that the *absolute* volume of government spending has increased greatly. Government expenditures on goods and services to-

---

[4]Most business subsidies are "concealed" in the form of low-interest loans, loan guarantees, tax concessions, or the public provision of facilities at prices less than costs.

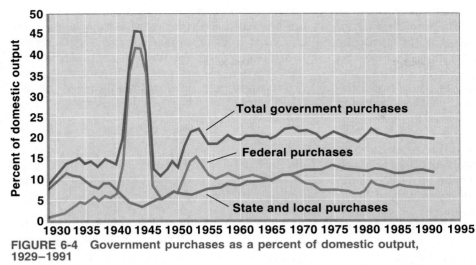

FIGURE 6-4 Government purchases as a percent of domestic output, 1929–1991

Government purchases rose relative to domestic output over the 1929–1940 period, only to increase dramatically during World War II. Since the early 1950s total government purchases have been approximately 20 percent of the domestic output.

taled $1087 billion in 1991 as compared to only $9 billion in 1929!

When transfer payments are added, our impression of government's role and its growth change considerably. Transfers have grown rapidly since the 1960s, rising from $29 billion or 5 percent of the domestic output in 1960, to $759 billion or 13 percent of the domestic output in 1991. The net result is that tax revenues required to finance both government purchases *and* transfers are equal to approximately one-third of the domestic output. In 1990 an average tax bill of about $13,000 was imposed on every family in the United States. In 1991 the average taxpayer spent about 2 hours and 49 minutes of each 8-hour workday to pay taxes. However, the size of our public sector is small compared to other industrialized countries. Taxes in Sweden, Norway, France, Great Britain, and West Germany are 51, 46, 45, 39, and 37 percent of domestic output respectively, compared to about 30 percent in the United States.

Some Causes

Let's now consider some specific factors which account for the historical growth and present size of government spending and taxes.

1 War and Defense   Hot and cold wars have tended to sustain Federal expenditures at high levels for the past four decades. War, national defense, and military-space research are among the major causes of the growth of government spending and taxation which has occurred since 1940.

2 Population Growth   There are over twice as many Americans today as there were a scant sixty years ago. This means there are more people for whom public goods and services must be provided. Even with a constant level of government spending per person, total government spending would have increased dramatically in recent decades.

3 Urbanization and the Demand for Public Goods
The increasing urbanization of our economy has necessitated massive expenditures on streets, public transportation facilities, police and fire protection, and sewers. Also, the public has demanded more and better public goods and services to "match" the rising standard of living provided by the private sector of the economy. We want bigger and better highways to accommodate more and better automobiles. We seek more and better educational facilities to upgrade the labor force for the more demanding jobs of private industry.

4 Environmental Quality Population growth and urbanization have contributed to serious and well-publicized problems of environmental quality. Society has become highly aware that the production and consumption of vast quantities of goods can lead to serious external or spillover costs in air, water, and land pollution. Government has inherited a central role in coping with these environmental problems.

5 Egalitarianism Since the mid-1960s there has occurred a sharp expansion of programs designed to alleviate poverty and reduce income inequality. Social security, unemployment compensation, welfare, Medicare, food stamps, and public housing are examples. These programs accounted for about 3 percent of domestic output twenty years ago. They now require approximately 13 percent of domestic output.

FEDERAL FINANCE

Now we will disaggregate the public sector into Federal, state, and local units of government to compare their expenditures and taxes. Table 6-1 tells the story for the Federal government.

Federal Expenditures

Although Table 6-1 reveals a wide variety of Federal expenditures, three important areas of spending stand out: (1) income security, (2) national defense, and (3) interest on the public debt. The *income security* category reflects the myriad income-maintenance programs for the aged, the disabled, the unemployed, the handicapped, the medically indigent, and families with

no breadwinner. *National defense* constitutes about one-fourth of the Federal budget and underscores the high costs of military preparedness. *Interest on the public debt* has grown dramatically in recent years because the public debt itself has grown. The remaining categories of expenditures listed in Table 6-1 are largely self-explanatory.

Federal Receipts

The receipts side of Table 6-1 clearly shows that the personal income tax, payroll taxes, and the corporate income tax are the basic revenue getters, accounting for 45, 37, and 9 cents of each dollar collected.

Personal Income Tax The **personal income tax** is the kingpin of our national tax system and merits special comment. This tax is levied on *taxable income,* that is, on the incomes of households and unincorporated businesses after certain exemptions ($2,150 for each household member) and deductions (business expenses, charitable contributions, home mortgage interest payments, certain state and local taxes) are taken into account.

The Federal personal income tax is a *progressive tax,* that is, people with higher incomes pay a larger percentage of their income as taxes than do persons with lower incomes. The progressivity is achieved through a system of higher tax rates which apply to successive layers or brackets of income.

Columns 1 and 2 of Table 6-2 portray the mechanics of the income tax for a married couple filing a joint return. Note that the 15 percent rate applies to all taxable income up to $34,000, at which point any *additional* income up to $82,150 is taxable at the 28 percent rate.

TABLE 6-1 The Federal budget, 1990

Tax receipts	Billions of dollars	Percent of total	Expenditures	Billions of dollars	Percent of total
Personal income tax	$ 467	45	Income security	$ 494	39
Payroll taxes	380	37	National defense	299	24
Corporate income taxes	94	9	Interest on public debt	184	15
Excise taxes	35	3	Commerce, housing, and transportation	97	8
Customs duties	17	2	Education, training, and health	96	8
Estate and gift taxes	12	1	Agriculture, natural resources, and environment	46	4
All other	26	3	All other (net)	36	3
Total receipts	$1031	100	Total expenditures	$1252	100

Source: Economic Report of the President. Because of rounding, figures may not add up to totals.

TABLE 6-2 **Federal personal income tax rates, 1991***

(1) Total taxable income	(2) Marginal tax rate (4) ÷ (3)	(3) Change in income Δ(1)	(4) Change in taxes Δ(5)	(5) Total tax	(6) Average Tax rate (5) ÷ (1)
$ 0	0%	—	—	—	—
34,000	15	$34,000	$ 5,100	$ 5,100	15%
82,150	28	48,150	13,482	18,582	22.6
Over 82,150	31	—	—	—	—

*Data are for a married couple filing a joint return.

Any additional taxable income above $82,150 is taxed at 31 percent.

The tax rates shown in column 2 of Table 6-2 are marginal tax rates. A **marginal tax rate** is the tax paid on additional or incremental income. By definition, it is the *increase* in taxes paid (column 4) divided by the *increase* in income (column 3). Thus, if our couple's taxable income increased from $0 to $34,000 the increase in taxes paid would be $5,100 (=.15 × $34,000) as shown in column 4. If the couple's taxable income rose by an additional $48,150 (column 3)—that is, from $34,000 to $82,150—a higher marginal tax rate of 28 percent would apply so that an additional tax of $13,482 (=.28 × $48,150) would have to be paid (column 4).

The marginal tax rates of column 2 overstate the personal income tax bite because the rising rates apply only to income falling within each successive tax bracket. To get a better picture of the tax burden one must consider average tax rates. The **average tax rate** is the total tax paid divided by total taxable income. In column 6 of Table 6-2 for the $0 to $34,000 tax bracket the average tax rate is $5,100 (column 4) divided by $34,000 (column 1) or 15 percent, the same as the marginal tax rate. But the couple earning $82,150 does *not* pay 28 percent of its income as taxes as the marginal tax rate would suggest. Rather, its average tax rate is only about 22.6 percent (=$18,582 ÷ $82,150). The reason is that the first $34,000 of income it taxed at 15 percent and only the next $48,150 is subject to the 28 percent rate. You should calculate the average tax rate for a couple earning $182,500. What we observe here is that, if the marginal tax rate is higher than the average tax rate, the average tax rate will rise.[5]

By definition, a tax whose average tax rate rises as income increases is called a *progressive tax*. Such a tax claims both a larger absolute amount and a larger proportion of income as income rises. Thus we can say

that our current personal income tax is mildly progressive.

Payroll Taxes Social security contributions, or **payroll taxes,** are the premiums paid on the compulsory insurance plans—old age insurance and Medicare—provided for by existing social security legislation. These taxes are paid by both employers and employees. Improvements in, and extensions of, our social security programs, plus growth of the labor force, have resulted in very significant increases in payroll taxes in recent years. In 1992 employees and employers each paid a tax of 7.65 percent on the first $55,500 of an employee's annual earnings.

Corporate Income Tax The Federal government also taxes corporate income. This **corporate income tax** is levied on a corporation's profits—the difference between its total revenue and its total expenses. The basic rate is 34 percent, which applies to annual profits over $335,000. A firm with profits of $1,335,000 would pay corporate income taxes of $340,000. Firms making annual profits less than $335,000 are taxed at lower rates.

Excise Taxes Commodity or consumption taxes may take the form of **sales taxes** or **excise taxes.** The difference between the two is basically one of coverage. Sales taxes fall on a wide range of products, whereas excises are taxes on a small, select list of commodities. As Table 6-1 suggests, the Federal government collects excise taxes on such commodities as alcoholic beverages, tobacco, and gasoline. Beginning in 1991 a new excise tax applies to certain luxury goods. A 10 percent tax is now levied on that portion of the price above $30,000 for cars, $100,000 for boats, $250,000 for aircraft, and $10,000 for furs and jewelry. If your rich uncle were to buy you a $60,000 Mercedes for graduation, he would have to pay a tax of $3,000. The Federal government does *not* levy a general sales tax; sales taxes are the bread and butter of most state governments.

[5]The arithmetic is the same as what you may have encountered in school. You must get a score on an additional or "marginal" examination higher than your existing average grade to pull your average up!

TABLE 6-3   Consolidated budget of all state governments, 1990

Tax receipts	Billions of dollars	Percent of total	Expenditures	Billions of dollars	Percent of total
Sales, excise, and gross receipts taxes	$147	49	Public welfare	$ 83	25
Personal income taxes	96	32	Education	75	23
Corporate income taxes	22	7	Highways	44	13
Property taxes	6	2	Health and hospitals	42	13
Death and gift taxes	4	1	Public safety	30	9
Licenses, permits, and others	25	8	All others	59	18
Total receipts	$300	100	Total expenditures	$333	100

Source: Bureau of the Census, State Government Finances in 1990. Because of rounding, figures may not add up to totals.

STATE AND LOCAL FINANCE

While the Federal government finances itself largely through personal and corporate income taxation and payroll taxes, state and local governments rely heavily on sales and property taxes, respectively. Although there is considerable overlap in the types of expenditures made by the three levels of government, public welfare is the main outlay of state governments, followed closely by education. For local governments, education is the dominant expenditure.

State Expenditures and Receipts

Note in Table 6-3 that the basic sources of tax revenue at the state level are sales and excise taxes, which account for about 49 percent of all state tax revenues. State personal income taxes, which entail much more modest rates than those of the Federal government, are the second most important source of revenue. Taxes on corporate income, property, inheritances,

and licenses and permits constitute the remainder of state tax revenue.

On the expenditure side, the major outlays of state governments are for (1) public welfare, (2) education, (3) highway maintenance and construction, and (4) health and hospitals.

Note that the budget statement shown in Table 6-3 contains aggregated data, telling us little about the finances of individual states. States vary tremendously in the types of taxes employed. Thus, although personal income taxes are a major source of revenue for all state governments combined, four states do not use the personal income tax. Furthermore, great variations in the size of tax receipts and disbursements exist among the states.

Local Expenditures and Receipts

The receipts and expenditures shown in Table 6-4 are for all units of local government, including counties, municipalities, townships, and school districts. One major source of revenue and a single basic use of reve-

TABLE 6-4   Consolidated budget of all local governments, 1990

Tax receipts	Billions of dollars	Percent of total	Expenditures	Billions of dollars	Percent of total
Property taxes	$150	75	Education	$217	43
Sales and excises	31	15	Welfare, health, and hospitals	66	13
Personal and corporate income taxes	11	6	Environment and housing	56	11
Licenses, permits, and others	9	4	Public safety	50	10
			Transportation	34	7
			All others	81	16
Total receipts	$201	100	Total expenditures	$504	100

Source: Bureau of the Census, Government Finances in 1989–1990. Because of rounding, figures may not add up to totals.

LAST WORD

LOTTERIES: FACTS AND CONTROVERSIES

State lotteries, which began in 1963, are a potentially important source of public revenue. What are the characteristics of lotteries? And what are the arguments for and against this means of enhancing state revenues?

In 1990 some 33 states and the District of Columbia had lotteries which sold over $20 billion worth of tickets. The average lottery returns about 50 percent of its gross revenues to ticket purchasers as prizes and 40 percent goes to the state treasury. The remaining 10 percent is for designing and promoting the lottery and for commissions to retail outlets which sell tickets. Although states sponsoring lotteries currently obtain only 3 to 4 percent of their total revenues in this way, per capita sales of lottery tickets increased by 12 percent per year over the 1975–1989 period.

Lotteries have been controversial. Critics make the following arguments. First, the 40 percent of gross revenues from lotteries which goes to the state governments is in effect a 40 percent tax on ticket purchases. This tax is higher than the taxes on cigarettes and liquor. Furthermore, research indicates that the "lottery tax" is highly regressive in that there is little relationship between ticket purchases and household incomes. This means that low-income families spend a larger proportion of their incomes on lotteries than do high-income families. The 10 percent of the adults who patronize lotteries most heavily account for one-half of total ticket sales. Second, critics argue that it is ethically wrong for the state to sponsor gambling. Gambling is generally regarded as immoral and, in other forms, is illegal in most states. It is also held that lotteries may whet the appetite for gambling and generate compulsive gamblers who will impoverish themselves and their families. Third, lotteries may be sending the message that luck and fate—rather than education, hard work, and saving and investing—are the route to success and wealth in America.

But there are counterarguments. It is contended,

in the first place, that lottery revenue should not be regarded as a tax. Tax collections are compulsory and involve coercion; the purchase of a lottery ticket is voluntary and entails free consumer choice. A second and related argument is that within wide limits it is not appropriate to make moral judgments about how people should spend their incomes. Individuals allegedly achieve the maximum satisfaction from their incomes by spending without interference. If some people derive satisfaction from participating in lotteries, they should be free to do so. Third, faced with tax revenue shortfalls and intense pressure not to raise taxes, lotteries are a relatively painless source of revenue to finance important state services such as education and welfare programs. Finally, lotteries are competitive with illegal gambling and thereby may be socially beneficial in curtailing the power of organized crime.

Two observations seem certain at the moment. One is that total lottery revenue will continue to increase. More and more states are establishing lotteries and people seem to enjoy gambling, particularly when they feel their losses are being used for "good causes." The other point is that this source of revenue will remain controversial.

Source: Based on Charles T. Clotfelter and Philip J. Cook, "On the Economics of State Lotteries," *Journal of Economic Perspectives,* Fall, 1990, pp. 105–119.

nue stand out: The bulk of the revenue received by local government comes from **property taxes** and most local revenue is spent for education. Other, less important sources of funds and types of disbursements are self-explanatory.

The gaping deficit shown in Table 6-4 is largely removed when nontax resources of income are taken into account: In 1990 the tax revenues of local govern-

ments were supplemented by some $209 billion in intergovernmental grants from Federal and state governments. Furthermore, local governments received an additional $52 billion as proprietary income, that is, as revenue from government-owned hospitals and utilities. Finally, lotteries—the subject of this chapter's Last Word—are a growing source of nontax revenue for two-thirds of the states.

♦ *Government purchases are about 20 percent of the domestic output; the addition of transfers increases government spending to almost one-third of domestic output.*

♦ *Income security and national defense are the main Federal expenditures; personal income, payroll, and corporate income taxes are the primary sources of revenue.*

♦ *States rely primarily on sales and excise taxes for revenue; their spending is largely for education, welfare, and health.*

♦ *Education is the dominant expenditure for local governments and most of their revenue is derived from property taxes.*

Fiscal Federalism

Historically, the tax collections of both state and local governments have fallen substantially short of their expenditures. These revenue shortfalls are largely filled by Federal transfers or grants. It is not uncommon for 15 to 20 percent of all revenue received by state and local governments to come from the Federal government. In addition to Federal grants to state and local governments, the states also make grants to local governmental units. This system of intergovernmental transfers is called **fiscal federalism.** Concern over large and persistent Federal budget deficits has precipitated declines in Federal grants in recent years, causing state and local governments to increase tax rates, impose new taxes, and restrain expenditures.

CHAPTER SUMMARY

1 Government enhances the operation of the market system by **a** providing an appropriate legal and social framework, and **b** acting to maintain competition.

2 Government alters the distribution of income by direct market intervention and through the tax-transfer system.

3 Spillovers or externalities cause the equilibrium output of certain goods to vary from the optimal output. Spillover costs result in an overallocation of resources which can be corrected by legislation or specific taxes. Spillover benefits are accompanied by an underallocation of resources which can be corrected by subsidies to either consumers or producers.

4 Government must provide public goods because such goods are indivisible and entail benefits from which nonpaying consumers cannot be excluded.

5 The manipulation of taxes and its expenditures is one basic means by which government can reduce unemployment and inflation.

6 The circular flow model helps us envision how government performs its redistributional, allocative, and stabilizing functions.

7 Although the absolute level of total government purchases of goods and services has increased greatly, such purchases have been about 20 percent of the domestic output in the entire post-World War II period.

8 Government purchases are exhaustive or resource-absorbing; transfer payments are not. Government purchases and transfers combined amount to about one-third of the domestic output.

9 Wars and national defense, population growth, urbanization, environmental problems, and egalitarianism have been among the more important causes of the historical growth of the public sector.

10 The main categories of Federal spending are for income security, national defense, and interest on the public debt; revenues come primarily from personal income, payroll, and corporate income taxes.

11 The primary sources of revenue for the states are sales and excise taxes; public welfare, education, highways, and health and hospitals are the major state expenditures.

12 At the local level, most revenue comes from the property tax, and education is the most important expenditure.

13 Under our system of fiscal federalism, state and local tax revenues are supplemented by sizable revenue grants from the Federal government.

TERMS AND CONCEPTS

monopoly	public or social goods	personal income tax	corporate income tax
spillover costs and spillover benefits	free-rider problem	marginal and average tax rates	sales and excise taxes
exclusion principle	government purchases	payroll taxes	property taxes
	transfer payments		fiscal federalism

QUESTIONS AND STUDY SUGGESTIONS

1 Carefully evaluate this statement: "The public, as a general rule . . . gets less production in return for a dollar spent by government than from a dollar spent by private enterprise."

2 Enumerate and briefly discuss the main economic functions of government.

3 Explain why, in the absence of spillovers, equilibrium and optimal outputs are identical in competitive markets. What divergences arise between equilibrium and optimal output when a spillover costs and b spillover benefits are present? How might government correct for these discrepancies? "The presence of spillover costs suggests underallocation of resources to that product and the need for governmental subsidies." Do you agree? Explain how zoning and seat belt laws might be used to deal with a problem of spillover costs.

4 UCLA researchers have concluded that injuries caused by firearms cost about $429 million a year in hospital expenses alone. Because the majority of those shot are poor and without insurance, almost 86 percent of hospital costs must be borne by taxpayers. Use your understanding of externalities to recommend appropriate policies.

5 What are the basic characteristics of public goods? Explain the significance of the exclusion principle. By what means does government provide public goods?

6 Use your understanding of the characteristics of private and public goods to determine whether the following should be produced through the market system or provided by government: a bread; b street lighting; c bridges; d parks; e swimming pools; f medical care; g mail delivery; h housing; i air traffic control; j libraries.

7 Explain how government might manipulate its expenditures and tax revenues to reduce a unemployment and b the rate of inflation.

8 "Most governmental actions simultaneously affect the distribution of income, the allocation of resources, and the levels of unemployment and prices." Use the circular flow model to confirm this assertion for each of the following: a the construction of a new high school in Blackhawk County; b a 2 percent reduction in the corporate income tax; c an expansion of preschool programs for disadvantaged children; d a $50 billion increase in spending for space research; e the levying of a tax on air polluters; and f a $1 increase in the minimum wage.

9 Draw a production possibilities curve with public goods on the vertical axis and private goods on the horizontal axis. Assuming the economy is initially operating on the curve, indicate the means by which the production of public goods might be increased. How might the output of public goods be increased if the economy is initially functioning at a point inside the curve?

10 Describe and account for the historical growth of the public sector of the economy. In your response carefully distinguish between government purchases and transfer payments.

11 What is the most important source of revenue and the major type of expenditure at the Federal level? At the state level? At the local level?

12 Briefly describe the mechanics of the Federal personal income tax. Use the concepts of marginal and average tax rates to explain why it is a progressive tax.

13 Assume that the structure of a personal income tax is such that you would pay a tax of $2000 if your taxable income was $16,000 and a tax of $3000 if your taxable income was $20,000. What is the average tax rate at the $16,000 and $20,000 levels of taxable income? What marginal tax rate applies to taxable income which falls between $16,000 and $20,000? Is this tax progressive? Explain.

14 Calculate the average and marginal tax rates for the following table. Is this tax progressive? How do you know? What generalization can you offer concerning the relationship between marginal and average tax rates?

Income	Tax	Average tax rate	Marginal tax rate
$ 0	$ 0	_____	
100	10	_____	_____
200	30	_____	_____
300	60	_____	_____
400	100	_____	_____
500	150	_____	_____

15 The Federal government recently increased its excise taxes on gasoline, alcoholic beverages, and tobacco. What effect might these increases have on the revenues which states receive from their excises on these same products?

16 What is "fiscal federalism"? Why does it exist?

PART

2

National Income, Employment, and Fiscal Policy

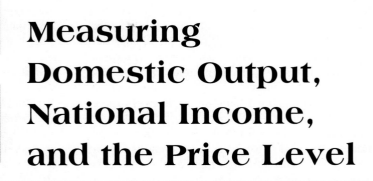

CHAPTER 7

Measuring Domestic Output, National Income, and the Price Level

"**P**ersonal Consumption Expenditures Surge" "Private Domestic Investment Stagnates" "Gross Domestic Product Up 3.4 Percent" "Personal Income Continues To Fall" "Price Level Rises 0.8 Percent for Month"

These are typical headlines in the business and economics sections of the news. Many readers skip these articles, concluding that they are too technical, and therefore of limited interest.

The goal of this chapter is to ensure that you are not one of those readers. The potential payoff from this chapter is large. Upon completing it, you will have learned the basics of how government statisticians and accountants measure and record the levels of domestic output, national income, and prices for the entire United States. Moreover, you will acquire an understanding of important terms such as gross domestic product, net domestic product, national income, personal income, disposable income, and the price level. Finally, this chapter will extend your vocabulary in a way that will aid your comprehension of the macroeconomics in subsequent chapters.

Our specific approach is as follows: First, we explain why it is important to be able to measure the performance of the economy. Second, the key measure of domestic output—gross domestic product or GDP—is defined. We show that GDP can be measured either from the vantage point of expenditures on output or by the income generated from the production of that output. Third, several other important measures of output and income are derived from GDP and their meanings explained. Fourth, we show how the overall level of prices—the price level—is measured. Fifth, we demonstrate how GDP can be adjusted for changes in the price level—that is, for inflation or deflation—so changes in the physical amount of the nation's production are more accurately reflected. Finally, some limitations of our measures of domestic output and national income are surveyed.

THE IMPORTANCE OF MACROECONOMIC MEASUREMENT

Our present aim is to define and understand a group of so-called social or national income accounting concepts which measure the overall production performance of the economy. We do so because national income accounting does for the economy as a whole what private accounting does for the individual business enterprise or, for that matter, for the household. The business executive is vitally interested in knowing how well his or her firm is doing, but the answer is not always immediately discernible.

Measurement of a firm's flows of income and expenditures is needed to assess its operations for the current year. With this information, the executive can gauge the firm's economic health. If things are going well, the accounting data can be used to explain this success. Costs might be down or sales and product prices up, resulting in large profits. If things are going badly, accounting measures can be employed to discover immediate causes. And by examining the accounts over a period of time, the executive can detect growth or decline of profits for the firm and indications of the immediate causes. All this information helps the executive make intelligent business decisions.

A system of **national income accounting** operates in much the same way for the economy as a whole:

1 It allows us to keep a finger on the economic pulse of the nation. The various measures which make up our national income accounting system permit us to measure the level of production in the economy at some point in time and explain the immediate causes of that level of performance.

2 By comparing national income accounts over a period of time, we can plot the long-run course which the economy has been following; the growth or stagnation of the economy will show up in the national income accounts.

3 Finally, information supplied by national income accounts provides a basis for the formulation and application of public policies to improve the performance of the economy; without national income accounts, economic policy would be based on guesswork. *National income accounting allows us to keep tabs on the economic health of society and formulate policies which will improve that health.*

What are these accounting measures?

GROSS DOMESTIC PRODUCT

There are many conceivable measures of the economic well-being of society. But the best available indicator of an economy's health is its annual total output of goods and services or, as it is sometimes called, the economy's aggregate output. There are two closely related basic national income accounting measures of the total output of goods and services: gross national product and gross domestic product. Both measure *the total market value of all final goods and services produced in the economy in one year.* The difference is in how the "economy" is defined.

Gross national product (GNP) consists of the total output produced by land, labor, capital, and entrepreneurial talent supplied by Americans, whether these resources are located in the United States or abroad. Thus, for example, the share of output (income) produced by an American working in France is included in our GNP. Conversely, the share of output (income) produced in the United States by foreign-owned resources is excluded from our GNP.

On the other hand, **gross domestic product** (GDP) comprises the value of the total goods and services produced within the boundaries of the United States, whether by American or foreign-supplied resources. For instance, the full value of the autos produced at a Japanese-owned Nissan factory in the United States, including profits, is a part of American GDP. Conversely, profits earned by an American-owned IBM plant in France are excluded from our GDP.

Most nations use GDP as the chief measure of their output. In 1992 the United States switched from GNP accounting to GDP accounting. Thus, our focus will be on GDP.

In discussing GDP, we will see that all goods *produced* in a particular year may not be *sold;* some may be added to inventories. Any increase in inventories must therefore be included in determining GDP, since GDP measures all current production, whether or not it is sold. Our definition of GDP is very explicit and merits considerable comment.

A Monetary Measure

Note, first, that GDP measures the market value of annual output; it is a monetary measure. Indeed, it must be if we are to compare the heterogeneous collections of goods and services produced in different years and get a meaningful idea of their relative worth. If the

TABLE 7-1 Comparing heterogeneous outputs by using money prices (hypothetical data)

Year	Annual outputs	Market values
1	3 oranges and 2 apples	3 at 20 cents + 2 at 30 cents = $1.20
2	2 oranges and 3 apples	2 at 20 cents + 3 at 30 cents = $1.30

economy produces three oranges and two apples in year 1 and two oranges and three apples in year 2, in which year is output greater? We cannot answer this question until price tags are attached to the various products as indicators of society's evaluation of their relative worth.

The problem is resolved in Table 7-1, where the money price of oranges is 20 cents and the price of apples is 30 cents. Year 2's output is greater than year 1's, because society values year 2's output more highly; society is willing to pay more for the collection of goods produced in year 2 than for goods produced in year 1.

Avoiding Double Counting

To measure total output accurately, all goods and services produced in any given year must be counted once, but not more than once. Most products go through a series of production stages before reaching a market. As a result, parts or components of most products are bought and sold many times. To avoid counting several times the parts of products that are sold and resold, GDP includes only the market value of final goods and ignores transactions involving intermediate goods.

By **final goods** we mean goods and services being purchased for final use and not for resale or further processing or manufacturing. Transactions involving

intermediate goods refer to purchases of goods and services for further processing and manufacturing or for resale. The sale of final goods is *included* and the sale of intermediate goods is *excluded* from GDP. Why? Because the value of final goods already includes all intermediate transactions involved in their production. To count intermediate transactions separately would be **double counting** and an exaggerated estimate of GDP.

To clarify this point, suppose there are five stages of production in getting a wool suit manufactured and to the consumer, who, of course, is the ultimate or final user. As Table 7-2 indicates, firm A, a sheep ranch, provides $60 worth of wool to firm B, a wool processor. Firm A pays out the $60 it receives in wages, rents, interest, and profits. Firm B processes the wool and sells it to firm C, a suit manufacturer, for $100. What does firm B do with this $100? As noted, $60 goes to firm A, and the remaining $40 is used by B to pay wages, rents, interest, and profits for the resources needed in processing the wool. The manufacturer sells the suit to firm D, a clothing wholesaler, who in turn sells it to firm E, a retailer, and then, at last, it is bought for $250 by a consumer, the final user. At each stage, the difference between what a firm has paid for the product and what it receives for its sale is paid out as wages, rent, interest, and profits for the resources used by that firm in helping to produce and distribute the suit.

TABLE 7-2 Value added in a five-stage production process (hypothetical data)

(1) Stage of production	(2) Sales value of materials or product	(3) Value added
	0	
Firm A, sheep ranch	$ 60	$60(= $ 60 − $ 0)
Firm B, wool processor	100	40(= 100 − 60)
Firm C, suit manufacturer	125	25(= 125 − 100)
Firm D, clothing wholesaler	175	50(= 175 − 125)
Firm E, retail clothier	250	75(= 250 − 175)
Total sales values	$710	
Value added (total income)		$250

How much should we include in GDP in accounting for the production of this suit? Just $250, the value of the final product. This figure includes all the intermediate transactions leading up to the product's final sale. It would be a gross exaggeration to sum all the intermediate sales figures and the final sales value of the product in column 2 and add the entire amount, $710, to GDP. This would be a serious case of double counting, that is, counting the final product *and* the sale and resale of its various parts in the multistage productive process. The production and sale of the suit has generated $250, not $710, worth of output and income.

To avoid double counting, national income accountants are careful to calculate only the *value added* by each firm. **Value added** is the market value of a firm's output *less* the value of the inputs which it has purchased from others. Thus, in column 3 of Table 7-2 the value added of firm B is $40, the difference between the $100 value of its output and the $60 it paid for the inputs provided by firm A. By adding together the values added by the five firms in Table 7-2 the total value of the suit can be accurately determined. Similarly, by calculating and summing the values added by all firms in the economy, we can determine the GDP, that is, the market value of total output.

GDP Excludes Nonproduction Transactions

GDP measures the annual production of the economy. In doing so, the many nonproduction transactions which occur each year must be carefully excluded. *Nonproduction transactions* are of two major types: (1) purely financial transactions, and (2) secondhand sales.

Financial Transactions Purely financial transactions are of three general types: public transfer payments, private transfer payments, and the buying and selling of securities.

1 We have already mentioned *public transfer payments* (Chapter 5). These are the social security payments, welfare payments, and veterans' payments which government makes to particular households. The basic characteristic of public transfer payments is that recipients make no contribution to *current* production in return for them. Thus, to include them in GDP would be to overstate this year's production.

2 *Private transfer payments*—for example, a university student's monthly subsidy from home or an occasional gift from a wealthy relative—do not entail production but simply the transfer of funds from one private individual to another.

3 *Security transactions*—buying and selling stocks and bonds—are also excluded from GDP. Stock market transactions merely involve swapping paper assets. The amount spent on these assets does not directly involve current production. Only the services provided by the security broker are included in GDP. Note, however, that sales of *new* issues of stocks and bonds transfer money from savers to businesses which often spend the proceeds on capital goods. Thus, these transactions may indirectly contribute to spending, which does account for output.

Secondhand Sales The reason for excluding secondhand sales from GDP is that such sales either reflect no *current* production, or they involve double counting. If you sell your 1982 Ford to a friend, this transaction would be excluded in determining GDP because no current production is involved. Including the sales of goods produced some years ago in this year's GDP would be an exaggeration of this year's output. Similarly, if you purchased a brand new Ford and resold it a week later to your neighbor, we would still exclude the resale transaction from the current GDP. When you originally bought the new car, its value was included in GDP then. To include its resale value would be to count it twice.

Two Sides to GDP: Spending and Income

We now must consider how the market value of total output—or for that matter, any single unit of output—is measured. Returning to Table 7-2, how can we measure, for example, the market value of a suit?

First, we can determine how much a consumer, the final user, spends in obtaining it. Second, we can add up all the wage, rental, interest, and profit incomes created in its production. This second approach is the value-added technique discussed in Table 7-2.

The final-product and value-added approaches are two ways of looking at the same thing. *What is spent on a product is received as income by those who contributed to its production.* Indeed, Chapter 3's circular flow model demonstrated this concept. If $250 is spent on the suit, that is necessarily the total amount of income derived from its production. You can verify this by noting the incomes generated by firms A, B, C, D, and E in Table 7-2 are $60, $40, $25, $50, and $75 respectively, and total $250.

TABLE 7-3 **The output and income approaches to GDP**

Output, or expenditures, approach		Income, or allocations, approach
Consumption expenditures by households		**Nonincome charges or allocations**
plus		plus
Investment expenditures by businesses		**Wages**
plus	= GDP =	plus
Government purchases of goods and services		**Rents**
plus		plus
Expenditures by foreigners		**Interest**
		plus
		Profits
		minus
		GNP-GDP adjustment

This equality of the expenditure for a product and the income derived from its production is guaranteed, because profit income serves as a balancing item. Profit—or loss—is the income remaining after wage, rent, and interest incomes have been paid by the producer. If the wage, rent, and interest incomes which the firm must pay in getting the suit produced are less than the $250 expenditure for the suit, the difference will be the firm's profits.[1] Conversely, if wage, rent, and interest incomes exceed $250, profits will be negative, that is, losses will be realized, to balance the expenditure on the product and the income derived from its production.

This reasoning is also valid for the output of the economy as a whole. There are two different ways of looking at GDP: One is to see GDP as the sum of all the expenditures involved in taking that total output off the market. This is called the *output,* or **expenditures, approach.** The other views it in terms of the income derived or created from the production of the GDP. This is called the *earnings,* or *allocations,* or **income, approach** to the determination of GDP.

GDP can be determined either by adding up all that is spent to buy this year's total output or by summing up all the incomes derived from the production of this year's output. Putting this in the form of a simple equation, we can say that

$$\left.\begin{array}{l}\text{Amount spent to}\\\text{purchase this year's}\\\text{total output}\end{array}\right\} = \left\{\begin{array}{l}\text{money income}\\\text{derived from}\\\text{production of}\\\text{this year's output}\end{array}\right.$$

This is more than an equation: It is an identity. Buying (spending money) and selling (receiving money in-

come) are two aspects of the same transaction. *What is spent on a product is income to those who have contributed their human and property resources in getting that product produced and to market.*

For the economy as a whole, we can expand the above identity to read as in Table 7-3. This summary statement shows that all final goods produced in the American economy are purchased either by the three domestic sectors—households, businesses, and government—or by foreign consumers. It also demonstrates that, aside from a few complicating factors, discussed later, the total receipts which businesses acquire from the sale of total output are allocated among resource suppliers as wage, rent, interest, and profit income. Using this summary as a point of reference, we next examine in detail the meaning and significance of the types of expenditures and the incomes derived from them.

THE EXPENDITURES APPROACH TO GDP

To determine GDP through the expenditures approach, we must add up all types of spending on finished or final goods and services. But our national income accountants have more precise terms for the different types of spending than those in Table 7-3. We examine these precise terms and their meanings next.

Personal Consumption Expenditures (C)

What we have called "consumption expenditures by households" is **personal consumption expenditures** to national income accountants. It includes ex-

---

[1] The term "profits" is used here in the accounting sense to include both normal profits and economic profits as defined in Chapter 5.

penditures by households on *durable consumer goods* (automobiles, refrigerators, video recorders), *nondurable consumer goods* (bread, milk, beer, cigarettes, shirts, toothpaste), and *consumer expenditures for services* (of lawyers, doctors, mechanics, barbers). We will use the letter *C* to designate the total of these expenditures.

Gross Private Domestic Investment (I_g)

This term refers to all investment spending by American business firms. Investment spending includes three things:

1 All final purchases of machinery, equipment, and tools by business enterprises
2 All construction
3 Changes in inventories

This is more than we have ascribed to the term "investment" thus far. Hence, we must explain why each of these three items is included under the general heading of gross private domestic investment.

The reason for including the first group of items is apparent. This simply restates our original definition of investment spending as the purchase of tools, machinery, and equipment.

The second item—all construction—merits explanation. Clearly, building a new factory, warehouse, or grain elevator is a form of investment. But why include residential construction as investment rather than consumption? Because apartment buildings are investment goods which, like factories and grain elevators, are income-earning assets. Other residential units which are rented are for the same reason investment goods. Furthermore, owner-occupied houses are classified as investment goods because they could be rented out to yield a money income return, even though the owner may not do so. For these reasons all residential construction is considered as investment.

Finally, changes in inventories are counted as investment because an increase in inventories is, in effect, "unconsumed output," and that precisely is what investment is!

Inventory Changes as Investment Because GDP is designed to measure total current output, we must include in GDP any products which are produced *but not sold* this year. If GDP is to be an accurate measure of total production, it must include the market value of any additions to inventories which accrue during the year. If we excluded an increase in inventories, GDP

would understate the current year's total production. If businesses have more goods on their shelves and in warehouses at year's end than they had at the start, the economy has produced more than it has purchased during this year. This increase in inventories must be added to GDP as a measure of *current* production.

What about a decline in inventories? This must be subtracted in figuring GDP, because in this situation the economy sells a total output which exceeds current production, the difference being reflected in inventory reduction. Some of the GDP taken off the market this year reflects not current production but, rather, a drawing down of inventories on hand at the beginning of this year. And inventories on hand at the start of any year's production represent the production of previous years. Consequently, a decline in inventories in any given year means that the economy has purchased more than it has produced during the year. Rephrased, society has purchased all of this year's output plus some of the inventories inherited from previous years' production. Because GDP is a measure of the *current* year's output, we must omit any purchases of past production, that is, any drawing down of inventories, in determining GDP.[2]

Noninvestment Transactions We have discussed what investment is; it is equally important to emphasize what it is not. Specifically, investment does *not* refer to the transfer of paper assets or secondhand tangible assets. The buying of stocks and bonds is excluded from the economist's definition of investment, because such purchases merely transfer the ownership of existing assets. The same holds true of the resale of existing assets.

Investment is the construction or manufacture of *new* capital assets. The creation of these earning assets gives rise to jobs and income, not the exchange of claims to existing capital goods.

Gross versus Net Investment We have broadened our concepts of investment and investment goods to include purchases of machinery and equipment, all construction, and changes in inventories. Now let's focus our attention on the three modifiers, "gross," "private," and "domestic," which national income ac-

---

[2]Both *planned* and *unplanned* changes in inventories are included as part of investment. In the former, firms may intentionally increase their inventories because aggregate sales are growing. In the latter, an unexpected drop in sales may leave firms with more unsold goods (larger inventories) than intended.

countants use in describing investment. The second and third terms tell us, respectively, that we are talking about spending by private business enterprises as opposed to governmental (public) agencies, and that the investment is in America—as opposed to abroad.

The term "gross," however, cannot be disposed of so easily. **Gross private domestic investment** includes production of *all* investment goods—those which replace machinery, equipment, and buildings used up in the current year's production *plus* any net additions to the economy's stock of capital. In short, gross investment includes both replacement and added investment. On the other hand, the term **net private domestic investment** refers only to the added investment in the current year.

A simple example will make the distinction clear. In 1991 our economy produced about $725 billion worth of capital goods. However, in the process of producing the GDP in 1991, the economy used up some $623 billion worth of machinery and equipment. Thus, our economy added $102 (or $725 minus $623) billion to its stock of capital in 1991. Gross investment was $725 billion in 1991, but net investment was only $102 billion. The difference between the two is the value of the capital used up or depreciated in the production of 1991's GDP.

Net Investment and Economic Growth The relationship between gross investment and *depreciation*—the amount of the nation's capital worn out or used up in a particular year—is a good indicator of whether our economy is expanding, static, or declining. Figure 7-1 illustrates these cases.

1 Expanding Economy When gross investment exceeds depreciation (Figure 7-1a), the economy is expanding in that its productive capacity—measured by its stock of capital goods—is growing. More simply, net investment is a positive figure in an expanding economy. For example, as noted above, in 1991 gross investment was $725 billion, and $623 billion worth of capital goods was consumed in producing that year's GDP. Our economy ended 1991 with $102 billion more capital goods than it had on hand at the start of the year. Bluntly stated, we made a $102 billion addition to our "national factory" in 1991. Increasing the supply of capital goods is a basic means of expanding the productive capacity of the economy (Chapter 2).

2 Static Economy A stationary or static economy is one in which gross investment and depreciation are equal (Figure 7-1b). The economy is standing pat; it produces just enough capital to replace what is consumed in producing the year's output—no more, no less. Example: During World War II, the Federal government purposely restricted private investment to free resources to produce war goods. In 1942 gross private investment and depreciation (replacement investment) were each about $10 billion and thus net investment was about zero. At the end of 1942 our stock of capital was about the same as at the start of that year. Our economy was stationary; its production facilities failed to expand.

3 Declining Economy A declining economy arises whenever gross investment is less than depreciation, that is, when the economy uses up more capital in a year than it produces (Figure 7-1c). Under these circumstances net investment will be a negative figure—the economy will be *disinvesting*. Depressions foster such circumstances. During bad times, when production and employment are at a low ebb, the nation has a greater productive capacity than it is currently using. There is little or no incentive to replace depreciated capital equipment, much less add to the existing stock. Depreciation is likely to exceed gross investment, with the result that the nation's stock of capital is less at the end of the year than it was at the start.

This was the case during the heart of the Great Depression. In 1933 gross investment was only $1.6 billion, while the capital consumed during that year was $7.6 billion. Net disinvestment was therefore $6 billion. That is, net investment was a minus $6 billion, indicating that the size of our "national factory" shrunk during that year.

We will use the symbol I for domestic investment spending and attach the subscript g when referring to gross and n when referring to net investment.

Government Purchases (G)

This classification of expenditures *includes* all governmental spending, Federal, state, and local, on the finished products of businesses and all direct purchases of resources—labor, in particular—by government. However, it *excludes* all government transfer payments, because such outlays, as previously noted, do not reflect any current production but merely transfer governmental receipts to certain specific households. The letter G will indicate **government purchases.**

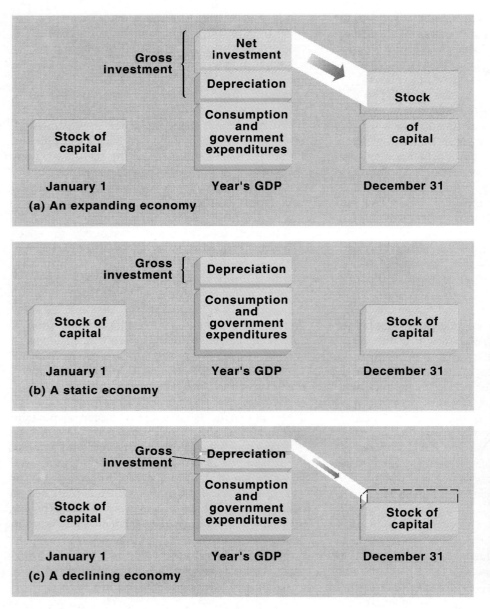

FIGURE 7-1 Expanding, static, and declining economies

In an expanding economy (a), gross investment exceeds depreciation, which means that the economy is making a net addition to its stock of capital facilities. In a static economy (b), gross investment precisely replaces the capital facilities depreciated in producing the year's output, leaving the stock of capital goods unchanged. In a declining economy (c), gross investment is insufficient to replace the capital goods depreciated by the year's production. As a result, the economy's stock of capital declines.

Net Exports (X_n)

How do American international trade transactions enter into national income accounting? We can best explain it in this way: On the one hand, we are trying to add up all spending in American markets which accounts for or induces the production of goods and services in the American economy.

Spending by foreigners on American goods will account for American output just as will spending by Americans. Thus, we must add in what foreigners spend on American goods and services—that is, we must add in the value of American exports—in determining GDP by the expenditures approach.

On the other hand, we must recognize that a portion of consumption, investment, and government purchases is for goods which have been imported, that is, produced abroad, and therefore does *not* reflect production activity in the United States. The value of imports is subtracted to avoid overstating total production in the United States.

TABLE 7-4 **The income statement for the economy, 1991** *(in billions of dollars)*

Receipts: expenditures approach		Allocations: income approach	
Personal consumption expenditures *(C)*	$3887	Consumption of fixed capital	$623
Gross private domestic investment *(I_g)*	725	Indirect business taxes	521
Government purchases *(G)*	1087	Compensation of employees	3388
Net exports *(X_n)*	−27	Rents	−13
		Interest	481
		Proprietors' income	380
		Corporate income taxes	120
		Dividends	138
		Undistributed corporate profits	47
		Gross national product	$5684
		Less: Net American income earned abroad	12
Gross domestic product	$5672	Gross domestic product	$5672

Source: U.S. Department of Commerce data. Because of rounding, details may not add up to totals.

Rather than treat these two items—American exports and imports—separately, our national income accountants merely take the difference between the two. Thus, net exports of goods and services or, more simply, **net exports,** *is the amount by which foreign spending on American goods and services exceeds American spending on foreign goods and services.*

If foreigners buy $45 billion worth of American exports and Americans buy $35 billion worth of foreign imports in a given year, net exports would be *plus* $10 billion. We must emphasize that our definition of net exports might result in a negative figure. If foreigners spend $30 billion on American exports and Americans spend $40 billion on foreign imports, our "excess" of foreign spending over American spending is *minus* $10 billion. Note in Table 7-4 that in 1991 Americans in fact spent $27 billion more on foreign goods and services than foreigners spent on American goods and services, a matter which will receive our attention in later chapters.

The letter X_n will designate net exports.

$C + I_g + G + X_n = GDP$

These four categories of expenditures—personal consumption expenditures *(C)*, gross private domestic investment *(I_g)*, government purchases *(G)*, and net exports *(X_n)*—are comprehensive. They include all possible types of spending. Added together, they measure the market value of the year's output or, in other words, the GDP. That is,

$$C + I_g + G + X_n = GDP$$

For 1991 (Table 7-4):
$$\$3887 + \$725 + \$1087 - \$27 = \$5672$$

THE INCOME APPROACH TO GDP[3]

How was this $5672 billion of expenditure allocated or distributed as income? It would be simple if we could say that total expenditures on the economy's annual output flow to households as wage, rent, interest, and profit incomes. However, the picture is complicated by two *nonincome charges* against the value of total output (GDP). These are (1) consumption of fixed capital, and (2) indirect business taxes. Also, a complication arises because some of the recorded wage, rent, interest, and profit income comes from resources supplied by Americans abroad.

Depreciation: Consumption of Fixed Capital

The useful life of most capital equipment extends far beyond the year of purchase. Actual expenditures for capital goods and their productive life are not synchronized in the same accounting period. To avoid gross understatement of profit and therefore of total income in the year of purchase and overstatement of profit and total income in succeeding years, individual businesses

[3]Some instructors may choose to omit this section because the expenditures approach is more relevant for the analysis of Chapters 9–12.

estimate the useful life of their capital goods and allocate the total cost of such goods more or less evenly over the life of the machinery. The annual charge which estimates the amount of capital equipment used up in each year's production is called "depreciation." Depreciation is a bookkeeping entry designed to yield a more accurate statement of profit income and hence total income of a firm in each year.

If profits and total income for the economy as a whole are to be stated accurately, a gigantic depreciation charge must be made against the total receipts of the business sector. This depreciation charge is called **consumption of fixed capital.** This is exactly what it is—an allowance for capital goods which have been "consumed" in producing this year's GDP. This huge depreciation charge constitutes the previously noted difference between gross and net investment (I_g and I_n).

For present purposes, the significance of this charge is that part of the business sector's receipts is *not* available for income payments to resource suppliers. Part of the receipts—that is, part of the value of production—is a cost of production which reduces business profits. But, unlike other costs of production, depreciation does not add to anyone's income. In real terms, meaning in terms of physical goods and services, the consumption of fixed capital tells us that a portion of this year's GDP must be set aside to replace the machinery and equipment used up in its production. Not all of GDP can be consumed as income by society without impairing the economy's stock of production facilities.

Indirect Business Taxes

The second complicating nonincome charge arises because government levies certain taxes, called **indirect business taxes,** which business firms treat as costs of production and therefore add to the prices of the products they sell. Such taxes include general sales taxes, excises, business property taxes, license fees, and customs duties. Assume a firm produces a product designed to sell at $1. As we have seen, production of this item creates an equal amount of wages, rental, interest, and profit income. But now government imposes a 5 percent sales tax on all products sold at retail. The retailer adds this 5 percent to the price of the product, raising its price from $1 to $1.05 and thereby shifting the burden of the sales tax to consumers.

This $.05 of tax must be paid to government before the remaining $1 can be paid to households as wage, rent, interest, and profit incomes. Furthermore, this flow of indirect business taxes to government is not earned income, because government contributes nothing directly to the production of the good in return for these tax receipts. For this reason we must exclude indirect business taxes when figuring the total income earned by the factors of production. Part of the value of the annual output reflects the indirect business taxes passed along to consumers as higher product prices. This part of the value of the nation's output is *not* available as either wages, rents, interest, or profits.

Consumption of fixed capital and indirect business taxes account for the nonincome allocations listed in Table 7-3. What remains are wages, rents, interest, profits, and a GNP–GDP adjustment. But national income statisticians need a more detailed breakdown of wages and profits than we have discussed thus far.

Compensation of Employees

This largest income category comprises primarily the wages and salaries paid by businesses and government to suppliers of labor. It also includes an array of wage and salary supplements, in particular, payments by employers into social insurance and into a variety of private pension, health, and welfare funds for workers. These wage and salary supplements are part of the employer's cost of obtaining labor and are treated as a component of the firm's total wage payments.

Rents

Rents consist of income payments received by households which supply property resources. Rents were negative in 1991 because depreciation exceeded rental revenue.

Interest

Interest refers to money income payments flowing from private businesses to the suppliers of money capital. For reasons noted later, interest payments made by government are excluded from interest income.

Proprietors' Income

What we have loosely termed "profits" is also broken into two basic accounts: *proprietors' income* or income of unincorporated businesses, and *corporate profits.* Proprietors' income refers to the net income of sole proprietorships, partnerships, and cooperatives. Corporate profits cannot be dismissed so easily, because corporate earnings may be distributed in several ways.

Corporate Profits

Generally, three things happen with corporate profits:

1 A part will be claimed by, and therefore flow to, government as *corporate income taxes.*

2 A part of the remaining corporate profits will be paid out to stockholders as *dividends.* Such payments flow to households, which are the ultimate owners of all corporations.

3 What remains of corporate profits after both corporate income taxes and dividends have been paid is called *undistributed corporate profits.* These retained corporate earnings, along with consumption of fixed capital, are invested currently or in the future in new plants and equipment, increasing the real assets of the investing businesses.

Net American Income Earned Abroad

When we add employee compensation, rents, interest, proprietors' income, and corporate profits we get the national income earned by American-supplied resources, whether here or abroad. Adding the two nonincome charges to this total yields gross national product (GNP), not GDP. Therefore, to get gross *domestic* product we have to subtract from GNP the *net* income which Americans earned abroad. This net income earned abroad—or net output produced by Americans there—is determined by subtracting total income payments to the rest of the world from total income receipts from the rest of the world. Thus, *net* income from abroad can be either positive or negative. In 1991 it was a positive $12 billion, meaning that American-supplied resources produced and earned more abroad than foreign-owned resources produced and earned in the United States. Subtracting this positive amount from GNP, in 1991 we get:

	Billions
Gross national product	$5684
Net American income earned abroad	−12
Gross domestic product	$5672

Table 7-4 summarizes our discussions of both the expenditure and income approaches to GDP. You will note that this is a gigantic income statement for the economy as a whole. The left-hand side tells us what the economy produced in 1991 and the total revenue derived from that production. The right-hand side indicates how the income derived from the production of 1991's GDP was allocated.

OTHER SOCIAL ACCOUNTS

Our discussion has centered on GDP as a measure of the economy's annual output. However, there are related social accounting concepts of equal importance which can be derived from GDP. Our plan of attack in identifying these concepts will be to start with GDP and make a series of adjustments—subtractions and additions—necessary to the derivation of the related social accounts. We have already mentioned the first two of these adjustments.

Net Domestic Product (NDP)

GDP as a measure of total output has an important defect: It gives us a somewhat exaggerated picture of this year's production. *It fails to make allowance for that part of this year's output needed to replace the capital goods used up in the year's production.*

Example: Using hypothetical figures, suppose that on January 1, 1993, the economy had $100 billion worth of capital goods on hand. Assume also that during 1993, $40 billion worth of this equipment and machinery is used up in producing a GDP of $800 billion. Thus, on December 31, 1993, the stock of capital goods on hand stands at only $60 billion.

Does the GDP figure of $800 billion measure what this year's production adds to society's well-being? In fact, it would be much more accurate to subtract from the year's GDP the $40 billion worth of capital goods used to replace the machinery and equipment consumed in producing that GDP. This leaves a *net* output figure of $800 minus $40, or $760 billion.

Net output is a better measure of the production available for consumption and additions to the capital stock than is *gross* output. In our system of social accounting, we derive **net domestic product** (NDP) by subtracting the consumption of fixed capital, which measures replacement investment or the value of the capital used up in a year's production, from GDP. Hence, in 1991:

	Billions
Gross domestic product	$5672
Consumption of fixed capital...................	−623
Net domestic product........................	$5049

NDP, then, is GDP adjusted for depreciation charges. It measures the total annual output which the entire economy—households, businesses, governments, and foreigners—might consume without impairing our capacity to produce in ensuing years.

Adjusting Table 7-4 from GDP to NDP is straightforward. On the income side, we just strike out consumption of fixed capital. The other items should add up to a NDP of $5049 billion. On the expenditure side, one must change *gross* private domestic investment to *net* private domestic investment by subtracting replacement investment as measured by the consumption of fixed capital from the former figure. In 1991, a gross investment figure of $725 billion less a depreciation charge of $623 billion results in a net private domestic investment figure of $102 billion and therefore a NDP of $5049 billion.

National Income (NI)

In analyzing certain problems, it is useful to know how much American resource suppliers earned for their contributions of land, labor, capital, and entrepreneur-

ial talent. **National income** is all income *earned* by American-owned resources, whether located here or abroad. To determine national income, two adjustments to NDP must be made.

1 Net output produced (net income earned) by American-supplied resources abroad must be *added* to NDP. That is, we want a measure of all income earned by Americans, not just the domestic income they earned within the borders of the United States.
2 Indirect business taxes must be *subtracted* from NDP. Recall that government contributes nothing directly to production in return for the indirect business tax revenues it receives; government is not an economic resource. This amount is not part of payments to resources, and therefore is not part of national income.

In 1991:

	Billions
Net domestic product	$5049
Net American income earned abroad	+12
Indirect business taxes	−521
National income	$4540

National income can be thought of as how much it costs society to obtain its national output. NI can be obtained through the income approach by directly adding up employee compensation, rent, interest, proprietors' income, and corporate profits. You should check this by referring to Table 7-4.

Personal Income (PI)

Personal income (income *received*) and national income (income *earned*) are likely to differ because some income which is earned—social security contributions (payroll taxes), corporate income taxes, and undistributed corporate profits—is not actually received by households. Conversely, some income which is received—transfer payments—is not currently earned. Recall that transfer payments are made up of such items as (1) old age and survivors' insurance payments and unemployment compensation, both of which stem from our social security program; (2) welfare payments; (3) a variety of veteran's payments such as educational allowances and disability payments; (4) payments out of private pension and welfare programs; and (5) interest payments paid by government and by consumers.[4]

In moving from national income as a measure of income earned to personal income as an indicator of income actually received, we must subtract from national income those three types of income which are earned but not received and add income received but not currently earned.

	Billions
National income (income earned)	$4540
Social security contributions	−527
Corporate income taxes	−120
Undistributed corporate profits	−47
Transfer payments	+988
Personal income (income received)	$4834

Disposable Income (DI)

Disposable income is personal income less personal taxes. *Personal taxes* are comprised of personal income taxes, personal property taxes, and inheritance taxes, the first of the three being by far the most important. This adjustment is as follows:

	Billions
Personal income (income received before personal taxes)	$4834
Personal taxes	−616
Disposable income (income received after personal taxes)	$4218

Disposable income is the amount of income which households have to dispose of as they see fit. Basically, their choices are two. Remembering that economists conveniently define saving as "that part of disposable income not spent on consumer goods," it follows that households divide their disposable income between consumption and saving.

[4]Why treat interest payments on government bonds as income *not* currently earned, particularly when interest on the bonds of private firms is included in national income as earned income? The rationale is that much of the debt has been incurred in connection with (1) war and defense and (2) recessions. Unlike public deficits to finance airports or highways, deficits stemming from the military and recessions yield no production assets (services) to the economy. Hence, interest paid on such debt does *not* reflect the generation of any current output or income. Similar reasoning underlies the inclusion of interest payments by consumers as a part of transfer payments.

We have derived four additional social accounting concepts from GDP:

  Net domestic product (NDP), the market value of the annual output net of consumption of fixed capital

  National income (NI), income earned by American-supplied factors of production for their current contributions to production, or the resource costs entailed in getting the year's national output produced

  Personal income (PI), income received by households before personal taxes

  Disposable income (DI), income received by households less personal taxes

The relationships between GDP, NDP, NI, PI, and DI are summarized in Table 7-5.

The Circular Flow Revisited

Figure 7-2 is a synthesis of the expenditures and income approaches to GDP. As a more realistic and more complex expression of the circular flow model of the economy (Chapters 3 and 6), this figure merits your careful study.

Starting at the GDP rectangle in the upper left-hand corner, the expenditures side of GDP is shown by the blue arrows. Immediately to the right of the GDP rectangle are the nine allocations of GDP and then the various additions and subtractions which are needed in

TABLE 7-5 The relationships between GDP, NDP, NI, PI, and DI in 1991

	Billions
Gross domestic product (GDP)	$5672
Consumption of fixed capital	−623
Net domestic product (NDP)	$5049
Net American income earned abroad	+12
Indirect business taxes	−521
National income (NI)	$4540
Social security contributions	−527
Corporate income taxes	−120
Undistributed corporate profits	−47
Transfer payments	+988
Personal income (PI)	$4834
Personal taxes	−616
Disposable income (DI)	$4218

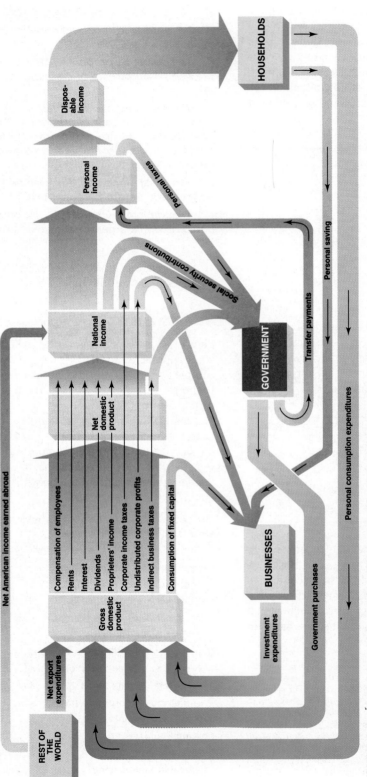

FIGURE 7-2 National output and the flows of expenditure and income

This figure is an elaborate circular flow diagram which fits the expenditures and allocations sides of GDP to one another. The income or allocations flows are shown in red; the expenditure flows, in green. You should trace through the income and expenditures flows, relating them to the five basic national income accounting measures.

the derivation of NDP, NI, and PI. All allocations or income flows are depicted by red arrows. Note the flow of personal taxes out of PI and the division of DI between consumption and personal saving in the household sector. In the government sector the flows of revenue in the form of four basic types of taxes are denoted on the right; on the left, government disbursements take the form of purchases of goods and services and transfers. The position of the business sector is such as to emphasize, on the left, investment expenditures and, on the right, the three major sources of funds for business investment.

Finally, observe the role of the rest of the world in the flow diagram. Spending by people abroad on our exports adds to our GDP, but a part of our consumption, government, and investment expenditures buy imported products rather than domestically produced goods. The flow emanating from "Rest of the World" shows that we handle this complication by calculating *net* exports (exports minus imports). Recall that this may be a positive or a negative amount. Also, note that *net* American income earned abroad (positive or negative) is added to national income.

The major virtue of Figure 7-2 is that it simultaneously portrays the expenditure and income aspects of GDP, fitting the two approaches to one another. These flows of expenditure and income are part of a continuous, repetitive process. Cause and effect are intermingled: Expenditures give rise to income, and out of this income arise expenditures, which again flow to resource owners as income, and so forth.

A final point: The table inside the covers of this book contains a useful historical summary of the national income accounts and related statistics.

MEASURING THE PRICE LEVEL

Thus far we have focused chiefly on domestic output and national income. We now consider how the price level is measured.

Measurement of the price level is significant for two reasons.

1 It is meaningful to know how much the price level has changed, if at all, from one period to another. That is, we must be aware of whether and to what extent inflation (a rising price level) or deflation (a falling price level) has occurred.

2 Because GDP is the market value, or total money value, of all final goods and services produced in a year, money values are used as the common measure when summing a heterogeneous output into a meaningful total. The value of different years' output (GDPs) can be meaningfully compared only if the value of money itself does not change.

Price Indexes

The price level is stated as an index number. A **price index** measures the combined price of a particular collection of goods and services, called a "market basket," in a *given* period relative to the combined price of an identical or similar group of goods and services in a *reference* period. This point of reference, or benchmark, is called the "base year." More formally,

$$\text{Price index in a given year} = \frac{\text{price of market basket in a given year}}{\text{price of the same market basket in the base year}} \times 100$$

By convention the price ratio between the given year and the base year is multiplied by 100. For example, a price ratio of $2/1$ ($=2$) is expressed as an index number of 200. Similarly, a price ratio of, say $1/3$ ($=.33$), is expressed as 33.

The Federal government computes indexes of the prices of several different collections or market baskets of goods and services. The best known of these indexes is the consumer price index (CPI), which measures the prices of a fixed market basket of some 300 consumer goods and services purchased by a "typical" urban consumer. The CPI is considered in detail in this chapter's Last Word.

The GDP price index or the **GDP deflator,** however, is more useful than the CPI for measuring the overall price level. The GDP deflator is broader than the CPI in that the GDP deflator includes not only the prices of consumer goods and services, but also the prices of investment goods, goods and services purchased by government, and goods and services which enter into world trade. For this reason, the GDP deflator is the price index associated with adjusting money or nominal GDP for price changes. **Nominal GDP** is output valued in terms of the prices existing at the time the output is produced.[5]

---

[5]Price indexes in addition to the CPI and the GDP deflator are the *producer price index,* which measures the prices of 3200 commodities at the point of their first commercial sale; the *export price index,* which provides a measure of price changes for all products sold by U.S. businesses to foreign buyers; and the *import price index,* which measures price changes of goods purchased from other countries.

Computing a GDP Price Index

Table 7-6 gives an example of how a GDP price index or deflator can be computed in a particular year for a hypothetical economy. Observe from column 1 that in 1993 this economy produces only four goods: pizzas (a consumption good); industrial robots (a capital good); paper clips (a good purchased by government); and computer disks (an export good). Suppose that in 1993 the outputs of the four goods are 2, 1, 1, and 1 units, respectively, as shown in column 2. Furthermore, assume that the per unit prices of these four products in 1993 are those shown in column 3. The total price (cost) of the 1993 output therefore is $64, an amount found by summing the expenditures on each of the four goods (column 4).

Now, let's arbitrarily select 1987 as our reference or base year to establish a price index for 1993. The 1987 prices of the components of the 1993 output are listed in column 5 of Table 7-6. From columns 5 and 3, we observe that the prices of pizza and paper clips were lower in 1987 than in 1993, the price of robots was higher, and the price of computer disks did not change. Most importantly, the total price (cost) of the 1993 output—shown at the bottom of column 6—was $50 in 1987 rather than $64 as in 1993. This tells us that the 1993 output would have cost $50 if 1987 prices had persisted. To determine the 1993 price index, we divide the 1993 price of the market basket ($64) by the 1987 price of that same collection of goods ($50). The quotient is then multiplied by 100 to express the price index in its conventional form.

$$\text{GDP price index}_{1993} = \frac{\text{price of market basket}_{1993}}{\text{price of 1993 market basket in the base year}_{1987}} \times 100$$

More concretely,

$$\text{GDP price index}_{1993} = \frac{\$64}{\$50} \times 100 = 128$$

The price index for 1993 is 128. This index value may be thought of as the price level for 1993.

These steps can be used to calculate the price level for all years in a series of years. For example, the price index in the 1987 base year is found by discovering the price of the particular collection of goods and services produced in 1987 and comparing this price to the price of that same market basket in the base year. However, in this special case, the "given year" and the "reference year" are the same. That is,

$$\text{GDP price index}_{1987} = \frac{\text{price of market basket}_{1987}}{\text{price of market basket}_{1987}} \times 100$$

The GDP price index for the 1987 base year therefore is 100. In effect, we automatically set the price index at 100 in the base year.

Likewise, if we wanted to know the GDP price index for 1950, we would determine 1950 output and then estimate what that same or a similar collection of goods and services would have cost in the 1987 base year. If prices on the 1950 output had quadrupled between 1950 and 1987, the price ratio of the market basket would be $\frac{1}{4}$ ($=.25$) and the 1950 GDP price index would be 25 ($=.25 \times 100$).

Once a GDP price index has been constructed for each year in a series of years, comparisons of price levels between years is possible. First example: If the price indexes for 1993 and 1987 are 128 and 100, respectively, we can calculate that the price level increased by 28 percent [$=(128 - 100)/100$] between

TABLE 7-6 **Computing a GDP price index for 1993** *(hypothetical data)*

(1) Product	(2) Quantities in market basket in 1993	(3) Prices of 1993 market basket in 1993	(4) Expenditures on 1993 market basket in 1993 (3) × (2)	(5) Prices of 1993 market basket in 1987 (base year)	(6) Expenditures on 1993 market basket in 1987 (5) × (2)
Pizzas	2	$12	$24	$ 5	$10
Robots	1	18	18	20	20
Paper clips	1	8	8	6	6
Computer disks	1	14	14	14	14
Total price (cost)			$64		$50
GDP price index 1993			$128 \left(= \frac{\$64}{\$50} \times 100\right)$		

the two years. Second example: If, as suggested by our previous illustration, the price index for 1950 is 25, we can say that the price level rose by 412 percent [(128 − 25)/25] between 1950 and 1993. Third example: if the price index fell from 100 in 1987 to 98 in 1988, we would know that the price level declined by 2 percent [= (98 − 100)/100].

Conclusions: The GDP price index compares the price of each year's output to the price of that same output in the base year or reference year. A series of price indexes for various years enables us to compare price levels between years. An increase in the GDP price index from one year to the next constitutes *inflation;* a decrease in the price index constitutes *deflation.*

NOMINAL AND REAL GDP

Inflation or deflation complicates gross domestic product because GDP is a price-times-quantity figure. The raw data from which the national income accountants estimate GDP are the total sales figures of business firms; however, these figures include changes in *both* the quantity of output *and* the level of prices. This means that a change in either the quantity of total physical output or the price level will affect the size of GDP. However, it is the quantity of goods produced and distributed to households which affects their standard of living, not the size of the price tags on these goods. The hamburger of 1970 which sold for 65 cents yielded the same satisfaction as will an identical hamburger selling for $2.00 in 1993.

The situation facing our social accountants is this: In gathering statistics from financial reports of businesses and deriving GDP in various years, government accountants come up with nominal GDP figures. They do *not* know directly to what extent changes in price, on the one hand, and changes in quantity of output, on the other, have accounted for the given increases in nominal GDP. For example, they would not know directly if a 4 percent increase in nominal GDP resulted from a 4 percent rise in output and zero inflation, a zero percent change in output and 4 percent inflation, or some other combination of changes in output and the price level, say, a 2 percent increase in output and 2 percent inflation. The problem is one of adjusting a price-times-quantity figure so it will accurately reflect changes in physical output or quantity, not changes in prices.

Fortunately, national income accountants have resolved this difficulty: They *deflate* GDP for rising prices and *inflate* it when prices are falling. These adjustments give us a picture of GDP for various years *as if* prices and the value of the dollar were constant. A GDP figure which reflects current prices, that is, which is *not* adjusted for changes in the price level, is alternatively called *unadjusted, current dollar, money,* or *nominal GDP.* Similarly, GDP figures which are inflated or deflated for price level changes measure *adjusted, constant dollar,* or **real GDP.**

The Adjustment Process

The process for adjusting current dollar or nominal GDP for inflation or deflation is straightforward. The GDP deflator for a specific year tells us the ratio of that year's prices to the prices of the same goods in the base year. The GDP deflator or GDP price index therefore can be used to inflate or deflate nominal GDP figures. The outcome of this adjustment is that GDP for each year gets expressed in real terms: in other words, *as if* base year prices prevailed. *The simplest and most direct method of deflating or inflating a year's nominal GDP is to express that year's index number in decimal form, and divide it into the nominal GDP.* This yields the same result as the more complex procedure of dividing nominal GDP by the corresponding index number and multiplying the quotient by 100. In equation form:

$$\frac{\text{Nominal GDP}}{\text{price index (in hundredths)}} = \text{real GDP}$$

To illustrate in terms of Table 7-6, in 1993 nominal GDP is $64 and the price index for that year is 128 (= 1.28 in hundredths). Real GDP in 1993, therefore, is:

$$\frac{\$64}{1.28} = \$50$$

In summary, the real GDP figures measure the value of total output in the various years *as if* the prices of the products had been constant from the reference or base year throughout all the years being considered. Real GDP thus shows the market value of each year's output measured in terms of constant dollars, that is, dollars which have the same value, or purchasing power, as the base year. Real GDP is clearly superior to nominal GDP as an indicator of the economy's production performance.

Inflating and Deflating

Table 7-7 is a "real-world" illustration of the **inflating** and **deflating** process. Here we are taking actual nomi-

TABLE 7-7 Adjusting GDP for changes in the price level *(selected years, in billions of dollars)*

(1) Year	(2) Nominal, or unadjusted, GDP	(3) Price level index,* percent (1987 = 100)	(4) Real, or adjusted, GDP, 1987 dollars
1960	$ 513.4	26.0	$1974.6 (= 513.4 ÷ 0.260)
1965	702.7	28.4	_____
1970	1010.7	35.1	$2879.5 (= 1010.7 ÷ 0.351)
1975	1585.9	49.2	_____
1980	2708.0	71.7	$3776.8 (= 2708.0 ÷ 0.717)
1983	3405.0	87.2	$3904.8 (= 3405.0 ÷ 0.872)
1985	4038.7	94.4	_____
1986	4268.6	96.9	$4405.2 (= 4268.6 ÷ 0.969)
1987	4539.9	100.0	$4539.9 (= 4539.9 ÷ 1.000)
1988	4900.4	103.9	_____
1989	5244.0	108.4	$4837.6 (= 5244.0 ÷ 1.084)
1990	5513.8	112.9	$4883.1 (= 5513.8 ÷ 1.129)
1991	5671.8	117.0	$4847.7 (= 5671.8 ÷ 1.170)

*U.S. Department of Commerce implicit price deflators.

Source: U.S. Department of Commerce data.

nal GDP figures for selected years and adjusting them with an index of the general price level for these years to obtain real GDP. Note that the base year is 1987.

Because the long-run trend has been for the price level to rise, the problem is one of increasing, or *inflating,* the pre-1987 figures. This upward revision of nominal GDP acknowledges that prices were lower in years prior to 1987 and, as a result, nominal GDP figures understated the real output of those years. Column 4 indicates what GDP would have been in all these selected years if the 1987 price level had prevailed.

The rising price level has caused the nominal GDP figures for the post-1987 years to overstate real output; hence, these figures must be reduced, or *deflated,* as in column 4, to gauge what GDP would have been in 1988, 1990, and so on, if 1987 prices had actually prevailed. In short, while the *nominal* GDP figures reflect both output and price changes, the *real* GDP figures allow us to estimate changes in real output, because the real GDP figures, in effect, hold the price level constant.

Example: For 1991 nominal GDP was $5671.8 billion and the price index was 117.0 or 17.0 percent higher than 1987. To compare 1991's GDP with 1987's we express the 1991 index in hundredths (1.170) and divide it into the nominal GDP of $5671.8 as shown in column 4. The resulting real GDP of $4847.7 is directly comparable to the 1987 base year's GDP because both reflect only changes in output and *not* price level changes. You should trace through the computations involved in deriving the real GDP figures given in Table 7-7 and also determine real GDP for years 1965, 1975, 1985, 1988, for which the figures have been purposely omitted.

QUICK REVIEW 7-3

▪ *A price index compares the combined price of a specific market basket of goods and services in a particular year to the combined price of the same basket in a base year.*

▪ *Nominal GDP is output valued at current prices; real GDP is output valued at constant prices (base year prices).*

▪ *A year's nominal GDP can be adjusted to real GDP by dividing nominal GDP by the GDP price index (expressed in hundredths).*

GDP AND SOCIAL WELFARE

GDP is a reasonably accurate and extremely useful measure of domestic economic performance. It is not, and was never intended to be, an index of social welfare. GDP is merely a measure of the annual volume of market-oriented activity.

> . . . any number of things could make the Nation better off without raising its real [GDP] as measured today: we might start the list with peace, equality of opportunity, the elimination of injustice and violence, greater brotherhood among Americans of different racial and ethnic backgrounds, better understanding between parents and children and between husbands and wives, and we could go on endlessly.[6]

Nevertheless, it is widely held that there should be a strong positive correlation between real GDP and social welfare, that is, greater production should move society toward "the good life." Thus, we must understand some of the shortcomings of GDP—some reasons why it might understate or overstate real output and why more output will not necessarily make society better off.

Nonmarket Transactions

Certain production transactions do not appear in the market. Hence, GDP as a measure of the market value of output fails to include them. Standard examples include the production services of a homemaker, the efforts of the carpenter who repairs his or her own home, or the work of the erudite professor who writes a scholarly but nonremunerative article. Such transactions are *not* reflected in the profit and loss statements of business firms and therefore escape the national income accountants, causing GDP to be understated. However, some quantitatively large nonmarket transactions, such as that portion of farmers' output which farmers consume themselves, are estimated by national income accountants.

Leisure

Over many years, leisure has increased very significantly. The workweek declined from about 53 hours at the turn of the century to approximately 40 hours by the end of World War II. Since then the workweek has declined more slowly and is currently about 35 hours. In addition, the expanded availability of paid vacations, holidays, and leave time has reduced the work year. This increased leisure has had a positive effect upon our well-being. Our system of social accounting under-

---

[6]Arthur M. Okun, "Social Welfare Has No Price Tag," *The Economic Accounts of the United States: Retrospect and Prospect* (U.S. Department of Commerce, July 1971), p. 129.

states our well-being by not directly recognizing this. Nor do the accounts reflect the satisfaction—the "psychic income"—which people derive from their work.

Improved Product Quality

GDP is a quantitative rather than a qualitative measure. It does not accurately reflect improvements in product quality. This is a shortcoming: quality improvement clearly affects economic well-being as much as does the quantity of goods. To the extent that product quality has improved over time, GDP understates improvement in our material well-being.

Composition and Distribution of Output

Changes in the composition and the allocation of total output among specific households may influence economic welfare. GDP, however, reflects only the size of output and does not tell us anything about whether this collection of goods is "right" for society. A switchblade knife and a Beethoven compact disc, both selling for $14.95, are weighted equally in the GDP. And some economists feel that a more equal distribution of total output would increase national economic well-being. *If these economists are correct, a future trend toward a less unequal distribution of GDP would enhance the economic welfare of society. A more unequal future distribution would have the reverse effect.*

Conclusion: GDP measures the size of the total output but does not reflect changes in the composition and distribution of output which might also affect the economic well-being of society.

Per Capita Output

For many purposes the most meaningful measure of economic well-being is per capita output. Because GDP measures the size of total output, it may conceal or misrepresent changes in the standard of living of individual households in the economy. For example, GDP may rise significantly, but if population is also growing rapidly, the per capita standard of living may be relatively constant or may even be declining.

This is the plight of many of the less developed countries. India's domestic output grew at about 4.3 percent per year over the 1965–1989 period. But annual population growth exceeded 2 percent, resulting in a meager annual increase in per capita output of only 1.8 percent.

LAST WORD

THE CONSUMER PRICE INDEX

The consumer price index is the most widely reported measure of inflation; therefore, it is important to have some knowledge of its characteristics and limitations.

The consumer price index (CPI) measures changes in the prices of a "market basket" of some 300 goods and services purchased by urban consumers. The composition of this market basket was determined on the basis of a survey of the spending patterns of urban consumers over the 1982–1984 period. The index is a "fixed-weight" index in that the composition of the market basket is the same in each year as in the base period (1982–1984).

The "fixed-weight" approach used to construct the CPI differs from the technique used to construct the GDP deflator discussed in this chapter. We previously indicated that the GDP deflator is found by establishing the market basket on the basis of the composition of output in *each* particular year and then determining what the price of that same composition of goods would have been in the base year (Table 7-6). Hence, the composition of the market basket used to construct the GDP index changes from year to year. But in the case of the CPI, the composition of the market basket is fixed in the base period and is assumed not to change from one period to another. The reason for this assumption is that the purpose of the CPI is to measure changes in the costliness of a constant standard of living. There are two well-known problems associated with the CPI which lead critics to conclude that this price index overstates increases in the cost of living.

Consumers in fact do change their spending patterns—the composition of the market basket changes—particularly in response to changes in relative prices. If the price of beef rises, consumers will substitute away from beef and buy fish, veal, or mutton instead. This means that over time consumers are buying a market basket which contains more of the relatively low-priced and less of the relatively high-priced goods and services. The fixed-weight CPI assumes these substitutions have not occurred and it therefore overstates the actual cost of living.

The CPI does not take qualitative improvements into account. To the extent that goods and services have improved since 1982–1984, their prices should be higher. Thus we ought to pay more for medical care today than in the early 1980s because it is generally of higher quality. The same can be said for computers, automobile tires, stereos, and many other items. The CPI, however, assumes all of the increase in the money or nominal value of the market basket is due solely to inflation rather than quality improvements. Again, the CPI tends to overstate the rate of inflation.

In general, economists feel that the CPI overstates the rate of inflation, perhaps by a significant margin. So

GDP and the Environment

There are undesirable and much publicized "gross domestic by-products" accompanying the production and growth of the GDP such as dirty air and water, automobile junkyards, congestion, noise, and other forms of environmental pollution. Clearly, the costs of pollution affect our economic well-being adversely.

These spillover costs associated with the production of the GDP are not now deducted from total output and, hence, GDP overstates our national economic welfare. Ironically, as GDP increases, so does pollution and the extent of this overstatement. As put by one economist, "The ultimate physical product of economic life is garbage."[7] A rising GDP means more garbage—more environmental pollution. In fact, under existing ac-

what? The major consequence is that this overstatement may contribute to ongoing inflation because the incomes of large numbers of people are tied directly or indirectly to changes in the CPI. For example, some 40 million social security recipients have their monthly check tied or "indexed" to the CPI. And an estimated 6 million workers have cost-of-living adjustments (COLAs) in their collective bargaining agreements. When prices rise, their money wages automatically increase to further fuel inflation. Furthermore, the wage expectations and demands of virtually all workers—union or nonunion, blue- or white-collar—are linked to the cost of living as measured by the CPI. Thus the CPI is not merely a vehicle for measuring the problem of inflation; it may be part of the problem!

Another consequence of an overstated CPI stems from the "indexing" of personal income tax brackets. This indexing—or adjusting tax brackets upward to account for the rate of inflation—was begun in 1985 to resolve an inequity in the personal income tax. Specifically, the intent of indexing is to prevent inflation from pushing households into higher tax brackets even though their real incomes have not increased. For example, a 10 percent increase in your *nominal* income might put you in a higher marginal tax bracket and increase the proportion of your income paid in taxes. But if product prices are also rising by 10 percent, your *real* or inflation-adjusted income has remained constant. The result would be an unintended redistribution of real income from taxpayers to the Federal government. The purpose of indexing tax brackets was to prevent this redistribution. However, to the extent that the CPI *overstates* inflation, indexing will reduce government's tax share. The Federal government will be deprived of substantial amounts of tax revenue and real income will be redistributed from government to taxpayers.

counting procedures, when a manufacturer pollutes a river and government spends to clean it up, the cleanup expense is added to the GDP while the pollution is not subtracted!

[7]See the delightful and perceptive essay "Fun and Games with the Gross National Product" by Kenneth E. Boulding, in Harold W. Helfrich, Jr. (ed.), *The Environmental Crisis* (New Haven: Yale University Press, 1970), p. 162.

The Underground Economy

Economists agree that there is a relatively large and perhaps expanding underground or subterranean sector in our economy. Some participants in this sector engage in illegal activities such as gambling, loansharking, prostitution, and the narcotics trade. These may well be "growth industries." Obviously, persons receiving income from such illegal businesses choose to conceal their incomes.

Most participants in the underground economy are in legal activities, but do not fully report their incomes to the Internal Revenue Service (IRS). A waiter or waitress may underreport tips from customers. A businessperson may record only a portion of sales receipts for the tax collector. A worker who wants to retain unemployment compensation or welfare benefits may obtain an "off the books" or "cash only" job so there is no record of his or her work activities. As inflation and high tax burdens squeeze real disposable incomes, the incentive to receive income in forms (for example, cash and barter) which cannot be readily discovered by the IRS is strengthened.

Although there is no consensus on the size of the underground economy, most estimates suggest that it is between 5 to 15 percent of the recorded GDP. In 1991, that meant official GDP was understated by between $284 and $851 billion. If this additional income had been taxed at a 20 percent average tax rate, the Federal budget deficit for 1991 would have declined from $269 billion to between a $212 billion and a $99 billion deficit.

There is also some evidence to suggest that the underground economy has been growing relative to the legal economy. If so, then national income accounts will increasingly understate our economy's performance and growth through time.

Finally, to the extent that a proportion of the population is involved in illegal activities or in legal activities where income is concealed, our official unemployment statistics will be overstated. This may pose a problem for policy makers. If the existence of the underground economy distorts such basic economic indicators as GDP and the unemployment rate, policies based on these indicators may be inappropriate and harmful. Thus an understated GDP and an overstated unemployment rate might prompt policy makers to stimulate the economy. But, as we will find in Chapter 12, the stimulus may cause unwanted inflation rather than increases in real output and employment.

CHAPTER SUMMARY

1 Gross domestic product (GDP), a basic measure of society's economic performance, is the market value of all final goods and services produced within the United States in a year. Intermediate goods, nonproduction transactions, and secondhand sales are purposely excluded in calculating GDP.

2 GDP may be calculated by summing total expenditures on all final output or by summing the income derived from the production of that output.

3 By the expenditures approach GDP is determined by adding consumer purchases of goods and services, gross investment spending by businesses, government purchases, and net exports; $GDP = C + I_g + G + X_n$.

4 Gross investment can be divided into **a** replacement investment (required to maintain the nation's stock of capital at its existing level), and **b** net investment (the net increase in the stock of capital). Positive net investment is associated with a growing economy; negative net investment with a declining economy.

5 By the income or allocations approach GDP is calculated as the sum of compensation to employees, rents, interest, proprietors' income, corporate income taxes, dividends, undistributed corporate profits, *plus* the two nonincome charges (capital consumption allowance and indirect business taxes) and *minus* net American income earned abroad.

6 Other important national income accounting measures are derived from GDP. Net domestic product (NDP) is GDP less the consumption of fixed capital. National income (NI) is total income earned by American resource suppliers; it is found by adding net American income earned abroad and subtracting indirect business taxes from NDP. Personal income (PI) is the total income paid to households prior to any allowance for personal taxes. Disposable income (DI) is personal income after personal taxes have been paid. DI measures the amount of income households have available to consume or save.

7 Price indexes are computed by comparing the price of a specific collection or "market basket" of output in a given period to the price (cost) of the same market basket in a base period and multiplying the outcome (quotient) by 100. The GDP deflator is the price index associated with adjusting nominal GDP to account for inflation or deflation and thereby obtaining real GDP.

8 Nominal (current dollar) GDP measures each year's output valued in terms of the prices prevailing in that year. Real (constant dollar) GDP measures each year's output in terms of the prices which prevailed in a selected base year. Because it is adjusted for price level changes, real GDP measures the level of production activity.

9 The various national income accounting measures exclude nonmarket and illegal transactions, changes in leisure and product quality, the composition and distribution of output, and the environmental effects of production. Nevertheless, these measures are reasonably accurate and very useful indicators of the nation's economic performance.

TERMS AND CONCEPTS

national income accounting	**value added**	**government purchases**	**personal income**
gross national product	**expenditures and income approaches**	**net exports**	**disposable income**
gross domestic product	**personal consumption expenditures**	**consumption of fixed capital**	**price index**
final and intermediate goods	**gross and net private domestic investment**	**indirect business taxes**	**GDP deflator**
double counting		**net domestic product**	**nominal GDP**
		national income	**real GDP**
			inflating and deflating

QUESTIONS AND STUDY SUGGESTIONS

1 "National income statistics are a powerful tool of economic understanding and analysis." Explain this statement. "An economy's output is its income." Do you agree?

2 Why do national income accountants include only final goods in measuring total output? How do GDP and NDP differ?

3 What is the difference between gross private domestic investment and net private domestic investment? If you were to determine net domestic product through the expenditures approach, which of these two measures of investment spending would be appropriate? Explain.

4 Why are changes in inventories included as part of investment spending? Suppose inventories declined by $1 billion during 1993. How would this affect the size of gross private domestic investment and gross domestic product in 1993? Explain.

5 The following is a list of domestic output and national income figures for a given year. All figures are in billions. The ensuing questions ask you to determine the major national income measures by both the expenditure and income methods. Answers derived by each approach should be the same.

Personal consumption expenditures	$245
Net American income earned abroad	4
Transfer payments	12
Rents	14
Consumption of fixed capital (depreciation)	27
Social security contributions	20
Interest	13
Proprietors' income	33
Net exports	3
Dividends	16
Compensation of employees	223
Indirect business taxes	18
Undistributed corporate profits	21
Personal taxes	26
Corporate income taxes	19
Corporate profits	56
Government purchases	72
Net private domestic investment	33
Personal saving	16

    a   Using the above data, determine GDP and NDP by both the expenditure and income methods.
    b   Now determine NI (1) by making the required additions and subtractions from GDP, and (2) by adding up the types of income which comprise NI.
    c   Make those adjustments of NI required in deriving PI.
    d   Make the required adjustments from PI (as determined in 5c) to obtain DI.

6 Use the concepts of gross and net investment to distinguish between an expanding, a static, and a declining economy. "In 1933 net private domestic investment was minus $6 billion. This means in that particular year the economy produced no capital goods at all." Do you agree? Explain: "Though net investment can be positive, negative, or zero, it is quite impossible for gross investment to be less than zero."

7 Define net exports. Explain how the United States' exports and imports each affect domestic production. Suppose foreigners spend $7 billion on American exports in a given year and Americans spend $5 billion on imports from abroad in the same year. What is the amount of America's net exports? Explain how net exports might be a negative amount.

8 Given the following national income accounting data, compute   **a** GDP, **b** NDP, and   **c** NI. All figures are in billions.

Compensation of employees	$194.2
U.S. exports of goods and services	13.4
Consumption of fixed capital	11.8
Government purchases	59.4
Indirect business taxes	14.4
Net private domestic investment	52.1
Transfer payments	13.9
U.S. imports of goods and services	16.5
Personal taxes	40.5
Net American income earned abroad	2.2
Personal consumption expenditures	219.1

9 Why do national income accountants compare the market value of the total outputs in various years rather than actual physical volumes of production? Explain. What problem is posed by any comparison over time of the market values of various total outputs? How is this problem resolved?

10 Suppose that in 1974 the total output of a hypothetical economy consisted of three goods—X, Y, and Z—produced in the following quantities: X = 4, Y = 1, Z = 3. Also suppose that in 1974 the prices of X, Y, and Z were as follows: X = $3, Y = $12, and Z = $5. Finally, assume that in 1987 the prices of these goods were X = $5, Y = $10, and Z = $10. Determine the GDP price index for 1974, using 1987 as the base year. By what percent did the price level rise between 1974 and 1987?

11 The following table shows nominal GDP and an appropriate price index for a group of selected years. Compute real GDP. Indicate in each calculation whether you are inflating or deflating the nominal GDP data.

Year	Nominal GDP, billions	Price level index, percent (1987 = 100)	Real GDP, billions
1959	$ 494.2	25.6	$_____
1964	648.0	27.7	$_____
1967	814.3	30.3	$_____
1973	1349.6	41.3	$_____
1978	2232.7	60.3	$_____
1988	4900.4	103.9	$_____

12 Which of the following are included in deriving this year's GDP? Explain your answer in each case.
    a   Interest on an AT&T bond
    b   Social security payments received by a retired factory worker
    c   The services of a painter in painting the family home

d   The income of a dentist

e   The money received by Smith when he sells a 1983 Chevrolet to Jones

f   The monthly allowance which a college student receives from home

g   Rent received on a two-bedroom apartment

h   The money received by Mac when he resells this year's model Plymouth to Ed

i   Interest received on government bonds

j   A 2-hour decline in the length of the workweek

k   The purchase of an AT&T bond

l   A $2 billion increase in business inventories

m   The purchase of 100 shares of GM common stock

n   The purchase of an insurance policy

o   Wages paid to a domestic servant

p   The market value of a homemaker's services

q   The purchase of a Renaissance painting by a public art museum

13 What would be the most likely effect on real GDP of each of the following: a a law mandating an increase in the workweek from 40 hours to 50 hours for every able-bodied adult;   b legalization of all activities currently undertaken in the underground economy; and   c a $1 million increase in the production of burglar alarms offset by a $1 million decline in the provision of prenatal health care services?

Would society's well-being in each of these situations change in the same direction as the change in real GDP? Explain.

Macroeconomic Instability: Unemployment and Inflation

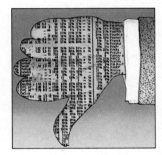

In an ideal economy, real GDP would expand over time at a brisk, steady pace. Additionally, the price level, as measured by the GDP deflator or the consumer price index, would remain constant or only rise slowly. The result would be neither significant unemployment nor inflation. Several periods of U.S. history fit this pattern. But experience shows that steady economic growth, full employment, and a stable price level cannot be taken for granted. Recent cases in point: (1) The inflation rate skyrocketed to 13.5 percent in 1980. (2) During a sixteen-month period in the early 1980s, real output fell by 3.5 percent. (3) Three million more people were unemployed in 1982 than in 1980. (4) The annual inflation rate rose from 1.9 percent in 1986 to 4.8 percent in 1989. (5) In mid-1990, output in the U.S. economy turned downward for the eighth time since 1950.

In this and the next several chapters we explore the problem of achieving macroeconomic stability, or more specifically, steady economic growth, full employment, and price stability. The present chapter proceeds as follows: First, we establish an overview of the business cycle—the periodic fluctuations in output, employment, and price level which characterize our economy. Then we look in more detail at unemployment. What are the various types of unemployment? How is unemployment measured? Why is unemployment an economic problem? Finally, we examine inflation—a serious problem which plagued us throughout the 1970s and into the early 1980s. What are inflation's causes and consequences?

OVERVIEW OF THE BUSINESS CYCLE

Our society seeks economic growth *and* full employment *and* price level stability along with other less quantifiable goals (Chapter 1). The broad spectrum of American economic history reflects remarkable economic growth. Technological progress, rapid increases in productive capacity, and a standard of living which is among the highest in the world are strategic facets of the dynamic character in our economy.

The Historical Record

But our long-run economic growth has not been steady; it has been interrupted by periods of economic

129

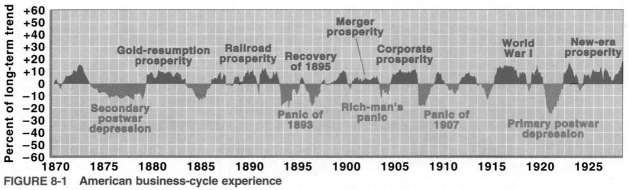

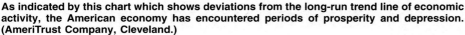

FIGURE 8-1 American business-cycle experience

As indicated by this chart which shows deviations from the long-run trend line of economic activity, the American economy has encountered periods of prosperity and depression. (AmeriTrust Company, Cleveland.)

instability as Figure 8-1 reveals. Periods of rapid economic expansion have sometimes been marred by inflation. At other times, expansion has given way to recession and depression, that is, falling levels of employment and output. On a few occasions—most notably in the 1970s and early 1980s— we have experienced a rising price level and abnormally high unemployment simultaneously. In short, the long-term trend of economic growth has been interrupted and complicated by both unemployment and inflation.

Phases of the Cycle

The term **business cycle** refers to the recurrent ups and downs in the level of economic activity which extend over several years. Individual business cycles vary substantially in duration and intensity. Yet all display common phases which are variously labeled by different economists. Figure 8-2 shows the several phases of a stylized business cycle.

1 Peak We begin our explanation with a cyclical **peak** at which business activity has reached a temporary maximum such as the middle peak in Figure 8-2. Here the economy is at full employment and the domestic output is also at or very close to capacity. The price level is likely to rise during this cyclical phase.

2 Recession The peak is followed by a **recession,** which is a period of decline in total output, income, employment, and trade, lasting six months or longer. This downturn is marked by widespread contractions of business in many sectors of the economy. But, be-

cause many prices in our economy are downwardly inflexible, the price level is likely to fall only if the recession is severe and prolonged—that is, if a depression occurs. An old one-liner is: "When your neighbor loses his job, it's a recession; when you lose your job it's a depression."

3 Trough The **trough** of the recession or depression is where output and employment "bottom out" at their lowest levels. The trough phase of the cycle may be short-lived or quite long.

FIGURE 8-2 The business cycle

Economists distinguish between four phases of the business cycle and recognize that the duration and strength of each phase is highly variable. A recession, for example, need not always entail serious and prolonged unemployment. Nor need a cyclical peak always entail full employment.

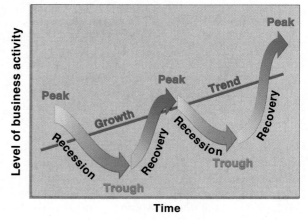

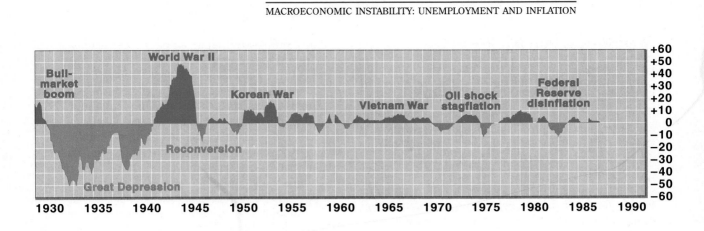

4 Recovery Finally, in the **recovery** phase the economy's levels of output and employment expand toward full employment. As recovery intensifies, the price level may begin to rise before the realization of full employment and full capacity production.

Despite common phases, specific business cycles vary greatly in duration and intensity. Indeed, some economists prefer to talk of business *fluctuations,* rather than *cycles,* because cycles imply regularity while fluctuations do not. The Great Depression of the 1930s resulted in a 40 percent decline in real GDP over a three-year period and seriously undermined business activity for an entire decade. By comparison, our more recent recessions—detailed in Table 8-1—have been minor in both intensity and duration.

Causation: A First Glance

Historically, economists have suggested many theories to explain fluctuations in business activity. Some center on innovation, contending that major innova-

tions such as the railroad, the automobile, or synthetic fibers have great impact on investment and consumption spending and therefore on output, employment, and the price level. But these major innovations occur irregularly and thus contribute to the variability of economic activity.

Other economists have explained the business cycle in terms of political and random events, as suggested by some of the labeling in Figure 8-1. Wars, for example, can be economically very disruptive. A virtually insatiable demand for war goods during hostilities can generate a period of overfull employment and sharp inflation, frequently followed by an economic slump when peace returns and military spending plummets. Still other economists view the cycle as a purely monetary phenomenon. When government creates too much money, an inflationary boom is generated; a relative paucity of money will precipitate a declining output and unemployment.

Despite these diverse opinions, most economists believe that the immediate determinant of the levels of domestic output and employment is the level of total or aggregate expenditures. In a largely market-directed economy, businesses produce goods and services only if they can be sold profitably. If total spending is low, most businesses will not find it profitable to produce a large volume of goods and services. Hence, output, employment, and the level of incomes will all be low. A higher level of total spending will mean that more production will be profitable; thus, output, employment, and incomes will all be higher also. Once the economy reaches full employment, real output becomes fixed and added spending will simply pull up the price level. Later in this chapter we will find that the relationship between aggregate spending and the price level is more complex and that, in fact, inflation may arise from causes other than a change in total spending.

TABLE 8-1 United States recessions since 1950

Period	Duration in months	Depth (decline in real output)
1953–54	10	−3.0%
1957–58	8	−3.5
1960–61	10	−1.0
1969–70	11	−1.1
1973–75	16	−4.3
1980	6	−3.4
1981–82	16	−2.6
1990–?1991	8	

Source: NBER and Federal Reserve Bank of Boston.

Noncyclical Fluctuations

Not all changes in business activity result from the business cycle. There can be **seasonal variations** in business activity. For example, pre-Christmas and pre-Easter buying rushes cause considerable fluctuations each year in the tempo of business activity, particularly in the retail industry. Agriculture, the automobile industry, construction—all are subject to some degree of seasonality.

Business activity is also subject to a **secular trend**—its expansion or contraction over a long period of years, for example, 25, 50, or 100 years. We note here that the long-run secular trend for American capitalism has been one of rather remarkable expansion (Chapter 19). For present purposes, the importance of this long-run expansion is that the business cycle involves fluctuations in business activity around a long-run growth trend. Note that in Figure 8-1 cyclical fluctuations are measured as deviations from the secular growth trend and that the stylized cycle of Figure 8-2 is drawn against a trend of growth.

Cyclical Impact: Durables and Nondurables

The business cycle is pervasive; it is felt in virtually every nook and cranny of the economy. The interrelatedness of the elements of the economy allows few, if any, to escape the cold hand of depression or the fever of inflation. However, various individuals and various segments of the economy are affected in different ways and degrees by the business cycle.

Insofar as production and employment are concerned, service industries and industries producing nondurable consumer goods are somewhat insulated from the most severe effects of recession. And, of course, recession actually helps some firms such as pawnbrokers and law firms specializing in bankruptcies! Who is hit hardest by recession? Those firms and industries producing capital goods and consumer durables. The construction industry is particularly vulnerable. Industries and workers producing housing and commercial buildings, heavy capital goods, farm implements, automobiles, refrigerators, gas ranges, and similar products bear the brunt of bad times. Conversely, these "hard goods" industries are stimulated most by expansion. Two facts help explain the vulnerability of these industries to the business cycle.

1 Postponability Within limits, purchase of hard goods is postponable. As the economy slips into bad times, producers frequently put off the acquisition of more modern production facilities and construction of new plants. The business outlook simply does not warrant increases in the stock of capital goods. The firm's present capital facilities and buildings will likely still be usable and in excess supply. In good times, capital goods are usually replaced before they completely depreciate. When recession strikes, however, business firms patch up their outmoded equipment and make it do. As a result, investment in capital goods will decline sharply. Some firms, having excess plant capacity, may not even bother to replace all the capital which they are currently consuming. Net investment for them may be a negative figure.

Much the same holds true for consumer durables. When recession occurs and the family must trim its budget, plans for the purchases of durables such as major appliances and automobiles often first feel the ax. People will repair their old appliances and cars rather than buy new models. Food and clothing—consumer nondurables—are a different story. A family must eat and clothe itself. These purchases are much less postponable. True, to some extent the quantity and certainly the quality of these purchases will decline, but not so much as with durables.

2 Monopoly Power Most industries producing capital goods and consumer durables are industries of high concentration, where a small number of large firms dominate the market. As a result, these firms have sufficient monopoly power to temporarily resist lowering prices by restricting output in the face of a declining demand. Consequently, the impact of a fall in demand centers primarily on production and employment. The reverse is true in nondurable, or soft, goods industries, which are for the most part highly competitive and characterized by low concentration. Price declines cannot be resisted in such industries, and the impact of a declining demand falls to a greater extent on prices than on the levels of production.

Figure 8-3 provides historical evidence on this point. It shows the percentage declines in price and quantity which occurred in ten selected industries as the economy fell from peak prosperity in 1929 to the depth of depression in 1933. Generally, high-concentration industries make up the top half of the table and low-concentration industries the bottom half. Note the drastic production declines and relatively modest price declines of the high-concentration industries on the one hand, and the large price declines and relatively small output declines which took place in the low-concentration industries on the other.

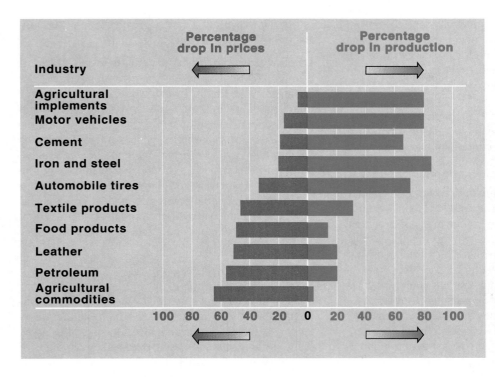

FIGURE 8-3 Relative price and production declines in ten industries, 1929–1933

The high-concentration industries shown in the top half were characterized by relatively small price declines and large declines in output during the early years of the Great Depression. In the low-concentration industries of the bottom half, price declines were relatively large, and production fell by relatively small amounts. [Gardiner C. Means, *Industrial Prices and Their Relative Flexibility* (Washington, 1953), p. 8.]

QUICK REVIEW 8-1

∳ **The long-term secular trend of real domestic output has been upward in the United States.**

∳ **The typical business cycle has four phases: peak, recession, trough, and recovery.**

∳ **Industries producing capital goods and consumer durables normally suffer greater output and employment declines during recession than do service and nondurable consumer goods industries.**

Armed with this thumbnail sketch of the business cycle, let's now examine unemployment and inflation in more detail.

UNEMPLOYMENT

"Full employment" is hard to define. A person might initially interpret it to mean that everyone who is in the labor market—100 percent of the labor force—is employed. But such is not the case; some unemployment is normal or warranted.

Types of Unemployment

In defining full employment, we first distinguish among several different types of unemployment.

Frictional Unemployment Given freedom to choose occupations and jobs, at any time some workers will be "between jobs." Some will be in the process of voluntarily switching jobs. Others will have been fired and are seeking reemployment. Still others will be temporarily laid off from their jobs because of seasonality (for example, bad weather in the construction industry) or model changeovers (as in the automobile industry). And there will be some workers, particularly young people, searching for their first jobs. As these people find jobs or are called back from temporary layoffs, other job seekers and temporarily laid-off workers will replace them in the "unemployment pool." Therefore, even though the specific individuals who are unemployed for these reasons change from month to month, this type of unemployment persists.

Economists use the term **frictional unemployment**—which consists of *search unemployment* and *wait unemployment*—for the group of workers who are either searching for jobs or waiting to take jobs in the near future. The adjective "frictional" correctly implies that the labor market does not operate perfectly and instantaneously—that is, without friction—in matching workers and jobs.

Frictional unemployment is regarded as inevitable and, at least in part, desirable. This is so because many workers who are voluntarily "between jobs" are moving from low-paying, low-productivity jobs to higher-paying, higher-productivity positions. This means more income for workers and a better allocation of labor resources—and therefore a larger real output—for the economy as a whole.

Structural Unemployment Frictional unemployment shades into a second category, called **structural unemployment.** Here, economists use the term "structural" in the sense of "compositional." Important changes occur over time in the "structure" of consumer demand and in technology, which in turn alter the "structure" of the total demand for labor. Because of such changes, some skills will be in less demand or may even become obsolete. Demand for other skills will expand, including new skills which previously did not exist. Unemployment results because the composition of the labor force does not respond quickly or completely to the new structure of job opportunities. As a result, some workers find they have no readily marketable talents; their skills and experience have been rendered obsolete and unwanted by changes in technology and consumer demand. Similarly, the geographic distribution of jobs constantly changes. Witness the migration of industry and employment opportunities from the Snow Belt to the Sun Belt over the past two decades.

Examples: (1) Years ago, highly skilled glassblowers were thrown out of work by the invention of bottle-making machines. (2) More recently, unskilled and inadequately educated blacks have been dislodged from agriculture in the south as a result of the mechanization of agriculture. Many of these workers have migrated to northern cities and have suffered prolonged unemployment because of insufficient skills. (3) An American shoe worker, unemployed because of import competition, cannot become, say, a computer programmer without considerable retraining and perhaps also geographic relocation. (4) Finally, many oil-field workers in the "oil-patch" states of the United States found themselves structurally unemployed when the world price of oil declined dramatically in the 1980s. Less drilling and other oil-related activity took place, and widespread layoffs resulted.

The distinction between frictional and structural unemployment is hazy. The key difference is that frictionally unemployed workers have salable skills, whereas structurally unemployed workers are not readily reemployable without retraining, additional education, and possibly geographic relocation. Frictional unemployment is more short-term, while structural unemployment is more long-term, and therefore regarded as more serious.

Cyclical Unemployment **Cyclical unemployment** is unemployment caused by the recession phase of the business cycle, that is, by a deficiency of aggregate or total spending. As the overall demand for goods and services decreases, employment falls, and unemployment rises. For this reason, cyclical unemployment is sometimes called *deficient-demand unemployment.* During the recession year 1982, for example, the unemployment rate rose to 9.7 percent. This compares to a 6.7 percent unemployment rate in the recession year 1991. Cyclical unemployment at the depth of the Great Depression in 1933 was about 25 percent of the labor force.

Defining "Full Employment"

Full employment does *not* mean zero unemployment. Economists regard frictional and structural unemployment as essentially unavoidable; hence, "full employment" is defined as something less than employment of 100 percent of the labor force. Specifically, the **full-employment unemployment rate** is equal to the total of frictional and structural unemployment. Stated differently, the full-employment unemployment rate is achieved when cyclical unemployment is zero. The full-employment rate of unemployment is alternatively referred to as the **natural rate of unemployment.** The real level of domestic output associated with the natural rate of unemployment is called the economy's **potential output.** That is, the economy's potential output is the real output forthcoming when the economy is "fully employed."

From a slightly different vantage point the full or natural rate of unemployment results when labor markets are in balance in the sense that the number of job seekers equals the number of job vacancies. The natural rate of unemployment is some positive amount because it takes time for frictionally unemployed job seekers to find appropriate job openings. And, regarding the structurally unemployed, it also takes time to achieve the skills and geographic relocation needed for reemployment. If the number of job seekers exceeds available vacancies, labor markets are not in balance; there is a deficiency of aggregate demand and cyclical unemployment is present. On the other hand, if aggregate demand is excessive a "shortage" of labor will arise; the number of job vacancies will exceed the number of workers seeking employment. In this situation the actual rate of unemployment is below the natural rate. Unusually "tight" labor markets such as this are associated with inflation.

The concept of the natural rate of unemployment merits elaboration in two respects.

1 The term does *not* mean that the economy will always operate at the natural rate and thereby realize its potential output. We have already suggested in our brief discussion of the business cycle that the economy frequently operates at an unemployment rate in excess of the natural rate. On the other hand, the economy may on rare occasions achieve an unemployment rate lower than the natural rate. For example, during World War II, when the natural rate was 3 or 4 percent, the pressure of wartime production resulted in an almost unlimited demand for labor. Overtime work was common as was "moonlighting" (holding more than one job). The government also froze some people working in "essential" industries in their jobs, reducing frictional unemployment. The actual rate of unemployment was below 2 percent in the entire 1943–1945 period and actually dropped to 1.2 percent in 1944. The economy was producing beyond its potential output, but incurred considerable inflationary pressure in the process.

2 The natural rate of unemployment itself is *not* immutable, but rather is subject to revision because of the shifting demographics of the labor force or institutional changes (changes in society's laws and customs). For example, in the 1960s it was believed that this unavoidable minimum of frictional and structural unemployment was about 4 percent of the labor force. In other words, full employment was said to exist when 96 percent of the labor force was employed. But today, economists generally agree that the natural rate of unemployment is about 5 to 6 percent.

Why is the natural rate of unemployment higher today than in the 1960s? First, the demographic makeup of the labor force has changed. Young workers—who traditionally have high unemployment rates—have become relatively more important in the labor force. Second, institutional changes have occurred. For example, our unemployment compensation program has been expanded both in terms of numbers of workers covered and size of benefits. This is important because, by cushioning the economic impact of unemployment, unemployment compensation permits unemployed workers to engage in a more leisurely job search, thereby increasing frictional unemployment and the overall unemployment rate.

Measuring Unemployment

The controversy over the full employment rate of unemployment is complicated by problems encountered in the actual measurement of the rate of unemployment. Figure 8-4 is a helpful starting point. The total

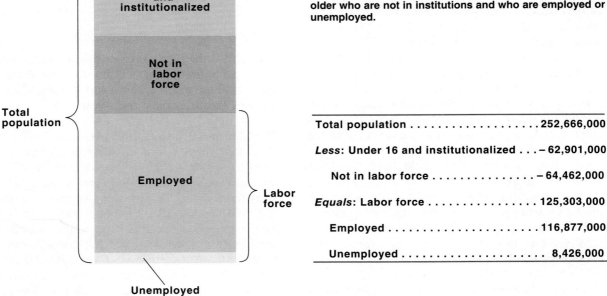

FIGURE 8-4 The labor force, employment, and unemployment, 1991

The labor force consists of persons sixteen years of age or older who are not in institutions and who are employed or unemployed.

Total population	252,666,000
Less: Under 16 and institutionalized . . .	– 62,901,000
Not in labor force	– 64,462,000
Equals: Labor force	125,303,000
Employed	116,877,000
Unemployed	8,426,000

population is divided into three broad groups. One group comprises those under 16 years of age and people who are institutionalized, for example, in mental hospitals or correctional institutions. These people are not considered to be potential members of the labor force.

A second group, labeled "not in labor force," are adults who are potential workers, but for some reason —they are homemakers, in school, or retired—are not employed and are not seeking work.

The remaining group is the **labor force,** which constituted about 50 percent of the total population in 1991. The labor force is essentially all people who are able and willing to work. Both those who are employed and those who are unemployed but actively seeking work are counted as being in the labor force. The *unemployment rate* is the percentage of the labor force which is unemployed:

$$\frac{\text{Unemployment}}{\text{rate}} = \frac{\text{unemployment}}{\text{labor force}} \times$$

In 1991 the unemployment rate was

$$6.7\% = \frac{8,426,000}{125,303,000} \times 100$$

Unemployment rates for selected years between 1929 and 1991 are provided on the inside covers of this book.

The Bureau of Labor Statistics (BLS) attempts to determine who is employed and who is not by conducting a nationwide random survey of some 60,000 households each month. A series of questions is asked regarding which members of the household are working, unemployed and looking for work, not looking for work, and so on. Despite the careful sampling and interview techniques used, the data collected from this survey have been subjected to a number of criticisms.

1 Part-time Employment The official data include all part-time workers as fully employed. In 1991 about 16 million people worked part time because of personal choice. Another 6 million part-time workers either wanted to work full time, but could not find suitable full-time work, or were on short hours because of a temporary slack in consumer demand. These last two groups of workers were, in effect, partially employed and partially unemployed. By counting them as fully employed the official BLS data tend to *understate* the unemployment rate.

2 Discouraged Workers One must be actively seeking work to be counted as unemployed. An unem-

ployed individual who is not actively seeking employment is classified as "not in the labor force." The problem is that there is a sizable number of workers who, after unsuccessfully seeking employment for a time, become discouraged and drop out of the labor force. The number of **discouraged workers** is larger during recession than prosperity, an estimated 1.25 million people fell into this category in 1991. By not counting discouraged workers as unemployed, official data tend to *understate* the unemployment rate.

3 False Information Alternatively, the unemployment rate may be *overstated* in that some respondents who are not working may claim they are looking for work, even though that is not the case. These individuals will be classified as "unemployed," rather than "not in the labor force." A person's motivation for giving this false information is that unemployment compensation or welfare benefits may depend on professed job pursuit. The presence of the underground economy (Chapter 7) may also cause the official unemployment rate to be overstated. Someone fully employed in the South Florida drug traffic or "running numbers" for the Chicago Mafia is likely to identify himself as "unemployed."

The main point is that, although the unemployment rate is a basic consideration in policy making, it has certain shortcomings. And, while the unemployment rate is one of the best measures of the economic condition of the nation, it is not an infallible barometer of our economic health.

Economic Cost of Unemployment

Problems in measuring the unemployment rate and defining the full-employment unemployment rate do not negate the fact that above-normal unemployment involves great economic and social costs.

GDP Gap and Okun's Law The basic economic cost of unemployment is forgone output. *When the economy fails to generate enough jobs for all who are able and willing to work, potential production of goods and services is irretrievably lost.* In terms of Chapter 2's analysis, unemployment keeps society from moving to its production possibilities curve. Economists measure this sacrificed output in terms of the **GDP gap,** the amount by which *actual GDP* falls short of *potential GDP.* Potential GDP is determined by assuming that the natural rate of unemployment exists and projecting the economy's "normal" growth rate. Figure 8-5 shows the GDP

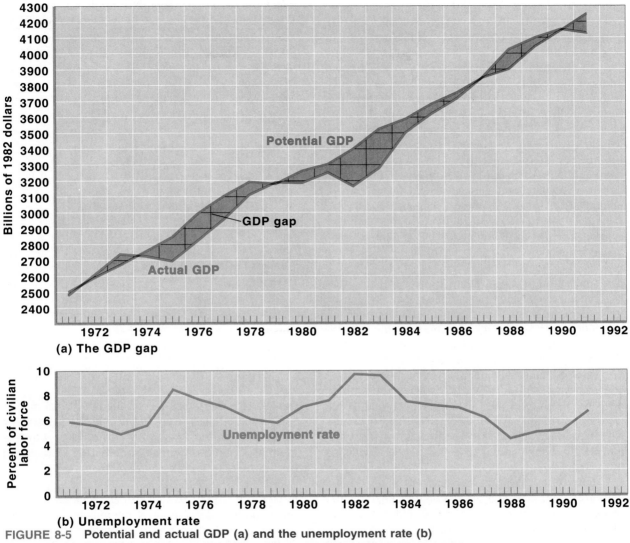

FIGURE 8-5   Potential and actual GDP (a) and the unemployment rate (b)

The difference between potential and actual GDP is the GDP gap. The GDP gap measures the output which the economy sacrifices because it fails to use fully its productive potential. Note that a high unemployment rate means a large GDP gap. [*Economic Report of the President* and Robert J. Gordon, *Macroeconomics,* 5th ed. (New York: HarperCollins, 1990).]

gap for recent years and underscores the close correlation between the actual unemployment rate (Figure 8-5b) and the GDP gap (Figure 8-5a). The higher the unemployment rate, the larger the GDP gap.

The well-known macroeconomist Arthur Okun quantified the relationship between the unemployment rate and the GDP gap. This relationship, known as **Okun's law,** indicates that *for every 1 percent that the actual unemployment rate exceeds the natural rate, a $2\frac{1}{2}$ percent GDP gap occurs.* This $1:2\frac{1}{2}$, or $2:5$, unemploy-

ment rate–GDP gap link permits calculation of the absolute loss of output associated with any unemployment rate. For example, in 1983 the unemployment rate was $9\frac{1}{2}$ percent, or $3\frac{1}{2}$ percent over the then-assumed 6 percent natural rate. Multiplying this $3\frac{1}{2}$ percent by Okun's $2\frac{1}{2}$ figure indicates that the 1983 GDP gap was $8\frac{3}{4}$ percent. Stated differently, 1983's GDP would have been $8\frac{3}{4}$ percent larger than it actually was had the full employment rate of unemployment been realized. Applying this $8\frac{3}{4}$ percent loss to 1983's $3405 billion nominal GDP, we find that the economy sacrificed almost $298 billion (=$3405 × 8¾ percent) of output because the natural rate of unemployment was not achieved.

On the other hand, observe in Figure 8-5 that on occasion the economy's actual output can exceed its potential output. We have already mentioned that this state of affairs existed during World War II when unemployment rates fell below 2 percent. Extra shifts of workers were employed, capital equipment was used beyond its designed capacity, and overtime work and moonlighting were common. We observe in Figure 8-5 that an economic boom caused actual GDP to exceed potential GDP in 1973, creating a "negative" GDP gap. Potential GDP can occasionally be exceeded, but the excess of actual over potential GDP cannot be sustained indefinitely.

Unequal Burdens Aggregate figures conceal the fact that the cost of unemployment is unequally distributed. An increase in the unemployment rate from 6 to, say, 9 or 10 percent would be more tolerable if every worker's hours of work and wage income were reduced proportionately. But this is not the case.

Table 8-2 contrasts unemployment rates for various labor market groups for 1982, in which there was a deep recession, and the full-employment year 1989. Observation of the large variance in the rates of unemployment *within each year* and comparison of the rates *between* the two years yields several generalizations.

1 Occupation White-collar workers enjoy lower unemployment rates and are less vulnerable to unemployment during recessions than blue-collar workers. This is because white-collar workers are employed in less cyclically vulnerable industries (services and non-durable goods) or are self-employed. Also, businesses are less inclined to lay off the more-skilled white-collar workers in whom they have large training investments.

2 Age Teenagers incur much higher unemployment rates than do adults. Teenagers have low skill levels, more frequently quit their jobs, are more frequently discharged from jobs, and often have little geographic mobility. Many unemployed teenagers are new labor-market entrants searching for their first job.

3 Race The unemployment rate for blacks—both adults and teenagers—has been roughly *twice* that of whites. A number of explanatory factors may be at work here including discrimination in education and

TABLE 8-2 Unemployment rates by demographic group: recession (1982) and full employment (1989)

Demographic group	Unemployment rate, 1982 (%)	Unemployment rate, 1989 (%)
Overall	9.7	5.3
Occupation		
Blue-collar	14.2	7.3
White-collar	5.2	3.9
Age		
16–19	23.2	15.0
Black, 16–19	48.0	32.4
White, 16–19	20.4	12.7
Males, 20+	8.8	4.5
Females, 20+	8.3	4.7
Race		
Black	18.9	11.4
White	8.6	4.5
Gender		
Female	9.4	5.4
Male	9.9	5.2
Duration		
15 weeks or more	3.2	1.1

Source: Economic Report of the President; Employment and Earnings.

the labor market, the concentration of blacks in less-skilled (blue-collar) occupations, and the geographic isolation of blacks in central-city areas where employment opportunities for new labor-market entrants are minimal.

4 Gender Male and female unemployment rates are quite comparable. The lower unemployment rate for women in the 1982 recession year reflects the fact that male workers are dominant in such cyclically vulnerable hard-goods industries as automobiles, steel, and construction.

5 Duration A final generalization is that the number of persons unemployed for long periods—fifteen weeks or more—as a percentage of the labor force is much less than the unemployment rate. But this figure rises significantly during recessions. The "long-term" unemployed were only 1.1 percent of the labor force in 1989 compared to the overall 5.3 percent unemployment rate. A very large proportion of unemployment is of relatively short duration. But also observe that the "long-term" unemployed were 3.2 percent of the labor force in the 1982 recession, implying a significant amount of economic hardship.

Noneconomic Costs

Severe cyclical unemployment is more than an economic malady; it is a social catastrophe as well. Depression means idleness. And idleness means loss of skills, loss of self-respect, a plummeting of morale, family disintegration, and sociopolitical unrest. It is no exaggeration to say that:

> A job gives hope for material and social advancement. It is a way of providing one's children a better start in life. It may mean the only honorable way of escape from the poverty of one's parents. It helps to overcome racial and other social barriers. In short . . . a job is the passport to freedom and to a better life. To deprive people of jobs is to read them out of our society.[1]

History makes it clear that severe unemployment leads to rapid and sometimes violent social and political change. Witness the movement to the left of American political philosophy during the Depression of the 1930s. The Depression-inspired New Deal was a veritable revolution in American political and economic thinking. Witness also Hitler's ascent to power against a background of unemployment. Furthermore, the high unemployment among blacks and other minorities unquestionably has been an important cause of the unrest and violence periodically plaguing cities in America and elsewhere. At a more mundane level, research links increases in suicides, homicides, cardiovascular mortality, and mental illness to high unemployment.

International Comparisons

Unemployment rates vary greatly among nations over specific periods. The major reason for these differences is that nations have different natural rates of unemployment and also may be in different phases of their business cycles. Figure 8-6 shows unemployment rates approximating U.S. measurement concepts for five industrialized nations for recent years. Historically, the United States has had higher unemployment rates than most industrially advanced nations. But this general pattern changed in the 1980s. Observe that the U.S. unemployment rate was below the rates in England, Germany, and France in several years during the 1980s.

[1]Henry R. Reuss, *The Critical Decade* (New York: McGraw-Hill Book Company, 1964), p. 133.

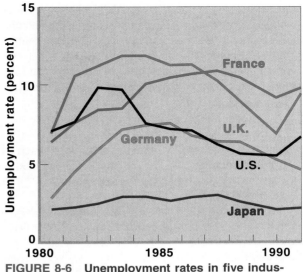

FIGURE 8-6   Unemployment rates in five industrial nations, 1980–1991

The unemployment rate in the United States has been below that in France, the United Kingdom, and Germany in several of the past eleven years. (*Economic Report of the President.*)

QUICK REVIEW 8-2

⬩   *Unemployment is of three general types: frictional, structural, and cyclical.*

⬩   *The natural unemployment rate is estimated to be between 5 and 6 percent.*

⬩   *Society loses domestic output—goods and services—when cyclical unemployment occurs.*

⬩   *Blue-collar workers, teenagers, and blacks bear a disproportionate burden of unemployment.*

INFLATION: DEFINED AND MEASURED

We now turn to inflation as an aspect of macroeconomic instability. The problems posed by inflation are more subtle than those of unemployment and are somewhat more difficult to grasp.

The Meaning of Inflation

Inflation is a rising general level of prices. This does not mean that *all* prices are necessarily rising. Even during periods of rather rapid inflation, some prices may be relatively constant and others actually falling. For example, although the United States experienced high rates of inflation in the 1970s and early 1980s, the prices of video recorders, digital watches, and personal computers actually declined. Indeed, as we will see, one of the troublesome aspects of inflation is that prices rise very unevenly. Some streak upward; others ascend at a more leisurely pace; others do not rise at all.

Measuring Inflation

Inflation is measured by price index numbers such as those introduced in Chapter 7. Recall that a price index measures the general level of prices in reference to a base period.

To illustrate, the consumer price index uses 1982–1984 as the base period in which that period's price level is set equal to 100. In 1991 the price index was approximately 136. This means that prices were 36 percent higher in 1991 than in 1982–1984, or that a given collection of goods which cost $100 in 1982–1984 cost $136 in 1991.

The *rate* of inflation can be calculated for any given year by subtracting last year's (1990) price index from this year's (1991) index, dividing that difference by last year's (1990) index, and multiplying by 100 to express it as a percentage. For example, the consumer price index was 130.7 in 1990 and 136.2 in 1991. The rate of inflation for 1991 is derived as follows:

$$\text{Rate of inflation} = \frac{136.2 - 130.7}{130.7} \times 100 = 4.2\%$$

The so-called **rule of 70** provides a different perspective for gaining a quantitative appreciation of inflation. It permits quick calculation of the number of years it takes the price level to double. We divide the number 70 by the annual rate of inflation:

$$\text{Approximate number of years required to double} = \frac{70}{\text{percentage annual rate of increase}}$$

For example, a 3 percent annual rate of inflation will double the price level in about $23 (= 70 \div 3)$ years. Inflation of 8 percent per year will double the price level in about $9 (= 70 \div 8)$ years. Inflation at 12 percent will double the price level in only about 6 years. Note that the rule of 70 is generally applicable in that it will allow you, for example, to estimate how long it will take for real GDP *or* your savings account to double.

With these facts in mind, we next examine the historical record of inflation in the United States and compare annual inflation rates internationally for a recent period. Then we will survey the causes of inflation and its consequences.

The Facts of Inflation

Figure 8-7 surveys inflation in the United States since 1920. The figures shown are annual increases in the consumer price index, which is constructed using a base period of 1982–1984. That is, the CPI for the 1982–1984 period is arbitrarily set at 100. Although most of you have grown up in an "age of inflation," observe that our economy has not always been inflation-prone. The price level was remarkably stable in the prosperous 1920s and declined—that is, *deflation* occurred—during the early years of the Great Depression of the 1930s. Prices then rose sharply in the immediate post–World War II period (1945–1948). However, overall price stability characterized the 1951–1965 period in which the average annual increase in the price level was less than $1\frac{1}{2}$ percent. But the inflation which took hold in the late 1960s and surged ahead in the 1970s introduced Americans to double-digit inflation. In 1979 and 1980 the price level rose at 12 to 13 percent annual rates. By the end of the 1980s, the inflation rate had settled into a 4–5 percent annual range. Specific annual rates of inflation can be found on the inside covers of this textbook.

Inflation is not a distinctly American institution. Virtually all industrial nations have experienced this problem. Figure 8-8 traces the post-1980 annual inflation rates of the United States, the United Kingdom, Japan, France, and Germany. Observe that inflation in the United States has been neither unusually high nor low relative to inflation in these other industrial countries.

Some nations have had double-digit, triple-digit, or still higher annual rates of inflation in recent years. In 1990, for example, the annual inflation rate in Greece was 20 percent; in Poland, 586 percent; and in Yugoslavia, 583 percent. Several Latin American nations experienced astronomical rates of inflation in 1990: Brazil, 2938 percent; Argentina, 2314 percent; and Peru, 7482 percent! The Peruvian inti, worth 7 cents when introduced in 1986, was worth less than two-thousandths of a penny in 1990.

Causes: Theories of Inflation

Economists distinguish between two types of inflation.

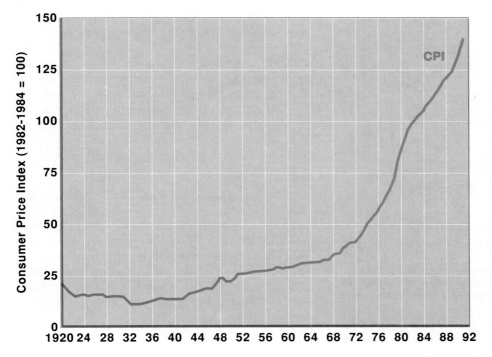

FIGURE 8-7 Price level behavior in the United States since 1920

The price stability of the 1920s and the deflation of the 1930s gave way to sharp inflation in the immediate post-World War II period. The 1951–1965 period was characterized by a reasonably stable price level, but the period since 1965 has clearly been an "age of inflation." (Bureau of Labor Statistics.)

1 Demand-Pull Inflation Traditionally, changes in the price level have been attributed to an excess of total demand. The economy may attempt to spend beyond its capacity to produce; it may seek some point beyond its production possibilities curve. The business sector cannot respond to this excess demand by expanding real output because all available resources are already fully employed. This excess demand will bid up the prices of the fixed real output, causing **demand-pull inflation.** The essence of demand-pull inflation is often expressed as "too much money chasing too few goods."

But the relationship between total demand, on the one hand, and output, employment, and the price level, on the other, is more complex than these comments suggest. Figure 8-9 will help unravel these complications.

Range 1 In *range 1* total spending—the sum of consumption, investment, government, and net export spending—is so low that domestic output is far short of its maximum full-employment level. In other words, a substantial GDP gap exists. Unemployment rates are high and businesses have much idle production capacity. Now assume that total demand increases. Real domestic output will rise and the unemployment rate will fall, but there will be little or no increase in the price level. Large amounts of idle human and property re-

FIGURE 8-8 Inflation rates in five industrial nations, 1980–1991

Inflation rates in the United States over the past eleven years have neither been extraordinarily high nor low relative to rates in other industrial nations. (*Economic Report of the President.*)

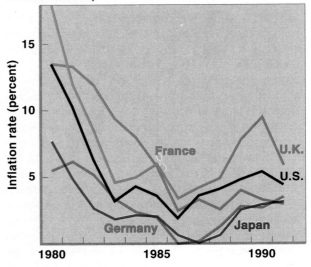

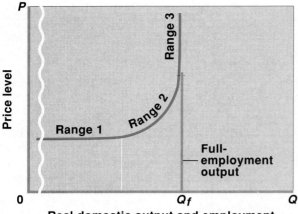

FIGURE 8-9   The price level and the level of employment

As aggregate expenditures increase, the price level generally begins to rise before full employment is reached. At full employment, additional spending tends to be purely inflationary.

sources can be put back to work at their *existing* prices. An unemployed worker does not ask for a wage increase during a job interview!

In terms of Chapter 4's demand and supply analysis, the usual price-raising effects of the assumed increases in demand do not occur because supply is a horizontal line. The increases in the amount of labor and other resources supplied are possible because idle resources are available and the additional production is profitable. The net result is large output-increasing effects and no price-increasing effects.

Range 2   As demand continues to rise, the economy enters *range 2* where it approaches full employment and is closer to fully using its available resources. But note that, before full employment is achieved, the price level may begin to rise. As production expands, supplies of idle resources do not vanish simultaneously in all sectors and industries of the economy. Bottlenecks develop in some industries even though most have excess production capacity. Some industries are using fully their production capacity before others and cannot respond to further increases in demand for their products by increasing output. So their prices rise. As labor markets tighten, some types of labor become fully employed and their money wages rise. This increases production costs and prompts businesses to increase their prices. Finally, as full employment is approached, firms will be forced to employ less efficient (less productive) workers and this contributes to rising costs and prices. The inflation which occurs in range 2

is sometimes called *premature inflation* because it occurs before the economy reaches full employment.

Range 3   As total spending increases into *range 3,* full employment occurs in all sectors of the economy. Industries in the aggregate can no longer respond to increases in demand with increases in output. Real domestic output is at a maximum and further increases in demand will cause demand-pull inflation. Total demand in excess of society's capacity to produce pulls the price level upward.

Reprise: Chapter 7's distinction between nominal and real GDP is helpful at this point. So long as the price level is constant (range 1), increases in nominal and real GDP are identical. But with premature inflation (range 2), nominal GDP is rising faster than real GDP, so nominal GDP must be "deflated" to measure changes in physical output. With pure inflation (range 3), nominal GDP is rising—perhaps rapidly—but real GDP is constant.

2 Cost-Push or Supply-Side Inflation   Inflation may also arise on the supply or cost side of the market. During several periods in our recent economic history the price level has risen despite rather widespread evidence that aggregate demand was not excessive. We have experienced periods when output and employment were both *declining* (evidence of a deficiency of total demand), while at the same time the general price level was *increasing*.

The theory of **cost-push inflation** explains rising prices in terms of factors which raise **per unit production cost.** Per unit production cost is the average cost of a particular level of output. This average cost is found by dividing the total cost of resource inputs by the amount of output produced. That is,

$$\text{Per unit production cost} = \frac{\text{total input cost}}{\text{units of output}}$$

Rising per unit production costs in the economy squeeze profits and reduce the amount of output firms are willing to supply at the existing price level. As a result, the economywide supply of goods and services declines. This decline in supply drives up the price level. Hence, under this scenario, costs are *pushing* the price level upward, rather than demand *pulling* it upward, as with demand-pull inflation.

Two sources of cost-push inflation are increases in nominal wages and increases in the prices of nonwage inputs such as raw materials and energy.

Wage-Push Variant The wage-push variant of cost-push inflation theorizes that, under some circumstances, unions may be a source of inflation. That is, unions exert some control over nominal wage rates through collective bargaining. Suppose major unions demand and receive large increases in wages. Let's also assume that these wage gains set the standard for wage increases paid to many nonunion workers. If the economywide wage gains are excessive relative to any offsetting factors such as rises in output per hour, then employers will experience rising per unit production costs. Producers will respond by reducing the amount of goods and services offered for sale. Assuming no change in demand, this decline in supply will result in an increase in the price level. Because the culprit is an excessive increase in nominal wages, this type of inflation is called the *wage-push variant* of cost-push inflation.

Supply-Shock Variant A second major variant of cost-push inflation, labeled *supply shock,* traces rising production costs—and therefore product prices—to abrupt, unanticipated increases in the costs of raw materials or energy inputs. The dramatic run-ups of imported oil prices in 1973–1974 and again in 1979–1980 are good illustrations. As energy prices rose during these periods, the costs of producing and transporting virtually every product in the economy increased. Rapid cost-push inflation ensued.

Complexities

The real world is much more complex than our simple distinction between demand-pull and cost-push inflation suggests. In practice it is difficult to distinguish between the two types of inflation. For example, suppose a boost in health care spending occurs which increases total spending, causing demand-pull inflation. As the demand-pull stimulus works its way through product and resource markets, individual firms find their wage costs, material costs, and fuel prices rising. From their perspective they must raise their prices because production costs have risen. Although inflation in this case is clearly demand-pull, it appears to be cost-push to many business firms. It is not easy to label inflation as demand-side or supply-side without knowing the ultimate source—the original cause—of price and wage increases.

Cost-push and demand-pull inflation differ in another important respect. Demand-pull inflation will continue so long as there is excess total spending. On the other hand, cost-push inflation automatically is self-limiting; it will die out or cure itself. Reduced supply will decrease real domestic output and employment and these declines will constrain further cost increases. Cost-push inflation generates a recession and the recession inhibits additional cost increases. This process will be addressed in more detail in Chapter 17.

QUICK REVIEW 8-3

✦ *Inflation is a rising general level of prices, measured as a percentage change in a price index.*

✦ *The United States' inflation rate has been within the middle range of rates of other advanced industrial nations, and far below the rates experienced by some nations.*

✦ *Demand-pull inflation occurs when total spending exceeds the economy's ability to provide goods and services at the existing price level; total spending pulls the price level upward.*

✦ *Cost-push inflation occurs when factors such as excessive wage increases and rapid increases in raw material prices drive up per unit production costs; higher costs push the price level upward.*

REDISTRIBUTIVE EFFECTS OF INFLATION

Our attention now shifts from causes to effects. We first consider how inflation capriciously redistributes income; second, we examine possible effects on the domestic output.

As we will see, the relationship between the price level and the domestic output is ambiguous. Historically, real output and the price level have risen and fallen together. In the past two decades or so, however, on several occasions real output has fallen while prices have continued to rise. We will dodge this issue for a moment by assuming that real output is constant and at the full-employment level. By holding real output and income constant we can better isolate the effects of inflation on the distribution of that income. Assuming that the size of the national income pie is fixed, how does inflation affect the size of the slices going to different income receivers?

To answer this question we must understand the difference between money or nominal income and real income.[2] *Money* or **nominal income** is the number of

---

[2]Chapter 7's distinction between nominal and real GDP is pertinent and you may want to review the "inflating" and "deflating" process involved in converting nominal GDP to real GDP (Table 7-7).

dollars one receives as wages, rent, interest, or profits. **Real income** measures the amount of goods and services nominal income can buy.

Clearly, if your nominal income increases faster than the price level, your real income will rise. Conversely, if the price level increases faster than your nominal income, your real income will decline. The change in one's real income can be approximated through this formula:

$$\begin{array}{ccc} \text{Percentage} & \text{percentage} & \text{percentage} \\ \text{change in} = & \text{change in} & - \text{ change in} \\ \text{real income} & \text{nominal income} & \text{price level} \end{array}$$

Thus, if your nominal income rises by 10 percent in a given year and the price level rises by 5 percent in the same period, your real income will *increase* by about 5 percent. Conversely, a 5 percent increase in nominal income accompanied by 10 percent inflation will *decrease* your real income by approximately 5 percent.[3]

The point is this: While inflation reduces the purchasing power of the dollar—the amount of goods and services a dollar will buy—it does not necessarily follow that a person's real income will fall. The purchasing power of the dollar declines whenever inflation occurs; a decline in your real income or standard of living occurs only when your nominal income fails to keep pace with inflation.

Finally, note that the redistribution effects of inflation are quite different, depending on whether or not it is expected. With **anticipated inflation,** an income receiver *may* be able to take steps to avoid or lessen the adverse effects which inflation would otherwise have on real income. The generalizations which immediately follow assume the presence of **unanticipated inflation.** We will then modify our generalizations by taking the anticipation of inflation into account.

---

[3]A more precise calculation follows Chapter 7's process for changing nominal GDP to real GDP. Hence,

$$\text{Real income} = \frac{\text{nominal income}}{\text{price index (in hundredths)}}$$

Thus, in our first illustration, if nominal income rises by 10 percent from $100 to $110 and the price level (index) increases by 5 percent from 100 to 105, then real income has increased as follows:

$$\frac{\$110}{1.05} = \$104.76$$

The 5 percent increase in real income shown by the simple formula in the text is a good approximation of the 4.76 percent yielded by our more complex formula.

Fixed-Nominal-Income Receivers

Our distinction between nominal and real incomes shows that *inflation penalizes people who receive relatively fixed nominal incomes.* Restated, inflation redistributes income away from fixed income receivers toward others in the economy. The classic case is the elderly couple living on a private pension or annuity which provides a fixed amount of nominal income each month. The pensioner who retired in 1978 on what appeared to be an adequate pension finds by 1991 that the purchasing power of that pension had been cut by one-half.

Similarly, landlords who receive lease payments of fixed dollar amounts will be hurt by inflation as they receive dollars of declining value over time. To a lesser extent some white-collar workers, some public sector employees whose income is dictated by fixed pay scales, and families living on fixed levels of welfare and other transfer income will be victims of inflation. Note, however, that Congress has *indexed* social security benefits; social security payments are tied to the consumer price index to prevent erosion from inflation.

Some people living on flexible incomes *may* benefit from inflation. The nominal incomes of such households may spurt ahead of the price level, or cost of living, with the result that their real incomes are enhanced. Workers in expanding industries and represented by vigorous unions may keep their nominal wages apace with, or ahead of, the rate of inflation.

On the other hand, some wage earners are hurt by inflation. Those in declining industries or without strong, aggressive unions may find that the price level skips ahead of their money incomes.

Business executives and other profit receivers *might* benefit from inflation. *If* product prices rise faster than resource prices, business receipts will grow at a faster rate than costs. Thus some profit incomes will outdistance the rising tide of inflation.

Savers

Inflation also hurts savers. *As prices rise, the real value, or purchasing power, of a nest egg of savings will deteriorate.* Savings accounts, insurance policies, annuities, and other fixed-value paper assets once adequate to meet rainy-day contingencies or provide for a comfortable retirement decline in real value during inflation. The simplest case is the individual who hoards money as a cash balance. For example, a $1000 cash balance would have lost one-half its real value between 1967 and 1977. Of course, most forms of savings earn interest. But the value of savings will still decline if the rate of inflation exceeds the rate of interst.

Example: A household may save $1000 in a certificate of deposit (CD) in a commercial bank or savings and loan association or buy a $1000 bond at 6 percent interest. But if inflation is 13 percent (as in 1980), the real value or purchasing power of that $1000 will be cut to about $938 at the end of the year. That is, the saver will receive $1060 (equal to $1000 plus $60 of interest), but deflating that $1060 for 13 percent inflation means that the real value of $1060 is only about $938 (equal to $1060 divided by 1.13.)

Debtors and Creditors

Inflation also redistributes income by altering the relationship between debtors and creditors. *Unanticipated inflation benefits debtors (borrowers) at the expense of creditors (lenders)*. Suppose you borrow $1000 from a bank, to be repaid in two years. If in that time the general level of prices were to double, the $1000 which you repay will have only half the purchasing power of the $1000 originally borrowed. True, if we ignore interest charges, the same number of dollars is repaid as was borrowed. But because of inflation, each of these dollars will now buy only half as much as it did when the loan was negotiated. As prices go up, the value of the dollar comes down. Thus, because of inflation, the borrower is given "dear" dollars but pays back "cheap" dollars. The inflation of the past few decades has been a windfall to those who purchased homes in, say, the mid-1960s with fixed-interest-rate mortgages. On the one hand, inflation has greatly reduced the real burden of their mortgage indebtedness. On the other hand, the nominal value of housing has increased more rapidly than the overall price level.

The Federal government, which has amassed $3600 billion of public debt over the decades, has also been a major beneficiary of inflation. Historically, the Federal government has regularly paid off its loans by taking out new ones. Inflation has permitted the Treasury to pay off its loans with dollars which have less purchasing power than the dollars it originally borrowed. Nominal national income and therefore tax collections rise with inflation; the amount of public debt owed does not. Thus, inflation reduces the real burden of the public debt to the Federal government. Given

that inflation benefits the Federal government in this way, some economists have wondered out loud whether society can really expect government to be particularly zealous in its efforts to halt inflation.

In fact, some nations such as Brazil once used inflation so extensively to reduce the real value of their debts that lenders now force them to borrow money in U.S. dollars or in some other relatively stable currency instead of their own currency. This prevents them from using domestic inflation as a means of subtly "defaulting" on their debt. Any inflation which they generate will reduce the value of their own currencies, but not the value of the dollar-denominated debt they must pay back.

Anticipated Inflation

The redistributive effects of inflation will be less severe or even eliminated if transactors (1) anticipate inflation and (2) have the capacity to adjust their nominal incomes to reflect expected price level changes. For example, the prolonged inflation which began in the late 1960s prompted many unions in the 1970s to insist on labor contracts with **cost-of-living adjustment (COLA)** clauses to automatically adjust workers incomes for inflation.

Similarly, the redistribution of income from lender to borrower which we just observed might be altered *if* inflation is anticipated. Suppose a lender (perhaps a commercial bank or savings and loan) and a borrower (a household) both agree that 5 percent is a fair rate of interest on a one-year loan, *provided* the price level is stable. But assume inflation has been occurring and both lender and borrower agree it is reasonable to anticipate a 6 percent increase in the price level over the next year. If the bank lends the household $100 at 5 percent, the bank will be paid back $105 at the end of the year. But if 6 percent inflation does occur during the year, the purchasing power of that $105 will have been reduced to about $99. The *lender* will in effect have paid the *borrower* $1 to use the lender's money for a year.

The lender can avoid this curious subsidy by charging an *inflation premium*, which means increasing the interest rate by the amount of the anticipated inflation. By charging 11 percent the lender will receive back $111 at the end of the year which, adjusted for the 6 percent inflation, has the real value or purchasing power of about $105. Here there is a mutually agreeable transfer of purchasing power from borrower to lender of $5, or 5 percent, for the use of $100 for one year. Note that savings and loan institutions have developed variable-interest-rate mortgages to protect themselves from the adverse effects of inflation. Incidentally, these examples imply that, rather than being a cause of inflation, high nominal interest rates may be a consequence of inflation.

Our illustration shows the difference between the real rate of interest, on the one hand, and the money or nominal rate of interest, on the other. The **real interest rate** *is the percentage increase in purchasing power that the lender receives from the borrower.* In our example the real interest rate is 5 percent. The **nominal interest rate** *is the percentage increase in money that the lender receives.* The nominal rate of interest is 11 percent in our example. The difference in these two concepts is that the real interest rate is adjusted or "deflated" for the rate of inflation while the nominal interest rate is not. Stated differently, the nominal interest rate is the sum of the real interest rate plus the premium paid to offset the expected rate of inflation.

Addenda

Three final points must be mentioned.

1 Not surprisingly, the effects of deflation are substantially the reverse of those of inflation. *Assuming no change in total output,* those with fixed money incomes will find their real incomes enhanced. Creditors will benefit at the expense of debtors. And savers will discover the purchasing power of their savings has grown because of falling prices.

2 The fact that any given family may be an income earner, a holder of financial assets, and an owner of real assets simultaneously will likely cushion the redistributive impact of inflation. If the family owns fixed-value monetary assets (savings accounts, bonds, and insurance policies), inflation will lessen their real value. But that same inflation may increase the real value of any property assets (a house, land) which the family owns. In short, many families are simultaneously hurt and benefited by inflation. All these effects must be considered before we can conclude that the family's net position is better or worse because of inflation.

3 The final point is that the redistributive effects of inflation are *arbitrary;* they occur regardless of society's goals and values. Inflation lacks a social conscience and takes from some and gives to others, whether they be rich, poor, young, old, healthy, or infirm.

OUTPUT EFFECTS OF INFLATION

We have assumed thus far that the economy's real output is fixed at the full-employment level. As a result, the redistributive effects of inflation and deflation have been in terms of some groups gaining absolutely at the expense of others. *If* the size of the pie is fixed and inflation causes some groups to get larger slices, other groups must necessarily get smaller slices. But, in fact, the level of domestic output may vary as the price level changes. The size of the pie itself may vary.

There is much uncertainty and disagreement as to whether inflation will be accompanied by a rising or a falling real domestic output. We will consider three scenarios, the first associating inflation with an expanding output and the remaining two with a declining output.

Stimulus of Demand-Pull Inflation

Some economists argue that full employment can only be achieved if some modest amount of inflation is tolerated. They base their reasoning on Figure 8-9. We know that the levels of real domestic output and employment depend on aggregate spending. If spending is low, the economy will operate in range 1. In this range there is price level stability, but real domestic output is substantially below its potential and the unemployment rate is high. If aggregate spending now increases so that the economy moves into range 2, we find society must accept a higher price level—some amount of inflation—to achieve these higher levels of real domestic output and the accompanying lower unemployment rates. If further increases in aggregate spending pull the economy into range 3, that spending will be purely inflationary because the full-employment or capacity level of real domestic output will have been reached.

The critical point is that in range 2 there appears to be a tradeoff between output (including employment) and inflation. Some moderate amount of inflation must be accepted if we are to realize high levels of output and employment. The high levels of spending which give us higher levels of output and low unemployment rates also cause some inflation. Stated differently, an inverse relationship may exist between the inflation rate and the unemployment rate.

This scenario has been criticized in recent years. Many economists feel that any tradeoff between the inflation rate and the unemployment rate is a transitory or short-run phenomenon at best and there is no such tradeoff in the long run. This controversy will be explored in detail in Chapter 17.

Cost-Push Inflation and Unemployment

There is an equally plausible set of circumstances in which inflation might cause output and employment both to *decline*. Suppose the level of total spending is initially such that the economy is enjoying full employment *and* price level stability. If cost-push inflation now occurs, the amount of real output which the existing level of total demand will buy will be reduced. That is, a given level of total spending will only be capable of taking a smaller real output off the market when cost-push pressures boost the price level. Hence, real output will fall and unemployment will rise.

Economic events of the 1970s support this scenario. In late 1973 the Organization of Petroleum Exporting Countries (OPEC) became effective and exerted its market power to quadruple the price of oil. The cost-push inflationary effects generated rapid price level increases in the 1973–1975 period. At the same time the unemployment rate rose from slightly less than 5 percent in 1973 to 8.5 percent in 1975. Similar outcomes occurred in 1979–1980 in response to a second OPEC oil price shock.

Hyperinflation and Breakdown

Some economists express anxiety over our first scenario. They are fearful that the mild, "creeping" inflation which might initially accompany economic recovery may snowball into a more severe **hyperinflation.** This term is reserved for extremely rapid inflation whose ultimate impact on domestic output and employment can be devastating. The contention is that, as prices persist in creeping upward, households and businesses will expect them to rise further. So, rather than let their idle savings and current incomes depreci-

ate, people are induced to "spend now" to beat anticipated price rises. Businesses do the same in buying capital goods. Action based on this "inflationary psychosis" intensifies pressure on prices, and inflation feeds on itself.

Furthermore, as the cost of living rises, labor demands and gets higher nominal wages. Indeed, unions may seek wage increases sufficient not only to cover last year's price level increase but also to compensate for inflation anticipated during the future life of their new collective bargaining agreement. Prosperity is not a good time for business firms to risk strikes by resisting such demands. Business managers recoup their rising labor costs by boosting the prices they charge consumers. And for good measure, businesses may jack prices up an extra notch or two to be sure that profit receivers keep abreast or ahead of the inflationary parade. As the cost of living moves upward as a result of these price increases, labor once again has an excellent excuse to demand another round of substantial wage increases. But this triggers another round of price increases. The net effect is a cumulative *wage-price inflationary spiral.* Nominal-wage and price rises feed on each other, and this creeping inflation bursts into galloping inflation.

Aside from disruptive redistributive effects, hyperinflation can precipitate economic collapse. Severe inflation encourages a diversion of effort toward speculative, and away from productive, activity. Businesses may find it increasingly profitable to hoard both materials and finished products in anticipation of further price increases. But, by restricting the availability of materials and products relative to the demand for them, such actions will intensify inflationary pressures. Rather than invest in capital equipment, businesses and individual savers may purchase nonproductive wealth—jewels, gold and other precious metals, real estate, and so forth—as hedges against inflation.

In the extreme, as prices shoot up sharply and unevenly, normal economic relationships are disrupted. Business owners do not know what to charge for their products. Consumers do not know what to pay. Resource suppliers will want to be paid with actual output, rather than with rapidly depreciating money. Creditors will avoid debtors to escape the repayment of debts with cheap money. Money becomes virtually worthless and ceases to do its job as a measure of value and medium of exchange. The economy may literally be thrown into a state of barter. Production and exchange grind toward a halt, and the net result is eco-

LAST WORD

THE STOCK MARKET AND MACROECONOMIC INSTABILITY

How, if at all, do changes in stock prices relate to the macroeconomy?

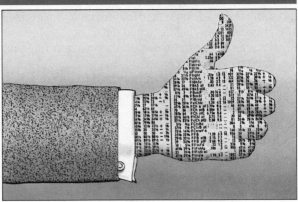

Financial investors daily buy and sell the stock certificates of hundreds of corporations. These corporations pay dividends—a portion of their profits—to the owners of their stock shares. The price of a particular company's stock is determined by supply and demand. Individual stock prices generally rise and fall in concert with the collective expectations for each firm's profits. Greater profits normally result in higher dividends to the owners of the stock, and in anticipation of these higher dividends, financial investors are willing to pay more for the stock.

Stock market averages such as the Dow Jones industrial average—the average price of the stocks of a selected list of major United States industrial firms—are closely watched and reported. It is not uncommon for these price averages to change over periods of time, or even to rise or fall sharply during a single day. Some of you will remember "Black Monday," October 19, 1987, when the Dow Jones industrial average experienced a record one-day fall of roughly 20 percent. About $500 billion in stock market wealth evaporated in a single day!

The volatility of the stock market raises an important question: Do changes in stock price averages *cause* macroeconomic instability? There are linkages between the stock market and the economy which might lead us to think the answer to this question is "Yes." Consider a sharp decline in stock prices. Feeling poorer, owners of stock may respond by reducing their spending on goods and services. Because it is less attractive to raise funds by issuing new shares of stock, firms may react by cutting back on their purchases of new capital goods. Research studies find, however, that the consumption and investment impacts of stock price changes are relatively mild. Therefore, although stock price averages do influence total spending, the stock market is *not* a major cause of recession or inflation.

A related question thus emerges: Even though changes in stock prices do not *cause* significant changes in domestic output and the price level, might not they *predict* such changes? That is, if stock market values are based on expected profits, wouldn't we expect rapid changes in stock price averages to forecast changes in future business conditions? Indeed, stock prices often *do* fall prior to recessions and rise prior to expansions. For this reason stock prices are among a group of eleven variables which constitute an index of leading indicators (Last Word, Chapter 12). This index often provides a useful clue to the future direction of the economy. But taken alone, stock market prices are not a reliable predictor of changes in domestic output. Stock prices have fallen rapidly in some instances with no recession following. Black Monday itself did not produce a recession during the following two years. In other instances, recessions have occurred with no prior decline in stock market prices.

In summary, the relationship between stock market prices and the macroeconomy is quite loose. Changes in stock prices are not a major source of macroeconomic instability nor are they reliable in forecasting business recessions or expansions.

nomic, social, and very possibly political chaos. Hyperinflation has precipitated monetary collapse, depression, and sociopolitical disorder.

Unfortunately, history reveals a number of examples which fit this gloomy scenario. Consider the effects of World War II on price levels in Hungary and Japan:

The inflation in Hungary exceeded all known records of the past. In August, 1946, 828 octillion (1 followed by 27 zeros) depreciated pengös equaled the value of 1 prewar pengö. The price of the American dollar reached a value of 3×10^{22} (3 followed by 22 zeros) pengös. Fishermen and farmers in 1947 Japan used scales to weigh currency and change, rather than bothering to count it. Prices rose some 116 times in Japan, 1938 to 1948.[4]

The German inflation of the 1920s was also catastrophic:

> The German Weimar Republic is an extreme example of a weak government which survived for some time through inflationary finance. On April 27, 1921, the German government was presented with a staggering bill for reparations payments to the Allies of 132 billion gold marks. This sum was far greater than what the Weimar Republic could reasonably expect to raise in taxes. Faced with huge budget deficits, the Weimar government simply ran the printing press to meet its bills.
>
> During 1922, the German price level went up 5,470 percent. In 1923, the situation worsened; the German price level rose 1,300,000,000,000 times. By October of 1923, the postage on the lightest letter sent from Germany to the United States was 200,000 marks. Butter cost 1.5 million marks per pound, meat 2 million marks, a loaf of bread 200,000 marks, and an egg 60,000 marks. Prices increased so rapidly that waiters changed the prices on the menu several times during the course of a lunch. Sometimes customers had to pay double the price listed on the menu when they ordered.
>
> Photographs of the period show a German housewife starting the fire in her kitchen stove with paper money and children playing with bundles of paper money tied together into building blocks.[5]

A closing word of caution is in order. Such dramatic hyperinflations as those just documented are almost invariably the consequence of imprudent expansion of the money supply by government. Given appropriate public policies, there is no reason why mild or creeping inflation need become hyperinflation.

CHAPTER SUMMARY

1 Our economy has been characterized by fluctuations in domestic output, employment, and the price level. Although characterized by common phases—peak, recession, trough, recovery—business cycles vary greatly in duration and intensity.

2 Although the business cycle has been explained in terms of such ultimate causal factors as innovations, political events, and money creation, it is generally agreed that the level of total spending is the immediate determinant of domestic output and employment.

3 All sectors of the economy are affected by the business cycle, but in varying ways and degrees. The cycle has greater output and employment ramifications in the capital goods and durable consumer goods industries than it does in services and nondurable goods industries. Over the cycle, price fluctuations are greater in competitive than in monopolistic industries.

4 Economists distinguish between frictional, structural, and cyclical unemployment. The full-employment or natural rate of unemployment is currently believed to be between 5 and 6 percent. The accurate measurement of unemployment is complicated by the existence of part-time and discouraged workers.

5 The economic cost of unemployment, as measured by the GDP gap, consists of the goods and services which society forgoes when its resources are involuntarily idle. Okun's law suggests that every 1 percent increase in unemployment above the natural rate gives rise to a $2\frac{1}{2}$ percent GDP gap.

6 Unemployment rates and inflation rates vary greatly among nations. Unemployment rates differ because nations have different natural rates of unemployment and often are in different phases of their business cycles. Inflation and unemployment rates in the United States recently have been in the middle range compared to rates in other industrial nations.

7 Economists discern both demand-pull and cost-push (supply-side) inflation. Two variants of cost-push inflation are wage-push inflation and inflation caused by a supply shock.

8 Unanticipated inflation arbitrarily redistributes income at the expense of fixed-income receivers, creditors, and savers. If inflation is anticipated, individuals and businesses may be able to take steps to lessen or eliminate adverse redistributive effects.

9 The demand-pull theory of inflation suggests that some inflation may be necessary if the economy is to realize high levels of output and employment. However, the cost-push theory of inflation indicates that inflation may be accompanied by declines in real output and employment. Hyperinflation, usually associated with injudicious government policy, might undermine the monetary system and precipitate economic collapse.

---

[4]Theodore Morgan, *Income and Employment,* 2d ed. (Englewood Cliffs, N.J.: Prentice-Hall, Inc., 1952), p. 361.

[5]Raburn M. Williams, *Inflation! Money, Jobs, and Politicians* (Arlington Heights, Ill.: AHM Publishing Corporation, 1980), p. 2.

TERMS AND CONCEPTS

business cycle
peak, recession,
    trough, and recovery
    phases
seasonal variations
secular trend
frictional, structural,
    and cyclical
    unemployment

full-employment
    unemployment rate
natural rate of
    unemployment
potential output
labor force
discouraged workers
GDP gap

Okun's law
rule of 70
demand-pull and cost-
    push inflation
per unit production
    cost
nominal and real
    income

anticipated versus
    unanticipated
    inflation
cost-of-living
    adjustment (COLA)
nominal and real
    interest rates
hyperinflation

QUESTIONS AND STUDY SUGGESTIONS

1 What are the major phases of the business cycle? How long do business cycles last? How do seasonal variations and secular trends complicate measurement of the business cycle? Why does the business cycle affect output and employment in durable goods industries more severely than in industries producing nondurables?

2 Why is it difficult to determine the full-employment unemployment rate? Why is it difficult to distinguish between frictional, structural, and cyclical unemployment? Why is unemployment an economic problem? What are the consequences of the "GDP gap"? What are the noneconomic effects of unemployment?

3 Given that there exists an unemployment compensation program which provides income for those out of work, why worry about unemployment?

4 Use the following data to calculate **a** the size of the labor force and **b** the official unemployment rate. Total population, 500; population under 16 years of age and institutionalized, 120; not in labor force, 150; unemployed, 23; part-time workers looking for full-time jobs, 10.

5 Explain how an *increase* in your nominal income and a *decrease* in your real income might occur simultaneously. Who loses from inflation? From unemployment? If you had to choose between **a** full employment with a 6 percent annual rate of inflation or **b** price stability with an 8 percent unemployment rate, which would you select? Why?

6 If the price index was 110 last year and is 121 this year, what was this year's rate of inflation? What is the "rule of 70"? How long would it take for the price level to double if inflation persisted at **a** 2, **b** 5, and **c** 10 percent per year?

7 Carefully describe the relationship between total spending and the levels of output and employment. Explain the relationship between the price level and increases in total spending as the economy moves from substantial unemployment to moderate unemployment and, finally, to full employment.

8 Explain how severe "hyperinflation" might lead to a depression.

9 Evaluate as accurately as you can how each of the following individuals would be affected by unanticipated inflation of 10 percent per year:

    a   a pensioned railroad worker

    b   a department-store clerk

    c   a UAW assembly-line worker

    d   a heavily indebted farmer

    e   a retired business executive whose current income comes entirely from interest on government bonds

    f   the owner of an independent small-town department store

10 A noted television comedian once defined inflation as follows: "Inflation? That means your money today won't buy as much as it would have during the depression when you didn't have any." Is his definition accurate?

11 Assume that in a given year the natural rate of unemployment is 5 percent and the actual rate of unemployment is 9 percent. Use Okun's law to determine the size of the GDP gap in percentage point terms. If the nominal GDP is $500 billion in that year, how much output is being forgone because of unemployment?

9

Aggregate Demand and Aggregate Supply

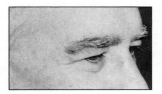

In Chapter 7 we discovered how domestic output and national income are measured. We also learned how a price index is constructed and used to compare price levels from one period to the next. In addition, the price index permitted us to convert nominal GDP to real GDP and thus meaningfully to compare GDP in various years. In Chapter 8 we saw how real GDP, employment, and the price level have fluctuated over time. We also described the economic impacts of changes in real GDP and the price level.

It is now time to shift the emphasis from description to analysis by building on the definitions and facts in Chapters 7 and 8. The present chapter introduces basic tools to help organize our thinking about macroeconomic theories and controversies. First, we discuss the need to look at a market in the aggregate—that is, to combine individual markets into a single market. Next, the concepts of aggregate demand and aggregate supply are introduced. The shapes of the aggregate demand and aggregate supply curves will be explained and forces causing them to shift will be outlined. We will then consider the equilibrium levels of prices and real domestic output. Finally, the effects of shifts in the aggregate demand and aggregate supply curves on the price level and the size of real domestic output are explored.

This chapter is a skeletal introduction to aggregate demand and supply. The "bare bones" model presented here will be fleshed out as we proceed through Parts 2, 3, and 4. In fact, you may want to review this chapter after completion of Part 4. While the skeletal framework in this chapter will help you understand the discussion in the following chapters, similarly, the discussion in the ensuing chapters will expand and reinforce your grasp of the basic model presented here.

THE NEED FOR AN AGGREGATE MODEL

In Chapter 4 we examined in detail the demand and supply curves for single products. We were interested in discovering how market demand and supply for particular goods establish each product's equilibrium price and quantity. That model was then used to show how equilibrium prices and quantities change in response to changes in one or more of the determinants of supply and demand.

Single-product demand and supply models such as those in Chapter 4 are particularly useful for understanding differences in the prices and outputs of various products and services. They help us comprehend why the equilibrium price of a donut is considerably less than the equilibrium price of a diamond, why the price of a barrel of oil is less than the price of a barrel of perfume, and why the annual expenditure on oil is greater than the annual expenditure on diamonds, perfume, and donuts combined. The single-product model also helps explain why equilibrium prices and quantities of some individual products change from one period to the next. For example, it helps explain why the price of medical care has increased relative to other prices over the past two decades, or why production of personal computers has risen tremendously since their introduction in the late 1970s.

Nevertheless, the single-product demand and supply model leaves several important economic questions unanswered. What causes prices in general to rise or fall? Why does the overall price level remain relatively constant during some periods only to surge upward in others? What determines the sum of all the equilibrium quantities in specific product markets within a nation—the country's real domestic output? Why does real domestic output recede from previous levels in some years while in others it grows rapidly?

To answer these questions we must combine—or aggregate—all individual markets in the economy into a single overall market. We must combine the thousands of individual prices—of pizzas, industrial robots, corn, personal computers, crankshafts, donuts, diamonds, oil, perfume, and so forth—into a single aggregate price or a price level. Similarly, we must merge the equilibrium quantities of individual products and services into a single entity called real domestic output. Combining all the prices of individual products and services into a price level, as well as merging all the equilibrium quantities into real domestic output, is called **aggregation.** The combined prices (the price level) and the merged equilibrium quantities (real domestic output) are each referred to as **aggregates.**

The labels on our graph in the simple macroeconomic model therefore become the *price level* (on the vertical axis), not the price of a single product; and *real domestic output* (on the horizontal axis), not the quantity of a specific product. With these labels in mind, we now examine aggregate demand and aggregate supply.

AGGREGATE DEMAND

Aggregate demand *is a schedule, graphically represented as a curve, which shows the various amounts of goods and services—the amounts of real domestic output—which domestic consumers, businesses, government, and foreign buyers collectively will desire to purchase at each possible price level.* Other things being equal, the lower the price level, the larger will be the real domestic output these entities will want to purchase. Conversely, the higher the price level, the smaller will be the domestic output they desire to buy. Thus, the relationship between the price level and the amount of real domestic output collectively demanded is inverse or negative.

Aggregate Demand Curve

The inverse relationship between the price level and domestic output is apparent in Figure 9-1. Observe that the aggregate demand curve slopes downward and to the right as does the demand curve for an individual product.

Why so? Curiously, the rationale is *not* the same as that which applies to the demand for a single product. That explanation centered on income and substitution effects. When the price of an individual product falls, the consumer's (constant) money income will enable him or her to purchase more of the product (the income effect). And, as price falls, the consumer wants to buy more of the product because it becomes relatively less expensive than other goods (the substitution effect).

But these explanations do not work when we are dealing with aggregates. In Figure 9-1 prices in general are falling as we move down the aggregate demand curve so the rationale for the substitution effect (a product becoming cheaper relative to all other products) is not applicable. Similarly, while an individual's demand curve for a specific product assumes the consumer's income to be fixed, the aggregate demand curve im-

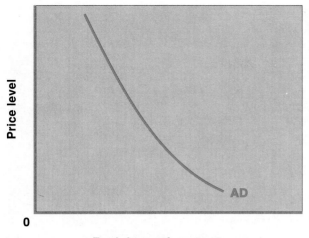

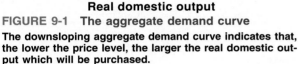

FIGURE 9-1   The aggregate demand curve

The downsloping aggregate demand curve indicates that, the lower the price level, the larger the real domestic output which will be purchased.

plies varying aggregate incomes. As we move up the aggregate demand curve we move to higher price levels. But, recalling our circular flow model, higher prices paid for goods and services will flow to resources suppliers as expanded wage, rent, interest, and profit incomes. As a result, an increase in the price level does *not* necessarily mean a decline in the nominal income of the economy as a whole.

If substitution and income effects do not explain the downsloping aggregate demand curve, what then is the rationale for a downsloping curve? The rationale rests primarily on three factors: (1) the wealth, or real balances, effect; (2) the interest-rate effect; and (3) the foreign purchases effect.

Wealth Effect   The first reason why the aggregate demand curve is downsloping involves the **wealth** or **real balances effect.** A higher price level will reduce the real value or purchasing power of the public's accumulated financial assets. In particular, the real value of assets with fixed money values such as savings accounts or bonds will diminish. Because of the erosion of purchasing power of such assets, the public will be poorer in real terms and will retrench on its spending. A household might buy a new car or a sailboat if the purchasing power of their financial asset balances is, say, $50,000. But if inflation erodes the purchasing power of these asset balances to $30,000, the family may defer its purchase. Conversely, a decline in the

price level will increase the real value or purchasing power of one's wealth and increase spending.

Interest-Rate Effect   The **interest-rate effect** suggests that the rationale for the downsloping aggregate demand curve lies in the impact of the changing price level on interest rates and in turn on consumption and investment spending. As the price level rises so will interest rates, and rising interest rates will reduce certain kinds of consumption and investment spending.

Elaboration: *The aggregate demand curve assumes that the supply of money in the economy is fixed.* When the price level increases, consumers will need more money for purchases and businesses will similarly require more money to meet their payrolls and purchase other needed inputs. In short, a higher price level will increase the demand for money.

Given a fixed supply of money, this increase in demand will drive up the price paid for the use of money. That price is the interest rate. Higher interest rates will curtail interest-sensitive expenditures by businesses and households. A firm expecting a 10 percent return on a potential purchase of a capital good will find that purchase profitable when the interest rate is, say, only 7 percent. But the purchase is unprofitable and will not be made when the interest rate has risen to, say, 12 percent. Similarly, an increase in the interest rate will make some consumers decide *not* to purchase houses or automobiles. To summarize: A higher interest rate curtails certain interest-sensitive business and consumer expenditures.

Conclusion: A higher price level—by increasing the demand for money and the interest rate—reduces the amount of real output demanded.

Foreign Purchases Effect   We found in Chapter 7's discussion of national income accounting that imports (American purchases of foreign goods) and exports (foreign purchases of American goods) are important components of total spending. The volumes of our imports and exports depend on, among other things, relative price levels here and abroad. Thus, if the price level rises in the United States relative to foreign countries, American buyers will purchase more imports at the expense of American goods. Similarly, foreigners will buy fewer American goods, reducing American exports. In short, other things being equal, a rise in our domestic price level will increase our imports and reduce our exports, thereby reducing the net exports (exports minus imports) component of aggregate demand in the United States.

Conclusion: The **foreign purchases effect** of a price-level increase results in a decline in the aggregate amount of American goods and services demanded. Conversely, a relative decline in our price level will reduce our imports and increase our exports, thereby increasing the net exports component of American aggregate demand.

Determinants of Aggregate Demand

Thus far we have found that changes in the price level cause changes in the level of spending by domestic consumers, businesses, government, and foreign buyers in such a way that we can predict changes in the amount of real domestic output. That is, an increase in the price level, *other things being equal,* will decrease the quantity of real output demanded. Conversely, a decrease in the price level will increase the amount of real output desired. This relationship is represented graphically as point-to-point movements along a stable aggregate demand curve. However, if one or more of those "other things" change, the entire aggregate demand curve shifts positions. We refer to those "other things" as **determinants of aggregate demand;** they "determine" the location of the aggregate demand curve.

To understand what causes changes in domestic output, you must distinguish between *changes in the quantity of real output demanded* caused by changes in the price level and *changes in aggregate demand* caused by changes in one or more of the determinants of aggregate demand. Recall that we drew a similar distinction when discussing single-product demand curves in Chapter 4.

As shown in Figure 9-2, an increase in aggregate demand is depicted by the rightward movement of the curve from AD_1 to AD_2. This shift indicates that, at each price level, the desired amount of real goods and services is larger than before. Alternatively, a decrease in aggregate demand is shown as the leftward shift of the curve from AD_1 to AD_3. This shift tells us that people desire to buy less real output at each price level than previously.

To repeat: The changes in aggregate demand shown in the figure occur when changes occur in one or more of the factors previously assumed to be constant. These determinants of aggregate demand, or *aggregate demand shifters,* are listed in Table 9-1. Let's examine each element of the table in the order shown.

Consumer Spending Independently of changes in the price level, domestic consumers collectively may

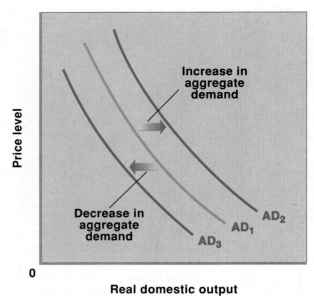

FIGURE 9-2 Changes in aggregate demand

A change in one or more of the determinants of aggregate demand listed in Table 9-1 will change aggregate demand. An increase in aggregate demand is shown as the rightward shift of the AD curve from AD_1 to AD_2; a decrease in aggregate demand, as a leftward shift from AD_1 to AD_3.

alter their purchases of American-produced real output. When this happens the entire aggregate demand curve shifts. It shifts leftward as from AD_1 to AD_3 in Figure 9-2 when consumers buy less output than before at each possible price level; it moves rightward as from AD_1 to AD_2 when they buy more at each possible price level.

Changes in one or more of several non-price-level factors may change consumer spending and therefore

TABLE 9-1 Determinants of aggregate demand: factors that shift the aggregate demand curve

1 **Change in consumer spending**
  a **Consumer wealth**
  b **Consumer expectations**
  c **Consumer indebtedness**
  d **Taxes**

2 **Change in investment spending**
  a **Interest rates**
  b **Profit expectations on investment projects**
  c **Business taxes**
  d **Technology**
  e **Degree of excess capacity**

3 **Change in government spending**

4 **Change in net export spending**
  a **National income abroad**
  b **Exchange rates**

shift the aggregate demand curve. As indicated in Table 9-1, these factors are real consumer wealth, consumer expectations, consumer indebtedness, and taxes.

Consumer Wealth Consumer wealth is all the assets owned by consumers, including financial assets such as stocks and bonds and physical assets such as houses and land. A sharp decline in the real value of consumer assets encourages people to save more (buy fewer products) to restore their wealth. The resulting decline in consumer spending will decrease aggregate demand—that is, shift the aggregate demand curve leftward. Conversely, an increase in the real value of consumer wealth will increase consumption spending at each price level; the aggregate demand curve will shift rightward.

Important warning: We are *not* referring here to the previously discussed "wealth effect" or "real balances effect," which assumes a fixed aggregate demand curve and results from a change in the price level. In contrast, the change in real wealth addressed here is independent of a change in the price level; it is a *non-price-level factor* which shifts the entire aggregate demand curve. An example would be a sharp increase in stock prices which increases consumer wealth, even though the price level has not changed. Similarly, a sharp decline in the real value of houses and land reduces consumer wealth, independent of changes in the general price level.

Consumer Expectations Changes in expectations about the future usually change consumer spending. When people expect their future real income to rise, they spend more of their current income. Present consumption spending increases (present saving falls), and the aggregate demand curve shifts rightward. Conversely, an expectation that real income will decline in the future reduces present consumption spending and therefore reduces aggregate demand.

Similarly, a widely held expectation of surging future inflation increases aggregate demand today, because consumers buy products before prices escalate. Conversely, expectations of lower price levels in the near future may reduce present consumption in that people postpone some of their present consumption to take advantage of the future lower prices.

Consumer Indebtedness Consumers with high levels of indebtedness from past buying sprees financed by installment loans may be forced to cut present spending to pay off existing consumer debt. The result

is a decline in consumption spending and a leftward shift of the aggregate demand curve. Conversely, when consumers' indebtedness is relatively low, their present consumption spending increases. This produces an increase in aggregate demand.

Taxes A reduction in personal income tax rates increases take-home income and increases consumer purchases at each possible price level. That is, tax cuts shift the aggregate demand curve rightward. Tax increases, on the other hand, reduce consumption spending and shift the aggregate demand curve leftward.

Investment Spending Investment spending—the purchase of capital goods—is a second determinant of aggregate demand. A decline in the amount of new capital goods desired by businesses at each price level will shift the aggregate demand curve leftward. Conversely, an increase in the desired amount of investment goods will increase aggregate demand. Let's consider the factors which can alter the level of investment spending as listed in Table 9-1.

Interest Rates All else being equal, an increase in the interest rate caused by a factor other than a change in the price level will lower investment spending and reduce aggregate demand. We are *not* referring here to the so-called "interest-rate effect" occurring due to a change in the price level. Instead, we are referring to a change in the interest rate resulting from, say, a change in the nation's money supply. An increase in the money supply tends to reduce the interest rate and thereby increases investment. Conversely, a decrease in the supply of money increases the interest rate and reduces investment.

Profit Expectations on Investment Projects Improved profit expectations on investment projects will increase the demand for capital goods and shift the aggregate demand curve rightward. For example, an anticipated rise in spending by consumers may in turn improve the profit expectations of possible investment projects. Alternatively, if the profit outlook on possible investment projects dims because of an expected decline in consumer spending, investment spending will decline. Consequently, aggregate demand will also decline.

Business Taxes An increase in business taxes will reduce after-tax profits from corporate investment and will reduce investment spending and aggregate demand. Conversely, tax reductions increase after-tax profits from corporate investment, increase investment spending, and push the aggregate demand curve rightward.

Technology New and improved technologies stimulate investment spending and increase aggregate demand. Example: Recent advances in the high-tech fields of microbiology and electronics have spawned new labs and production facilities to exploit the new technologies.

Degree of Excess Capacity A rise in excess capacity —unused existing capital—will retard the demand for new capital goods and reduce aggregate demand. Firms operating factories at well below capacity have little incentive to build new factories. Alternatively, when firms collectively discover that their excess capacity is dwindling, they build new factories and buy more equipment. Hence, investment spending rises and the aggregate demand curve shifts to the right.

Government Spending Government's desire to buy goods and services is a third determinant of aggregate demand. An increase in government purchases of domestic output at each price level will increase aggregate demand so long as tax collections and interest rates do not change as a result. An example would be a decision by government to revitalize the interstate highway system. Conversely, a reduction in government spending, such as a cutback in government spending on military hardware, will reduce aggregate demand.

Net Export Spending The final determinant of aggregate demand is net export spending. When foreign consumers change their purchases of U.S. goods independently of changes in our price level, the American aggregate demand curve shifts as well. We again specify "independent of changes in our price level" to distinguish clearly from changes in spending associated with the foreign purchases effect. That effect helps explain why a change in the American price level produces a change in real U.S. output. In discussing aggregate demand shifters we instead address changes in net exports caused by factors other than changes in the price level. Increases in net exports (exports minus imports) caused by these other factors push our aggregate demand curve rightward. The logic behind this proposition is as follows. First, a higher level of American exports constitutes an increased *foreign demand*

for American goods. Second, a reduction of our imports implies an increased *domestic demand* for American-produced products.

The non-price-level factors which alter net exports are primarily national income abroad and exchange rates.

National Income Abroad Rising national income in a foreign nation increases the foreign demand for U.S. goods and consequently increases aggregate demand in America. As income levels rise in a foreign nation, its citizens can afford to buy both more products made at home *and* made in the United States. Our exports therefore rise in step with increases in the national income levels of our trading partners. Declines in national income abroad have the opposite effect: Our net exports decline, shifting the aggregate demand curve leftward.

Exchange Rates A change in the exchange rate between the dollar and other currencies is a second factor affecting net exports and hence aggregate demand. Suppose the dollar price of yen rises, which means the *dollar depreciates* in terms of the yen. Viewed differently, the yen price of dollars falls, meaning the *yen appreciates.* The new relative values of dollars and yen means consumers in Japan can obtain *more* dollars with any particular number of yen. Similarly, consumers in the United States will obtain *fewer* yen for each dollar. As a result, Japanese consumers will discover that American goods are cheaper in terms of yen. American consumers meanwhile will find that fewer Japanese products can be purchased with a given number of dollars. With respect to our *exports,* a $30 pair of American-made blue jeans now might be bought for 2880 yen compared to 3600 yen. And in terms of our *imports,* a Japanese watch might now cost $225 rather than $180. In these circumstances our exports will rise and imports will fall. This increase in net exports translates into an increase in U.S. aggregate demand. You are urged to think through the opposite scenario in which the dollar appreciates (yen depreciates).

QUICK REVIEW 9-1

♪ *Aggregate demand reflects an inverse relationship between the price level and the amount of real domestic output demanded.*

♪ *Changes in the price level produce wealth, interest-rate, and foreign purchases effects which explain the downward slope of the aggregate demand curve.*

♦ *Changes in one or more of the determinants of aggregate demand (Table 9-1) alter the amounts of real domestic output demanded at each price level; they shift the aggregate demand curve.*

♦ *An increase in aggregate demand is shown as a rightward shift of the aggregate demand curve; a decrease entails a leftward shift of the curve.*

AGGREGATE SUPPLY

Aggregate supply *is a schedule, graphically represented by a curve, showing the level of real domestic output available at each possible price level.* Higher price levels create an incentive for enterprises to produce and sell additional output. Lower price levels cause reductions in output. As a result, the relationship between the price level and the amount of domestic output businesses offer for sale is direct or positive.

Aggregate Supply Curve

In macroeconomics there is disagreement over the nature and shape of the aggregate supply curve. But for our purposes, it will be useful to think of the aggregate supply curve as comprising three distinct segments or ranges. We also assume that the aggregate supply curve itself does not shift when the price level changes.

The three segments of the aggregate supply curve are identified as (1) the Keynesian (horizontal), (2) the intermediate (upsloping), and (3) the classical (vertical) range. Let's examine these three ranges and explain the rationale for each. Our explanations are essentially those which you are already familiar with from our discussion of Figure 8-9. The shape of the aggregate supply curve reflects what happens to per unit production costs as the domestic output expands or contracts. Recall from Chapter 8 that per unit production cost is found by dividing the total cost of the inputs (resources) used by the quantity of output. In other words, the per unit production cost of a particular level of output is the average cost of that output.

Keynesian (Horizontal) Range In Figure 9-3 Q_f designates the full-employment or potential level of real domestic output first introduced in Chapter 8. Recall that the natural rate of unemployment occurs at this output level. Observe that the horizontal range of aggregate supply comprises real levels of domestic output which are substantially less than the full-employment output Q_f. Hence, the horizontal range implies

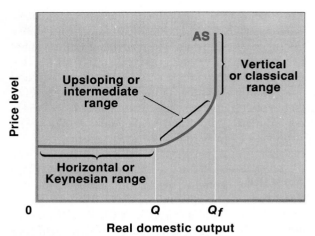

FIGURE 9-3 The aggregate supply curve
The aggregate supply curve shows the level of real domestic output which will be produced at various price levels. It comprises three ranges: (a) a horizontal or Keynesian range where the price level remains constant as domestic output varies; (b) a vertical or classical range where real domestic output is constant at the full-employment level and the price level can vary; and (c) an intermediate range where both real output and the price level are variable.

that the economy is in a severe recession or depression and that large amounts of unused machinery and equipment and unemployed workers are available. These idle resources—both human and property—can be put back to work with little or no upward pressure on the price level. As domestic output expands over this range no shortages or production bottlenecks will be incurred to cause prices to rise. A worker unemployed for two or three months will hardly expect a wage increase when recalled to his or her job. Because producers can acquire labor and other inputs at stable prices, production costs will not rise as output is expanded and so there is no reason to raise product prices.

Conversely, this horizontal range also implies that, if real domestic output contracts, product and resource prices will be downwardly inflexible. That means real output and employment will fall, but product prices and wages will remain rigid. Indeed, as explained in Chapter 8, real output and employment will decline in this range *because* prices and wages are assumed to be inflexible.

This horizontal range has been dubbed the **Keynesian range** after the famous English economist John Maynard Keynes (pronounced "canes"), the subject of this chapter's Last Word. Keynes—whose theory of employment is discussed in the next two chapters—examined the functioning of capitalistic economies against the backdrop of the Great Depression of the 1930s when unemployment in the United States was as high as 25 percent. In this lamentable economic condition there was ample room to expand production without fear of higher production costs or higher prices. Conversely, Keynes held that declines in real domestic output and employment would *not* be cushioned by price and wage reductions.

Classical (Vertical) Range　At the other extreme, we find that the economy reaches full employment or a natural rate of unemployment at a real domestic output of Q_f. The economy is at a point *on* Chapter 2's production possibilities curve and in the short term no further increase in real output is attainable. Any further increase in the price level will fail to elicit additional real output because the economy is already operating at capacity. At full employment individual firms may try to expand production by bidding resources away from other firms. But the resources and additional production one firm gains will be lost by some other firm. Resource prices (costs) and ultimately product prices will rise because of this process, but real domestic output will remain unchanged.

Two diverse points must be made concerning the vertical range of the aggregate supply curve.

1　This range is associated with classical economics —also to be discussed in the next chapter—which concludes there are forces inherent in a market economy which cause full employment to be the norm. Hence, the vertical range is also known as the **classical range** of the aggregate supply curve.

2　"Full employment" and "full-employment real output" are slippery concepts. This is true not merely because the "full employment or natural unemployment rate" is difficult to quantify (Chapter 8), but also because hours of work and the size of the labor force can sometimes be expanded beyond what is normal. Recall from Figure 8-5 that periodically actual GDP exceeds potential GDP. Thus, in a highly prosperous economy daily working hours and the workweek can be extended. Workers can also engage in "moonlighting," the practice of holding more than one job.

Example: During World War II a 10-hour workday and a six-day workweek were common. Many workers, after their normal workday at a regular job, would work a partial or full night shift in a defense plant. Women and young persons, who would not ordinarily have worked, joined the labor force in response to patriotic appeals and high wages. But for our purposes we assume there is some specific level of real output which corresponds to full employment.

Intermediate (Upsloping) Range　Finally, in the **intermediate range** between Q and Q_f an expansion of real output is accompanied by a rising price level. One reason is that the aggregate economy is in fact comprised of innumerable product and resource markets *and* full employment is not reached evenly or simultaneously in various sectors or industries. As the economy expands in the QQ_f real output range, the high-tech computer industry, for example, may encounter shortages of skilled workers while the automobile or steel industries are still faced with substantial unemployment. Similarly, in certain industries raw-material shortages or similar production bottlenecks may begin to appear. Expansion also means some firms will be forced to use older and less efficient machinery as they approach capacity production. Also, less capable workers may be hired as output expands. For all of these reasons, per unit production costs rise and firms must receive higher product prices for production to be profitable. Thus, in the intermediate range a rising real output is accompanied by a higher price level.

As we have noted, the shape of the aggregate supply curve is a matter of controversy. We will find in later chapters that some economists—called *classical* or *new classical economists*—contend the curve is vertical throughout, implying that a change in aggregate demand will be relatively harmless because it only affects the price level while leaving output and employment unchanged. Other economists—known as *Keynesians* —argue that the aggregate supply curve is either horizontal or upsloping and therefore that decreases in aggregate demand have adverse and very costly effects on output and employment.

Determinants of Aggregate Supply

Our discussion of the shape of the aggregate supply curve revealed that real domestic output increases as the economy moves from left to right through the Keynesian and intermediate ranges of aggregate supply. These changes in output result from *movements along* the aggregate supply curve and must be distinguished from *shifts* in the aggregate supply curve itself. An existing aggregate supply curve identifies the relationship between the price level and real domestic output, *other things being equal.* But when one or more of these "other things" change, the aggregate supply curve itself shifts.

The shift of the curve from AS_1 to AS_2 in Figure 9-4 shows an *increase* in aggregate supply. Over the intermediate and classical range of the aggregate supply curves, this shift is rightward, indicating that businesses collectively will produce more real output at each price level than previously. Over the Keynesian range of the aggregate supply curves, an increase in aggregate supply can best be thought of as a decline in the price level at each level of domestic output (a downward shift of aggregate supply). For convenience we will refer to an increase in aggregate supply as a "rightward" shift of the curve rather than a "rightward or a downward" shift. Conversely, the shift of the curve from AS_1 to AS_3 will be referred to as a "leftward shift," indicating a *decrease* in aggregate supply. That is, businesses now will produce less real output at each price level than before (or charge higher prices at each level of output).

Table 9-2 summarizes the "other things" which shift the aggregate supply curve when they change. These factors are called the **determinants of aggregate supply** because they collectively "determine" or establish the location of the aggregate supply curve. These determinants have one thing in common: When

TABLE 9-2   Determinants of aggregate supply: factors that shift the aggregate supply curve

1 **Change in input prices**
 a **Domestic resource availability**
   a_1 **land**
   a_2 **labor**
   a_3 **capital**
   a_4 **entrepreneurial ability**
 b **Prices of imported resources**
 c **Market power**
2 **Change in productivity**
3 **Change in legal-institutional environment**
 a **Business taxes and subsidies**
 b **Government regulation**

they change, per unit production costs also change. We established in earlier chapters that the supply decisions of businesses are made on the basis of production costs and revenues. Businesses are profit seekers and profits arise from the difference between product prices and per unit production costs. Producers respond to higher prices for their products—that is, to higher price levels—by increasing their real output. And, production bottlenecks mean that per unit production costs rise as output expands toward full employment. For this reason the aggregate supply curve slopes upward in its intermediate range.

The point is that there are factors *other than changes in real domestic output* which alter per unit production costs (see Table 9-2). When one or more change, per unit production costs change at each price level and the aggregate supply curve shifts positions. Specifically, decreases in per unit production costs of this type shift the aggregate supply curve rightward. Conversely, increases in per unit production costs shift the aggregate supply curve leftward. *When per unit production costs change for reasons other than a change in domestic output, firms collectively alter the amount of domestic output they produce at each price level.*

We now examine how changes in the aggregate supply shifters listed in Table 9-2 affect per unit production costs and thereby shift the aggregate supply curve.

Input Prices   Input or resource prices—to be distinguished from the output prices comprising the price level—are an important determinant of aggregate supply. All else being equal, higher input prices increase per unit production costs and therefore reduce aggregate supply. Lower input prices produce just the opposite result. The following factors influence input prices:

FIGURE 9-4   Changes in aggregate supply

A change in one or more of the determinants of aggregate supply listed in Table 9-2 will cause a change in aggregate supply. An increase in aggregate supply is shown as a rightward shift of the AS curve from AS_1 to AS_2; a decrease in aggregate supply, as a leftward shift from AS_1 to AS_3.

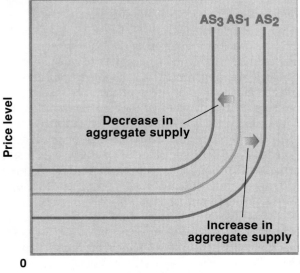

domestic resource availability, the prices of imported resources, and market power.

Domestic Resource Availability We noted in Chapter 2 that a society's production possibilities curve shifts outward when the resources available to it increase. Rightward shifts in the production possibilities curve translate into rightward shifts of our aggregate supply curve. Increases in the supply of domestic resources lower input prices and, as a result, per unit production costs fall. Thus, at any given price level, firms collectively will produce and offer for sale more real domestic output than before. Conversely, declines in resource supplies increase input prices and shift the economy's aggregate supply curve to the left.

How might changes in the availability of land, labor, capital, and entrepreneurial resources work to shift the aggregate supply curve? Several examples will help answer this question.

Land Land resources might become more available through discoveries of mineral deposits, irrigation of land, or new technical innovations which permit us to transform what were previously "nonresources" into valuable factors of production. An increase in the supply of land resources lowers the price of land inputs and thus lowers per unit production costs. For example, the recent discovery that widely available materials at low temperatures can act as superconductors of electricity is expected eventually to reduce per unit production costs by reducing electricity loss during transmission. This lower price of electricity will increase aggregate supply.

Two examples of reductions in land resources availability may also be cited: (1) the widespread depletion of the nation's underground water through irrigation, and (2) the nation's loss of topsoil through intensive farming. Eventually, each of these problems may increase input prices and shift the aggregate supply curve leftward.

Labor About 75 percent of all business costs are wages or salaries. All else being equal, changes in wages thus have a significant impact on per unit production costs and on the location of the aggregate supply curve. An increase in the availability of labor resources reduces the price of labor; a decrease raises labor's price. Examples: The influx of women into the labor force during the past two decades placed a downward pressure on wages and expanded American aggregate supply. Emigration of employable workers

from abroad also has historically increased the availability of labor in the United States.

Conversely, the great loss of life during World War II greatly diminished the postwar availability of labor in the United States, tending to raise per unit production costs. Currently, the AIDS epidemic threatens to reduce the supply of labor and thus diminish the nation's aggregate supply of real output.

Capital Aggregate supply tends to increase when society adds to its stock of capital. Such an addition would happen if society saved more of its income and directed the savings toward purchase of capital goods. In much the same way, an improvement in the quality of capital reduces production costs and increases aggregate supply. For example, businesses over the years have replaced poor quality equipment with new, superior equipment.

Conversely, aggregate supply will decline when the quantity and quality of the nation's stock of capital diminish. Example: In the depths of the Great Depression of the 1930s, our capital stock deteriorated because new purchases of capital were insufficient to offset the normal wearing out and obsolescence of plant and equipment.

Entrepreneurial Ability Finally, the amount of entrepreneurial ability available to the economy can change from one period to the next and shift the aggregate supply curve. Recent media focus on individuals who have amassed fortunes through entrepreneurial efforts might conceivably increase the number of people who have entrepreneurial aspirations, tending to shift the aggregate supply curve rightward.

Prices of Imported Resources Just as foreign demand for American goods contributes to our aggregate demand, the importation of resources from abroad adds to our aggregate supply. Resources add to our productive capacity whether they be domestic or imported. Imported resources reduce input prices and therefore decrease the per unit cost of producing American real domestic output. Generally, a decrease in the prices of imported resources expands our aggregate supply; an increase in the prices of these resources reduces our aggregate supply.

Exchange rate fluctuations are a factor which periodically alter the price of imported resources. Suppose that the dollar price of foreign currency falls—that is, the dollar appreciates—enabling American firms to obtain more foreign currency with each American dollar. This means that American producers face a lower dollar price of imported resources. Under these conditions, American firms would expand their imports of foreign resources and realize reductions in per unit production costs at each level of output. Falling per unit production costs of this type shift the American aggregate supply curve to the right.

Conversely, an increase in the dollar price of foreign currency—dollar depreciation—raises the prices of imported resources. As a result, our imports of these resources fall, our per unit production costs jump upward, and our aggregate supply curve moves leftward.

Market Power   A change in the degree of market power or monopoly power held by sellers of resources can also affect input prices and aggregate supply. *Market power* is the ability to set a price above that which would occur in a competitive situation. The rise and fall of OPEC's market power during the past two decades is a good illustration. The tenfold increase in the price of oil that OPEC achieved during the 1970s permeated our economy, drove up per unit production costs, and jolted the American aggregate supply curve leftward. Conversely, a substantial reduction in OPEC's market power during the mid-1980s reduced the cost of manufacturing and transporting products, and as a direct result, increased American aggregate supply.

A change in union market power also can be expected to affect the location of the aggregate supply curve. Some observers believe that unions experienced growing market power in the 1970s, resulting in union wage increases which widened the gap between union and nonunion workers. This higher pay may well have increased per unit production costs and produced leftward shifts of aggregate supply. Alternatively, union market power greatly waned during the 1980s. Consequently, in many industries the price of union labor fell, resulting in lower per unit production costs. The result was an increase in aggregate supply.

Productivity   Productivity relates a nation's level of real output to the quantity of input used to produce that output. In other words, **productivity** is a measure of average output, or of real output per unit of input:

$$\text{Productivity} = \frac{\text{real output}}{\text{input}}$$

An increase in productivity means that more real domestic output can be obtained from the amount of resources—or inputs—currently available.

How does an increase in productivity affect the aggregate supply curve? We first need to discover how a change in productivity alters per unit production costs. Suppose real domestic output in a hypothetical economy is 10 units, the input quantity needed to produce that quantity is 5, and the price of each input unit is $2. Productivity—output per input—is 2 ($=10/5$). The per unit cost of output would be found through the following formula:

$$\text{Per unit production cost} = \frac{\text{total input cost}}{\text{units of output}}$$

In this case, per unit cost is $1, found by dividing $10 of input cost ($=\$2 \times 5$ units of input) by 10 units of output.

Now suppose that real domestic output doubles to 20 units, while the input price and quantity remain constant at $2 and 5 units. That is, suppose productivity rises from 2 ($=10/5$) to 4 ($=20/5$). Because the total cost of the inputs stays at $10 ($=\$2 \times 5$ units of input), the per unit cost of the output falls from $1 to $.50 ($=\$10$ of input cost/20 units of output).

By reducing per unit production costs, an increase in productivity will shift the aggregate supply curve rightward; conversely, a decline in productivity will increase per unit production costs and shift the aggregate supply curve leftward.

We will discover in Chapter 19 that productivity growth is a major factor explaining the secular expansion of aggregate supply in the United States and the corresponding growth of real domestic output. The use of more machinery and equipment per worker, improved production technology, a better-educated and trained labor force, and improved forms of business enterprises have interacted to raise productivity, all else being equal, and increase aggregate supply.

Legal-Institutional Environment   Changes in the legal-institutional setting in which businesses collectively operate may alter per units costs of output and shift the aggregate supply curve. Two categories of changes of this type are (1) changes in taxes and subsidies, and (2) changes in the extent of regulation.

Business Taxes and Subsidies   Higher business taxes, such as sales, excise, and social security taxes, increase per unit costs and reduce aggregate supply in much the same way as a wage increase. Example: An increase in the social security taxes paid by businesses will increase production costs and reduce aggregate supply. Similarly, a business subsidy—a payment or tax break by government to firms—reduces production costs and increases aggregate supply. Example: During the 1970s, the government subsidized producers of energy from alternative sources such as wind, oil shale, and solar power. The purpose was to reduce production costs and encourage development of energy sources which might substitute for oil and natural gas. To the extent that these subsidies were successful, the aggregate supply curve moved rightward.

Government Regulation It is usually costly for businesses to comply with government regulations. Hence, regulation increases per unit production costs and shifts the aggregate supply curve leftward. "Supply-side" proponents of deregulation of the economy have argued forcefully that, by increasing efficiency and reducing paperwork associated with complex regulations, deregulation will reduce per unit costs. In this way, the aggregate supply curve purportedly will shift rightward. Conversely, increases in regulation raise production costs and reduce aggregate supply.

QUICK REVIEW 9-2

◆ *The aggregate supply curve has three distinct ranges: the horizontal Keynesian range, the upsloping intermediate range, and the vertical classical range.*

◆ *In the intermediate range, per unit production costs and therefore the price level rise as output expands toward its potential.*

◆ *By altering per unit production costs independent of changes in the level of output, changes in one or more of the determinants of aggregate supply (Table 9-2) shift the location of the aggregate supply curve.*

◆ *An increase in aggregate supply is shown as a rightward shift of the aggregate supply curve; a decrease by a leftward shift of the curve.*

EQUILIBRIUM: REAL OUTPUT AND THE PRICE LEVEL

We found in Chapter 4 that the intersection of the demand for and supply of a particular product will determine the equilibrium price and output of that good. Similarly, as we see in Figure 9-5a and b (Key Graph) the intersection of the aggregate demand and aggregate supply curves determines the **equilibrium price level** and **equilibrium real domestic output.**

In Figure 9-5a note where aggregate demand crosses aggregate supply in its intermediate range. We find that the equilibrium price level and level of real domestic output are P_e and Q_e, respectively. To illustrate why P_e is the equilibrium price and Q_e is the equilibrium level of real domestic output, suppose that the price level were P_1 rather than P_e. We observe from the aggregate supply curve that price level P_1 would entice businesses to produce at most real output level Q_1. How much real output would domestic consumers, businesses, government, and foreign buyers wish to purchase at P_1? We see from the aggregate demand curve that the answer is Q_2. Competition among buyers to purchase the available real output of Q_1 will drive up the price level to P_e. As arrows in Figure 9-5a indicate, the rise in the price level from P_1 to P_e encourages *producers* to increase their real output from Q_1 to Q_e and simultaneously causes *buyers* to scale back their desired level of purchases from Q_2 to Q_e. When equality occurs between the amount of real domestic output produced and the amount purchased, as it does at P_e, the economy has achieved equilibrium.

In Figure 9-5b aggregate demand intersects aggregate supply in the Keynesian range where aggregate supply is perfectly horizontal. In this particular case the price level does *not* play a role in bringing about the equilibrium level of real domestic output. To understand why, first observe that the equilibrium price and real output levels in Figure 9-5b are P_e and Q_e. If the business sector had produced a larger domestic output, such as Q_2, it could not dispose of that output. Aggregate demand would be insufficient to take the domestic output off the market. Faced with unwanted inventories of goods, businesses would reduce their production to the equilibrium level of Q_e—shown by the leftward pointing arrow—and the market would clear. Conversely, if firms had only produced domestic output of Q_1, businesses would find that their inventories of goods would quickly diminish because sales of output would exceed production. Businesses would react by increasing production and domestic output would rise to equilibrium as shown by the rightward pointing arrow.

CHANGES IN EQUILIBRIUM

Now we will shift the aggregate demand and aggregate supply curves and observe the effects on real domestic output (and therefore on employment) and the price level.

KEY GRAPH

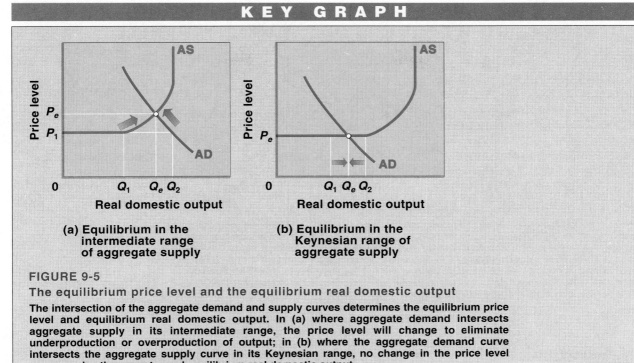

(a) Equilibrium in the intermediate range of aggregate supply

(b) Equilibrium in the Keynesian range of aggregate supply

FIGURE 9-5

The equilibrium price level and the equilibrium real domestic output

The intersection of the aggregate demand and supply curves determines the equilibrium price level and equilibrium real domestic output. In (a) where aggregate demand intersects aggregate supply in its intermediate range, the price level will change to eliminate underproduction or overproduction of output; in (b) where the aggregate demand curve intersects the aggregate supply curve in its Keynesian range, no change in the price level accompanies the move toward equilibrium real domestic output.

Shifting Aggregate Demand

Suppose households and businesses decide to increase their spending, thereby shifting the aggregate demand curve to the right. Our list of determinants of aggregate demand (Table 9-1) provides several possible reasons for this decision. Perhaps consumers become more optimistic in their expectations about future economic conditions. These favorable expectations might stem from new American technological advances which promise to increase the competitiveness of our products in both domestic and world markets and therefore to increase future real income. As a result, consumers would consume more (save less) of their current incomes. Similarly, firms anticipate that future business conditions will enhance profits from current investments in new capital. They increase their investment spending to enlarge their productive capacities. As shown in Figure 9-6, the precise effects of an *increase* in aggregate demand depend on whether the economy is currently in the Keynesian,

intermediate, or classical range of the aggregate supply curve.

In the Keynesian range of Figure 9-6a, where there is high unemployment and much unused production capacity, the effect of an increase in aggregate demand (AD_1 to AD_2) brings about a large increase in real domestic output (Q_1 to Q_2) and employment with no increase in the price level (P_1). In the classical range of Figure 9-6b, where labor and capital are fully employed, an increase in aggregate demand (AD_5 to AD_6) would affect the price level only, increasing it from P_5 to P_6. Real domestic output will remain at the full-employment level Q_f. In the intermediate range of Figure 9-6c an increase in aggregate demand (AD_3 to AD_4) will raise both real domestic output (Q_3 to Q_4) *and* the price level (P_3 to P_4).

The price level increases associated with aggregate demand increases in both the classical and intermediate ranges of the aggregate supply curve constitute **demand-pull inflation** because shifts in aggregate demand are pulling up the price level.

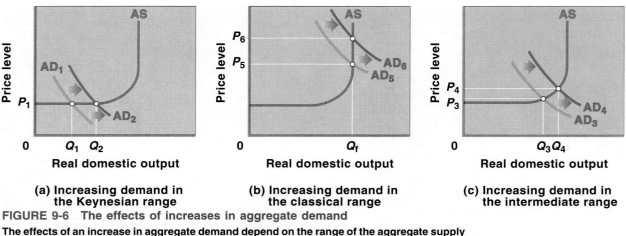

FIGURE 9-6   The effects of increases in aggregate demand

The effects of an increase in aggregate demand depend on the range of the aggregate supply curve in which it occurs. (a) An increase in aggregate demand in the Keynesian (horizontal) range will increase real domestic output, but leave the price level unaffected. (b) In the classical (vertical) range an increase in aggregate demand will increase the price level, but real domestic output cannot increase beyond the full-employment level. (c) An increase in demand in the intermediate range will increase both real domestic output and the level of prices. The increases in aggregate demand shown in (b) and (c) depict demand-pull inflation.

A Ratchet Effect?

What of *decreases* in aggregate demand? Our model predicts that in the Keynesian range real domestic output will fall and the price level will remain unchanged. In the classical range prices fall and real output remains at the full-employment level. In the intermediate range the model suggests that both real domestic output and the price level will diminish.

But an important complicating factor raises serious doubts about the predicted effects of declines in aggregate demand in the classical and intermediate ranges. The reverse movements of aggregate demand —from AD_6 to AD_5 in Figure 9-6b and from AD_4 to AD_3 in Figure 9-6c—may *not* restore the initial equilibrium positions, at least in the short term. The complication is that many prices—both of products and resources—are "sticky" or inflexible in a downward direction. What goes up in economics need not come down—at least not down to its original level. Hence, some economists envision a **ratchet effect** at work (a ratchet is a mechanism which cranks a wheel forward but not backward).

Graphical Depiction   The workings of the ratchet effect are shown in Figure 9-7. If aggregate demand increases from AD_1 to AD_2, the economy moves from the $P_1 Q_1$ equilibrium at *a* in the Keynesian range to the

new $P_2 Q_f$ equilibrium at *b* in the classical range. But while prices readily move up, they do not easily come down, at least not in the short term. Thus if aggregate demand should reverse itself and decrease from AD_2 to AD_1, the economy will *not* return to the original equilibrium position at *a*. Rather, the new, higher price level of P_2 will persist—prices have been ratcheted up from P_1 to P_2—and the decline in aggregate demand will therefore move the economy to equilibrium at *c*. The price level remains at P_2 and real domestic output has fallen all the way to Q_2.

Stated differently, the initial increase in aggregate demand and the downward inflexibility of prices have ratcheted the Keynesian range of the aggregate supply curve up from the P_1 to the P_2 price level. The original aggregate supply curve was $P_1 ab$AS; the new aggregate supply curve is $P_2 c$AS. There is an asymmetry in the aggregate supply schedule in that its horizontal range shifts upward readily and quite rapidly when aggregate demand is expanding, but shifts downward slowly or not at all when aggregate demand declines.

Causes   The reasons for downward price inflexibility are complex.

1   Wages—which typically constitute 75 percent or more of a firm's total costs—often are inflexible downward, at least temporarily. Given this inflexibility, it is difficult for firms to reduce their prices and remain

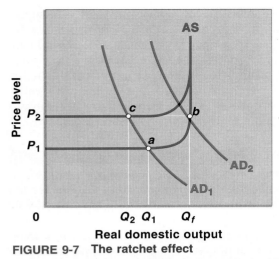

FIGURE 9-7   The ratchet effect

An increase in aggregate demand from AD_1 to AD_2 will move the equilibrium position from *a* to *b* with real domestic output rising from Q_1 to Q_f and the price level from P_1 to P_2. But if prices are inflexible downward, then a decline in aggregate demand from AD_2 to AD_1 will not return the economy to its original equilibrium at *a*. Rather, the new equilibrium will be at *c* with the price level remaining at P_2 and output falling below the original level to Q_2. The ratchet effect means that the aggregate supply curve has changed from P_1abAS to P_2cAS.

profitable. But why are wages inflexible? One reason is that part of the labor force works under contracts prohibiting wage cuts for the duration of the contract. It is not uncommon for collective bargaining agreements in major industries to run for three years. Similarly, wages and salaries of nonunion workers are usually adjusted once a year, rather than quarterly or monthly.

2   Wage inflexibility is reinforced because employers may *not* want to reduce wage rates. The reasons are at least twofold. On the one hand, lower wages may adversely affect worker morale and labor productivity (output per worker). While lower wages lower labor cost per unit of output, lower worker productivity increases unit labor costs. An employer might rightly fear that the latter might more than counterbalance the former so that a lower wage rate increases, rather than reduces, labor cost per unit of production.

3   Furthermore, most employers have an "investment" in the training and experience of their present labor forces. If they cut wages in the face of a decline in aggregate demand, they could expect to lose workers more or less randomly—both some highly trained and some relatively unskilled workers could be expected to quit. When highly trained workers find jobs with other firms, the present employer forgoes any chance of getting a return on the investment made in their training. A better option might be to maintain wages and lay off workers on the basis of seniority. Generally, workers with less seniority who are laid off will also be the less skilled workers in whom the employer's training investment is least.

4   Note also that the minimum wage imposes a legal floor under the wages of the least skilled workers. The important point is that, if production costs are downwardly inflexible, so too will be product prices.

5   Another reason for the downward stickiness of prices stems from the fact that in many industries firms have sufficient monopolistic power to resist price cuts for a time when demand declines. A glance back at Figure 8-3 may be helpful. Despite the catastrophic decline in aggregate demand that occurred between 1929 and 1933, firms in the agricultural implements, motor vehicle, cement, iron and steel, and similar industries had a remarkable capacity to resist price cuts, accepting large declines in production and employment as an alternative.

Controversy   Not all economists are persuaded that the ratchet effect remains relevant today. These critics point to declining power of unions in the United States and large wage cuts in several basic industries following the 1981–1982 recession as evidence of increased downward wage flexibility. They also note that growing foreign competition has undermined monopoly power and the accompanying ability of firms to resist price cuts in the face of falling demand. But defenders of the ratchet effect question whether these recent institutional changes have altered the basic historical pattern. Since 1950 the price level has fallen in only a single year—1955. Meanwhile, the economy has experienced eight recessions during this period (Table 8-1).

Shifting Aggregate Supply

Two hypothetical situations will help illustrate the effects of a change in aggregate supply on the equilibrium price level and level of real domestic output.

First, suppose that foreign suppliers impose dramatic increases in the prices of our imported oil as OPEC did in 1973–1974 and again in 1979–1980. The higher energy prices permeate the world economy, driving up the cost of producing and distributing virtually every domestically produced product and imported resource. Thus, domestic per unit costs of production rise at each output level. The American aggregate supply curve therefore shifts leftward, as

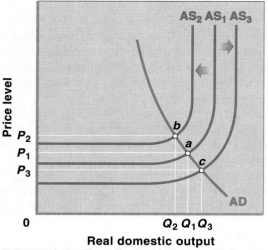

FIGURE 9-8 The effects of changes in aggregate supply

A leftward shift in aggregate supply from AS_1 to AS_2 will cause cost-push inflation in that the price level increases from P_1 to P_2. Real domestic output will fall from Q_1 to Q_2. A rightward shift of aggregate supply from AS_1 to AS_3 will increase the real domestic output from Q_1 to Q_3 and reduce the price level from P_1 to P_3.

Observe that the shift in the aggregate supply curve involves a change in the full-employment level of real domestic output; in particular, a rightward shift of the curve signifies economic growth and indicates that the economy's potential output has increased. In terms of Chapter 2, the economy's production possibilities curve has moved to the right, reflected in the rightward shift of the aggregate supply curve in Figure 9-8.

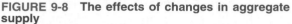

QUICK REVIEW 9-3

◗   **The equilibrium price level and amount of real domestic output are determined at the intersection of the aggregate demand and aggregate supply curves.**

◗   **Increases in aggregate demand in the upsloping and vertical ranges of aggregate supply cause demand-pull inflation.**

◗   **The price level is "sticky" or inflexible in a downward direction in the short run.**

◗   **Decreases in aggregate supply cause cost-push inflation.**

◗   **Increases in aggregate supply expand real domestic output; they result in economic growth.**

shown by the movement from AS_1 to AS_2 in Figure 9-8. The price level increase occurring here is clearly **cost-push inflation** (Chapter 8).

Note that, given aggregate demand, the effects of a leftward shift in aggregate supply are doubly bad. When aggregate supply shifts from AS_1 to AS_2, real domestic output will decline from Q_1 to Q_2 *and* the price level will rise from P_1 to P_2. That is, the economy will move from *a* to *b*. Falling employment and inflation will occur.

Alternatively, suppose that one of the factors in Table 9-2 changes so that aggregate supply increases. Specifically, suppose the economy experiences a sharp increase in productivity which is not matched by increases in higher paychecks for workers. Or, perhaps a liberalization of immigration laws increases the supply of labor and pulls wage rates down. Or, finally, maybe lower business tax rates reduce per unit costs (a tax is a cost as viewed by a business), shifting the aggregate supply curve rightward. In Figure 9-8 the shift in the aggregate supply from AS_1 to AS_3 indicates an increase in real output from Q_1 to Q_3 and assuming downward price and wage flexibility, a simultaneous decline in the price level from P_1 to P_3. In brief, the economy moves from *a* to *c*.

UNANSWERED QUESTIONS: LOOKING AHEAD

Our aggregate demand and aggregate supply model is a useful framework for developing a more detailed and comprehensive understanding of macroeconomics. However, this model raises many questions. Are there features of the economy which ensure that the aggregate demand curve always intersects the aggregate supply curve in the classical range? That is, are there automatic mechanisms which ensure full employment of the nation's resources (Chapter 10)? What economic principles underlie the less-than-full-employment equilibrium implied by an intersection of aggregate demand and aggregate supply in the Keynesian and intermediate ranges of aggregate supply (Chapters 10 and 11)? What, if anything, can the government do to keep aggregate demand from periodically declining and producing widespread unemployment (Chapter 12)?

Still other questions are: What role do money, the banking system, and the Federal Reserve play in determining the location of the aggregate demand curve and the macroeconomic health of the economy (Chapters 13 through 15)? Have government policies to manage aggregate demand contributed to macro-

LAST WORD

JOHN MAYNARD KEYNES (1883–1946)

The English economist John Maynard Keynes is regarded as the originator of modern macroeconomics.

In 1935 George Bernard Shaw received a letter from John Maynard Keynes in which Keynes asserted, "I believe myself to be writing a book on economic theory which will largely revolutionize . . . the way the world thinks about economic problems." And, in fact, Keynes' *The General Theory of Employment, Interest, and Money* (1936) did revolutionize economic analysis and established Keynes as one of the most brilliant and influential economists of all time.

The son of an eminent English economist, Keynes was educated at Eton and Cambridge. While his early interests were in mathematics and probability theory, Keynes ultimately turned to economics.

Keynes was far more than an economist: He was an incredibly active, many-sided man who also played such diverse roles as principal representative of the Treasury at the World War I Paris Peace Conference, deputy for the Chancellor of the Exchequer, a director of the Bank of England, trustee of the National Gallery, chairman of the Council for the Encouragement of Music and the Arts, bursar of King's College, Cambridge, editor of the *Economic Journal*, chairman of the *Nation* and later the *New Statesman* magazines, and chairman of the National Mutual Life Assurance Society. He also ran an investment company, organized the Camargo Ballet (his wife, Lydia Lopokova, was a renowned star of the Russian Imperial Ballet), and built (profitably) the Arts Theatre at Cambridge.*

In addition, Keynes found time to amass a $2 million personal fortune by speculating in stocks, international currencies, and commodities. He was also a

leading figure in the "Bloomsbury group," an *avant-garde* group of intellectual luminaries who greatly influenced the artistic and literary standards of England.

Most importantly, Keynes was a prolific scholar. His books encompassed such widely ranging topics as probability theory, monetary economics, and the economic consequences of the World War I peace treaty. His *magnum opus*, however, was the *General Theory*, which has been described by John Kenneth Galbraith as "a work of profound obscurity, badly written and prematurely published." Yet the *General Theory* attacked the classical economists' contention that recession will automatically cure itself. Keynes' analysis suggested that recession could easily spiral downward into a depression. Keynes claimed that modern capitalism contained no automatic mechanism which would propel the economy back toward full employment. The economy might languish for many years in depression. Indeed, the massive unemployment of the worldwide depression of the 1930s seemed to provide sufficient evidence that Keynes was right. His basic policy recommendation—a startling one in view of the balanced-budget sentiment at the time—was for government in these circumstances to increase its spending to induce more production and put the unemployed back to work.

*E. Ray Canterbery, *The Making of Economics*, 3d ed. (Belmont, Calif.: Wadsworth Publishing Company, 1987), p. 126.

---

economic stability, or, conversely, have they produced the very instability they are designed to counter (Chapter 16)? What set of aggregate demand and supply circumstances explains periods of "stagflation"—simultaneous rising inflation and recession (Chapter 17)? Where do Federal budget deficits and the national debt fit into this overall framework (Chapter 18)? And, finally, what are the facts and issues of economic growth—rises of real domestic output and income—and what policies might generate faster growth (Chapter 19)?

Our answers to these and a host of related questions will form the heart of our ensuing study of macroeconomics.

CHAPTER SUMMARY

1 For purposes of analysis we consolidate—or aggregate—the outcomes from the enormous number of individual product markets into a composite market in which key variables are the price level and the level of real domestic output. This is accomplished through an aggregate demand–aggregate supply model of the economy.

2 The aggregate demand curve shows the level of real domestic output which the economy will purchase at each possible price level.

3 The rationale for the downsloping aggregate demand curve is based on the wealth or real balances effect, the interest-rate effect, and the foreign purchases effect. The wealth or real balances effect indicates that inflation will reduce the real value or purchasing power of fixed-value financial assets held by households, causing them to retrench on their consumer spending. The interest-rate effect indicates that, given the supply of money, a higher price level will increase the demand for money, thereby increasing the interest rate and reducing consumption and investment purchases which are interest-rate sensitive. The foreign purchases effect suggests that a change in the United States' price level relative to other countries will change the net exports component of American aggregate demand in the opposite direction.

4 The determinants of aggregate demand are spending by domestic consumers, businesses, government, and foreign buyers. Changes in the factors listed in Table 9-1 cause changes in spending by these groups and shift the aggregate demand curve.

5 The aggregate supply curve shows the levels of real domestic output which will be produced at various possible price levels.

6 The shape of the aggregate supply curve depends on what happens to per unit production costs—and therefore to the prices which businesses must receive to cover costs and make a profit—as real domestic output expands. The Keynesian range of the curve is horizontal because, with substantial unemployment, production can be increased without per unit cost or price increases. In the intermediate range, per unit costs increase as production bottlenecks appear and less efficient equipment and workers are employed. Prices must therefore rise as real domestic output is expanded. The classical range coincides with full employment; real domestic output is at a maximum and cannot be increased, but the price level will rise in response to an increase in aggregate demand.

7 As indicated in Table 9-2, the determinants of aggregate supply are input prices, productivity, and the legal-institutional environment. All else being equal, a change in one of these factors will change per unit production costs at each level of output and therefore alter the location of the aggregate supply curve.

8 The intersection of the aggregate demand and aggregate supply curves determines the equilibrium price level and real domestic output.

9 Given aggregate supply, increases in aggregate demand will **a** increase real domestic output and employment but not alter the price level in the Keynesian range; **b** increase both real domestic output and the price level in the intermediate range; and **c** increase the price level but not change real domestic output in the classical range.

10 The ratchet effect is at work when prices are flexible upward, but relatively inflexible downward. An increase in aggregate demand will raise the price level, but in the short term, prices cannot be expected to fall when demand decreases.

TERMS AND CONCEPTS

aggregation	foreign purchases effect	Keynesian, classical,	equilibrium price level
aggregates	determinants of	and intermediate	equilibrium real
aggregate demand	aggregate demand	ranges of the	domestic output
wealth or real balances	aggregate supply	aggregate supply	demand-pull inflation
effect	determinants of	curve	ratchet effect
interest-rate effect	aggregate supply	productivity	cost-push inflation

QUESTIONS AND STUDY SUGGESTIONS

1 Why is the aggregate demand curve downsloping? Specify how your explanation differs from the rationale behind the downsloping demand curve for a single product.

2 Explain the shape of the aggregate supply curve, accounting for the differences between the Keynesian, intermediate, and classical ranges of the curve.

3 Suppose that the aggregate demand and supply schedules for a hypothetical economy are as shown below:

Amount of real domestic output demanded, billions	Price level (price index)	Amount of real domestic output supplied, billions
$100	300	$400
200	250	400
300	200	300
400	150	200
500	150	100

a   Use these sets of data to graph the aggregate demand and supply curves. What will be the equilibrium price level and level of real domestic output in this hypothetical economy? Is the equilibrium level of real domestic output also the full-employment level of real domestic output? Explain.

b   Why will a price level of 150 *not* be an equilibrium price level in this economy? Why *not* 250?

c   Suppose that buyers desire to purchase $200 billion of extra real domestic output at each price level. What factors might cause this change in aggregate demand? What is the new equilibrium price level and level of real domestic output? Over what range of the aggregate supply curve—Keynesian, intermediate, or classical—has equilibrium changed?

4 Suppose that the hypothetical economy in question 3 had the following relationship between its real domestic output and the input quantities necessary for producing that level of output:

Input quantity	Real domestic output
150.0	400
112.5	300
75.0	200

a   What is the level of productivity in this economy?
b   What is the per unit cost of production if the price of each input is $2?
c   Assume that the input price increases from $2 to $3 with no accompanying change in productivity. What is the new per unit cost of production? In what direction would the $1 increase in input price push the aggregate supply curve? What effect would this shift in aggregate supply have on the price level and the level of real domestic output?
d   Suppose that the increase in input price had *not* occurred but instead that productivity had increased by 100 percent. What would be the new per unit cost of production? What effect would this change in per unit production cost have on the aggregate supply curve? What effect would this shift in aggregate supply have on the price level and the level of real domestic output?

5 Will an increase in the American price level relative to price levels in other nations shift our aggregate demand curve? If so, in what direction? Explain. Will a decline in the dollar price of foreign currencies shift the American aggregate supply curve rightward or simply move the economy along an existing aggregate supply curve? Explain.

6 What effects might each of the following have on aggregate demand or aggregate supply? In each case use a diagram to show the expected effects on the equilibrium price level and level of real domestic output. Assume that all other things remain constant.

a   A widespread fear of depression on the part of consumers
b   A large purchase of wheat by Russia
c   A 5-cent increase in the excise tax on gasoline
d   A reduction in interest rates at each price level
e   A cut in Federal spending for higher education
f   The expectation of a rapid rise in the price level
g   The complete disintegration of OPEC, causing oil prices to fall by one-half
h   A 10 percent reduction in personal income tax rates
i   An increase in labor productivity
j   A 12 percent increase in nominal wages
k   Depreciation in the international value of the dollar
l   A sharp decline in the national incomes of our western European trading partners
m   A decline in the percentage of the American labor force which is unionized

7 What is the relationship between the production possibilities curve discussed in Chapter 2 and the aggregate supply curve discussed in this chapter?

8 Other things being equal, what effect will each of the following have on the equilibrium price level and level of real domestic output:

a   An increase in aggregate demand in the classical range of aggregate supply
b   An increase in aggregate supply (assume prices and wages are flexible)
c   An equal increase in both aggregate demand and aggregate supply
d   A reduction in aggregate demand in the Keynesian range of aggregate supply
e   An increase in aggregate demand and a decrease in aggregate supply
f   A decrease in aggregate demand in the intermediate range of aggregate supply (assume prices and wages are inflexible downward)

9 In the accompanying diagram assume that the aggregate demand curve shifts from AD_1 in year 1 to AD_2 in year 2, only to fall back to AD_1 in year 3. Locate the new year 3 equilibrium position on the assumption that prices and wages are **a** completely flexible and **b** completely rigid downward. Which of the two equilibrium positions is more desirable? Which is more realistic? Explain why the price level might be ratcheted upward when aggregate demand increases.

10 "Unemployment can be caused by a leftward shift of aggregate demand or a leftward shift of aggregate supply." Do you agree? Explain. In each case, specify price level effects.

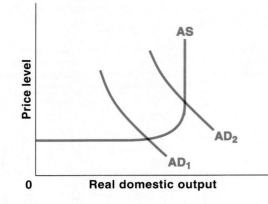

CHAPTER 10

Classical and Keynesian Theories of Employment

In preceding chapters we gained some familiarity with macroeconomic theory and problems through the concepts of aggregate demand and supply. In this and the next chapter we will expand our understanding of macroeconomic principles.

First, we will contrast the extreme forms of classical and Keynesian employment theories and thus clarify Chapter 9's designations of the classical (vertical) and Keynesian (horizontal) ranges of the aggregate supply curve. The comparison is a vivid one. Classical economics suggests that full employment is the norm of a market economy and that a laissez faire policy is best. Keynesian economics holds that unemployment is characteristic of laissez faire capitalism, and activist government policies are required to avoid the wastes of idle resources. We have seen that the market system can provide for an efficient allocation of resources (Chapter 5). The question now is: Can it also achieve and maintain full employment of available resources?

After contrasting these two widely divergent views, our second objective will be to examine the tools of Keynesian employment theory in greater detail. The Keynesian view has dominated macroeconomics since the Great Depression and, with many modifications and embellishments, is the core of modern mainstream macroeconomics. In Chapter 11 we use the tools developed in this chapter to demonstrate how the equilibrium levels of real domestic output and employment are determined in the Keynesian model. This model also explains a curious phenomenon: An initial change in spending ultimately produces a multiple change in national income and domestic output. At the end of Chapter 11, we link the Keynesian analysis directly back to the aggregate demand and aggregate supply model introduced in Chapter 9. Therefore, in subsequent chapters we can bring each of these related perspectives to bear in examining government stabilization policies.

SIMPLIFICATIONS

Four simplifying assumptions will help us achieve our objectives:

1 Although our analysis eventually will involve an "open economy" in which there are international trade transactions, initially we assume a "closed economy." Our discussion in this chapter will deal with the domestic economy, deferring complications arising from exports and imports until midway through Chapter 11.

2 Government will be ignored until Chapter 12, thereby permitting us in Chapters 10 and 11 to determine whether or not laissez faire capitalism can achieve and maintain full employment.

3 Although saving actually occurs in both the business and household sectors of the economy, we will for convenience speak as if all saving were personal saving.

4 For simplicity we will assume that depreciation and *net* American income earned abroad are zero.

Two implications of these assumptions are noteworthy: First, we found in Chapter 7 that there are four components of aggregate spending: consumption, investment, government purchases, and net exports. Our assumptions 1 and 2 mean that, for the moment, we are concerned only with consumption and investment.

Second, assumptions 2 through 4 permit us to treat gross domestic product (GDP), national income (NI), personal income (PI), and disposable income (DI) as being equal. All the items which in practice distinguish them from one another are due to depreciation, net American income earned abroad, government (taxes and transfer payments), and business saving (see Table 7-5). This means if $500 billion worth of goods and services is produced as GDP, exactly $500 billion worth of DI is received by households to split between consumption and saving.

THE CLASSICAL THEORY OF EMPLOYMENT

Until the Great Depression of the 1930s, many prominent economists of the nineteenth and early twentieth centuries—now called classical economists[1]—felt that the market system would ensure full employment of the economy's resources. It was acknowledged that

[1]Most notable among this group of classical economists are David Ricardo, John Stuart Mill, F. Y. Edgeworth, Alfred Marshall, and A. C. Pigou.

now and then abnormal circumstances such as wars, political upheavals, droughts, speculative crises, and gold rushes would arise to push the economy from the path of full employment (see Figure 8-1). But when these deviations occurred, automatic adjustments within the market system would soon restore the economy to the full-employment level of output.

Classical employment theory is not simply an artifact of economic thought. A few modern economists have reformulated, revitalized, and extended the work of these nineteenth- and twentieth-century economists to generate a "new" classical economics. Indeed, Chapter 16's discussions of monetarism and rational expectations theory explain currently held views of macroeconomics which have strong intellectual roots in classical theory.

The **classical theory of employment** was grounded on two basic concepts:

1 Underspending—that is, a level of spending insufficient to purchase a full-employment output—was most unlikely to occur.

2 Even if a deficiency of total spending were to occur, price-wage (including interest-rate) adjustments would result quickly and ensure that the decline in total spending would *not* entail declines in real output, employment, and real incomes.

Say's Law

Classical theory's denial of the possibility of underspending was based in part on Say's law. **Say's law** is the disarming notion that the very act of producing goods generates an amount of income exactly equal to the value of the goods produced. The production of any output would automatically provide the income needed to take that output off the market. *Supply creates its own demand.*[2]

The essence of Say's law can be understood most easily in terms of a barter economy. A shoemaker, for example, produces or *supplies* shoes as a means of buying or *demanding* the shirts and stockings produced by other craftsmen. The shoemaker's supply of shoes *is* his demand for other goods. And so it allegedly is for other producers and for the entire economy: Demand must be the same as supply! In fact, the circular flow model of the economy and national income accounting both suggest something of this sort. Income generated from the production of any level of total output would, *when spent,* be just sufficient to provide a matching total demand. Assuming that the composition of output is in

[2]Attributed to the nineteenth-century French economist J. B. Say.

accord with consumer preferences, all markets would be cleared of their outputs. It would seem that all business owners need do to sell a full-employment output is to produce that output; Say's law guarantees there will be sufficient consumption spending for its successful disposal.

Saving: A Complicating Factor

However, there is one obvious omission in this simple application of Say's law. Although it is an accepted truism that output gives rise to an identical amount of nominal income (Chapter 7), there is no guarantee that the recipients of this income will spend it all. Some income might be saved (not spent) and therefore not reflected in product demand. Saving would constitute a break, or "leakage," in the income-expenditure flows and would undermine the effective operation of Say's law. Saving is a withdrawal of funds from the income stream which will cause consumption expenditures to fall short of total output. If households saved part of their incomes, supply would not create its own demand. Saving would cause a deficiency of consumption. The consequence would be unsold goods, cutbacks in production, unemployment, and falling incomes.

Saving, Investment, and the Interest Rate

But the classical economists argued that saving would not really result in a deficiency of total demand, because every dollar saved would be invested by businesses. Investment would occur to compensate for any deficiency of consumer spending; investment would fill any consumption "gap" caused by saving. Business firms, after all, do not plan to sell their entire output to consumers, but rather produce much of total output in the form of capital goods for sale to one another. Investment spending by businesses is a supplement or an addition to the income-expenditure stream which may fill any consumption gap arising from saving. Thus, if businesses as a group intend to invest as much as households want to save, Say's law will hold and the levels of domestic output and employment will remain constant. Whether or not the economy could achieve and sustain a level of spending sufficient to provide a full-employment level of output and income therefore would depend on whether businesses were willing to invest enough to offset the amount households want to save.

Classical economists argued that capitalism contained a very special market—the *money market*—which would guarantee an equality of saving and investment plans and therefore full employment. That is,

the money market—and, more specifically, the *interest rate* (the price paid for the use of money)—would ensure that dollars which leaked from the income-expenditure stream as saving would automatically reappear as dollars spent on investment goods.

The rationale underlying the saving and investment equating adjustments of the interest rate was simple and quite plausible. The classical economists contended that, other things being equal, households normally prefer to consume rather than save. Consumption of goods and services satisfies human wants; idle dollars do not. Hence, it was reasoned that consumers would save only if someone would pay them a rate of interest as a reward for their thriftiness. The greater the interest rate, the more dollars saved; that is, the saving (supply-of-dollars) curve of households would be upsloping, as shown by *S* in Figure 10-1a.

And who would pay for the use of saving? None other than investors—business owners who seek (demand) money capital to replace and enlarge their plants and stocks of capital equipment. Because the interest rate is a cost to borrowing businesses, they will be more willing to borrow and invest at low than at high interest rates. Thus, the investment (demand-for-dollars) curve of businesses is downsloping, as shown by *I* in Figure 10-1a.

Classical economists concluded that the money market, in which savers supply dollars and investors demand dollars, would establish an equilibrium price for the use of money—an equilibrium interest rate—at which the quantity of dollars saved (supplied) would equal the number of dollars invested (demanded).

In terms of Figure 10-1a, the interest rate would be r and the amounts of saving and investment both would be q. Saving, said the classicists, does not really constitute a break in the income-expenditure stream or a fatal flaw in Say's law, because the interest rate will cause every dollar saved to get into the hands of investors and be spent on capital equipment. Therefore, an increase in thriftiness is no cause for social concern; it simply shifts the supply-of-saving curve to the right, from S to S' in Figure 10-1b. Although saving will momentarily exceed investment and perhaps cause some temporary unemployment, the surplus of saving will drive the interest rate down to a new and lower equilibrium level, r'. And this lower interest rate will expand the volume of investment spending until it again equals the amount of saving at q', thereby preserving full employment.

In short, changes in the interest rate would guarantee the operation of Say's law even in an economy in which substantial saving occurs. As the classical econ-

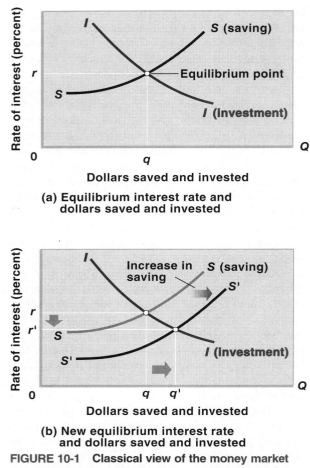

(a) Equilibrium interest rate and dollars saved and invested

(b) New equilibrium interest rate and dollars saved and invested

FIGURE 10-1   Classical view of the money market
The classical economists believed that the saving plans of households would be reflected in a supply-of-dollars curve *S* and the investment plans of businesses in a demand-for-dollars curve *I* in the money market. In (a) the equilibrium interest rate *r*, the price paid for the use of money, would equate the amounts households and businesses planned to save and invest, thereby guaranteeing a full-employment level of spending. In (b) an increase in desired saving at each interest rate results in a rightward shift of the supply-of-dollars curve to *S'*. The equilibrium interest rate therefore falls to *r'* and the new equilibrium amounts of dollars saved and invested increases to *q'*. At *q'* the amounts of saving and investment are again equal and the full-employment level of spending is again assured.

omists saw it, the economy was like a gigantic bathtub in which the volume of water measured the levels of output and employment. Any leakage down the drain of saving would be returned to the tub through the spigot of investment. This had to be the case, because the interest rate connected the drainpipe and the spigot!

Price-Wage Flexibility

The classical economists bolstered their conclusion that full employment is the norm of capitalism with the argument that the level of output which businesses can sell depends not only on the level of total spending but also on the level of product prices. Even if the interest rate should somehow temporarily fail to equate the amounts which households wanted to save with the investment intentions of businesses, any resulting decline in total spending would be offset by proportionate declines in the price level. That is, $40 will buy four shirts at $10, but $20 will buy the same number of shirts provided their price falls to $5. Hence, if households temporarily saved more than businesses were willing to invest, the resulting decline in total spending would not result in a prolonged decline in real output, real income, and the level of employment *if* product prices declined in proportion to the decline in expenditures.

And, according to classical economists, this is precisely what would happen. Competition among sellers would ensure price flexibility. As declines in product demand became general, competing producers would lower their prices to dispose of accumulating surpluses. The result of "excess" saving would be to lower prices; and lower prices, by increasing the real value or purchasing power of the dollar, would permit nonsavers to obtain more goods and services with their current money incomes. Saving would therefore lower prices, but not output and employment.

"But," skeptics have asked, "doesn't this ignore the resource market? Although businesses can sustain sales in the face of declining demand by accepting lower product prices, won't they find it unprofitable to do so? As product prices decline, won't resource prices—particularly wage rates—have to decline significantly so businesses can produce *profitably* at the now lower prices?" Classical economists replied that wage rates must and would decline. General declines in product demand would be mirrored in declines in the demand for labor and other resources. The immediate result would be a surplus of labor, that is, unemployment, at the wage rate prevailing prior to these declines in the demand for labor. However, though not willing to employ all workers at the original wage rates, producers would find it profitable to employ these workers at lower wage rates. The demand for labor, in other words, is downsloping; those workers unable to locate employment at the old higher wage rates could find jobs at the new lower wage rates.

Would workers be willing to accept lower wage rates? Competition among unemployed workers, according to the classical economists, would force them to do so. In competing for scarce jobs, idle workers would bid down wage rates until these rates (wage costs to employers) were so low that employers would once again find it profitable to hire all available workers. This would happen at the new lower equilibrium wage rate. The classical economists therefore concluded that *involuntary unemployment* was impossible. Anyone who was willing to work at the market-determined wage rate could readily find employment. Competition in the labor market ruled out involuntary idleness.

Classical Theory and Laissez Faire

In the classical view these market system adjustments —fluctuations in the interest rate on the one hand, and **price-wage flexibility** on the other—were fully capable of maintaining full employment in a capitalistic economy. Working together, the classical economists felt, the two adjustment mechanisms made full employment a foregone conclusion. They came to embrace capitalism as a self-regulating economy in which full employment was the norm. Capitalism was capable of "running itself." Government assistance in operating the economy was unnecessary—nay, harmful. In an economy capable of achieving both full production and full employment, governmental interference could only be a detriment to its efficient operation. The logic of the classical theory led to the conclusion that a laissez faire economic policy was desirable.

KEYNESIAN ECONOMICS

One embarrassing fact persistently denied the validity of the classical theory of employment—recurring periods of prolonged unemployment and inflation. While one might explain a minor recession, such as the brief downswings of 1924 and 1927, in terms of wars and similar external considerations, serious and prolonged downswings, such as the Great Depression of the 1930s, were not easily rationalized. There is a remarkable inconsistency between a theory which concludes that unemployment is virtually impossible and the actual occurrence of a ten-year siege of very substantial unemployment. And so various economists came to criticize both the rationale and the underlying assumptions of classical employment theory. They tried to find a better, more realistic explanation of those forces which determine the level of employment.

Finally, in 1936 the renowned English economist John Maynard Keynes, whom you met in Chapter 9's Last Word, set forth a new explanation of the level of employment in capitalistic economies. In his *General Theory of Employment, Interest, and Money*,[3] Keynes attacked the foundations of classical theory and, in doing so, touched off a major revolution in economic thinking on macroeconomic questions. Although Keynes fathered modern employment theory, many others have since refined and extended his work. In this and following chapters, we explore Keynesian employment theory, or **Keynesian economics,** as it stands today.

Keynesian employment theory contrasts sharply with the classical position. Its blunt conclusion in its extreme form is that capitalism does *not* contain any mechanisms capable of guaranteeing full employment. The economy might come to rest—that is, reach an aggregate output equilibrium—with either considerable unemployment or substantial inflation. Full employment is more of an accident than a norm. Capitalism is *not* a self-regulating system capable of perpetual prosperity; it cannot be depended on to "run itself."

Furthermore, economic fluctuations should not be associated exclusively with external forces such as wars, droughts, and similar abnormalities. Rather, the causes of unemployment and inflation lie mainly in the failure of certain fundamental economic decisions—in particular, saving and investment decisions—to be completely synchronized in a capitalistic system. In addition, product prices and wages tend to be downwardly inflexible; extended and costly periods of recession will prevail before significant declines in prices and wages occur. Internal, in addition to external, forces contribute to economic instability.

Keynesians back these sweeping contentions by rejecting the very mechanisms on which the classical position is grounded—the interest rate and price-wage adjustments.

The Unlinking of Saving and Investment Plans

Keynesian theory rejects Say's law by seriously questioning the ability of the interest rate to match the saving and investment plans of households and businesses. The fact that modern capitalism is amply

[3]New York: Harcourt, Brace & World, Inc., 1936.

endowed with an elaborate money market and a wide variety of financial institutions does not diminish this skepticism about the interest rate as a mechanism capable of connecting the saving drain and the investment spigot. Keynesians find untenable the classical contention that business firms would invest more when households increased their rates of saving. After all, does not more saving mean less consumption? Can we really expect business planners to expand their capital facilities as the markets for their products shrink? More generally, the Keynesian view holds that savers and investors formulate their saving and investment plans for different reasons which, in the case of saving, are largely unrelated to the rate of interest.

Savers and Investors are Differently Motivated

Saving decisions are motivated by diverse considerations. Some save to make large purchases which exceed any single paycheck; households save for down payments on houses and to buy automobiles or television sets. Some saving is solely for the convenience of having liquid funds readily available to take advantage of any extraordinarily good buys which may occur. Or saving may provide for future needs of individuals and their families: Households save for the future retirement of the family breadwinner or to provide a college education for their children. Saving may be a precautionary, rainy-day measure—a means of protection against such unpredictable events as prolonged illness and unemployment. Or saving may be merely a deeply ingrained habit practiced on an almost automatic basis with no specific purposes in mind. Much saving is highly institutionalized or contractual: for example, payments for life insurance and annuities or participation in a "bond-a-month" program.

The basic point is that none of these diverse motives for saving is particularly sensitive to the interest rate. In fact, Keynesians argue that one can readily pose a situation in which, contrary to the classical conception (Figure 10-1), saving is *inversely* related to the interest rate. For example, if a family seeks to provide an annual retirement income of $12,000 from saving, it will need to save $200,000 if the interest rate is 6 percent, but only $100,000 if the interest rate is 12 percent.

In the Keynesian view, the primary determinant of both saving and consumption is the level of national income.

Why do businesses purchase capital goods? The motivation for investment spending, as we will see, is complex. The interest rate—the cost of obtaining money capital to invest—*is* a consideration in formulating investment plans, but it is *not* the only factor. The rate of profit which business firms expect to realize on the investment is also a crucial determinant of the amounts they desire to invest. Furthermore, during a major recession or depression, profit expectations may be so bleak that investment will be low and possibly declining despite substantial reductions in the interest rate. Interest rate reductions may not stimulate investment spending when it is most needed.

Money Balances and Banks

Keynesian employment theory sees the classical concept of the money market (Figure 10-1) as oversimplified and therefore incorrect in another sense. Specifically, the classical money market assumes that current saving is the only source of funds for the financing of investment. Keynesian economics holds that there are two other sources of funds which can be made available in the money market: (1) the accumulated money balances—cash and checking account money—held by households, and (2) lending institutions which can add to the money supply.

Keynesian theory stipulates that the public holds money balances not merely to negotiate day-to-day transactions, but also as a form of accumulated wealth not held in savings accounts in banks. The important point here is that, by drawing down or decumulating a portion of these money balances and offering these dollars to investors, a supply of funds in excess of current saving can be made available in the money market. Similarly, as we will find in Chapter 14, when lending institutions make loans, they add to the money supply. Lending by banks and other financial institutions, therefore, is also a means of augmenting current saving as a source of funds for investment.

The consequence is that a reduction in the money balances held by households *and* bank lending can lead to an amount of investment which is in excess of current saving. This implies that Say's law is invalid and that output, employment, and the price level can fluctuate. More specifically, we will see that an excess of investment over saving results in an increase in total spending which has an expansionary effect on the economy. If the economy is initially in recession, output and employment will increase; if the economy is already at full employment, the added spending will cause demand-pull inflation.

Conversely, classical theory is incorrect in assuming that all current saving will appear in the money market. If (1) households add some of their current saving to their money balances rather than channel it into the money market, or (2) some current saving is used to retire outstanding bank loans and these funds are not loaned to someone else, then the amount of funds made available in the money market will be less than that shown by the classical saving curve in Figure 10-1. This suggests that the amount of current saving will exceed the amount invested. Again, Say's law does not hold and macroeconomic instability will result. In this case the excess of saving over investment will mean a decline in total demand which is contractionary; output and employment will tend to fall.

To summarize: *The Keynesian position is that saving and investment plans can be at odds and thereby can result in fluctuations in total output, total income, employment, and the price level.* It is largely a matter of chance that households and businesses will desire to save and invest identical amounts. Keynesian economists feel they are better plumbers than their classical predecessors by recognizing that the saving drain and the investment spigot are *not* connected.

The Discrediting of Price-Wage Flexibility

But what of the second aspect of the classical position—the contention that downward price-wage adjustments will eliminate the unemployment effects of a decline in total spending?

Existence Modern Keynesians recognize that some prices and wages are flexible downward. In the early 1980s some prices fell and large numbers of workers were forced to accept wage freezes, wage cuts, and reduced fringe benefits. Causal factors included (1) back-to-back recessions, one of which was so severe as to bring about the highest unemployment rates since the 1930s; (2) enhanced foreign competition; and (3) deregulation of the airlines and trucking industries. But Keynesians argue that wage-price flexibility does not exist to the overall degree necessary for ensuring the restoration of full employment in the face of a decline in aggregate demand. The market system of capitalism has never been perfectly competitive; it is riddled by market imperfections and circumscribed by practical and political obstacles working against downward price-wage flexibility. In terms of Chapter 9's discussion of the ratchet effect, Keynesians argue that monopolistic producers have both the ability and desire to resist falling product prices as demand declines. And in resource markets, strong labor unions are equally persistent in holding the line against wage cuts.

Union collective bargaining agreements shield wages from downward adjustment for the two- or three-year duration of these contracts. In nonunion labor markets wages usually are adjusted only once a year. Furthermore, employers are often wary of wage cuts, recognizing adverse effects on worker morale and productivity. In short, as a practical matter, downward price-wage flexibility cannot be expected to offset the unemployment effects of a decline in aggregate demand.

Usefulness Even if price-wage declines accompanied a contraction of total spending, these declines might not reduce unemployment. The volume of total money demand cannot remain constant as prices and wages decline. Lower prices and wages necessarily mean lower nominal incomes, and lower nominal incomes in turn entail further reductions in total spending. The net result is likely to be little or no change in the depressed levels of output and employment.

Keynesians point out that the classicists were tripped up in their reasoning by the fallacy of composition. Because any particular group of workers typically buys only a small amount of what it produces, the product and therefore labor demand curves of a single firm can be regarded as independent of any wage (income) changes accorded its own workers. In other words, a decline in its wage rate will move a *single firm* down its stable labor demand curve and result in more employment. But this reasoning, argue Keynesian economists, does not apply to the economy as a whole, to general wage cuts. Wages are the major source of income in the economy. Widespread wage declines will therefore result in declines in incomes and also declines in the demand for both products and the labor used in producing them. The result is that employers will hire little or no additional labor after the general wage cuts. What holds true for a single firm—a wage cut for its employees will not adversely affect labor demand—is not true for the economy as a whole—general wage cuts *will* lower money incomes, causing the demand for products and labor to decline generally.

CLASSICS AND KEYNES: AD-AS RESTATEMENT

These two views of the macroeconomic world—classical and Keynesian—can be meaningfully restated and compared in their crude or extreme forms in terms of Chapter 9's aggregate demand and aggregate supply curves.

Classical View

The classical view is that the aggregate supply curve is vertical and therefore exclusively determines the level of real domestic output. On the other hand, the downsloping aggregate demand curve is stable and solely establishes the price level.

Vertical Aggregate Supply Curve The classical position sees the aggregate supply curve as a vertical line as shown in Figure 10-2a. This is why we referred to the vertical portion of our aggregate supply curve in Chapter 9 as the "classical range." The vertical aggregate supply curve, remember, is located where the natural or full-employment rate of unemployment is being realized. According to the classical economists, the economy will operate at its full-employment level of output, Q_f, for the reasons previously discussed: Say's law, flexible interest rates, and responsive prices and wages. We stress that classical economists believe that Q_f does *not* change in response to changes in the price level. Observe, for example, that as the price level falls in Figure 10-2a from P_1 to P_2, real domestic output remains firmly anchored at Q_f.

But, you might argue, this stability of output seems at odds with Chapter 4's upsloping supply curves for individual products. There we found that lower prices would make production less profitable and cause producers to offer *less* output and presumably employ *fewer* workers. The classical response to your argument is that input costs would fall along with product prices to leave *real* profits unchanged and therefore output unchanged.

Consider a simplified illustration. Suppose we have a one-firm economy in which the firm's owner must receive a *real* profit of $20 to be induced to produce the full-employment output of, say, 100 units. Recall from Chapter 8 that what ultimately counts is the *real* reward one receives and not the level of prices. Suppose the owner's only input (aside from personal entrepreneurial talent) is 10 units of labor hired at $8 per worker for a total wage cost of $80 (=10 × $8). Also suppose the 100 units of output sell for $1 per unit so that total revenue is $100 (=100 × $1). This firm's *nominal* profit is $20 (=$100 − $80) and, using the $1 price to designate the base price index of 100 percent, its *real* profit is also $20 (=$20 ÷ 1.00). Well and good; full employment is achieved. But suppose that the price level declines by one-half. Would our producer still realize the $20 of real profits needed to induce the production of a 100-unit full-employment output?

The classical answer is Yes. Now that product price is only $.50, total revenue will only be $50 (=100 × $.50). But the cost of 10 units of labor will be

FIGURE 10-2 **Classical and Keynesian views of the macroeconomy**

According to classical theory (a), aggregate supply will determine the full-employment level of real domestic output while aggregate demand will establish the price level. Aggregate demand normally is stable, but if it should decline, say, as shown from AD₁ to AD₂, the price level will quickly fall from P_1 to P_2 to eliminate the temporary excess supply of *ab* and to restore full employment at *c*. The Keynesian view (b) is that aggregate demand is unstable and that price and wages are downwardly inflexible. An AD₁ to AD₂ decline in aggregate demand has no effect on the price level. Rather, real output falls from Q_f to Q_u and can remain at this equilibrium indefinitely.

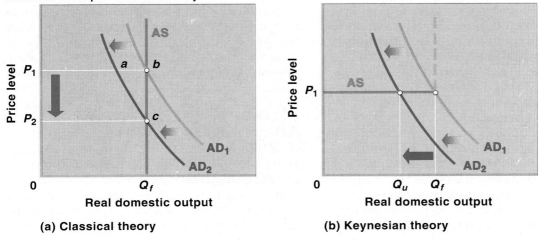

(a) Classical theory

(b) Keynesian theory

reduced to $40 (=$10 \times 4) because the wage rate will be halved. Although *nominal* profits fall to $10 (=$50 - 40), *real* profits remain at $20. In other words, by dividing money profits of $10 by the new price index (expressed as a decimal) we obtain *real* profits of $20 (=$10 \div .50$).

Generalization: With perfectly flexible wages there would be no change in the real rewards and therefore the production or output behavior of businesses. Under conditions of perfect wage flexibility, a change in the price level will not cause the economy to stray from its full-employment position.

Stable Aggregate Demand The classical economists theorized that money underlies aggregate demand. Specifically, the amount of real domestic output which can be purchased depends on (1) the quantity of money households and businesses possess and (2) the purchasing power or real value of that money as determined by the price level. Recall that the purchasing power of the dollar simply refers to the real quantity of goods and services a dollar will buy. Thus as we move down the vertical axis of Figure 10-2a the price level is falling. This means that the purchasing power of each dollar increases and therefore the given quantity of money can purchase a larger quantity of real output. If the price level declined by one-half, a given quantity of money would now purchase a real domestic output which is twice as large. Given a fixed money supply, the price level and real domestic output are inversely related.

And what of the *location* of the aggregate demand curve? According to the classical economists, aggregate demand will be reasonably stable if the nation's monetary authorities maintain a constant supply of money. Given aggregate supply, increases in the supply of money will shift the aggregate demand curve rightward and spark demand-pull inflation; reductions in the supply of money will shift the curve leftward and trigger deflation. The key to price-level stability then, according to the classical economists, is to control the nation's money supply to prevent unwarranted shifts in aggregate demand.

A final observation: Even if there are declines in the money supply and therefore in aggregate demand, the economy depicted in Figure 10-2a will *not* experience unemployment. Admittedly, the immediate effect of a decline in aggregate demand from AD_1 to AD_2 is an excess supply of output in that the aggregate output of goods and services exceeds aggregate spending by the amount *ab*. But, given the presumed downward flexibility of product and resource prices, this excess supply will reduce product prices along with workers' wages and the prices of other inputs. As a result, the price level will quickly decline from P_1 to P_2 until the amounts of output demanded and supplied are brought once again into equilibrium, this time at *c*. While the price level has fallen from P_1 to P_2, the level of real domestic output remains at the full-employment level.

Keynesian View

As noted earlier, the core of the Keynesian theory is that, at least in the short run, product prices and wages are downwardly inflexible, resulting in what is graphically represented as a horizontal aggregate supply curve. Additionally, aggregate demand is subject to periodic changes caused by changes in one or more of the determinants of aggregate demand (Table 9-1). Let's explore these two points in terms of Figure 10-2b.

1 Horizontal Aggregate Supply Curve (to Full-Employment Output) The downward inflexibility of prices and wages discussed first in Chapter 9 translates to a horizontal aggregate supply curve as shown in Figure 10-2b. Here, a decline in real domestic output from Q_f to Q_u will have no impact on the price level. Conversely, an increase in domestic output from Q_u to Q_f will also leave the price level unchanged. A "Keynesian range" of the aggregate supply curve therefore extends from zero real domestic output rightward to the full-employment or potential output Q_f. Once full employment is reached, according to Keynesians, the aggregate supply curve becomes vertical. This view is shown by the vertical line extending upward from the horizontal aggregate supply curve at Q_f.

2 Unstable Aggregate Demand Keynesian economists view aggregate demand as being unstable from one period to the next, even if there are no changes in the supply of money. In particular, the investment component of aggregate demand fluctuates, thereby altering the location of the aggregate demand curve. Suppose, for example, that aggregate demand in Figure 10-2b declines from AD_1 to AD_2. The sole impact of this change in aggregate demand will be on output and employment in that real domestic output falls from Q_f to Q_u while the price level remains constant at P_1. Moreover, Keynesians believe that unless there is a fortuitous offsetting increase in aggregate demand, real domestic output may remain at Q_u, which is below the full-employment level Q_f. Active macroeconomic policies of aggregate demand management by government are essential to avoid the wastes of recession and depression.

Classical Theory

✦ *The classical theory of employment is grounded in Say's law, the classical interest rate mechanism, and downwardly flexible prices and wages.*

✦ *The aggregate supply curve is vertical at the full-employment level of output; the aggregate demand curve is stable if the money supply is constant.*

✦ *Government macroeconomic policies are unnecessary and counterproductive; automatic, built-in mechanisms provide for full-employment output.*

Keynesian Theory

✦ *Keynesian analysis unlinks saving and investment plans and discredits downward price-wage flexibility, implying that changes in aggregate spending, output, and employment are likely.*

✦ *The aggregate supply curve is horizontal; the aggregate demand curve is unstable largely because of the volatility of investment.*

✦ *Active macroeconomic policies by government are necessary to mitigate recessions or depressions.*

TOOLS OF KEYNESIAN EMPLOYMENT THEORY

According to Keynesian economics, how are the levels of output and employment determined in modern capitalism? *The amount of goods and services produced and therefore the level of employment depend directly on the level of total or aggregate expenditures.* Subject to the economy's productive potential as determined by the scarce resources available to it, businesses will produce the level of output they can profitably sell. Both workers and machinery are idled when there are no markets for the goods and services they can produce. Aggregate expenditures and total output and employment vary directly with each other.

Aggregate expenditures can best be understood in terms of the four components of GDP discussed in Chapter 7: consumption, investment, government purchases, and net exports. Our plan of attack is to analyze the consumption and investment components of aggregate expenditures in the rest of this chapter. In Chapter 11 we derive the Keynesian private sector model of equilibrium GDP and employment, with net exports included. Chapter 12 adds government expenditures (along with taxes) to the model.

We preface our discussion with two other comments.

1 Unless specified otherwise we assume that the economy is operating within the horizontal Keynesian range of the aggregate supply curve. That is, the economy is presumed to have a substantial amount of excess productive capacity and unemployed labor so that an increase in aggregate demand will increase real output and employment, but *not* the price level.

2 In the Keynesian model we develop the notion of *aggregate expenditures,* which shows the relationship between real domestic output and national income, on the one hand, and the economy's total spending, on the other. This contrasts with the macro model we have used thus far in which *aggregate demand* portrays the relationship between real domestic output and the price level. In Chapter 11 we reconcile Chapter 9's aggregate demand–aggregate supply model and the Keynesian expenditures-output model which we now begin to construct.

CONSUMPTION AND SAVING

In terms of absolute size, consumption is the main component of aggregate expenditures (Chapter 7). It is therefore important to understand the major determinants of consumption spending. Recall that economists define personal saving as "not spending" or "that part of disposable income (DI) which is not consumed." In other words, disposable income equals consumption plus saving. Hence, in examining the determinants of consumption we are also simultaneously exploring the determinants of saving.

Income-Consumption and Income-Saving Relationships

Many considerations influence the level of consumer spending. But common sense and available statistical data both suggest that the most important determinant of consumer spending is income—in particular, disposable income. And, of course, since saving is that part of disposable income not consumed, DI is also the basic determinant of personal saving.

Consider some recent historical data. In Figure 10-3 each dot indicates the consumption–disposable income relationship for each year since 1960 and the green line is fitted to these points. Consumption is directly related to disposable income and, indeed, households clearly spend most of their income.

But we can say more. The gray 45-degree line is added to the diagram as a point of reference. Because this line bisects the 90-degree angle formed by the vertical and horizontal axes of the graph, each point on the 45-degree line must be equidistant from the two axes. We can therefore regard the vertical distance from any point on the horizontal axis to the 45-degree line as either consumption *or* disposable income. If we regard it as disposable income, then the amount (the vertical distance) by which the actual amount consumed in any given year falls short of the 45-degree guideline indicates the amount of saving in any particular year. For example, in 1991 consumption was $3887 billion, and disposable income was $4218 billion; hence, saving in 1991 was $331 billion. Disposable income less consumption equals saving. By observing these vertical distances as we move to the right in Figure 10-3, we note that saving also varies directly with the level of disposable income. Not shown in Figure 10-3 is the fact that in years of very low income, for example, some of

the worst years of the Great Depression, consumption exceeded disposable income. The dots for these depression years would be located *above* the 45-degree line. Households actually consumed in excess of their current incomes by *dissaving,* that is, by going into debt and liquidating previously accumulated wealth.

In summary, Figure 10-3 suggests that (1) households consume most of their disposable income and (2) both consumption and saving are directly related to the income level.

The Consumption Schedule

Figure 10-3 displays historical data; it shows us how much households *actually did consume* (and save) at various levels of DI over a period of years. For analytical purposes we need to show an income-consumption relationship—a consumption schedule—which indicates the various amounts households *plan* to consume at various possible levels of disposable income which might prevail at some specific *point in time.* A hypothetical **consumption schedule** of the type we require for analysis is shown in columns 1 and 2 of Table 10-1 and is plotted in Figure 10-4a (Key Graph). This consumption schedule reflects the consumption–disposable income relationship suggested by the em-

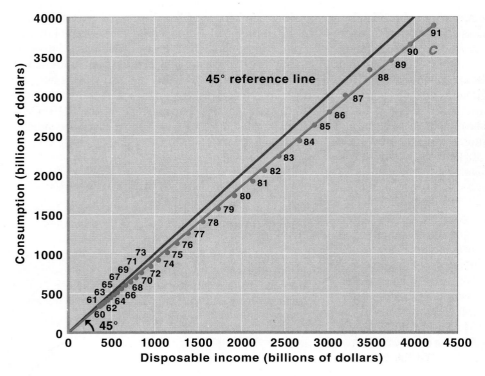

FIGURE 10-3
Consumption and disposable income, 1960–1991

Each dot in this figure shows consumption and disposable income in a given year. The *C* line generalizes on the relationship between consumption and disposable income. It indicates a direct relationship and that households consume the bulk of their incomes.

TABLE 10-1 Consumption and saving schedules *(hypothetical data; columns 1 through 3 in billions)*

(1) Level of output and income (GDP = DI)	(2) Consumption, C	(3) Saving, S (1) − (2)	(4) Average propensity to consume (APC) (2)/(1)	(5) Average propensity to save (APS) (3)/(1)	(6) Marginal propensity to consume (MPC) Δ(2)/Δ(1)*	(7) Marginal propensity to save (MPS) Δ(3)/Δ(1)*
(1) $370	$375	$−5	1.01	−.01		
					.75	.25
(2) 390	390	0	1.00	.00		
					.75	.25
(3) 410	405	5	.99	.01		
					.75	.25
(4) 430	420	10	.98	.02		
					.75	.25
(5) 450	435	15	.97	.03		
					.75	.25
(6) 470	450	20	.96	.04		
					.75	.25
(7) 490	465	25	.95	.05		
					.75	.25
(8) 510	480	30	.94	.06		
					.75	.25
(9) 530	495	35	.93	.07		
					.75	.25
(10) 550	510	40	.93	.07		

*The Greek letter Δ, delta, means "a change in."

pirical data of Figure 10-3, and is consistent with many empirical family budget studies. The relationship is direct—as common sense would suggest—and we note that households will spend a *larger proportion* of a small disposable income than of a large disposable income.

The Saving Schedule

It is a simple task to derive a **saving schedule.** Because disposable income equals consumption plus saving (DI = C + S), we need only subtract consumption (column 2) from disposable income (column 1) to find the amount saved (column 3) at each level of DI. That is, DI − C = S. Hence, columns 1 and 3 of Table 10-1 constitute the saving schedule, plotted in Figure 10-4b. Note that there is a direct relationship between saving and DI but that saving constitutes a smaller proportion (fraction) of a small DI than of a large DI. If households consume a smaller and smaller proportion of DI as DI goes up (column 4), they must save a larger and larger proportion (column 5).

Remembering that each point on the 45-degree line indicates a point where DI equals consumption, we see that dissaving would occur at the relatively low DI of, say, $370 billion (row 1), where consumption is actually $375 billion. Households will consume more than their current incomes by drawing down accumulated savings or by borrowing. Graphically, the vertical distance of the consumption schedule *above* the 45-degree line is equal to the vertical distance of the saving schedule *below* the horizontal axis at the $370 billion level of output and income (see Figure 10-4a and b). In this instance, each of these two vertical distances measures the $5 billion of *dissaving* which occurs at the $370 billion income level.

The **break-even income** is at the $390 billion income level (row 2). This is the level at which households consume their entire incomes. Graphically, the consumption schedule cuts the 45-degree line, and the saving schedule cuts the horizontal axis (saving is zero) at the break-even income level. At all higher incomes, households will plan to save part of their income. The vertical distance of the consumption schedule *below* the 45-degree line measures this saving, as does the vertical distance of the saving schedule *above* the horizontal axis. For example, at the $410 billion level of income (row 3), both these distances indicate $5 billion worth of saving (see Figure 10-4a and b).

Average and Marginal Propensities

Columns 4 to 7 of Table 10-1 show additional characteristics of the consumption and saving schedules.

APC and APS That fraction, or percentage, of any given total income which is consumed is called the **average propensity to consume** (APC), and that fraction of any total income which is saved is the **average propensity to save** (APS). That is,

$$APC = \frac{\text{consumption}}{\text{income}}$$

KEY GRAPH

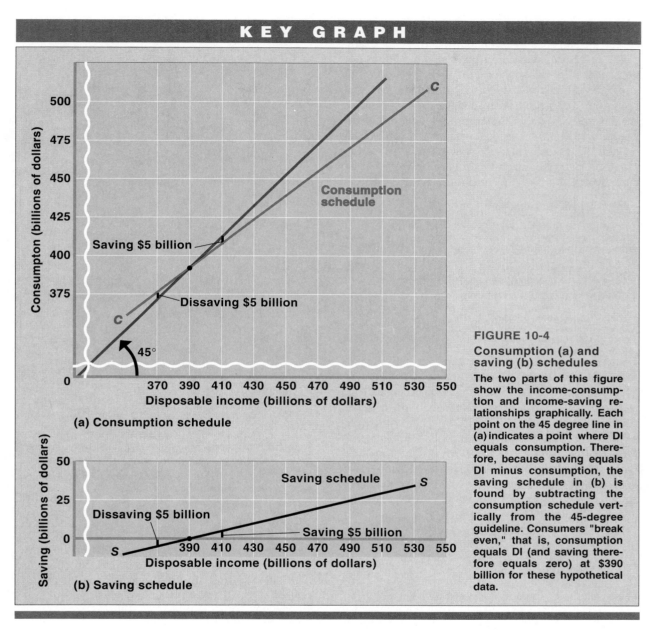

FIGURE 10-4

Consumption (a) and saving (b) schedules

The two parts of this figure show the income-consumption and income-saving relationships graphically. Each point on the 45 degree line in (a) indicates a point where DI equals consumption. Therefore, because saving equals DI minus consumption, the saving schedule in (b) is found by subtracting the consumption schedule vertically from the 45-degree guideline. Consumers "break even," that is, consumption equals DI (and saving therefore equals zero) at $390 billion for these hypothetical data.

and

$$APS = \frac{\text{saving}}{\text{income}}$$

For example, at the $470 billion level of income (row 6) in Table 10-1, the APC is $\frac{450}{470} = \frac{45}{47}$, or about 96 percent, while the APS is $\frac{20}{470} = \frac{2}{47}$, or about 4 percent. By calculating the APC and APS at each of the ten levels of DI shown in Table 10-1, we find that the APC falls and the APS rises as DI increases. This quantifies a point just

made: The fraction of total DI which is consumed declines as DI rises, a change that makes it necessary for the fraction of DI which is saved to rise as DI rises.

Because disposable income is either consumed or saved, the sum of the fraction of any level of DI which is consumed plus the fraction which is saved (not consumed) must exhaust that level of income. In short, APC + APS = 1. Columns 4 and 5 of Table 10-1 illustrate this point.

NATIONAL INCOME, EMPLOYMENT, AND FISCAL POLICY

MPC and MPS The fact that households consume a certain portion of some given total income—for example, $\frac{45}{47}$ of a $470 billion disposable income—does not guarantee they will consume the same proportion of any *change* in income which they might receive. The proportion, or fraction, of any change in income which is consumed is called the **marginal propensity to consume** (MPC), marginal meaning "extra" or "a change in." Or, alternatively stated, the MPC is the ratio of a *change* in consumption to the *change* in income which brought the consumption change about:

$$MPC = \frac{\text{change in consumption}}{\text{change in income}}$$

Similarly, the fraction of any change in income which is saved is the **marginal propensity to save** (MPS). The MPS is the ratio of a *change* in saving to the *change* in income which brought it about:

$$MPS = \frac{\text{change in saving}}{\text{change in income}}$$

Thus, if disposable income is currently $470 billion (row 6) and household incomes rise by $20 billion to $490 billion (row 7), we find that they will consume $\frac{15}{20}$, or $\frac{3}{4}$, and save $\frac{5}{20}$, or $\frac{1}{4}$, of that increase in income (see columns 6 and 7 of Table 10-1). In other words, the MPC is $\frac{3}{4}$, or .75, and the MPS is $\frac{1}{4}$, or .25. *The sum of the MPC and the MPS for any given change in disposable income must always be 1.* Consuming and saving out of extra income is an either-or proposition; that fraction of any change in income which is not consumed is, by definition, saved. Therefore the fraction consumed (MPC) plus the fraction saved (MPS) must exhaust the whole increase in income:

$$MPC + MPS = 1$$

In our example .75 plus .25 equals 1.

MPC and MPS as Slopes The MPC is the numerical value of the slope of the consumption schedule and the MPS is the numerical value of the slope of the saving schedule. We know from the appendix to Chapter 1 that the slope of any line can be measured by the ratio of the vertical change to horizontal change involved in moving from one point to another on that line.

In Figure 10-5 we highlight the slopes of the consumption and saving lines derived from Table 10-1 by enlarging relevant portions of Figures 10-4a and 10-4b. Observe that consumption changes by $15 billion (vertical change) for each $20 billion change in disposable income (horizontal change); the slope of the consump-

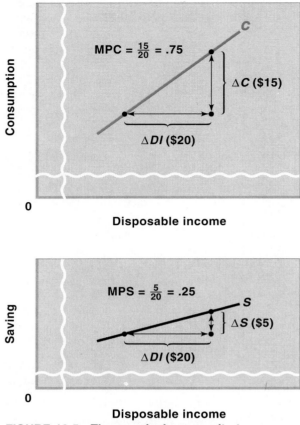

FIGURE 10-5 The marginal propensity to consume and the marginal propensity to save
The MPC is the slope of the consumption schedule and the MPS is the slope of the saving schedule.

tion line is .75 (=$15/$20)—the value of the MPC. Saving changes by $5 billion (vertical change) for every $20 billion change in disposable income (horizontal change). The slope of the saving line therefore is .25 (=$5/$20), which is the value of the MPS.

Nonincome Determinants of Consumption and Saving

The level of disposable income is the basic determinant of the amounts households will consume and save, just as price is the basic determinant of the quantity demanded of a single product. Recall that changes in determinants other than price, such as consumer tastes, incomes, and so forth (Chapter 4), will shift the demand curve for a given product. Similarly, certain determinants might cause households to consume more or less at each possible level of DI and thereby change the locations of the consumption and saving schedules. These factors are familiar to us because they were mentioned in a slightly different context in our discussion of aggregate demand in Chapter 9. There we focused on the downward slope of the aggregate demand curve and the factors which shift that curve. Here we see how these factors alter the consumption–disposable income and savings–disposable income relationships shown in Figure 10-4.

1 Wealth Generally, the greater the amount of wealth households have accumulated, the larger will be the amount of consumption and the smaller the amount of saving out of any level of current income. By *wealth* we mean both real assets (a house, automobiles, television sets, and other durables) and financial assets (cash, savings accounts, stocks, bonds, insurance policies, pensions) which households own. Households save—refrain from consumption—to accumulate wealth. Other things being equal, the more wealth households have accumulated, the weaker the incentive to save to accumulate additional wealth. An increase in wealth shifts the saving schedule downward and the consumption schedule upward.

Example: The dramatic stock market crash of 1929 significantly decreased the financial wealth of many families almost overnight and was undoubtedly a factor in explaining the low levels of consumption in the depressed 1930s. More recent example: The general decline in real estate values during 1989 and 1990 eroded household wealth and contributed to a retrenchment of consumer spending.

For the most part, however, the amount of wealth held by households only changes modestly from year to year and therefore does not typically account for large shifts in the consumption and saving schedules.

2 Price Level An increase in the price level shifts the consumption schedule downward; a decrease in the price level shifts it upward. This generalization is closely related to our discussion of wealth as a determinant of consumption because changes in the price level change the *real value* or *purchasing power* of certain types of wealth. Specifically, the real value of financial assets whose values are fixed in money terms will vary inversely with changes in the price level. This, of course, is the *wealth* or *real balances effect* which you encountered in Chapter 9.

Example: Suppose you own a $10,000 government bond. If the price level increases by, say, 10 percent, the real value of your $10,000 financial asset will decrease by approximately 10 percent. Because your real financial *wealth* has been reduced, you will be less inclined to consume out of current *income*. Conversely, a decrease in the price level will increase your real financial wealth and induce you to consume more of your current income.

Note that, whenever we draw (locate) a particular consumption or saving schedule as in Figure 10-4, we are implicitly assuming a constant price level. This means that the horizontal axis of that figure measures *real* disposable income, as opposed to nominal or money, disposable income.

3 Expectations Household expectations concerning future prices, money incomes, and the availability of goods may have a significant impact on current spending and saving. Expectations of rising prices and product shortages trigger more spending and less saving currently. This shifts the consumption schedule upward and the saving schedule downward. It is natural for consumers to seek to avoid paying higher prices or having to "do without." Expected inflation and expected shortages induce people to "buy now" to escape higher future prices and bare shelves. The expectation of rising money incomes in the future also tends to make consumers freer in their current spending. Conversely, expected price declines, anticipations of shrinking incomes, and the feeling that goods will be abundantly available may induce consumers to retrench on consumption and build up savings.

4 Consumer Indebtedness The level of consumer debt can also affect the willingness of households to consume and save out of current income. If households are in debt to the degree that, say, 20 or 25 percent of their current incomes are committed to installment payments on previous purchases, consumers may well retrench on current consumption to reduce indebtedness. Conversely, if consumer indebtedness is relatively low, households may consume at an unusually high rate by increasing this indebtedness.

5 Taxation In Chapter 12, where consumption will be plotted against before-tax income, we will find that changes in taxes will shift the consumption and saving schedules. Specifically, we will discover that taxes are paid partly at the expense of consumption *and* partly at the expense of saving. Therefore, an *increase* in taxes will shift *both* the consumption and saving schedules *downward*. Conversely, a tax reduction will be partly consumed and partly saved by households. Thus a tax *decrease* will shift *both* the consumption and saving schedules *upward*.

Shifts and Stability

Three final, related points are relevant to our discussion of the consumption and saving schedules.

1 Terminology The movement from one point to another on a given stable consumption schedule (for example, a to b on C_0 in Figure 10-6a) is called a *change in the amount consumed.* The sole cause of this change is a change in the level of disposable income. On the other hand, a *change in the consumption schedule* refers to an upward or downward shift of the entire schedule—for example, a shift from C_0 to C_1 or to C_2 in Figure 10-6a. A relocation of the consumption schedule is caused by changes in any one or more of the nonincome determinants just discussed. A similar distinction in terminology applies to the saving schedule in Figure 10-6b.

2 Schedule Shifts Insofar as the first four nonincome determinants of consumption are concerned, the consumption and saving schedules will shift in opposite directions. If households decide to consume *more* at each possible level of disposable income, they want to save *less,* and vice versa. Graphically, if the consumption schedule shifts upward from C_0 to C_1 in Figure 10-6, the saving schedule will shift downward from S_0 to S_1. Similarly, a downshift in the consumption schedule from C_0 to C_2 means an upshift in the saving schedule from S_0 to S_2. As just noted, the exception to this involves the fifth nonincome determinant—taxation. Households will consume less *and* save less to pay higher taxes. Thus, a tax increase will lower *both* consumption and saving schedules, whereas a tax cut will shift *both* schedules upward.

3 Stability Economists generally agree that, aside from deliberate governmental actions designed to shift them, the consumption and saving schedules are generally stable. This may be because consumption-saving decisions are strongly influenced by habit or because the nonincome determinants are diverse and changes in them frequently work in opposite directions and therefore tend to be self-canceling.

FIGURE 10-6 Shifts in the consumption (a) and saving (b) schedules

A change in any one or more of the nonincome determinants will cause the consumption and saving schedules to shift. If households consume more at each level of DI, they are necessarily saving less. Graphically this means that an upshift in the consumption schedule (C_0 to C_1) entails a downshift in the saving schedule (S_0 to S_1). Conversely, if households consume less at each level of DI, they are saving more. A downshift in the consumption schedule (C_0 to C_2) is reflected in an upshift of the saving schedule (S_0 to S_2).

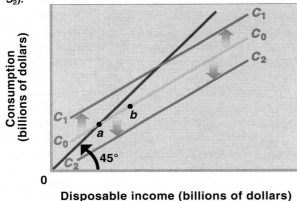

(a) Consumption schedule

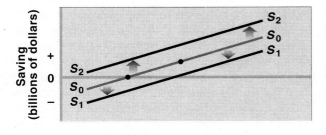

(b) Saving schedule

INVESTMENT

We now turn to investment, the second component of private spending. Recall that investment refers to expenditures on new plants, capital equipment, machinery, and so forth. There are two basic determinants of the level of net investment spending: (1) the expected rate of net profits businesses hope to realize from investment spending, and (2) the interest rate.

Expected Rate of Net Profit

Investment spending is guided by the profit motive; the business sector buys capital goods only when it expects such purchases to be profitable. Suppose the owner of a small cabinetmaking shop is considering investing in a new sanding machine which costs $1000 and has a useful life of only one year. The new machine will presumably increase the firm's output and sales revenue. Specifically, suppose that the *net* expected revenue (that is, net of such operating costs as power, lumber, labor, certain taxes, and so forth) from the machine is $1100. In other words, after operating costs have been accounted for, the remaining expected net revenue is sufficient to cover the $1000 cost of the machine and leave a return of $100. Comparing this $100 return or profit with the $1000 cost of the machine, we find that the expected *rate* of net profit on the machine is 10 percent (=$100/$1000).

The Real Interest Rate

There is one important cost associated with investing which our example has ignored. That, of course, is the interest rate—the financial cost the firm must pay to borrow the *money* capital required to purchase the *real* capital (the sanding machine).

Our generalization is this: If the expected rate of net profits (10 percent) exceeds the interest rate (say, 7 percent), it will be profitable to invest. But if the interest rate (say, 12 percent) exceeds the expected rate of net profits (10 percent), it will be unprofitable to invest.

But what if the firm does *not* borrow, but rather finances the investment internally out of funds saved from past profits? The role of the interest rate as a cost in investing in real capital remains valid. By using this money to invest in the sander, the firm incurs an opportunity cost (Chapter 2) in the sense that it forgoes the interest income it could have realized by lending the funds to someone else.

Note that the *real* rate of interest, rather than the nominal rate, is crucial in making investment deci-sions. Recall from Chapter 8 that the nominal interest rate is expressed in terms of dollars of current value, while the real interest rate is stated in terms of dollars of constant or inflation-adjusted value. In other words, the real interest rate is the nominal rate less the rate of inflation. In our sanding machine illustration we implicitly assumed a constant price level so that all our data, including the interest rate, were in real terms.

But what if inflation is occurring? Suppose a $1000 investment is estimated to yield a real (inflation-adjusted) expected rate of net profits of 10 percent and the nominal interest rate is 15 percent. At first, one would say the investment is unprofitable and should not be made. But assume now there is ongoing inflation of 10 percent per year. This means that the investor will be paying back dollars with approximately 10 percent less in purchasing power. While the nominal interest rate is 15 percent, the real rate is only 5 percent (=15 percent − 10 percent). Comparing this 5 percent real interest rate with the 10 percent expected real rate of net profits, we find that the investment *is* profitable and should be undertaken.

Investment-Demand Curve

We now move from a single firm's investment decision to an understanding of the total demand for investment goods by the entire business sector. Assume every firm in the economy has estimated the expected rate of net profits from all relevant investment projects and these data have been collected. These estimates can now be *cumulated*—that is, successively summed—by asking: How many dollars' worth of investment projects entail an expected rate of net profit of, say, 16 percent or more? Of 14 percent or more? Of 12 percent or more? And so on.

Suppose there are no prospective investments which will yield an expected net profit of 16 percent or more. But there are $5 billion of investment opportunities with an expected rate of net profits between 14 and 16 percent; an *additional* $5 billion yielding between 12 and 14 percent; still an *additional* $5 billion yielding between 10 and 12 percent; and an *additional* $5 billion in each successive 2 percent range of yield down to and including the 0 to 2 percent range.

By *cumulating* these figures we obtain the data of Table 10-2, which are shown graphically by the **investment-demand curve** in Figure 10-7. Note in Table 10-2 that the number opposite 12 percent, for example, tells us there are $10 billion worth of investment opportunities which will yield an expected net profit of 12 percent *or more;* the $10 billion, in other words, in-

TABLE 10-2 Profit expectations and investment
(hypothetical data)

Expected rate of net profit (in percent)	Amount of investment (billions of dollars per year)
16%	$ 0
14	5
12	10
10	15
8	20
6	25
4	30
2	35
0	40

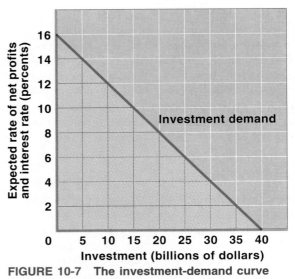

FIGURE 10-7 The investment-demand curve

The investment-demand curve for the economy is derived by arraying all relevant investment projects in descending order of their expected rate of net profitability and applying the rule that investment should be undertaken up to the point at which the interest rate is equal to the expected rate of net profits. The investment-demand curve is downsloping, reflecting an inverse relationship between the interest rate (the financial price of investing) and the aggregate quantity of capital goods demanded.

cludes the $5 billion of investment which will yield an expected return of 14 percent or more *plus* the $5 billion which is expected to yield between 12 and 14 percent.

Given this cumulated information on expected net profit rates of all possible investment projects, we again introduce the real interest rate or financial cost of investing. We know from our sanding machine example that an investment project will be undertaken provided its expected net profit rate exceeds the real interest rate. Let's apply this reasoning to Figure 10-7. If we assume that rate of interest is 12 percent, we find that $10 billion of investment spending will be profitable, that is, $10 billion worth of investment projects entail an expected net profit rate of 12 percent or more. Stated differently, at a financial "price" of 12 percent, $10 billion worth of investment goods will be demanded. Similarly, if the interest rate were lower at, say, 10 percent, then an additional $5 billion of investment projects would become profitable and the total amount of investment goods demanded would be $15 billion (=$10 + $5). At an interest rate of 8 percent, a further $5 billion of investment would become profitable and the total demand for investment goods would be $20 billion. At 6 percent, investment would be $25 billion. And so forth.

By applying the rule that all investment projects should be undertaken up to the point at which the expected rate of net profit equals the interest rate, we discover that the curve of Figure 10-7 is the investment-demand curve. Various possible financial prices of investing (various real interest rates) are shown on the vertical axis and the corresponding quantities of investment goods demanded are revealed on the horizontal axis. By definition, any line or curve embodying such data is the investment-demand curve. Consistent with our product and resource demand curves of Chapter 4, observe the *inverse* relationship between the interest rate (price) and the amount of spending on investment goods (quantity demanded).

This conception of the investment decision allows us to anticipate an important aspect of macroeconomic policy. We will find in our discussion of monetary policy in Chapter 15 that by changing the supply of money, government can alter the interest rate. This is done primarily to change the level of investment spending. At any point in time, business firms in the aggregate have a wide variety of investment projects under consideration. If interest rates are high, only those projects with the highest expected rate of net profit will be undertaken. Hence, the level of investment will be small. As the interest rate is lowered, projects whose expected rate of net profit is less will also become commercially feasible and the level of investment will rise.

A final point: Assuming a fixed supply of money, a change in the price level will influence the amount of investment through the *interest-rate effect* described in Chapter 9. A rise in the price level will increase the amount of money that consumers and businesses desire to have available for purchasing the higher-priced output. That is, if prices rise by, say 10 percent, then people will want to have 10 percent more money in their billfolds and checking accounts. With a fixed supply of money, this increase in the demand for money balances elevates the price of money—the interest rate—which, in turn, reduces investment. Likewise, lower price levels reduce the demand for money balances, decrease the interest rate, and bolster investment.

Shifts in Investment Demand

In discussing the consumption schedule, we noted that, although disposable income is the key determinant of the amount consumed, there are other factors which affect consumption. These "nonincome determinants," you will recall, cause shifts in the consumption schedule. So it also is with the investment-demand schedule. Given the expected rates of net profit of various possible investments, Figure 10-7 portrays the interest rate as the main determinant of investment.

But other factors or variables determine the location of the investment-demand curve. We will examine several of the more important "noninterest determinants" of investment demand, noting how changes in these determinants might shift the investment-demand curve. Note that any factor which increases the expected net profitability of investment will shift the investment-demand curve to the right. Conversely, anything which decreases the expected net profitability of investment will shift the investment-demand curve to the left.

1 Acquisition, Maintenance, and Operating Costs As our sanding machine example revealed, the initial costs of capital goods, along with the estimated costs of operating and maintaining those goods, are important considerations in gauging the expected rate of net profitability of any particular investment. To the extent that these costs rise, the expected rate of *net* profit from prospective investment projects will fall, shifting the investment-demand curve to the left. Conversely, if these costs decline, expected net profit rates will rise, shifting the investment-demand curve to the right. Note that the wage policies of unions may affect the investment-demand curve because wage rates are a major operating cost for most firms.

2 Business Taxes Business owners look to expected profits *after taxes* in making their investment decisions. Hence, an increase in business taxes will lower profitability and shift the investment-demand curve to the left; a tax reduction will shift it to the right.

3 Technological Change Technological progress—the development of new products, improvements in existing products, the creation of new machinery and production processes—is a basic stimulus to investment. The development of a more efficient machine, for example, will lower production costs or improve product quality, increasing the expected rate of net profit from investing in the machine. Profitable new products—mountain bikes, digital tape players, high-resolution television, legal drugs, and so on—induce a flurry of investment as firms tool up for expanded production. In short, a rapid rate of technological progress shifts the investment-demand curve to the right, and vice versa.

4 The Stock of Capital Goods on Hand Just as the stock of consumer goods on hand affects household consumption-saving decisions, so the stock of capital goods on hand influences the expected profit rate from additional investment in a given industry. To the extent that a given industry is well stocked with productive facilities and inventories of finished goods, investment will be retarded in that industry. Obviously, such an industry will be amply equipped to fulfill present and future market demand at prices which yield mediocre profits. If an industry has enough, or even excessive, productive capacity, the expected rate of profit from further investment in the industry will be low, and therefore little or no investment will occur. Excess productive capacity shifts the investment-demand curve to the left; a relative scarcity of capital goods shifts it to the right.

5 Expectations We noted earlier that business investment is based on *expected* profits. Capital goods are durable—they may have a life expectancy of ten or twenty years—and thus the profitability of any capital investment will depend on business planners' expectations of the *future* sales and *future* profitability of the product which the capital helps produce. Business expectations may be based on elaborate forecasts of future business conditions which incorporate a number of "business indicators." Nevertheless, such elusive and difficult-to-predict factors as changes in the domestic political climate, the thrust of foreign affairs, population growth, and stock market conditions must be taken into account on a subjective or intuitive basis. For present purposes we note that, if business executives are optimistic about future business conditions, the investment-demand curve will shift to the right; a pessimistic outlook will shift it to the left.

QUICK REVIEW 10-3

♦ *A specific investment will be undertaken if the expected rate of net profits exceeds the real interest rate.*

♦ *The investment demand curve shows the expected rates of net profits for various levels of total investment.*

♦ *Total investment is established where the real interest rate and the expected rate of net profits on investment are equal.*

♦ *The investment demand curve shifts when changes occur in the costs of capital goods, business taxes, technology, the stock of capital goods on hand, and business expectations.*

Investment and Income

To add the investment decisions of businesses to the consumption plans of households (Chapter 11), we must express investment plans in terms of the level of disposable income (DI), or GDP. That is, we will construct an **investment schedule** showing the amounts which business firms as a group plan or intend to invest at each possible level of income or output. Such a schedule will mirror the investment plans or intentions of business owners and managers in the same way the consumption and saving schedules reflect the consumption and saving plans of households.

TABLE 10-3 The investment schedule *(hypothetical data; in billions)*

(1) Level of output and income	(2) Investment, I_g	(3) Investment, I'_g
$370	$20	$10
390	20	12
410	20	14
430	20	16
450	20	18
470	20	20
490	20	22
510	20	24
530	20	26
550	20	28

We assume that business investment is geared to long-term profit expectations as influenced by technological progress, population growth, and so forth, and therefore is *autonomous* or independent of the level of current disposable income or domestic output. Specifically, suppose that the investment-demand curve is as shown in Figure 10-7 *and* that the current rate of interest is 8 percent. This means that the business sector will find it profitable to spend $20 billion on investment goods. In Table 10-3, columns 1 and 2, we are assuming that this level of investment will be forthcoming at every level of income. The I_g line in Figure 10-8 shows this graphically.

This assumed independence of investment and income is admittedly a simplification. A higher level of business activity may *induce* additional spending on

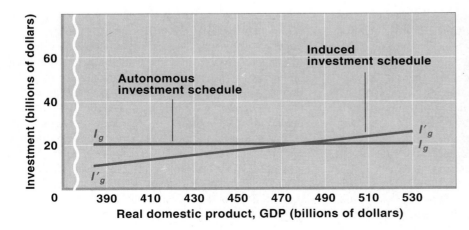

FIGURE 10-8 The investment schedule: two possibilities

Our discussion will be facilitated by employing the investment schedule I_g, which assumes that the investment plans of businesses are independent or autonomous of the current level of income. Actually, the investment schedule may be slightly upsloping, as suggested by I'_g.

capital facilities, as suggested by columns 1 and 3 of Table 10-3 and I_g in Figure 10-8. There are at least two reasons why investment might vary directly with income. First, investment is related to profits; much investment is financed internally out of business profits. Therefore, it is very plausible that as disposable income and GDP rise, so will business profits and therefore the level of investment. Second, at low levels of income and output, the business sector will have excess production capacity; many industries will have idle machinery and equipment and therefore little incentive to purchase additional capital goods. But, as the level of income rises, this excess capacity disappears and firms are inclined to add to their stock of capital goods. Our simplification, however, is not too unrealistic and will greatly facilitate later analysis.

Instability of Investment

In contrast to the consumption schedule, the investment schedule is unstable. Proportionately, investment is the most volatile component of total spending. Figure 10-9 shows the volatility of investment and also makes clear that this variability is substantially greater than that of GDP. These data also suggest that our simplified treatment of investment as being independent of domestic output (Figure 10-8) is essentially realistic; investment spending does not closely follow GDP.

Some of the more important factors explaining the variability of investment follow:

1 Durability Because of their durability, capital goods have a rather indefinite useful life. Within limits, purchases of capital goods are discretionary and therefore postponable. Older equipment or buildings can be scrapped and entirely replaced, on the one hand, or patched up and used for a few more years, on the other. Optimism about the future may prompt business planners to replace their older facilities, that is, to modernize their plants, and this will call for a high level of investment. A less optimistic view, however, may lead to very small amounts of investment as older facilities are repaired and kept in use.

2 Irregularity of Innovation We have indicated that technological progress is a major determinant of investment. New products and processes provide a major stimulus to investment. However, history suggests that major innovations—railroads, electricity, automobiles, computers, and so forth—occur quite ir-

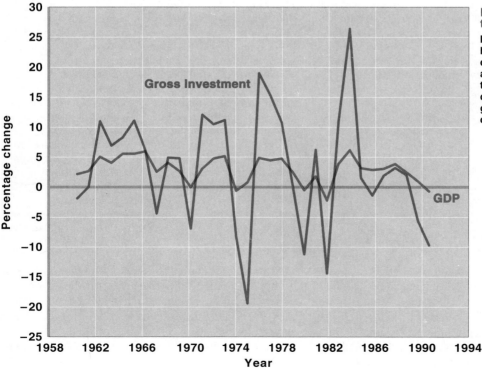

FIGURE 10-9 The volatility of investment

Investment spending is highly volatile. In comparing changes in real investment and real GDP, we observe that the annual percentage changes in investment are greater than the percentage changes in GDP.

LAST WORD

THE SHARE ECONOMY: MAKING WAGES FLEXIBLE

Can greater downward wage flexibility be achieved to soften the impact of a decline in aggregate demand on employment? MIT's Martin Weitzman has offered a proposal to achieve this goal.*

Our comparisons of the classical and the Keynesian conceptions of the macroeconomy suggest that, if wages are stable, employment will tend to be unstable and vice versa. Most modern economists recognize that long-term union contracts, among other considerations, make wages downwardly inflexible at least in the short run. Hence, the declines in labor demand which accompany recession have their primary effect on employment. Professor Weitzman's proposal seeks to increase the downward flexibility of wage rates so that the functioning of labor markets corresponds more closely with the classical model and thereby results in greater employment stability.

In essence Weitzman's proposal is that some portion of wages should be tied directly to the firm's profitability; some part of worker compensation should be in the form of profit sharing. For example, instead of paying workers a guaranteed wage rate of $10 per hour, Weitzman suggests that workers be guaranteed $5 per hour (the base wage) and additional compensation equal to some predetermined percentage of the firm's profits (the share wage). Total compensation (base wage + share wage) may exceed or fall short of $10 per hour, depending on the firm's economic fortunes.

How would employment be affected by such a plan? Assume initially that workers are receiving $10 per hour—$5 in the form of a guaranteed wage and another $5 as profit-sharing compensation. Now suppose a recession occurs and the employer's sales and

profits both decline. As a result, the $5 of profit-sharing income will fall and might decline to zero so that actual wages paid by the firm fall from $10 to $5. Given the new depressed demand for labor, the firm would clearly choose to hire more workers under Weitzman's proposal where wages have now fallen to $5, than if they were fixed at $10.

There are a number of criticisms of the profit-sharing wage plan. For example, it has been argued that the plan might jeopardize the historical wage gains of labor and result in exploitative wages. A further criticism is that with lower guaranteed wages employers will be inclined to adopt production techniques which involve the use of relatively more labor and relatively less capital. Because the amount of capital equipment per worker is critical to labor productivity and economic growth, the long-run expansion of real GDP might be impaired. At a more pragmatic level there is the fundamental question as to whether workers will accept the prospect of more jobs and greater employment stability in exchange for a reduced wage guarantee. It should be noted, however, that a growing number of union and nonunion labor contracts *do* contain profit-sharing arrangements. Hence, although a full-blown share economy seems improbable, profit-sharing appears to be an idea which is spreading.

*Martin L. Weitzman, *The Share Economy* (Cambridge, Mass.: Harvard University Press, 1984).

regularly, and when they do occur, these innovations induce a vast upsurge or "wave" of investment spending which in time recedes. A classic illustration is the widespread acceptance of the automobile in the 1920s. This event not only brought about substantial increases in investment in the automobile industry itself, but also induced tremendous amounts of investment in

such related industries as steel, petroleum, glass, and rubber, not to mention public investment in streets and highways. But when investment in these related industries was ultimately "completed"—that is, when enough capital facilities had been created to meet the needs of the automobile industry—total investment leveled off.

3 Variability of Profits We know that business owners and managers invest only when they feel it will be profitable to do so and that, to a significant degree, the expectation of future profitability is influenced by the size of current profits. Current profits, however, are themselves highly variable (line 13 of the table on the inside covers provides information on undistributed corporate profits). Thus, the variability of profits contributes to the volatile nature of the incentive to invest. Furthermore, the instability of profits may also cause investment fluctuations, because profits are a major source of funds for business investment. American businesses tend to prefer this internal source of financing to increases in external debt or stock issue. In short, expanding profits give business planners both greater incentives and greater means to invest; declining profits have the reverse effects. The fact that actual profits are variable adds to the instability of investment.

4 Variability of Expectations We have already discussed how the durability of capital equipment results in the making of investment decisions on the basis of *expected* net profit. Now, while there is a tendency for business firms to project current business conditions into the future, it is equally true that expectations are sometimes subject to radical revision when some event or combination of events suggests a significant change in future business conditions. What kinds of events make business confidence so capricious? Changes in the domestic political climate, changes in energy developments, changes in population growth and therefore in anticipated market demand, court decisions in key labor or antitrust cases, legislative actions, strikes, changes in governmental economic policies, and a host of similar considerations may give rise to substantial shifts in business optimism or pessimism.

The stock market merits specific comment in this regard. Business planners frequently look to the stock market as an index or barometer of the overall confidence of society in future business conditions; a rising "bull" market signifies public confidence in the business future, whereas a falling "bear" market implies a lack of confidence. The stock market, however, is a highly speculative market, and initially modest changes in stock prices can be seriously intensified by participants who jump on the bandwagon by buying when prices begin to rise and by selling when stock prices start to fall. Furthermore, by affecting the amount of proceeds gained through offerings of new stock, upsurges and slumps in stock values also affect the level of investment—that is, the amount of capital goods purchased.

For these and similar reasons, we can correctly associate most fluctuations in output and employment with changes in investment. In terms of Figure 10-8, we can think of this volatility as being reflected in frequent and substantial upward and downward shifts in the investment schedule.

CHAPTER SUMMARY

1 Classical employment theory envisioned laissez faire capitalism as being capable of providing virtually continuous full employment. This analysis was based on Say's law and the ability of the money market to equate saving and investment.

2 Classical economists argued that because supply creates its own demand, general overproduction was improbable. This conclusion was held to be valid even when saving occurred, because the money market, or more specifically, the interest rate, would automatically synchronize the saving plans of households and the investment plans of businesses.

3 Classical employment theory also held that even if temporary declines in total spending occurred, these declines would be compensated for by downward price-wage adjustments in such a way that real output, employment, and real income would not decline.

4 Keynesian employment theory rejects the notion that the interest rate would equate saving and investment by pointing out that savers and investors make their saving and investment decisions for different reasons—reasons which, for savers, are largely unrelated to the interest rate. Furthermore, because of changes in **a** the public's holdings of money balances, and **b** loans made by banks and other financial institutions, the supply of funds may exceed or fall short of current saving, and saving and investment will not be equal.

5 Keynesian economists discredit price-wage flexibility on both practical and theoretical grounds. They argue that **a** union and business monopolies, minimum-wage legislation, and a host of related factors have virtually eliminated the possibility of substantial price-wage reductions, and **b** price-wage cuts will lower total income and therefore the demand for labor.

6 Classical economist see **a** a vertical aggregate supply curve which establishes the level of output, and **b** a stable aggregate demand curve which establishes the price level; Keynesians see **a** a horizontal aggregate supply curve at

less-than-full-employment levels of output, and **b** an inherently unstable aggregate demand curve.

7 The basic tools of Keynesian employment theory are the consumption, saving, and investment schedules, which show the various amounts that households intend to consume and save and that businesses plan to invest at the various possible income-output levels, given a particular price level.

8 The locations of the consumption and saving schedules are determined by such factors as **a** the amount of wealth owned by households; **b** the price level; **c** expectations of future income, future prices, and product availability; **d** the relative size of consumer indebtedness; and **e** taxation. The consumption and saving schedules are relatively stable.

9 The *average* propensities to consume and save show the proportion or fraction of any level of *total* income consumed and saved. The *marginal* propensities to consume and save show the proportion or fraction of any *change* in total income consumed or saved.

10 The immediate determinants of investment are **a** the expected rate of net profit and **b** the real rate of interest.

The economy's investment-demand curve can be determined by cumulating investment projects and arraying them in descending order according to their expected net profitability and applying the rule that investment will be profitable up to the point at which the real interest rate equals the expected rate of net profit. The investment-demand curve reveals an inverse relationship between the interest rate and the level of aggregate investment.

11 Shifts in the investment-demand curve can occur as the result of changes in **a** the acquisition, maintenance, and operating costs of capital goods; **b** business taxes; **c** technology; **d** the stocks of capital goods on hand; and **e** expectations.

12 We make the simplifying assumption that the level of investment determined by the current interest rate and the investment-demand curve does not vary with the level of GDP.

13 The durability of capital goods, the irregular occurrence of major innovations, profit volatility, and the variability of expectations all contribute to the instability of investment spending.

TERMS AND CONCEPTS

classical theory of employment	**Keynesian economics**	**average propensities to consume and save**	**marginal propensities to consume and save**
Say's law	**consumption and saving schedules**	**investment-demand curve**	**investment schedule**
price-wage flexibility	**break-even income**		

QUESTIONS AND STUDY SUGGESTIONS

1 Explain the classical economists' conclusion that Say's law would prevail even in an economy where substantial saving occurred. What arguments have Keynesian economists used in attacking the classical view that Say's law would result in sustained full employment?

2 "Unemployment can be avoided so long as businesses are willing to accept lower product prices, and workers to accept lower wage rates." Critically evaluate.

3 Use the aggregate demand–aggregate supply model to compare classical and Keynesian interpretations of **a** the aggregate supply curve, and **b** the aggregate demand curve. Which model do you think is more realistic?

4 Precisely how are the APC and the MPC different? Why must the sum of the MPC and the MPS equal 1? What are the basic determinants of the consumption and saving schedules? Of your own level of consumption?

5 Explain precisely what relationships are shown by **a** the consumption schedule, **b** the saving schedule,

c the investment-demand curve, and **d** the investment schedule.

6 Explain how each of the following will affect the consumption and saving schedules or the investment schedule:

a A decline in the amount of government bonds which consumers are holding

b The threat of limited, nonnuclear war, leading the public to expect future shortages of consumer durables

c A decline in the real interest rate

d A sharp decline in stock prices

e An increase in the rate of population growth

f The development of a cheaper method of manufacturing pig iron from ore

g The announcement that the social security program is to be restricted in size of benefits

h The expectation that mild inflation will persist in the next decade

i An 8 percent reduction in the price level

7 Explain why an upshift in the consumption schedule typically involves an equal downshift in the saving schedule. What is the exception?

8 Complete the accompanying table.

Level of output and income (GDP = DI)	Consumption	Saving	APC	APS	MPC	MPS
$240	$_____	$−4	___	___	___	___
260	_____	0	___	___	___	___
280	_____	4	___	___	___	___
300	_____	8	___	___	___	___
320	_____	12	___	___	___	___
340	_____	16	___	___	___	___
360	_____	20	___	___	___	___
380	_____	24	___	___	___	___
400	_____	28	___	___	___	___

a Show the consumption and saving schedules graphically.

b Locate the break-even level of income. How is it possible for households to dissave at very low income levels?

c If the proportion of total income consumed decreases and the proportion saved increases as income rises, explain both verbally and graphically how the MPC and MPS can be constant at various levels of income.

9 What are the basic determinants of investment? Explain the relationship between the real interest rate and the level of investment. Why is the investment schedule less stable than the consumption and saving schedules?

10 Assume there are no investment projects in the economy which yield an expected rate of net profit of 25 percent or more. But suppose there are $10 billion of investment projects yielding expected net profit of between 20 and 25 percent; another $10 billion yielding between 15 and 20 percent; another $10 billion between 10 and 15 percent; and so

forth. Cumulate these data and present them graphically, putting the expected rate of net profit on the vertical axis and the amount of investment on the horizontal axis. What will be the equilibrium level of aggregate investment if the real interest rate is **a** 15 percent, **b** 10 percent, and **c** 5 percent? Explain why this curve is the investment-demand curve.

11 Advanced analysis: Linear equations (see appendix to Chapter 1) for the consumption and saving schedules take the general form $C = a + bY$ and $S = -a + (1 - b)Y$, where C, S, and Y are consumption, saving, and national income, respectively. The constant a represents the vertical intercept, and b is the slope of the consumption schedule.

a Use the following data to substitute specific numerical values into the consumption and saving equations.

National income (Y)	Consumption (C)
$ 0	$ 80
100	140
200	200
300	260
400	320

b What is the economic meaning of b? Of $(1 - b)$?

c Suppose the amount of saving which occurs at each level of national income falls by $20, but that the values for b and $(1 - b)$ remain unchanged. Restate the saving and consumption equations for the new numerical values and cite a factor which might have caused the change.

12 Advanced analysis: Suppose that the linear equation for consumption in a hypothetical economy is $C = 40 + .8Y$. Also suppose that income (Y) is $400. Determine **a** the marginal propensity to consume, **b** the marginal propensity to save, **c** the level of consumption, **d** the average propensity to consume, **e** the level of saving, and **f** the average propensity to save.

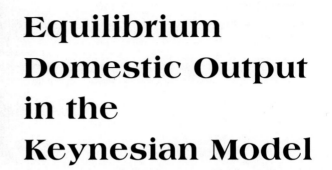

Equilibrium Domestic Output in the Keynesian Model

There is a chance that sometime during your lifetime you or a member of your family will experience a layoff because of a decline in total spending. A greater likelihood is that you will live through a period in which total spending suddenly surges, sharply increasing domestic output, national income, and total employment.

In this chapter we continue our development of the Keynesian aggregate expenditures model—a model which helps us understand cyclical changes in total spending, output, income, and employment. We first use the consumption, saving, and investment schedules developed in Chapter 10 to explain the equilibrium levels of output, income, and employment. Next, we will analyze *changes* in the equilibrium levels of output, income, and employment brought about by changes in investment spending. Then, the foreign sector is added to the model to show how exports and imports affect the macroeconomy. The final section reconciles our newly developed aggregate expenditures model with Chapter 9's aggregate demand and supply model.

Until government is included in our discussion in Chapter 12, we continue to assume no depreciation, no *net* American income earned abroad, no government, and no business saving. Recall that these assumptions permit us to equate GDP and DI. In addition, unless explicitly indicated to the contrary, we assume that the price level is constant. In other words, the economy is presumed to be operating within the Keynesian (horizontal) range of the aggregate supply curve. Hence, our analysis will be in terms of *real* domestic output as opposed to *nominal* domestic output.

Note that in this and the next chapter we deal with a *model* of the economy designed to clarify the basic determinants of the levels of output and employment. The specific numbers employed are only illustrative; they are not intended to measure the real world.

196

EXPENDITURES-OUTPUT APPROACH

In determining and explaining the equilibrium level of output, we employ two closely interrelated approaches: the **aggregate expenditures–domestic output** (or $C + I_g = $ GDP) **approach** and the **leakages-injections** (or the $S = I_g$) **approach.** Let's first discuss the aggregate expenditures–domestic output approach, using both simple arithmetic data and graphical analysis.

Tabular Analysis

Table 11-1 combines the income-consumption and income-saving data of Table 10-1 and the simplified income-investment data of columns 1 and 2 in Table 10-3.

Domestic Output Column 2 of Table 11-1 is the total or domestic output schedule for the economy. It indicates the various possible levels of total output—that is, the various possible real GDPs—which the business sector of the economy might produce. *Producers are willing to offer each of these ten levels of output in the expectation that they will receive an identical amount of receipts of income from its sale.* For example, the business sector will produce $370 billion worth of output, thereby incurring $370 billion worth of costs (wages, rents, interest, and profit), only if businesses expect that this output can be sold for $370 billion worth of receipts. Some $390 billion worth of output will be of-

fered if businesses feel this output can be sold for $390 billion. And so it is for all the other possible levels of output.

Aggregate Expenditures The total, or aggregate, expenditures schedule is shown in column 6 of Table 11-1. It shows the total amount which will be spent at each possible output-income level. In the closed private sector of the economy, the aggregate expenditures schedule shows the amount of consumption and planned gross investment spending $(C + I_g)$ forthcoming at each output-income level. Our initial focus is on *planned* or intended investment as shown in column 5 of Table 11-1. Later analysis will reveal that imbalances in aggregate expenditures and real domestic output will result in unplanned or unintended investment in the form of inventory changes (Column 7).

Equilibrium GDP Of the ten possible levels of GDP in Table 11-1, which one will be the equilibrium level? Which level of total output will the economy be capable of sustaining?

   The equilibrium level of output is that output whose production will create total spending just sufficient to purchase that output. In other words, the equilibrium level of GDP is where the total quantity of goods produced (GDP) is equal to the total quantity of goods purchased $(C + I_g)$. Examination of the domestic output schedule of column 2 and the aggregate expenditures schedule of column 6 indicates that this equality exists only at

TABLE 11-1 Determination of the equilibrium levels of employment, output, and income: the closed private sector (*hypothetical data*)

(1) Possible levels of employment, millions	(2) Real domestic output (and income) (GDP = DI),* billions	(3) Consumption, C, billions	(4) Saving, S, billions	(5) Investment, I_g, billions	(6) Aggregate expenditures $(C + I_g)$, billions	(7) Unintended investment (+) or disinvestment (−) in inventories	(8) Tendency of employment, output, and incomes
(1) 40	$370	$375	$−5	$20	$395	$−25	Increase
(2) 45	390	390	0	20	410	−20	Increase
(3) 50	410	405	5	20	425	−15	Increase
(4) 55	430	420	10	20	440	−10	Increase
(5) 60	450	435	15	20	455	−5	Increase
(6) 65	470	450	20	20	470	0	Equilibrium
(7) 70	490	465	25	20	485	+5	Decrease
(8) 75	510	480	30	20	500	+10	Decrease
(9) 80	530	495	35	20	515	+15	Decrease
(10) 85	550	510	40	20	530	+20	Decrease

*If depreciation and net American income earned abroad are zero, government is ignored, and it is assumed that all saving occurs in the household sector of the economy, GDP as a measure of domestic output is equal to NI, PI, and DI. This means that households receive a DI equal to the value of total output.

the $470 billion level of GDP (row 6). This is the only level of output at which the economy is willing to spend precisely the amount necessary to take that output off the market. Here the annual rates of production and spending are in balance. There is no overproduction, which results in a piling up of unsold goods and therefore cutbacks in the production rate. Nor is there an excess of total spending, which draws down inventories and prompts increases in the rate of production. In short, there is no reason for businesses to alter this rate of production; $470 billion is therefore the **equilibrium GDP.**

Disequilibrium To enhance our understanding of the meaning of the equilibrium level of GDP, let's examine other possible levels of GDP to see why they cannot be sustained.

At the $410 billion level of GDP (row 3), businesses would find that if they produced this output, the income created would give rise to $405 billion in consumer spending. Supplemented by $20 billion of planned investment, total expenditures ($C + I_g$) would be $425 billion, as shown in column 6. The economy provides an annual rate of spending more than sufficient to purchase the current $410 billion rate of production. Because businesses are producing at a lower rate than buyers are taking goods off the shelves, an unintended decline in business inventories of $15 billion would occur (column 7) if this situation were sustained. But businesses will adjust to this imbalance between aggregate expenditures and domestic output by stepping up production. A higher rate of output will mean more jobs and a higher level of total income. In short, if aggregate expenditures exceed the domestic output, the latter will be pulled upward.

By making the same comparisons of GDP (column 2) and $C + I_g$ (column 6) at all other levels of GDP below the $470 billion equilibrium level, we find that the economy wants to spend in excess of the level at which businesses are willing to produce. The excess of total spending at all these levels of GDP will drive GDP upward to the $470 billion level.

The reverse is true at all levels of GDP above the $470 billion equilibrium level. Businesses will find that the production of these total outputs fails to generate the levels of spending needed to take them off the market. Being unable to recover their costs, businesses will cut back on production.

To illustrate: At the $510 billion level of output (row 8), business managers will find there is insufficient spending to permit the sale of that output. Of the $510

billion worth of income which this output creates, $480 billion is received back by businesses as consumption spending. Though supplemented by $20 billion worth of planned investment spending, total expenditures ($500 billion) fall $10 billion short of the $510 billion quantity produced. If this imbalance persisted, $10 billion of inventories would pile up (column 7). But businesses will react to this unintended accumulation of unsold goods by cutting back on the rate of production. This decline in GDP will mean fewer jobs and a decline in total income. You should verify that deficiencies of total spending exist at all other levels of GDP in excess of the $470 billion level.

The equilibrium level of GDP exists where the total output, measured by GDP, and aggregate expenditures, $C + I_g$, are equal. Any excess of total spending over total output will drive GDP upward. Any deficiency of total spending will pull GDP downward.

Graphical Analysis

The same analysis can be shown in a simple graph. In Figure 11-1 (Key Graph) the **45-degree line** (used in Chapter 10 to delineate graphically how disposable income is divided between consumption and saving) now takes on increased significance. Recall that the special property of the 45-degree line is that at any point on the line, the value of what is being measured on the horizontal axis (in this case GDP) is equal to the value of what is being measured on the vertical axis (here it is aggregate expenditures or $C + I_g$). Having discovered in our tabular analysis that the equilibrium level of domestic output is determined where $C + I_g$ equals GDP, we can say that the 45-degree line in Figure 11-1 is a graphical statement of this equilibrium condition.

Next, we must add the aggregate expenditures schedule to Figure 11-1. To do this we graph the consumption schedule of Figure 10-4a and add to it *vertically* the constant $20 billion amount from Figure 10-8, which, we assume, businesses plan to invest at each possible level of GDP. More directly, we can plot the $C + I_g$ data of column 6 in Table 11-1. Observe that the aggregate expenditures line shows total spending rising with domestic output and national income, but that expenditures do not rise as much as income. This is so because the marginal propensity to consume—the slope of line C—is less than 1. Because the aggregate expenditures line $C + I_g$ is parallel to the consumption line, the slope of the aggregate expenditures line equals the MPC and is also less than 1. A part of any

KEY GRAPH

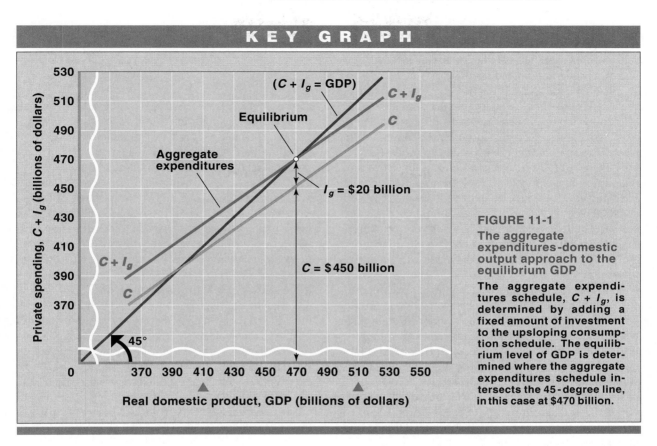

FIGURE 11-1

The aggregate expenditures-domestic output approach to the equilibrium GDP

The aggregate expenditures schedule, $C + I_g$, is determined by adding a fixed amount of investment to the upsloping consumption schedule. The equilibrium level of GDP is determined where the aggregate expenditures schedule intersects the 45-degree line, in this case at $470 billion.

increase in national income will *not* be spent; it will be saved. For our particular data, aggregate expenditures rise by $15 billion for every $20 billion increase in domestic output and national income because $5 billion of each $20 billion income increment is saved.

The equilibrium level of GDP is that GDP which corresponds to the intersection of the aggregate expenditures schedule and the 45-degree line. This intersection locates the only point at which aggregate expenditures (on the vertical axis) are equal to GDP (on the horizontal axis). Because our aggregate expenditures schedule is based on the data of Table 11-1, we once again find that equilibrium output is $470 billion. Observe that consumption at this output is $450 billion and investment is $20 billion.

It is evident from Figure 11-1 that no levels of GDP above the equilibrium level are sustainable, because $C + I_g$ falls short of GDP. Graphically, the aggregate expenditures schedule lies *below* the 45-degree line. For example, at the $510 billion GDP level, $C + I_g$ is only $500 billion. Inventories of unsold goods rise to undesired levels, prompting businesses to readjust

production sights downward in the direction of the $470 billion output level.

Conversely, at all possible levels of GDP less than $470 billion, the economy desires to spend in excess of what businesses are producing. $C + I_g$ exceeds the value of the corresponding output. Graphically, the aggregate expenditures schedule lies *above* the 45-degree line. At the $410 billion GDP, for example, $C + I_g$ totals $425 billion. Inventories decline as the rate of spending exceeds the rate of production, prompting businesses to raise their production sights toward the $470 billion GDP. Unless there is some change in the location of the aggregate expenditures line, the $470 billion level of GDP will be sustained indefinitely.

LEAKAGES-INJECTIONS APPROACH

The expenditures-output approach to determining GDP spotlights total spending as the immediate determinant of the levels of output, employment, and income. Though the leakages-injections approach is less direct, it does have the advantage of underscoring the reason $C + I_g$ and GDP are unequal at all levels of output except the equilibrium level.

The essence of the leakages-injections approach is this: Under our simplifying assumptions we know that the production of any level of domestic output will generate an identical amount of disposable income. But we also know a part of that income may be saved—that is, *not* consumed—by households. Saving therefore represents a *leakage,* withdrawal, or diversion of potential spending from the income-expenditures stream. The consequence of saving is that consumption falls short of total output or GDP; hence, by itself consumption is insufficient to take the domestic output off the market, and this fact would seem to set the stage for a decline in total output.

However, the business sector does not intend to sell its entire output to consumers; some domestic output will consist of capital or investment goods sold within the business sector. Investment can therefore be thought of as an *injection* of spending into the income-expenditures stream which supplements consumption; stated differently, investment is a potential offset to, or replacement for, the leakage of saving.

If the leakage of saving exceeds the injection of investment, then $C + I_g$ will fall short of GDP and this level of GDP will be too high to be sustained. Any GDP where saving exceeds investment will be an above-equilibrium GDP. Conversely, if the injection of investment exceeds the leakage of saving, then $C + I_g$ will be greater than GDP and GDP will be driven upward. Any GDP where investment exceeds saving will be a below-equilibrium GDP. Only where $S = I_g$—where the leakage of saving is exactly offset by the injection of investment—will aggregate expenditures equal the domestic output. And we know that this equality defines the equilibrium GDP.

In the closed private economy assumed here, there are only one leakage (saving) and one injection (investment). In general terms, a *leakage* is any use of income other than its expenditure on domestically produced output. In the more realistic models which follow (the section on international trade in this chapter and Chapter 12), we will need to incorporate the additional leakages of imports and taxes into our analysis.

Similarly, an *injection* is any supplement to consumer spending on domestic production. Again, in later models we must add injections of exports and government purchases to our discussion. But for now we need only compare the single leakage of saving with the sole injection of investment to assess the impact on GDP.

Tabular Analysis

The saving schedule (columns 2 and 4) and the investment schedule (columns 2 and 5) of Table 11-1 are pertinent. Our $C + I_g$ = GDP approach has led us to conclude that all levels of GDP less than $470 billion are unstable because the corresponding $C + I_g$ exceeds these GDPs, driving GDP upward. A comparison of the amounts households and businesses want to save and invest at each of the below-equilibrium GDP levels explains the excesses of total spending. In particular, at each of these relatively low GDP levels, businesses plan to invest more than households want to save.

For example, at the $410 billion level of GDP (row 3), households will save only $5 billion, thereby spending $405 of their $410 billion incomes. Supplemented by $20 billion of business investment, aggregate expenditures ($C + I_g$) are $425 billion. Aggregate expenditures exceed GDP by $15 billion (=$425 − $410) *because* the amount businesses plan to invest at this level of GDP exceeds the amounts households save by $15 billion. The fact is that a very small leakage of saving at this relatively low income level will be more than compensated for by the relatively large injection of investment spending which causes $C + I_g$ to exceed GDP and induce GDP upward.

Similarly, all levels of GDP above the $470 billion level are also unstable, because here GDP exceeds $C + I_g$. The reason for this insufficiency of aggregate expenditures lies in the fact that at all GDP levels above $470 billion, households will want to save in excess of the amount businesses plan to invest. The saving leakage is not replaced or compensated for by the injection of investment.

For example, households will choose to save at the high rate of $30 billion at the $510 billion GDP (row 8). Businesses, however, will plan to invest only $20 billion at this GDP. This $10 billion excess of saving over planned investment will cause total spending to fall $10 billion short of the value of total output. Specifically, aggregate expenditures are $500 billion and real GDP is $510 billion. This deficiency will reduce GDP.

Again we verify that the equilibrium GDP is $470 billion. Only at this level are the saving desires of households and the investment plans of businesses equal. Only when businesses and households attempt to invest and save at equal rates—where the leakages and injections are equal—will $C + I_g$ = GDP. Only here will the annual rates of production and spending be in balance; only here will unplanned changes in inventories be absent. One can think of it in this way: If saving were zero, consumer spending would always be sufficient to clear the market of any given GDP; consumption would equal GDP. But saving can and does occur, causing consumption to fall short of GDP. Only when businesses are willing to invest at the same rate at which households save will the amount by which consumption falls short of GDP be precisely counterbalanced.

Graphical Analysis

The leakages-injections approach to determining the equilibrium GDP can be demonstrated graphically, as in Figure 11-2. Here we have combined the saving schedule of Figure 10-4b and the investment schedule of Figure 10-8. The numerical data for these schedules are repeated in columns 2, 4, and 5 of Table 11-1. We see the equilibrium level of GDP is at $470 billion, where the saving and investment schedules intersect. Only here do businesses and households invest and save at the same rates; therefore, only here will GDP and $C + I_g$ be equal.

At all higher levels of GDP, households will save at a higher rate than businesses plan to invest. The fact that the saving leakage exceeds the investment injection causes $C + I_g$ to fall short of GDP, driving GDP

downward. At the $510 billion GDP, for example, saving of $30 billion will exceed investment of $20 billion by $10 billion, with the result that $C + I_g$ is $500 billion, $10 billion short of GDP.

At all levels of GDP below the $470 billion equilibrium level, businesses will plan to invest more than households save. Here the injection of investment exceeds the leakage of saving so that $C + I_g$ exceeds GDP, driving the latter upward. To illustrate: At the $410 billion level of GDP the $5 billion leakage of saving is more than compensated for by the $20 billion that businesses plan to invest. The result is that $C + I_g$ exceeds GDP by $15 billion, inducing businesses to produce a larger GDP.

PLANNED VERSUS ACTUAL INVESTMENT

We have emphasized that discrepancies in saving and investment can occur and bring about changes in the equilibrium GDP. Now we must recognize that, in another sense, saving and investment must always be equal! This apparent contradiction concerning the equality of saving and investment is resolved when we distinguish between **planned investment** and saving (which need not be equal) and **actual investment** and saving (which by definition must be equal). The catch is that *actual investment consists of both planned and unplanned investment (unplanned changes in inventory*

FIGURE 11-2   The leakages-injections approach to the equilibrium GDP

A second approach is to view the equilibrium GDP as determined by the intersection of the saving (S) and the planned investment (I_g) schedules. Only at the point of equilibrium will households plan to save the amount businesses want to invest. It is the consistency of these plans which equates GDP and $C + I_g$.

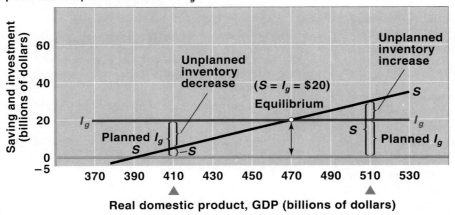

investment), and unplanned investment acts as a balancing item which always equates the actual amounts saved and invested in any period of time.

Disequilibrium and Inventories

Consider, for example, the $490 billion above-equilibrium GDP (row 7 of Table 11-1). What would happen if businesses produced this output, thinking they could sell it? At this level, households save $25 billion of their $490 billion DI, so consumption is only $465 billion. *Planned* investment (column 5) is $20 billion; businesses plan or desire to buy $20 billion worth of capital goods. This means aggregate expenditures ($C + I_g$) are $485 billion, and sales therefore fall short of production by $5 billion. This extra $5 billion of goods is retained by businesses as an *unintended* or *unplanned* increase in inventories (column 7). It is unintended because it results from the failure of total spending to take total output off the market. Remembering that, by definition, changes in inventories are a part of investment, we note the *actual* investment of $25 billion ($20 planned *plus* $5 unintended or unplanned) equals saving of $25 billion, even though saving exceeds *planned* investment by $5 billion. Businesses, being unwilling to accumulate unwanted inventories at this annual rate, will cut back production.

Now look at the below-equilibrium $450 billion output (row 5 of Table 11-1). Because households save only $15 billion of their $450 billion DI, consumption is $435 billion. Planned investment by businesses is $20 billion, so aggregate expenditures are $455 billion. Sales exceed production by $5 billion. This is so because an unplanned decline in business inventories has occurred. Businesses have unintentionally *dis*invested $5 billion in inventories (column 7). Note once again that *actual* investment is $15 billion ($20 planned *minus* $5 unintended or unplanned) and equal to saving of $15 billion, even though *planned* investment exceeds saving by $5 billion. This unplanned decline in investment in inventories due to the excess of sales over production will induce businesses to increase the GDP by expanding production.

To summarize: At all *above-equilibrium* levels of GDP (where saving exceeds planned investment), actual investment and saving are equal because of unintended increases in inventories which, by definition, are included as a part of actual investment. Graphically (Figure 11-2), the unintended inventory increase is measured by the vertical distance by which the saving schedule lies above the (planned) investment schedule.

At all *below-equilibrium* levels of GDP (where planned investment exceeds saving), actual investment will be equal to saving because of unintended decreases in inventories which must be subtracted from planned investment to determine actual investment. These unintended inventory declines are shown graphically as the vertical distance by which the (planned) investment schedule lies above the saving schedule.

Achieving Equilibrium

These distinctions are important because they correctly suggest that *it is the equality of planned investment and saving which determines the equilibrium level of GDP.* We can think of the process by which equilibrium is achieved as follows:

1 A difference between saving and planned investment causes a difference between the production and spending plans of the economy as a whole.

2 This difference between aggregate production and spending plans results in unintended investment or disinvestment in inventories.

3 As long as unintended investment in inventories persists, businesses will revise their production plans downward and thereby reduce the GDP. Conversely, as long as unintended disinvestment in inventories exists, firms will revise their production plans upward and increase the GDP. Both types of movements in GDP are toward equilibrium because they bring about the equality of planned investment and saving.

4 Only where planned investment and saving are equal will the level of GDP be in equilibrium; that is, only where planned investment equals saving will there be no unintended investment or disinvestment in inventories to drive the GDP downward or upward. Note in column 7 of Table 11-1 that only at the $470 billion equilibrium GDP is there no unintended investment or disinvestment in inventories.

QUICK REVIEW 11-1

◆ *In a closed private economy, equilibrium GDP occurs where aggregate expenditures equal real domestic output ($C + I_g = GDP$).*

◆ *Alternatively, equilibrium GDP is established where planned investment equals saving ($I_g = S$).*

◆ *Actual investment consists of planned investment plus unplanned changes in inventories and is always equal to saving.*

◆ *At equilibrium GDP, changes in inventories are zero; no unintended investment or disinvestment occurs.*

CHANGES IN EQUILIBRIUM GDP AND THE MULTIPLIER

Thus far, we have been concerned with explaining the equilibrium levels of total output and income. But we saw in Chapter 8 that the GDP of American capitalism is seldom stable; rather, it is characterized by long-run growth and punctuated by cyclical fluctuations. Let's turn to the questions of *why* and *how* the equilibrium level of real GDP fluctuates.

The equilibrium level of GDP will change in response to changes in the investment schedule or the saving-consumption schedules. Because investment spending generally is less stable than the consumption-saving schedules, we will assume that changes in the investment schedule occur.

The impact of changes in investment can be seen through Figure 11-3a and b. Suppose the expected rate of net profit on investment rises (shifting the investment-demand curve of Figure 10-7 to the right) *or* the

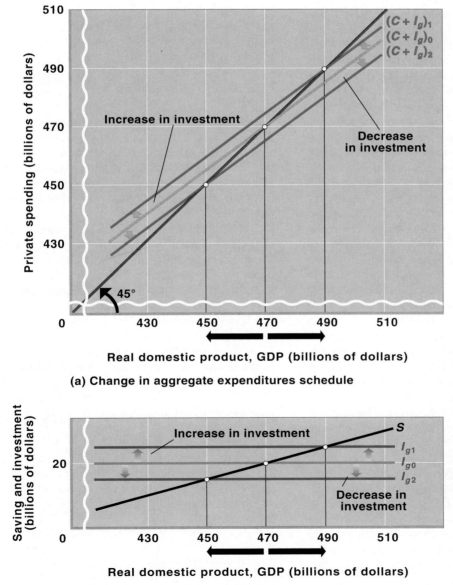

(a) Change in aggregate expenditures schedule

(b) Change in investment schedule

FIGURE 11-3 Changes in the equilibrium GDP caused by shifts in (a) the aggregate expenditures schedule and (b) the investment schedule

An upshift in the aggregate expenditures schedule from, say, $(C + I_g)_0$ to $(C + I_g)_1$ will increase the equilibrium GDP. Conversely, a downshift in the aggregate expenditures schedule from, say, $(C + I_g)_0$ to $(C + I_g)_2$ will lower the equilibrium GDP. In the saving-investment figure an upshift in the investment schedule (I_{g0} to I_{g1}) will raise, and a downshift (I_{g0} to I_{g2}) will lower, the equilibrium GDP.

NATIONAL INCOME, EMPLOYMENT, AND FISCAL POLICY

interest rate falls (moving down the stable curve). As a result, investment spending increases by, say, $5 billion. This is indicated in Figure 11-3a by an upward shift in the aggregate expenditures schedule from $(C + I_g)_0$ to $(C + I_g)_1$, and in Figure 11-3b by an upward shift in the investment schedule from I_{g0} to I_{g1}. In each of these portrayals the consequence is a rise in the equilibrium GDP from $470 to $490 billion.

Conversely, if the expected rate of net profit from investment decreases *or* the interest rate rises, a decline in investment spending of, say, $5 billion will occur. This is shown by the downward shift of the investment schedule from I_{g0} to I_{g2} in Figure 11-3b and the aggregate expenditures schedule from $(C + I_g)_0$ to $(C + I_g)_2$ in Figure 11-3a. In each case, these shifts cause the equilibrium GDP to fall from the original $470 billion level to $450 billion. You should verify these conclusions in terms of Table 11-1 by substituting $25 billion and then $15 billion for the $20 billion planned investment figure in column 5 of the table.

Incidentally—and at the risk of getting ahead of ourselves—the indicated $5 billion changes in investment may be the direct result of economic policy. Looking back at Table 10-2, we find that the initial $20 billion level of investment is associated with an 8 percent interest rate. *If* the economy is in a recession, the monetary authorities may purposely negotiate a reduction in the interest rate to 6 percent (by increasing the money supply), causing a $5 billion increase in investment and thereby in aggregate expenditures to stimulate the economy.

Conversely, *if,* with the initial $20 billion of investment, the economy faces a demand-pull inflation problem, the monetary authorities may increase the interest rate to 10 percent (by reducing the money supply), thereby reducing investment and aggregate expenditures to constrain the inflation. Monetary policy—changing the money supply to alter interest rates and aggregate expenditures—is the subject of Chapter 15.

Changes in the consumption-saving schedules will have similar effects. If households want to consume more (save less) at each level of GDP, the aggregate expenditures schedule will shift upward and the saving schedule downward in Figure 11-3a and b, respectively. In either portrayal these shifts will mean an increase in the equilibrium GDP. If households want to consume less (save more) at each possible GDP, the resulting drop in the consumption schedule and the increase in the saving schedule will reduce the equilibrium GDP.

The Multiplier Effect

You may have noticed a curious feature of these examples: A $5 billion change in investment spending led to a $20 billion change in the output-income level. This surprising result is called the **multiplier effect** or, more simply, the *multiplier.* Specifically, the multiplier is the ratio of a change in equilibrium GDP to the initial change in (investment) spending which caused that change in real GDP. That is:

$$\text{Multiplier} = \frac{\text{change in real GDP}}{\text{initial change in spending}}$$

In this case the multiplier is 4 (change of GDP of 20 ÷ change in investment of 5). Or, by rearranging our equation, we can say that:

$$\text{Change in GDP} = \text{multiplier} \times \frac{\text{initial change in}}{\text{spending}}$$

Three points about the multiplier must be made here.
1   The "initial change in spending" is usually associated with investment spending because investment is the most volatile component of aggregate expenditures (Figure 10-9). But changes in consumption, government purchases, or exports also are subject to the multiplier effect.
2   The "initial change in spending" refers to an upshift or downshift in the aggregate expenditures schedule due to an upshift or downshift in one of its components. In Figure 11-3b we find that real GDP has increased by $20 billion because the investment schedule has shifted upward by $5 billion from I_{g0} to I_{g1}.
3   Implicit in our second point is that the multiplier is a two-edged sword working in both directions. A small increase in spending can give rise to a multiple increase in GDP, or a small decrease in spending can be magnified into a much larger decrease in GDP by the multiplier. Note carefully the effects of the shift in $(C + I_g)_0$ to $(C + I_g)_1$ or to $(C + I_g)_2$ and I_{g0} to I_{g1} or to I_{g2} in Figure 11-3a and b.

Rationale   The multiplier is based on two facts.
1   The economy is characterized by repetitive, continuous flows of expenditures and income through which dollars spent by Smith are received as income by Jones.

Any change in income will cause both consumption and saving to vary in the same direction as, and by a fraction of, the change in income.

It follows that an initial change in the rate of spending will cause a spending chain reaction which, although of diminishing importance at each successive step, will cumulate to a multiple change in GDP.

The rationale underlying the multiplier effect is illustrated numerically in Table 11-2. Suppose a $5 billion increase in investment spending occurs. Graphically, this is the upshift of the aggregate expenditures schedule by $5 billion in Figure 11-3a and the upshift of the investment schedule from $20 to $25 billion in Figure 11-3b. We continue to assume that the MPC is .75 and the MPS is .25. Also, we suppose that the economy is initially in equilibrium at $470 billion.

The initial increase in investment generates an equal amount of wage, rent, interest, and profit income because spending and receiving of income are two sides of the same transaction. How much consumption will be induced by this $5 billion increase in the incomes of households? We find the answer by applying the marginal propensity to consume of .75 to this change in income. Thus, the $5 billion increase in income raises consumption by $3.75 (=.75 × $5) billion and saving by $1.25 (=.25 × $5) billion, as shown in columns (2) and (3) of Table 11-2. The $3.75 billion spent is received by other households as income (second round). These households consume .75 of this $3.75 billion or $2.81 billion, and save .25 of it, or $0.94 billion. The $2.81 billion consumed flows to still other households as income (third round). This process continues.

Figure 11-4, which is derived from Table 11-2, shows the cumulative effects of the various rounds of the multiplier process. Observe that each round *adds* the [orange] blocks to national income and GDP. The cumulation of the additional income in each round—the sum of the [orange] blocks—constitutes the total change in income or GDP. Though the spending and respending effects of the initial increase in investment diminish with each successive round of spending, the cumulative increase in the output-income level will be $20 billion if the process is carried through to the last dollar. The $5 billion increase in investment will therefore increase the equilibrium GDP by $20 billion, from $470 to $490 billion. Hence, the multiplier is 4 (=$20 billion ÷ $5 billion).

It is no coincidence that the multiplier effect ends at the point where exactly enough saving has been generated to offset the initial $5 billion increase in investment spending. Only then will the disequilibrium created by the investment increase be corrected. In this case, GDP and total incomes must rise by $20 billion to create $5 billion in additional saving to match the $5 billion increase in investment spending. Income must increase by four times the initial excess of investment over saving, because households save one-fourth of any increase in their incomes (that is, the MPS is .25). As noted, in this example the multiplier—the number of times the ultimate increase in income exceeds the initial increase in investment spending—is 4.

The Multiplier and the Marginal Propensities You may have sensed from Table 11-2 some relationship between the MPS and the size of the multiplier. The fraction of an increase in income saved—that is, the MPS—determines the cumulative respending effects of any initial change in I_g, G, X_n or C, and therefore the multiplier. Specifically, *the size of the MPS and the size of the multiplier are inversely related*. The smaller the fraction of any change in income saved, the greater the respending at each round and, therefore, the greater the multiplier. If the MPS is .25, as in our example, the multiplier is 4. If the MPS were .33, the multiplier

TABLE 11-2 **The multiplier: a tabular illustration** *(hypothetical data; in billions)*

	(1) *Change in income*	*(2)* *Change in consumption (MPC = .75)*	*(3)* *Change in saving (MPS = .25)*
Assumed increase in investment	$ 5.00	$ 3.75	$1.25
Second round	3.75	2.81	0.94
Third round	2.81	2.11	0.70
Fourth round	2.11	1.58	0.53
Fifth round	1.58	1.19	0.39
All other rounds	4.75	3.56	1.19
Totals	$20.00	$15.00	$5.00

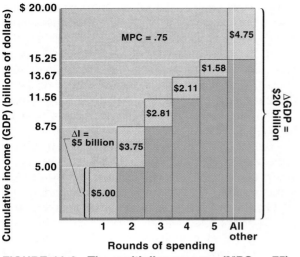

FIGURE 11-4 The multiplier process (MPC = .75)

An initial change in investment spending of $5 billion creates an equal $5 billion of new income in round 1. Households spend $3.75 (=.75 × $5) billion of this new income, creating $3.75 of added income in round 2. Of this $3.75 of new income, households spend $2.81 (=.75 × $3.75) billion and income rises by that amount in round 3. The cumulation of such income increments over the entire process eventually results in a total change of income and GDP of $20 billion. The multiplier therefore is 4 (=$20 billion ÷ $5 billion).

would be 3. If the MPS were .2, the multiplier would be 5.

Look again at Table 11-1 and Figure 11-3b. Initially the economy is in equilibrium at the $470 billion level of GDP. Now businesses increase investment by $5 billion so that planned investment of $25 billion exceeds saving of $20 billion at the $470 billion level. This means $470 billion is no longer the equilibrium GDP. By how much must gross domestic product or national income rise to restore equilibrium? By enough to generate $5 billion of additional saving to offset the $5 billion increase in investment. Because households save $1 out of every $4 of additional income they receive (MPS = .25), GDP must rise by $20 billion—four times the assumed increase in investment—to create the $5 billion of extra saving necessary to restore equilibrium. Hence, the multiplier is 4. If the MPS were .33, GDP would only have to rise by $15 billion (three times the increase in investment) to generate $5 billion of additional saving and restore equilibrium, and the multiplier therefore would be 3. But if the MPS were .20, GDP would have to rise by $25 billion for an extra $5 billion of saving to be forthcoming and equilibrium to be restored, yielding a multiplier of 5.

Furthermore, recall that the MPS measures the slope of the saving schedule. In terms of the leakages-injections ($S = I_g$) approach, this means that if the MPS is relatively large (say, .5) and the slope of the saving schedule is therefore relatively steep (.5), any given upward shift in investment spending will be subject to a relatively small multiplier. For example, a $5 billion increase in investment will entail a new point of intersection of the S and I_g schedules only $10 billion to the right of the original equilibrium GDP. The multiplier is only 2. But if the MPS is relatively small (say, .10), the slope of the saving schedule will be relatively gentle. Therefore, a $5 billion upward shift in the investment schedule will provide a new intersection point some $50 billion to the right of the original equilibrium GDP. The multiplier is 10 in this case. You should verify these two examples by drawing appropriate saving and investment diagrams.

We can summarize these and all other possibilities by merely saying that *the multiplier is equal to the reciprocal of the MPS.* The reciprocal of any number is the quotient you obtain by dividing 1 by that number. We can say:

$$\text{The multiplier} = \frac{1}{\text{MPS}}$$

This formula provides a shorthand method of determining the multiplier. All you need to know is the MPS to calculate the size of the multiplier. Recall, too, from Chapter 10 that since MPC + MPS = 1, it follows that MPS = 1 − MPC. Therefore, we can also write our multiplier formula as

$$\text{The multiplier} = \frac{1}{1 - \text{MPC}}$$

Significance of the Multiplier The significance of the multiplier is that a relatively small change in the investment plans of businesses or the consumption-saving plans of households can trigger a much larger change in the equilibrium level of GDP. The multiplier magnifies the fluctuations in business activity initiated by changes in spending.

As illustrated in Figure 11-5, the larger the MPC (the smaller the MPS), the greater will be the multiplier. For example, if the MPC is .75 and the multiplier is therefore 4, a $10 billion decline in planned investment will reduce the equilibrium GDP by $40 billion. But if the MPC is only .67 and the multiplier is 3, the same $10 billion drop in investment will cause the equilibrium GDP to fall by only $30 billion. This makes

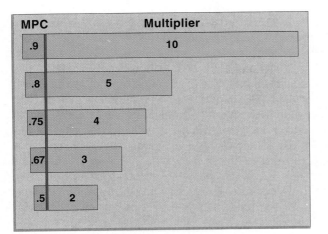

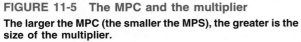

FIGURE 11-5   The MPC and the multiplier

The larger the MPC (the smaller the MPS), the greater is the size of the multiplier.

sense intuitively: A large MPC means the chain of induced consumption shown in Figure 11-4 dampens down slowly and thereby cumulates to a large change in income. Conversely, a small MPC (a large MPS) causes induced consumption to decline quickly so the cumulative change in income is small.

Generalizing the Multiplier   The multiplier concept as presented here is sometimes called the *simple multiplier* because it is based on a simple model of the economy. In terms of the $\dfrac{1}{\text{MPS}}$ formulation, the simple multiplier reflects only the leakage of saving. But, as noted earlier, in the real world successive rounds of income and spending can also be dampened down by other leakages in the form of imports and taxes. In addition to the leakage into saving, some portion of income at each round would be siphoned off as additional taxes, and

another part would be used to purchase additional goods from abroad. The result of these additional leakages is that the $\dfrac{1}{\text{MPS}}$ statement of the multiplier can be generalized by changing the denominator to read "fraction of the change in income which is not spent on domestic output" or "fraction of the change in income which leaks, or is diverted, from the income-expenditure stream." The more realistic multiplier which results when all these leakages—saving, taxes, and imports—are taken into account is called the *complex multiplier*. The Council of Economic Advisers, which advises the President on economic matters, has estimated the complex multiplier for the United States to be about 2.

Paradox of Thrift

A curious irony—dubbed the **paradox of thrift**—is suggested by the leakages-injections approach to GDP determination and by our analysis of the multiplier. The paradox is that if society attempts to save more, it may end up actually saving the same amount.

Suppose I_g and S_1 in Figure 11-6 are the current investment and saving schedules which determine a $470 billion equilibrium GDP. Now assume that households, perhaps anticipating a recession, attempt to save $5 billion more at each income level to provide a nest egg against the expected bad times. This attempt to save more is reflected in an upward shift of the saving schedule from S_1 to S_2. But this very upshift creates an excess of saving over planned investment at the current $470 billion equilibrium output. And we know that the multiplier effect will cause this small increase in saving (decline in consumption) to be reflected in a much larger—$20 billion (=$5 × 4) in this case—*decline* in equilibrium GDP.

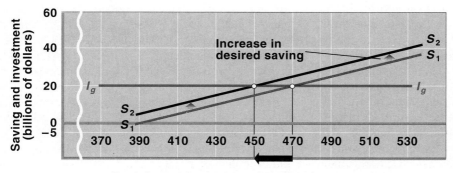

FIGURE 11-6   The paradox of thrift

Unless offset by an upshift in the planned investment schedule, any attempt by households to save more (S_1 to S_2) will be frustrated by a multiple decline in the equilibrium GDP.

There is a paradox here in several different senses.

1 At the new $450 billion equilibrium GDP, households are saving the same amount they did at the original $470 billion GDP. Society's attempt to save more has been frustrated by the multiple decline in the equilibrium GDP which that attempt itself caused.

2 This analysis suggests that thrift, which has always been held in high esteem in our economy, can be a social vice. From the individual point of view, a penny saved may be a penny earned. But from the social point of view, a penny saved is a penny not spent and therefore causes a decline in someone's income. The act of thrift may be virtuous from the individual's viewpoint but disastrous from the social standpoint because of its potential undesirable effects on total output and employment.

3 It is ironic, if not paradoxical, that households may be most strongly induced to save more (consume less) at the very time when increased saving is most inappropriate and economically undesirable, that is, when the economy seems to be backsliding into recession. Someone fearing the loss of his or her job will hardly be inclined to go on a spending spree. In our scenario more saving has made an anticipated recession a reality.

But the paradox of thrift and its implication that saving is socially undesirable must be altered in two important respects.

1 Assume the economy is initially experiencing rather pronounced demand-pull inflation. That is, the economy is operating, not in the horizontal Keynesian range, but in the vertical classical range of the aggregate supply curve. Here the economy is producing at full employment and an excess of aggregate demand is pulling up the price level. If households saved more (consumed less) in this situation, aggregate demand would shift leftward and the rate of inflation would be reduced. Look back at Figure 9-6b once again. Assume that the aggregate demand curve is initially at AD_6 with the price level at P_6. An increase in saving will reduce aggregate demand to, say, AD_5 and the price level would decline toward P_5. In this case more saving is socially desirable because it restrains inflation.

2 Recall from our discussion of Figure 2-4 that, other things being equal, an economy which saves *and invests* a larger proportion of its domestic output will achieve a higher rate of economic growth. A higher rate of saving frees resources from consumption uses so that they *may* be allocated to the production of more investment goods. This additional machinery and equipment enhances the nation's future productive capacity. Thus, if we make the classical assumption that the money market effectively links saving and investment decisions (recall Figure 10-1), then the upshift in the saving schedule from S_1 to S_2 in Figure 11-6 would be matched by an equal upshift in the investment schedule so that the equilibrium level of GDP would remain at $470 billion. In this case real output and employment would be unchanged but the composition of output would include more investment goods and fewer consumer goods. The result would be a more rapid rate of future economic growth. If rapid growth is a desired social goal, additional saving in this scenario would clearly be virtuous when matched by an equal increase in investment.

EQUILIBRIUM VERSUS FULL-EMPLOYMENT GDP

We now turn from the task of explaining to that of evaluating the equilibrium GDP.

The $470 billion equilibrium GDP embodied in our analysis (Table 11-1 and Figures 11-1 and 11-2) may or may not entail full employment. The aggregate expenditures schedule might well lie above or below that which would intersect the 45-degree line at the full-employment noninflationary level of output. Indeed, we have assumed thus far that production occurs in the less-than-full-employment Keynesian range of the aggregate supply curve.

Recessionary Gap

Assume in Figure 11-7a that the full-employment noninflationary level of domestic output is $490 billion. Suppose, too, that the aggregate expenditures schedule is at $(C + I_g)_1$, which is the aggregate expenditures schedule developed and employed in this chapter. This schedule intersects the 45-degree line to the left of the full-employment output, causing the economy's aggregate production to fall $20 billion short of its capacity production. In terms of Table 11-1, the economy is failing to employ 5 million of its 70 million available workers and, as a result, is sacrificing $20 billion worth of output.

The amount by which aggregate expenditures fall short of the full-employment level of GDP is called the **recessionary gap** simply because this deficiency of spending has a contractionary or depressing impact on the economy. Note in Table 11-1 that, assuming the full-employment GDP is $490 billion, the correspond-

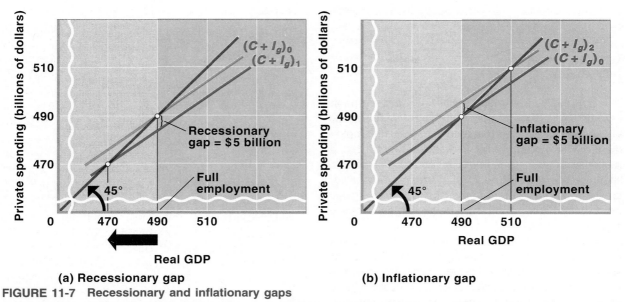

FIGURE 11-7 Recessionary and inflationary gaps

The equilibrium and full-employment GDPs may not coincide. A recessionary gap, shown in (a), is the amount by which aggregate expenditures fall short of the noninflationary full-employment GDP. It will cause a multiple decline in real GDP. The inflationary gap in (b) is the amount by which aggregate expenditures exceed the noninflationary full-employment level of GDP. This gap will cause demand-pull inflation.

ing level of total expenditures is only $485 billion. The recessionary gap is $5 billion, the amount by which the aggregate expenditures schedule would have to shift upward to realize the full-employment noninflationary GDP. Graphically, the recessionary gap is the *vertical* distance by which the aggregate expenditures schedule $(C + I_g)_1$ lies below the full-employment point on the 45-degree line. Because the relevant multiplier is 4, we observe a $20 billion differential (equal to the recessionary gap of $5 billion *times* the multiplier of 4) between the equilibrium GDP and the full-employment GDP. This $20 billion gap is the GDP gap which we encountered in Figure 8-5.

Inflationary Gap

If aggregate expenditures are at $(C + I_g)_2$ in Figure 11-7b, a demand-pull inflationary gap will exist. Specifically, the amount by which aggregate spending exceeds the full-employment level of GDP is called an **inflationary gap.** In this case, a $5 billion inflationary gap exists, as shown by the *vertical* distance between $(C + I_g)_2$ and the full-employment point on the 45-degree line. The inflationary gap is the amount by which the aggregate expenditures schedule would

have to shift downward to realize the full-employment noninflationary GDP.

The effect of this inflationary gap—this excess demand—will be to pull up the prices of the economy's fixed physical volume of production. Businesses as a whole cannot respond to the $5 billion in excess demand by expanding their real outputs, so *demand-pull inflation* will occur; nominal GDP will rise, but real GDP will not.

INTERNATIONAL TRADE AND EQUILIBRIUM OUTPUT

Thus far our aggregate expenditures model has ignored international trade by assuming a closed economy. We now acknowledge the existence of exports and imports and the fact that **net exports** (exports minus imports) may be either positive or negative in a particular period. A glance at line 4 on the inside covers of this book will reveal that net exports in some years have been positive (exports > imports) and in other years negative (imports > exports). Observe that net exports in 1975 were a *positive* $14 billion, for example, while in 1987 they were a *negative* $143 billion.

How do net exports—that is, exports and imports —relate to aggregate expenditures?

Net Exports and Aggregate Expenditures

Recall from Chapters 7 and 9 that—like consumption, investment, and government purchases—exports (X) give rise to domestic production, income, and employment. Even though goods and services produced in response to such spending are sent abroad, foreign spending on American goods increases production and creates jobs and incomes in the United States. Exports must therefore be added as a new component of aggregate expenditures.

Conversely, when an economy is open to international trade, part of its consumption and investment spending will be for imports (M), that is, for goods and services produced abroad rather than in the United States. In order not to overstate the value of domestic production, we must reduce the sum of consumption and investment expenditures for the portions expended on imported goods. Thus, in measuring aggregate expenditures for domestic goods and services, we must subtract expenditures on imports.

In short, for a private nontrading or closed economy, aggregate expenditures are $C + I_g$. But for a trading or open economy, aggregate spending is $C + I_g + (X - M)$. Or, recalling that net exports (X_n) equals $(X - M)$, we can say that aggregate expenditures for a private, open economy are $C + I_g + X_n$.

TABLE 11-3 **Two net export schedules** *(hypothetical data; in billions)*

(1) Level of GDP	(2) Net exports X_{n1} ($X > M$)	(3) Net exports X_{n2} ($X < M$)
$370	$+5	$−5
390	+5	−5
410	+5	−5
430	+5	−5
450	+5	−5
470	+5	−5
490	+5	−5
510	+5	−5
530	+5	−5
550	+5	−5

The Net Export Schedule

Table 11-3 shows two potential net export schedules for the hypothetical economy characterized by the data presented in Table 11-1. Similar to consumption and investment schedules, a net export schedule lists the amount of a particular expenditure—in this case net exports—which will occur at each level of GDP. The net export schedule X_{n1} (columns 1 and 2) tells us that exports exceed imports by $5 billion at each level of GDP. Perhaps exports are $15 billion, for example, while imports are $10 billion. The schedule X_{n2} (columns 1 and 3) reveals that imports are $5 billion higher than exports. That is, perhaps imports are $15 billion while exports are $10 billion. To simplify our discussion we assume in both cases that net exports are autonomous or independent of GDP.[1]

The two net export schedules from Table 11-3 are plotted in Figure 11-8b. Schedule X_{n1} reveals that a *positive* $5 billion of net exports are associated with each level of GDP. Conversely, X_{n2} is below the horizontal axis and shows that net exports are a *negative* $5 billion.

Net Exports and Equilibrium GDP

The aggregate expenditures schedule labeled $C + I_g$ in Figure 11-8a is identical to the one found in Table 11-1 and Figure 11-1. That is, $C + I_g$ reflects the combined consumption and gross investment expenditures which will occur at each level of GDP. The equilibrium level of GDP will be $470 billion when there is no foreign sector. Recall that this equilibrium level of output is determined at the intersection of the $C + I_g$ schedule and the 45-degree reference line; only there will aggregate expenditures equal GDP.

But net exports can be either positive or negative. Hence, exports and imports need not be neutral in their effect on the equilibrium level of GDP. How will each of the net export schedules presented in Figure 11-8b affect equilibrium GDP?

---

[1]Although our *exports* depend on *foreign* incomes and are thus independent of American GDP, our *imports* do vary directly with our own *domestic* national income. Just as our domestic consumption varies directly with our GDP, so do our purchases of foreign goods. As our GDP rises, American households buy not only more Pontiacs and more Pepsi but also Porsches and Perrier. However, for now we will ignore the resulting complications of the positive relationship between imports and American GDP.

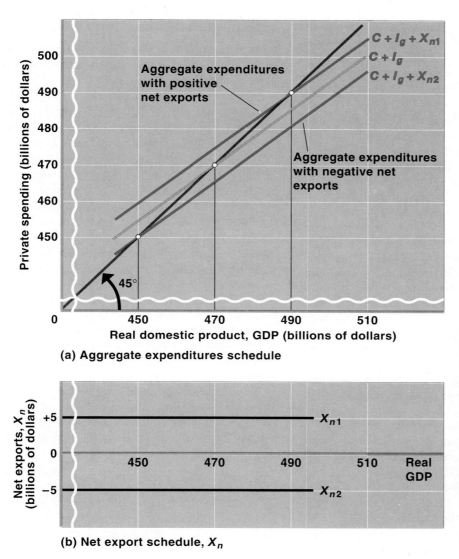

(a) Aggregate expenditures schedule

(b) Net export schedule, X_n

FIGURE 11-8   Net exports and the equilibrium GDP

Positive net exports such as shown by the net export schedule X_{n1} in (b) elevate the aggregate expenditures schedule in (a) from the closed-economy level of $C + I_g$ to the open-economy level of $C + I_g + X_{n1}$. Negative net exports such as depicted by the net export schedule X_{n2} in (b) lower the aggregate expenditures schedule in (a) from the closed-economy level of $C + I_g$ to the open-economy level of $C + I_g + X_{n2}$.

Positive Net Exports   First, suppose the net export schedule for our hypothetical economy is X_{n1}. The $5 billion of additional net export expenditures by foreigners are accounted for by adding $5 billion to the $C + I_g$ schedule in Figure 11-8a. Restated, aggregate expenditures at each level of GDP are $5 billion higher than indicated by the $C + I_g$ schedule alone. The aggregate expenditures schedule for the open economy thus becomes $C + I_g + X_{n1}$. The presence of international trade has increased equilibrium GDP from $470 billion in the simplified closed economy to $490 billion in the more realistic open economy. You should verify that the new equilibrium GDP is $490 billion by adding $5

billion to each level of aggregate expenditures in Table 11-1 and then determining where $C + I_g + X_n$ equals GDP.

Generalization: *Positive net exports increase aggregate expenditures beyond what they would be in a closed economy and thus have an expansionary effect on domestic GDP.* In this case, adding net exports of $5 billion has increased GDP by $20 billion, implying a multiplier of 4.

Negative Net Exports   An extension of our line of reasoning enables us to determine the impact of negative net exports on equilibrium GDP. If net exports are

X_{n2} as shown in Figure 11-8b, rather than X_{n1}, $5 billion of net export spending by foreigners must be subtracted from the aggregate expenditure schedule $C + I_g$ to establish aggregate expenditures for the open economy. The $5 billion of negative net exports mean that our hypothetical economy is importing $5 billion more of goods than it is selling abroad. The aggregate expenditures schedule shown as $C + I_g$ in Figure 11-8a therefore has overstated the expenditures on *domestic* output at each level of GDP. We must reduce the sum of consumption and investment expenditures by the $5 billion net amount expended on imported goods. For example, if imports are $15 billion and exports are $10 billion, we must subtract the $5 billion of *net* imports (= −$5 billion of net exports) from the combined domestic consumption and investment expenditures.

After we subtract $5 billion from the $C + I_g$ schedule in Figure 11-8a, the relevant aggregate expenditures schedule becomes $C + I_g + X_{n2}$ and equilibrium GDP falls from $470 to $450. Again, a change in net exports of $5 billion has resulted in a fourfold change in GDP, telling us that the multiplier is 4. Confirmation of the new equilibrium GDP can be obtained by subtracting $5 billion from aggregate expenditures at each level of GDP in Table 11-1 and ascertaining the new equilibrium GDP.

A corollary to our first generalization emerges: *Negative net exports reduce aggregate expenditures relative to what they would be in the closed economy and hence have a contractionary effect on domestic GDP.* Imports add to the stock of goods available in the economy, but they diminish domestic GDP by reducing expenditures on domestically produced products.

Our generalizations concerning positive and negative net exports and equilibrium GDP allow us to conclude that a decline in net exports—that is, a decrease in exports or an increase in imports—decreases aggregate expenditures and has a contractionary effect on domestic GDP. Conversely, an increase in net exports —the result of either an increase in exports or a decrease in imports—increases aggregate expenditures and has an expansionary effect on domestic GDP. These changes may be in terms of real GDP or the price level, depending on where the economy initially is located relative to its potential output. For example, if the full employment level of GDP in Figure 11-8a is $470 billion, then a rise of net exports from zero to $5 billion will create an inflationary gap of $5 billion, *not* a real GDP increase of $20 billion as implied in our earlier discussion.

International Economic Linkages

Our analysis of net exports and domestic GDP permits us to demonstrate how circumstances or policies abroad can affect our domestic GDP.

Prosperity Abroad   A rising level of national income among our trading partners will enable us to sell more of our goods abroad, thus raising our net exports and increasing our domestic GDP. We should be interested in the prosperity of our trading partners because their good fortune enables them to buy more imports. These purchases stimulate our exports and transfer some of their prosperity to us.

Tariffs   Suppose our trading partners impose high tariffs on American goods to reduce their imports and stimulate production in their economies. But their imports are our exports. When they restrict their imports to stimulate *their* economies, they are reducing our exports and depressing *our* economy. We may retaliate by imposing trade barriers on their products. If so, their exports will decline and their net exports may be unchanged or even fall. In the Great Depression of the 1930s various nations, including the United States, imposed trade barriers in the hope of reducing domestic unemployment. But rounds of retaliation simply throttled world trade and made the world depression worse.

Exchange Rates   Depreciation of the dollar relative to other currencies (Chapters 4 and 9) will permit people abroad to obtain more dollars per unit of their currencies. The price of American goods in terms of these currencies will fall, stimulating purchases of our exports. Conversely, American consumers will find they need more dollars to buy foreign goods and consequently will reduce their spending on imports. The resulting higher American exports and lower imports will increase our net exports and expand our GDP.

Whether depreciation of the dollar raises real GDP or produces inflation depends crucially on the initial location of the economy relative to its full-employment level of output. If the economy initially is operating below its productive capacity, the depreciation of the dollar and the resulting rise in net exports will increase real GDP. Alternatively, if the economy initially is fully employed, the depreciation of the dollar and higher level of net exports will cause domestic inflation.

Finally, while this last example has been cast in terms of a depreciation of the dollar, you should think through the impact that an *appreciation* of the dollar will have on net exports and equilibrium GDP.

QUICK REVIEW 11-2

❡ *The multiplier is the principle that initial changes in spending can cause magnified changes in national income and GDP.*

❡ *The higher the marginal propensity to consume (the lower the marginal propensity to save), the larger is the simple multiplier.*

❡ *Society may not always be successful in attempts to save more because reduced consumption can cause GDP and national income to fall.*

❡ *In the Keynesian model, a recessionary gap is the amount by which the aggregate expenditures line must increase for the economy to realize full employment GDP; the inflationary gap is the amount by which the aggregate expenditures line must decrease for the economy to end demand-pull inflation.*

❡ *Positive net exports increase aggregate expenditures on domestic output and increase equilibrium GDP; negative net exports decrease aggregate expenditures on domestic output and reduce equilibrium GDP.*

RECONCILING TWO MACRO MODELS

Our final challenge is to reconcile the Keynesian model of this chapter which shows the relationship between *aggregate expenditures* and real GDP and which assumes a constant price level with Chapter 9's model which portrays the relationship between real GDP and the *price level*. The Keynesian model, developed during the massive unemployment of the 1930s, assumes that an increase in aggregate expenditures will bring about an increase in domestic output at the existing or "going" price level. In contrast, the aggregate demand–aggregate supply model indicates that the price level will rise as aggregate demand increases in the intermediate and classical ranges of the aggregate supply curve. To repeat: The Keynesian expenditures-output analysis is a *constant* price level model; the aggregate demand–aggregate supply analysis is a *variable* price level model.

Deriving the AD Curve

By using familiar concepts and ideas we can forge an important link between our two models by showing how shifts in the aggregate expenditures schedule caused by price level changes permit us to trace out or locate a given downsloping aggregate demand curve.

Wealth Effect We know from Chapter 10 that there is an inverse relationship between the location of the consumption schedule and the price level. An increase in the price level causes the consumption schedule— and therefore the aggregate expenditures schedule— to shift downward and vice versa. A primary reason is the *real balances* or *wealth effect* introduced in Chapter 9. An increase in the price level reduces the real value or purchasing power of people's wealth. To restore the value of their wealth, people must save more and therefore consume less. At the higher price level the consumption schedule and therefore the aggregate expenditures schedule will shift downward and real GDP will fall.

Conversely, a decline in the price level increases the real value of people's wealth. When individuals are wealthier they are more inclined to consume and less inclined to save out of current real income. At the lower price level the consumption and aggregate expenditures curves shift upward and real GDP rises.

Interest-Rate Effect We also know from Chapter 10 that there is an inverse relationship between the location of the investment schedule (Table 10-3 and Figure 10-8) and the price level. An increase in the price level, all else being equal, will increase the interest rate, which in turn will shift the investment and aggregate expenditures schedules downward. This *interest-rate effect,* remember, works as follows: More money will be needed for purchases at the higher price level and, given a fixed supply of money, the increase in money demand will boost the interest rate and reduce investment expenditures. Conversely, a decline in the price level will reduce the demand for money, lower the interest rate, and elevate the investment and aggregate expenditures schedules. Lower price levels will be associated with greater aggregate expenditures and higher equilibrium levels of real GDP.

Foreign Purchases Effect Finally, there is an inverse relationship between the price level and the net export schedule. An increase in the price level will shift the net export schedule downward and thus reduce

KEY GRAPH

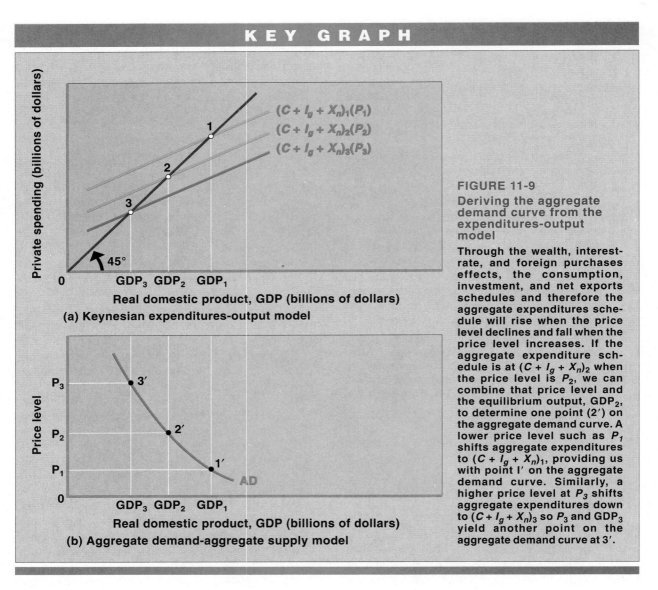

(a) Keynesian expenditures-output model

(b) Aggregate demand-aggregate supply model

FIGURE 11-9

Deriving the aggregate demand curve from the expenditures-output model

Through the wealth, interest-rate, and foreign purchases effects, the consumption, investment, and net exports schedules and therefore the aggregate expenditures schedule will rise when the price level declines and fall when the price level increases. If the aggregate expenditure schedule is at $(C + I_g + X_n)_2$ when the price level is P_2, we can combine that price level and the equilibrium output, GDP_2, to determine one point (2′) on the aggregate demand curve. A lower price level such as P_1 shifts aggregate expenditures to $(C + I_g + X_n)_1$, providing us with point I′ on the aggregate demand curve. Similarly, a higher price level at P_3 shifts aggregate expenditures down to $(C + I_g + X_n)_3$ so P_3 and GDP_3 yield another point on the aggregate demand curve at 3′.

aggregate expenditures and equilibrium GDP. Other things being equal, higher prices for American goods will reduce U.S. export sales abroad and increase our imports of relatively cheaper foreign products. American net exports, aggregate expenditures on American goods, and American GDP will all fall due to this *foreign purchases effect*. A lower American price level, on the other hand, will produce the opposite effects.

Combined Models The aggregate demand curve of the variable price-level model merely relates the various possible price levels to the corresponding equilibrium GDPs. Note in **Figure 11-9 (Key Graph)** that we

can "stack" our Keynesian model of Figure 11-9a and the aggregate demand–aggregate supply model of Figure 11-9b vertically because real domestic output is being measured on the horizontal axis of both models. Now we can start in the top diagram with the aggregate expenditures schedule $(C + I_g + X_n)_2$. The price level relevant to this aggregate expenditures schedule is P_2 as shown in parentheses to remind us of that fact. From this information we can plot the equilibrium real domestic output, GDP_2, and the corresponding price level of P_2. This gives us one point—namely 2′—on Figure 11-9b's aggregate demand curve.

We can now go through the same procedure but

assume that the price level is lower at P_1. We know that, other things being equal, a lower price level will: (1) increase the value of wealth, boosting consumption expenditures; (2) reduce the interest rate, promoting investment expenditures; and (3) reduce imports and increase exports, increasing net export expenditures. Consequently, the aggregate expenditures schedule will rise from $(C + I_g + X_n)_2$ to, say, $(C + I_g + X_n)_1$, giving us equilibrium at GDP_1. In Figure 11-9b we locate this new price level–real domestic output combination, P_1 and GDP_1, at point 1′.

Similarly, now suppose the price level increases from the original P_2 level to P_3. The real value of wealth falls, the interest rate rises, exports fall, and imports rise. Consequently, the consumption, investment, and net export schedules fall, shifting the aggregate expenditures schedule downward from $(C + I_g + X_n)_2$ to $(C + I_g + X_n)_3$ where real output is GDP_3. This lets us locate a third point on Figure 11-9b's aggregate demand curve, namely point 3′ where the price level is P_3 and real output is GDP_3.

In summary, a decrease in the price level shifts the aggregate expenditures schedule upward and increases real GDP. An increase in the price level shifts the aggregate expenditures schedule downward, reducing real GDP. The resulting price level–real GDP combinations yield various points such as 1′, 2′, and 3′, which locate a given downsloping aggregate demand curve.

Shifting the AD Curve

We know from Chapter 10 that the price level (and its impact on the real value of wealth, the interest rate, and net exports) is only one of many factors which might shift the aggregate expenditures schedule. For example, the consumption component of aggregate expenditures might be affected by expectations, consumer debt, or tax changes. And the investment component might be altered by changes in profit expectations, technological change, business taxes, and so forth. Likewise, the net export component of aggregate expenditures might be influenced by changes in exchange rates, tariff policies, and changes in levels of GDP and income in foreign nations.

What happens if we *hold the price level constant* and consider shifts in aggregate expenditures caused by these determinants of consumption, investment, and net exports? The answer is that the entire aggregate demand curve will shift rightward or leftward. (These aggregate demand shifters were discussed in Chapter 9 and summarized in Table 9-1.)

In Figure 11-10 we begin with the aggregate expenditures schedule at $(C + I_g + X_n)_1$ in the top diagram, yielding a real domestic output of GDP_1. Assume now that more optimistic business expectations cause investment to increase so that the aggregate expenditures schedule rises from $(C + I_g + X_n)_1$ to $(C + I_g + X_n)_2$. (The parenthetical P_1's remind us that in this case the price level is assumed to be constant.) The result will be a multiplied increase in real GDP from GDP_1 to GDP_2. In the lower graph this is reflected in an

FIGURE 11-10 Shifts in the aggregate expenditures schedule and in the aggregate demand curve

In (a) we assume that some determinant of consumption, investment, or net exports other than the price level shifts the aggregate expenditures schedule from $(C + I_g + X_n)_1$ to $(C + I_g + X_n)_2$, thereby increasing real domestic output from GDP_1 to GDP_2. In (b) we find that the aggregate demand counterpart of this is a rightward shift of the aggregate demand curve from AD_1 to AD_2 which is just sufficient to show the same increase in real output as in the expenditures-output model. We previously summarized the "aggregate demand shifters" in Table 9-1.

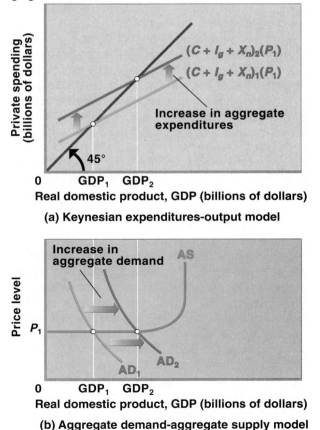

(a) Keynesian expenditures-output model

(b) Aggregate demand-aggregate supply model

increase in aggregate demand from AD_1 to AD_2 which shows the same multiplied increase in real GDP from GDP_1 to GDP_2. *The initial increase in investment shown as the upward shift of the aggregate expenditures curve in the top graph has shifted the AD curve in the lower graph by a horizontal distance equal to the change in investment times the multiplier.* Notice that this change in real GDP is associated with the constant price level P_1 because we are in the horizontal Keynesian range of the aggregate supply curve.

Multiplier with Price Level Changes

Thus far our two macro models seem compatible. The aggregate demand curve can be derived from the Keynesian model (Figure 11-9) and the multiplied effect of an initial change in some component of aggregate spending can be seen in both models (Figure 11-10). The two models part company, however, when changes in aggregate expenditures and aggregate demand cause price level changes.

In Figure 11-11, which restates and extends Figure 11-10b, we see that the previously discussed shift in aggregate demand from AD_1 to AD_2 occurs in the horizontal Keynesian range of aggregate supply. In other words, the economy is assumed to be in recession with ample excess productive capacity and a high unemployment rate. Therefore, businesses are willing to produce more output *at existing prices*. Any change in aggregate demand over this range is translated fully into a change in real GDP and employment while the price level remains constant. In the Keynesian range of aggregate supply a "full-strength" multiplier is at work.

If the economy is in the intermediate or classical range of the aggregate supply curve, part or all of any initial increase in aggregate demand will be dissipated in inflation and therefore *not* reflected in increased real output and employment. In Figure 11-11 the shift of aggregate demand from AD_2 to AD_3 is of the same magnitude as the AD_1 to AD_2 shift, but look what happens. Because we are now in the intermediate range of the aggregate supply curve, a portion of the increase in aggregate demand is dissipated in inflation as the price level rises from P_1 to P_2. Thus real GDP rises to only GDP'. If the aggregate supply curve had been horizontal, the AD_2 to AD_3 shift would have increased real domestic output to GDP_3. But inflation has weakened the multiplier so that the actual increase is to GDP' which is only about half as much.

Our conclusions are twofold. First, *for any given initial increase in aggregate demand, the resulting increase in real GDP will be smaller the larger the increase*

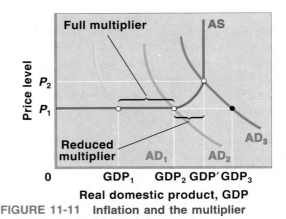

FIGURE 11-11 Inflation and the multiplier

The aggregate demand–aggregate supply model allows us to envision how inflation reduces the size of the multiplier. For the AD_1 to AD_2 increase in aggregate demand the price level is constant and the multiplier is at full strength. Although the increase in aggregate demand from AD_2 to AD_3 is of equal magnitude, it is partly dissipated in inflation (P_1 to P_2) and real output therefore only increases from GDP_2 to GDP'.

in the price level. Price level increases weaken the multiplier. You should sketch an increase in demand equal to the AD_2 to AD_3 shift in the vertical classical range to confirm that this increase in spending would be entirely dissipated in inflation. There would be no multiplier because real GDP would be unchanged. Our second, more general conclusion is that *the aggregate expenditures–output model is not sufficient to explain situations where changes in aggregate expenditures (and hence in aggregate demand) cause the price level to change.*

QUICK REVIEW 11-3

✦ *A change in the price level alters the location of the aggregate expenditures schedule through the wealth, interest rate, and foreign purchases effects.*

✦ *The aggregate demand curve is derived from the aggregate expenditures model by allowing the price level to change and observing the effect on the aggregate expenditures schedule and thus on equilibrium GDP.*

✦ *Holding the price level constant, increases in consumption, investment, and net export expenditures shift the aggregate expenditures schedule upward and the aggregate demand curve to the right.*

✦ *Price level increases occurring in the upsloping intermediate range of aggregate supply weaken the multiplier.*

LAST WORD

SQUARING THE ECONOMIC CIRCLE

Humorist Art Buchwald examines the multiplier.

WASHINGTON—The recession hit so fast that nobody knows exactly how it happened. One day we were the land of milk and honey and the next day we were the land of sour cream and food stamps.

This is one explanation.

Hofberger, the Chevy salesman in Tomcat, Va., a suburb of Washington, called up Littleton, of Littleton Menswear & Haberdashery, and said, "Good news, the new Novas have just come in and I've put one aside for you and your wife."

Littleton said, "I can't, Hofberger, my wife and I are getting a divorce."

"I'm sorry," Littleton said, "but I can't afford a new car this year. After I settle with my wife, I'll be lucky to buy a bicycle."

Hofberger hung up. His phone rang a few minutes later.

"This is Bedcheck the painter," the voice on the other end said. "When do you want us to start painting your house?"

"I changed my mind," said Hofberger. "I'm not going to paint the house."

"But I ordered the paint," Bedcheck said. "Why did you change your mind?"

"Because Littleton is getting a divorce and he can't afford a new car."

That evening when Bedcheck came home his wife said, "The new color television set arrived from Gladstone's TV Shop."

"Take it back," Bedcheck told his wife.

"Why?" she demanded.

"Because Hofberger isn't going to have his house painted now that the Littletons are getting a divorce."

The next day Mrs. Bedcheck dragged the TV set in its carton back to Gladstone. "We don't want it."

Gladstone's face dropped. He immediately called his travel agent, Sandstorm. "You know that trip you had scheduled for me to the Virgin Islands?"

"Right, the tickets are all written up."

"Cancel it. I can't go. Bedcheck just sent back the color TV set because Hofberger didn't sell a car to Lit-

tleton because they're going to get a divorce and she wants all his money."

Sandstorm tore up the airline tickets and went over to see his banker, Gripsholm. "I can't pay back the loan this month because Gladstone isn't going to the Virgin Islands."

Gripsholm was furious. When Rudemaker came in to borrow money for a new kitchen he needed for his restaurant, Gripsholm turned him down cold. "How can I loan you money when Sandstorm hasn't repaid the money he borrowed?"

Rudemaker called up the contractor, Eagleton, and said he couldn't put in a new kitchen. Eagleton laid off eight men.

Meanwhile, General Motors announced it was giving a rebate on its new models. Hofberger called up Littleton immediately. "Good news." he said, "even if you are getting a divorce, you can afford a new car."

"I'm not getting a divorce," Littleton said. "It was all a misunderstanding and we've made up."

"That's great," Hofberger said. "Now you can buy the Nova."

"No way," said Littleton. "My business has been so lousy I don't know why I keep the doors open."

"I didn't realize that," Hofberger said.

"Do you realize I haven't seen Bedcheck, Gladstone, Sandstorm, Gripsholm, Rudemaker or Eagleton for more than a month? How can I stay in business if they don't patronize my store?"

Source: Art Buchwald, "Squaring the Economic Circle," *Cleveland Plain Dealer,* February 22, 1975. Reprinted by permission.

Looking Ahead

What's next? In Chapter 12 we will embellish our expenditures-output and aggregate demand and supply models by moving from a private sector economy to a mixed economy in which government expenditures and taxes are considered. Our main mission will be to explain how government might alter its expenditures and tax collections to alleviate either unemployment or inflation.

CHAPTER SUMMARY

1 For a closed private economy the equilibrium level of GDP is where aggregate expenditures and domestic output are equal or, graphically, where the $C + I_g$ line intersects the 45-degree line. At any GDP greater than equilibrium GDP, domestic output will exceed aggregate spending, resulting in unintended investment in inventories, depressed profits, and eventual declines in output, employment, and income. At any below-equilibrium GDP, aggregate expenditures will exceed domestic output, resulting in unintended disinvestment in inventories, substantial profits, and eventual increases in GDP.

2 A complementary leakages-injections approach determines equilibrium GDP at the point where the amount households save and the amount businesses plan to invest are equal. This is at the point where the saving and planned investment schedules intersect. Any excess of saving over planned investment will cause a shortage of total spending, forcing GDP to fall. Any excess of planned investment over saving will cause an excess of total spending, inducing GDP to rise. These changes in GDP will in both cases correct the indicated discrepancies in saving and planned investment.

3 Shifts in the saving-consumption schedules or in the investment schedule will cause the equilibrium output-income level to change by several times the amount of the initial change in spending. This multiplier effect accompanies both increases and decreases in spending. The simple multiplier is equal to the reciprocal of the marginal propensity to save.

4 The paradox of thrift is the notion that the attempt of society to save more, as reflected in an upshift of the saving schedule, may be frustrated by the multiple decline in the equilibrium GDP which will ensue. If demand-pull inflation exists, however, more saving will reduce the price level. Furthermore, if the additional saving is invested, the equilib-

rium GDP will be unchanged and the economy will realize a more rapid rate of growth.

5 The equilibrium level of GDP and the full-employment noninflationary GDP need not coincide. The amount by which aggregate expenditures fall short of the full-employment GDP is called the recessionary gap; this gap prompts a multiple decline in real GDP. The amount by which aggregate expenditures exceed the full-employment GDP is the inflationary gap; it causes demand-pull inflation.

6 Positive net exports increase aggregate expenditures and thus increase American GDP; negative net exports decrease aggregate expenditures and therefore reduce American GDP. Increases in exports or decreases in imports have an expansionary effect on GDP while decreases in exports or increases in imports have a contractionary effect on GDP.

7 The downsloping aggregate demand curve can be derived from the expenditures-output model by varying the price level and determining how the consequent changes in aggregate expenditures alter the equilibrium level of real domestic output. Shifts in the aggregate demand curve are associated with shifts in the aggregate expenditures curve caused by non-price-level factors that alter consumption, investment, or net export spending.

8 Assuming a constant price level, the aggregate demand–aggregate supply model would show the same multiplied change in real GDP as portrayed in the expenditures-output model.

9 In the intermediate and classical ranges of the aggregate supply curve the aggregate demand–aggregate supply model tells us that the multiplier will be weakened because a portion of any increase in aggregate demand will be dissipated in inflation.

TERMS AND CONCEPTS

aggregate expenditures–
   domestic output
   approach
equilibrium GDP
	leakages-injections
	   approach
	45-degree line
	multiplier effect
		planned and actual
		   investment
		paradox of thrift
			recessionary and
			   inflationary gaps
			net exports

QUESTIONS AND STUDY SUGGESTIONS

1 Explain graphically the determination of the equilibrium GDP by **a** the aggregate expenditures–domestic output approach and **b** the leakages-injections approach for the private sector of a closed economy. Why must these two approaches

always yield the same equilibrium GDP? Explain why the intersection of the aggregate expenditures schedule and the 45-degree line determines the equilibrium GDP.

CHAPTER ELEVEN ＊ 219

2 Assuming the level of investment is $16 billion and independent of the level of total output, complete the following table and determine the equilibrium level of output and income which the private sector of this closed economy would provide.

Possible levels of employment, millions	Real domestic output (GDP = DI), billions	Consumption, billions	Saving, billions
40	$240	$244	$_____
45	260	260	_____
50	280	276	_____
55	300	292	_____
60	320	308	_____
65	340	324	_____
70	360	340	_____
75	380	356	_____
80	400	372	_____

a If this economy has a labor force of 70 million, will there exist an inflationary or a recessionary gap? Explain the consequences of this gap.

b Will an inflationary or a recessionary gap exist if the available labor force is only 55 million? Trace the consequences.

c What are the sizes of the MPC and the MPS?

d Use the multiplier concept to explain the increase in the equilibrium GDP which will occur as the result of an increase in planned investment spending from $16 to $20 billion.

3 Using the consumption and saving data given in question 2 and assuming the level of investment is $16 billion, what are the levels of saving and planned investment at the $380 billion level of domestic output? What are the levels of saving and actual investment? What are saving and planned investment at the $300 billion level of domestic output? What are the levels of saving and actual investment? Use the concept of unintended investment to explain adjust-

ments toward equilibrium from both the $380 and $300 billion levels of domestic output.

4 "Planned investment is equal to saving at all levels of GDP; actual investment equals saving only at the equilibrium GDP." Do you agree? Explain. Critically evaluate: "The fact that households may save more than businesses want to invest is of no consequence, because events will in time force households and businesses to save and invest at the same rates."

5 What effect will each of the changes designated in question 6 at the end of Chapter 10 have on the equilibrium level of GDP? Explain your answers.

6 What is the simple multiplier effect? What relationship does the MPC bear to the size of the multiplier? The MPS? What will the multiplier be when the MPS is 0, .4, .6, and 1? When the MPC is 1, .90, .67, .50, and 0? How much of a change in GDP will result if businesses increase their level of investment by $8 billion and the MPC in the economy is .80? If the MPC is .67? Explain the difference between the simple and the complex multiplier.

7 Explain the paradox of thrift. What is its significance? "One's view of the social desirability of saving depends on whether one assumes a Keynesian or classical view of the macroeconomy." Do you agree?

8 The data in columns 1 and 2 of the table below are for a closed economy.

a Use columns 1 and 2 to determine the equilibrium GDP for the closed economy.

b Now open this economy for international trade by including the export and import figures of columns 3 and 4. Calculate net exports and determine the equilibrium GDP for the open economy. Explain why equilibrium GDP differs from the closed economy.

c Given the original $20 billion level of exports, what would be the equilibrium GDP if imports were $10 billion larger at each level of GDP? Or $10 billion smaller at each level of GDP? What generalization concerning the level of imports and the equilibrium GDP is illustrated by these examples?

d What is the size of the multiplier in these examples?

(1) Real domestic output (GDP = DI), billions	(2) Aggregate expenditures, closed economy, billions	(3) Exports, billions	(4) Imports, billions	(5) Net exports, billions	(6) Aggregate expenditures, open economy, billions
$200	$240	$20	$30	$_____	$_____
250	280	20	30	_____	_____
300	320	20	30	_____	_____
350	360	20	30	_____	_____
400	400	20	30	_____	_____
450	440	20	30	_____	_____
500	480	20	30	_____	_____
550	520	20	30	_____	_____

9 Using appropriate diagrams, reconcile the Keynesian aggregate expenditures model and the aggregate demand–aggregate supply model. Explain the following two statements:

a "The Keynesian model is an unemployment model; the aggregate demand—aggregate supply model is an inflation model."

b "The Keynesian model can explain demand-pull inflation, but the aggregate demand–aggregate supply model is needed to explain cost-push inflation."

10 Explain how an upsloping aggregate supply curve might weaken the multiplier effect.

11 Advanced analysis: Assume the consumption schedule for the economy is such that $C = 50 + 0.8Y$. As-sume further that investment and net exports are autono-mous (indicated by I_{g0} and X_{n0}); that is, planned investment and net exports are independent of the level of income and in the amount $I_g = I_{g0} = 30$ and $X_n = X_{n0} = 10$. Recall also that in equilibrium the amount of domestic output produced (Y) is equal to the aggregate expenditures $(C + I_g + X_n)$, or $Y = C + I_g + X_n$.

a Calculate the equilibrium level of income for this economy. Check your work by putting the consumption, investment, and net export schedules in tabular form and determining the equilibrium income.

b What will happen to equilibrium Y if $I_g = I_{g0} = 10$? What does this tell you about the size of the multiplier?

CHAPTER 12

Fiscal Policy

In 1964 the Johnson administration implemented legislation to cut tax rates without simultaneously reducing government spending. This legislation was initiated earlier by the Kennedy administration.

During the Vietnam war, the Johnson administration placed a 10 percent surcharge on corporate and individual income taxes.

Between 1982 and 1984 the Reagan administration cut personal income tax rates by 25 percent.

In 1990 the Bush administration put in place a tax-spending package designed to reduce the Federal budget deficit by $500 billion over a five-year period.

What is the logic of these fiscal actions? Why might government raise or lower tax rates independently of changes in its spending? Under what conditions does it make sense for government to alter the level of its spending even though tax rates remain fixed?

To answer these important questions we must add the public sector to the analysis of the equilibrium GDP developed in Chapters 10 and 11. Recall that the consumption, investment, and import-export decisions of households and businesses are based on private self-interest and that the outcome of these decisions may be either recession or inflation.

In contrast, government is an instrument of society as a whole; within limits government's decisions on spending and taxing can be altered to influence the equilibrium GDP in terms of the general welfare. In particular, we saw in Chapter 6 that a fundamental function of the public sector is to stabilize the economy. This stabilization is achieved in part through the manipulation of the public budget—government spending and tax collections—for the expressed purpose of increasing output and employment or reducing the rate of inflation. Indeed, one of the basic notions of mainstream economics is that government has an obligation to behave in his way.

Specific goals of this chapter are to:
1 Analyze the impact of government purchases and taxes on the GDP.
2 Explain how some degree of economic stability is built into our tax system.
3 Survey shortcomings and problems in the application of fiscal policy.

221

LEGISLATIVE MANDATES

The idea that government fiscal actions can exert an important stabilizing influence on the economy began to gain widespread acceptance during the depression of the 1930s. Keynesian employment theory played a major role in emphasizing the importance of remedial fiscal measures.

Employment Act of 1946   In 1946, when the end of World War II recreated the specter of unemployment, the Federal government formalized in law its area of responsibility in promoting economic stability. The **Employment Act of 1946** proclaims:

> The Congress hereby declares that it is the continu-
> ing policy and responsibility of the Federal Govern-
> ment to use all practicable means consistent with its
> needs and obligations and other essential considera-
> tions of national policy, with assistance and coopera-
> tion of industry, agriculture, labor and State and
> local governments, to coordinate and utilize all its
> plans, functions, and resources for the purpose of
> creating and maintaining, in a manner calculated to
> foster and promote free competitive enterprise and
> the general welfare, conditions under which there
> will be afforded useful employment opportunities,
> including self-employment, for those able, willing,
> and seeking to work and to promote maximum em-
> ployment, production, and purchasing power.

The Employment Act of 1946 is a landmark in American socioeconomic legislation in that it commits the Federal government to take positive action through monetary and fiscal policy to maintain economic stability.

CEA and JEC   Responsibility for fulfilling the purposes of the act rests with the executive branch; the President must submit an annual Economic Report describing the current state of the economy and making appropriate policy recommendations. The act also established a **Council of Economic Advisers** (CEA) to assist and advise the President on economic matters, and a *Joint Economic Committee* (JEC) of the Congress, which has investigated a wide range of economic problems of national interest. In its advisory capacity as "the President's intelligence arm in the eternal war against the business cycle," the CEA and its staff gather and analyze relevant economic data and use them to make forecasts; to formulate programs and policies designed to fulfill the goals of the Employment Act; and to "educate" the President, the Congress, and the general public on problems and policies relevant to the nation's economic health.

DISCRETIONARY FISCAL POLICY

Discretionary fiscal policy is the deliberate manipulation of taxes and government spending by the Congress to alter real domestic output and employment, control inflation, and stimulate economic growth.

Simplifying Assumptions

To keep our discussion as clear as possible, the following simplifying assumptions are made.

1   We continue to employ the simplified investment and net export schedules, where levels of investment and net exports are independent of the level of GDP. Furthermore, we suppose initially that net exports are zero.

2   We assume that the initial impact of government purchases is such that they neither depress nor stimulate private spending. That is, government purchases will not cause any upward or downward shifts in the consumption and investment schedules.

3   It is presumed that the government's net tax revenues—total tax revenues less "negative taxes" in the form of transfer payments—are derived entirely from personal taxes. Although DI will fall short of PI by the amount of government's tax revenues, GDP, NI, and PI will remain equal.

4   We assume initially that a fixed amount of taxes is collected regardless of the level of GDP.

5   We suppose initially that the price level is constant. Changes in aggregate expenditures or aggregate demand will have their full effect on real output and employment rather than being dissipated wholly or in part by a changing price level. Stated differently, the economy is presumed to be functioning within the horizontal Keynesian range of the aggregate supply curve.

6   Finally, let's assume that the impact of fiscal policy is confined to the demand side of the macroeconomy; there are no intended or unintended effects upon aggregate supply.

These assumptions will give us a simple and uncluttered view of how changes in government spending and taxes influence the economy. Most of these assumptions will be dropped as we examine the complications and shortcomings fiscal policy often encounters in the real world.

In our discussion of the private sector of the economy, we implicitly assumed that government purchases of goods and services (G) and tax revenues (T) were both zero. Now we suppose that G and T each increase from zero to, say, $20 billion, and note the individual impact of each and then the combined impact of the two.

Government Purchases and Equilibrium GDP

Suppose government decides to purchase $20 billion worth of goods and services regardless of the level of GDP.

Tabular Example   Table 12-1 shows the impact on the equilibrium GDP in terms of arithmetic data. Columns 1 through 4 are carried over from Table 11-1 for the private closed economy, in which the equilibrium GDP was $470 billion. The only new wrinkles are the additions of net exports (exports minus imports) in column 5 and government purchases in column 6. By adding government purchases to private spending ($C + I_g + X_n$), we get a new, higher level of aggregate expenditures as shown in column 7. Comparing columns 1 and 7, we find that aggregate expenditures and domestic output are equal at a higher level of GDP; specifically, equilibrium GDP has increased from $470 (row 6) to $550 billion (row 10). *Increases in public spending, like increases in private spending, will boost the aggregate expenditures schedule in relation to the 45-degree line and result in a higher equilibrium GDP.*

Note, too, that government spending is subject to the multiplier. A $20 billion increase in government purchases has increased equilibrium GDP by $80 billion (=$550 billion minus $470 billion). The multiplier in this example is 4.

This $20 billion increase in government spending is *not* financed by increased tax revenues. We will find momentarily that increased taxes reduce the equilibrium GDP. Stated differently, government spending must entail budget deficits to have the expansionary impact just described. Indeed, Keynes's basic policy recommendation was deficit spending by government to overcome recession or depression.

In terms of the leakages-injections approach, government purchases—like investment and exports—are an injection of spending. Leakages of savings and imports cause consumption of domestic output to fall short of domestic disposable income, creating a potential spending gap. This gap may be filled by injections of investment, exports, and government purchases. Observe in Table 12-1 that the $550 billion equilibrium level of GDP (row 10) occurs where $S + M = I_g + X + G$. That is, when taxes are assumed to be zero, $40 + 10 = 20 + 10 + 20$.

Graphical Analysis   Figure 12-1 shows graphically the impact of government purchases. In Figure 12-1a we add government purchases, G, vertically to the level of private spending, $C + I_g + X_n$. The aggregate expenditures schedule (private plus public) now has been increased to $C + I_g + X_n + G$, resulting in the indicated $80 billion increase in equilibrium GDP.

TABLE 12-1   The impact of government purchases on equilibrium GDP (*hypothetical data*)

(1) Real domestic output and income (GDP = DI), billions	(2) Consumption, C, billions	(3) Saving, S, billions	(4) Investment, I_g, billions	(5) Net exports, X_n, billions		(6) Government purchases, G, billions	(7) Aggregate expenditures ($C + I_g + X_n + G$), billions, or (2) + (4) + (5) + (6)
				Exports, X	Imports, M		
(1) $370	$375	$−5	$20	$10	$10	$20	$415
(2) 390	390	0	20	10	10	20	430
(3) 410	405	5	20	10	10	20	445
(4) 430	420	10	20	10	10	20	460
(5) 450	435	15	20	10	10	20	475
(6) 470	450	20	20	10	10	20	490
(7) 490	465	25	20	10	10	20	505
(8) 510	480	30	20	10	10	20	520
(9) 530	495	35	20	10	10	20	535
(10) 550	510	40	20	10	10	20	550

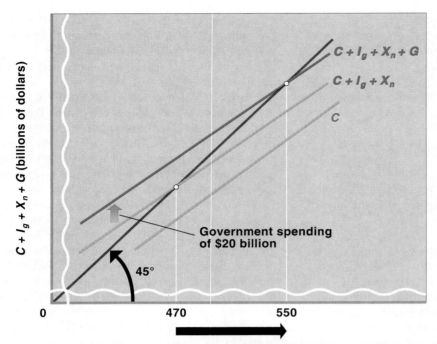

Real domestic product, GDP (billions of dollars)

(a) Aggregate expenditures-domestic output approach

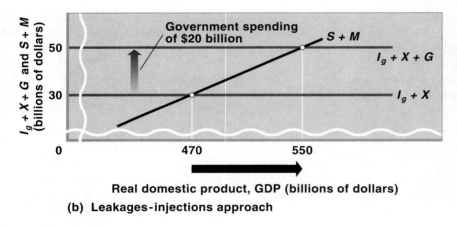

Real domestic product, GDP (billions of dollars)

(b) Leakages-injections approach

FIGURE 12-1 Government spending and the equilibrium GDP

(a) *The aggregate expenditures–domestic output approach.* The addition of government expenditures G to our analysis raises the aggregate expenditures $(C + I_g + X_n + G)$ schedule and increases the equilibrium level of GDP as would an increase in C, I_g, or X_n. Note that changes in government spending are subject to the multiplier effect. (b) *Leakages-injections approach.* In terms of the leakages-injections approach, government spending supplements private investment and net export spending $(I_g + X_n + G)$, increasing the equilibrium GDP.

Figure 12-1b shows the same change in the equilibrium GDP in terms of the leakages-injections approach. Like investment and exports, government spending is an offset to the leakage of saving and imports. With G added to our discussion, the equilibrium level of GDP is now determined at the point where the amount households save and import is offset exactly by the amount businesses plan to invest and export *plus* the amount government desires to spend on goods and services. Assuming there are no taxes, the equilibrium

GDP is determined by the intersection of the $S + M$ schedule and the $I_g + X + G$ schedule. Note that both approaches indicate the same new $550 billion equilibrium GDP.

A *decline* in government spending G will cause the aggregate expenditures schedule to fall in Figure 12-1a and the $I_g + X + G$ schedule to fall in Figure 12-1b. In either case the result is a multiple *decline* in the equilibrium GDP. You should verify that, if government spending were to decline from $20 to $10 billion, the equilibrium GDP would fall by $40 billion, that is, from $550 to $510 billion, implying a multiplier of 4.

Taxation and Equilibrium GDP

But government also collects tax revenues. How do tax collections affect the equilibrium level of GDP? To answer this question in the simplest way, we assume that government imposes a **lump-sum tax** which, by definition, is *a tax of a constant amount or, more precisely, a tax which yields the same amount of tax revenue at each level of GDP.* Suppose the lump-sum tax is $20 billion so that government obtains $20 billion of tax revenue at each and every level of GDP. What is the impact of government's increasing tax collections from zero to $20 billion at each level of GDP?

Tabular Example Table 12-2 is relevant. Taxes are inserted as column 2 and we note in column 3 that disposable (after-tax) income is less than GDP by the amount of the taxes. DI has been reduced by $20 billion—the amount of the taxes—at each level of GDP. Because DI is made up of consumer spending and saving, a decline in DI will lower both consumption and saving. But by how much will each decline? The MPC and MPS hold the answer: The MPC tells us what fraction of a decline in DI will come at the expense of consumption, and the MPS indicates what fraction of a drop in DI will come at the expense of saving. Observing that the MPC equals .75 (=15/20) and the MPS equals .25 (=5/20), we can conclude that if government collects $20 billion in taxes at each possible level

of GDP, the amount of consumption at each level of GDP will drop by $15 billion (.75 × $20 billion), and the amount of saving at each level of GDP will fall by $5 billion (.25 × $20 billion).

Observe in columns 4 and 5 of Table 12-2 that the amounts of consumption and saving *at each level of GDP* are $15 and $5 billion smaller, respectively, than in Table 12-1. Thus, for example, before the imposition of taxes, where GDP equaled DI, consumption was $420 billion and saving $10 billion at the $430 billion level of GDP (row 4 of Table 12-1). After taxes are imposed, DI is $410 billion, $20 billion short of the $430 billion GDP, with the result that consumption is only $405 billion and saving is $5 billion (columns 4 and 5 of Table 12-2).

To summarize: *Taxes cause DI to fall short of GDP by the amount of the taxes. This decline in DI reduces both consumption and saving at each level of GDP. The sizes of the declines in C and S are determined by the MPC and the MPS.* Specifically, multiply the tax increase ($20 billion) by the MPC (.75) to determine the decrease in consumption ($15 billion). Similarly, multiply the tax increase ($20 billion) by the MPS (.25) to determine the decrease in saving ($5 billion).

What is the effect upon equilibrium GDP? We calculate aggregate expenditures again as shown in column 9 of Table 12-2. Note that aggregate spending is $15 billion less at each level of domestic output than it was in Table 12-1. The reason is that after-tax consumption, designated by C_a, is $15 billion less at each level of GDP. Comparing domestic output and aggregate expenditures in columns 1 and 9, we see the aggregate

TABLE 12-2 Determination of the equilibrium levels of employment, output, and income: private and public sectors (*hypothetical data*)

(1) Real domestic output and income (GDP = NI = PI), billions	(2) Taxes, T, billions	(3) Disposable income, DI, billions, or (1) − (2)	(4) Consumption, C_a, billions	(5) Saving, S_a, billions, or (3) − (4)	(6) Investment, I_g, billions	(7) Net exports, X_n, billions Exports, X	Imports, M	(8) Government expenditures, G, billions	(9) Aggregate expenditures ($C_a + I_g + X_n + G$), billions, or (4) + (6) + (7) + (8)
(1) $370	$20	$350	$360	$−10	$20	$10	$10	$20	$400
(2) 390	20	370	375	−5	20	10	10	20	415
(3) 410	20	390	390	0	20	10	10	20	430
(4) 430	20	410	405	5	20	10	10	20	445
(5) 450	20	430	420	10	20	10	10	20	460
(6) 470	20	450	435	15	20	10	10	20	475
(7) 490	20	470	450	20	20	10	10	20	490
(8) 510	20	490	465	25	20	10	10	20	505
(9) 530	20	510	480	30	20	10	10	20	520
(10) 550	20	530	495	35	20	10	10	20	535

amounts produced and purchased are equal only at the $490 billion GDP (row 7). Observe that the $20 billion lump-sum tax has caused equilibrium GDP to fall by $60 billion from $550 billion (row 10 in Table 12-1) to $490 billion (row 7 in Table 12-2).

Our alternative leakages-injections approach confirms this result. Taxes, like saving and imports, are a leakage from the domestic income-expenditures stream. Saving, importing, and paying taxes are all uses of income which do not involve domestic consumption. Consumption will now fall short of domestic output—creating a potential spending gap—in the amount of after-tax saving and imports *plus* taxes. This gap may

be filled by planned investment, exports, and government purchases. Hence, our new equilibrium condition for the leakages-injections approach is: After-tax saving, S_a, plus imports plus taxes equals planned investment plus exports plus government purchases. Symbolically, $S_a + M + T = I_g + X + G$. You should verify in Table 12-2 that this equality of leakages and injections is fulfilled *only* at the $490 billion GDP (row 7).

Graphical Analysis The impact of the $20 billion increase in taxes is shown in Figure 12-2a and b. In Figure 12-2a the $20 billion *increase* in taxes shows up as a

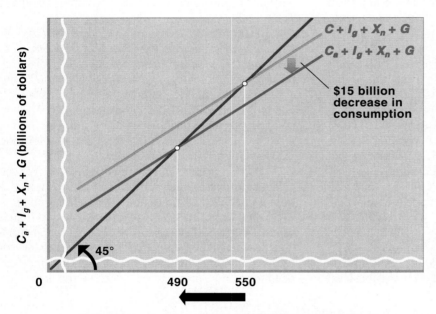

(a) Aggregate expenditures-domestic output approach

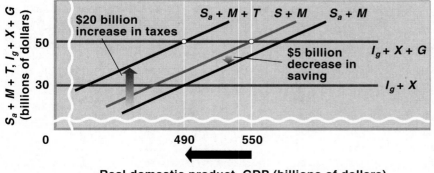

(b) Leakages-injections approach

FIGURE 12-2   Taxes and the equilibrium GDP

(a) ***The aggregate expenditures–domestic output approach.*** If the MPC is .75, the imposition of $20 billion of taxes will lower the consumption schedule by $15 billion and cause a decline in the equilibrium GDP. (b) ***The leakages-injections approach.*** Here taxes have a twofold effect. First, with an MPS of .25, the imposition of taxes of $20 billion will reduce disposable income by $20 billion and saving by $5 billion at each level of GDP. This is shown by the shift from S (saving before taxes) + M to S_a (saving after taxes) + M. Second, the $20 billion of taxes is an additional $20 billion leakage at each GDP level, giving us $S_a + M + T$. By adding government, the equilibrium condition changes from $S + M = I_g + X$ to $S_a + M + T = I_g + X + G$.

$15 (*not* $20) billion *decline* in the aggregate expenditures ($C_a + I_g + X_n + G$) schedule. Under our simplifying assumption that all taxes are personal income taxes, this decline in aggregate expenditures is solely the result of a decline in the consumption component of the aggregate expenditures schedule. The equilibrium GDP shifts from $550 billion to a $490 billion level as a result of this tax-caused drop in consumption. *Increases in taxes will lower the aggregate expenditures schedule relative to the 45-degree line and cause the equilibrium GDP to fall.*

Consider now the leakages-injections approach: The analysis here is slightly more complex because the imposition of $20 billion in taxes has a twofold effect in Figure 12-2b.

1 The taxes reduce DI by $20 billion and, with the MPS at .25, cause saving to fall by $5 billion at each level of GDP. In Figure 12-2b this is shown as a shift from $S + M$ (saving before taxes plus imports) to $S_a + M$ (saving after taxes plus imports).

2 The $20 billion in taxes as such appears as a $20 billion additional leakage at each GDP level which must be added to $S_a + M$ (not $S + M$), giving us $S_a + M + T$.

Equilibrium now exists at the $490 billion GDP, where the total amount which households save plus imports plus the amount of taxes government intends to collect are equal to the total amount businesses plan to invest plus exports plus the amount of government purchases. The equilibrium condition for the leakages-injections approach now is $S_a + M + T = I_g + X + G$. Graphically, the intersection of the $S_a + M + T$ and the $I_g + X + G$ schedules determines the equilibrium GDP.

A *decrease* in existing taxes will increase the aggregate expenditures schedule as a result of an upward shift in the consumption schedule in Figure 12-2a. In Figure 12-2b a tax cut will reduce the $S_a + M + T$ schedule. The result in either case is a multiple *increase* in the equilibrium GDP. You should employ both the expenditures-output and the leakages-injections approaches to confirm that a tax reduction of $10 billion (from the present $20 to $10 billion) will increase the equilibrium GDP from $490 to $520 billion.

Balanced-Budget Multiplier

Note an important and curious point about our tabular and graphical illustrations. *Equal increases in government spending and taxation increase the equilibrium GDP. That is, if G and T are each increased by a particu-lar amount, the equilibrium level of domestic output will rise by that same amount.* In our example the $20 billion increases in G and T increase the equilibrium GDP by $20 billion (from $470 to $490 billion).

The rationale for this **balanced-budget multiplier** is revealed in our example. A change in government spending has a more powerful effect on aggregate expenditures than does a tax change of the same size. Government spending has a *direct* and unadulterated impact upon aggregate expenditures. Government spending is a component of aggregate expenditures and, when government purchases increase by $20 billion as in our example, the aggregate expenditures schedule shifts upward by the entire $20 billion.

But a change in taxes affects aggregate expenditures *indirectly* by changing disposable income and thereby changing consumption. Specifically, our lump-sum tax increase shifts the aggregate expenditures schedule downward only by the amount of the tax *times* the MPC. That is, a $20 billion tax increase shifts the aggregate expenditures schedule downward by $15 billion (=$20 billion × .75).

The overall result is a *net* upward shift of the aggregate expenditures schedule of $5 billion which, subject to a multiplier of 4, boosts GDP by $20 billion. This $20 billion increase in GDP is equal to the size of the initial increase in government expenditures and taxes. *The balanced budget multiplier is 1.*

The fact that the balanced budget multiplier is 1 is shown in Figure 12-3. Given the MPC of .75, the tax increase of $20 billion reduces disposable income by $20 billion and decreases consumption expenditures by $15 billion. The $15 billion decline in consumption expenditures *reduces* GDP by $60 billion (=$15 billion × the multiplier of 4). However, observe in Figure 12-3 that the increase in government expenditures of $20 billion *increases* GDP by $80 billion (=$20 billion × the multiplier of 4). Hence, the equal increases of taxes and government expenditures of $20 billion yield a *net* increase of GDP of $20 billion (=$80 billion − $60 billion). *Equal increases in G and T expand GDP by an amount equal to the increase in G and T.* You should experiment to verify that the balanced-budget multiplier is valid regardless of the sizes of the marginal propensities to consume and save.

Fiscal Policy over the Cycle

Our discussion suggests how fiscal policy might be used to help stabilize the economy. The fundamental purpose of fiscal policy is to eliminate unemployment

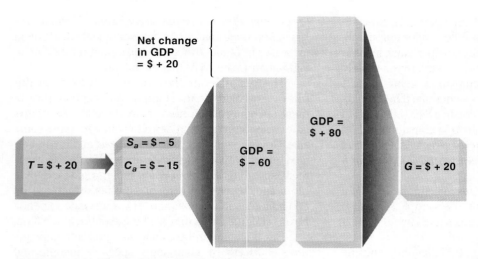

**Net change
in GDP
= $ + 20**

$T = \$ + 20$

$S_a = \$ - 5$

$C_a = \$ - 15$

**GDP =
$ - 60**

**GDP =
$ + 80**

$G = \$ + 20$

FIGURE 12-3 The balanced-budget multiplier

The balanced-budget multiplier is 1. An equal increase in taxes and government expenditures will increase GDP by an amount equal to the increase in the amount of government expenditures and taxes. Given an MPC of .75, a tax increase of $20 billion will reduce disposable income by $20 billion and lower consumption expenditures by $15 billion. Because the multiplier is 4, GDP will therefore decline by $60 billion. The $20 billion increase in government expenditures, however, will produce a more than offsetting increase in GDP of $80 billion. The net increase in GDP will be $20 billion, which equals the amount of the increase in government expenditures and taxes.

or inflation. When recession exists, an **expansionary fiscal policy** is in order. This entails (1) increased government spending, *or* (2) lower taxes, *or* (3) a combination of the two. In other words, if the budget is balanced at the outset, fiscal policy should move toward a government budget *deficit* during recession or depression.

Conversely, when demand-pull inflation is present, a restrictive or **contractionary fiscal policy** is appropriate. A contractionary policy is composed of (1) decreased government spending, *or* (2) higher taxes, *or* (3) a combination of these two policies. Fiscal policy should move toward a *surplus* in the government's budget when the economy is faced with the problem of controlling inflation.

Keep in mind, however, that not only does the difference between government spending and taxes (the size of a deficit or surplus) affect the GDP, but so does the absolute size of the budget. In our illustration of the balanced-budget multiplier, increases in *G* and *T* of $20 billion increased GDP by $20 billion. If *G* and *T* had both increased by only $10 billion, equilibrium GDP would only have risen by $10 billion.

Financing Deficits and Disposing of Surpluses

Given the size of a deficit, its expansionary effect on the economy will depend upon the method by which it is financed. Similarly, given the size of a surplus, its deflationary impact will depend on its disposition.

Borrowing versus New Money There are two different ways by which the Federal government can finance a deficit: by borrowing from (selling interest-bearing bonds to) the public, or by issuing new money to its creditors. The impact on aggregate expenditures will be different in each case.

1 Borrowing If the government goes into the money market and borrows, it will be competing with private business borrowers for funds. This added demand for funds will drive the equilibrium interest rate upward. We know from Chapter 10 that investment spending is inversely related to the interest rate. Government borrowing therefore will increase the interest rate and "crowd out" some private investment spending and interest-sensitive consumer spending.

2 Money Creation If deficit spending is financed by issuing new money, crowding-out of private expenditures can be avoided. Federal spending can increase without any adverse effect on investment or consumption. Thus, we can conclude that *the creation of new money is a more expansionary way of financing deficit spending than is borrowing.*

Debt Retirement versus Idle Surplus Demand-pull inflation calls for fiscal action by government which will result in a budget surplus. However, the anti-inflationary effect of this surplus depends on what government does with it.

1 Debt Reduction Since the Federal government has an outstanding debt of some $3.6 trillion, it is logical that government should use a surplus to retire outstanding debt. The anti-inflationary impact of a surplus, however, may be reduced somewhat by paying off debt. In retiring debt held by the general public, the government transfers its surplus tax revenues back into the money market, causing the interest rate to fall and thereby stimulating investment and consumption.

2 Impounding On the other hand, government can realize a greater anti-inflationary impact from its budgetary surplus by impounding the surplus funds, that is, by allowing them to stand idle. An impounded surplus means that the government is extracting and withholding purchasing power from the income-expenditure stream. If surplus tax revenues are not reinjected into the economy, there is no possibility of some portion of the surplus being spent. There is no chance that the funds will create inflationary pressure to offset the deflationary impact of the surplus itself. We conclude that *the impounding of a budgetary surplus is more contractionary than the use of the surplus to retire public debt.*

Policy Options: *G* or *T*?

Is it preferable to use government spending or taxes to eliminate recessionary and inflationary gaps? The answer depends to a considerable extent upon one's view as to whether the public sector is too large or too small. "Liberal" economists, who think the public sector needs to be enlarged to meet various failures of the market system (Chapter 6), can recommend that aggregate expenditures should be expanded during recessions by increasing government purchases *and* that aggregate expenditures should be constrained during inflationary periods by increasing taxes.

Conversely, "conservative" economists, who contend that the public sector is overly large and inefficient, can advocate that aggregate expenditures be increased during recessions by cutting taxes *and* that aggregate expenditures be reduced during inflation by cutting government spending. An active fiscal policy designed to stabilize the economy can be associated with either an expanding or a contracting public sector.

QUICK REVIEW 12-1

✦ **The Employment Act of 1946 commits the Federal government to take positive actions to promote "maximum employment, production, and purchasing power."**

✦ **Government purchases shift the aggregate expenditures schedule upward and raise equilibrium GDP.**

✦ **Taxation reduces disposable income, lowers consumption spending and saving, shifts the aggregate expenditures schedule downward, and reduces equilibrium GDP.**

✦ **The balanced-budget multiplier is 1.**

✦ **Expansionary fiscal policy involves increases in government spending, reductions in taxes, or some combination of the two; contractionary fiscal policy entails the opposite actions.**

NONDISCRETIONARY FISCAL POLICY: BUILT-IN STABILIZERS

To some degree appropriate changes in relative levels of government expenditures and taxes occur automatically. This so-called automatic or *built-in stability* is not included in our discussion of discretionary fiscal policy because we assumed a simple lump-sum tax whereby the same amount of tax revenue was collected at each level of GDP. Built-in stability arises because in reality our net tax system (net taxes equal taxes minus transfers and subsidies) is such that *net tax revenues[1] vary directly with GDP.*

Virtually all taxes will yield more tax revenue as GDP rises. In particular, personal income taxes have progressive rates and result in more than proportionate increases in tax collections as GDP expands. Furthermore, as GDP increases and more goods and services are purchased, revenues from corporate income taxes and sales and excise taxes will increase. And, similarly, payroll tax payments increase as economic

---

[1]From now on, we will use the term "taxes" in referring to net taxes.

expansion creates more jobs. Conversely, when GDP declines, tax receipts from all these sources will decline. Transfer payments (or "negative taxes") behave in precisely the opposite way. Unemployment compensation payments, welfare payments, and subsidies to farmers all *decrease* during economic expansion and *increase* during a contraction.

Automatic or Built-In Stabilizers

Figure 12-4 helps us understand how the tax system gives rise to built-in stability. Government expenditures G are given and assumed to be independent of the level of GDP; expenditures are decided on at some fixed level by Congress. But Congress does *not* determine the *level* of tax revenues; rather, it establishes tax *rates*. Tax revenues then vary directly with the level of GDP which the economy actually realizes. The direct relationship between tax revenues and GDP is shown in the upsloping T line.

The economic importance of this direct relationship between tax receipts and GDP comes into focus when we remember two things.

1 Taxes are a leakage or withdrawal of potential purchasing power from the economy.

2 It is desirable from the standpoint of stability to increase leakages or withdrawals of purchasing power when the economy is moving toward inflation and to diminish these withdrawals when the economy is tending to slump.

In other words, the kind of tax system portrayed in Figure 12-4 builds some stability into the economy by

FIGURE 12-4   Built-in stability

If tax revenues vary directly with GDP the deficits which will occur automatically during recession will help alleviate that recession. Conversely, the surpluses which occur automatically during expansion will assist in offsetting possible inflation.

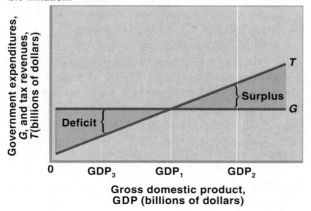

automatically bringing about changes in tax revenues and therefore in the public budget which tend to counter both inflation and unemployment. Generally speaking, a **built-in stabilizer** is *anything which increases the government's deficit (or reduces its surplus) during a recession and increases its surplus (or reduces its deficit) during inflation without requiring explicit action by policy makers.* As Figure 12-4 clearly reveals, this is precisely what our tax system does.

As GDP rises during prosperity, tax revenues *automatically* increase and, because they are a leakage, restrain the economic expansion. In other words, as the economy moves toward a higher GDP, tax revenues automatically rise and move the budget from a deficit toward a surplus.

Conversely, as GDP falls during recession, tax revenues *automatically* decline and this reduction in leakages cushions the economic contraction. With a falling GDP, tax receipts decline and move the public budget from a surplus toward a deficit. In terms of Figure 12-4, the low level of income GDP_3 will automatically give rise to an expansionary budget deficit; the high and perhaps inflationary income level GDP_2 will automatically generate a contractionary budget surplus.

It is clear from Figure 12-4 that the size of the automatic budget deficits or surpluses and therefore built-in stability depends on the responsiveness of changes in taxes to changes in GDP. If tax revenues change sharply as GDP changes, the slope of line T in the figure will be steep and the vertical distances between T and G—the deficits or surpluses—will be large. Alternatively, if tax revenues change very little when GDP changes, the slope will be gentle and built-in stability will be low.

Said differently, the steepness of T in Figure 12-4 depends on the type of tax system in place. If the tax system is **progressive,** meaning the average tax rate (=tax revenue/GDP) rises with GDP, the T line will be steeper than if the tax system is **proportional** or **regressive.** A proportional tax system is one in which the average tax rate remains constant as GDP rises; in a regressive tax system the average tax rate falls as GDP rises. Tax revenues will rise with GDP under progressive and proportional tax systems and may either rise, fall, or remain the same when GDP increases under a regressive system. But the relevant generalization is this: *The more progressive the tax system, the greater is the economy's built-in stability.*

Changes in public policies or laws which alter the progressivity of the net tax system (taxes minus transfers and subsidies) therefore affect the degree of built-in stability. The tax system became less progressive between 1977 and 1985. Built-in stability fell because social security taxes, which are regressive, rose substantially. Also, in the early 1980s the Federal government "indexed" the personal income tax. Indexing means that income tax brackets are widened each year to adjust for inflation. Before indexing, inflation would push taxpayers into higher marginal tax brackets and thus increase government's tax revenues.

The tax system has become more progressive since 1986. The Tax Reform Act of 1986 greatly reduced the highest marginal tax rates, but also removed tax breaks used by the wealthy. Subsequent tax changes have increased the share of total taxes paid by the wealthy. The Council of Economic Advisers concludes that tax progressivity and therefore the degree of built-in stability is similar to that in the mid-1970s.

The built-in stability provided by our tax system has reduced the severity of business fluctuations. But built-in stabilizers can only diminish, *not* correct, major changes in equilibrium GNP. Discretionary fiscal policy—changes in tax rates and expenditures—therefore may be needed to correct inflation or recession of any appreciable magnitude.

Full-Employment Budget

Built-in stability—the fact that tax revenues vary directly with GDP—makes it hazardous to use the **actual budget** surplus or deficit in any given year as an index of the government's fiscal stance. Suppose the economy is at full employment at GDP_1 in Figure 12-4 and the budget is in balance. Now, assume that C_a or I_g or X_n declines, causing a recession at GDP_3. The government, let's assume, takes no discretionary fiscal action; therefore, the G and T lines remain in the positions shown in the diagram. As the economy moves to GDP_3, tax revenues fall and, with government expenditures unaltered, a deficit occurs. But this **cyclical deficit** is clearly *not* the result of positive countercyclical fiscal actions by the government; rather it is the byproduct of fiscal inaction as the economy slides into a recession.

We cannot gain a meaningful picture of the government's fiscal posture—whether Congress was appropriately manipulating taxes and expenditures—by viewing the historical record of budgetary deficits or surpluses. The actual budget surplus or deficit reflects not only possible discretionary decisions about spending and taxes (as shown in the locations of the G and T lines in Figure 12-4), but also the level of equilibrium GDP (where the economy is operating on the horizontal axis of Figure 12-4). Given that tax revenues vary

with GDP, the problem of comparing deficits or surpluses in year 1 and year 2 is that the level of GDP may be vastly different in each of the two years.

Economists have resolved this problem through the concept of a full-employment budget. The **full-employment budget** *measures what the Federal budgetary surplus or deficit would be if the economy were to operate at full employment throughout the year.* Figure 12-5 compares the full-employment budget and the actual budget as percentages of domestic output since 1955. Two features stand out.

1 In many years the sizes of the actual budget deficits or surpluses greatly differed from the sizes of the deficits or surpluses of the full-employment budget. Consider 1961 and 1962, years of above-normal unemployment and sluggish economic growth. A look at the actual budget deficits in these years implies that government was appropriately engaged in an expansionary fiscal policy. But the full-employment budget data tell us that this was *not* the case. The full-employment budget data indicate that, *if* the economy had been at full employment, there would have been a budgetary surplus. Our fiscal policy in 1961 and 1962 was in fact contractionary, and this was partially responsible for the less-than-full-employment levels of domestic output, the consequent poor tax harvests, and the deficits which occurred in the actual budgets for 1961 and 1962.

Also, consider 1969, a year when tax revenues were flowing into the Federal government at a rapid pace because inflation was occurring and the unemployment rate was *less* than the full-employment unemployment rate. Note that even though the actual budget was in surplus, the full-employment budget was in deficit. How could this be? If the unemployment rate were at the higher full-employment level, tax revenues would have been much lower, and given the level of government spending the budget would have been in deficit. Fiscal policy was mildly stimulative in 1969 even though the actual budget was in surplus.

2 Both the actual and full-employment budgets have been in deficit over the past few decades. The last surplus in the actual budget occurred in 1969; the last surplus in the full-employment budget occurred in 1962. In the mid- and late 1980s there were large actual and full-employment budget deficits. These latter budget deficits were also called **structural deficits.** A large portion of the actual deficits during this period did not result from automatic deficiencies in tax revenues brought forth by below-full-employment domestic output and income; they were not mainly cyclical deficits. Rather, they resulted from structural imbalances

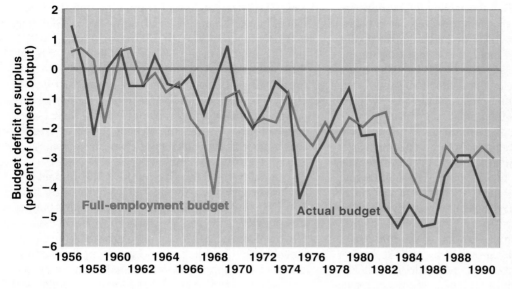

FIGURE 12-5 The full-employment budget and the actual budget

Full-employment budget deficits and surpluses often are different in size from actual budget deficits and surpluses. The full-employment budget surplus or deficit is a better indicator of the government's fiscal posture than is the actual surplus or deficit.

between government spending and tax revenues caused by large cuts in tax rates early in the 1980s and increases in government expenditures. The year 1989 is a case in point. Although the economy had achieved full employment, a large full-employment budget deficit occurred. This structural deficit implied an expansionary fiscal policy.

We might logically wonder why the combination of full employment and an expansionary fiscal policy in 1989 did not touch off demand-pull inflation. One important reason was that net exports $(X - M)$ were highly negative. By reducing aggregate expenditures on domestic GDP, the negative net exports canceled the expansionary effects of the large deficit in the full-employment budget.

QUICK REVIEW 12-2

◆ **Tax revenues automatically increase during economic expansions and decrease during recessions; transfers automatically decrease during expansions and increase during recessions.**

◆ **Automatic changes in taxes and transfers add a degree of built-in stability to the economy.**

◆ **The full-employment budget compares government spending to the tax revenues that would accrue if there were full employment; it is more useful than the actual budget in revealing the status of fiscal policy.**

◆ **Full-employment budget deficits are also called structural deficits, as distinct from cyclical deficits.**

PROBLEMS, CRITICISMS, AND COMPLICATIONS

Unfortunately, there is a great deal of difference between fiscal policy on paper and fiscal policy in practice. Let's examine specific problems which may be encountered in enacting and applying appropriate fiscal policy.

Problems of Timing

Several problems of timing may arise in connection with fiscal policy.

1 Recognition Lag The recognition lag refers to the time which elapses between the beginning of a recession or inflation and the certain awareness that it is actually happening. It is difficult to predict accurately the future course of economic activity. Although forecasting tools such as the index of leading indicators (see this chapter's Last Word) provide clues as to the direction of the economy, the economy may be four or six months into a recession or inflation before that fact shows up in relevant statistics and is acknowledged.

2 Administrative Lag The wheels of democratic government are often slow in turning. There will typically be a significant lag between the time that the need for fiscal action is recognized and the time that action is actually taken. The $11 billion tax cut which became law in February of 1964 was first proposed to President Kennedy by the Council of Economic Advisers in 1961, and in turn proposed by him in late 1962. The 1968 surcharge on personal and corporate incomes was enacted approximately a year after it was requested by President Johnson. Indeed, Congress has on occasion taken so much time in adjusting fiscal policy that the economic situation has turned around in the interim, rendering the policy action completely inappropriate.

3 Operational Lag   There will also be a lag between the time that fiscal action is taken by Congress and the time that action affects output, employment, or the price level. Although changes in tax rates can be put into effect quickly, government spending on public works—the construction of dams, interstate highways, and so forth—requires long planning periods and even longer periods of construction. Such spending is of questionable usefulness in offsetting short—for example, six- to eighteen-month—periods of recession. Because of these kinds of problems, discretionary fiscal policy has come to rely increasingly on tax changes.

Political Problems

Fiscal policy is created in the political arena and this greatly complicates its use in stabilizing the economy.

1 Other Goals   Recall that economic stability is *not* the sole objective of government spending and taxing policies. Government is also concerned with the provision of public goods and services and the redistribution of income (Chapter 6). A classic example occurred during World War II when government spending for military goods rose dramatically, causing strong and persistent inflationary pressures in the early 1940s. The defeat of Nazi Germany and Japan was simply a higher priority goal than achieving price level stability.

Also note that fiscal policies of state and local governments are frequently procyclical. Unlike the Federal government, most state and local governments face constitutional or other legal requirements to balance their budgets. Thus, like households and private businesses, state and local governments increase expenditures during prosperity and cut them during recession. During the Great Depression of the 1930s, most of the increase in Federal spending was offset by decreases in state and local spending. During the recent recession of 1990–1991, many state and local governments had to increase tax rates, impose new taxes, and reduce spending to offset falling tax revenues resulting from the reduced personal income and spending of their citizens.

2 Expansionary Bias?   Rhetoric to the contrary, deficits tend to be politically attractive and surpluses politically painful. That is, there may well be a political bias in favor of deficits; fiscal policy may have an expansionary-inflationary bias. Tax reductions are politically popular, and so are increases in government spending, provided that the given politician's constituents share liberally in the benefits. But higher taxes upset voters and reducing government expenditures can be politically precarious. For example, it might well be political suicide for a farm-state senator to vote for tax increases and against agricultural subsidies. Figure 12-5 is informative. In the 1965–1967 period we find the full-employment budget shifting significantly toward deficits or, in other words, to an expansionary posture. Yet in each of those three years the unemployment rate was below 4 percent and the price level was rising. The proper fiscal stance should have been one of restraint, not stimulus.

3 A Political Business Cycle?   Some economists stress that the overriding goal of politicians is not necessarily to act in the interests of the national economy, but rather to get reelected. A few economists have put forth the notion of a **political business cycle.** They argue that politicians might manipulate fiscal policy to maximize voter support, even though their fiscal decisions tend to *destabilize* the economy. According to this view, fiscal policy, as we have described it, may be corrupted for political purposes and cause economic fluctuations.

The populace, it is assumed, takes economic conditions into account in voting. Incumbents are penalized at the polls if economic conditions are depressed; they are rewarded if the economy is prosperous. As an election approaches, the incumbent administration (aided by an election-minded Congress) will cut taxes and increase government spending. Not only will these actions be popular per se, but the resulting stimulus to the economy will push all the critical economic indicators in proper directions. Output and real incomes will rise; unemployment will fall; and the price level will be relatively stable. As a result, incumbents will enjoy a very cordial economic environment in which to stand for reelection.

But after the election, continued expansion of the economy is reflected increasingly in a rising price level and less in growing real incomes. Growing public concern over inflation will prompt politicians to invoke a contractionary fiscal policy. Crudely put, a "made-in-Washington" recession will be engineered by trimming government spending and increasing taxes to restrain inflation. This recession will not hurt incumbents because the next election is still two or three years away and the critical consideration for most voters is the performance of the economy in the year or so before the election. Indeed, the recession provides a new starting point from which fiscal policy can again be used to generate another expansion in time for the next election campaign.

This possible perversion of fiscal policy is both highly disturbing and inherently difficult to document. Although empirical evidence is mixed and inconclusive, there is some evidence to support this political theory of the business cycle.

Crowding-Out Effect

We now move from practical problems in the application of fiscal policy to a basic criticism of fiscal policy itself. The essence of the **crowding-out effect** is that an expansionary (deficit) fiscal policy will increase the interest rate and reduce investment spending, weakening or canceling the stimulus of the fiscal policy.

Assume the economy is in recession and government invokes discretionary fiscal policy in the form of an increase in government spending. Government now enters the money market to finance the deficit. The resulting increase in the demand for money raises the interest rate, the price paid for borrowing money. Because investment spending varies inversely with the interest rate (review Figure 10-7), some investment will be choked off or crowded out.[2] In terms of Figure 12-1 an increase (upshift) in the government component of aggregate expenditures may cause a decrease (downshift) in the private investment component. If investment fell by the same amount as the increase in government spending, then fiscal policy would be completely ineffective.

While few would question the logic involved, there is disagreement as to the size of the crowding-out effect. Some economists argue that there will be little crowding-out when there is considerable unemployment. Their rationale is that, given a recession, the stimulus provided by an increase in government spending can be expected to improve business profit expectations which are an important determinant of the location of the investment-demand curve (Figure 10-7). If the investment-demand curve does shift rightward, then investment spending need not fall—it may even increase—even though interest rates are higher.

Another relevant consideration concerns monetary policy, which we discuss in detail in later chapters. The monetary authorities may increase the supply of money by just enough to offset the deficit-caused increase in the demand for money. In this case the equilibrium interest rate would not change and the crowding-out effect would be zero. In the 1980s the monetary authorities restrained the growth of the money supply and, consequently, the crowding-out effects of the large deficits of the 1980s may have been quite large. In comparison, in the 1960s the monetary authorities were strongly disposed to stabilize interest rates. They consequently would increase the money supply in response to higher interest rates occasioned by government borrowing. As a result, crowding-out was probably inconsequential.

Offsetting Saving

A few prominent economists theorize that deficit spending is offset by an equal increase in private saving. Supposedly, people recognize that today's deficit spending will eventually require higher taxes for themselves or their heirs. People allegedly increase their present saving (reduce their current consumption) in anticipation of these higher taxes. A budget deficit—*public dissaving*—therefore produces an increase in *private saving*. This concept is termed the **Ricardian equivalence theorem,** named after British economist David Ricardo who first suggested it in the early 1800s. More formally, the theorem states that financing a deficit by borrowing has the same effect on GDP as financing it through a present tax increase.

In terms of Figures 12-1 and 12-2, the increase in aggregate expenditures expected from the rise in government spending or decline in taxes is partially or fully offset by a downward shift of the consumption schedule (upward shift of the saving schedule). Aggregate expenditures and real GDP therefore do not expand as predicted by the Keynesian model. Fiscal policy is either rendered totally ineffective or is severely weakened.

---

[2]Some interest-sensitive consumption spending—for example, automobile purchases—may also be crowded out.

Although research continues on this topic, mainstream economists reject this line of reasoning as unrealistic and contrary to historical evidence. For example, they point out that the large budget deficits of the 1980s were accompanied by *declines*—not increases—in the national saving rate.

Aggregate Supply and Inflation

Our discussion of complications and criticisms of fiscal policy has thus far been entirely demand-oriented. We now consider a supply-side complication. The point to remember is that given an upsloping aggregate supply curve, some portion of the potential effect of an expansionary fiscal policy on real output and employment may be dissipated in the form of inflation. This idea was stressed in Figure 11-11 and is not new to you.

Graphical Portrayal: Crowding-Out and Inflation

It will be helpful here to portray fiscal policy and its complications in the context of the aggregate demand–aggregate supply model. We suppose in Figure 12-6a that there exists a noninflationary full-employment

level of GDP which is at $490 billion. Note that our aggregate supply curve eliminates the intermediate range so that up to full employment the price level is perfectly constant, but after full employment is achieved the classical range prevails so that any further increase in aggregate demand would be purely inflationary.

We begin with aggregate demand at AD_1 which gives us an unemployment equilibrium at $470 billion. This, you may recall, was the private sector equilibrium of Table 11-1. Assume now that an expansionary fiscal policy is undertaken which shifts the aggregate demand curve rightward by $20 billion to AD_2 and the economy therefore achieves full employment without inflation at $490 billion. We know from our previous discussion of discretionary fiscal policy in terms of Tables 12-1 and 12-2 and Figure 12-3 that the expansionary effect of the balanced-budget multiplier when G and T are each $20 billion would be sufficient to achieve this $20 billion increase in equilibrium GDP. You should verify that an increase in G of $5 billion *or* a decrease in T of $6⅔ billion would bring about the same expansionary effect. In any event, with no offsetting or complicating factors at work this "pure and simple" expansionary fiscal policy moves the economy from recession to full employment.

FIGURE 12-6 Fiscal policy: the effects of crowding-out, the net export effect, and inflation

Given a simplified aggregate supply curve, we observe in (a) that fiscal policy is uncomplicated and works at full strength. In (b) it is assumed that some amount of private investment is crowded out by the expansionary fiscal policy so that fiscal policy is weakened. In (c) a more realistic aggregate supply curve reminds us that, when the economy is close to full employment, part of the impact of an expansionary fiscal policy will be reflected in inflation rather than in increases in real output and employment. Finally, in (d)—the same graph as (b)—we assume that fiscal policy increases the interest rate, which attracts foreign financial capital to the United States. The dollar therefore appreciates and our net exports fall, thus weakening the expansionary fiscal policy.

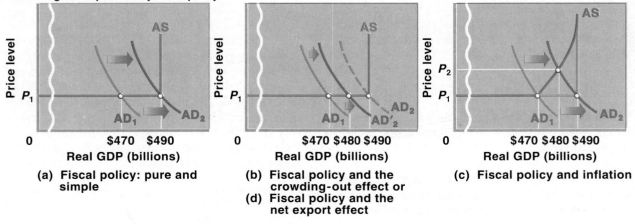

(a) Fiscal policy: pure and simple

(b) Fiscal policy and the crowding-out effect or
(d) Fiscal policy and the net export effect

(c) Fiscal policy and inflation

In Figure 12-6b we muddy the waters by adding the crowding-out effect. While fiscal policy is expansionary and designed to shift aggregate demand from AD_1 to AD_2, some investment may be crowded out so that aggregate demand ends up at AD_2'. Equilibrium GDP increases to only $480 rather than the desired $490 billion. *The crowding-out effect may weaken fiscal policy.*

In Figure 12-6c we switch to a more realistic aggregate supply curve which includes an intermediate range. We ignore the crowding-out effect so that the expansionary fiscal policy is successful in shifting aggregate demand from AD_1 to AD_2. If the aggregate supply curve was shaped as in Figure 12-6a and b, full employment would now be realized at $490 billion and the price level would remain at P_1. But we find that the presence of the upsloping intermediate range on the aggregate supply curve causes a part of the increase in aggregate demand to be dissipated in higher prices with the result that the increase in real GDP is diminished. Specifically, the price level rises from P_1 to P_2 and real domestic output increases to only $480 billion.

In terms of our aggregate expenditures model (Figures 12-1 and 12-2), an expansionary fiscal policy may not increase aggregate expenditures by the full amount of the increase in government expenditures (or the increase in consumption associated with the reduction of a lump-sum tax). If the price level rises— as it does when the aggregate supply curve is upsloping—the increase in government expenditures will be partially offset by declines in consumption, investment, and net export expenditures. These declines result respectively from the wealth, interest-rate, and foreign purchases effects created by the higher domestic price level. That is, the aggregate demand curve in Figure 12-6c shifts from AD_1 to AD_2, but we move upward along AD_2 to the new equilibrium price level and level of real domestic output because of the upsloping aggregate supply curve. Demand-side fiscal policy does not escape the realities imposed by the aggregate supply curve.

Fiscal Policy in the Open Economy

Additional complications arise when we allow for the fact that our economy is a component of the broader world economy.

Shocks Originating from Abroad Events and policies abroad that affect our net exports have an impact on our economy. Our economy is susceptible to unforeseen international *aggregate demand shocks* which can alter our GDP and render our fiscal actions inappropriate.

Suppose we are in a recession and have changed government expenditures and taxes to levels which bolster aggregate demand and GDP without igniting inflation (as from AD_1 to AD_2 in Figure 12-6a). Now suppose that the economies of our major trading partners unexpectedly and abruptly begin to expand rapidly. Greater employment and rising incomes in those nations translate into more purchases of American goods. Our net exports rise, aggregate demand increases too rapidly, and we experience demand-pull inflation. Had we known in advance that our net exports would rise significantly, we would have enacted a less expansionary fiscal policy. The point is that our growing participation in the world economy brings with it the *complications* of mutual interdependence as well as the *gains* from specialization and trade.

Net Export Effect An effect which we will call the **net export effect** may work through international trade to reduce the effectiveness of fiscal policy. We concluded in our discussion of the crowding-out effect that an expansionary fiscal policy might boost interest rates, thus reducing *investment* and weakening fiscal policy. Now we need to ascertain what effect such an increase in the interest rate might have on our *net exports* (exports minus imports).

Suppose we invoke an expansionary fiscal policy which brings with it a higher interest rate. The higher interest rate will attract financial capital from abroad where interest rates presumably are unchanged. But foreign financial investors must acquire U.S. dollars before buying the desired American securities. We know that an increase in the demand for a commodity— in this case dollars—will raise its price. So the price of dollars will rise in terms of foreign currencies; in other words, the dollar will appreciate.

What will be the impact of this dollar appreciation on our net exports? Because more units of foreign currencies are needed to buy our goods, foreigners will see our exports as being more expensive; hence, our exports will decline. Conversely, Americans, who can now exchange their dollars for more units of foreign currencies, will buy more imports. The consequence of this scenario is that net export expenditures in the United States will diminish and our expansionary fiscal policy will be partially negated.[3]

---

[3]The appreciation of the dollar will also reduce the dollar price of foreign resources such as oil imported to the United States. As a result, aggregate supply will increase and part of the contractionary net export effect described here may be offset.

Returning to our aggregate demand and supply analysis in Figure 12-6b, now labeled d, will clarify this point. An expansionary fiscal policy designed to increase aggregate demand from AD_1 to AD_2 may hike the domestic interest rate and ultimately reduce our net exports through the process just described. The decline in the net export component of aggregate demand will partially offset the expansionary fiscal policy. The aggregate demand curve will shift rightward from AD_1 to AD_2', *not* to AD_2, and equilibrium GDP will increase from $470 to $480, *not* to $490. Hence, the net export effect of fiscal policy joins our other factors of timing, political problems, crowding-out, Ricardian effects, and inflation in complicating the "management" of aggregate demand.

Table 12-3 summarizes the net export effect resulting from fiscal policy. Specifically, column 1 reviews the analysis just discussed (Figure 12-6d). But note that the net export effect works in both directions. By reducing the domestic interest rate, a *contractionary* fiscal policy tends to *increase* net exports. In this regard, you should follow through the analysis in column 2 of Table 12-3 and relate it to the aggregate demand–aggregate supply model.

TABLE 12-3 Fiscal policy and the net export effect

(1) Expansionary fiscal policy	(2) Contractionary fiscal policy
Problem: Recession, slow growth	**Problem:** Inflation
↓	↓
Expansionary fiscal policy	Contractionary fiscal policy
↓	↓
Higher domestic interest rate	Lower domestic interest rate
↓	↓
Increased foreign demand for dollars	Decreased foreign demand for dollars
↓	↓
Dollar appreciates	Dollar depreciates
↓	↓
Net exports decline (aggregate demand decreases, partially offsetting the expansionary fiscal policy)	Net exports increase (aggregate demand increases, partially offsetting the contractionary fiscal policy)

QUICK REVIEW 12-3

♦ **Time lags and political problems complicate fiscal policy.**

♦ **The crowding-out effect indicates that an expansionary fiscal policy may increase the interest rate and reduce investment spending.**

♦ **A few economists adhere to the Ricardian equivalence theorem which holds that deficit spending creates expectations of future tax increases and therefore is offset dollar-for-dollar by increases in private saving.**

♦ **The upsloping range of the aggregate supply curve means that part of an expansionary fiscal policy may be dissipated in inflation.**

♦ **Fiscal policy may be weakened by an accompanying net export effect which works through changes in a the interest rate, b the international value of the dollar, and c exports and imports.**

Supply-Side Fiscal Policy

While we have seen how movements along the aggregate supply curve can complicate the operation of fiscal policy, we now turn to the possibility of a more direct link between fiscal policy and aggregate supply. Economists now recognize that fiscal policy—especially tax changes—*may* alter aggregate supply and affect the price level–real output outcomes of a change in fiscal policy.

Suppose in Figure 12-7 that aggregate demand and aggregate supply are presently at AD_1 and AS_1 so

---

FIGURE 12-7 Supply-side effects of fiscal policy

The traditional view is that tax cuts will increase aggregate demand as from AD_1 to AD_2, thereby increasing both real domestic output (Q_1 to Q_2) and the price level (P_1 to P_2). If the tax reductions induce favorable supply-side effects, aggregate supply will shift rightward as from AS_1 to AS_2. This allows the economy to realize an even larger output (Q_3 as compared to Q_2) and a lower price level (P_3 as compared to P_2).

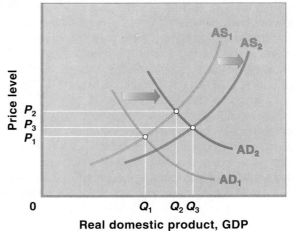

LAST WORD

THE LEADING INDICATORS

One tool policy makers use to forecast the future direction of real GDP is a monthly index of a group of variables which in the past has provided advance notice of changes in GDP.

"Index of Leading Indicators Falls for Third Month— Recession Feared"; "Index of Leading Indicators Surges Again"; "Decline in Stock Market Drags Down Index of Leading Indicators." Headlines such as these appear regularly in the business sections of our major newspapers. The focus of these articles is the Commerce Department's weighted average—or composite index—of eleven economic variables which has historically reached its peak or trough in advance of the corresponding turns in the business cycle. Changes in the index of leading indicators thus provide a clue to the future direction of the economy and may therefore shorten the length of the "recognition lag" associated with the implementation of macroeconomic policy.

Let's examine the eleven components of the index of leading indicators in terms of a predicted *decline* in GDP, keeping in mind that the opposite changes forecast a *rise* in GDP.

1 Average workweek Decreases in the length of the average workweek of production workers in manufacturing foretell declines in future manufacturing output and GDP.

2 Initial claims for unemployment insurance Higher first-time claims for unemployment insurance

are associated with falling employment and subsequently sagging production.

3 New orders for consumer goods A slump in the number of orders received by manufacturers for consumer goods portends reduced future production—a decline in GDP.

4 Stock market prices Declines in stock prices often are reflections of expected declines in corporate sales and profits. Furthermore, lower stock prices diminish consumer wealth, leading consumers to cut back on their spending. Lower stock market values

---

that the equilibrium level of real GDP is Q_1 and the price level is P_1. Assume further that it is felt that the level of unemployment associated with Q_1 is too high and that an expansionary fiscal policy is therefore invoked in the form of a tax cut. We know that the demand-side effect is to increase aggregate demand from AD_1 to, say, AD_2. This shift increases real GDP to Q_2, but also boosts the price level to P_2.

How might tax cuts affect aggregate supply? Some economists—appropriately labeled supply-side economists—feel strongly that tax reductions will shift the aggregate supply curve significantly to the right. Lower taxes will increase disposable incomes, thus increasing household saving. Similarly, tax reductions on businesses will increase the profitability of investment. In

brief, lower taxes will increase the volumes of both saving and investment, increasing the rate of capital accumulation. Stated differently, the size of our "national factory"—our productive capacity—will grow more rapidly than otherwise.

Furthermore, lower personal income tax rates also increase after-tax wages—the price paid for work— and stimulate work incentives. Many people not already in the labor force will offer their services now that after-tax wages are higher. Those already in the labor force will want to work longer hours and take fewer vacations.

Lower tax rates are also a prod to risk takers. Individuals and businesses will be more willing to risk their energies and financial capital on new production meth-

also make it less attractive for firms to issue new shares of stock as a way to raise funds for investment. Hence, declines in stock prices can bring forth declines in aggregate demand and GDP.

5 Contracts and orders for new plant and equipment A drop in orders for capital equipment and other investment goods implies reduced future aggregate demand and domestic output.

6 Building permits for houses Decreases in the number of building permits taken out for new homes augur future declines in investment and therefore the distinct possibility that GDP will fall.

7 Vendor performance Somewhat ironically, better performance by sellers of inputs in supplying buyers in a timely fashion indicates slackening business demand and potentially falling GDP.

8 Change in unfilled orders of durable goods Decreases in the dollar amounts of unfilled orders of durable manufactured goods imply falling aggregate demand and therefore ensuing declines in GDP.

9 Change in sensitive raw material prices Declines in certain sensitive raw material prices often precede declines in domestic output.

10 The money supply Decreases in the money supply are associated with falling GDP. The components of the money supply and its role in the macro economy are the subjects of Chapters 13 through 16.

11 Index of consumer expectations Declines in consumer confidence indicated by this index compiled by the University of Michigan's Survey Research Center foreshadow curtailed consumption expenditures and eventual declines in domestic output.

None of these factors *alone* consistently predicts the future course of the economy. It is not unusual in any month, for example, for one or two of the indicators to be decreasing while the other indicators are increasing. Rather, changes in the *weighted average*—or composite index—of the eleven components are what in the past have provided advance notice of a change in the direction of GDP. The rule of thumb is that three successive monthly declines or increases in the index indicate the economy will soon turn in that same direction.

Although the composite index has correctly signaled business fluctuations on numerous occasions, it has not been an infallible sentinel. At times the index has provided false warnings of recessions which have never happened. In other instances, recessions have so closely followed the downturn in the index that policy makers have not had sufficient time to make use of the "early" warning. Moreover, changing structural features of the economy on occasion have rendered the existing index obsolete and have necessitated its revision.

Given these caveats, the index of leading indicators can best be thought of as a useful but not totally reliable signaling device which authorities must employ with considerable caution in formulating macroeconomic policy.

---

ods and new products when lower tax rates promise a larger potential after-tax reward.

Through all these avenues, lower taxes will shift aggregate supply to the right as from AS_1 to AS_2 in Figure 12-7, reducing inflation and further increasing real GDP. This supply-side rationale for increasing aggregate supply was the basis for the Reagan administration tax cuts in the 1980s.

Supply-siders also contend that lower tax *rates* need not result in lower tax *revenues*. In fact, lower tax rates that cause a substantial expansion of domestic output and income can be expected to generate increases in tax revenues. This enlarged tax base will enhance total tax revenues even though tax rates are lower. Thus, while the mainstream view is that a reduction in

tax rates will reduce tax revenues and increase budget deficits, the supply-side view is that tax rate reductions can be structured to increase tax revenues and reduce deficits.

Most economists are cautious concerning the supply-side effects of tax cuts. First, they feel that the hoped-for positive effects of a tax reduction on incentives to work, save and invest, and bear risks are not nearly as strong as supply-siders believe. Second, any rightward shifts of the aggregate supply curve are likely to be realized over an extended period of time, while the demand-side impact will be more immediate. The controversies surrounding supply-side economics will resurface in Chapter 17.

CHAPTER SUMMARY

1   Government responsibility for achieving and maintaining full employment is set forth in the Employment Act of 1946. The Council of Economic Advisers (CEA) was established to advise the President on policies appropriate to fulfilling the goals of the act.

2   Increases in government spending expand, and decreases contract, the equilibrium GDP. Conversely, increases in taxes reduce, and decreases expand, the equilibrium GDP. Appropriate fiscal policy therefore calls for increases in government spending and decreases in taxes—a budget deficit—to correct for unemployment. Decreases in government spending and increases in taxes—a budget surplus—are appropriate fiscal policy for correcting demand-pull inflation.

3   The balanced-budget multiplier indicates that equal increases in government spending and taxation will increase the equilibrium GDP by the amount of the increases in government expenditures and taxes.

4   Built-in stability refers to the fact that net tax revenues vary directly with the level of GDP. Therefore, during a recession, the public budget automatically tends toward a stabilizing deficit; conversely, during expansion, the budget automatically tends toward an anti-inflationary surplus. Built-in stability lessens, but does not correct, undesired changes in the GDP.

5   The full-employment budget measures what the Federal budgetary surplus or deficit would be *if* the economy operated at full employment throughout the year. The full-employment budget is a more meaningful indicator of the government's fiscal posture than its actual budgetary surplus or deficit.

6   The enactment and application of appropriate fiscal policy are subject to certain problems and questions. Some of the most important are these: **a** Can the enactment and application of fiscal policy be better timed to maximize its effectiveness in heading off economic fluctuations?   **b** Can the economy rely on Congress to enact appropriate fiscal policy?   **c** An expansionary fiscal policy may be weakened if it crowds out some private investment spending.   **d** Do people increase their saving in anticipation of the future higher taxes they think deficit spending will entail?   **e** Some of the effect of an expansionary fiscal policy may be dissipated in inflation.   **f** Fiscal policy may be rendered ineffective or inappropriate by unforeseen events occurring within the world economy. Also, fiscal policy may precipitate changes in exchange rates which weaken its effects.   **g** Supply-side economists contend that traditional fiscal policy fails to consider the effects of tax changes on aggregate supply.

TERMS AND CONCEPTS

Employment Act of 1946	**balanced-budget multiplier**	**progressive, proportional, and regressive tax systems**	**cyclical and structural deficits**
Council of Economic Advisers	**expansionary and contractionary fiscal policy**	**actual and full-employment budgets**	**crowding-out effect**
discretionary fiscal policy	**built-in stabilizers**		**Ricardian equivalence theorem**
lump-sum tax	**political business cycle**		**net export effect**

QUESTIONS AND STUDY SUGGESTIONS

1   Explain graphically the determination of equilibrium GDP through both the aggregate expenditures–domestic output approach and the leakages-injections approach for the private sector. Now add government spending and taxation, showing the impact of each on the equilibrium GDP. Explain how discretionary fiscal policy can be used to alleviate inflation and offset a recession.

2   Refer to the tabular data for question 2 at the end of Chapter 11. Now, assuming investment is $16 billion, incorporate government into the table by assuming that it plans to tax and spend $20 billion at each possible level of GDP. Assume net exports are zero, all taxes are personal taxes,

and that government spending does not induce shifts in the consumption and investment schedules. Explain the changes in the equilibrium GDP which the addition of government entails.

3   What is the balanced-budget multiplier? Demonstrate the balanced-budget multiplier in terms of your answer to question 2. Explain: "Equal increases in government spending and tax revenues of *n* dollars will increase the equilibrium GDP by *n* dollars." Does this hold true regardless of the size of the MPS?

4   Explain how both "conservative" and "liberal" economists might support an activist fiscal policy.

5 Explain the functioning of the built-in stabilizers. Can you suggest ways to strengthen built-in stability?

6 Define the "full-employment budget" and explain its significance. How does it differ from the "actual budget"? What is the difference between a cyclical deficit and a structural deficit?

7 Briefly state and evaluate the major problems encountered in enacting and applying fiscal policy. Explain the notion of a political business cycle. What is the crowding-out effect and why is it relevant to fiscal policy? In what respect is the net export effect similar to the crowding-out effect? Do you think people increase their saving in anticipation of the future higher taxes they think deficit spending will eventually entail?

8 Comment on the following statement: "When faced with inflation, mainstream economists recommend higher taxes to restrain demand, while supply-side economists recommend lower taxes to increase aggregate supply."

9 Demonstrate graphically the potential effects of a tax *increase* on aggregate demand and aggregate supply.

10 Using Figure 12-4 as a basis for your response, explain the stabilizing or destabilizing effects of fiscal policy if a constitutional amendment requiring an annually balanced budget were passed.

11 Use Figure 12-4 to explain why a deficit increase which causes the economy to expand might be partly self-liquidating. In requesting a tax cut in the early 1960s President Kennedy said, "It is a paradoxical truth that tax rates are too high today and tax revenues are too low and the soundest way to raise tax revenues in the long run is to cut tax rates now." Was his rationale correct?

12 **Advanced analysis:** Assume that, in the absence of any taxes, the consumption schedule for an economy is as shown below:

GDP, billions	Consumption, billions
$100	$120
200	200
300	280
400	360
500	440
600	520
700	600

a Graph this consumption schedule and note the size of the MPC.

b Assume now a lump-sum (regressive) tax system is imposed in such a way that the government collects $10 billion in taxes at all levels of GDP. Calculate the tax rate at each level of GDP. Graph the resulting consumption schedule and compare the MPC and the multiplier with that of the pretax consumption schedule.

c Now suppose a proportional tax system with a 10 percent tax rate is imposed instead of the regressive system. Calculate the new consumption schedule, graph it, and note the MPC and the multiplier.

d Finally, impose a progressive tax system such that the tax rate is zero percent when GDP is $100, 5 percent at $200, 10 percent at $300, 15 percent at $400, and so forth. Determine and graph the new consumption schedule, noting the effect of this tax system on the MPC and the multiplier.

e Explain why the proportional and progressive tax systems contribute to greater economic stability, while the regressive system does not. Demonstrate graphically.

13 **Advanced analysis:** We can add the public sector to the private economy model of question 11 at the end of Chapter 11 as follows. Assume $G = G_0 = 28$ and $T = T_0 = 30$. Because of the presence of taxes, the consumption schedule, $C = 50 + 0.8Y$, must be modified to read $C_a = 50 + 0.8(Y - T)$, where the term $(Y - T)$ is disposable (after-tax) income. Assuming all taxes are on personal income, investment remains $I_g = I_{g0} = 30$. Net exports are again independent of the level of income, that is, $X_n = X_{n0} = 10$. Using the equilibrium condition $Y = C_a + I_g + X_n + G$, determine the equilibrium level of income. Explain why the addition of the public budget with a slight surplus *increases* the equilibrium income. Now substitute $T = 0.2Y$ for $T = T_0 = 30$, and solve again for the level of income.

PART 3

Money, Banking, and Monetary Policy

13 Money and Banking

Money—one of our truly great inventions—constitutes a most fascinating aspect of economics.

"Money bewitches people. They fret for it, and they sweat for it. They devise most ingenious ways to get it, and most ingenuous ways to get rid of it. Money is the only commodity that is good for nothing but to be gotten rid of. It will not feed you, clothe you, shelter you, or amuse you unless you spend it or invest it. It imparts value only in parting. People will do almost anything for money, and money will do almost anything for people. Money is a captivating, circulating, masquerading puzzle."[1]

Money is also one of the most crucial elements of economics. It is much more than a passive component of the economic system—a mere tool for facilitating the economy's operation. When operating properly, the monetary system is the life-blood of the circular flows of income and expenditure which typify all economies. A well-behaved money system is conducive to both full production and full employment. Conversely, a malfunctioning monetary system can make major contributions to severe fluctuations in the economy's levels of output, employment, and prices, *and* can distort the allocation of resources.

In this chapter we are concerned with the nature and functions of money and the basic institutions of the American banking system. Chapter 14 examines the methods by which individual commercial banks and the banking system as a whole can vary the money supply. In Chapter 15 we discuss how the central banks of the economy attempt to regulate the supply of money to promote full employment and price level stability. Finally, Chapter 16 focuses on *monetarism*, a view which contends that the money supply is *the* key determinant of output, employment, and the price level.

We begin the present chapter with a review of the functions of money. Next, attention shifts to the supply of money as we pose the rather complicated question:

[1]Federal Reserve Bank of Philadelphia, "Creeping Inflation," *Business Review,* August 1957, p. 3.

What constitutes money in our economy? Third, we consider what "backs" the supply of money in the United States. Fourth, the demand for money is explained. Fifth, we combine the supply of money and the demand for money to portray and explain the market for money. Finally, the institutional structure and recent difficulties of the American financial system will be discussed.

THE FUNCTIONS OF MONEY

What is money? Money is what money does. Anything that performs the functions of money is money. There are three functions of money:

1 Medium of Exchange First and foremost, money is a **medium of exchange;** it is usable in buying and selling goods and services. A worker in a bagel bakery does not want to be paid 200 bagels per week. Nor does the bagel bakery wish to receive, say, fresh fish for its bagels. However, money is readily acceptable as payment. It is a convenient social invention which allows resource suppliers and producers to be paid with a "good" (money) which can be used to buy any one of the full range of goods and services available in the marketplace. As a medium of exchange, money allows society to escape the complications of barter. And by providing a convenient way of exchanging goods, money allows society to gain the advantages of geographic and human specialization (Figure 3-1).

2 Measure of Value Money is also a **measure of value.** Society finds it convenient to use the monetary unit as a yardstick for measuring the relative worth of heterogeneous goods and resources. Just as we measure distance in miles or kilometers, we gauge the value of goods and services in terms of dollars. This has distinct advantages. With a money system, we need not state the price of each product in terms of all other products for which it might possibly be exchanged; we need not state the price of cows in terms of corn, crayons, cigars, Chevrolets, croissants, or some other product. This use of money as a common denominator means that the price of each product need be stated *only* in terms of the monetary unit. It permits transactors to readily compare the relative worth of various commodities and resources. Such comparisons facilitate rational decision making. Recall from Chapter 7 the necessity of using money as a measure of value in calculating the size of the GDP. Money is also used as a measure of value for transactions involving future payments. Debt obligations of all kinds are measured in terms of money.

3 Store of Value Finally, money serves as a **store of value.** Because money is the most liquid—that is, the most spendable—of all assets, it is a very convenient form in which to store wealth. Most methods of holding money do not yield monetary returns such as one gets by storing wealth in the form of real assets (property) or paper assets (stocks, bonds, and so forth). However, money does have the advantage of being immediately usable by a firm or a household in meeting any and all financial obligations.

THE SUPPLY OF MONEY

Basically, anything which is generally acceptable as a medium of exchange *is* money. Historically, such diverse items as whales' teeth, elephant tail bristles, circular stones, nails, slaves (yes, human beings), cattle, beer, cigarettes, and pieces of metal have functioned as media of exchange. As we will see, in our economy the debts of governments and of commercial banks and other financial institutions are currently employed as money.

Defining Money: *M*1

Neither economists nor public officials agree on what specific items constitute the economy's money supply. Narrowly defined—and designated as *M*1—the money supply is composed of two items:
1   Currency, that is, coins and paper money in the hands of the nonbank public.
2   All checkable deposits, that is, deposits in commercial banks and various "thrift" or savings institutions on which checks can be drawn.[2]

Coins and paper money are debts of government and governmental agencies. Checking accounts represent debts of the commercial bank or savings institu-

[2]In the ensuing discussion of the definitions of money several of the quantitatively less significant components are not explicitly discussed in order to sidestep a maze of details. For example, travelers' checks are included in the *M*1 money supply. Reference to the statistical appendix of any recent *Federal Reserve Bulletin* will provide you with more comprehensive definitions.

tion. Let's comment briefly on the components of the *M*1 money supply (Table 13-1).

Currency: Coins + Paper Money   From copper pennies to silver dollars, coins are the "small change" of our money supply. Coins are a very small portion of the total money supply; they constitute only 2 or 3 percent of the total $866 billion *M*1 money supply. Coins are essentially "convenience money" which permit us to make all kinds of very small purchases.

All coins in circulation in the United States are **token money.** This simply means that the **intrinsic value**—the value of the bullion (metal) contained in the coin itself—is less than the face value of the coin. This is purposely the case to avoid the melting down of token money for profitable sales as bullion. If our 50-cent pieces each contained 75 cents' worth of silver bullion, it would be highly profitable to melt these coins for sale as bullion. Despite the illegality of such a procedure, 50-cent pieces would disappear from circulation. This is one of the potential defects of commodity money: Its worth as a commodity may come to exceed its worth as money, ending its functioning as a medium of exchange.

Much more quantitatively significant than coins, paper money constitutes about 28 percent of the economy's *M*1 money supply. All of this $240 or so billion of paper currency is in the form of **Federal Reserve Notes,** which are issued by the Federal Reserve Banks with the authorization of Congress. A quick glance at

any currency in your wallet will reveal the words "Federal Reserve Note" at the top of the face of the bill and the Reserve Bank of issue in the circle to the left.

Checkable Deposits   The safety and convenience of using checks have made checking accounts the most important type of money in the United States. You would not think of stuffing $4896.47 in bills and coins in an envelope and dropping it in a mailbox to pay a debt; but to write and mail a check for a large sum is commonplace. A check must be endorsed (signed on the reverse side) by the person cashing it; the drawer of the check subsequently receives the canceled check as an endorsed receipt attesting to the fulfillment of the obligation. Similarly, because the writing of a check requires endorsement by the drawer, the theft or loss of your bankbook is not nearly so calamitous as if you lost an identical amount of currency. It is, furthermore, more convenient to write a check in many cases than to transport and count out a large sum of currency. For all these reasons, *checkbook money* has become the dominant form of money in our economy. In terms of dollar volume, about 90 percent of all transactions are carried out by checks.

It might seem strange that checking accounts are part of the money supply. But the reason for their inclusion is clear: Checks, which are nothing more than a means for transferring the ownership of deposits in banks and other financial institutions, are generally acceptable as a medium of exchange. True, as a stop at

TABLE 13-1   Alternative money definitions for the United States: *M*1, *M*2, and *M*3

Money definition or concept	Absolute amount (in billions)	Percentage of concept		
		M1	M2	M3
Currency (coins and paper money)	$ 261	30%	8%	6%
plus Checkable deposits	605*	70	18	15
*equals M*1	$ 866	100%		
plus Noncheckable savings deposits	448		13	11
plus Small time deposits	1176*		35	28
plus Money market deposit accounts (MMDAs)	548		16	13
plus Money market mutual fund balances (MMMFs)	353		10	9
*equals M*2	$3391		100%	
plus Large time deposits	752*			18
*equals M*3	$4143			100%

*These figures include other quantitatively smaller components.

Source: Federal Reserve Bulletin, November 1991, p. A13. Data are for August 1991.

most gas stations will verify, checks are somewhat less generally accepted than currency. But, for practically all major purchases, sellers willingly accept checks as a means of payment. Furthermore, such deposits can be immediately converted into paper money and coins on demand; checks drawn on these deposits are for all practical purposes the equivalent of currency.

To summarize:

Money, $M1$ = currency + checkable deposits

Institutions Offering Checkable Deposits Table 13-1 shows that **checkable deposits** are clearly the largest component of the $M1$ money supply. By glancing ahead at Figure 13-4 we find that many financial institutions offer checkable deposits in the United States.

1   Commercial banks are the mainstays of the system. They accept the deposits of households and businesses and use these financial resources to extend a wide variety of loans. Commercial bank loans provide short-term working capital to businesses and farmers, finance consumer purchases of automobiles and other durable goods, and so on.

2   The commercial banks are supplemented by a variety of other financial institutions—savings and loan associations (S&Ls), mutual savings banks, and credit unions—which are collectively designated as **thrift** or **savings institutions** or, more simply, "thrifts." **Savings and loan associations** and **mutual savings banks** marshal the savings of households and businesses which are then used, among other things, to finance housing mortgages. **Credit unions** accept the deposits of "members"—usually a group of individuals who work for the same company—and lend these funds to finance installment purchases.

The checkable deposits of banks and thrifts go by various exotic names—demand deposits, NOW (negotiable order of withdrawal) accounts, ATS (automatic transfer service) accounts, and share draft accounts. Nevertheless, they are all similar in that depositors can write checks on them whenever, and in whatever amount, they choose.

Qualification   A technical qualification of our definition of money must be added: Currency and checkable deposits owned by government (the Treasury) and by the Federal Reserve Banks, commercial banks, or other financial institutions are excluded. A paper dollar in the hands of John Doe obviously constitutes just $1 of the money supply. But, if we counted dollars held by banks as part of the money supply, the same $1 would count for $2 when deposited in a bank. It would count for a $1 demand deposit owned by Doe and also for $1 worth of currency resting in the bank's vault. This problem of double counting can be avoided by excluding currency resting in banks (and currency redeposited in the Federal Reserve Banks or other commercial banks) in determining the total money supply.

The exclusion of currency held by, and demand deposits owned by, government is somewhat more arbitrary. The major reason for this exclusion is that it permits us better to gauge the money supply and rate of spending in the private sector of the economy apart from spending initiated by government policy.

Near-Monies: $M2$ and $M3$

Near-monies are certain highly liquid financial assets such as noncheckable savings accounts, time deposits, and short-term government securities which, although they do not directly function as a medium of exchange, can be readily and without risk of financial loss converted into currency or checkable deposits. Thus, on demand you may withdraw currency from a **noncheckable savings account** at a commercial bank or thrift institution. Or, alternatively, you may request that funds be transferred from a noncheckable savings account to a checkable account.

As the term implies, **time deposits** only become available to a depositor at maturity. For example, a 90-day or 6-month time deposit is only available without penalty when the designated period expires. Although time deposits are somewhat less liquid than noncheckable savings accounts, they can be taken as currency or shifted into checkable accounts when they mature.

Alternatively, you can withdraw funds quickly from a **money market deposit account (MMDA).** These are interest-bearing accounts offered by banks and thrifts, which pool individual deposits to buy a variety of short-term securities. MMDAs have minimum balance requirements and limit how often money can be withdrawn. Or, through a telephone call, you can redeem shares in a **money market mutual fund (MMMF)** offered through a financial investment company. These companies use the combined funds of individual shareholders to buy short-term credit instruments such as certificates of deposit and U.S. government securities.

M2   Thus our monetary authorities offer a second and broader definition of money:

$$\text{Money, } M2 = \frac{M1 + \text{noncheckable savings}}{\text{deposits} + \text{small (less than}}$$
$$\$100,000) \text{ time deposits}$$
$$+ \text{ MMDAs} + \text{MMMFs}$$

In other words, **M2** includes (1) the medium of exchange items (currency and checkable deposits) which compose $M1$ plus (2) other items such as noncheckable savings deposits, small time deposits, money market deposit accounts, and individual money market mutual fund balances. These latter deposits can be quickly and without loss converted into currency and checkable deposits. Table 13-1 shows that the addition of noncheckable savings deposits, small time deposits, MMDAs, and MMMFs yields an $M2$ money supply of $3391 billion as compared to an $M1$ figure of $866 billion.

M3 A third "official" definition, **M3,** recognizes that large ($100,000 or more) time deposits—usually owned by businesses as certificates of deposit—are also easily convertible into checkable deposits. There is a going market for these certificates and they can therefore be sold (liquidated) at any time, although perhaps at the risk of a loss. The addition of these large time deposits to $M2$ yields a still broader definition of money:

$$\text{Money, } M3 = \frac{M2 + \text{large } (\$100,000 \text{ or}}{\text{more) time deposits}}$$

Consulting Table 13-1 again, we find that the $M3$ money supply rises to $4143 billion.

Finally, there are still other slightly less liquid assets such as certain government securities (for example, Treasury bills and U.S. savings bonds) which can be easily converted into $M1$ money. There exists a whole spectrum of assets which vary slightly from one another in terms of their liquidity or "moneyness."

Which definition of money shall we adopt? The simple $M1$ definition has a notable virtue: It includes only items *directly* and *immediately* usable as a medium of exchange. For this reason it is the most-cited statistic in discussions of the money supply. However, for some purposes economists prefer the broader $M2$ definition. For example, $M2$ is used as one of the eleven trend variables in the index of leading indicators (Last Word, Chapter 12). And what of $M3$ and still broader definitions of money? These definitions are so inclusive that many economists question their usefulness.

We will adopt the narrow M*1 definition of money in our discussion and analysis, unless stated otherwise.* Bear in mind that the important principles which apply to $M1$ are also applicable to $M2$ and $M3$ in that $M1$ is a component in these broader measures.

Near-Monies: Implications

Aside from complicating our definition of money, the existence of near-monies is important for several related reasons.

1 Spending Habits The highly liquid assets affect people's consuming-saving habits. Usually, the greater the amount of financial wealth people hold as near-monies, the greater is their willingness to spend out of their money incomes.

2 Stability Conversion of near-monies into money or vice versa can affect the economy's stability. For example, during the prosperity-inflationary phase of the business cycle, a significant conversion of noncheckable deposits into checkable deposits or currency adds to the money supply and, if not offset, could enhance inflationary pressures. Such conversions can complicate the task of the monetary authorities in controlling the money supply and the level of economic activity.

3 Policy The specific definition of money adopted is important for purposes of monetary policy. For example, the money supply as measured by $M1$ might be constant, while money defined as $M2$ might be increasing. Now, if the monetary authorities feel it is appropriate to have an expanding supply of money, acceptance of our narrow $M1$ definition would call for specific actions to increase currency and checkable deposits. But acceptance of the broader $M2$ definition would suggest that the desired expansion of the money supply is already taking place and that no specific policy action is required.

Credit Cards

You may wonder why credit cards—Visa, MasterCard, American Express, Discover, and so forth—have been ignored in our discussion of how money is defined. After all, credit cards are a convenient means of making purchases. The answer is that credit cards are *not* really money, but rather a means of obtaining a short-term loan from the commercial bank or other financial institution which has issued the card.

When you purchase a box of cassettes with a credit card, the issuing bank will reimburse the store. Then later you reimburse the bank. You pay an annual fee for the services provided and, if you repay the bank in installments, you pay a sizable interest charge. Credit cards, in short, are a means of deferring or postponing payment for a short period of time. Your purchase of cassettes is not actually complete until you have paid your credit-card bill.

It is worth noting, however, that credit cards—and, indeed, all other forms of credit—allow individuals and businesses to "economize" in the use of money. Credit cards permit you to have less currency and checkable deposits on hand for transactions. Stated differently, credit cards facilitate the synchronization of your expenditures and your receipt of income, thereby reducing the cash and checkable deposits you must hold.

QUICK REVIEW 13-1

♦ *Money serves as a medium of exchange, a measure of value, and a store of value.*

♦ *The narrow M1 definition of money includes currency and checkable deposits.*

♦ *Thrift institutions as well as commercial banks now offer accounts on which checks can be written.*

♦ *The M2 definition of money includes M1 plus noncheckable savings deposits, small (less than $100,000) time deposits, money market deposit accounts, and money market mutual fund balances; M3 consists of M2 plus large time deposits (more than $100,000).*

WHAT "BACKS" THE MONEY SUPPLY?

This is a slippery question; any reasonably complete answer is likely to be at odds with the preconceptions many of us hold about money.

Money as Debt

The major components of the money supply—paper money and checkable deposits—are debts, or promises to pay. *Paper money is the circulating debt of the Federal Reserve Banks. Checkable deposits are the debts of commercial banks and thrift institutions.*

Furthermore, paper currency and checkable deposits have no intrinsic value. A $5 bill is just a piece of paper, and a checkable deposit is merely a bookkeeping entry. And coins, we know, have an intrinsic value less than their face value. Nor will government redeem the paper money you hold for anything tangible, such as gold. In effect, we have chosen to "manage" our money supply to provide the amount of money needed for that particular volume of business activity which will foster full employment, price level stability, and a healthy rate of economic growth.

Most economists feel that management of the money supply is more sensible than linking it to gold or any other commodity whose supply might arbitrarily and capriciously change. A large increase in the nation's gold stock as the result of new gold discovery or a breakthrough in the extraction of gold from ore might increase the money supply far beyond the amount needed to transact a full-employment level of business activity, and therefore cause inflation. Conversely, the historical decline in domestic gold production could reduce the domestic money supply to the point where economic activity was choked off and unemployment and a retarded growth rate resulted.

The point is that paper money cannot be converted into a fixed amount of gold or some other precious metal but is exchangeable only for other pieces of paper money. The government will swap one paper $5 bill for another bearing a different serial number. That is all you can get if you ask the government to redeem some of your paper money. Similarly, check money cannot be exchanged for gold but only for paper money, which, as we have just seen, will not be redeemed by the government for anything tangible.

Value of Money

If currency and checkable deposits have no intrinsic characteristics which give them value *and* if they are not backed by gold or other precious metals, then why are they money? What gives a $20 bill or a $100 checking account entry its value? A reasonably complete answer to these questions involves three points.

1 Acceptability Currency and checkable deposits are money simply because they are accepted as money. By virtue of long-standing business practice, currency and checkable deposits perform the basic function of money; they are acceptable as a medium of exchange. Suppose you swap a $20 bill for a shirt or blouse at a clothing store. Why does the merchant accept this piece of paper in exchange for that product? The merchant accepts paper money because he or she is confident that others will also be willing to accept it in exchange for goods and services. The merchant knows that paper money can purchase the services of clerks, acquire products from wholesalers, and pay the rent on the store. We accept paper money in exchange because we are confident it will be exchangeable for real goods and services when we choose to spend it.

2 Legal Tender   Our confidence in the acceptability of paper money is partly a matter of law; currency has been designated as **legal tender** by government. This means that paper currency must be accepted in the payment of a debt or the creditor forfeits both the privilege of charging interest and the right to sue the debtor for nonpayment. Put more bluntly, the acceptability of paper dollars is bolstered by the fact that government says these dollars are money. The paper money in our economy is basically **fiat money;** it is money because the government says it is, not because of redeemability in terms of some precious metal. The general acceptability of currency is also bolstered by the willingness of government to accept it in the payment of taxes and other obligations due the government.

Lest we be overimpressed by the power of government, it should be noted that the fact that paper currency is generally accepted in exchange is decidedly more important than government's legal tender decree in making these pieces of paper function as money. Indeed, the government has *not* decreed checks (which are also fiat money) to be legal tender, but they nevertheless successfully perform the vast bulk of the economy's exchanges of goods, services, and resources. The fact that a governmental agency—the Federal Deposit Insurance Corporation (FDIC)—insures the deposits of commercial banks and S&Ls undoubtedly contributes to the willingness of individuals and businesses to use checkable deposits as a medium of exchange.

3 Relative Scarcity   Basically, the value of money, like the economic value of anything else, is a supply and demand phenomenon. That is, money derives its value from its scarcity relative to its usefulness. The usefulness of money lies in its unique capacity to be exchanged for goods and services, either now or in the future. The economy's demand for money thus depends on its total dollar volume of transactions in any given time period plus the amount of money individuals and businesses want to hold for possible future

transactions. Given a reasonably constant demand for money, the value or "purchasing power" of the monetary unit will be determined by the supply of money.

Money and Prices

The real value or purchasing power of money is the amount of goods and services a unit of money will buy. When money rapidly loses its purchasing power, it rapidly loses its role as money.

Value of the Dollar   The amount a dollar will buy varies inversely with the price level; *a reciprocal relationship exists between the general price level and the value of the dollar.* Figure 13-1 shows this inverse relationship. When the consumer price index or "cost-of-living" index goes up, the purchasing power of the dollar necessarily goes down, and vice versa. Higher prices lower the value of the dollar because more dollars will be needed to buy a given amount of goods and services. Conversely, lower prices increase the purchasing power of the dollar because you will need fewer dollars to obtain a given quantity of goods and services. If the price level doubles, the value of the dollar will decline by one-half, or 50 percent. If the price level falls by one-half, or 50 percent, the purchasing power of the dollar will double.

The arithmetic of the relationship between the price level and the value of the dollar is as follows. If we let P equal the price level expressed as an index number (in hundredths) and D equal the value of the dollar, then our reciprocal relationship is

$$D = \frac{1}{P}$$

If the price level P equals 1.00, then the value of the dollar D is 1.00. But, if P rises from 1.00 to 1.20, D will be 0.833, meaning a 20 percent increase in the price level will reduce the value of the dollar by 16.67 percent. Check your understanding of this reciprocal relationship by determining the value of D and its percentage rise when P falls by 20 percent to 0.80.

Inflation and Acceptability   We noted in Chapter 8 several situations in which a nation's currency became worthless and unacceptable in exchange. With few exceptions these were circumstances where government issued so many pieces of paper currency that the value of each of these units of money was almost totally undermined. The infamous post-World War I inflation in Germany is a notable example. In December of 1919

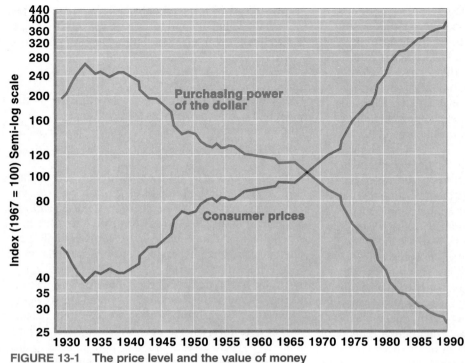

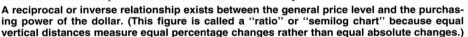

FIGURE 13-1   The price level and the value of money

A reciprocal or inverse relationship exists between the general price level and the purchasing power of the dollar. (This figure is called a "ratio" or "semilog chart" because equal vertical distances measure equal percentage changes rather than equal absolute changes.)

there were about 50 billion marks in circulation. Four years later this figure had expanded to 496,585,345,900 billion marks! The result? The German mark in 1923 was worth an infinitesimal fraction of its 1919 value.[3]

How might inflation and the accompanying decreases in the value of a nation's currency affect the acceptability of paper currency as money? Households and businesses will accept paper currency as a medium of exchange so long as they know they can spend it without any noticeable loss in its purchasing power. But, with spiraling inflation, this is not the case. Runaway inflation, such as Germany incurred in the early 1920s and several Latin-American nations faced in the 1980s, may significantly depreciate the value of money between the time of its receipt and its expenditure. Money will be "hot" money. It is as if the government were constantly taxing away the purchasing power of dollars. Rapid depreciation of the value of the dollar may cause it to cease functioning as a medium of ex-

[3]Frank G. Graham, *Exchange, Prices and Production in Hyperinflation Germany, 1920–1923* (Princeton, N.J.: Princeton University Press, 1930), p. 13.

change. Businesses and households may refuse to accept paper money in exchange because they do not want to bear the loss in its value which will occur while it is in their possession. (All this despite the fact that government says the paper currency is legal tender!) Without an acceptable medium of exchange, the economy will revert to inefficient barter.

Similarly, people will use money as a store of value so long as there is no unreasonable deterioration in the value of those stored dollars because of inflation. And the economy can effectively employ the monetary unit as a measure of value only when its purchasing power is relatively stable. A yardstick of value subject to drastic shrinkage no longer permits buyers and sellers to establish the terms of trade clearly. When the value of the dollar is declining rapidly, sellers will not know what to charge and buyers will not know what to pay for various goods and services.

Managing Money

The major "backing" of paper money is the government's ability to keep the value of money reasonably stable. This entails (1) appropriate fiscal policy, as explained in Chapter 12 and (2) intelligent management or regulation of the money supply, as noted above. Businesses and households accept paper money in exchange for goods and services so long as it commands a roughly equivalent amount of goods and services when they in turn spend it. In our economy a blending of legislation, government policy, and social practice serves as a bulwark against any imprudent expansion of the money supply which might seriously jeopardize money's value in exchange.

What we have said with respect to paper currency also applies to checking account money. In this case money is the debt of commercial banks and thrift institutions. Your checking account of $200 merely means that your bank or thrift is indebted to you for that number of dollars. You can collect this debt in one of two ways. You can go to the bank or thrift and demand paper currency for your checkable deposit; this simply amounts to changing the debts you hold from the debts of a bank or thrift to government-issued debts. Or, and this is more likely, you can "collect" the debt which the bank or savings institution owes you by transferring this claim by check to someone else.

For example, if you buy a $200 coat from a store, you can pay for it by writing a check, which transfers your bank's indebtedness from you to the store. Your bank now owes the store the $200 it previously owed to you. The store accepts this transfer of indebtedness (the check) as a medium of exchange because it can convert it into currency on demand or can transfer the debt to others in making purchases of its choice. Thus, checks, as means of transferring the debts of banks and thrifts, are acceptable as money because of the ability of banks and thrifts to honor these claims.

In turn, the ability of banks and thrifts to honor claims against them depends on their not creating too many of these claims. We will see that a decentralized system of private, profit-seeking banks does not contain sufficient safeguards against the creation of too much check money. Hence, the American banking and financial system has substantial centralization and governmental control to guard against the imprudent creation of checkable deposits.

Caution: This does not mean that in practice the supplies of currency and checkable-deposit money have always been judiciously controlled to achieve a high degree of economic stability. Indeed, many economists allege that most of the inflationary woes we have encountered historically are largely the consequence of imprudent increases in the money supply.

QUICK REVIEW 13-2

✦ In the United States and other advanced economies, all money is essentially the debts of government, commercial banks, and thrift institutions.

✦ These debts efficiently perform the functions of money so long as their value, or purchasing power, is relatively stable.

✦ The value of money is not rooted in carefully defined quantities of precious metals (as in the past), but rather, in the amount of goods and services money will purchase in the marketplace.

✦ Government's responsibility in stabilizing the value of the monetary unit involves (1) the application of appropriate fiscal policies, and (2) effective control over the supply of money.

THE DEMAND FOR MONEY

Our emphasis thus far has been on what constitutes the supply of money and how the money supply is "backed." We now turn to the demand for money. Our earlier discussion of the functions of money suggests two basic reasons why the public wants to hold money.

Transactions Demand, D_t

The first reason is that people want money as a medium of exchange—to conveniently negotiate the purchase of goods and services. Households must have enough money on hand to buy groceries and pay mortgage and utility bills until the next paycheck. Similarly, businesses need money to pay for labor, materials, power, and so on. Money demanded for all such purposes is called the **transactions demand** for money.

Not surprisingly, the basic determinant of the amount of money demanded for transaction purposes is the level of nominal GDP. The larger the total money value of all goods and services exchanged in the economy, the larger will be the amount of money needed to negotiate these transactions. *The transactions demand for money varies directly with nominal GDP.* Note that we specify *nominal* GDP. Households and firms will want more money for transactions purposes if *either* prices rise *or* real output increases. In both instances there will be a larger dollar volume of transactions to negotiate.

In Figure 13-2a (Key Graph) the relationship between the transactions demand for money, D_t, and the interest rate is graphed. Because the transactions demand for money depends on the level of nominal GDP

KEY GRAPH

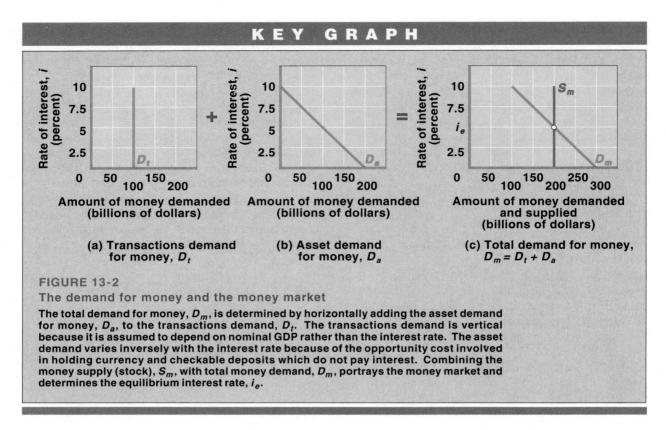

FIGURE 13-2

The demand for money and the money market

The total demand for money, D_m, is determined by horizontally adding the asset demand for money, D_a, to the transactions demand, D_t. The transactions demand is vertical because it is assumed to depend on nominal GDP rather than the interest rate. The asset demand varies inversely with the interest rate because of the opportunity cost involved in holding currency and checkable deposits which do not pay interest. Combining the money supply (stock), S_m, with total money demand, D_m, portrays the money market and determines the equilibrium interest rate, i_e.

and is independent of the interest rate, we show the transactions demand as a vertical line. For simplicity we assume the amount of money demanded for transactions is unrelated to changes in the interest rate. That is, higher interest rates will not reduce the amount of money demanded for transactions.[4]

We have located the transactions demand at $100 billion arbitrarily, but a rationale can be provided. For example, if each dollar held for transactions purposes is spent on the average three times per year *and* nominal GDP is assumed to be $300 billion, then the public would need $100 billion of money to purchase that GDP.

Asset Demand, D_a

The second reason for holding money is rooted in money's function as a store of value. People may hold their financial assets in many forms—for example, as corporate stocks, private or government bonds, or as *M*1 money. Hence, there is an **asset demand** for money.

What determines the asset demand for money? First, we must recognize that each of the various forms in which our financial assets may be held has advantages and disadvantages. To simplify, let's compare holding bonds with holding money as an asset. The advantages of holding money are its liquidity and lack of risk. Money is the most liquid of all assets in that it is immediately usable in making purchases. Money is an especially attractive asset to be holding when the prices of goods, services, and other financial assets are expected to decline. When the price of a bond falls, the bondholder will suffer a loss if the bond must be sold before maturity. There is no such risk with holding money.

The disadvantage of holding money as an asset is that, compared to holding bonds, one does *not* earn interest income or, in the case of an interest-bearing checking account, earn as much interest income as on bonds or noncheckable deposits. And idle currency earns no interest at all. Some banks and thrifts require

[4]This is a simplification. We would also expect the amount of money held by businesses and households to negotiate transactions to vary inversely with the interest rate. When interest rates are high, consumers and businesses will try to reduce the amount of money held for transactions purposes to have more funds to put into interest-earning assets.

minimum-sized checkable deposits for the depositor to be paid interest; hence, many depositors do not achieve these minimum deposit balances and therefore earn no interest. The interest paid on checkable deposits which exceed the required minimums is less than that paid on bonds and the various noncheckable deposits.

Knowing this, the problem is deciding how much of your financial assets to hold as, say, bonds and how much as money. The solution depends primarily upon the rate of interest. By holding money a household or business incurs an opportunity cost (Chapter 2); interest income is forgone or sacrificed. If a bond pays 10 percent interest, then it costs $10 per year of forgone income to hold $100 as cash or in a noninterest checkable account. It is no surprise that *the asset demand for money varies inversely with the rate of interest.* When the interest rate or opportunity cost of holding money as an asset is low, the public will choose to hold a large amount of money as assets. Conversely, when the interest rate is high, it is costly to "be liquid" and the amount of assets held in the form of money will be small. Stated differently, when it is expensive to hold money as an asset, people will hold less of it; when money can be held cheaply, people will hold more of it. This inverse relationship between the interest rate and the amount of money people will want to hold as an asset is shown by D_a in Figure 13-2b.

Total Money Demand, D_m

As shown in Figure 13-2c, the **total demand** for money, D_m, can be found by adding the asset demand horizontally to the transactions demand. (The vertical blue line in Figure 13-2a represents the transactions demand to which Figure 13-2b's asset demand has been added.) The resulting downsloping line represents the total amount of money the public will want to hold for transactions and as an asset at each possible interest rate. Also note that a change in the nominal GDP—working through the transactions demand for money—will shift the total money demand curve. Specifically, an increase in nominal GDP will mean that the public will want to hold a larger amount of money for transactions purposes and this will shift the total money demand curve to the right. For example, if nominal GDP increases from $300 to $450 billion and we continue to suppose that the average dollar held for transactions is spent three times per year, then the transactions demand line will shift from $100 to $150 billion. Thus the total money demand curve will lie $50 billion further to the right at each possible interest rate

than formerly. Conversely, a decline in nominal GDP will shift the total money demand curve to the left.

THE MONEY MARKET

We can combine the demand for money with the supply of money to portray the **money market** and determine the equilibrium rate of interest. In Figure 13-2c we have drawn a vertical line, S_m, to represent the money supply. The money supply is shown as a vertical line because we assume our monetary authorities and financial institutions have provided the economy with some particular *stock* of money, such as the $M1$ total shown in Table 13-1. Just as in a product or resource market (Chapter 4), the intersection of money demand and money supply determines equilibrium price. The "price" in this case is the equilibrium interest rate, that is, the price paid for the use of money.

If disequilibrium existed in the money market, how would the money market achieve equilibrium? Consider Figure 13-3, which replicates Figure 13-2c and adds two alternative supply-of-money curves.

FIGURE 13-3 Restoring equilibrium in the money market

A decrease in the supply of money creates a temporary shortage of money in the money market. People and institutions attempt to gain more money by selling bonds. The supply of bonds therefore increases, which reduces bond prices and raises interest rates. At higher interest rates, people reduce the amount of money they wish to hold. Hence, the amount of money supplied and demanded once again is equal at the higher interest rate. An increase in the supply of money creates a temporary surplus of money, resulting in an increase in the demand for bonds and higher bond prices. Interest rates fall and equilibrium is reestablished in the money market.

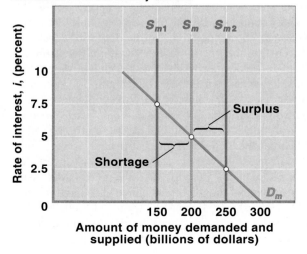

1　Suppose that the supply of money is reduced from $200 billion, shown as S_m, to $150 billion, designated as S_{m1}. Note that the quantity of money demanded exceeds the quantity supplied by $50 billion at the previous equilibrium interest rate of 5 percent. In this case, people will attempt to make up for the shortage of money by selling some of the financial assets they own (we assume for simplicity that these assets are bonds). But one person's receipt of money through the sale of a bond is another person's loss of money through the purchase of that bond. Overall, there is only $150 billion of money available. The collective attempt to get more money by selling bonds will increase the supply of bonds relative to demand in the bond market and drive down bond prices.

Generalization: *Lower bond prices are associated with higher interest rates.* (Last Word, Chapter 5.) To clarify this point, suppose that a bond with no expiration date pays a fixed $50 annual interest and is selling for its face value of $1000. The interest yield on this bond is 5 percent. That is:

$$\frac{\$50}{\$1000} = 5\%$$

Now suppose the price of this bond falls to $667 because of the previously described increased supply of bonds. The $50 fixed annual interest payment will now yield $7\frac{1}{2}$ percent to whomever buys the bond:

$$\frac{\$50}{\$667} = 7\frac{1}{2}\%$$

Because all borrowers must compete by offering to pay lenders interest yields similar to those available on bonds, a higher general interest rate emerges. In Figure 13-3 the interest rate rises from 5 percent at the money supply of $200 billion to $7\frac{1}{2}$ percent when the money supply is $150 billion. This higher interest rate raises the opportunity cost of holding money and reduces the amount of money firms and households want to hold. Specifically, the amount of money demanded declines from $200 billion at the 5 percent interest rate to $150 billion at the $7\frac{1}{2}$ percent interest rate. The money market is back into equilibrium: The quantity of money demanded and supplied are each $150 billion at the $7\frac{1}{2}$ percent interest rate.

2　Conversely, an increase in the supply of money from $200 billion ($S_m$) to $250 billion ($S_{m2}$) will result in a surplus of money of $50 billion at the initial 5 percent interest rate. People will try to rid themselves of money by purchasing more bonds. But one person's expenditure of money is another person's receipt of money. The collective attempt to buy more bonds will increase the demand for bonds and pull bond prices upward.

Corollary: *Higher bond prices are associated with lower interest rates.* In terms of our example, the $50 interest payment on a bond now priced at, say, $2000, will yield a bond buyer only $2\frac{1}{2}$ percent:

$$\frac{\$50}{\$2000} = 2\frac{1}{2}\%$$

The point is that interest rates in general will fall as people unsuccessfully attempt to reduce their money holdings below $250 billion by buying bonds. In this case, the interest rate will fall to a new equilibrium at $2\frac{1}{2}$ percent. Because the opportunity cost of holding money now is lower—being liquid is less expensive—consumers and businesses will increase the amount of currency and checkable deposits they are willing to hold from $200 billion to $250 billion. Once again equilibrium in the money market is restored: The quantities of money demanded and supplied are each $250 billion at an interest rate of $2\frac{1}{2}$ percent.

In Chapter 15 we will discover how monetary policy attempts to change the money supply so as to alter the equilibrium real interest rate. A higher interest rate will reduce investment and consumption spending, a lower rate will increase investment and consumption spending, and either situation ultimately affects the levels of real output, employment, and prices.

QUICK REVIEW 13-3

◆　**People hold money for transaction and asset purposes.**

◆　**The total demand for money includes the transaction and asset demands; it graphs as an inverse relationship between the interest rate and the quantity of money demanded.**

◆　**The equilibrium interest rate is determined by money demand and supply; it occurs where people are willing to hold the exact amount of money being supplied by the monetary authorities.**

◆　**Bond prices and interest rates are inversely related.**

THE UNITED STATES FINANCIAL SYSTEM

In the past two decades the financial sector of our economy has undergone sweeping changes and it is fair to say that the financial system is currently in a state of flux. Early regulatory legislation rather rigidly defined the mission or kind of business various financial institutions could conduct. For example, commercial banks provided checking accounts and made business and consumer loans. Savings and loan associations accepted savings deposits and provided these savings for mortgage lending. But a combination of competitive pressures, innovation, and deregulation in the recent past has expanded the functions of the various financial institutions and blurred the traditional distinctions between them.

The **Depository Institutions Deregulation and Monetary Control Act** (DIDMCA) of 1980 attempted to cope with these realities by reducing or eliminating many of the historical distinctions between commercial banks and various thrift institutions. Most important for present purposes, DIDMCA permitted all depository institutions to offer checkable deposits. But in extending the privilege of offering checkable deposits to the thrifts, DIDMCA requires in turn that the thrifts be subject to the same limitations on the creation of checkable deposits that apply to commercial banks. With these introductory observations in mind, let's examine the overall framework of our financial system.

Centralization and Regulation

Although the trend has been toward deregulation of the financial system, considerable centralization and governmental control remain. This centralization and regulation has historical roots. It became painfully apparent rather early in American history that, like it or not, centralization and public control were essential for an efficient banking system. Congress became increasingly aware of this about the turn of the twentieth century. Decentralized banking fostered the inconvenience and confusion of a heterogeneous currency, monetary mismanagement, and a money supply inappropriate to the needs of the economy. "Too much" money can precipitate dangerous inflationary problems; "too little" money can stunt the economy's growth by hindering the production and exchange of goods and services. The United States and innumerable foreign countries have learned through bitter experience that a decentralized, unregulated banking system is not likely to provide that particular money supply which is most conducive to the welfare of the economy as a whole.

An unusually acute money panic in 1907 was the straw that broke Congress's back. A National Monetary Commission was established to study the monetary and banking problems of the economy and to out-

line a course of action for Congress. The end result was the Federal Reserve Act of 1913.

Structure of the Federal Reserve System

The monetary control system which has developed under the frequently amended Federal Reserve Act and DIDMCA is sketched in Figure 13-4. We must understand the nature and roles of the various segments which compose the banking system and the relationships the parts bear to one another.

Board of Governors   The kingpin of our money and banking system is the **Board of Governors** of the Federal Reserve System ("the Fed"). The seven members of this Board are appointed by the President with the confirmation of the Senate. Terms are long—fourteen years—and staggered so that one member is replaced every two years. The intention is to provide the Board with continuity, experienced membership, and autonomy or independence. The Board is staffed by appointment rather than elections as a way to divorce monetary policy from partisan politics.

The Board of Governors exercises general supervision and control over the operation of the money and banking system of the nation. The Board chairman is the most powerful central banker in the world. The Board's actions, which are to be in the public interest and designed to promote the general economic welfare, are made effective through certain control techniques which alter the money supply (Chapter 15).

Two important bodies assist the Board of Governors in determining basic banking policy.

1   The **Federal Open Market Committee** (FOMC), made up of the seven members of the Board plus five of the presidents of the Federal Reserve Banks, sets the System's policy on the purchase and sale of government bonds in the open market. These open-market operations are the most significant technique by which monetary authorities can affect the money supply (Chapter 15).

2   The **Federal Advisory Council** is composed of twelve prominent commercial bankers, one selected annually by each of the twelve Federal Reserve Banks. The Council meets periodically with the Board of Governors to voice its views on banking policy. However, as its name indicates, the Council is purely advisory; it has no policy-making powers.

The Fed is essentially an independent institution. It cannot be abolished or rendered ineffective by presidential whim, nor can its role and functions be altered

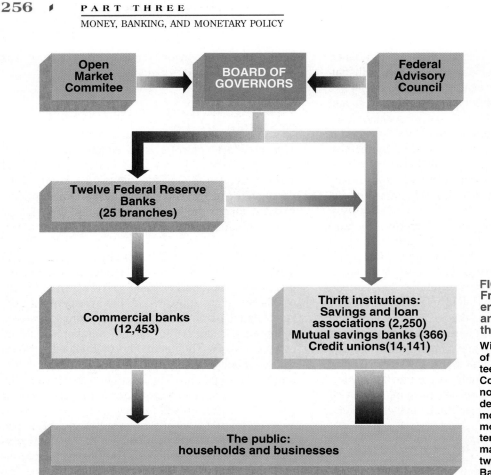

FIGURE 13-4
Framework of the Federal Reserve System and its relationship to the public

With the advice and counsel of the Open Market Committee and the Federal Advisory Council, the Board of Governors makes the basic policy decisions which provide monetary control of our money and banking systems. These decisions are made effective through the twelve Federal Reserve Banks.

by Congress except by specific legislative action. As noted, the long terms of the Board's members are designed to provide them with security and isolate them from political pressures.

The independence of the Fed has been a matter of ongoing controversy. Proponents of independence contend that the Fed must be protected from political pressures if it is to perform effectively the difficult and highly technical task of managing the money supply. Furthermore, it is argued that it is politically expedient for Congress and the executive branch to invoke expansionary fiscal policies—tax cuts and special-interest spending win votes—and there is thus a need for an independent monetary authority to guard against consequent inflation.

Opponents of an independent Fed argue that it is undemocratic to have such a powerful agency whose members are not directly subject to the will of the people. Also, because the legislative and executive

branches of government bear ultimate responsibility for the economic well-being of the nation, they should be able to manipulate *all* the policy tools essential to the economy's health. Why should Congress and the administration be responsible for the consequences of policies they do not fully control? Critics cite instances of the Fed using monetary policy to counter the effects of fiscal policy.

You will be able to clarify your own position on this issue after we have analyzed the working of monetary policy in Chapter 15.

The Twelve Federal Reserve Banks The twelve **Federal Reserve Banks** have three major characteristics. They are (1) central banks, (2) quasi-public banks, and (3) bankers' banks.

1 Central Banks Most nations have one central bank, for example, Britain's Bank of England or Ger-

FIGURE 13-5 The twelve Federal Reserve Districts

The Federal Reserve System divides the United States into twelve districts, each of which has one central bank and in some instances one or more branches of the central bank. Hawaii and Alaska are included in the twelfth district. *(Federal Reserve Bulletin.)*

many's Bundesbank. The United States has twelve! This partly reflects our geographic size and economic diversity and the fact that we have a large number of commercial banks. It also is the result of a political compromise between proponents of centralization and advocates of decentralization.

Figure 13-5 locates the twelve Federal Reserve Banks and indicates the district each serves. Through these central banks the basic policy directives of the Board of Governors are made effective. The Federal Reserve Bank of New York City is by far the most important of these central banks. The development of modern communication and transportation facilities has undoubtedly lessened the geographic need for a system of regional banks.

2 Quasi-Public Banks The twelve Federal Reserve Banks are quasi-governmental banks. They reflect an interesting blend of private ownership and public control. The Federal Reserve Banks are owned by the member banks in their districts. Upon joining the Federal Reserve System, commercial banks are required to purchase shares of stock in the Federal Reserve Bank in their district. But the basic policies which the Federal Reserve Banks pursue are set by a governmental body—the Board of Governors. The central banks of American capitalism are privately owned but governmentally controlled. And the owners control neither the officials of the central banks nor their policies.

The fact that the Federal Reserve Banks are essentially public institutions is vitally important to under-

standing their operation. In particular, the Federal Reserve Banks are *not* motivated by profits, as are private enterprises. The policies followed by the central banks are those perceived by the Board of Governors to promote the well-being of the economy as a whole. Hence, the activities of the Federal Reserve Banks will frequently be at odds with the profit motive.[5] Also, the Federal Reserve Banks do not compete with commercial banks. With rare exceptions, the Federal Reserve Banks do not deal with the public, but rather, with the government and the commercial banks.

3 Bankers' Banks Finally, the Federal Reserve Banks are frequently called "bankers' banks." This is a shorthand way of saying that the Federal Reserve Banks perform essentially the same functions for depository institutions as depository institutions perform for the public. Just as banks and thrifts accept the deposits of and make loans to the public, so the central banks accept the deposits of and make loans to banks and thrifts. But the Federal Reserve Banks have a third function which banks and thrifts do not perform: the function of issuing currency. Congress has authorized the Federal Reserve Banks to put into circulation Federal Reserve Notes, which constitute the economy's paper money supply.

[5]Though it is not their basic goal, the Federal Reserve Banks have actually operated profitably, largely as the result of Treasury debts held by them. Part of the profits has been used to pay dividends to member banks on their holdings of stock; the bulk of the remaining profits has been turned over to the United States Treasury.

Commercial Banks The workhorses of the American financial system are its 12,453 **commercial banks.** Roughly two-thirds of these are **state banks,** that is, private banks operating under state charters. The remaining one-third received their charters from the Federal government, that is, they are **national banks.**

Thrift Institutions Thrift institutions are regulated by agencies which are separate and apart from the Board of Governors and the Federal Reserve Banks. Thus, for example, the operation of savings and loan associations is regulated and monitored by the Treasury Department's Office of Thrift Supervision. But, as we have noted, DIDMCA expanded the lending authority of all thrifts, so that S&Ls and mutual saving banks can now make consumer and business loans.

DIDMCA also has made S&Ls and other depository institutions subject to monetary control by the Federal Reserve System. In particular, thrifts now must meet the same reserve requirements as commercial banks, *and* they now can borrow from the Fed. We will find in Chapter 15 that the changing of reserve requirements and the terms under which depository institutions can borrow from the Federal Reserve Banks are two basic means by which the Board of Governors controls the supply of money. In Figure 13-4 we have noted with mauve arrows that the thrift institutions are partially subject to the control of the Board of Governors and the central banks in that decisions concerning monetary policy will affect the thrifts along with the commercial banks.

Fed Functions and the Money Supply

The Fed performs a wide variety of functions.[6]

1 Reserves The Federal Reserve Banks hold deposits, called *reserves,* which are made by banks and thrifts. We will find in Chapter 15 that these deposits are of strategic importance in managing the economy's money supply.

2 Check Collection Another important function of the Fed is to provide the mechanism for the collection of checks. If Sarah writes a check on her Salem bank or thrift to Sam who deposits it in his San Diego bank or thrift, how does the San Diego bank collect the check against the Salem bank? Answer: The Fed handles it in two or three days by adjusting the aforementioned reserves of the two banks.

3 Fiscal Agents The Federal Reserve Banks act as fiscal agents for the Federal government. The government collects huge sums through taxation, spends equally astronomical amounts, and sells and redeems bonds. The government avails itself of the Fed's facilities in carrying out these activities.

4 Supervision The Fed supervises the operations of member banks. Periodic bank examinations assess member bank profitability; ascertain that banks perform in accordance with the myriad regulations to which they are subject; and uncover questionable practices or fraud.[7]

5 Control of Money Supply Finally—and most important of all—the Federal Reserve System has ultimate responsibility for regulating the supply of money. *The major task of the Federal Reserve authorities is to manage the money supply in accordance with the needs of the economy as a whole.* This task involves making that amount of money available which is consistent with high and rising levels of output and employment and a relatively constant price level. Whereas all the other functions are of a more-or-less routine or service nature, the goal of correctly managing the money supply entails making basic and unique policy decisions of a nonroutine character. Chapter 15 discusses Federal Reserve monetary policy and its effectiveness. But before we turn to that subject we must explore how banks create money (Chapter 14).

BANK AND THRIFT FAILURES

We have established that the past decade has been a time of great change in the financial industry. Financial innovations have blurred the lines separating banks, thrifts, and mutual fund companies. Legislation has

---

[6]For a detailed look at the service functions of the Federal Reserve Banks, see Board of Governors of the Federal Reserve System, *The Federal Reserve System: Purposes and Functions.* 7th ed. (1984), chaps. 1, 2, 7.

[7]The Federal Reserve is not alone in the task of supervision. The individual states supervise all banks which they charter. The Comptroller of the Currency supervises all national banks and the Office of Thrift Supervision oversees all thrifts. Finally, the Federal Deposit Insurance Corporation has the power to supervise all banks and thrifts whose deposits it insures.

ended restrictions on maximum interest rates payable on customer deposits. Gone are the days when bankers joked about the 3-6-3 rule: 3 percent interest to savers, 6 percent interest from borrowers, and 3 o'clock to the golf course.

Financial innovation and deregulation have enhanced competition among financial institutions and undoubtedly increased productive and allocative efficiency (Chapter 2). Deregulation and competition, however, have also produced an unpleasant and costly side effect: a rising tide of bank and thrift failures. As we see in Table 13-2, more than 2000 banks and thrifts have failed since 1980. Saving and loan associations (S&Ls) accounted for most of the approximately 1000 insolvent thrifts.

We know that business failures are normal, everyday occurrences in competitive market economies; they are a means of eliminating persistent and significant economic inefficiencies. Many observers believe there are too many banks and thrifts and that a major consolidation of the financial industry is required. So why are bank and thrift failures of special concern? There are two reasons.

1 Banks and thrifts are collectively and in some cases individually instrumental to the monetary system underlying the financial health of the entire economy. These financial institutions hold the money deposits of businesses and households, and as we will discover in Chapter 14, create the major portion of the nation's money supply by making loans to the public. Several of the banks and thrifts which failed in the late 1980s and early 1990s were large financial institutions. Without timely governmental action their collapse might have threatened the regional or even the national economy.

2 Bank and thrift failures present a special problem for taxpayers. The Federal government has in effect pledged its full credit to back checking and savings deposits in insured banks and thrifts. For this reason it has agreed to pay a large portion of the losses resulting from bank and thrift failures. The bill to taxpayers for bailing out the S&L industry has been estimated to be $500 billion over a forty-year period. That would mean tax payments of $5000 for each American household!

Commercial Bank Difficulties

Although a handful of large commercial banks failed in the early 1980s, bank failures throughout the rest of the 1980s consisted mainly of small institutions operating in agricultural and energy-producing regions. Poor crop prices and declines in oil and natural gas prices resulted in significant loan defaults and consequent bank failures in regions where the economy depends on these products. Regional recessions and falling local real estate prices in the late 1980s added to the problems facing banks and forced several to close.

The national recession beginning in the summer of 1990 struck a more generalized blow, producing significant losses in some major banks and causing several financially troubled banks to fail. One such bank was the relatively large Bank of New England. In 1991 the Bush administration moved to shore up the bank deposit insurance fund by granting the Federal Deposit Insurance Corporation (FDIC) authority to borrow from the government. Nevertheless, the banking industry remains generally sound, and most large banks are expected to again prosper as the economy recovers.

Savings and Loan Collapse

Of greater concern and magnitude, however, has been the collapse of the savings and loan industry. Specifically, one-third of 3000 S&Ls existing in 1987 are no longer in business. The reasons for S&L failures are somewhat complex and therefore require careful consideration.

Deregulation and Competition Deregulation of the banking and thrift industry in the early 1980s contributed to the S&L crisis by removing the S&Ls' previ-

TABLE 13-2 Bank and thrift failures, 1980–1991

Year	Banks	Thrifts
1980	10	3
1981	10	11
1982	10	28
1983	42	71
1984	79	27
1985	124	34
1986	145	49
1987	206	48
1988	221	220
1989	207	327
1990	169	215
1991	124	142

Source: Federal Deposit Insurance Corporation and Resolution Trust Corporation.

LAST WORD

THE MYSTERY OF THE MISSING MONEY*

The Federal Reserve cannot account for $196 billion of paper money it has issued over the years.

About $1038 worth of currency is now in circulation for each of the 252 million Americans. Meanwhile, government estimates that people and businesses in the United States hold only $260 of currency per capita. That leaves $778 per capita, or a total of $196 billion, missing. Where has this currency gone?

Some observers suggest that people lie about how much currency they are holding. This "solution" to the mystery of the missing money is unpersuasive. Why lie? The surveys which supply the data are anonymous.

Perhaps drug dealers and other participants in the underground economy are holding the missing money. In particular, some analysts point to the growing volume of circulating $100 bills as supporting this view. The problem with this theory is that only about 12 percent of the drug money seized by the Customs Service has been $50 and $100 bills.

Are businesses holding more money and not reporting it? Not likely. Businesses put cash to work earning interest. The Federal Reserve estimates that business holdings account for only one-half of the nation's overall $260 per capita currency holdings.

Could the proliferation of automatic bank machines shed light on this mystery? By making it more convenient to get cash, these machines could mean people are holding more unreported cash than previously. However, bank cash machines also make currency *replenishment* easier, reducing the need to hold as much cash in any particular day. Furthermore, credit cards and checks have reduced cash holdings.

---

ously protected role. Before the 1980s, banking laws had carved out a near monopoly for the S&Ls on home mortgage loans. When the government lifted interest rate ceilings on deposits in banks and thrifts, competition drove up the interest on deposits. Many S&Ls were caught holding fixed-rate, long-term mortgages issued at interest rates far below those now needed to maintain and attract deposits. S&Ls responded to the resulting losses by using the provisions of new thrift legislation to shift their lending toward riskier commercial, consumer, and real estate loans which earned higher interest rates.

Deposit Insurance Banks and thrifts pay premiums to the FDIC to insure the deposits they hold. In 1980 the Federal government increased deposit insurance from $40,000 to $100,000 per account. The main purpose of deposit insurance is to prevent "bank panics"— sudden and massive deposit withdrawals by worried customers. Such bank panics destabilized the econ-

omy in the early 1930s and contributed to the Great Depression.

Somewhat ironically, deposit insurance—designed to *add* stability to the financial system—inadvertently contributed to the worsening S&L problem. As with all insurance, deposit insurance creates a **moral hazard problem.** *This problem is that insuring an individual against risk of loss reduces the insured's incentive to prevent the loss from occurring.* In last-chance attempts to salvage their enterprises, financially troubled S&Ls began to offer extraordinarily high interest rates to attract deposits away from competing institutions. Knowing that accounts of $100,000 or less were fully insured, savers directed their funds to these financially shaky S&Ls. These S&Ls began making risky high-interest loans to attempt to earn interest returns above those being paid on their expensive, newly acquired funds.

In brief, deposit insurance enabled shaky S&Ls to attract funds by removing the incentive for depositors

So where *is* the missing money? Although not certain, the Federal Reserve believes that people abroad hold more than half of the unrecorded United States currency. In Argentina, for example, an estimated $5 billion to $7 billion in American cash is circulating freely. The Polish government recently estimated that $5 billion of cash is in circulation in Poland.

United States currency flows abroad when Americans buy imports. It also flows out of the United States when Americans send dollars to relatives living in other countries. The United States profits when American dollars stay in other nations. The cost of printing a dollar is less than 3 cents, and hence the United States makes more than 97 cents on each dollar which is sent abroad and not returned. It's like American Express selling traveler's checks which never get cashed.

But there is a bigger potential benefit from a world economic perspective. The availability of a stable, reliable currency, wherever people use it, enables transactions which might not otherwise occur. In brief, dollar holdings may overcome special monetary problems in some foreign nations, increasing real output there and thus worldwide.

*Adapted from Robert D. Hershey, Jr.: "Billions Elude Dollar Tally; Is Currency in Use Abroad?" *The New York Times*, Tuesday, February 20, 1990, p. D1. Updated.

to direct funds toward healthy financial institutions. It also encouraged S&Ls to gamble with insured deposits, or to incur more risk than would otherwise be prudent for their stockholders. If the risky ventures paid off, shareholders would win. If the loans defaulted and caused the S&Ls to collapse, the government insurance fund, not S&L shareholders, would pay for the losses by depositors.

Loan Defaults and Fraud   Major defaults on many of these risky loans forced several large S&Ls into bankruptcy. Particularly hard hit were savings and loans in Texas and other "oil patch" states. Loan defaults in these areas increased rapidly as oil prices fell and economic conditions worsened. Speculative loans on office buildings and other real estate went into default. Furthermore, the looser banking regulations provided a convenient opportunity for some S&L officers to defraud their failing institutions. As indicated in Table 13-2, more than 1000 S&Ls failed in the late 1980s and

early 1990s. Federal investigators have now detected criminal conduct in 40 percent of these failed S&Ls.

The Thrift Bailout and Future Reform

The losses at S&Ls eventually plunged the S&L deposit insurance fund severely into the red, forcing government to face the crisis. In August 1989 the Financial Institutions Reform, Recovery, and Enforcement Act (FIRREA) became law. The new law established the **Resolution Trust Corporation** and directed it to oversee the closing or sale of all failed S&Ls. The total cost for the first ten years is estimated to be $160 billion, most of it paid by taxpayers. As previously indicated, the forty-year cost may reach $500 billion.

The FIRREA also placed deposit insurance for the thrifts and banks under FDIC control. It increased premiums paid by banks and thrifts for deposit insurance and raised the thrift's capital requirements—the percentage of their assets financed by owners—to match those of banks. The law also for the first time permitted S&Ls to accept deposits from commercial businesses. Finally, FIRREA directs the Federal Reserve to allow bank holding companies to acquire healthy S&Ls.

FIRREA may be only the first phase of an overall reform of the banking industry. In 1991 the Bush administration proposed sweeping reform legislation designed to foster further competition within the financial services industry and perhaps to hasten the perceived need for consolidation. Among its provisions, the proposal would limit deposit insurance to single accounts, permit interstate banking, and allow banks to own brokerage houses and insurance companies (and vice versa). Although some of these provisions met with Congressional resistance, apparently the revolution in banking first begun a decade or so ago has yet to run its full course.

QUICK REVIEW 13-4

◆   *The Federal Reserve System consists of the Board of Governors, twelve Federal Reserve Banks, commercial banks, and thrift institutions.*

◆   *The Federal Reserve's major role is to regulate the supply of money in the economy.*

◆   *The 1980s and early 1990s have witnessed a sharp rise in the number of bank and thrift failures.*

◆   *The government has bailed out failed savings and loan associations using taxpayer dollars.*

CHAPTER SUMMARY

1 Anything that functions as **a** a medium of exchange, **b** a measure of value, and **c** a store of value is money.

2 The Federal Reserve System recognizes three "official" definitions of the money supply. *M*1 is currency and checkable deposits; *M*2 is *M*1 plus noncheckable savings deposits, small (less than $100,000) time deposits, money market deposit accounts, and money market mutual fund balances; and *M*3 is *M*2 plus large ($100,000 or more) time deposits. In our analysis we concentrate on *M*1 since its components are immediately spendable.

3 Money, which is essentially the debts of government and depository institutions (commercial banks and thrift institutions), has value because of the goods and services which it will command in the market. Maintenance of the purchasing power of money depends largely on the effectiveness with which government manages the money supply.

4 The total demand for money consists of the transactions and asset demands for money. The transactions demand varies directly with nominal GDP; the asset demand varies inversely with the interest rate. The money market combines the demand for money with the money supply to determine the equilibrium interest rate.

5 Disequilibriums in the money market are corrected through changes in bond prices. As bond prices change, interest rates move in the opposite direction. At the equilibrium interest rate, bond prices are stable and the amounts of money demanded and supplied are equal.

6 The American banking system is composed of **a** the Board of Governors of the Federal Reserve System, **b** the twelve Federal Reserve Banks, and **c** some 12,453 commercial banks and 16,757 thrift institutions. The Board of Governors is the basic policy-making body for the entire banking system. The directives of the Board are made effective through the twelve Federal Reserve Banks, which are simultaneously **a** central banks, **b** quasi-public banks, and **c** bankers' banks.

7 The major functions of the Federal Reserve System are **a** to hold the deposits or reserves of commercial banks and other depository institutions, **b** to provide facilities for the rapid collection of checks, **c** to act as fiscal agent for the Federal government, **d** to supervise the operations of member banks, and **e** to regulate the supply of money in terms of the best interests of the economy as a whole.

8 There has been a rising number of bank and thrift failures in the 1980s and early 1990s. The collapse of major S&Ls resulted from deregulation and competition, the moral hazard problem associated with deposit insurance, loan defaults by borrowers, and criminal conduct. The government bailout of failed S&Ls may eventually cost taxpayers $500 billion.

TERMS AND CONCEPTS

medium of exchange	**savings and loan associations**	**legal tender**	**Federal Open Market Committee**
measure of value	**credit unions**	**fiat money**	**Federal Advisory Council**
store of value	**near-monies**	**transactions, asset, and total demand for money**	**Federal Reserve Banks**
M1, M2, M3	**noncheckable savings accounts**	**money market**	**commercial banks**
token money	**time deposits**	**Depository Institutions Deregulation and Monetary Control Act**	**state banks**
intrinsic value	**MMDA (money market deposit account)**	**Board of Governors**	**national banks**
Federal Reserve Notes	**MMMF (money market mutual fund)**		**moral hazard problem**
checkable deposits			**Resolution Trust Corporation**
thrift or savings institutions			
mutual savings banks			

QUESTIONS AND STUDY SUGGESTIONS

1 Describe how drastic inflation can undermine the ability of money to perform its three basic functions.

2 What are the disadvantages of commodity money? What are the advantages of **a** paper money and **b** check money as compared with commodity money?

3 "Money is only a bit of paper or a bit of metal that gives its owner a lawful claim to so much bread or beer or diamonds or motorcars or what not. We cannot eat money, nor drink money, nor wear money. It is the goods that money can buy that are being divided up when money is divided up."[8] Evaluate and explain.

[8]George Bernard Shaw, *The Intelligent Woman's Guide to Socialism and Capitalism* (New York: Brentano's, Inc., 1982), p. 9. Used by permission of the Public Trustee and the Society of Authors.

4 Fully evaluate and explain the following statements:

a "The invention of money is one of the great achievements of the human race, for without it the enrichment that comes from broadening trade would have been impossible."

b "Money is whatever society says it is."

c "When prices of everything are going up, it is not because everything is worth more, but because the dollar is worth less."

d "The difficult questions concerning paper [money] are . . . not about its economy, convenience or ready circulation but about the amount of the paper which can be wisely issued or created, and the possibilities of violent convulsions when it gets beyond bounds."[9]

e "In most modern industrial economies of the world the debts of government and of commercial banks are used as money."

5 What items constitute the $M1$ money supply? What is the most important component of the $M1$ money supply? Why is the face value of a coin greater than its intrinsic value? Distinguish between $M2$ and $M3$. What are near-monies? Of what significance are they? What arguments can you make for including savings deposits in a definition of money?

6 What "backs" the money supply in the United States? What determines the value of money? Who is responsible for maintaining the value of money? Why is it important to be able to alter the money supply? What is meant by **a** "sound money" and **b** "52-cent dollar"?

7 What is the basic determinant of **a** the transactions demand and **b** the asset demand for money? Explain how these two demands might be combined graphically to determine total money demand. How is the equilibrium interest rate determined in the money market? How might **a** the expanded use of credit cards, **b** a shortening of worker pay periods, and **c** an increase in nominal GDP affect the transactions demand for money and the equilibrium interest rate?

8 Suppose that a bond having no expiration date has a face value of $10,000 and annually pays a fixed amount of interest of $800. Compute and enter in the space provided either the interest rate which a bond buyer could secure at each of the bond prices listed or the bond price at each of the interest rates shown. What generalization can be drawn from the completed table?

Bond price	Interest rate %
$ 8,000	
	8.9
$10,000	
$11,000	
	6.2

9 Assume the money market is initially in equilibrium and that the money supply is now increased. Explain the adjustments toward a new equilibrium interest rate. Will bond prices be higher at the new equilibrium rate of interest? What effects would you expect that interest-rate change to have on the levels of output, employment, and prices? Answer the same questions for a decrease in the money supply.

10 What is the major responsibility of the Board of Governors? Discuss the major characteristics of the Federal Reserve Banks. Of what significance is the fact that the Federal Reserve Banks are quasi-public? Do you think the Fed should be an independent institution?

11 What are the two basic functions of commercial banks and thrift institutions? State and briefly discuss the major functions of the Federal Reserve System.

12 Explain the "moral hazard problem" associated with insurance and relate this problem to the collapse of major savings and loan associations during the late 1980s and early 1990s.

[9]F. W. Taussig, *Principles of Economics,* 4th ed. (New York: The Macmillan Company, 1946), pp. 247–248.

CHAPTER 14

How Banks Create Money

If you get a chance to visit Washington, D.C., you might enjoy touring the United States Bureau of Printing and Engraving. There, thousands of large sheets containing more than $22 million of Federal Reserve Notes roll off the printing presses daily. After machines cut the sheets into individual bills, employees ship the currency to the twelve Federal Reserve Banks for distribution.

We are all fascinated by large sums of currency. But, rather than currency, people use checkable deposits of commercial banks and thrift institutions for most of their transactions. The amount of these deposits far exceeds the amount of currency banks hold. Who creates these checkable deposits? The answer is loan officers at commercial banks. Their tools? Computers and computer printers! The revelation that bankers create money sounds like something "Sixty Minutes" or a congressional committee should investigate. But, in truth, banking authorities are well aware that banks create checking deposit money. In fact, the Federal Reserve *relies* on banks to create a large portion of the nation's money supply.

Because the bulk of all checkable deposits are the demand deposits of commercial banks, this chapter will explain how commercial banks can *create* demand deposit money. Specifically, we explain and compare the money-creating abilities of (1) a *single* commercial bank which is part of a multibank system, and (2) the commercial banking *system* as a whole. Throughout our discussion recall that thrift institutions also provide checkable deposits. Therefore the term "depository institution" is readily substitutable for "commercial bank" in this and the following chapter. Similarly, the term "checkable deposit" can be substituted for "demand deposit."

THE BALANCE SHEET OF A COMMERCIAL BANK

An understanding of the basic items on a bank's balance sheet, and how various transactions change these

items, will give us a valuable analytical tool for grasping the workings of our monetary and banking systems.

A **balance sheet** is a statement of assets and claims summarizing the financial position of a firm—in this case a commercial bank—at some point in time.

264

Every balance sheet has one overriding virtue. By definition, it must balance, because each and every known *asset,* being something of economic value, will be claimed by someone. Can you think of an asset—something of monetary value—which no one claims? A balance sheet balances because the value of assets equals the amount of claims against them. The claims shown on a balance sheet are divided into two groups: the claims of the owners of a firm against the firm's assets, called *net worth,* and the claims of nonowners, called *liabilities.* Thus, a balance sheet balances because

Assets = liabilities + net worth

A balance-sheet approach to our study of the money-creating ability of commercial banks is valuable in two specific respects.
1   A bank's balance sheet provides a convenient point of reference from which we can introduce new terms and concepts in an orderly manner.
2   The use of balance sheets allows us to quantify certain strategic concepts and relationships which would defy comprehension if discussed in verbal terms alone.

HISTORY AS PROLOGUE: THE GOLDSMITHS

We are about to use balance sheets to explain how a **fractional reserve system of banking** operates. The characteristics and working of such a system can be better understood by considering a bit of economic history.

When the ancients began to use gold in making transactions, it became apparent that it was both unsafe and inconvenient for consumers and merchants to carry gold and have it weighed and assessed for purity every time a transaction was negotiated. It therefore became commonplace to deposit one's gold with goldsmiths whose vaults or strongrooms could be used for a fee. Upon receiving a gold deposit, the goldsmith would issue a receipt to the depositor. Soon goods were traded for the goldsmiths' receipts and the receipts became an early form of paper money.

At this point the goldsmiths—now embryonic bankers—used a 100 percent reserve system; their circulating paper money receipts were fully backed by gold. But, given the public's acceptance of the goldsmiths' receipts as paper money, the goldsmiths became aware that the gold they stored was rarely redeemed. In fact, they found themselves in charge of "going concerns" where the amount of gold deposited in any week or month was likely to exceed the amount withdrawn.

It was only a matter of time until some particularly adroit goldsmith hit on the idea that paper money could be issued *in excess of* the amount of gold held. Goldsmiths would put these additional "receipts" redeemable in gold—paper money—into circulation by making interest-earning loans to merchants, producers, and consumers. Borrowers were willing to accept loans in this form because gold receipts were accepted as a medium of exchange.

At this juncture a *fractional reserve system* of banking came into being. If, for example, our ingenious goldsmith made loans equal to the amount of gold stored, then the total value of paper money in circulation would be twice the value of the gold. Reserves would be 50 percent of outstanding paper money.

A system of fractional reserve banking—the kind of system we have today—has two significant characteristics.

1 Money Creation and Reserves   Banks in such a system can *create money.* When our goldsmith made loans by giving borrowers paper money which was not fully backed by gold reserves, money was being created. The quantity of such money the goldsmith could create would depend on the amount of reserves it was deemed prudent to keep on hand. The smaller the amount of reserves deemed necessary, the larger the amount of paper money the goldsmith could create. Although gold is no longer used to "back" our money supply (Chapter 13), bank lending (money creation) today is constrained by the amount of reserves banks feel obligated, or are required, to keep.

2 Bank Panics and Regulation   Banks which operate on the basis of fractional reserves are vulnerable to bank "panics" or "runs." Our goldsmith who has issued paper money equal to twice the value of gold reserves cannot convert all that paper money into gold in the unlikely event all holders of that paper money appear simultaneously demanding gold. In fact, there are many instances of European and American banks being ruined by this unfortunate circumstance. However, a bank panic is highly unlikely *if* the banker's reserve and lending policies are prudent. Indeed, a basic reason why banking systems are highly regulated industries is to prevent bank runs.

A SINGLE COMMERCIAL BANK IN THE BANKING SYSTEM

We now will explore the money-creating potential of a single bank which is part of a multibank banking system. What accounts constitute a commercial bank's balance sheet? How does a single commercial bank create and destroy money? What factors govern the money-creating abilities of such a bank?

Formation of a Commercial Bank

For answers to these questions we must understand the ins and outs of a commercial bank's balance sheet and how certain elementary transactions affect that balance sheet. We start with the organization of a local commercial bank.

Transaction 1: The Birth of a Bank Suppose far-sighted citizens of the metropolis of Wahoo, Nebraska, decide that their town needs a new commercial bank to provide banking services for that growing community. Assuming these enterprising individuals can secure a state or national charter for their bank, they then turn to the task of selling, say, $250,000 worth of capital stock (equity shares) to buyers, both in and out of the community. These financing efforts meet with success and the Merchants and Farmers Bank of Wahoo now exists—at least on paper. How does the Wahoo bank's balance statement appear at its birth?

The new owners of the bank have sold $250,000 worth of shares of stock in the bank—some to themselves, some to other people. As a result, the bank now has $250,000 in cash on hand and $250,000 worth of capital stock outstanding. The cash is an asset to the bank and that cash held by a bank is sometimes called **vault cash** or *till money*. The outstanding shares of stock, however, constitute an equal amount of claims which the owners have against the bank's assets. The shares of stock are the net worth of the bank, though they are assets from the viewpoint of those who possess these shares. The bank's balance sheet would read:

BALANCE SHEET 1: WAHOO BANK		
Assets		**Liabilities and net worth**
Cash	$250,000	Capital stock $250,000

Transaction 2: Becoming a Going Concern The newly established board of directors must now get the newborn bank off the drawing board and make it a reality. First, property and equipment must be acquired. Suppose the directors, confident of the success of their venture, purchase a building for $220,000 and $20,000 worth of office equipment. This simple transaction changes the composition of the bank's assets. The bank now has $240,000 less in cash and $240,000 worth of new property assets. Using blue to denote those accounts affected by each transaction, we find that the bank's balance sheet at the end of transaction 2 appears as follows:

BALANCE SHEET 2: WAHOO BANK		
Assets		**Liabilities and net worth**
Cash	$ 10,000	Capital stock $250,000
Property	240,000	

Note that the balance sheet still balances, as indeed it must.

Transaction 3: Accepting Deposits Commercial banks have two basic functions: to accept deposits of money and to make loans. Now that our bank is operating, suppose that the citizens and businesses of Wahoo decide to deposit $100,000 in the Merchants and Farmers Bank. What happens to the bank's balance sheet?

The bank receives cash, which we know is an asset to the bank. Suppose this money is placed in the bank as demand deposits (checking accounts), rather than time deposits or savings accounts. These newly created demand deposits constitute claims which depositors have against the assets of the Wahoo bank. Thus the depositing of money in the bank creates a new liability account—demand deposits. The bank's balance sheet now looks like this:

BALANCE SHEET 3: WAHOO BANK		
Assets		**Liabilities and net worth**
Cash	$110,000	Demand deposits $100,000
		Capital stock 250,000

Note that, although there is no direct change in the total supply of money, a change in the composition of the economy's money supply has occurred as a result of transaction 3. Bank money, or demand deposits, have *increased* by $100,000 and currency held by the nonbank public has *decreased* by $100,000. Currency held by a bank, you will recall, is *not* part of the economy's money supply.

It is apparent that a withdrawal of cash will reduce the bank's demand-deposit liabilities and its holdings of cash by the amount of the withdrawal. This, too, changes the composition, but not the total supply, of money.

Transaction 4: Depositing Reserves in a Federal Reserve Bank All commercial banks and thrift institutions which provide checkable deposits must keep a **legal reserve** or, more simply, **reserves.** This legal reserve is *an amount of funds equal to a specified percentage of its own deposit liabilities which a member bank must keep on deposit with the Federal Reserve Bank in its district or as vault cash.* To simplify our discussion we suppose that our bank keeps its legal reserve *entirely* in the form of deposits in the Federal Reserve Bank of its district. But remember that in reality vault cash is counted as reserves and banks keep a significant portion of their reserves in this form.

The "specified percentage" of its deposit liabilities which the commercial bank must keep as reserves is known as the **reserve ratio.** That is exactly what it is—a ratio between the size of the reserves which the commercial bank must keep and the commercial bank's own outstanding deposit liabilities. This ratio is as follows:

$$\frac{\text{Reserve}}{\text{ratio}} = \frac{\text{commercial bank's required reserves}}{\text{commercial bank's demand-deposit liabilities}}$$

If the reserve ratio were $\frac{1}{10}$, or 10 percent, our bank, having accepted $100,000 in deposits from the public, would be obligated to keep $10,000 as reserves. If the ratio were $\frac{1}{5}$, or 20 percent, $20,000 of reserves would be required. If $\frac{1}{2}$, or 50 percent, $50,000 would be required, and so forth.

Historically, the Board of Governors had the authority to establish and vary the reserve ratio within limits legislated by Congress. The reserve ratio limits which now prevail are those shown in Table 14-1. A 3 percent reserve is required on the first $42.2 million of

TABLE 14-1 Reserve requirements of depository institutions

Type of deposit	Current requirement	Statutory limits
Checkable deposits		
$0–42.2 million	3%	3%
Over $42.2 million	10	8–14
Noncheckable nonpersonal savings and time deposits	0	0–9

Source: Federal Reserve. Data are for March 1992.

demand or other checkable deposits held by an institution. The reserve requirement on an institution's checkable deposits over $42.2 million is currently 10 percent, although the Board of Governors can vary this between 8 and 14 percent. Currently, no reserves must be kept against noncheckable nonpersonal (business) savings and time deposits. This ratio can be varied between 0 and 9 percent. Also, after consultation with appropriate congressional committees, the Federal Reserve may impose reserve requirements for 180 days in excess of those specified in Table 14-1.

To simplify the following discussion we suppose that the reserve ratio for commercial banks is $\frac{1}{5}$, or 20 percent, and that this requirement applies only to demand deposits. Although on the high side, the 20 percent figure is convenient to use in computations. And, because we are concerned with checkable (spendable) demand deposits, we ignore reserves on noncheckable savings and time deposits in our discussion. The point is that reserve requirements are *fractional,* meaning they are less than 100 percent. This consideration is vital in our analysis of the lending ability of the banking system.

The Wahoo bank will just be meeting the required 20 percent ratio between its deposit in the Federal Reserve Bank and its own deposit liabilities by depositing $20,000 in the Federal Reserve Bank. To distinguish this deposit from the public's deposits in commercial banks, we will use the term *reserves* in referring to those funds which commercial banks deposit in the Federal Reserve Banks.

But suppose that the directors of the Wahoo bank anticipate that their holdings of the public's demand deposits will grow in the future. Hence, instead of sending just the minimum amount, $20,000, they send an extra $90,000, for a total of $110,000. In so doing, the bank will avoid the inconvenience of sending additional reserves to the Federal Reserve Bank each time its own demand-deposit liabilities increase. And, as we will see, it is on the basis of extra reserves that banks can lend and thereby earn interest income.

Actually, of course, the bank would not deposit *all* its cash in the Federal Reserve Bank. However, because (1) banks as a rule hold vault cash only in the amount of $1\frac{1}{2}$ or 2 percent of their total assets, and (2) vault cash can be counted as reserves, we assume that all the bank's cash is deposited in the Federal Reserve Bank and therefore constitutes the commercial bank's total reserves. The cumbersome process of adding two assets—"cash" and "deposits in the Federal Reserve Bank"—to determine "reserves" is thereby avoided.

At the completion of this transaction, the balance sheet of the Merchants and Farmers Bank will appear as follows:

BALANCE SHEET 4: WAHOO BANK			
Assets		**Liabilities and net worth**	
Cash	$ 0	Demand	
Reserves	110,000	deposits	$100,000
Property	240,000	Capital stock	250,000

Several points relevant to this transaction merit comment:

1 Excess Reserves A note on terminology: The amount by which the bank's **actual reserves** exceed its **required reserves** is the bank's **excess reserves.**
That is,

$$\frac{\text{Excess}}{\text{reserves}} = \frac{\text{actual}}{\text{reserves}} - \frac{\text{required}}{\text{reserves}}$$

In this case,

Actual reserves	$110,000
Required reserves	−20,000
Excess reserves	$90,000

The only reliable way of computing excess reserves is to multiply the bank's demand-deposit liabilities by the reserve ratio to obtain required reserves ($100,000 times 20 percent equals $20,000), then to subtract this figure from the actual reserves listed on the asset side of the bank's balance sheet.

To understand this process, you should compute excess reserves for the bank's balance sheet as it stands at the end of transaction 4, assuming that the reserve ratio is (1) 10 percent, (2) $33\frac{1}{3}$ percent, and (3) 50 percent.

Because the ability of a commercial bank to make loans depends on the existence of excess reserves, this concept is crucial in grasping the money-creating ability of the banking system.

2 Control What is the rationale underlying the requirement that member banks deposit a reserve in the Federal Reserve Bank of their district? One might think that the basic purpose of reserves is to enhance the liquidity of a bank and protect commercial bank depositors from losses. In other words, reserves would constitute a ready source of funds from which commercial banks can meet large and unexpected withdrawals of cash by depositors.

But this reasoning breaks down under close scrutiny. Although historically reserves were seen as a source of liquidity and therefore protection for depositors, *legal,* or required, reserves cannot be used to meet unexpected cash withdrawals. If the banker's nightmare should materialize—everyone with demand deposits in the bank appearing at once to demand these deposits in cash—the banker could not draw upon required reserves to meet this "bank panic" without violating the legal reserve ratio and incurring the wrath and penalties of the Federal Reserve authorities. In practice, legal reserves are *not* an available pool of liquid funds on which commercial banks can rely in times of emergency.[1] In fact, even if legal reserves were accessible to commercial banks, they would not be sufficient to meet a serious "run" on a bank. As already noted, reserves are *fractional;* that is, demand deposits may be 10 or 20 times as large as a bank's required reserves.

Commercial bank depositors must be protected by other means. As noted in Chapter 13, periodic bank

---

[1]This amendment must be added: As depositors withdraw cash from a commercial bank, the bank's demand-deposit liabilities will decline. This lowers the absolute amount of required reserves which the bank must keep, freeing some of the bank's actual reserves for use in meeting cash withdrawals by depositors. To illustrate: Suppose a commercial bank has reserves of $20 and demand-deposit liabilities of $100. If the legal reserve ratio is 20 percent, all the bank's reserves are required. Now, if depositors withdraw, say, $50 worth of their deposits as cash, the bank will only need $10 as required reserves to support the remaining $50 of demand-deposit liabilities. Thus $10 of the bank's actual reserves of $20 are no longer required. The bank can draw on this $10 in helping to meet the cash withdrawals of its depositors. And, of course, if a bank goes out of business, all its reserves will be available to pay depositors and other claimants.

examinations are an important device for promoting prudent commercial banking practices. And banking laws restrict banks as to the kinds of assets they may acquire; for example, banks are generally prohibited from buying common stocks. Furthermore, insurance funds administered by the Federal Deposit Insurance Corporation (FDIC) exist to insure individual deposits in banks and thrifts up to $100,000.

If the purpose of reserves is not to provide for commercial bank liquidity, what is their function? *Control* is the basic answer. Legal reserves permit the Board of Governors to influence the lending ability of commercial banks. Chapter 15 will examine how the Board of Governors can invoke certain policies which either increase or decrease commercial bank reserves and affect the ability of banks to grant credit. The objective is to prevent banks from *over*extending or *under*extending bank credit. To the degree that these policies are successful in influencing the volume of commercial bank credit, the Board of Governors can help the economy avoid the business fluctuations which lead to bank runs, bank failures, and collapse of the monetary system. In this indirect way—controlling commercial bank credit and thereby stabilizing the economy— reserves function to protect depositors, not as a source of liquidity. Another function of reserves is to facilitate the collection or "clearing" of checks.

3 Asset and Liability Note there is an apparent accounting matter which transaction 4 entails. Specifically, *the reserve created in transaction 4 is an asset to the depositing commercial bank but a liability to the Federal Reserve Bank receiving it.* To the Wahoo bank the reserve is an asset; it is a claim which this commercial bank has against assets of another institution—the Federal Reserve Bank. To the Federal Reserve Bank this reserve is a liability, a claim which another institution—the Wahoo bank—has against it. Just as the demand deposit you get by depositing money in a commercial bank is an asset to you and a liability to your commercial bank, so the deposit or reserve which a commercial bank establishes by depositing money in a bankers' bank is an asset to the commercial bank and a liability to the Federal Reserve Bank. An understanding of this relationship is necessary in pursuing transaction 5.

Transaction 5: A Check Is Drawn Against the Bank
This is a significant and somewhat more complicated transaction. Suppose Clem Bradshaw, a Wahoo farmer who deposited a substantial portion of the $100,000 in

demand deposits which the Wahoo bank received in transaction 3, buys $50,000 worth of farm machinery from the Ajax Farm Implement Company of Beaver Crossing, Nebraska. Bradshaw very sensibly pays for this machinery by writing a $50,000 check, against his deposit in the Wahoo bank, to the Ajax company. We need to know (1) how this check is collected or cleared, and (2) the effect the collection of the check has on the balance sheets of the banks involved in the transaction.

To do this, we must consider the Wahoo bank (Bradshaw's bank), the Beaver Crossing bank (the Ajax Company's bank), and the Federal Reserve Bank of Kansas City.[2] For simplicity's sake, we deal only with changes which occur in those specific accounts affected by this transaction.

We trace this transaction in three related steps, keying the steps by letters to Figure 14-1.

a Bradshaw gives his $50,000 check, drawn against the Wahoo bank, to the Ajax company. Ajax deposits the check in its account with the Beaver Crossing bank. The Beaver Crossing bank increases Ajax's demand deposit by $50,000 when it deposits the check. Ajax is now paid off. Bradshaw is pleased with his new machinery, for which he has now paid.

b Now the Beaver Crossing bank has Bradshaw's check in its possession. This check is simply a claim against the assets of the Wahoo bank. The Beaver Crossing bank will collect this claim by sending this check—along with checks drawn on other banks—to the Federal Reserve Bank of Kansas City. Here a clerk will clear, or collect, this check for the Beaver Crossing bank by *increasing* its reserve in the Federal Reserve Bank by $50,000 and by *decreasing* the Wahoo bank's reserve by a like amount. The check is collected merely by making bookkeeping notations that the Wahoo bank's claim against the Federal Reserve Bank has been reduced by $50,000 and the Beaver Crossing bank's claim increased accordingly. Note these changes on the balance sheets in Figure 14-1.

c Finally, the Federal Reserve Bank sends the cleared check back to the Wahoo bank, and for the first time the Wahoo bank discovers that one of its depositors has drawn a check for $50,000 against his demand deposit. Accordingly, the Wahoo bank reduces Bradshaw's demand deposit by $50,000 and recognizes that the collection of this check has entailed a $50,000 de-

---

[2]Actually, the Omaha branch of the Federal Reserve Bank of Kansas City would handle the process of collecting this check.

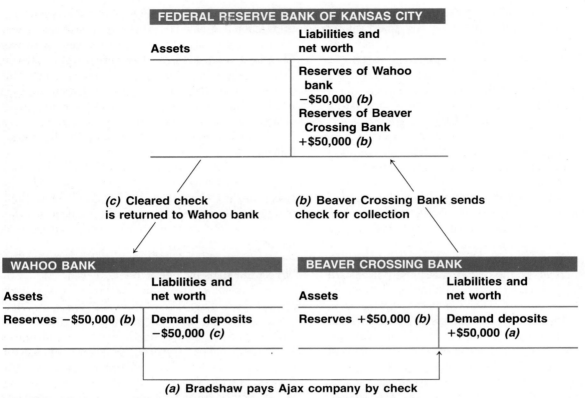

FIGURE 14-1   The collection of a check through a Federal Reserve Bank
The bank against which a check is drawn and cleared loses both reserves and deposits; the bank in which the check is deposited acquires reserves and deposits.

cline in its reserves at the Federal Reserve Bank. Note that the balance statements of all three banks will still balance. The Wahoo bank will have reduced both its assets and liabilities by $50,000. The Beaver Crossing bank will have $50,000 more in reserves and in demand deposits. Ownership of reserves at the Federal Reserve Bank will have changed, but total reserves will stay the same.

Whenever a check is drawn against a bank and deposited in another bank, collection of that check will entail a loss of both reserves and demand (checkable) deposits by the bank on which the check is drawn. Conversely, if a bank receives a check drawn on another bank, the bank receiving the check will, in the process of collecting it, have its reserves and deposits *increased* by the amount of the check. In our example, the Wahoo bank loses $50,000 in both reserves and deposits to the Beaver Crossing bank. But there is no loss of reserves or deposits for the banking system as a whole. What one bank loses another bank gains.

Bringing all the other assets and liabilities back into the picture, the Wahoo bank's balance sheet looks like this at the end of transaction 5:

BALANCE SHEET 5: WAHOO BANK			
Assets		**Liabilities and net worth**	
Reserves	$ 60,000	Demand deposits	$ 50,000
Property	240,000	Capital stock	250,000

You should verify that with a 20 percent reserve requirement, the bank's *excess* reserves now stand at $50,000.

Transaction 5 is reversible. If a check drawn against another bank is deposited in the Wahoo bank, the Wahoo bank will receive both reserves and deposits equal to the amount of the check as it is collected.

Money-Creating Transactions of a Commercial Bank

The next three transactions are particularly crucial because they explain (1) how a single commercial bank can literally create money by making loans, (2) how money is destroyed when loans are repaid, and (3) how banks create money by purchasing government bonds from the public.

Transaction 6: Granting a Loan In addition to accepting deposits, commercial banks grant loans to borrowers. What effect does commercial bank lending have on the balance sheet of a commercial bank?

Suppose that the Grisley Meat Packing Company of Wahoo decides that its is time to expand its facilities. Suppose, too, that the company needs exactly $50,000 —which, by some coincidence, just happens to be equal to the Wahoo bank's excess reserves—to finance this project.

The company approaches the Wahoo bank and requests a loan for this amount. The Wahoo bank knows the Grisley company's fine reputation and financial soundness and is convinced of its ability to repay the loan. So the loan is granted. The president of Grisley hands a promissory note—a high-class IOU—to the Wahoo bank. Grisley wants the convenience and safety of paying its obligations by checks. So, instead of receiving a bushel basket full of currency from the bank, Grisley will get a $50,000 increase in its demand deposit in the Wahoo bank. From the Wahoo bank's standpoint it has acquired an interest-earning asset (the promissory note) and has created demand deposits (a liability) to "pay" for this asset.

In short, Grisley has swapped an IOU for the right to draw an additional $50,000 worth of checks against its demand deposit in the Wahoo bank. Both parties are pleased. The Wahoo bank now possesses a new asset —an interest-bearing promissory note which it files under the general heading of "Loans." Grisley, sporting a fattened demand deposit, can now expand its operations.

At the moment the loan is negotiated, the Wahoo bank's position is shown by balance sheet 6a.

BALANCE SHEET 6a: WAHOO BANK (when loan is negotiated)			
Assets		**Liabilities and net worth**	
Reserves	$ 60,000	Demand	
Loans	50,000	deposits	$100,000
Property	240,000	Capital stock	250,000

All this looks innocent enough. But a closer examination of the Wahoo bank's balance statement will reveal a startling fact: *When a bank makes loans, it creates money.* The president of the Grisley company went to the bank with something which is *not* money—her IOU—and walked out with something that *is* money— a demand deposit.

Contrast transaction 6a with transaction 3 where demand deposits were created, but only by currency going out of circulation. There was a change in the *composition* of the money supply in that situation but no change in the total *supply* of money. But when banks lend, they create demand (checkable) deposits which *are* money. By extending credit the Wahoo bank has "monetized" an IOU. Grisley and the Wahoo bank have created and then swapped claims. The claim created by Grisley and given to the bank is not money; an individual's IOU is not generally acceptable as a medium of exchange. But the claim created by the bank and given to Grisley is money; checks drawn against a demand deposit are acceptable as a medium of exchange.

The bulk of the money used in our economy is created through the extension of credit by commercial banks. This checking account money may be thought of as "debts" of commercial banks and thrift institutions. Checks are bank "debts" in the sense that they are claims banks and thrifts promise to pay "on demand."

But there are important forces limiting the ability of a commercial bank to create demand deposits—that is, "bank money"—by lending. In the present case, the Wahoo bank can expect the newly created demand deposit of $50,000 to be a very active account. Grisley would not borrow $50,000 at, say, 7, 10, or 12 percent interest for the sheer joy of knowing funds were available if needed.

Assume that Grisley awards a $50,000 contract to the Quickbuck Construction Company of Omaha. Quickbuck, true to its name, completes the expansion job and is rewarded with a check for $50,000 drawn by Grisley against its demand deposit in the Wahoo bank. Quickbuck, with headquarters in Omaha, does *not* deposit this check in the Wahoo bank but instead deposits it in the Fourth National Bank of Omaha. Fourth National now has a $50,000 claim against the Wahoo bank. This check is collected in the manner described in transaction 5. As a result, the Wahoo bank *loses* both reserves and deposits equal to the amount of the check; Fourth National *acquires* $50,000 of reserves and deposits.

In summary, assuming a check is drawn by the borrower for the entire amount of the loan ($50,000) and given to a firm which deposits it in another bank, the Wahoo bank's balance sheet will read as follows *after the check has been cleared against it:*

BALANCE SHEET 6b: WAHOO BANK (after a check drawn on the loan has been collected)			
Assets		**Liabilities and net worth**	
Reserves	$ 10,000	Demand	
Loans	50,000	deposits	$ 50,000
Property	240,000	Capital stock	250,000

Note that after the check has been collected, the Wahoo bank barely meets the legal reserve ratio of 20 percent. The bank has *no excess reserves.* This poses an interesting question: Could the Wahoo bank have lent an amount greater than $50,000—an amount greater than its excess reserves—and still have met the 20 percent reserve requirement if a check for the full amount of the loan were cleared against it? The answer is "No."

For example, suppose the Wahoo bank had loaned $55,000 to the Grisley company. Collection of the check against the Wahoo bank would have lowered its reserves to $5,000 (=$60,000 − $55,000) and deposits would once again stand at $50,000 (=$105,000 −

$55,000). The ratio of actual reserves to deposits would now be $5,000/$50,000, or only 10 percent. The Wahoo bank could thus *not* have lent $55,000.

By experimenting with other figures over $50,000, you will find that the maximum amount the Wahoo bank could lend at the outset of transaction 6 is $50,000. This figure is identical with the amount of excess reserves the bank had available when the loan was negotiated. *A single commercial bank in a multibank banking system can lend only an amount equal to its initial preloan excess reserves.* When it lends, it faces the likelihood that checks for the entire amount of the loan will be drawn and cleared against the lending bank. A lending bank can anticipate the loss of reserves to other banks equal to the amount it lends.[3]

Transaction 7: Repaying a Loan If commercial banks create demand deposits—that is, money—when they make loans, is money destroyed when loans are repaid? The answer is "Yes." Using balance sheets 6b and 7, we see what happens when Grisley repays the $50,000 it borrowed.

To simplify, we (1) suppose the loan is repaid not in installments but rather in one lump sum two years after the date of negotiation, and (2) ignore interest charges on the loan. Grisley will write a check for $50,000 against its demand deposit, which we assume was $50,000 before the Grisley loan was negotiated. As a result, the Wahoo bank's demand-deposit liabilities decline by $50,000; Grisley has given up $50,000 worth of its claim against the bank's assets. In turn, the bank will surrender Grisley's IOU which it has been holding these many months. The bank and the company have reswapped claims. But the claim given up by Grisley is money; the claim it is repurchasing—its IOU—is not. The supply of money has therefore been reduced by $50,000; that amount of demand deposits has been destroyed, unaccompanied by an increase in the money supply elsewhere in the economy.

The fact that the Grisley company's IOU has been "demonetized" is shown in balance sheet 7. Observe that the Wahoo bank's demand deposits and loans have each returned to zero. Note that the decline in demand deposits increases the bank's holdings of excess reserves; this provides the basis for new loans to be made.

---

[3]Qualification: If some of the checks written on a loan are redeposited back in the lending bank by their recipients, then that bank will be able to lend an amount somewhat greater than its initial excess reserves.

BALANCE SHEET 7: WAHOO BANK (after loan has been repaid)

Assets		Liabilities and net worth	
Reserves	$ 10,000	Demand	
Loans	0	deposits	$ 0
Property	240,000	Capital stock	250,000

In the unlikely event Grisley repays the loan with cash, the supply of money will still decline by $50,000. In this case, Grisley would repurchase its IOU by handing over $50,000 in cash to the bank. Loans fall on the bank's balance sheet by $50,000 and cash increases by $50,000. Remember that we specifically excluded currency held by banks from the money supply because to include such cash would be double counting; it is apparent that this constitutes a $50,000 reduction in the supply of money.

Transaction 8: Buying Government Securities When a commercial bank buys government bonds from the public, the effect is substantially the same as lending. New money is created.

Assume that the Wahoo bank's balance sheet initially stands as it did at the end of transaction 5. Now suppose that, instead of making a $50,000 loan, the bank buys $50,000 of government securities from a securities dealer. The bank receives the interest-bearing bonds which appear on its balance statement as the asset "Securities" and gives the dealer an increase in its demand-deposit account. The Wahoo bank's balance sheet would appear as follows:

BALANCE SHEET 8: WAHOO BANK

Assets		Liabilities and net worth	
Reserves	$ 60,000	Demand	
Securities	50,000	deposits	$100,000
Property	240,000	Capital stock	250,000

Demand deposits, that is, the supply of money, have been increased by $50,000, as in transaction 6. *Commercial bank bond purchases from the public increase the supply of money in the same way as does lending to the public.* The bank accepts government bonds (which are not money) and gives the securities dealer an increase in its demand deposits (which is money).

Of course, when the securities dealer draws and clears a check for $50,000 against the Wahoo bank, the bank will lose both reserves and deposits in that amount and therefore will just be meeting the legal reserve requirement. Its balance sheet will now read precisely as in 6b except that "Securities" is substituted for "Loans" on the asset side.

Finally, the selling of government bonds to the public by a commercial bank—like the repayment of a loan—will reduce the supply of money. The securities buyer will pay by check and both "Securities" and "Demand deposits" (the latter being money) will decline by the amount of the sale.

Profits, Liquidity, and the Federal Funds Market

The relative importance of the various asset items on a commercial bank's balance sheet is the result of the banker's pursuit of two conflicting goals.

1 Profits One goal is profits. Commercial banks, like any other business, are seeking profits. This is why the bank wants to make loans and buy securities. These two items are the major earning assets of commercial banks.

2 Liquidity On the other hand, a commercial bank must seek safety. For a bank, safety lies in liquidity—specifically such liquid assets as cash and excess reserves. Banks must be on guard for depositors' transforming their demand deposits into cash. Similarly, more checks may be cleared against a bank than are cleared in its favor, causing a net outflow of reserves. Bankers thus seek a proper balance between prudence and profits. The compromise achieved determines the relative size of earning assets as opposed to highly liquid assets.

An interesting way banks can partly reconcile the goals of profits and liquidity is to lend temporary excess reserves held at the Federal Reserve banks to other commercial banks. Normal day-to-day flows of funds to banks rarely leave all banks with their exact levels of legally required reserves. Furthermore, funds held at the Federal Reserve banks are highly liquid, but they do not draw interest. Banks therefore lend these funds to other banks on an overnight basis as a way to earn additional interest without sacrificing long-term liquidity. Banks which borrow in this *Federal funds market*—the market for immediately available reserve balances at the Federal Reserve—do so because they find themselves temporarily short of required reserves. The interest rate paid on these overnight loans is called the **Federal funds rate.**

In terms of Figure 14-1, we would show an overnight loan of reserves from the Beaver Crossing bank to the Wahoo bank as a decrease in reserves at the Beaver Crossing bank and an increase in reserves at the Wahoo bank. Ownership of reserves at the Federal Reserve Bank of Kansas City will have changed, but total reserves there are not affected.

QUICK REVIEW 14-2

∮ **Banks create money when they make loans; money vanishes when bank customers pay off loans.**

∮ **New money is created when banks buy government bonds from the public; money disappears when banks sell government bonds to the public.**

∮ **Banks balance profitability and safety in determining their mix of earning assets and highly liquid assets.**

∮ **Banks borrow and lend temporary excess reserves on an overnight basis in the Federal funds market; the interest rate on these loans is the Federal funds rate.**

THE BANKING SYSTEM: MULTIPLE-DEPOSIT EXPANSION

Thus far we have seen that a single bank in a banking system can lend dollar for dollar with its excess reserves. The situation is different for all commercial banks taken as a group. We will find that *the commercial banking system can lend, that is, can create money, by a multiple of its excess reserves. This multiple lending is accomplished even though each bank in the system can only lend dollar for dollar with its excess reserves.*

The immediate task is to uncover how these seemingly paradoxical conclusions come about. To do this, we must keep our analysis uncluttered. Therefore, we will rely on three simplifying assumptions.

1 The reserve ratio for all commercial banks is 20 percent.

2 Initially all banks are exactly meeting this 20 percent reserve requirement. No excess reserves exist; all banks are "loaned up."

3 If any bank becomes able to increase its loans as a result of acquiring excess reserves, an amount equal to these excess reserves will be loaned to one borrower, who will write a check for the entire amount of the loan and give it to someone else, who deposits the check in another bank. This third assumption means the worst thing possible happens to any lending bank—a check for the entire amount of the loan is drawn and cleared against it in favor of another bank.

The Banking System's Lending Potential

To begin, suppose that a junkyard owner finds a $100 bill while dismantling a car which has been on the lot for years. He deposits the $100 in bank A, which adds the $100 to its reserves. Since we are recording only *changes* in the balance sheets of the various commercial banks, bank A's balance sheet will now appear as shown by the entries designated as (a_1):

BALANCE SHEET: COMMERCIAL BANK A			
Assets		**Liabilities and net worth**	
Reserves	$+100 ($a_1$) − 80 ($a_3$)	Demand deposits	$+100 ($a_1$) + 80 ($a_2$) − 80 ($a_3$)
Loans	+ 80 (a_2)		

Recall from transaction 3 that this $100 deposit of currency does *not* alter the money supply. While $100 of demand-deposit money comes into being, an offsetting $100 of currency is no longer in the hands of the public. What *has* happened is that bank A has acquired *excess reserves* of $80. Of the newly acquired $100 in reserves, 20 percent, or $20, must be earmarked to offset the new $100 deposit and the remaining $80 is excess reserves. Remembering that a single commercial bank can lend only an amount equal to its excess reserves, we conclude that bank A can lend a maximum of $80. When a loan for this amount is negotiated, bank A's loans will increase by $80, and the borrower will get an $80 demand deposit. We add these figures—designated as (a_2)—to bank A's balance sheet.

But now we must employ our third assumption: The borrower draws a check for $80—the entire amount of the loan—and gives it to someone who deposits it in another bank, bank B. As we saw in transaction 6, bank A *loses* both reserves and deposits equal to the amount of the loan (a_3). The net result of these transactions is that bank A's reserves now stand at $20 (=$100 − $80), loans at $80, and demand deposits are at $100 (=$100 + $80 − $80). When the dust has settled, bank A is just meeting the 20 percent reserve ratio.

Recalling transaction 5, bank B *acquires* both the reserves and the deposits which bank A has lost. Bank B's balance sheet looks like this (b_1):

BALANCE SHEET: COMMERCIAL BANK B

Assets		Liabilities and net worth	
Reserves	$+80 ($b_1$)	Demand	
	−64 (b_3)	deposits	$+80 ($b_1$)
Loans	+64 (b_2)		+64 (b_2)
			−64 (b_3)

When the check is drawn and cleared, bank A *loses* $80 in reserves and deposits and bank B *gains* $80 in reserves and deposits. But 20 percent, or $16, of bank B's newly acquired reserves must be kept as required reserves against the new $80 in demand deposits. This means that bank B has $64 (=$80 − $16) in excess reserves. It can therefore lend $64 ($b_2$). When the borrower draws a check for the entire amount and deposits it in bank C, the reserves and deposits of bank B both fall by the $64 ($b_3$). As a result of these transactions, bank B's reserves now stand at $16 (=$80 − $64), loans at $64, and demand deposits at $80 (=$80 + $64 − $64). After all this has occurred, bank B is just meeting the 20 percent reserve requirement.

We are off and running again. Bank C has acquired the $64 in reserves and deposits lost by bank B. Its balance statement appears as follows (c_1):

BALANCE SHEET: COMMERCIAL BANK C

Assets		Liabilities and net worth	
Reserves	$+64.00 ($c_1$)	Demand	
	−51.20 (c_3)	deposits	$+64.00 ($c_1$)
Loans	+51.20 (c_2)		+51.20 (c_2)
			−51.20 (c_3)

Exactly 20 percent, or $12.80, of this new reserve will be required, the remaining $51.20 being excess reserves. Hence, bank C can safely lend a maximum of $51.20. Suppose it does ($c_2$). And suppose the borrower draws a check for the entire amount and gives it to someone who deposits it in another bank (c_3).

Bank D—the bank receiving the $51.20 in reserves and deposits—now notes these changes on its balance sheet (d_1):

BALANCE SHEET: COMMERCIAL BANK D

Assets		Liabilities and net worth	
Reserves	$+51.20 ($d_1$)	Demand	
	−40.96 (d_3)	deposits	$+51.20 ($d_1$)
Loans	+40.96 (d_2)		+40.96 (d_2)
			−40.96 (d_3)

It can now lend $40.96 ($d_2$). The borrower draws a check for the full amount and deposits it in another bank (d_3).

Now, if we wanted to be particularly obnoxious, we could go ahead with this procedure by bringing banks E, F, G, H, . . . , N into the picture. We merely suggest that you check through computations for banks E, F, and G, to ensure you understand the procedure.

The nucleus of this analysis is summarized in Table 14-2. Data for banks E through N are supplied so you may check your computations. Our conclusion is startling: On the basis of the $80 in excess reserves (acquired by the banking system when someone deposited $100 of currency in bank A), the *entire commercial banking system* is able to lend $400. The banking system can lend by a multiple of 5 when the reserve ratio is 20 percent. Yet each single bank in the banking system is lending only an amount equal to its excess reserves. How do we explain these seemingly conflicting conclusions? Why is it that the *banking system* can lend by a multiple of its excess reserves, but *each individual bank* can only lend dollar for dollar with its excess reserves?

The answer is that reserves lost by a single bank are not lost to the banking system as a whole. The reserves lost by bank A are acquired by bank B. Those lost by B are gained by C. C loses to D, D to E, E to F, and so forth. Although reserves can be, and are, lost by *individual* banks in the banking system, there can be no loss of reserves for the banking *system* as a whole.

We reach the curious conclusion that an individual bank can only safely lend an amount equal to its excess reserves, but the commercial banking system can lend by a multiple of its excess reserves. This contrast, incidentally, is a fine illustration of why it is imperative that we keep the fallacy of composition (Chapter 1) firmly in mind. Commercial banks *as a group* can create money

TABLE 14-2 Expansion of the money supply by the commercial banking system

Bank	(1) Acquired reserves and deposits	(2) Required reserves	(3) Excess reserves, or (1) − (2)	(4) Amount which the bank can lend; new money created =(3)
Bank A	$100.00 ($a_1$)	$20.00	$80.00	$ 80.00 (a_2)
Bank B	80.00 (a_3, b_1)	16.00	64.00	64.00 (b_2)
Bank C	64.00 (b_3, c_1)	12.80	51.20	51.20 (c_2)
Bank D	51.20 (c_3, d_1)	10.24	40.96	40.96 (d_2)
Bank E	40.96	8.19	32.77	32.77
Bank F	32.77	6.55	26.22	26.22
Bank G	26.22	5.24	20.98	20.98
Bank H	20.98	4.20	16.78	16.78
Bank I	16.78	3.36	13.42	13.42
Bank J	13.42	2.68	10.74	10.74
Bank K	10.74	2.15	8.59	8.59
Bank L	8.59	1.72	6.87	6.87
Bank M	6.87	1.37	5.50	5.50
Bank N	5.50	1.10	4.40	4.40
Other banks	21.97	4.40	17.57	17.57
Total amount of money created				$400.00

by lending in a manner much different from that of the *individual banks* in that system.

The Monetary Multiplier

The rationale involved in this *demand-deposit multiplier,* or **monetary multiplier** is similar to that of the income multiplier discussed in Chapter 11. The income multiplier was based on the fact that the expenditures of one household are received as income by another; the deposit multiplier rests on the reality that the reserves and deposits lost by one bank are received by another bank. And, just as the size of the income multiplier is determined by the reciprocal of the MPS, that is, by the leakage into saving which occurs at each round of spending, so the deposit multiplier m is the reciprocal of the required reserve ratio R, that is, of the leakage into required reserves which occurs at each step in the lending process. In short,

$$\text{Monetary multiplier} = \frac{1}{\text{required reserve ratio}}$$

or, symbolically,

$$m = \frac{1}{R}$$

In this formula, m tells us the maximum amount of new demand-deposit money which can be created for a *single dollar* of excess reserves, given the value of R. To determine the maximum amount of new demand-deposit money, D, which can be created by the banking system on the basis of any given amount of excess reserves, E, we multiply the excess reserves by the monetary multiplier. That is,

$$\begin{array}{l}\text{Maximum} \\ \text{demand-deposit} \\ \text{expansion}\end{array} = \begin{array}{l}\text{excess} \\ \text{reserves}\end{array} \times \begin{array}{l}\text{monetary} \\ \text{multiplier}\end{array}$$

or, more simply,

$$D = E \times m$$

Thus, in our example of Table 14-2:

$$\$400 = \$80 \times 5$$

But keep in mind that, despite the similar rationale underlying the income and deposit multipliers, the former has to do with changes in income and the latter with changes in the supply of money.

Diagrammatic Summary Figure 14-2 summarizes the final outcome from our example of a multiple-deposit expansion of the money supply. The initial de-

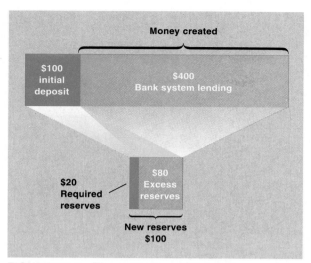

FIGURE 14-2 **The outcome of the money expansion process**

A deposit of $100 of currency into a checking account creates an initial demand deposit of $100. But if the reserve ratio is 20 percent, only $20 of reserves are legally required to support the $100 demand deposit. The $80 of excess reserves allows the banking system to create $400 of demand deposits through making loans. The $100 of reserves thus supports a total of $500 of money ($100 + $400).

posit of $100 of currency into the bank (lower box) creates an initial demand deposit of an equal amount (upper left box). Given our assumption of a 20 percent reserve ratio, however, only $20 of currency reserves are need to "back up" this $100 demand deposit. The excess reserves of $80 permit the creation of $400 of new demand deposits via the making of loans, correctly suggesting a monetary multiplier of 5. The $100 of new reserves thus supports a total supply of money of $500: $100 of initial demand deposit plus $400 of demand deposits created through lending.

You might experiment with these two teasers to test your understanding of multiple credit expansion by the banking system:

1   Rework the analysis in Table 14-2 (at least three or four steps of it) assuming the reserve ratio is 10 percent. What is the maximum amount of money the banking system could create upon acquiring $100 in new reserves and deposits? (No, the answer is not $800!)

2   Explain how a banking system which is "loaned up" and faced with a 20 percent reserve ratio might be forced to *reduce* its outstanding loans by $400 as a result of a $100 cash withdrawal from a demand deposit which forces the bank to draw down its reserves by $100.

Some Modifications

Our discussion of credit expansion has been a somewhat simplified one. There are certain complications which might modify the quantitative preciseness of our analysis.

Other Leakages   Aside from the **leakage** of required reserves at each step of the lending process, two other leakages of money from commercial banks might occur, thereby dampening the money-creating potential of the banking system.

1 **Currency Drains**   A borrower may request that part of his or her loan be paid in cash. Or the recipient of a check drawn by a borrower may present it at the bank to be redeemed partially or wholly in currency rather than added to the borrower's account. If the person who borrowed the $80 from bank A in our illustration asked for $16 of it in cash and the remaining $64 as a demand deposit, bank B would receive only $64 in new reserves (of which only $51.20 would be excess) rather than $80 (of which $64 was excess). This decline in excess reserves reduces the lending potential of the banking system accordingly. In fact, if the first borrower had taken the entire $80 in cash and if this currency remained in circulation, the multiple expansion process would have stopped then and there. But the convenience and safety of demand deposits make this unlikely.

2 **Excess Reserves**   Our analysis of the commercial banking system's ability to expand the money supply by lending is based on the supposition that commercial banks are willing to meet precisely the legal reserve requirement. To the extent that bankers hold excess reserves, the overall credit expansion potential of the banking system will be reduced. For example, suppose bank A, upon receiving $100 in new cash, decided to add $25, rather than the legal minimum of $20, to its reserves. Then it would lend only $75, rather than $80, and the money multiplier would be diminished accordingly.[4] In fact, the amount of excess reserves which banks have held in recent years has been very minimal. The explanation is very simple: Excess reserves earn

---

[4]Specifically, in our $m = \dfrac{1}{R}$ monetary multiplier, we now add to R, the required reserve ratio, the additional excess reserves which bankers choose to keep. For example, if banks want to hold additional excess reserves equal to 5 percent of any newly acquired demand deposits, then the denominator becomes .25 (equal to the .20 reserve ratio plus the .05 addition to excess reserves). The monetary multiplier is reduced from 5 to 1/.25, or 4.

LAST WORD

THE BANK PANICS OF 1930–1933

A series of bank panics in 1930–1933 resulted in a multiple contraction of the money supply.

In the early months of the Great Depression several financially weak banks became insolvent. As word spread that customers of these banks had lost their uninsured deposits, a general concern arose that something similar could happen at other banks. Depositors therefore began to withdraw funds—that is, "cash out" their accounts—at local banks, most of which had been financially healthy. In economic terminology, the initial failures of weak banks created negative externalities or spillover costs (Chapter 6) affecting healthy banks. More than 9000 banks failed within three years.

The massive conversion of checkable deposits to currency during 1930–1933 reduced the nation's money supply. The outflow of currency from banks meant the loss of bank reserves and a multiple decline of loans and checkable deposits. Also, banks "scrambled for liquidity" to meet anticipated further withdrawals by calling in loans and selling government securities to the public. Both actions enabled banks to increase their excess reserves—reserves which were *not* lent out. The lost deposits (reserves) and the scramble for liquidity collapsed the money supply through a reversal of the money expansion process shown in Table 14-2.

In 1933 President Franklin Roosevelt ended the bank panics by declaring a "national bank holiday,"

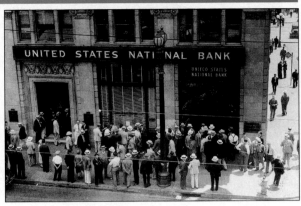

which closed all banks for a week and resulted in the federally insured deposit program. Meanwhile, the nation's money supply had plummeted by 25 percent, the largest such drop in American history. This decline in the money supply contributed to the nation's worst and longest depression.

Today, a multiple contraction of the money supply of the 1930–1933 magnitude is unthinkable. FDIC insurance has kept individual bank failures from becoming general bank panics. Also, while the Federal Reserve stood idly by during the bank panics of 1930–1933, today it would take immediate actions to maintain the banking system's reserves and the nation's money supply. These actions are the subject matter of Chapter 15.

---

no interest income for a bank; loans and investments do. Hence, our assumption that a bank will lend an amount equal to its excess reserves is reasonable and generally accurate.

Need for Monetary Control

Our illustration of the banking system's ability to create money rests on the assumption that commercial banks are willing to exercise their abilities to create money by lending and that households and businesses are willing to borrow. In reality the willingness of banks to lend on the basis of excess reserves varies cyclically, and therein lies the rationale for governmental control of the money supply to promote economic stability.

When prosperity reigns banks will expand credit to the maximum of their ability. Loans are interest-earning assets and in good times there is little fear of borrowers' defaulting. But, as we will find in Chapters 15 and 16, the money supply has an important effect on aggregate demand. By lending and thereby creating money to the maximum of their ability during prosperity, commercial banks may contribute to excessive aggregate demand and to inflation.

Conversely, if recession clouds appear on the economic horizon, bankers may hastily withdraw their invitations to borrow, seeking the safety of liquidity (excess reserves) even if it involves the sacrifice of potential interest income. Bankers may fear large-scale withdrawal of deposits by a panicky public and simultaneously doubt the ability of borrowers to repay. It is not too surprising that during some years of the Great Depression of the 1930s, banks had considerable excess reserves but lending was at a low ebb. The general point is that during recession banks may decrease the money supply by cutting back on lending. This contraction of the money supply will restrain aggregate demand and intensify the recession. A rapid shrinkage of the money supply contributed to the Great Depression of the 1930s, as this chapter's Last Word indicates.

We can conclude that profit-motivated bankers can be expected to vary the money supply to reinforce cyclical fluctuations. For this reason the Federal Reserve System has at its disposal certain policy instruments to control the money supply in an anticyclical, rather than procyclical, fashion. We turn to an analysis of these policy tools in Chapter 15.

CHAPTER SUMMARY

1 The operation of a commercial bank can be understood through its balance sheet, where assets are equal to liabilities plus net worth.

2 Modern banking systems are based on fractional reserves.

3 Commercial banks are required to keep a legal reserve deposit in a Federal Reserve Bank or as vault cash. This reserve is equal to a specified percentage of the commercial bank's demand-deposit liabilities. Excess reserves are equal to actual reserves minus required reserves.

4 Banks lose both reserves and demand deposits when checks are drawn against them.

5 Commercial banks create money—that is, demand deposits, or bank money—when they make loans. The creation of checkable deposits by bank lending is the most important source of money in our economy. Money is destroyed when loans are repaid.

6 The ability of a single commercial bank to create money by lending depends on the size of its *excess* reserves. Generally speaking, a commercial bank can lend only an amount equal to the size of its excess reserves. It is thus limited because, in all likelihood, checks drawn by borrowers will be deposited in other banks, causing a loss of reserves and deposits to the lending bank equal to the amount it has loaned.

7 Banks earn interest by making loans and purchasing bonds while they maintain liquidity by holding cash and excess reserves. Banks having temporary excess reserves often lend them on an overnight basis to banks which are short of required reserves. The interest rate paid on loans in this Federal funds market is called the Federal funds rate.

8 The commercial banking system as a whole can lend by a multiple of its excess reserves because the banking *system* cannot lose reserves, although individual banks can lose reserves to other banks in the system. The multiple by which the banking system can lend on the basis of each dollar of excess reserves is the reciprocal of the reserve ratio. This multiple credit expansion process is reversible.

9 The fact that profit-seeking banks would alter the money supply in a procyclical fashion underlies the need for the Federal Reserve System to control the money supply.

TERMS AND CONCEPTS

balance sheet	vault cash	actual, required, and	monetary multiplier
fractional reserve	legal reserves	excess reserves	leakage
system of banking	reserve ratio	Federal funds rate	

QUESTIONS AND STUDY SUGGESTIONS

1 Why must a balance sheet always balance? What are the major assets and claims on a commercial bank's balance sheet?

2 Why are commercial banks required to have reserves? Explain why reserves are assets to commercial banks but liabilities to the Federal Reserve Banks. What are excess reserves? How do you calculate the amount of excess reserves held by a bank? What is their significance?

3 "Whenever currency is deposited in a commercial bank, cash goes out of circulation and, as a result, the supply of money is reduced." Do you agree? Explain.

4 "When a commercial bank makes loans, it creates money; when loans are repaid, money is destroyed." Explain.

5 Explain why a single commercial bank can safely lend only an amount equal to its excess reserves but the commercial banking system can lend by a multiple of its excess reserves. Why is the multiple by which the banking system can lend equal to the reciprocal of its reserve ratio?

6 Assume that Jones deposits $500 in currency into her demand deposit in the First National Bank. A half-hour later Smith negotiates a loan for $750 at this bank. By how much and in what direction has the money supply changed? Explain.

7 Suppose the National Bank of Commerce has excess reserves of $8,000 and outstanding demand deposits of $150,000. If the reserve ratio is 20 percent, what is the size of the bank's actual reserves?

8 Suppose the Continental Bank has the following simplified balance sheet. The reserve ratio is 20 percent.

10 Suppose again that the Third National Bank has reserves of $20,000 and demand deposits of $100,000. The reserve ratio is 20 percent. The bank now sells $5,000 in securities to the Federal Reserve Bank in its district, receiving a $5,000 increase in reserves in return. How much excess reserves does the bank now have? Why does your answer differ (yes, it does!) from the answer to question 9?

11 Suppose a bank discovers its reserves will temporarily fall slightly short of those legally required. How might it remedy this situation through the Federal funds market? Next, assume the bank finds that its reserves will be substantially and permanently deficient. What remedy is available to this bank? Hint: Recall your answer to question 4.

12 Suppose that Bob withdraws $100 of cash from his checking account at Security Bank and uses it to buy a camera from Joe, who deposits the $100 in his checking account in Serenity Bank. Assuming a reserve ratio of 10 percent and no initial excess reserves, determine the extent to which **a** Security Bank must reduce its loans and demand deposits because of the cash withdrawal and **b** Serenity Bank can safely increase its loans and demand deposits because of the cash deposit. Have the cash withdrawal and deposit changed the money supply?

Assets		(1)	(2)	Liabilities and net worth		(1)	(2)
Reserves	$22,000	_____	_____	Demand			
Securities	38,000	_____	_____	deposits	$100,000	_____	_____
Loans	40,000	_____	_____				

a What is the maximum amount of new loans which this bank can make? Show in column 1 how the bank's balance sheet will appear after the bank has loaned this additional amount.

b By how much has the supply of money changed? Explain.

c How will the bank's balance sheet appear after checks drawn for the entire amount of the new loans have been cleared against this bank? Show this new balance sheet in column 2.

d Answer questions *a*, *b*, and *c* on the assumption that the reserve ratio is 15 percent.

13 Suppose the simplified consolidated balance sheet shown below is for the commercial banking system. All figures are in billions. The reserve ratio is 25 percent.

a How much excess reserves does the commercial banking system have? What is the maximum amount the banking system might lend? Show in column 1 how the consolidated balance sheet would look after this amount has been lent.

b Answer question 13a assuming that the reserve ratio is 20 percent. Explain the resulting difference in the lending ability of the commercial banking system.

Assets		(1)	Liabilities and net worth		(1)
Reserves	$ 52	_____	Demand		
Securities	48	_____	deposits	$200	_____
Loans	100	_____			

9 The Third National Bank has reserves of $20,000 and demand deposits of $100,000. The reserve ratio is 20 percent. Households deposit $5,000 in currency into the bank which is added to reserves. How much excess reserves does the bank now have?

14 What are banking "leakages"? How might they affect the money-creating potential of the banking system? Be specific.

15 Explain why there is a need for the Federal Reserve System to control the money supply.

CHAPTER 15

The Federal Reserve Banks and Monetary Policy

In Chapter 14 we focused on the money-creating ability of individual banks and the commercial banking system. Our discussion ended on a disturbing note: Unregulated commercial banking might contribute to cyclical fluctuations in business activity. That is, commercial banks will find it profitable to expand the supply of money during periods of demand-pull inflation and to restrict the money supply in seeking liquidity during depression.

In this chapter we will see how monetary authorities try to reverse the procyclical tendencies of the commercial banking system through a variety of control techniques. These procedures are the subject of numerous headlines in the financial pages of newspapers: "Bank Reserve Requirement Eased—First Change Since 1983" "Fed Aggressively Selling Bonds" "Fed Lowers Discount Rate to 5 Percent." What stories are these and similar headlines telling?

As in Chapter 14, our discussion is in terms of commercial banks because of their major role in creating demand-deposit money. However, throughout our discussion the term "depository institution" can be substituted for "commercial bank" and "checkable deposits" for "demand deposits."

The goals of this chapter are: First, the objectives of monetary policy and the roles of participating institutions are briefly discussed. Next, the balance sheet of the Federal Reserve Banks is surveyed, as it is through these central banks that monetary policy is largely implemented. Third, techniques of monetary control are analyzed in considerable detail. What are the major instruments of monetary control and how do they work? Fourth, the cause-effect chain through which monetary policy functions is detailed and the effectiveness of monetary policy is evaluated. Finally, a brief, but important, recapitulation of mainstream, Keynesian-based employment theory and policy is presented.

OBJECTIVES OF MONETARY POLICY

Before analyzing the techniques of monetary policy, we must clearly understand the objectives of monetary policy and identify the institutions responsible for formulating and implementing it.

Certain key points made in Chapter 13 merit reemphasis here. The Board of Governors of the Federal Reserve System is responsible for supervising and controlling the operation of our monetary and banking systems. This Board formulates basic policies which the banking system follows. Because it is a public body, the decisions of the Board of Governors are made in what it perceives to be the public interest. The twelve Federal Reserve Banks—the central banks of American capitalism—implement the policy decisions of the Board. You will recall that as quasi-public banks, the Federal Reserve Banks are not guided by the profit motive, but rather pursue measures the Board of Governors recommend.

However, to say that the Board follows policies which "promote the public interest" is not enough. We must pinpoint the goal of monetary policy. *The fundamental objective of* **monetary policy** *is to assist the economy in achieving a full-employment, noninflationary level of total output.* Monetary policy consists of altering the economy's money supply to stabilize aggregate output, employment, and the price level. Specifically, monetary policy entails increasing the money supply during a recession to stimulate spending and, conversely, restricting it during inflation to constrain spending.

The Federal Reserve Board alters the size of the nation's money supply by manipulating the size of excess reserves held by commercial banks. Excess reserves, you will recall, are critical to the money-creating ability of the banking system. The specific techniques the Board uses to change excess reserves in the banking system merit considerable discussion. Once we see how the Federal Reserve controls excess reserves and the money supply, we will turn to an explanation of how changes in the stock of money affect interest rates and aggregate expenditures.

CONSOLIDATED BALANCE SHEET OF THE FEDERAL RESERVE BANKS

Because monetary policy is implemented by the twelve Federal Reserve Banks, it is useful to consider the nature of the balance sheet of these banks. Some assets and liabilities found here differ considerably from those found on the balance sheet of a commercial bank. Table 15-1 is a simplified consolidated balance sheet which shows all the pertinent assets and liabilities of the twelve Federal Reserve Banks as of August 30, 1991.

Assets

Two major assets are important for our analysis.

1 Securities The securities shown are government bonds which Federal Reserve Banks have purchased. These bonds consist largely of debt instruments such as Treasury bills (short-term securities) and Treasury bonds (long-term securities) issued by the Federal government to finance past and present budget deficits. These securities are part of the public or national debt (Chapter 18). Some of these bonds may have been purchased directly from the Treasury, but most are bought in the open market from commercial banks or the public. Although these bonds are an important source of income to the Federal Reserve Banks, they

TABLE 15-1 Twelve Federal Reserve Banks' consolidated balance sheet, August 30, 1991 *(in millions)*

Assets		Liabilities and net worth	
Securities	$254,959	Reserves of commercial banks	$ 31,200
Loans to commercial banks	844	Treasury deposits	6,745
All other assets	63,960	Federal Reserve Notes (outstanding)	275,210
		All other liabilities and net worth	6,608
Total	$319,763	Total	$319,763

Source: Federal Reserve Bulletin, November 1991.

are not bought and sold purposely for income. Rather, they are bought and sold primarily to influence the size of commercial bank reserves and therefore their ability to create money by lending.

2 Loans to Commercial Banks　For reasons we will discuss soon, commercial banks occasionally borrow from Federal Reserve Banks. The IOUs which commercial banks give to these "bankers' banks" in negotiating loans are listed as loans to commercial banks. From the Federal Reserve Banks' point of view, these IOUs are assets, that is, claims against commercial banks which have borrowed from them. To commercial banks, these IOUs are liabilities. By borrowing in this way, commercial banks obtain increases in their reserves in exchange for IOUs.

Liabilities

On the liability side we find three major items.

1 Reserves of Commercial Banks　We are familiar with this account. It is an asset from the viewpoint of member banks but a liability to Federal Reserve Banks.

2 Treasury Deposits　Just as businesses and private individuals find it convenient and desirable to pay their obligations by check, so does the United States Treasury. It keeps deposits in the Federal Reserve Banks and draws checks on them to pay its obligations. To the Treasury such deposits are assets; to the Federal Reserve Banks they are liabilities. The Treasury creates and replenishes these deposits by depositing tax receipts and money borrowed from the public or the banks through the sale of bonds.

3 Federal Reserve Notes　Our paper money supply consists of Federal Reserve Notes issued by the Federal Reserve Banks. In circulation, these pieces of paper money constitute claims against assets of Federal Reserve Banks and are therefore treated by them as liabilities. Just as your own IOU is neither an asset nor a liability to you when it is in your own possession, so Federal Reserve Notes resting in the vaults of Federal Reserve Banks are neither an asset nor a liability. Only those notes in circulation are liabilities to the bankers' banks. These notes, which come into circulation through commercial banks, are not part of the money supply until they are in the hands of the public.

THE TOOLS OF MONETARY POLICY

With this cursory look at the Federal Reserve Banks' balance sheet, we can now explore how the Board of Governors of the Federal Reserve System can influence the money-creating abilities of the commercial banking system. There are three major instruments of monetary control which can be used by the Board of Governors to influence commercial bank reserves:
1　Open-market operations
2　Changing the reserve ratio
3　Changing the discount rate

Open-Market Operations

Open-market operations are the most important means the Fed uses to control the money supply. The term **open-market operations** refers to the buying and selling of government bonds by the Federal Reserve Banks in the open market—that is, the buying and selling of bonds from or to commercial banks and the general public. How do these purchases and sales of government securities affect the excess reserves of commercial banks?

Buying Securities　Suppose the Board of Governors orders the Federal Reserve Banks to buy government bonds in the open market. These securities can be purchased from commercial banks and the public. In either case the overall effect is basically the same—commercial bank reserves are increased.

From Commercial Banks　Let's trace the process Federal Reserve Banks use when buying government bonds *from commercial banks*. This transaction is a simple one.

　　a Commercial banks give up part of their holdings of securities to the Federal Reserve Banks.

　　b The Federal Reserve Banks pay for these securities by increasing the reserves of commercial banks by the amount of the purchase.

　　Just as the commercial bank may pay for a bond bought from a private individual by increasing the seller's demand deposit, so the bankers' bank may pay for bonds bought from commercial banks by increasing the banks' reserves. In short, the consolidated balance sheets of the commercial banks and the Federal Reserve Banks will change as follows:

FEDERAL RESERVE BANKS

Assets	Liabilities and net worth
+ Securities *(a)*	+ Reserves of commercial banks *(b)*
↑ *(a)* Securities |	| *(b)* Reserves ↓

COMMERCIAL BANKS

Assets	Liabilities and net worth
− Securities *(a)* + Reserves *(b)*	

The upward arrow shows that securities have moved from the commercial banks to the Federal Reserve Banks. Hence, we place a minus sign in front of "Securities" in the asset column of the balance sheet of the commercial banks. For the same reason, we place a plus sign in front of "Securities" in the asset column of the balance sheet of the Federal Reserve Banks.

The downward arrow indicates that the Federal Reserve Banks have provided reserves to the commercial banks. We therefore place a plus sign in front of "Reserves" in the balance sheet for the commercial banks. The plus sign in the liability column of the balance sheet of the Federal Reserve Banks indicates that commercial bank reserves have increased; they are a liability to the Federal Reserve Banks.

The most important aspect of this transaction is that, when Federal Reserve Banks purchase securities from commercial banks, the reserves—and therefore the lending ability—of the commercial banks are increased.

From the Public   If Federal Reserve Banks purchase securities *from the general public,* the effect on commercial bank reserves is substantially the same. Suppose that the Grisley Meat Packing Company has some negotiable government bonds which it sells in the open market to the Federal Reserve Banks. The transaction goes like this:

a Grisley gives up securities to the Federal Reserve Banks and gets in payment a check drawn by the Federal Reserve Banks on themselves.

b Grisley promptly deposits this check in its account with its Wahoo bank.

c The Wahoo bank collects this check against the Federal Reserve Banks by sending it to the Federal Reserve Banks for collection. As a result the Wahoo bank receives an increase in its reserves.

Balance sheet changes are as shown in the right column.

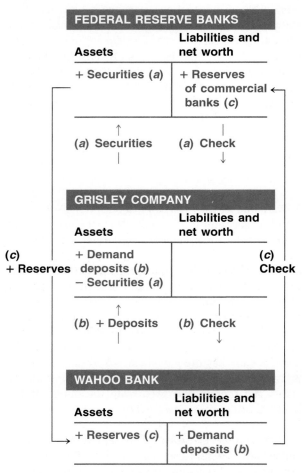

Two aspects of this transaction are noteworthy.

1   As with Federal Reserve purchases of securities directly from commercial banks, the reserves and lending ability of the commercial banking system have been increased. This is indicated by the plus sign in front of "Reserves," showing an increase in assets of the Wahoo bank.

2   In this instance the supply of money is directly increased by the central banks' purchase of government bonds, aside from any expansion of the money supply which may occur from the increase in commercial bank reserves. This direct increase in the money supply has taken the form of an increased amount of checking account money in the economy; thus the plus sign in front of demand deposits in the Wahoo bank. Because these demand deposits are an asset as viewed by Grisley, demand deposits have increased (plus sign) on Grisley's balance sheet.

There is a slight difference between the Federal Reserve Banks' purchases of securities from the commercial banking system and from the public. Assuming all commercial banks are "loaned up" initially, Federal Reserve bond purchases *from commercial banks* will increase actual reserves and excess reserves of commercial banks by the entire amount of the bond purchases. Thus, as shown in Figure 15-1, a $1000 bond purchase from a commercial bank would increase both the actual and excess reserves of the commercial bank by $1000.

On the other hand, Federal Reserve Bank purchases of bonds *from the public* increase actual reserves but also increase demand deposits. Thus, a $1000 bond purchase from the public would increase actual reserves of the "loaned up" banking system by $1000; but with a 20 percent reserve ratio, the excess reserves of the banking system would only amount to $800. In the case of bond purchases from the public, it is *as if* the commercial banking system had already used one-fifth, or 20 percent, of its newly acquired reserves to support $1000 worth of new demand-deposit money.

However, in each transaction the basic conclusion is the same: *When Federal Reserve Banks buy securities in the open market, commercial banks' reserves will be increased.* Assuming that the banks lend out their excess reserves, the nation's money supply will rise. Observe in Figure 15-1 that a $1000 purchase of bonds by the Federal Reserve will result in $5000 of additional money, regardless of whether the purchase was made from commercial banks or from the general public.

Selling Securities We should now suspect that Federal Reserve Bank sales of government bonds will reduce commercial bank reserves. Let's examine such sales.

To Commercial Banks Suppose the Federal Reserve Banks sell securities in the open market to *commercial banks:*

a Federal Reserve Banks give up securities which the commercial banks acquire.

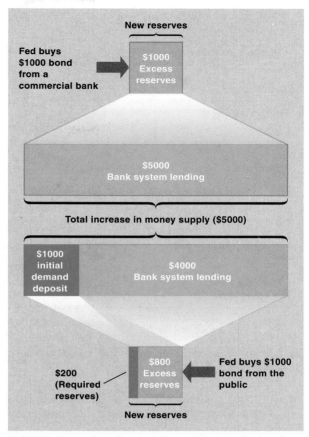

FIGURE 15-1 The Federal Reserve's purchase of bonds and the expansion of the money supply

Assuming all banks are "loaned up" initially, a Federal Reserve purchase of a $1000 bond from either a commercial bank or the public will increase the money supply by $5000 when the reserve ratio is 20 percent. In the top portion of the diagram, the purchase of a $1000 bond from a commercial bank creates $1000 of excess reserves which support an expansion of demand deposits of $5000 through making loans. In the lower portion, the purchase of a $1000 bond from the public creates only $800 of excess reserves, because $200 of reserves are required to "back up" the $1000 new demand deposit in the banking system. The commercial banks can therefore expand the money supply by $4000 by making loans. This $4000 of checking account money *plus* the initial new demand deposit of $1000 together equal $5000 of new money.

b Commercial banks pay for these securities by drawing checks against their deposits—that is, their reserves—in Federal Reserve Banks. The Federal Reserve Banks collect these checks by reducing the commercial banks' reserves accordingly.

The balance sheet changes appear as follows:

FEDERAL RESERVE BANKS

Assets	Liabilities and net worth
− Securities *(a)*	− Reserves of commercial banks *(b)*
(a) Securities ↓	*(b)* Reserves ↑

COMMERCIAL BANKS

Assets	Liabilities and net worth
− Reserves *(b)* + Securities *(a)*	

Note specifically the reduction in commercial bank reserves, as indicated by the minus signs before these entries.

To the Public If Federal Reserve Banks sell securities *to the public,* the overall effect will be substantially the same. Let's put the Grisley company on the buying end of government bonds which the Federal Reserve Banks are selling.

a The Federal Reserve Bank sells government bonds to Grisley, which pays with a check drawn on the Wahoo bank.

b The Federal Reserve Banks clear this check against the Wahoo bank by reducing its reserves.

c The Wahoo bank returns Grisley's check to it, reducing the company's demand deposit accordingly.

The balance sheets change as shown in the right column.

Note that Federal Reserve bond sales of $1000 to the commercial banking system reduce the system's actual and excess reserves by $1000. But a $1000 bond sale to the public reduces excess reserves by $800 because demand-deposit money is also reduced by $1000 by the sale. Since the commercial banking system has reduced its outstanding demand deposits by $1000, banks need keep $200 less in reserves.

In both variations of the Federal Reserve bond sale transaction, however, the conclusion is identical: *When Federal Reserve Banks sell securities in the open market,*

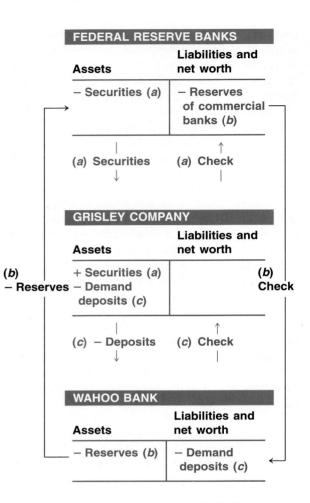

commercial bank reserves are reduced. If all excess reserves are presently lent out, this decline in commercial bank reserves will translate into a decline in the nation's money supply. In our example, a $1000 sale of government securities will result in a $5000 decline in the money supply irrespective of whether the sale was made to commercial banks or the general public. You can verify this by reexamining Figure 15-1 and tracing the effects of a *sale* of a $1000 bond by the Federal Reserve Banks either to commercial banks or the public.

What makes commercial banks and the public willing to sell government securities to, or buy them from, Federal Reserve Banks? The answer lies in the price of bonds and their interest rates. We know from Chapter 13 that bond prices and interest rates are inversely related. When the Federal Reserve buys government bonds, the demand for them will increase. Government bond prices will rise and their interest rates will decline. The higher bond prices and their lower interest rates will prompt bank and public holders of government bonds to sell them to the Federal Reserve Banks.

Conversely, when the Federal Reserve sells government bonds, the additional supply of bonds in the bond market will lower bond prices and raise their interest rates, making government bonds attractive purchases for banks and the public.

The Reserve Ratio

How can the Board of Governors influence the ability of commercial banks to lend through manipulation of the legal **reserve ratio?** A simple example will answer this query. Starting with row 2 of Table 15-2, suppose a commercial bank's balance sheet shows that reserves are $5000 and demand deposits $20,000. If the legal reserve ratio is 20 percent, the bank's *required* reserves are $4000. Since *actual* reserves are $5000, the *excess* reserves of this bank are $1000. On the basis of this $1000 of excess reserves, we saw that this single bank can lend $1000, but the banking system as a whole could create a maximum of $5000 in new checking account money by lending.

Raising the Reserve Ratio   Now, what if the Board of Governors raised the legal reserve ratio from 20 to 25 percent? (See row 3.) Required reserves would jump from $4000 to $5000, shrinking excess reserves from $1000 to zero. *Raising the reserve ratio increases the amount of required reserves banks must keep. Either banks lose excess reserves, diminishing their ability to create money by lending, or else they find their reserves deficient and are forced to contract checkable deposits and therefore the money supply.* In the case just cited, excess reserves are transformed into required reserves, and the money-creating potential of our *single bank* is re-

duced from $1000 to zero (column 6). The *banking system's* money-creating capacity declines from $5000 to zero (column 7).

What if the Board of Governors announced an increase in the legal reserve requirement to 30 percent? (See row 4.) The commercial bank would face the prospect of failing to meet this requirement. To protect itself against such an eventuality, the bank would be forced to lower its outstanding demand deposits and at the same time increase its reserves. To reduce its demand deposits, the bank could let outstanding loans mature and be repaid without extending new credit. To increase reserves, the bank might sell some of its security holdings, adding the proceeds to its reserves. Both actions will reduce the supply of money (see Chapter 14, transactions 6 and 8).

Lowering the Reserve Ratio   What would happen if the Board of Governors lowered the reserve ratio from the original 20 to 10 percent? (See row 1.) In this case, required reserves would decline from $4000 to $2000, and excess reserves would jump from $1000 to $3000. The single bank's lending or money-creating ability increases from $1000 to $3000 (column 6) and the banking system's money-creating potential expands from $5000 to $30,000 (column 7). *Lowering the reserve ratio changes required reserves to excess reserves and enhances the ability of banks to create new money by lending.*

Table 15-2 reveals that a change in the reserve ratio affects the money-creating ability of the *banking system* in two ways:

1   It affects the size of excess reserves.
2   It changes the size of the monetary multiplier.

For example, in raising the legal reserve ratio from 10 to 20 percent, excess reserves are reduced from $3000 to $1000 and the demand-deposit multiplier is

TABLE 15-2   The effects of changes in the reserve ratio on the lending ability of commercial banks (hypothetical data)

(1) Legal reserve ratio, percent	(2) Demand deposits	(3) Actual reserves	(4) Required reserves	(5) Excess reserves, or (3) − (4)	(6) Money-creating potential of single bank, = (5)	(7) Money-creating potential of banking system
(1) 10	$20,000	$5000	$2000	$ 3000	$ 3000	$ 30,000
(2) 20	20,000	5000	4000	1000	1000	5,000
(3) 25	20,000	5000	5000	0	0	0
(4) 30	20,000	5000	6000	−1000	−1000	−3,333

reduced from 10 to 5. The money-creating potential of the banking system declines from $30,000 (=$3000 × 10) to $5000 (=$1000 × 5).

Changing the reserve ratio is a potentially powerful technique of monetary control, but it is used only infrequently. Nevertheless, in 1992 the Federal Reserve reduced the reserve ratio from 12 to 10 percent.

The Discount Rate

One of the traditional functions of a central bank is to be a "lender of last resort." Central banks lend to commercial banks which are financially sound, but which have unexpected and immediate needs for additional funds. Thus, each Federal Reserve Bank will make short-term loans to commercial banks in its district.

When a commercial bank borrows, it gives the Federal Reserve Bank a promissory note or IOU drawn against itself and secured by acceptable collateral—typically United States government securities. Just as commercial banks charge interest on their loans, so do Federal Reserve Banks charge interest on loans they grant to commercial banks. This interest rate is called the **discount rate.**

As a claim against the commercial bank, the borrowing bank's promissory note is an asset to the lending Federal Reserve Bank and appears on its balance sheet as "Loans to commercial banks." To the commercial bank the IOU is a liability, appearing as "Loans from the Federal Reserve Banks" on the commercial bank's balance sheet.

In payment of the loan the Federal Reserve Bank will *increase* the reserves of the borrowing commercial bank. Since no required reserves need be kept against loans from Federal Reserve Banks, *all* new reserves acquired by borrowing from Federal Reserve Banks would be excess reserves. These changes are reflected in the balance sheets of the commercial banks and the bankers' banks as shown in the right column.

Note that this transaction is analogous to a private person's borrowing from a commercial bank (see Chapter 14, transaction 6).

The important point is that *commercial bank borrowing from the Federal Reserve Banks increases the reserves of commercial banks, enhancing their ability to extend credit to the public.*

The Board of Governors of the Federal Reserve System has the power to establish and manipulate the discount rate at which commercial banks can borrow from Federal Reserve Banks. From the commercial

FEDERAL RESERVE BANKS	
Assets	Liabilities and net worth
+ Loans to commercial banks ↑ IOUs	+ Reserves of commercial banks | + Reserves ↓

COMMERCIAL BANKS	
Assets	Liabilities and net worth
+ Reserves	+ Loans from the Federal Reserve Banks

banks' point of view, the discount rate is a cost entailed in acquiring reserves. When the discount rate is decreased, commercial banks are encouraged to obtain additional reserves by borrowing from Federal Reserve Banks. Commercial bank lending based on these new reserves will constitute an increase in the money supply.

Conversely, an increase in the discount rate discourages commercial banks from obtaining additional reserves through borrowing from the central banks. An increase in the discount rate therefore is consistent with the monetary authorities' desire to restrict the supply of money.

Easy Money and Tight Money

Suppose the economy is faced with unemployment and deflation. The monetary authorities correctly decide that an increase in the supply of money is needed to stimulate the volume of aggregate expenditures to help absorb idle resources. To induce an increase in the supply of money, the Board of Governors must expand the excess reserves of commercial banks. What specific policies will bring this about?

1 Buy Securities The Board of Governors should order Federal Reserve Banks to buy securities in the open market. These bond purchases will be paid for by increases in commercial bank reserves.

2 Reduce Reserve Ratio   The reserve ratio should be reduced, automatically changing required reserves into excess reserves and increasing the size of the money multiplier.

3 Lower Discount Rate   The discount rate should be lowered to induce commercial banks to add to their reserves by borrowing from Federal Reserve Banks.

This set of policy decisions is called an **easy money policy.** Its purpose is to make credit cheaply and easily available, so as to increase the volumes of aggregate expenditures and employment.

Suppose, on the other hand, excessive spending is pushing the economy into an inflationary spiral. The Board of Governors should attempt to reduce total spending by limiting or contracting the supply of money. The key to this goal lies in reducing the reserves of commercial banks. How is this done?

1 Sell Securities   Federal Reserve Banks should sell government bonds in the open market to tear down commercial bank reserves.

2 Increase Reserve Ratio   Increasing the reserve ratio will automatically strip commercial banks of excess reserves and decrease the size of the money multiplier.

3 Raise Discount Rate   A boost in the discount rate will discourage commercial banks from building up their reserves by borrowing at Federal Reserve Banks.

This group of directives is appropriately labeled a **tight money policy.** The objective is to tighten the supply of money to reduce spending and control inflationary pressures.

Relative Importance

Of the three major monetary controls, open-market operations clearly are the most important control mechanism. The reasons for this are worth noting.

The discount rate is less important than open-market operations for two interrelated reasons.

1   The amount of commercial bank reserves obtained by borrowing from the central banks is typically very small. On the average only 2 or 3 percent of bank reserves are acquired in this way. Indeed, open-market operations often induce commercial banks to borrow from Federal Reserve Banks. That is, to the extent that central bank bond sales leave commercial banks tem-

porarily short of reserves, commercial banks will be prompted to borrow from Federal Reserve Banks. Rather than being a primary tool of monetary policy, commercial bank borrowing from the Fed occurs largely in response to monetary policy as carried out by open-market operations.

2   While the manipulation of commercial bank reserves through open-market operations and the changing of reserve requirements are initiated by the Federal Reserve System, the discount rate depends on the initiative of commercial banks to be effective. For example, if the discount rate is lowered at a time when very few banks are inclined to borrow from Federal Reserve Banks, the lower rate will have little or no impact on bank reserves or the money supply.

Nevertheless, some economists point out that a change in the discount rate may have an important "announcement effect"; it may be a clear and explicit way of communicating to the financial community and the economy as a whole the intended direction of monetary policy. Other economists doubt this, arguing that changes in the discount rate are often "passive"; it is changed to keep it in line with other short-term interest rates, rather than to invoke a policy change.

What about changes in reserve requirements?

> Because the impact is so powerful, so blunt, so immediate, and so widespread, the Federal Reserve uses its authority to change reserve requirements only sparingly, particularly during tight money periods when increases in reserve requirements would be appropriate.[1]

The reluctance to increase reserve requirements undoubtedly is related to the fact that reserve balances earn no interest; thus, higher reserve requirements can have substantial adverse effects on bank profits.

But there are more positive reasons why open-market operations have evolved as the primary technique of monetary policy. This mechanism of monetary control has the advantage of flexibility—government securities can be purchased or sold in large or small amounts—and the impact on bank reserves is quite prompt. Yet, compared with reserve-requirement changes, open-market operations work subtly and less directly. Furthermore, quantitatively there is no question about the potential ability of the Federal Reserve Banks to affect commercial bank reserves through

---

[1]Lawrence S. Ritter and William L. Silber, *Money,* 5th ed. (New York: Basic Books, Inc., Publishers, 1984), p. 121.

bond sales and purchases. A glance at the consolidated balance sheet for the Federal Reserve Banks (Table 15-1) reveals very large holdings of government bonds ($255 billion), the sales of which could theoretically reduce commercial bank reserves from $31 billion to zero.

QUICK REVIEW 15-1

♪ *The objective of monetary policy is to help the economy achieve a full-employment, noninflationary level of domestic output.*

♪ *The Federal Reserve has three main instruments of monetary control, each of which works by changing the amount of excess reserves in the banking system.*

a   Open market operations (the Fed's buying and selling of government bonds to the banks and the public)

b   Changing the reserve ratio (the percent of deposit liabilities required as reserves)

c   Changing the discount rate (the interest rate the Federal Reserve Banks charge on loans to banks and thrifts).

♪ *Open-market operations are the Federal Reserve's most important monetary control mechanism.*

MONETARY POLICY, EQUILIBRIUM GDP, AND THE PRICE LEVEL

Although there is universal agreement that the Federal Reserve possesses the tools necessary to change the money supply, there is some disagreement on how changes in the money supply affect the economy. The traditional—or Keynesian—interpretation of how monetary policy works is our present subject. In Chapter 16 the monetarist perspective on monetary policy is examined in detail.

Cause-Effect Chain: Traditional View

Precisely how does monetary policy work toward the goal of full employment and price stability? The central factors and relationships are illustrated in Figure 15-2 (Key Graph).

Money Market   The diagram at the left shows the **money market,** where the demand for money curve, D_m, and the supply of money curve, S_m, are brought

together. Recall from Chapter 13 that the total demand for money is comprised of the transactions and the asset demands. The transactions demand is directly related to the level of economic transactions as reflected in the size of the nominal GDP. The asset demand is inversely related to the interest rate. Recall too that the interest rate is the opportunity cost of holding money as an asset; the higher the cost, the smaller the amount of money the public wants to hold. In Figure 15-2a the total demand for money is inversely related to the interest rate. In this presentation an increase in nominal GDP will shift D_m to the right; a decline in nominal GDP will shift D_m to the left.

We complete our portrayal of the money market by adding the money supply, S_m. The money supply is shown as a vertical line on the assumption that it is some fixed amount determined by the Board of Governors' policy independently of the interest rate. In other words, while monetary policy (the supply of money) helps determine the interest rate, the interest rate does not in turn determine the money supply.

Figure 15-2a tells us that, given the demand for money, if the supply of money is $150 billion, the equilibrium interest rate will be 8 percent. Recall from Chapter 10 that the real, not the nominal, rate of interest is critical for investment decisions. Hence, our discussion here assumes a constant price level and that the 8 percent interest rate portrayed in Figure 15-2a is the real rate of interest.

Investment   This 8 percent interest rate is projected off the investment-demand curve of Figure 15-2b. At this 8 percent interest rate it will be profitable for businesses to invest $20 billion. More investment will be forthcoming at an interest rate below 8 percent while less investment will occur if the interest rate is above 8 percent. Economists generally agree that the investment component of total spending is more likely to be affected by changes in the interest rate than is consumer spending. It is true, of course, that consumer purchases of automobiles—which depend heavily on installment credit—are sensitive to interest rates. But overall the interest rate is *not* a very crucial factor in determining how households divide their disposable income between consumption and saving.

The impact of changing interest rates on investment spending is great because of the large size and long-term nature of such purchases. Capital equipment, factory buildings, and warehouses are tremendously expensive purchases. In absolute terms, interest charges on funds borrowed for these purchases are considerable.

KEY GRAPH

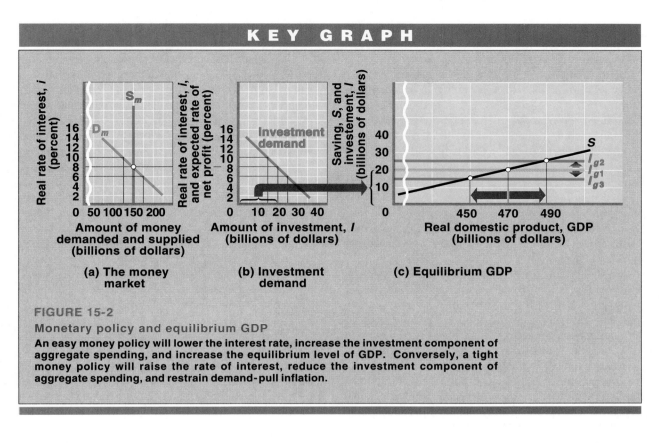

(a) The money market

(b) Investment demand

(c) Equilibrium GDP

FIGURE 15-2

Monetary policy and equilibrium GDP

An easy money policy will lower the interest rate, increase the investment component of aggregate spending, and increase the equilibrium level of GDP. Conversely, a tight money policy will raise the rate of interest, reduce the investment component of aggregate spending, and restrain demand-pull inflation.

Similarly, the interest cost on a house purchased on a long-term contract will be very large: A one-half percentage point change in the interest rate could easily amount to thousands of dollars on the total cost of a home.

Also, changes in the interest rate may affect investment spending by changing the relative attractiveness of capital equipment purchases and bond purchases. If the interest rate rises on bonds, then, given the profit expectations on capital goods purchases, businesses will be more inclined to use business savings to purchase securities than to buy capital equipment. Conversely, given profit expectations on investment spending, a fall in the interest rate makes capital goods purchases more attractive than bond ownership.

In brief, the impact of changing interest rates will be primarily on investment spending and, through this channel, on output, employment, and the level of prices. More specifically, as Figure 15-2b indicates, investment spending varies inversely with the interest rate.

Equilibrium GDP Finally, in Figure 15-2c the $20 billion of investment determined in Figure 15-2b is plugged into the simple leakages-injections model for the private closed economy to determine the equilibrium level of GDP. Observe that I_{g1} equals saving at the $470 billion level of GDP.

Effects of an Easy Money Policy

If the $470 billion of equilibrium GDP in Figure 15-2c entails widespread unemployment, the Federal Reserve would institute an *easy money policy.*

To increase the money supply the Federal Reserve Banks will take some combination of the following actions: (1) buy government securities from banks and the public in the open market, (2) lower the legal reserve ratio, or (3) lower the discount rate. The result will be an increase in excess reserves in the commercial banking system. Because excess reserves are the basis on which commercial banks can expand the money supply by lending, the nation's money supply likely will rise. An increase in the money supply will lower the interest rate, increasing investment and equilibrium GDP. The amount GDP increases will depend on the amount of the increase in investment and the size of the economy's income multiplier.

For example, if the full-employment GDP is $490 billion, an increase in the money supply from $150 to $175 billion will reduce the interest rate from 8 to 6 percent, as indicated in Figure 15-2a, and increase investment from $20 to $25 billion, as shown in Figure 15-2b. This $5 billion upshift of the investment schedule from I_{g1} to I_{g2} in Figure 15-2c, subject to the relevant income multiplier of 4, will increase equilibrium GDP from $470 billion to the desired $490 billion full-employment level.

Effects of a Tight Money Policy

Conversely, if the original $470 billion GDP generates demand-pull inflation, the Federal Reserve will institute a *tight money policy*.

The Federal Reserve Board will direct Federal Reserve Banks to undertake some combination of the following actions: (1) sell government securities to depository instutitions and the public in the open market, (2) increase the legal reserve ratio, or (3) increase the discount rate. Banks then will discover that their reserves are too low to meet the legal reserve ratio. How can depository institutions meet the reserve ratio when their demand deposits are too high relative to their reserves? The answer is they will need to reduce their demand deposits by refraining from issuing new loans as old loans are paid back. This will shrink money supply and increase the interest rate. The higher interest

rate will reduce investment, decreasing aggregate expenditures and restraining demand-pull inflation.

To illustrate: If the full-employment, noninflationary GDP is $450 billion, an inflationary gap of $5 billion will exist. At the $470 billion level of GDP, planned investment exceeds saving—and therefore aggregate expenditures exceed domestic output—by $5 billion. A decline in the money supply from $150 to $125 billion will increase the interest rate from 8 to 10 percent in Figure 15-2a and reduce investment from $20 to $15 billion in Figure 15-2b. The consequent $5 billion downshift in Figure 15-2c's investment schedule from I_{g1} to I_{g3} will equate planned investment and saving—and therefore aggregate expenditures and domestic output—at the $450 billion GDP, thereby eliminating the initial $5 billion inflationary gap.

Table 15-3 summarizes the traditional or Keynesian interpretation of how monetary policy works. We recommend that you study this table carefully.

Refinements and Feedbacks

The components of Figure 15-2 allow us to (1) appreciate some of the factors which determine the effectiveness of monetary policy and (2) note the existence of a "feedback" or "circularity" problem which complicates monetary policy.

Policy Effectiveness   Figure 15-2 indicates the magnitudes by which an easy or tight money policy will change the interest rate, investment, and the equilibrium GDP. These magnitudes are determined by the particular shapes of the demand for money and investment-demand curves. You might pencil in alternative curves to convince yourself that *the steeper the D_m curve, the larger will be the effect of any given change in the money supply on the equilibrium rate of interest. Furthermore, any given change in the interest rate will have a larger impact on investment—and hence on equilibrium GDP—the flatter the investment-demand curve.* In other words, a given change in quantity of money will be most effective when the demand for money curve is relatively steep and the investment-demand curve is relatively flat.

Conversely, a given change in the quantity of money will be relatively ineffective when the money-demand curve is flat and the investment-demand curve is steep. As we will find in Chapter 16, there is controversy as to the precise shapes of these curves and therefore the effectiveness of monetary policy.

TABLE 15-3   Monetary policy: Keynesian interpretation

(1) Easy money policy	(2) Tight money policy
Problem: unemployment and recession	**Problem:** inflation
Federal Reserve buys bonds, lowers reserve ratio, or lowers the discount rate	Federal reserve sells bonds, increases reserve ratio, or increases the discount rate
↓	↓
Money supply rises	Money supply falls
↓	↓
Interest rate falls	Interest rate rises
↓	↓
Investment spending increases	Investment spending decreases
↓	↓
Real GDP rises by a multiple of the increase in investment	Inflation declines

Feedback Effects   You may have sensed in Figure 15-2 a feedback or circularity problem which complicates monetary policy. The nature of this problem is as follows: By reading Figure 15-2 from left to right we discover that the interest rate, working through the investment-demand curve, is an important determinant of the equilibrium GDP. Now we must recognize that causation also runs the other way. The level of GDP is a determinant of the equilibrium interest rate. This link comes about because the transactions component of the money-demand curve depends directly on the level of nominal GDP.

How does this feedback from Figure 15-2c to 15-2a affect monetary policy? It means that the increase in the GDP which an easy money policy brings about will *increase* the demand for money, partially offsetting the interest-reducing effect of the easy money policy. Conversely, a tight money policy will reduce the nominal GDP. But this will *decrease* the demand for money and dampen the initial interest-increasing effect of the tight money policy. This feedback is also at the core of a policy dilemma, as we will see later.

Monetary Policy: AD-AS Framework

We can further refine our understanding of monetary policy by our aggregate demand–aggregate supply model. As with fiscal policy (Chapter 12), monetary policy is subject to constraints implicit in the aggregate supply curve. The cause-effect chain presented in Figure 15-2 and Table 15-3 indicates that monetary policy primarily affects investment spending and, therefore, real output and the price level. The AD-AS model, and the aggregate supply curve in particular, explains how the change in investment may be divided between changes in real output and changes in the price level.

Consider Figure 15-3. You may recall from Chapter 9 that in locating a given aggregate demand curve we assume that the money supply is fixed. An increase in the money supply lowers the interest rate and increases investment spending, which along with consumption, net exports, and government spending is one of the determinants of aggregate demand. The AD curve shifts rightward by a horizontal distance equal to the change in investment times the income multiplier. An increase in the money supply will permit consumers, firms, and government to purchase a larger real output at any given price level.

Conversely, by increasing the interest rate and reducing investment, a reduction in the money supply

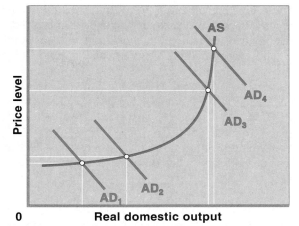

FIGURE 15-3   Monetary policy and the AD-AS model

An easy money policy in the near-horizontal Keynesian range of the aggregate supply curve has its primary effect on real output and employment rather than the price level. In the near-vertical classical range easy money would be inappropriate because it would cause inflation and bring about little or no increase in real output and employment. The effect of tight money on the economy is complicated by the downward stickiness of prices and wages.

shifts the AD curve leftward. The participants in the economy will not wish to buy as much real GDP at any given price level.

We thus note in Figure 15-3 that, if the economy is in the near-horizontal Keynesian or recession range of the aggregate supply curve, an easy money policy will shift the aggregate demand curve rightward as from AD$_1$ to AD$_2$ and have a large impact on real domestic output and employment and little or no effect on the price level.

But if the economy was already at or near to full employment, an increase in aggregate demand would have little or no effect on real output and employment. It would, however, cause a substantial increase in the price level. This is shown in Figure 15-3 by the shift of aggregate demand from AD$_3$ to AD$_4$ in the near-vertical range of the aggregate supply curve. Needless to say, an easy money policy would be inappropriate when the economy was at or near full employment. Figure 15-3 underscores the reason why: It would be highly inflationary.

You should analyze (1) an easy money policy in the intermediate range of aggregate supply and (2) a tight money policy in all three ranges. In analyzing tight money you also should distinguish between the case where prices are assumed to be flexible downward and where they are inflexible (recall Figure 9-7's ratchet effect). If prices are sticky in the short run but more flexible over time, then the short-run and long-run effects of a tight money policy may be different.

EFFECTIVENESS OF MONETARY POLICY

How well does monetary policy work? The effectiveness of monetary policy is subject to some debate.

Strengths of Monetary Policy

Most economists regard monetary policy as an essential component of our national stabilization policy. Indeed, several specific points can be made on behalf of monetary policy.

1 Speed and Flexibility   In comparison with fiscal policy, monetary policy can be quickly altered. We have seen (Chapter 12) that the application of appropriate fiscal policy may be seriously delayed by congressional deliberations. In contrast, the Open Market Committee of the Federal Reserve Board can literally buy or sell securities on a daily basis and affect the money supply and interest rates.

2 Isolation from Political Pressure   Since members of the Federal Reserve Board are appointed for 14-year terms, they are not subject to intense lobbying and pressure to remain elected. Thus the Board, more easily than Congress, can engage in politically unpopular policies which might be necessary for the long-term health of the economy. Additionally, monetary policy itself is a more subtle and more politically conservative measure than fiscal policy. Changes in government spending directly affect the allocation of resources and, of course, tax changes can have extensive political ramifications. By contrast, monetary policy works by a more subtle route and therefore seems to be more politically palatable.

3 Monetarism   In Chapter 16 we will examine in some detail the controversy over the relative effectiveness of monetary policy and fiscal policy. We merely note here that, although most economists view both fiscal and monetary policies as useful stabilization techniques, some economists—called *monetarists*—feel that changes in the money supply are the key determinants of the level of economic activity.

Shortcomings and Problems

It must be recognized, however, that monetary policy has certain limitations and encounters a number of real-world complications.

1 Cyclical Asymmetry   If pursued vigorously enough, tight money can actually destroy commercial banking reserves to the point where banks are forced to contract the volume of loans. This means a contraction of the money supply. But an easy money policy suffers from a "You can lead a horse to water, but you can't make him drink" problem. An easy money policy can only see to it that commercial banks have the excess reserves needed to make loans. It cannot guarantee that the banks' loans will actually be negotiated and the supply of money increased. If commercial banks, seeking liquidity, are unwilling to lend, the easy money policy efforts of the Board of Governors will be to little avail. Similarly, the public can frustrate the intentions of the Federal Reserve by deciding not to borrow excess reserves. Additionally, the money that the Federal Reserve Banks interject into the system through buying bonds from the public conceivably can be used by the public to pay off existing loans.

This cyclical asymmetry has not created a major difficulty for monetary policy except during severe depression. During more normal times, higher excess reserves translate into added lending and therefore to an increase in the money supply.

2 Changes in Velocity   From a monetary point of view (Chapter 16), total expenditures may be regarded as the money supply *multiplied* by the **velocity of money,** that is, the number of times per year the average dollar is spent on goods and services. If the money supply is $150 billion, total spending will be $600 billion if velocity is 4, but only $450 billion if velocity is 3.

Although the issue is controversial, some economists feel that velocity has a habit of changing in the opposite direction from the money supply, tending to offset or frustrate policy-instigated changes in the money supply. During inflation, when the money supply is restrained by policy, velocity may increase. Conversely, when policy measures are taken to increase the money supply during recession, velocity may very well fall.

Velocity might behave in this manner because of the asset demand for money. We know that an easy money policy, for example, means an increase in the supply of money relative to the demand for it and therefore a reduction in the interest rate (Figure 15-2a). But now that the interest rate—the opportunity cost of holding money as an asset—is lower, the public will hold larger money balances. This means dollars move from hand to hand—from households to businesses and back again—less rapidly. In technical terms, the velocity of money has declined. A reverse sequence of events may cause a tight money policy to induce an increase in velocity.

3 The Investment Impact Some economists doubt that monetary policy has as much impact on investment as Figure 15-2 implies. The combination of a relatively flat money-demand curve and a relatively steep investment-demand curve will mean that a given change in the money supply will not elicit a very large change in investment and, thus, not a large change in the equilibrium GDP (Figure 15-2).

Furthermore, the operation of monetary policy as portrayed may be complicated, and at least temporarily offset, by unfavorable changes in the location of the investment-demand curve. For example, a tight money policy designed to drive up interest rates may have little impact on investment spending if the investment demand curve in Figure 15-2b at the same time shifts to the right because of business optimism, technological progress, or expectations of higher future prices of capital. Monetary policy will have to raise interest rates extraordinarily high under these circumstances to be effective in reducing aggregate expenditures. Conversely, a severe recession may undermine business confidence, collapse the investment-demand curve to the left, and frustrate an easy money policy.

The Target Dilemma

This brings us to one of the most difficult problems of monetary policy. Should the Fed attempt to control the money supply *or* the interest rate? This **target dilemma** arises because monetary authorities cannot simultaneously stabilize both.

The Policy Dilemma To understand this dilemma, review the money market diagram of Figure 15-2a.

Interest Rate Assume the Fed's policy target is to stabilize the interest rate because interest rate fluctuations destabilize investment spending and, working through the income multiplier, destabilize the economy. Now suppose expansion of the economy increases nominal GDP and increases the transactions

demand, and therefore the total demand, for money. As a result, the equilibrium interest rate will rise. To stabilize the interest rate—that is, to bring it down to its original level—the Board of Governors would have to increase the supply of money. But this may turn a healthy recovery into an inflationary boom, the very thing that the Federal Reserve System wants to prevent.

A similar scenario can be applied to recession. As GDP falls, so will money demand and interest rates, provided that the money supply is unchanged. But to prevent interest rates from declining, the Board would have to reduce the money supply. This decline in the supply of money would contribute to a further contraction of aggregate expenditures and intensify the recession.

Money Supply What if the Fed's policy target is the money supply rather than the interest rate? Then the Fed must tolerate interest rate fluctuations which will contribute to instability in the economy. Simplified explanation: Assume in Figure 15-2a that the Fed achieves its desired money supply target of $150 billion. We know that any expansion of GDP will increase the demand for money and raise the interest rate. This higher interest rate may lower investment spending and choke off an otherwise healthy expansion. The point again is that the monetary authorities cannot simultaneously stabilize both the money supply and the interest rate.

Recent Policy Focus

Because an interest rate target and a money supply target cannot be realized simultaneously, a controversy exists as to which target, if either, is preferable. In recent years the Fed has taken a pragmatic, middle-of-the-road position, sometimes paying close attention to interest rates and other times focusing more on the money supply. This flexible approach has been manifested in several ways.

1 After the stock market crash of October 1987, the Fed promptly used open-market operations to pump reserves into the banking system to meet the immediate needs of the financial community and to stem a possible decline in consumer and business expenditures. This infusion of money occurred even though the economy was nearing full employment.

2 The Federal Reserve has shown flexibility in measuring the tightness or easiness of its monetary policy. During the 1980s thrifts and banks developed interest-

bearing checkable deposits which are included in *M*1. But transfer of funds from noncheckable savings deposits—particularly from *M*2—to interest-bearing checking accounts caused *M*1 to balloon. This meant people were using part of *M*1 more like savings balances than checking balances. Thus, the relationship between changes in *M*1 and nominal GDP broke down, and *M*1 became far less reliable as a target for monetary policy. In 1988 the Fed shifted its focus from *M*1 to *M*2 in setting its targets for monetary growth.

3   Aiming to increase aggregate demand to lift the economy from recession, the Federal Reserve aggressively targeted interest rates in 1991. Specifically, its open-market operations were designed to drive down the Federal funds rate to a specific level. Recall from Chapter 14 that the Federal funds rate is the interest rate banks charge one another on overnight loans to meet reserve requirements. This interest rate provides information to the Fed about the looseness or tightness of its monetary policy.

Interest rates in general, including the **prime interest rate**—the rate banks charge their most creditworthy customers—rise and fall with the Federal funds rate. When the Fed buys bonds from banks and the public, total reserves and excess reserves in the banking system rise, making it cheaper for banks to borrow reserves from one another. That is, the Federal funds rate falls. We know that increases in reserves in the banking system also increase bank lending to the public and therefore raise the money supply. As the money supply rises, the prime rate falls, increasing investment spending, aggregate demand, and GDP.

TABLE 15-4   Monetary policy and the net export effect

(1) *Easy money policy*	(2) *Tight money policy*
Problem: recession, slow growth	**Problem:** Inflation
Easy money policy (lower interest rate) ↓	Tight money policy (higher interest rate) ↓
Decreased foreign demand for dollars ↓	Increased foreign demand for dollars ↓
Dollar depreciates ↓	Dollar appreciates ↓
Net exports increase (increase in aggregate demand)	Net exports decrease (decrease in aggregate demand)

In summary, the Fed's recent policies have been both activist and pragmatic. It has actively changed the money supply and interest rates according to how it has perceived the needs of the economy. It has paid careful attention to both interest rates and the money supply without adhering strictly to either target.

QUICK REVIEW 15-2

◗   *The Federal Reserve is engaging in an easy money policy when it increases the money supply to reduce interest rates and increase investment spending and real GDP; it is engaging in a tight money policy when it reduces the money supply to increase interest rates and reduce investment spending and inflation.*

◗   *The steeper the money demand curve and the flatter the investment demand curve, the larger is the impact of a change in the money supply on the economy.*

◗   *The strengths of monetary policy include (1) speed and flexibility and (2) political acceptability; weaknesses are (1) potential inadequacy during recession and (2) offsetting changes in velocity.*

◗   *The Fed faces a target dilemma because it cannot simultaneously stabilize both the money supply and interest rates over the course of a business cycle.*

Monetary Policy and the International Economy

In Chapter 12 we established that linkages among economies of the world complicate domestic fiscal policy. These linkages also relate to monetary policy.

Net Export Effect   We saw in Chapter 12 that an expansionary fiscal (deficit) policy will increase the demand for money and boost the domestic interest rate. The higher interest rate will increase foreign financial investment in the United States, strengthening the demand for dollars in the foreign exchange market and boosting the international price of the dollar. This currency *appreciation* will produce lower net exports and hence weaken the stimulus of the fiscal policy (Figure 12-6d).

Will an easy money policy have a similar effect? As outlined in column 1 of Table 15-4, the answer is "No." An easy or expansionary money policy designed to alleviate recession will indeed produce a **net export effect,** but its direction will be exactly opposite to that of an expansionary fiscal policy. An easy money policy will reduce the domestic interest rate rather than increase it. The lower interest rate will discourage the inflow of financial capital to the United States. Hence, the demand for dollars in foreign exchange markets will fall, causing the dollar to *depreciate* in value. It will now take more dollars to buy, say, a Japanese yen or a French franc. All foreign goods are now more expensive to Americans and, conversely, American goods are cheaper to foreigners. Our imports will thus fall and our exports will rise, or, in short, our net exports will increase. As a result, aggregate expenditures and equilibrium GDP will expand in the United States.[2]

Conclusion: Unlike an expansionary fiscal policy which *reduces* net exports, an easy money policy *increases* net exports. *Exchange rate changes in response to interest rate changes in the United States strengthen domestic monetary policy.* This conclusion holds equally for a tight money policy which we know increases the domestic interest rate. In this regard you are urged to follow through the analysis in column 2 of Table 15-4.

Macro Stability and the Trade Balance   Returning to Table 15-4, assume that, in addition to domestic macroeconomic stability, a widely held economic goal is that the United States should achieve an approximate balance in the dollar value of its exports and imports. That is, we should achieve a balance in our international trade. In simple terms, we want to "pay our way" in international trade by earning from our exports an amount of money sufficient to finance our imports.

Consider column 1 of Table 15-4 once again, but now suppose that initially the United States has a very large balance of international trade *deficit,* which means our imports substantially exceed our exports so we are *not* paying our own way in world trade. By following through our cause-effect chain in column 1 we find that an easy money policy lowers the international value of the dollar so that our exports increase and our imports decline. This increase in net exports works to correct the assumed initial balance of trade deficit.

Conclusion: *The easy money policy which is appropriate for the alleviation of unemployment and sluggish growth is compatible with the goal of correcting a balance of trade deficit.* Conversely, if initially our exports were greatly in excess of our imports—that is, the United

States had a large balance of trade *surplus*—an easy money policy would aggravate the surplus.

Now consider column 2 of Table 15-4 and assume again that at the outset the United States has a large balance of trade deficit. In invoking a tight money policy to restrain inflation we would find that net exports would decrease, or, in other words, our exports would fall and imports would rise. This clearly means that the trade deficit would be enlarged.

Conclusion: *A tight money policy invoked to alleviate inflation conflicts with the goal of correcting a balance of trade deficit.* If our initial problem was that of a trade surplus, a tight money policy would tend to resolve that surplus.

Overall we find that an easy money policy alleviates a trade deficit and aggravates a trade surplus. Similarly, a tight money policy alleviates a trade surplus and aggravates a trade deficit. The point is that certain combinations of circumstances create conflicts or tradeoffs between the use of monetary policy to achieve domestic stability and the realization of balance in the nation's international trade.

RECAP: KEYNESIAN EMPLOYMENT THEORY AND POLICY

This is an opportune point to recapitulate and synthesize mainstream or Keynesian employment theory and associated stabilization policies. We want to better understand how the many analytical and policy aspects of macroeconomics discussed in this and the eight preceding chapters fit together. Figure 15-4 (Key Graph) provides the "big picture" we seek. The virtue of this diagram is that it shows how the many concepts and principles discussed relate to one another and how they constitute a coherent theory of what determines the level of resource use in a market economy. Note that those items which constitute, or are strongly influenced by, public policy are shown in red.

Reading from left to right in Figure 15-4, the key point is that the levels of output, employment, income, and prices are all directly related to the level of aggregate expenditures. The decisions of business firms to produce goods and therefore to employ resources depend on the total amount of money spent on these goods. To discover what determines the level of aggregate spending, we must examine its four major components.

[2]The depreciation of the dollar will also increase the price of foreign resources imported to the United States. Aggregate supply in the United States therefore will decline and part of the expansionary effect described here may be offset.

KEY GRAPH

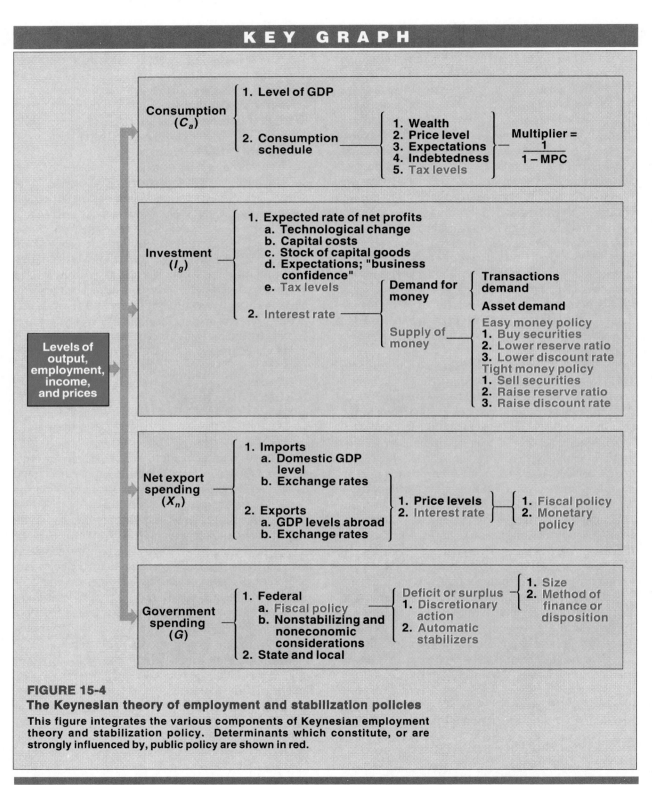

FIGURE 15-4

The Keynesian theory of employment and stabilization policies

This figure integrates the various components of Keynesian employment theory and stabilization policy. Determinants which constitute, or are strongly influenced by, public policy are shown in red.

$$C_a + I_g + X_n + G$$

The absolute level of consumption spending depends on the position of the consumption schedule and the level of gross domestic product or disposable income. Most economists are convinced that the consumption schedule is quite stable. Therefore, the absolute level of consumption spending usually can be thought of as changing in response to changes in GDP brought about by fluctuations in other components in aggregate expenditures. Furthermore, the slope of the consumption schedule, measured by the MPC (the marginal propensity to consume), is critical in determining the size of the multiplier.

Investment spending is a highly volatile component of aggregate spending and therefore likely to be a cause of fluctuations in the levels of output, employment, and prices. Note that both fiscal policy (taxes in particular) and monetary policy influence investment spending.

We know that net export spending is found by subtracting imports from exports. Both imports and exports are affected by exchange rates, while imports are influenced by the level of domestic GDP and exports by GDP levels in other nations. Exchange rates, in turn, depend on price levels and interest rates in various nations. By influencing the domestic price level and the interest rate, domestic fiscal and monetary policy thus affect exchange rates.

The government purchases component of aggregate expenditures differs from consumption, investment, and net exports in that it is determined directly by public policy. Consumption, investment, and net export decisions are made in the self-interest of household and business sectors. Government spending decisions, on the other hand, are made, at least in part, to fulfill society's interest in high levels of output and employment and a stable price level.

Fiscal and Monetary Policy

Fiscal policy refers to changes in government spending and tax revenues which are designed to eliminate either an inflationary or recessionary gap. Figure 15-4 clarifies the potential stabilizing role of government. Government spending, as one of the four major components of aggregate spending, directly affects output, employment, and the price level.

Tax policy, on the other hand, works indirectly through the consumption and investment components of total spending.[3] In particular, reductions in the personal income tax shift the consumption schedule upward; tax increases shift it downward. Cuts in the corporation income tax or other business taxes improve profit expectations, shift the investment-demand curve to the right, and stimulate investment; tax increases weaken profit expectations and reduce the willingness to invest.

Fiscal policy is both *discretionary* and *automatic*. The automatic or built-in stabilizers cause tax collections to vary directly with the level of national income. Discretionary policy consists of the changing of spending levels and the manipulation of tax rates or the tax structure by Congress to achieve greater stability in the economy. Keep in mind, however, that government expenditure and taxation policies are used not only to achieve macroeconomic stability, but also to achieve reallocations of resources and to redistribute income.

Monetary policy was just detailed in the discussion of Figure 15-2 and Table 15-3. Finally, we have seen that both fiscal and monetary policy can influence net exports by way of their effects on the domestic interest rate and price level.

Although we have treated fiscal and monetary policy separately, they are in fact interrelated and should be coordinated. This can be illustrated by referring again to Figure 15-2 and its feedback effects. The quantitative significance of, say, a given increase in government spending will depend on whether it is accompanied by an "accommodating" change in the money supply.

Suppose it is determined that the actual GDP is $25 billion short of the full-employment level and that the multiplier is 5. Other things being equal, a $5 billion increase in government purchases will move the economy to full employment. But in fact, other things—in particular, the interest rate—will not remain unchanged as the economy begins to expand under the impetus of additional spending (Figure 15-2c). As production and GDP expand, the transactions demand for money will increase and, given the supply of money, interest rates will rise (Figure 15-2a). The higher interest rates will "crowd out" some investment (Figure 15-2b) and partially offset the expansionary impact of

---

[3]In our earlier tabular (Table 12-2) and graphical (Figure 12-2) models of the economy, we made the simplifying assumption that all taxes were personal taxes and, therefore, tax changes only affected consumption.

LAST WORD

FOR THE FED, LIFE IS A METAPHOR

Paul Hellman points out that the popular press often depicts the Federal Reserve Board and its chairman Alan Greenspan as Captains Courageous.

The Federal Reserve Board leads a very dramatic life, or so it seems when one reads journalistic accounts of its activities. It loosens or tightens reins while riding herd on a rambunctious economy, goes to the rescue of an embattled dollar, tightens spigots on credit . . . you get the picture. For the Fed, life is a metaphor:

The Fed as mechanic The Fed sometimes must roll up its sleeves and adjust the economic machinery. The Fed spends a lot of time either tightening things or loosening things, or debating about whether to tighten or loosen.

Imagine a customer taking his car into Greenspan's Garage.

Normally calm, Skeezix Greenspan took one look at the car and started to sweat. This would be hard to fix—it was an economy car:

"What's the problem?" asked Greenspan.

"It's been running beautifully for over six years now," said the customer. "But recently it's been acting sluggish."

"These cars are tricky," said Greenspan. "We can always loosen a few screws, as long as you don't mind the side effects."

"What side effects?" asked the customer.

"Nothing at first," said Greenspan. "We won't even know if the repairs have worked for at least a year. After that, either everything will be fine, or your car will accelerate wildly and go totally out of control."

"Just as long as it doesn't stall," said the customer. "I hate that."

The Fed as warrior The Fed must fight inflation. But can it wage a protracted war? There are only seven Fed governors, including Greenspan—not a big army:

the increase in government spending. Unless the money supply is increased to keep the interest rate constant, the income multiplier effect of Chapters 11 and 12 will be diminished because of money market feedbacks which curtail investment and net export spending. Fiscal and monetary policies do not operate in isolation; effective stabilization policy presumes their careful coordination.

CHAPTER SUMMARY

1 Like fiscal policy, the goal of monetary policy is to assist the economy in achieving a full-employment, noninflationary level of total output.

2 For a consideration of monetary policy, the most important assets of the Federal Reserve Banks are securities and loans to commercial banks. The basic liabilities are the reserves of member banks, Treasury deposits, and Federal Reserve Notes.

3 The three major instruments of monetary policy are **a** open-market operations, **b** changing the reserve ratio, and **c** changing the discount rate.

4 Monetary policy operates through a complex cause-effect chain: **a** Policy decisions affect commercial bank reserves; **b** changes in reserves affect the money supply; **c** changes in the money supply alter the interest rate; and **d** changes in the interest rate affect investment, the equilib-

Gen. Greenspan sat in the war room plotting strategy. You never knew where the enemy would strike next—producer prices, retail sales, factory payrolls, manufacturing inventories.

Suddenly, one of his staff officers burst into the room: "Straight from the Western European front, sir—the dollar is under attack by the major industrial nations."

Greenspan whirled around toward the big campaign map. "We've got to turn back this assault!" he said.

"Yes sir." The officer turned to go.

"Hold it!" Greenspan shouted. Suddenly, his mind reeled with conflicting data. A strong dollar was good for inflation, right? Yes, but it was bad for the trade deficit. Or was it the other way around? Attack? Retreat? Macroeconomic forces were closing in.

"Call out the Reserve!" he told the officer.

"Uh . . . we are the Reserve," the man answered.

The Fed as the fall guy

Inflation isn't the only tough customer out there. The Fed must also withstand pressure from administration officials who are regularly described as "leaning heavily" on the Fed to ease up and relax. This always sounds vaguely threatening:

Alan Greenspan was walking down a deserted street late one night. Suddenly a couple of thugs wearing pin-stripes and wingtips cornered him in a dark alley.

"What do you want?" Greenspan asked.

"Just relax," said one.

"How can I relax?" asked Greenspan. "I'm in a dark alley talking to thugs."

"You know what we mean," said the other. "Ease up on the federal funds rate—or else."

"Or else what?" asked Greenspan.

"Don't make us spell it out. Let's just say that if anything unfortunate happens to the gross [domestic] product, I'm holding you personally responsible."

"Yeah," added the other. "A recession could get real painful."

The Fed as cosmic force

The Fed may be a cosmic force. After all, it does satisfy the three major criteria—power, mystery, and a New York office. Some observers even believe the Fed can control the stock market, either by action, symbolic action, anticipated action, or non-action. But saner heads realize this is ridiculous—the market has always been controlled by sunspots.

I wish we could get rid of all these romantic ideas about the Federal Reserve. If you want to talk about the Fed, keep it simple. Just say the Fed is worried about the money. This is something we all can relate to.

rium GDP, and the price level. Table 15-3 draws together all the basic notions relevant to the application of easy and tight money policies.

5   The advantages of monetary policy include its flexibility and political acceptability. Further, monetarists feel that the supply of money is the single most important determinant of the level of domestic output.

6   Monetary policy is subject to a number of limitations and problems. **a** The excess reserves which an easy money policy provides may not be used by banks to expand the supply of money. **b** Policy-instigated changes in the supply of money may be partially offset by changes in the velocity of money. **c** The impact of monetary policy will be lessened if the money-demand curve is flat and the investment-demand curve is steep. The investment-demand curve may also shift, negating monetary policy.

7   Monetary authorities face a policy dilemma in that they can stabilize interest rates *or* the money supply, but not both. Recent monetary policy has been pragmatic, focusing on the health of the economy and not on stabilizing either interest rates or the money supply exclusively. The Fed has focused on both $M2$ and the Federal funds rate in setting its policy.

8   The impact of an easy money policy on domestic GDP is strengthened by an accompanying increase in net exports precipitated by a lower domestic interest rate. Likewise, a tight money policy is strengthened by a decline in net exports. In some situations, there may be a tradeoff between the use of monetary policy to affect the international value of the dollar and thus to correct a trade imbalance and the use of monetary policy to achieve domestic stability.

9   Figure 15-4 provides a summary statement of mainstream or Keynesian employment theory and policy and merits your careful study.

TERMS AND CONCEPTS

monetary policy	reserve ratio	easy and tight money	target dilemma
open-market	discount rate	policies	prime interest rate
operations	money market	velocity of money	net export effect

QUESTIONS AND STUDY SUGGESTIONS

1 Use commercial bank and Federal Reserve Bank balance sheets to demonstrate the impact of each of the following transactions on commercial bank reserves:

a Federal Reserve Banks purchase securities from private businesses and consumers.

b Commercial banks borrow from Federal Reserve Banks.

c The Board of Governors reduces the reserve ratio.

2 Suppose you are a member of the Board of Governors of the Federal Reserve System. The economy is experiencing a sharp and prolonged inflationary trend. What changes in a the reserve ratio, b the discount rate, and c open-market operations would you recommend? Explain in each case how the change you advocate would affect commercial bank reserves, the money supply, interest rates, and aggregate expenditures.

3 In the table below you will find simplified consolidated balance sheets for the commercial banking system and the twelve Federal Reserve Banks. In columns 1 through 3, indicate how the balance sheets would read after each of the three ensuing transactions is completed. Do not cumulate your answers; that is, analyze each transaction separately, starting in each case from the given figures. All accounts are in billions of dollars.

a Suppose a decline in the discount rate prompts commercial banks to borrow an additional $1 billion from the Federal Reserve Banks. Show the new balance-sheet figures in column 1.

b The Federal Reserve Banks sell $3 billion in securities to the public, who pay for the bonds with checks. Show the new balance-sheet figures in column 2.

c The Federal Reserve Banks buy $2 billion of securities from commercial banks. Show the new balance-sheet figures in column 3.

d Now review each of the above three transactions, asking yourself these three questions: (1) What change, if any, took place in the money supply as a

Consolidated balance sheet:
all commercial banks

		(1)	(2)	(3)
Assets:				
Reserves	$ 33	_____	_____	_____
Securities	60	_____	_____	_____
Loans	60	_____	_____	_____
Liabilities and net worth:				
Demand deposits	$150	_____	_____	_____
Loans from the Federal Reserve Banks	3	_____	_____	_____

Consolidated balance sheet:
twelve Federal Reserve banks

		(1)	(2)	(3)
Assets:				
Securities	$60	_____	_____	_____
Loans to commercial banks	3	_____	_____	_____
Liabilities and net worth:				
Reserves of commercial banks	$33	_____	_____	_____
Treasury deposits	3	_____	_____	_____
Federal Reserve Notes	27	_____	_____	_____

direct and immediate result of each transaction? (2) What increase or decrease in commercial banks' reserves took place in each transaction? (3) Assuming a reserve ratio of 20 percent, what change in the money-creating potential of the commercial banking *system* occurred as a result of each transaction?

4 What is the basic objective of monetary policy? Describe the cause-effect chain through which monetary policy is made effective. Using Figure 15-2 as a point of reference, discuss how **a** the shapes of the demand for money and investment-demand curves and **b** the size of the MPS influence the effectiveness of monetary policy. How do feedback effects influence the effectiveness of monetary policy?

5 Evaluate the overall effectiveness of monetary policy. Why have open-market operations evolved as the primary means of controlling commercial bank reserves? Discuss the specific limitations of monetary policy.

6 Explain the observation that the Fed cannot simultaneously stabilize interest rates and the money supply. Explain why the target of stable interest rates might contribute to ongoing inflation.

7 Summarize the Keynesian theory of employment and show in detail how monetary and fiscal policies might affect the various components of aggregate expenditures.

8 Suppose the Federal Reserve decides to engage in a tight money policy as a way to reduce demand-pull inflation. Use the aggregate demand–aggregate supply model to show the intent of this policy for a closed economy. Next, introduce the open economy and explain how changes in the international value of the dollar might affect the location of your aggregate demand curve.

9 Design an antirecession stabilization policy, involving both fiscal and monetary policies, which is consistent with **a** a relative decline in the public sector, **b** greater income equality, and **c** a high rate of economic growth. Explain: "Truly effective stabilization policy presumes the coordination of fiscal and monetary policy."

PART

4

Problems and Controversies in Macro- economics

CHAPTER 16

Alternative Views: Monetarism and Rational Expectations

The Keynesian conception of employment theory and stabilization policy, summarized in the discussion represented by Figure 15-4, has dominated the thinking of most economists in all market-oriented industrial economies since World War II. In the United States, Democratic and Republican administrations alike have basically accepted these precepts, if not the Keynesian label.

In the past two decades, however, this theory has been challenged by alternative conceptions of macroeconomics, particularly monetarism and rational expectations theory (RET). Each of these schools of macroeconomic thinking is led by its own set of distinguished scholars. Five Nobel Prize winners—Paul Samuelson, Franco Modigliani, and Robert Solow of MIT; James Tobin of Yale; and Lawrence Klein of Pennsylvania—are members of the older generation of Keynesian spokesmen. Younger economists whose scholarship fits within the Keynesian tradition include Alan Blinder of Princeton, Stanley Fisher of MIT, and Robert Gordon of Northwestern.

The University of Chicago's Milton Friedman is the intellectual leader of the *monetarist school.* Winner of the 1976 Nobel Prize in economics, Friedman's pioneering empirical and theoretical research asserts that the role of money in determining the level of economic activity and the price level is much greater than suggested by early Keynesian theory.

The leading contributors to the *rational expectations theory* (RET)—a facet of the so-called *new classical economics*—are Chicago's Robert Lucas, Stanford's Thomas Sargent, and Harvard's Robert Barro.

The primary purpose of this chapter is to present monetarism and RET and compare them with Keynesianism. In Chapter 17, we will continue the debate over stabilization policy along with analysis of the problem of simultaneous inflation and unemployment. In Chapter 18, issues surrounding the troublesome budget deficits and the public debt are explored. Part 4 concludes with Chapter 19, which examines the important problem of maintaining economic growth.

BASIC DIFFERENCES

We begin by contrasting Keynesian economics and monetarism. For comparison, it first will be useful to characterize Keynesianism and monetarism in their polar forms. In reality, we will discover the lines between many contemporary Keynesians and monetarists are not so clearly drawn. But at the extreme, Keynesians and monetarists have different views on the inherent stability of capitalistic economies. They also have important ideological differences, particularly on the role of government.

Keynesians:
Instability and Intervention

Keynesians believe that capitalism and, more particularly, the free-market system suffer from inherent shortcomings. Most important for our discussion is the Keynesian contention that the private sector contains no mechanism to ensure macroeconomic stability. Imbalances of planned investment and saving *do* occur and the result is business fluctuations—periodic episodes of inflation or unemployment.

In particular, many markets are noncompetitive so that prices and wages are inflexible downward. Fluctuations in aggregate expenditures therefore affect primarily output and employment rather than prices. According to Keynesians, government can and should play a positive, activist role in stabilizing the economy; discretionary fiscal and monetary policies are needed to alleviate the economic ups and downs which would otherwise characterize the economy's course.

Monetarists:
Stability and Laissez Faire

The **monetarist** view is that markets are highly competitive and that a competitive market system provides the economy with a high degree of macroeconomic stability. Monetarism has its intellectual roots in Chapter 10's classical economics which argues that the price and wage flexibility which competitive markets provide would cause fluctuations in aggregate expenditures to alter product and resource prices rather than output and employment. Thus the market system would provide substantial macroeconomic stability *were it not for governmental interference with the functioning of the economy.*

The problem, as the monetarists see it, is that government has fostered and promoted downward wage-price inflexibility through the minimum-wage law, pro-union legislation, farm price supports, pro-business monopoly legislation, and so forth. The free-market system could provide substantial macroeconomic stability, but, despite good intentions, government interference has undermined this capability. Furthermore, monetarists argue that government has contributed to the instability of the system—to the business cycle—through its clumsy and mistaken attempts to achieve greater stability through *discretionary* fiscal and monetary policies.

Given the above comments, it is no surprise that monetarists have a strong *laissez faire* or free-market orientation. Governmental decision making is held to be bureaucratic, inefficient, harmful to individual incentives, and frequently characterized by policy mistakes which destabilize the economy. Furthermore, centralized decision making by government inevitably erodes individual freedoms.[1] The public sector should be kept to the smallest possible size.

Keynesians and monetarists therefore are opposed in their conceptions of the private and public sectors. To the Keynesian, the instability of private investment causes the economy to be unstable. Government plays a positive role by applying appropriate stabilization medicine. To the monetarist, government has harmful effects on the economy. Government creates rigidities which weaken the capacity of the market system to provide substantial stability and it embarks on monetary and fiscal measures which, although well intentioned, aggravate the very instability they are designed to cure.

THE BASIC EQUATIONS

Keynesian economics and monetarism each build their analysis upon specific equations.

The Aggregate Expenditures Equation

As indicated in previous chapters, Keynesian economics focuses on aggregate spending and its components. Recall that the basic Keynesian equation is:

$$C_a + I_g + X_n + G = \text{GDP} \tag{1}$$

---

[1]Friedman's philosophy is effectively expounded in two of his books: *Capitalism and Freedom* (Chicago: The University of Chicago Press, 1962); and with Rose Friedman, *Free to Choose* (New York: Harcourt Brace Jovanovich, 1980).

This theory says that the aggregate amount of after-tax consumption, gross investment, net exports, and government spending determines the total value of the goods and services sold. In equilibrium, $C_a + I_g + X_n + G$ (aggregate expenditures) is equal to GDP (domestic output).

Equation of Exchange

Monetarism, as the label suggests, focuses on money. The fundamental equation of monetarism is the **equation of exchange:**

$$MV = PQ \qquad (2)$$

where M is the supply of money; V is the income **velocity of money,** that is, the number of times per year the average dollar is spent on final goods and services; P is the price level or, more specifically, the average price at which each unit of physical output is sold; and Q is the physical volume of goods and services produced.

The label "equation of exchange" is easily understood. The left side, MV, represents the total amount *spent* by purchasers of output, while the right side, PQ, represents the total amount *received* by sellers of that output.

> The difference between the two approaches can be compared with two ways of looking at the flow of water through a sewer pipe—say, at the rate of 6000 gallons per hour. A neo-Keynesian investigator might say that the flow of 6000 gallons an hour consisted of 3000 gallons an hour from a paper mill, 2000 gallons an hour from an auto plant, and 1000 gallons an hour from a shopping center. A monetarist investigator might say that the sewer flow of 6000 gallons an hour consisted of an average of 200 gallons in the sewer at any one time with a complete turnover of the water 30 times every hour.[2]

Both the Keynesian and monetarist approaches are useful and insightful in understanding macroeconomics. In fact, the Keynesian equation can be readily "translated" into monetarist terms. According to the monetarist approach, total spending is the supply of money multiplied by its velocity. In short, MV is the monetarist counterpart of equilibrium $C_a + I_g + X_n + G$. Because MV is the total amount spent on final goods in one year, it is necessarily equal to nominal GDP. Furthermore, nominal GDP is the sum of the physical outputs of various goods and services (Q) multiplied

by their respective prices (P). That is, GDP = PQ. Thus, we can restate the Keynesian $C_a + I_g + X_n + G$ = GDP equation in nominal terms as the monetarist equation of exchange, $MV = PQ$.[3] The two approaches are two ways of looking at much the same thing. But the critical question remains: Which theory more accurately portrays macroeconomics and therefore is the better basis for economic policy?

Spotlight on Money

The Keynesian equation puts money in a secondary role. Indeed, the Keynesian conception of monetary policy entails a rather lengthy transmission mechanism (Chapter 15). This mechanism is shown in Figure 16-1a. A change in monetary policy alters the nation's supply of money. The change in the money supply affects the interest rate, which affects the level of investment. When the economy initially is operating at less than capacity, changes in investment affect nominal GDP ($= PQ$) by changing real output (Q) through the income multiplier effect. Alternatively, when the economy is achieving full employment, changes in investment affect nominal GDP by altering the price level (P).

Keynesians contend there are many loose links in this cause-effect chain with the result that monetary policy is an uncertain and relatively weak stabilization tool compared with fiscal policy. Some of the weaknesses of monetary policy were cited in Chapter 15. For example, recall from Figure 15-2 that monetary policy will be relatively ineffective if the demand for money curve is flat and the investment-demand curve is steep. Also, the investment-demand curve may shift adversely so that the impact of a change in the interest rate on investment spending is muted or offset. Nor will an easy money policy be very effective if banks and other depository institutions are not anxious to lend or the public eager to borrow.

Monetarists believe that money and monetary policy are much more important in determining the level of economic activity than do the Keynesians. *Monetarists hold that changes in the money supply are the single most important factor in determining the levels of output, employment, and prices.* They see a different cause-effect chain between the supply of money and the level

---

[2]Werner Sichel and Peter Eckstein, *Basic Economic Concepts* (Chicago: Rand McNally College Publishing Company, 1974), p. 344.

[3]Technical footnote: There is an important conceptual difference between the Keynesian $C_a + I_g + X_n + G$ and the MV component of the equation of exchange. Specifically, the former indicates planned or *intended* expenditures, which equal actual expenditures only in equilibrium. MV, on the other hand, reflects *actual* spending.

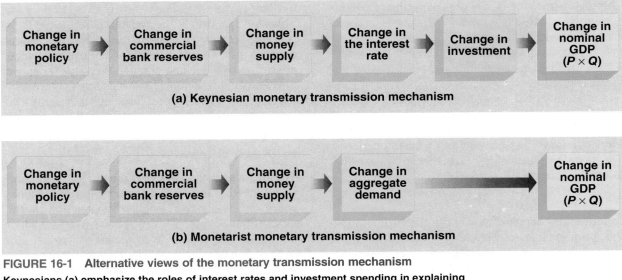

FIGURE 16-1 **Alternative views of the monetary transmission mechanism**

Keynesians (a) emphasize the roles of interest rates and investment spending in explaining
how changes in the money supply affect nominal GDP. On the other hand, monetarists (b)
contend that changes in the money supply cause direct changes in aggregate demand and
thereby changes in nominal GDP.

of economic activity than the Keynesian model suggests. Rather than limiting the effect of an increase in money to bond purchases and consequent declines in the interest rate, monetarists theorize that an increase in the money supply drives up the demand for all assets—real or financial—as well as for current output. Under conditions of full employment, the prices of all these items will rise. Monetarists also contend that the velocity of money is stable—meaning that it does not fluctuate wildly and does not change in response to a change in the money supply itself. Thus, changes in the money supply will have a predictable effect on the level of nominal GDP ($= PQ$). More precisely, an increase in M will increase P or Q, or some combination of both P and Q; a decrease in M will produce the opposite effects.

Monetarists believe that, although a change in M may cause short-run changes in real output and employment as market adjustments occur, the long-run impact of a change in M will be on the price level. Monetarists think the private economy is inherently stable and tends to operate at the full-employment level of output. The exact level of that full-employment output depends on such "real" factors as the quantity and quality of labor, capital, and land and upon technology (Chapter 19). For present purposes the point is that, if Q is constant at the economy's capacity output, then changes in M will lead to changes in P.

Monetarism implies a more direct transmission mechanism than does the Keynesian model. Observe in Figure 16-1b that monetarists view changes in the money supply as producing direct changes in aggregate demand which alter nominal GDP. We know from previous discussion that monetarists contend that changes in the money supply affect all components of aggregate demand, not just investment. Furthermore, changes in aggregate demand allegedly affect nominal GDP in the long run primarily through changes in the price level, not through changes in real output.

VELOCITY: STABLE OR UNSTABLE?

A critical theoretical issue in the Keynesian–monetarist debate centers on the question of whether the velocity of money, V, is stable. Note that, as used here, the word "stable" is *not* synonymous with the word "constant." Monetarists are well aware that velocity is higher today than in 1945. Shorter pay periods, greater use of credit cards, and faster means of making payments have increased velocity since 1945. These factors have enabled people over the years to reduce their cash and checkbook holdings relative to the size of the nominal GDP.

What monetarists mean when they say that velocity is stable is that the factors which alter velocity change gradually and predictably. Changes in velocity from one year to the next thus can be easily anticipated. Moreover, velocity does *not* change in response to changes in the supply of money itself.

If velocity is stable, the equation of exchange tells us that monetarists are indeed correct in claiming that a direct predictable relationship exists between the money supply and nominal GDP $(= PQ)$.

Suppose M is 100, V is 1, and nominal GDP is 100. Also assume velocity increases annually at a stable rate of 2 percent. Using the equation of exchange, we can predict that a 5 percent annual growth rate of the money supply will result in about a 7 percent increase in nominal GDP. M will increase from 100 to 105, V will rise from 1 to 1.02, and nominal GDP will increase from 100 to about 107 ($= 105 \times 1.02$).

But if V is not stable, the Keynesian contention that money plays only a secondary role in macroeconomics is valid. If V is variable and unpredictable from one period to another, the link between M and PQ will be loose and uncertain. In particular, a steady growth of M will not necessarily translate into a steady growth of nominal GDP.

Monetarists: *V* Is Stable

What rationale do monetarists offer for their contention that V is stable? Basically, they argue that people have a stable desire to hold money relative to holding other financial and real assets and buying current output. The factors which determine the amount of money people and businesses wish to hold at any given time are independent of the supply of money. Most importantly, the amount of money the public will want to hold will depend on the level of nominal GDP.

Consider a simple example. Suppose that, when the level of nominal GDP is $400 billion, the amount of money the public wants or *desires* to hold to negotiate the purchase of this output is $100 billion. (This implies that V is 4.) If we further assume that the *actual* supply of money is $100 billion, we can say that the economy is in equilibrium with respect to money; the *actual* amount of money supplied equals the amount the public *desires* to hold.

In the monetarist view an increase in the money supply of, say, $10 billion will upset this equilibrium in that the public will now be holding more money or liquidity than it wants to hold; the actual amount of money being held exceeds the desired amount. The natural reaction of the public (households and businesses) is to restore its desired balance of money relative to other items such as stocks and bonds, factories and equipment, houses and automobiles, and clothing and toys. The public has more money than it wants; the way to get rid of money is to buy things. But one person's spending of money leaves more cash in someone else's checkable deposit or billfold. That person, too, tries to "spend down" excess cash balances.

The collective attempt to reduce cash balances will increase aggregate demand, which will boost the nominal GDP. Because velocity is 4—the typical dollar is spent four times per year—nominal GDP must rise by $40 billion. When nominal GDP reaches $440 billion, the *actual* money supply of $110 billion again will be the amount which the public *desires* to hold, and by definition equilibrium will be reestablished. Spending on goods and services will increase until nominal GDP has increased sufficiently to restore the original equilibrium relationship between nominal GDP and the money supply. In fact, the relationship GDP/M defines V. A stable relationship between GDP and M means a stable V.

Keynesians: *V* Is Unstable

In the Keynesian view the velocity of money is variable and unpredictable. This position can best be understood in reference to the Keynesian conception of the demand for money (Chapter 13). The Keynesian view is that money is demanded, not only to use in negotiating transactions, but also to hold as an asset. Money demanded for *transactions* purposes will be "active" money, which is changing hands and circulating through the income-expenditures stream. In other words, transactions dollars have some positive velocity; the average transactions dollar may be spent, say, six times per year and thereby negotiate $6 worth of transactions. In this case V is 6 for each transactions dollar.

But money demanded and held as an *asset* is "idle" money; these dollars do *not* flow through the income-expenditures stream and therefore their velocity is zero. It follows that the overall velocity of the entire money supply will depend on how it is divided between transactions and asset balances. The greater the relative importance of "active" transactions balances, the larger will be V. Conversely, the greater the relative significance of "idle" asset balances, the smaller will be V.

Given this framework, Keynesians discredit the monetarist transmission mechanism—the allegedly dependable relationship between changes in M and changes in GDP—by arguing that a significant portion of any increase in the money supply may go into asset balances, *causing V to fall.* In the very extreme case, assume *all* the increase in the money supply is held by the public as additional asset balances. That is, the public simply hoards the additional money and uses none of it for transactions. The money supply will have increased, but velocity will decline by an offsetting amount so that there will be no effect on the size of nominal GDP.

We can consider the Keynesian position on a more advanced level by referring back to Figure 13-2. Note that the relative importance of the asset demand for money varies inversely with the rate of interest. An *increase* in the money supply will *lower* the interest rate. Because it is now less expensive to hold money as an asset, the public will hold larger zero-velocity asset balances. Therefore, the overall velocity of the money supply will fall.

Conversely, a *reduction* in the money supply will *raise* the interest rate, increasing the cost of holding money as an asset. The resulting decline in asset balances will increase the overall velocity of money. *In the Keynesian view velocity varies (1) directly with the rate of interest and (2) inversely with the supply of money.* If this analysis is correct, the stable relationship between M and nominal GDP embodied in the monetarist's transmission mechanism does *not* exist because V will vary whenever M changes.

At this juncture we can more fully appreciate a point made at the end of Chapter 15 in discussing possible shortcomings of monetary policy. We indicated that V has the bad habit of changing in the opposite direction from M. Our present discussion reveals the cause-effect chain through which this might occur.

Empirical Evidence

The stability of V is an empirical question and an appeal to "the facts" would seem to settle the issue. However, the facts are not easy either to discern or to interpret.

Monetarists think that the weight of empirical evidence clearly supports their position. In Figure 16-2 the money supply and the nominal domestic output *(PQ)* are both plotted. Given that $MV = PQ$, the close correlation between M and PQ suggests that V is stable. Monetarists reason that the money supply is the critical causal force in determining nominal GDP; causation runs from M to nominal GDP.

But Keynesians offer two arguments by way of rebuttal.

1 They point out that by simple manipulation of $MV = PQ$, we find that $V = PQ/M = GDP/M$. That is, we can empirically calculate the value of V by dividing each year's nominal output (GDP) by the money supply. Keynesians contend that the resulting data, shown in Figure 16-3, repudiate the monetarist contention that V is stable. For example, observe that there was considerable year-to-year variation in velocity even during the so-called "steady" upward trend of velocity between 1945 and 1982. Also, note the markedly changed behavior of velocity since 1982. In several of these years velocity actually declined.

Keynesians also point out that the close correlation between the velocity of money and the interest rate shown in Figure 16-3 supports their analytical conclusion that velocity varies directly with the rate of interest. (The short-term interest rate used here is the rate on three-month Treasury bills.) Velocity, in the Keynesian view, is variable both cyclically and secularly and these variations downgrade the role of money as a determinant of output, employment, and the price level.

Keynesians add this reminder: Given the large size of the money supply, a small variation in velocity can have a substantial impact on nominal GDP. For example, assume M is \$300 billion and V is 5. A modest 10 percent increase in V will cause a \$150 billion increase in nominal GDP. That is, MV—and therefore PQ—are initially \$1500 billion (= \$300 × 5). Now, if V increases by 10 percent to 5.5, PQ will be \$1650 billion (= MV = 300 × 5.5). Stated in terms of the issue at hand, a very small variation in V can offset a large absolute change in M.

2 Keynesians respond to Figure 16-2 by noting that *correlation* and *causation* are quite different things. It is possible that the changes in nominal GDP in Figure 16-2 were caused by changes in aggregate expenditures $(C_a + I_g + X_n + G)$, as suggested by the Keynesian model. Perhaps a favorable change in business expectations increased investment. It is also possible that the indicated growth in the nominal domestic output prompted—indeed, necessitated—that businesses and consumers borrow more money over time from commercial banks to finance this rising volume of economic activity.

In other words, Keynesians claim that causation may run from aggregate expenditures *to* domestic output *to* the money supply, rather than from the money supply *to* aggregate demand *to* domestic output as

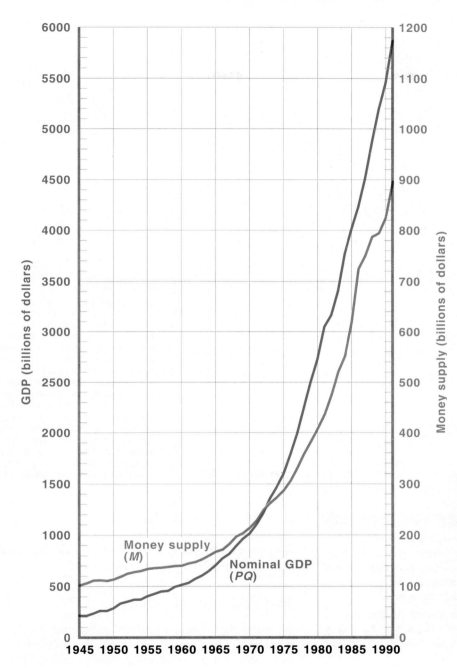

FIGURE 16-2   The money supply and GDP, 1945–1991

Monetarists cite the close positive correlation between the money supply and nominal GDP as evidence in support of their position that money is the critical determinant of economic activity and the price level. They assume that the money supply is the "cause" and the GDP is the "effect," an assumption which Keynesians question. Monetarists also feel that the close correlation between *M* and nominal GDP indicates that the velocity of money is stable. *(Economic Report of the President.)*

monetarists contend. The important point, argue Keynesians, is that the data of Figure 16-2 are as consistent with the Keynesian view as they are with the monetarist position.

The question of the stability of *V* remains a crucial point of conflict between Keynesians and monetarists. For example, the great instability of velocity during the past decade has led many monetarists to replace *M*1 velocity (Figure 16-3) in their models with the more stable velocity of the *M*2 money supply. Keynesians question whether a theory requiring periodic redefinitions of its key variable—the money supply—offers solid ground on which to establish macroeconomic policy.

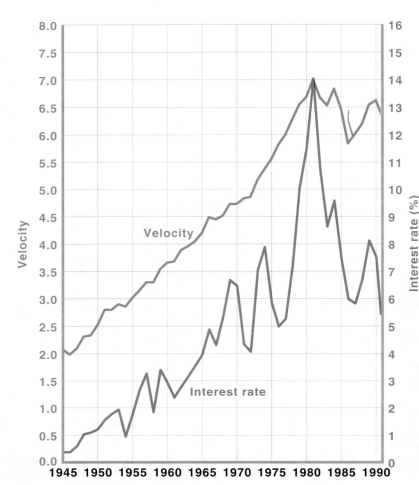

FIGURE 16-3 The velocity of money and the interest rate, 1945–1991

Keynesians argue that the velocity of money varies both cyclically and secularly. Hence, they conclude that any link between a change in the money supply and the subsequent change in nominal GDP is tenuous and uncertain. More specifically, Keynesians contend that velocity varies directly with the rate of interest because a lower interest rate will increase the size of zero-velocity asset balances and therefore lower the overall velocity of money. (Economic Report of the President.)

QUICK REVIEW 16-1

∮ *Keynesians view the economy as being inherently unstable and therefore requiring stabilization through active fiscal and monetary policies; monetarists see the economy as being relatively stable in the absence of government interference.*

∮ *Keynesians focus their analysis on the aggregate expenditures equation $(C_a + I_g + X_n + G = GDP)$ while monetarists base their analysis on the equation of exchange $(MV = PQ)$.*

∮ *Keynesians see changes in the money supply as working through changes in interest rates, investment, and aggregate expenditures; monetarists envision a direct link between the money supply, aggregate demand, and nominal GDP.*

∮ *Keynesians contend velocity $(V = PQ/M)$ varies directly with the interest rate and inversely with the money supply, whereas monetarists think velocity is relatively stable.*

POLICY DEBATES

Differences in Keynesian and monetarist theories spill over into the area of stabilization policy.

The Fiscal Policy Debate

Although Keynesians acknowledge the importance of monetary policy, they believe that fiscal policy is a more powerful and reliable stabilization device. This is implied by the basic equation of Keynesianism. Government spending is a direct component of aggregate expenditures. And taxes are only one short step removed, since tax changes allegedly affect consumption and investment in dependable and predictable ways.

Monetarists seriously downgrade or, in the extreme, reject fiscal policy as a stabilization device. They believe that fiscal policy is weak and ineffectual because of the **crowding-out effect** (Chapter 12). Monetarists' reasoning goes like this: Suppose government runs a budgetary deficit by selling bonds, that is, by borrowing from the public. By borrowing, government competes with private businesses for funds. Thus, government borrowing will increase the demand for money, raise the interest rate, and crowd out a substantial amount of private investment which otherwise would have been profitable. Hence, the net effect of a budget deficit on aggregate expenditures is unpredictable and, at best, modest.

Alternatively, the workings of the crowding-out effect can be seen from a more analytical perspective by referring back to Figure 15-2. Financing the government's deficit will increase the demand for money, shifting the D_m curve of Figure 15-2a to the right. Given the money supply, S_m, the equilibrium interest rate will rise. This increase in the interest rate will be relatively large, according to the monetarists, because the D_m curve is relatively steep.

Furthermore, monetarists believe that the investment-demand curve of Figure 15-2b is relatively flat; investment spending is very sensitive to changes in the interest rate. In short, the initial increase in the demand for money causes a relatively large rise in the interest rate which, projected off an interest-sensitive investment-demand curve, causes a large decline in the investment component of aggregate expenditures. The resulting large contractionary effect offsets the expansionary impact of the fiscal deficit and, on balance, the equilibrium GDP is unaffected. So sayeth Friedman: ". . . in my opinion, the state of the budget by itself has no significant effect on the course of nominal [money] income, on inflation, on deflation, or on cyclical fluctuations."[4]

Admittedly, if a deficit was financed by the issuing of new money, the crowding-out effect could be avoided and the deficit would be followed by economic expansion. *But,* the monetarists point out, the expansion would be due, *not* to the fiscal deficit per se, but rather, to the creation of additional money.

Keynesians, for the most part, do not deny that some investment may be crowded out. But they perceive the amount as being small, and conclude that the net impact of an expansionary fiscal policy on equilibrium GDP will be substantial. In terms of Figure 15-2, the extreme Keynesian view is that the demand for money curve is relatively flat and the investment-demand curve is steep. (You may recall that this combination tends to make monetary policy relatively weak and ineffective.) An increase in D_m will cause a very modest increase in the interest rate which, when projected off a steep investment-demand curve, will result in a very small decrease in the investment component of aggregate expenditures. In other words, little investment will be crowded out.

Keynesians *do* acknowledge that a deficit financed by creating new money will have a greater stimulus than one financed by borrowing. In terms of Figure 15-2a, for any given increase in D_m there is some increase in S_m which will leave the interest rate, and therefore the volume of investment, unchanged.

Monetary Policy: Discretion or Rules?

The Keynesian conception of monetary policy is that portrayed in Figure 15-2. As just noted, Keynesians believe that the demand for money curve is relatively flat and the investment-demand curve relatively steep, causing monetary policy to be a comparatively weak stabilization tool. We have also seen that, in contrast, monetarists contend that the money demand curve is very steep and the investment-demand curve quite flat, a combination which means that a change in the money supply has a powerful effect on the equilibrium level of nominal GDP. This is clearly in keeping with monetarism's fundamental contention that the money supply is the critical determinant of the level of economic activity and the price level.

However, strict monetarists do *not* advise use of easy and tight money policies to modify "downs" and "ups" of the business cycle. Professor Friedman contends that, historically, *discretionary* changes in the money supply made by monetary authorities have in fact been a *destabilizing* influence in the economy.

Examining the monetary history of the United States from the Civil War up to the establishment of the Federal Reserve System in 1913 and comparing this with the post-1913 record, Friedman concludes that, even if the economically disruptive World War II period is ignored, the latter (post-1913) period was clearly more unstable. Much of this decline in economic stability after the Federal Reserve System became effective is attributed to faulty decisions on the part of the monetary authorities. *In the monetarist view economic instability is more a product of monetary mismanagement than it is of any inherent destabilizers in the economy.* There are two important sources of monetary mismanagement.

[4]Statement by Friedman in Milton Friedman and Walter Heller, *Monetary vs. Fiscal Policy* (New York: W. W. Norton & Company, Inc., 1969), p. 51.

1 Irregular Time Lags There is the matter of *time lags.* Although the monetary transmission mechanism is direct, changes in the money supply affect nominal GDP only after a rather long and variable time period. Friedman's empirical work suggests that a change in the money supply may significantly change GDP in as short a period as six to eight months or in as long a period as two years. Because it is virtually impossible to predict the time lag involved in a given policy action, there is little chance of determining accurately when specific policies should be invoked or, in fact, which policy measure—easy or tight money—is appropriate.

Indeed, given the uncertain duration of this time lag, the use of discretionary monetary policy to "fine-tune" the economy for cyclical "ups" and "downs" may backfire and intensify these cyclical changes. For example, suppose an easy money policy is invoked because the various economic indicators suggest a mild recession. But assume now that within the ensuing six months the economy, for reasons unrelated to public policy actions, reverses itself and moves into the prosperity-inflationary phase of the cycle. At this point the easy money policy becomes effective and reinforces the inflation.

2 Interest Rate: Wrong Target Monetarists argue that monetary authorities have typically attempted to control interest rates to stabilize investment and therefore the economy. Recalling Chapter 15's discussion of the targeting dilemma, the problem with this is that the Board of Governors cannot simultaneously stabilize both the money supply and interest rates. Therefore, in trying to stabilize interest rates, the Fed might *destabilize* the economy.

Suppose the economy is coming out of a recession and is currently approaching full employment, with aggregate expenditures, output, employment, and the price level all increasing. This expanding volume of economic activity will increase the demand for money and therefore raise the interest rate. Now, if monetary authorities reason that their task is to stabilize interest rates, they will embark on an easy money policy. But this expansionary monetary policy will add to aggregate expenditures when the economy is already on the verge of an inflationary boom. The attempt to stabilize interest rates will fan existing inflationary fires and make the economy less stable. A similar scenario is applicable to an economy moving into a recession.

The Monetary Rule Monetarist moral: Monetary authorities should stabilize, not the interest rate, but the rate of growth of the money supply. Specifically, Friedman advocates legislating the **monetary rule** that the money supply be expanded each year at the same annual rate as the potential growth of our real GDP, meaning the supply of money should be increased steadily at 3 to 5 percent per year.

> Such a rule . . . would eliminate . . . the major cause of instability in the economy—the capricious and unpredictable impact of countercyclical monetary policy. As long as the money supply grows at a constant rate each year, be it 3, 4, or 5 percent, any decline into recession will be temporary. The liquidity provided by a constantly growing money supply will cause aggregate demand to expand. Similarly, if the supply of money does not rise at a more than average rate, any inflationary increase in spending will burn itself out for lack of fuel.[5]

Keynesian response: Despite a somewhat spotty record, it would be foolish to replace discretionary monetary policy with a monetary rule. Arguing that V is variable both cyclically and secularly, Keynesians contend that a constant annual rate of increase in the money supply could contribute to substantial fluctuations in aggregate expenditures and promote economic instability. Indeed, we concluded in Chapter 15 that wide fluctuations in interest rates and investment spending would accompany any shift from the interest rate target. As one Keynesian has quipped, the trouble with the monetary rule is that it tells the policy maker: "Don't do something, just stand there."

AD-AS Analysis

It is helpful to contrast monetarist and Keynesian views in terms of our earlier aggregate demand–aggregate supply model. By bringing aggregate supply into the picture we can see more clearly the implications of each model for real output and the price level. We can also further our understanding of policy differences.

Contrasting Portrayals Figure 16-4 portrays the monetarist perspective on the left and the Keynesian conception on the right. The key difference on the demand side, as we know, concerns the factors which will shift the aggregate demand curve. To monetarists the aggregate demand curve will shift rightward or leftward primarily because of an increase or decrease, respectively, in the money supply. Keynesians are more

[5]Lawrence S. Ritter and William L. Silber, *Money,* 5th ed. (New York: Basic Books, Inc., Publishers, 1984), pp. 141–142.

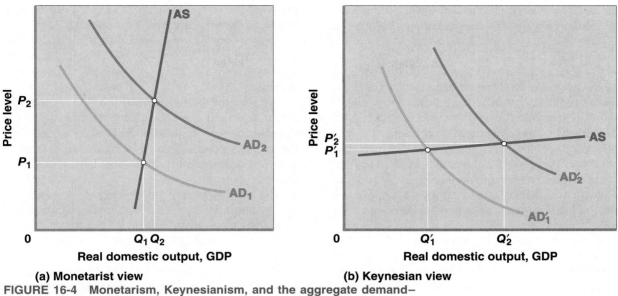

FIGURE 16-4   Monetarism, Keynesianism, and the aggregate demand–aggregate supply model

The monetarist view (a) is that the aggregate supply curve is relatively steep, which means that a change in aggregate demand will have a large effect on the price level but only cause a small change in real output and employment. The Keynesian conception (b) envisions a relatively flat aggregate supply curve which implies that a change in aggregate demand will cause large changes in real output and employment and small changes in the price level.

general, recognizing that in addition to changes in private spending both fiscal and monetary policy can shift the aggregate demand curve.

On the supply side we find that monetarists view the aggregate supply curve as being very steep or, in the long run, vertical, while Keynesians conceive of it as being quite flat, or in the extreme case, horizontal. This is nothing new to us as a glance back at Figure 9-3 will confirm. The aggregate supply curve presented there has a horizontal or near-horizontal "Keynesian" range and a vertical or near-vertical "classical" range. The flat Keynesian range reflects the belief that the economy can operate short of the full-employment or capacity level, while a near-vertical range mirrors the classical heritage of monetarism and the belief that flexible prices and wages continuously move the economy toward full employment.

Policy Implications   These different conceptions of the aggregate supply curve are important with respect to stabilization policy. In the monetarist view a change in aggregate demand affects primarily the price level and has little impact on real GDP. This conclusion derives from the assumption that, if the Federal Reserve adheres to a monetary rule, the economy will be oper-

ating near or at its full-employment output at all times. If policy makers attempt to use stabilization policy to increase real output and employment, their efforts will be largely in vain. As aggregate demand shifts from AD_1 to AD_2 in Figure 16-4a, we get a very modest increase in real output (Q_1 to Q_2) but a large increase in the price level (P_1 to P_2). The economy will pay a high "price" in terms of inflation to realize very modest increases in output and employment.

In comparison, the Keynesian conception indicates that an expansionary policy will have large effects on production and employment and little impact on the price level. This conclusion derives from the assumption that, because of its inherent instability, the private economy may be operating far below its productive potential. Thus in Figure 16-4b we find that the AD_1' to AD_2' increase in aggregate demand will entail a large increase in real output (Q_1' to Q_2') while eliciting only a small price level increase (P_1' to P_2'). To Keynesians, when the economy operates at less than its capacity, large gains in real output and employment can be obtained at only a small inflationary cost.

Once the economy has reached its full-employment level of output, the debate between Keynesians and monetarists largely ends. Both would agree that expansionary stabilization policies will produce demand-pull inflation in the classical range of aggregate supply.

Debate over the Monetary Rule The aggregate demand–aggregate supply model also can help clarify the debate over the monetarists' call for a monetary rule. In Figure 16-5 suppose the aggregate supply curve is vertical and the economy is initially operating at the Q_1 full-employment level of GDP. Observe that the aggregate supply curve shifts rightward from AS to AS', depicting a typical or average annual increase in potential real output. Such increases in aggregate supply result from real factors such as added resources and improved technology.

Monetarists argue that a monetary rule tying increases in the money supply to the typical rightward shift of the aggregate supply curve will ensure that the aggregate demand curve shifts rightward from AD to AD'. As a result, real GDP will rise from Q_1 to Q_2 and

the price level will remain constant at P_1. A monetary rule will allegedly promote price stability.

Keynesians dispute the close predictable link between changes in the money supply and changes in aggregate demand. They see two quite different scenarios.

1 During the period in question, the investment-demand curve (Figure 15-2b) may shift rapidly to the right because of optimistic business expectations. If so, the aggregate demand curve in Figure 16-5 will move to some point rightward of AD' and demand-pull inflation will occur. The monetary rule fails to accomplish its goal of maintaining price stability. According to Keynesians, a contractionary fiscal policy accompanied by a tight money policy can hold the rightward shift of aggregate demand to AD', thereby avoiding the inflation.

2 Suppose that, during the period in question, the investment-demand curve collapses leftward because of pessimistic business expectations. Aggregate demand will *not* increase from AD to AD' in Figure 16-5 and again the monetary rule flunks the price stability test: The price level falls from P_1 to P_2. By increasing aggregate demand to AD', argue Keynesians, an expansionary fiscal policy accompanied by an easy money policy can avoid the deflation. Or, if the price level is inflexible downward at P_1, expansionary stabilization policies can prevent the loss of potential output which otherwise would occur (Q_1Q_2).

FIGURE 16-5 The monetary rule and the aggregate demand–aggregate supply model

Monetarists favor a monetary rule which would fix the increase in the money supply over time to the average increase in real output. An increase in aggregate demand (AD to AD') thus would match an increase in aggregate supply (AS to AS') and the price level would remain constant. Keynesians counter that the monetary rule will not guarantee that aggregate demand will shift from AD to AD'. Because of instability within the private economy, aggregate demand may either shift to the right of AD', creating demand-pull inflation, or fail to shift all the way to AD', resulting in deflation. Hence, Keynesians argue that the discretionary use of stabilization policies is more likely to maintain price stability than is a monetary rule.

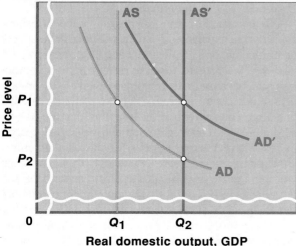

Real domestic output, GDP

QUICK REVIEW 16-2

♪   *In contrast to Keynesians, monetarists believe fiscal policy is weak and ineffectual because of a severe crowding-out effect.*

♪   *Monetarists see the money demand curve as being relatively steep and the investment-demand curve as relatively flat, implying that monetary policy has strong impacts on nominal GDP.*

♪   *Strict monetarists advocate that the Federal Reserve adhere to a monetary rule whereby it expands the money supply at a fixed annual rate approximating the growth of potential output.*

RATIONAL EXPECTATIONS THEORY

Keynesian economics and monetarism do not stand alone in the battle for the minds of economists, policy makers, and students. Developed largely since the mid-1970s, **rational expectations theory** (RET) has taken shape. Although several variants of RET have emerged, including Keynesian ones, we will discuss the version which has come to be associated with the *new classical economics.* (Other aspects of the new classical economics will be discussed in Chapter 17.) Our goal here is to relate RET to the debate over whether stabilization policy should be discretionary, as Keynesians argue, or based on rules, as monetarists contend. But first, some relevant background on RET will be useful.

Rational expectations theory follows the general thrust of economic theory in suggesting that people behave rationally. Market participants gather information and process it intelligently to form expectations about things in which they have a monetary stake. If financial investors, for instance, expect stock market prices to fall, they sell their shares in anticipation of that decline. The increased availability of stock in the market results in an immediate drop in prices offered per share. When consumers learn that a drought is expected to boost food prices, some of them purchase storable food products in advance of the price hike. These expectations cause an increase in market demand which in turn produces an increase in food prices before the food crop is even harvested.

But RET contains a second basic element which gives it its "new classical" flavor. Like the classical economics of Chapter 10, rational expectations theory assumes that all markets—both product and resource—are highly competitive. Therefore, wages and prices are flexible both upward and downward. Indeed, RET goes further by assuming that new information is quickly (in some cases instantaneously) taken into account in the demand and supply curves of such markets so that equilibrium prices and quantities quickly adjust to new events (technological change), market shocks (a drought or collapse of the OPEC oil cartel), or changes in public policies (a shift from tight to easy money). Both product and resource prices are highly flexible and change quickly as consumers, businesses, and resource suppliers change their economic behavior in response to new information.

POLICY FRUSTRATION

RET adherents contend that *the aggregate responses of the public to its expectations will render anticipated discretionary stabilization policies ineffective.* Consider monetary policy. Suppose monetary authorities announce that an easy money policy is in the offing. Purpose: To increase real output and employment. But based on past experience, the public anticipates that this expansionary policy will be accompanied by inflation and takes self-protective actions. Workers will press for higher nominal wages. Businesses will increase the prices of products. Lenders will raise interest rates.

All these responses are designed to prevent inflation from having anticipated adverse effects on the *real* incomes of workers, businesses, and lenders. But collectively this behavior raises wage and price levels and the increase in aggregate expenditures brought about by the easy money policy is completely dissipated in higher prices and wages. Therefore, real output and employment do *not* expand.

In Keynesian terms, the increase in real investment spending which the easy money policy was designed to generate (Figure 15-2) never materializes. The expected rate of net profit on investment remains unchanged in that the price of capital rises in lockstep with the prices of the extra production which the capital allows. Also, the nominal interest rate rises proportionately to the price level, thus leaving the real interest rate unchanged. No increase in real investment spending is forthcoming and no expansion of real GDP occurs.

In terms of the monetarists' equation of exchange, the easy money policy increases M and thus aggregate expenditures, MV. But the public's expectation of inflation elicits an increase in P by a percentage amount equal to the increase in MV. Despite the increased MV, real output, Q, and employment are therefore unchanged.

Note carefully what has occurred here. The decision to increase M was made to increase output and employment. But the public, acting on the expected effects of easy money, has taken actions which have frustrated or nullified the policy's goal. Easy money has been translated into inflation, rather than into desired increases in real output and employment. One can plausibly argue that the economy would have been better off if it had followed a steady money growth policy as suggested by the monetary rule. It was, after all, the government's discretionary easy money policy which prompted unions, businesses, and lenders to raise wages, prices, and interest rates. Why blame these groups for inflation, when the blame should be placed on government?

AD-AS Interpretation

We can better understand the RET contention of policy ineffectiveness by examining Figure 16-6. This diagram restates the classical model from Figure 10-2a. Here we portray the aggregate supply curve as being *vertical.*

Now, once again, assume an expansionary monetary policy shifts the aggregate demand curve rightward from AD_1 to AD_2. Why doesn't this increase in aggregate demand increase real output significantly (as in the Keynesian model of Figure 16-4b) or at least slightly (as in the monetarist model of Figure 16-4a)? According to RET, the answer is that consumers, businesses, and workers will anticipate that an expansionary policy means rising prices and will have built the expected effects into their market decisions concerning product prices, nominal wage rates, nominal interest rates, and so forth. Markets will instantaneously adjust, bringing the price level upward from P_1 to P_2. The economy does not move beyond output Q_1 be-

cause the price level rises by precisely the amount required to cancel any impact the expansionary policy might have had on real output and employment. The *combination* of rational expectations and instantaneous market adjustments—in this case upward wage, price, and interest rate flexibility—dooms the policy change to ineffectiveness. As aggregate demand expands from AD_1 to AD_2, the economy moves upward along the vertical aggregate supply curve directly from point *a* to point *b*. The only result is a higher price level; the *real* incomes of workers, businesses, lenders, and others are all unchanged because they have rationally anticipated the effects of public policy and have incorporated their expectations into market decisions to cause the resulting upshift of nominal wages, nominal profits, and nominal interest rates.

Presumably a decline in aggregate demand from AD_2 to AD_1 would have precisely the opposite effects. Instead of causing unemployment, the economy would move directly along the aggregate supply curve from *b* to *a*.

In the "old" classical theory there would be a period when a decline in aggregate demand would cause a temporary "lapse" from full employment until market adjustments were completed. The economy would first move from *b* to *c* in Figure 16-6, but then in time falling prices and wages would move the economy down AD_1 to full employment at point *a*. But in the RET version of the "new" classical economics, prices would adjust instantaneously to the anticipated policy so that the real output and employment would not deviate from Q_1. In other words, in the "old" classical economics changes in aggregate demand could cause short-run changes in output and employment. But the decision-making process and instantaneous market adjustments of the strict RET form of "new" classical economics preclude this.

Postscript: While RET supports monetarism in arguing for policy rules, it should be stressed that the rationales are quite different. According to the rational expectations theory, policy is ineffective, not because of policy errors or inability to time decisions properly, but because of public reaction to the expected effects of these policies. Monetarists are saying, in effect, that discretionary policy doesn't work because monetary authorities do not have enough information about time lags and such. RET supporters claim that discretionary policy is ineffective because the public has considerable knowledge concerning policy decisions and their impacts.

FIGURE 16-6 Rational expectations and the aggregate demand–aggregate supply model

Rational expectations theory implies that the aggregate supply curve is vertical. Strictly interpreted, the theory suggests that an increase in aggregate demand from, say, AD_1 to AD_2 will immediately result in an offsetting increase in the price level (P_1 to P_2) so that real domestic output will remain unchanged at Q_1. Conversely, a decline in aggregate demand from AD_2 to AD_1 will instantaneously reduce the price level from P_2 to P_1, leaving real domestic output and employment unchanged.

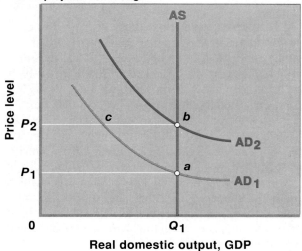

Evaluation

RET has caused a substantial stir in economics over the past two decades. Anyone exposed to RET thinking looks at the macroeconomy from a somewhat different perspective. The appeal of RET stems from at least two considerations. First, as with monetarism, RET is an option which might fill the void left by Keynesian economics' alleged inability to explain and correct by policy the simultaneous inflation and unemployment of the 1970s and early 1980s. Second, RET is strongly rooted in the theory of markets or, in other words, in microeconomics (defined in Chapter 1). Therefore, RET purports to provide linkages between macro- and microeconomics which economists have long sought.

But criticisms of RET are manifold and persuasive enough so that it is fair to say that at this point most economists do *not* subscribe to strict interpretations of RET. Three basic criticisms of RET follow.

1 Behavior Many economists question that people by and large are, or can be, as well-informed as RET assumes. Can we really expect households, businesses, and workers to understand how the economy works and what the impact will be of, say, the Fed's announced decision to increase its *M*2 money target growth rate from $3\frac{1}{2}$ to 5 percent per year? After all, economists who specialize in forecasting frequently mispredict the *direction* of changes in output, employment, and prices, much less correctly indicate the *amounts* by which such variables will change.

RET proponents counter that they are not suggesting that people always make *perfect* forecasts, but rather that they do not make consistent forecasting errors which can be exploited by policy makers. Furthermore, RET theorists point out that key decision-making institutions—large corporations, major financial institutions, and labor organizations—employ full-time economists to help anticipate impacts of newly implemented public policies. It allegedly is impossible to fool important decision-making institutions in the economy on a consistent basis. But the issue of whether people and institutions behave as RET suggests is highly controversial.

2 Sticky Prices A second main criticism of RET is that in reality markets—at least most markets—are *not* highly competitive and therefore do not adjust instantaneously (or even rapidly) to changing market conditions. While the stock market and certain commodity markets experience day-to-day or minute-to-minute price changes, many sellers can control within limits the prices they charge. When demand falls, for example, these sellers resist price cuts so that the impact is on output and employment (see Figure 9-7). This is particularly true of labor markets (Chapter 10) where union and individual contracts keep wages unresponsive to changing market conditions for extended periods. If markets adjust quickly and completely as RET suggests, how does one explain the decade of severe unemployment of the 1930s or the high $7\frac{1}{2}$ to $9\frac{1}{2}$ percent unemployment rates which persisted over the 1981–1984 period?

3 Policy and Stability A final criticism is that there is substantial domestic and international evidence to indicate that, contrary to RET predictions, economic policy does affect real GDP and employment. Thus, in the post-World War II period, when government has more actively invoked stabilization policies, fluctuations in real output have been less than in earlier periods.

ABSORPTION INTO THE MAINSTREAM

George Stigler, a Nobel Prize winning economist and historian of economic theory, stated: "New ideas [in economics] do not lead to the abandonment of the previous heritage; the new ideas are swallowed up by the existing corpus, which is thereafter a little different. And sometimes a little better."[6] As revolutionary as they were, Keynesian ideas themselves did not supplant the existing, micro-based economic heritage. Instead, economics simply incorporated the new macroeconomics within its expanded domain.

The controversies discussed in this chapter have been healthy because they have forced economists to rethink some of the fundamental aspects of macroeconomics. And as is true of many debates, considerable compromise and revision of positions have occurred. Although considerable disagreement remains—for example, the "rules" versus "discretion" debate—contemporary macroeconomics has absorbed several of the fundamental ideas of monetarism and RET. Three examples will help illustrate this point.

[6]George J. Stigler, *Five Lectures on Economic Problems* (London: Longmans, Green, 1949), p. 24.

LAST WORD

"*P*-STAR": A NEW TOOL FOR MONETARY POLICY?

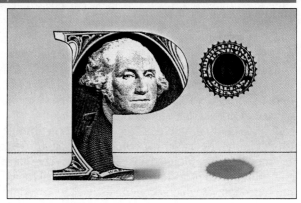

The Federal Reserve has devised an "experimental indicator" of future inflation based on the monetarist's equation of exchange. Will this indicator prove to be a useful tool for setting monetary policy?

An accurate indicator of future inflation has in the past eluded economists and thus made it difficult to formulate monetary policy. Now, however, a group of Federal Reserve economists believe they have found a reliable predictor of long-run inflation. These economists refer to their gauge of future inflation as "*P*-star," for the P^* term in the following equation:

$$P^* = \frac{M2 \times V^*}{Q^*}$$

The P^* in the equation is the predicted future price level. Recall from Chapter 13 that $M2$ is comprised of $M1$ *plus* noncheckable savings deposits, small (less than $100,000) time deposits, money market deposit accounts, and money market mutual fund balances. The V^* term measures the actual annual velocity of $M2$ over the past thirty-three years and Q^* is an estimate of the real potential GDP in the future, assuming the economy grows at a maximum noninflationary rate of 2.5 percent annually.

This formula is merely a variation of the equation of exchange ($MV = PQ$). If we multiply each side of the *P*-star equation by Q^* and reverse sides of the equation, we get: $M2 \times V^* = P^* \times Q^*$. Thus, the only new items here are the $M2$ term and the asterisks (stars). Proponents of the *P*-star theory use $M2$ rather than M (= $M1$) in the equation because their research shows that, although $M2$ velocity varies monthly and yearly, it has been constant at 1.65 over longer periods. This means that $1 dollar of $M2$ will change hands an average of 1.65 times per year over several years.

If, as the Federal Reserve research suggests, the

---

1 Money Matters There are very few economists today who would embrace the extreme Keynesian view that "money doesn't matter." Mainstream economics now incorporates the monetarist view that "money matters" in the economy. This fact is demonstrated by the emphasis we have given monetary policy in this book (Chapters 13–15). Changes in the money supply and interest rates are mainstream tools for pushing the economy toward full employment or pulling it back from expansionary booms and attendant inflation.

During the last half of the 1980s and early 1990s, government largely abandoned the use of discretionary fiscal policy because of large full-employment, or structural, deficits (Figure 12-5). On the one hand, elected officials deemed tax cuts or increases in government expenditure to be economically undesirable

under these conditions. On the other hand, tax increases and reductions in government expenditures were aimed at reducing the deficit, independently of the state of the economy. Thus, Federal Reserve monetary policy, not countercyclical fiscal policy, has recently carried the burden of stabilizing the economy.

Also, the mainstream has incorporated the monetarist precept that excessive growth of the money supply over long periods is a major source of rapid inflation. This consensus view is reflected in our previous discussions of demand-pull inflation (Chapter 8) and maintaining the domestic value of the dollar (Chapter 13).

In summary, mainstream macroeconomics has accepted a major part of monetarism—the importance of the money supply and monetary policy—while rejecting the monetary rule expounded by strict monetarism.

velocity of $M2$ is indeed *constant* over long periods, then the P-star equation can be useful for shaping monetary policy. If the predicted general level of future prices P^* exceeds the current price level P, then the Fed can expect inflation to rise. Thought of differently, $M2$ is growing too quickly relative to potential GDP, eventually causing inflation to increase. To counter this rising inflation the Fed should reduce the growth of $M2$ to boost interest rates and slow spending in the economy. Conversely, if P^* is less than P, the future rate of inflation will be less than the present rate. Depending on the present rate of inflation, an easy money policy might well be in order.

The Federal Reserve cautions that its P-star indicator is experimental and that it will need to test the theory for several years to determine its usefulness as a guide for long-term monetary policy. And, indeed, the new indicator has drawn considerable criticism. Detractors point out that $M2$ velocity is sensitive to changes in the interest rate and in any particular period need not match the *average* of $M2$ velocity over several past decades. They also point out that the growth rate of potential output Q^* need not be constant over time. Finally, research on historical data has found that P^* would have fared no better than other standard forecasting tools in predicting future inflation.

These criticisms aside, the new P-star indicator suggests the Federal Reserve will continue to pay close attention to $M2$ along with $M1$ and interest rates in conducting its monetary policy.

2 Crowding Out and Coordination   Thanks to the monetarists' emphasis on the crowding-out effect, mainstream economists now incorporate this idea within their analysis and are more fully aware of the wisdom of coordinating fiscal and monetary policy. If fiscal policy generates a crowding-out effect of some magnitude which diminishes the effectiveness of fiscal policy, then it is imperative that an appropriate monetary policy be applied simultaneously to negate any potential crowding out of private investment.

3 Expectations and Markets   Mainstream economists and policy makers are much more sensitive than previously as to how expectations might affect the economy and the outcome of a policy change. We have seen in previous chapters that expectations can shift the aggregate expenditures schedule in the Keynesian model and the aggregate demand curve in the AD-AS model. In Chapter 17 we emphasize the effects of expectations on aggregate supply.

Thanks to RET, mainstream economics increasingly searches for the links between microeconomics and macroeconomics. We are increasingly aware that what happens to the aggregate levels of output, employment, and prices depends on how individual product and resource markets function. Indeed, some Keynesians working at the frontier of economic knowledge incorporate rational expectation assumptions directly into their macro models. Unlike the new classical-based RET, however, these models also assume imperfect product and resource markets. Even in the presence of rational expectations, downward price and wage inflexibility lead to Keynesian conclusions: Instability *can* occur in the economy and fiscal and monetary policies *do* work.

Thus, monetarism and RET have both had a discernible impact on macro theory and policy. Disagreement among economists in this case has led to important new insights. An expanded and altered body of widely accepted macroeconomic principles has emerged and is a new base of common agreement among professionals and policy makers. The modern macroeconomics we have studied in previous chapters descends from Keynesian macroeconomics, but indeed it is somewhat different and no doubt better than it was before the monetarist and rational expectations critiques.

CHAPTER SUMMARY

The following statements contrast the strict Keynesian and monetarist positions on a number of critical points.

1 Basic differences: The *Keynesian* view is that the market system is largely noncompetitive and is therefore permissive of macroeconomic instability. An activist stabilization policy, centered on fiscal policy, is required to remedy this shortcoming. The *monetarist* view is that markets are highly competitive and conducive to macroeconomic stability. Monetarists favor a more *laissez faire* policy.

2 Analytical framework: To *Keynesians* the basic determinant of real output, employment, and the price level is the level of aggregate expenditures. Their basic equation is

$C_a + I_g + X_n + G$ = GDP. Components of aggregate expenditures are determined by a wide variety of factors which, for the most part, are unrelated to the supply of money. *Monetarism* focuses on the equation of exchange: $MV = PQ$. Because velocity V is basically stable, the critical determinant of real output and employment (Q) and the price level (P) is the supply of money (M).

3 **Fiscal policy:** The *Keynesian* position is that because **a** government spending is a component of aggregate expenditures and **b** tax changes have direct and dependable effects on consumption and investment, fiscal policy is a powerful stabilization tool. *Monetarists* argue that fiscal policy is weak and uncertain in its effects. Unless financed by an increase in the money supply, deficit spending will raise the interest rate and crowd out private investment spending.

4 **Monetary policy:** *Keynesians* argue that monetary policy entails a lengthy transmission mechanism, involving monetary policy decisions, bank reserves, the interest rate, investment, and finally the nominal GDP. Uncertainties at each step in the mechanism limit the effectiveness and dependability of monetary policy. Money matters, but its manipulation through monetary policy is not as powerful a stabilization device as fiscal policy. Specifically, the combination of a relatively flat demand for money curve and a relatively steep investment-demand curve makes monetary policy relatively ineffective. *Monetarists* believe that the relative stability of V indicates a rather dependable link between the money supply and nominal GDP. However, monetarists think that because of **a** variable time lags in becoming effective and **b** the incorrect use of the interest rate as a guide to policy, the application of discretionary monetary policy to "fine-tune" the economy is likely to fail. In practice, monetary policy has tended to destabilize the economy. Monetarists therefore recommend a monetary rule whereby the money supply is increased in accordance with the long-term growth of real GDP.

The following statements contain the essence of rational expectations theory (RET).

5 RET is based on two basic assumptions: **a** consumers, businesses, and workers understand how the economy works; are able to assess the future effects of policy and other changes; and adjust their decisions to further their own self-interests; **b** markets are highly competitive and prices and wages adjust quickly to changes in demand and supply.

6 RET holds that, when the public reacts to the expected effects of stabilization policy, the effectiveness of such policy will be negated. This theory therefore supports policy rules as opposed to discretionary policy.

7 Several aspects of monetarism and rational expectations have been incorporated into mainstream Keynesian-based macroeconomic analysis.

TERMS AND CONCEPTS

Keynesians	**equation of exchange**	**crowding-out effect**	**rational expectations**
monetarists	**velocity of money**	**monetary rule**	**theory**

QUESTIONS AND STUDY SUGGESTIONS

1 Explain: "The debate between Keynesians and monetarists is an important facet of the larger controversy over the role of government in our lives."

2 State and explain the basic equations of Keynesianism and monetarism. Can you "translate" the Keynesian equation into the monetarist equation?

3 In 1991 the money supply $(M1)$ was approximately $897 billion and the nominal GDP was about $5672 billion. What was the velocity of money in 1991? Figure 16-3 indicates that velocity increased steadily between the mid-1940s and 1982 and then leveled off or declined. Can you think of reasons to explain these trends?

4 What is the transmission mechanism for monetary policy according to **a** Keynesians and **b** monetarists? What significance do the two schools of thought apply to money and monetary policy as a determinant of economic activity? According to monetarism, what happens when the actual supply of money exceeds the amount of money which the public wants to hold?

5 Why do monetarists recommend that a "monetary rule" be substituted for discretionary monetary policy? Explain: "One cannot assess what monetary policy is doing by just looking at interest rates." Indicate how an attempt to stabilize interest rates can be destabilizing to the economy.

6 Answer the ensuing questions on the basis of the following information for a hypothetical economy in year 1: money supply = $400 billion; long-term annual growth of real GDP = 3 percent; velocity = 4. Assume that the banking system initially has no excess reserves and that the reserve requirement is 10 percent. Also, suppose that velocity is constant and that the economy initially is operating at its full employment level of output.

a   What is the level of nominal GDP in year 1 in this economy?

b   Suppose that the Federal Reserve adheres to the monetarist's rule through open-market operations. What amount of bonds will it have to sell to, or buy from, commercial depository institutions or the public between years 1 and 2 to meet its monetary rule?

7   Explain why monetarists assert fiscal policy is weak and ineffective. What specific assumptions do   **a** monetarists and   **b** strict Keynesians make with respect to the shapes of the demand for money and investment-demand curves? Why are the differences significant?

8   Indicate the precise relationship between the demand for money and the velocity of money. Discuss in detail: "The crucial issue separating Keynesians from monetarists is whether or not the demand for money is sensitive to changes in the rate of interest." Explain the Keynesian contention that a change in M is likely to be accompanied by a change in V in the opposite direction.

9   Explain and evaluate these statements in terms of the Keynesian–monetarist controversy:

> **a**   "If the national goal is to raise income, it can be achieved only by raising the money supply."

b   "The size of a Federal budget deficit is not important. What is important is how the deficit is financed."

c   "There is no reason in the world why, in an equation like $MV = PQ$, the V should be thought to be independent of the rate of interest. There is every plausible reason for the velocity of circulation to be a systematic and increasing function of the rate of interest."

d   "Monetarists assume that the PQ side of the equation of exchange is 'passive'; Keynesians assume it is 'active.'"

e   "If expectations are rational, then monetary policy cannot be used to stabilize production and employment. It only determines the price level."

10   Explain how rational expectations might impede discretionary stabilization policies. Relate Chapter 12's Ricardian equivalence theorem to the idea of RET. Do you favor discretionary policies or rules? Justify your position.

11   Use the aggregate demand–aggregate supply model to sketch graphically the   **a** monetarist,   **b** Keynesian, and   **c** rational expectations theories of the macroeconomy. Carefully compare the implications of each for public policy. In what respect, if any, does your RET portrayal differ from the "old" classical model of Figure 10-2a?

C H A P T E R
17

The Inflation–Unemployment Relationship

In Chapter 16 we presented the basic ideas of monetarism and the rational expectations theory (RET) and contrasted them with the mainstream Keynesian perspective. There we saw that, although mainstream economics has incorporated several of the insights of monetarism and RET, disputes remain on such matters as the degree of inherent instability in the economy and the effectiveness of active stabilization policy. This chapter continues our discussion of modern developments and controversies in macroeconomics by examining various explanations of the *simultaneous* occurrence of inflation and rising unemployment. By focusing attention on expectations, this chapter deepens our understanding of how the economy works. Our discussion also becomes more inclusive; in particular, we examine supply-side economics.

 This chapter's specific goals are as follows. First, we derive and examine the so-called *Phillips Curve,* which has been used historically to explain the apparent tradeoff between unemployment and inflation. Next, another theory—the *natural rate hypothesis*—is explored to analyze the economy's encounters with stagflation. Then, we advance our understanding of modern macroeconomics by exploring the distinction between short-run and long-run aggregate supply. This distinction permits us to augment our earlier analysis of demand-pull and cost-push inflation. Finally, policy proposals designed to deal with stagflation are discussed.

THE PHILLIPS CURVE

To start, we present some background which will help us better understand the description and analysis of the Phillips Curve.

Analytical and Historical Background

The Keynesian analysis of Chapters 10 through 12 focused on aggregate expenditures as the fundamental determinant of real domestic output and employment. The simplest Keynesian model implies that the economy may realize *either* unemployment (a recessionary gap) *or* inflation (an inflationary gap), but *not both* unemployment and inflation *simultaneously.*

 In the aggregate demand and supply model, the strict Keynesian analysis assumes a "reverse L"-shaped aggregate supply curve (Figure 10-2b). Over the horizontal (Keynesian) range of the aggregate supply curve, increases in aggregate demand expand real output and employment at a constant price level until full employment is achieved. Further increases in aggregate demand place the economy in the vertical (classical) range of aggregate supply, over which real output will remain constant, but inflation will occur. Presumably some "right" level of aggregate demand which intersects the aggregate supply curve precisely at the full-employment level of output would give us the best of all possible macroeconomic worlds: full employment *and* a stable price level (Q_f in Figure 10-2b).

This simple Keynesian model provides a generally satisfactory explanation of the economy's macro behavior over the four decades prior to the 1970s. The Great Depression, the World War II inflationary boom, and most of the macroeconomic ups and downs in the 1950s and 1960s can be interpreted and understood reasonably well within the context of Keynesian analysis.

But this situation changed in the 1970s. The coexistence of inflation and unemployment—indeed, the simultaneous occurrence of *increasing* unemployment and a *rising* price level—became common and was the central macroeconomic problem of the 1970s and early 1980s. There were two serious stagflationary episodes —1973–1975 and 1978–1980—which were not readily explainable through the simple Keynesian expenditures model. These unusual periods can be better understood, however, by (1) explicitly taking into account the more realistic *upsloping,* or intermediate range, of aggregate supply; and (2) allowing for leftward shifts of the aggregate supply curve.

The Phillips Curve: Concept and Data

The more realistic aggregate supply and demand model is shown in Figure 17-1. Recall that the aggregate demand curve slopes downward as a result of the wealth, interest rate, and foreign purchases effects. With respect to aggregate supply, we know that the three ranges of the curve—the horizontal Keynesian range, the upsloping intermediate range, and the vertical classical range—depend on what happens to production costs as real domestic output expands. The intersection of aggregate demand and aggregate supply determines real domestic output (and employment), on the one hand, and the price level, on the other.

In Figure 17-1 we perform a simple mental experiment. Suppose in a given period aggregate demand expands from AD_0 to AD_2. This shift might result from a change in any one of the determinants of aggregate demand discussed in Chapter 9. Businesses may de-

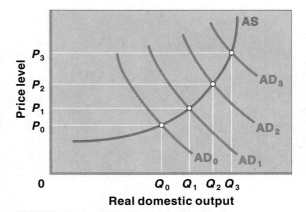

FIGURE 17-1 The effect of changes in aggregate demand on real domestic output and the price level

Comparing the effects of various possible increases in aggregate demand yields the conclusion that the larger the increase in aggregate demand, the greater will be the resulting inflation and the greater the increase in real domestic output. Because real domestic output and the unemployment rate are inversely related, we can generalize that, given aggregate supply, high rates of inflation should be accompanied by low rates of unemployment.

cide to buy more investment goods or government may decide to increase its expenditures to provide more public goods. Whatever the cause of the aggregate demand increase, the price level rises from P_0 to P_2 and real output expands from Q_0 to Q_2.

Now let's compare what would have happened if the increase in aggregate demand had been larger, say, from AD_0 to AD_3. The new equilibrium tells us that both the amount of inflation and the growth of real output would have been greater (and the unemployment rate thereby smaller). Similarly, suppose aggregate demand in our given year had only increased modestly from AD_0 to AD_1. We find that, compared with our original AD_0 to AD_2 shift, the amount of inflation and growth of real output would have been smaller (and the unemployment rate therefore larger).

The generalization from this mental experiment is that *the greater the rate of growth of aggregate demand, the greater will be the resulting inflation and the greater the growth of real domestic output (and the lower the unemployment rate).* Conversely, if aggregate demand grows more slowly, the smaller will be the resulting inflation and the slower the growth of real output (and the higher the unemployment rate). More simply, our generalization is that *high rates of inflation should be accompanied by low rates of unemployment and vice versa.* Figure 17-2a generalizes how the expected relationship should look.

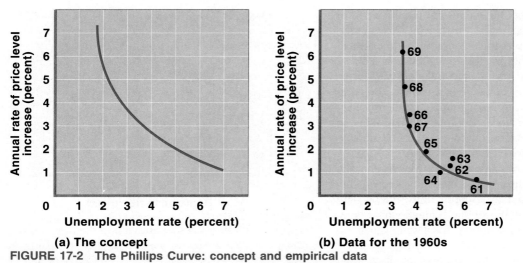

(a) The concept   **(b) Data for the 1960s**

FIGURE 17-2   The Phillips Curve: concept and empirical data

The Phillips Curve purported to show a stable relationship between the unemployment rate
and the rate of inflation. Because this relationship is inverse, there would presumably be a
tradeoff between unemployment and inflation. Data points for the 1960s seemed to confirm
the Phillips Curve concept. (Note: Inflation rates are on a December-to-December basis and
unemployment rates are for all workers, including resident members of the armed forces.)

Do the facts fit the theory? Empirical work by
economists in the late 1950s and 1960s verified the existence of this inverse relationship. It came to be known
as the **Phillips Curve**, named after A. W. Phillips, who
developed this concept in Great Britain. For example,
Figure 17-2b shows the relationship between the unemployment rate and the rate of inflation in the United
States for the 1961–1969 period. The green line generalizing on the data portrays the expected inverse relationship. Based on this kind of empirical evidence
economists believed that a stable, predictable tradeoff
existed between unemployment and inflation. Furthermore, national economic policy was predicated on the
existence of this tradeoff.

Logic of the Phillips Curve

How can the Phillips Curve be explained? What causes
the apparent tradeoff between full employment and
price level stability? Two sets of complementary considerations explain why inflation might occur before
full employment is realized.

1 Labor Market Imbalances   Given our derivation of
the Phillips Curve concept, it is no surprise that one set
of factors underlying the Phillips Curve is that which
Keynesians use to explain the intermediate range of
the aggregate supply curve. Certain imbalances—

"bottlenecks" and structural problems—arise in labor
markets as the economy expands toward full employment. "The" labor market in the United States in reality
comprises an extremely large number of individual
labor markets which are stratified and distinct both
occupationally and geographically. This labor market
diversity suggests the possibility that, as the economy
expands, full employment will *not* be realized simultaneously in each labor market. While full employment
and labor shortages may exist for some occupations
and areas, unemployment will persist for other occupations and regions. This disparity means that in an expanding economy, even though the overall unemployment rate may be, say 6½ or 7 percent, scarcities will
develop for specific kinds of labor and for labor in certain geographic areas, and wage rates of such workers
will rise. Rising wage rates mean higher costs and necessitate higher prices. The net result is rising prices
even though the economy as a whole is still operating
short of full employment.

It is fair to ask why labor market adjustments do
not eliminate these bottlenecks. Why, for example, do
not unemployed laborers become craftworkers? The
answer is that such shifts cannot be made with sufficient speed to eliminate labor market bottlenecks. The
training for a new occupation is costly in terms of both
time and money. Also, even if an unemployed laborer
has the ability, time, and money to acquire new skills

and relocate, an unemployed laborer in Kalamazoo may not be aware of the shortage of skilled craftworkers in Kenosha.

Then, too, artificial restrictions on the shiftability of workers sustain structural imbalances. For example, discrimination based on race, ethnic background, or gender can keep qualified workers from available positions. Similarly, licensing requirements and union restrictions on the number of available apprenticeships inhibit the leveling out of imbalances between specific labor markets.

In brief, labor market adjustments are neither sufficiently rapid nor complete enough to prevent production costs and product prices from rising *before* overall full employment is achieved.

2 Market Power A complementary explanation of the Phillips Curve is based on the assumption that labor unions and big businesses both possess significant monopoly or market power with which to raise wages and prices and that this power becomes easier to exert as the economy approaches full employment.

The "wage-push" inflationary scenario contends that, as the economy moves toward full employment, employers have more difficulty finding qualified new workers, and unions become more aggressive in their wage demands. Increasing prosperity also enhances the willingness of businesses to grant these demands. On the one hand, firms will hesitate to resist union demands and risk a costly strike at the very time business activity is becoming increasingly profitable. On the other hand, economic expansion provides a favorable environment in which monopoly power can be used to pass wage increases on to consumers in the form of higher product prices. The result is leftward *shifts* in the aggregate supply curve and a rising price level as the economy expands toward full employment.

Stabilization Policy Dilemma

If the Phillips Curve remains fixed as in Figure 17-2, policy makers are faced with a dilemma. Traditional fiscal and monetary policies merely alter aggregate demand. They do nothing to correct the labor market imbalances and market power which fuel inflation before full employment is attained. Specifically, the manipulation of aggregate demand through fiscal and monetary measures simply moves the economy *along* the given Phillips Curve. Hence, the expansionary fiscal policy and easy money policy which combine to boost aggregate demand and achieve a lower rate of

unemployment will simultaneously generate a higher rate of inflation. Conversely, a restrictive fiscal policy and a tight money policy can be used to reduce the rate of inflation, but only at the cost of a higher unemployment rate and more forgone production.

Policies to manage aggregate demand can be used to choose a point on the Phillips Curve, but such policies do not improve the "unemployment rate–inflation rate" tradeoff embodied in the curve. Given the presence of the Phillips Curve, it is impossible to achieve "full employment without inflation."

STAGFLATION: A SHIFTING PHILLIPS CURVE?

The concept of a stable Phillips Curve did not hold up very well during the 1970s and 1980s. Events of the 1970s and early 1980s were clearly at odds with the inflation rate–unemployment rate tradeoff embodied in the Phillips Curve. Figure 17-3 enlarges Figure 17-2b by adding data for the 1970–1991 period. The relatively clear-cut inverse relationship of the 1961–1969 period now becomes obscure and highly questionable.

Note in Figure 17-3 that in many years of the 1970s the economy experienced inflation and unemployment or, in a word, **stagflation.** Trace, for example, the data points for the 1972–1974 and 1977–1980 periods. At best, these more recent data suggest that the Phillips Curve shifted to less desirable positions where any given level of unemployment is accompanied by more inflation or, alternatively, each level of inflation is accompanied by more unemployment. The red and blue downsloping lines suggest such rightward shifts. At worst, the data imply there is no dependable tradeoff between unemployment and inflation.

Aggregate Supply Shocks

What caused the stagflation of the 1970s and early 1980s? One answer is that a series of cost shocks or **aggregate supply shocks** occurred. And the fact that these disturbances arose on the cost or supply side makes a difference. Remember that we derived the inverse relationship between the rate of inflation and the unemployment rate shown in Figure 17-2a by changing the level of *aggregate demand* in the intermediate range of the aggregate supply curve in Figure 17-1.

Now look at our cost-push inflation model graphed as Figure 17-4. Here a decrease (leftward shift) of *aggregate supply* causes the unemployment rate and the

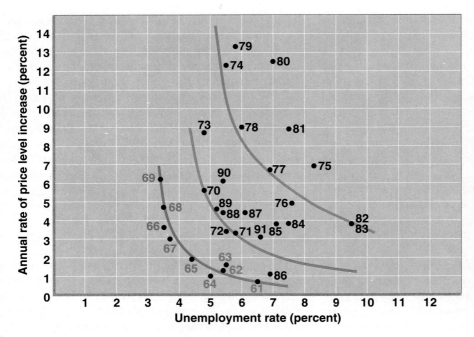

FIGURE 17-3 Inflation rates and unemployment rates, 1961–1991

Data points for the 1961–1991 period suggest no clear relationship between unemployment rates and rates of inflation. This raises questions as to the stability or existence of the Phillips Curve. Some economists think the curve shifted to the right in the 1970s and early 1980s as suggested by the red and blue curves. (Note: Inflation rates are on a December-to-December basis and unemployment rates are for all workers, including resident members of the armed forces.)

price level to vary *directly*. That is, both increase to give us stagflation. This, say Keynesian economists, is essentially what happened during 1973–1975 and again in 1978–1980.

FIGURE 17-4 Aggregate supply and stagflation

According to the mainstream interpretation, in 1973–1975 a series of supply shocks, including sharply increased energy costs, higher agricultural commodity prices, higher import prices, diminishing productivity growth, and inflationary expectations, shifted the aggregate supply curve leftward. The result was stagflation—a higher price level accompanied by a decline in real domestic output. A similar scenario occurred in 1978–1980.

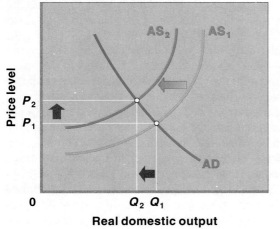

Let's consider the series of more-or-less random shocks which raised unit production costs and shifted the aggregate supply curve leftward, as from AS_1 to AS_2 in Figure 17-4, to generate the Great Stagflation of 1973–1975. More technically, we want to examine how changes in several of the determinants of aggregate supply (Chapter 9) contributed to stagflation.

1 OPEC and Energy Prices First and foremost, the effective functioning of the Organization of Petroleum Exporting Countries (OPEC) oil cartel resulted in a dramatic quadrupling of oil prices. The cost of producing and distributing virtually every good and service thus rose sharply.

2 Agricultural Shortfalls Severe worldwide agricultural shortfalls occurred in 1972 and 1973, particularly in Asia and the Soviet Union. In response, American agricultural exports expanded sharply, reducing domestic supplies of agricultural commodities. The resulting higher prices for raw agricultural products in the United States meant higher costs to the industrial sectors producing food and fiber products. These higher costs were passed on to consumers as higher prices.

3 Depreciated Dollar In the 1971–1973 period, the dollar was reduced in value to achieve greater balance in international trade and finance. Depreciation of the dollar means that it now takes more dollars to buy a unit of foreign money, which increases prices of all American imports. To the extent that American imports are production inputs, unit production costs increase and the aggregate supply curve shifts leftward.

4 Demise of Wage-Price Controls   In the 1971–1974 period the Nixon administration imposed wage and price controls which suppressed inflationary pressures in the economy. When these were abandoned in 1974, both businesses and input suppliers pushed up their prices rapidly to recoup the price increases they had been forced to forgo during the control period. This upsurge increased unit costs and product prices.

5 Productivity Decline   The stagflation episodes of the 1970s and early 1980s were not due solely to the four rather dramatic supply shocks just discussed. More subtle considerations involving productivity and expectations were also at work. The rate of growth of labor productivity—that is, the efficiency of labor— began to decline in the mid-1960s and continued to fall more-or-less persistently throughout the 1970s. This decline in the growth rate of output per worker-hour increased unit production costs. This is because an increase in unit labor costs (that is, labor cost per unit of output) approximates the difference between the increase in nominal-wage rates and the increase in labor productivity. More precisely:

$$\begin{matrix}\text{Percentage} \\ \text{change in} \\ \text{unit labor} \\ \text{costs}\end{matrix} \approx \begin{matrix}\text{percentage} \\ \text{change in} \\ \text{nominal-wage} \\ \text{rates}\end{matrix} - \begin{matrix}\text{percentage} \\ \text{change in} \\ \text{labor} \\ \text{productivity}\end{matrix} \quad (1)$$

For example, if hourly nominal wages are currently $5.00 and a worker produces 10 units per hour, unit labor costs will be $.50.

If nominal wages increase by 10 percent to $5.50 per hour and productivity also increases by 10 percent to 11 units per hour, then unit labor costs will be unchanged. That is, $5.00/10 = $5.50/11 = $.50. In our equation, 10 percent (change in nominal wages) *minus* 10 percent (change in productivity) *equals* no increase in unit labor costs.

Similarly, if nominal wages were to rise by 10 percent and labor productivity does not rise at all, unit labor costs would rise by 10 percent. That is, if the wage rate was $5.00 initially and output per hour was 10 units, labor costs would be $.50. But with wages now

$5.50 and output still at 10 units per hour, unit labor costs would now be $.55, which is a 10 percent increase. In our equation 10 percent *minus* zero percent *equals* a 10 percent increase in unit labor costs. Since labor costs are 70 to 80 percent of total production costs, product prices rise roughly in accord with increases in unit labor costs.

What we should consider from our simple equation when we think about stagflation is that, given the size of nominal-wage increases, a decline in the rate of growth of labor productivity will boost unit production costs and contribute to a leftward shift in the aggregate supply curve.

6 Inflationary Expectations and Wages   The inflation of the 1970s had its genesis in the inflation of the late 1960s which was caused by expanded military spending on the Vietnam war. By the early 1970s workers had been exposed to a period of accelerating inflation. As a result, nominal-wage demands of labor began to include the expectation of an increasing rate of inflation. Most employers, expecting to pass on higher wage costs in this context of mounting inflation, did not resist labor's demands for larger and larger increases in nominal wages. These nominal-wage increases would increase unit production costs and shift aggregate supply from AS_1 to AS_2 in Figure 17-4.

We can incorporate both **inflationary expectations** *and* declining labor productivity in equation (1) as causes of stagflation. If nominal wages are being pushed up at an accelerating rate and the growth rate of labor productivity is simultaneously falling, there will be a double impetus for unit labor costs—and ultimately product prices—to rise.

Synopsis   All these factors combined in the 1970s to adversely shift the aggregate supply curve to yield the worst possible macroeconomic world—falling output and rising unemployment combined with a rising price level (Figure 17-4). The numerical dimensions of the 1973–1975 stagflation were remarkable. The unemployment rate shot up from 4.8 percent in 1973 to 8.3 percent in 1975, contributing to a $47 billion *decline* in real GDP. In the same period the price level increased by 21 percent.

Like a bad dream, the 1973–1975 stagflation scenario essentially recurred in 1978–1980. In this instance an enormous $21 per barrel increase in oil prices was imposed by OPEC. Coupled with rising prices of agricultural commodities, the price level rose by 26 percent over the 1978–1980 period, while unemployment jumped from 6.0 to 7.5 percent. Real GDP grew by a very modest 2 percent annual rate over the three-year period.

Regardless of the causes of stagflation, it was clear to most economists in the 1970s that the Phillips Curve did not represent a stable relationship. There was evidence that adverse (leftward) shifts in aggregate supply were at work, which seemed to explain those unhappy occasions when the inflation rate and the unemployment rate increased simultaneously. To many economists the experience during the 1970s and early 1980s suggested that the Phillips Curve was shifting to the right and confronting the economy with higher rates of inflation and unemployment than previously.

Stagflation's Demise: 1982–1989

A return look at Figure 17-3 reveals a rather dramatic inward collapse of the inflation-unemployment points between 1982 and 1989. By 1989 the stagflation of the 1970s and early 1980s had nearly subsided. One important precursor to this favorable trend was the deep recession of 1981–1982, largely caused by an extremely tight money policy. The recession propelled the unemployment rate to 9.5 percent in 1982. Under conditions of extreme labor market slack, workers accepted smaller increases in their nominal wages—or in some cases wage reductions—to preserve their jobs. Firms, in turn, were forced to restrain price hikes to maintain their relative shares of a greatly diminished market.

Other significant factors were also at work. Intensive foreign competition throughout 1982–1989 suppressed wage and price hikes in several basic industries such as automobiles and steel. Deregulation of the airline and trucking industries also resulted in wage reductions or so-called "wage-givebacks." A decline in OPEC's monopoly power produced a stunning fall in the price of oil and its derivative products.

All of these factors combined to reduce unit production costs and hence shifted the aggregate supply curve rightward (as from AS_2 to AS_1 in Figure 17-4). Meanwhile, a record-long peacetime economic expansion created 17 million new jobs between 1982 and 1989. The previously high unemployment rate therefore fell dramatically from 9.5 percent in 1983 to 6.1 percent in 1987 and to 5.2 percent in 1989. Figure 17-3 reveals that the inflation-unemployment points for 1987–1989 are closer to the points associated with the Phillips Curve for the 1960s than are points in the late 1970s and early 1980s.

Like the situations in 1973–1974 and 1979–1980, unemployment and inflation moved in the *same* direction during some years within the 1983–1989 period. That is, unemployment and inflation did *not* move in opposite directions as implied by the Phillips Curve for the 1960s. During the Great Stagflation of the mid-1970s, inflation and unemployment simultaneously *increased;* during some of the years of the economic expansion of 1983–1989 inflation and unemployment simultaneously *declined.*

THE NATURAL RATE HYPOTHESIS

The standard explanation for the scattering of inflation rate-unemployment points to the right of the 1960s Phillips Curve is that a series of supply shocks shifted the aggregate supply curve *leftward,* moving the Phillips Curve rightward and upward as suggested in Figure 17-3. The inward collapse of inflation rate-unemployment points in the 1980s came about because of *rightward* shifts of the aggregate supply curve. This Keynesian view holds that a tradeoff between the inflation rate and the unemployment rate still exists, but that changes in aggregate supply may change the menu of inflation and unemployment choices—that is, may shift the Phillips Curve itself—during some abnormal periods.

A second explanation of simultaneously higher rates of unemployment and inflation, the **natural rate hypothesis,** is associated with new classical thinking. It questions the very existence of the concept of a downsloping Phillips Curve as portrayed in Figure 17-2. This view concludes that the economy is stable in the long run at the natural rate of unemployment. We know from Chapter 8 that the natural rate of unemployment is the rate achieved when the labor market experiences neither a shortage nor a surplus of workers. Alternatively stated, it is the rate of unemployment which exists when cyclical unemployment is zero.

According to the natural rate hypothesis, misguided full-employment policies, based on the incorrect assumption that a stable Phillips Curve *does* exist, will result in an increasing rate of inflation. The natural rate hypothesis has its empirical roots in Figure 17-3, where one can argue that a vertical line located at a presumed 6 percent natural rate of unemployment summarizes the inflation-unemployment "relationship" better than the traditional downsloping Phillips Curve. According to the natural rate hypothesis, any particular rate of inflation is compatible with the economy's natural rate of unemployment.

There are two variants of the natural rate interpretation of the inflation-unemployment data points shown in Figure 17-3: the adaptive expectations and rational expectations theories.

Adaptive Expectations Theory

One variant of the natural rate hypothesis is the **theory of adaptive expectations.** This theory is so named because it assumes that people form their expectations of future inflation on the basis of previous and present rates of inflation and only gradually change their expectations as experience unfolds. The adaptive expectations theory was advanced and popularized by Milton Friedman and is consistent with both the traditional monetarist and emerging new classical perspectives.

The adaptive expectations theory holds that there may be a short-run tradeoff between inflation and unemployment, but in the long run no such tradeoff exists. Any attempt to reduce the unemployment rate below the natural rate sets in motion forces which destabilize the Phillips Curve and shift it rightward. Hence, the adaptive expectations view distinguishes between a "short-run" and "long-run" Phillips Curve.

Short-Run Phillips Curve Consider Phillips Curve PC_1 in Figure 17-5. Suppose that the economy initially is experiencing a mild 3 percent rate of inflation and a natural rate of unemployment, which is assumed to be 6 percent. According to the adaptive expectations theory, such short-run curves as PC_1 exist because the actual rate of inflation is not always the same as the expected rate.

Establishing an additional point on Phillips Curve PC_1 will help clarify this notion. We begin at point a_1, where we assume that nominal wages are set on the expectation that the 3 percent rate of inflation will continue. But now suppose that government mistakenly judges the full-employment unemployment rate to be 4 percent instead of 6 percent. This misjudgment might occur because the economy temporarily achieved a 4 percent rate of unemployment in an earlier period. To achieve the targeted 4 percent rate of unemployment, suppose government invokes expansionary fiscal and monetary policy.

The resulting increase in aggregate demand boosts the rate of inflation to 6 percent. Given the level of money or nominal wages, *which were set on the expectation that the rate of inflation would continue to be 3*

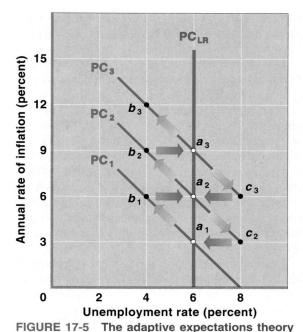

FIGURE 17-5   The adaptive expectations theory
The expansion of aggregate demand may temporarily increase profits and therefore output and employment (a_1 to b_1). But nominal wages will soon rise, reducing profits and thereby negating the short-run stimulus to production and employment (b_1 to a_2). Consequently, in the long run there is no tradeoff between the rates of inflation and unemployment; the long-run Phillips Curve is vertical. This suggests that Keynesian expansionary policies will generate increasing inflation rather than a lower rate of unemployment. On a more positive note, it also suggests that restrictive Keynesian stabilization policies can reduce inflation without creating permanent increases in unemployment.

percent, the higher product prices raise business profits. Firms respond to expanded profits by increasing output and therefore hiring more workers. In the short run, the economy moves to b_1, which, in contrast with a_1, entails a lower rate of unemployment (4 percent) and a higher rate of inflation (6 percent). This movement from a_1 to b_1 is generally consistent with our earlier interpretation of the Phillips Curve. Presumably, the economy has accepted some inflation as the "cost" of achieving a reduced level of unemployment. But the natural rate theorists interpret the movement from a_1 to b_1 quite differently. They see it as only a temporary manifestation of the following principle: *When the actual rate of inflation is higher than expected, the unemployment rate will fall.*

Long-Run Vertical Phillips Curve Point b_1 is *not* a stable equilibrium position, according to the adaptive expectations theory. Workers will recognize their nominal wages have not been rising as fast as inflation. They will therefore demand and receive nominal wage increases to restore their lost purchasing power. But, as nominal wages rise to restore the previous level of real wages existing at a_1, business profits will fall to their earlier level. This profit reduction means that the original motivation of businesses to increase output and employ more workers will disappear.

Unemployment then returns to its natural level at point a_2. Note, however, that the economy is now faced with a higher actual *and* expected rate of inflation—6 percent rather than 3 percent. Because the higher level of aggregate demand which originally moved the economy from a_1 to b_1 still exists, the inflation it engendered persists.

In view of the now-higher 6 percent expected rate of inflation, the short-run Phillips Curve shifts upward from PC_1 to PC_2. In brief, an "along-the-Phillips Curve" kind of movement from a_1 to b_1 on PC_1 is merely a short-run or transient phenomenon. In the long run—after nominal wages catch up with price level increases—unemployment will return to the natural rate at a_2 and a new short-run Phillips Curve PC_2 will exist at the higher expected rate of inflation.

This process may now be repeated. Government may reason that certain extraneous, chance events have frustrated its expansionist policies, and will try again. Policy measures are used to increase aggregate demand and the scenario repeats itself. Prices rise momentarily ahead of nominal wages, profits expand, and output and employment increase (a_2 to b_2). But, in time, workers now press for, and are granted, higher nominal wages to restore their level of real wages. Profits, therefore, fall to their original level, causing employment to gravitate back to the normal rate at a_3. Government's "reward" for trying to force the actual rate of unemployment below the natural rate is the perverse one of a still higher (9 percent) rate of inflation.

If we conceive of a_1b_1, a_2b_2, and a_3b_3 as a series of short-run Phillips Curves, the adaptive expectations theory says that, ironically, governmental attempts through policy to move along the short-run Phillips Curve (a_1 to b_1 on PC_1) *cause* the curve to shift to a *less* favorable position (PC_2, then PC_3, and so on). A stable Phillips Curve with the dependable series of unemployment rate–inflation rate tradeoffs which it implies does not exist.

There is, in fact, no *stable* rate of inflation (such as 6 percent at b_1) which can be accepted as the "cost" of reduced unemployment in the *long run*. To keep unemployment at the desired 4 percent level, government must *continually* expand the level of aggregate demand. The "cost" of a 4 percent unemployment rate is *not* a constant 6 percent annual rate of inflation at b_1, but rather an increasing rate of inflation, that is, an annual rate of inflation that increases from 6 percent (b_1) to 9 percent (b_2) to 12 percent (b_3), and so forth. Because accelerating inflation is unacceptable, the *long-run relationship* between unemployment and inflation is shown by the vertical line through a_1, a_2, and a_3. Any stable rate of inflation is consistent with the natural rate of unemployment. The Phillips Curve tradeoff portrayed earlier in Figure 17-2 does not exist.

Disinflation　This adaptive expectations scenario can be employed to explain **disinflation**—reductions in the rate of inflation—as well as inflation itself. Suppose in Figure 17-5 the economy is at point a_3 where the inflation rate is 9 percent and the unemployment rate is 6 percent. A significant decline in aggregate demand such as that associated with the 1981–1982 recession can be expected to reduce inflation below the 9 percent expected rate, say, to 6 percent. Business profits will fall because product prices are rising less rapidly than wages. The nominal wage increases, remember, were set on the assumption that the 9 percent rate of inflation would continue. In response to the profit decline, firms will reduce their employment and consequently the unemployment rate will rise. The economy will temporarily slide downward from point a_3 to c_3 along short-run Phillips Curve PC_3. According to the natural rate theorists, *when the actual rate of inflation is lower than the expected rate, the unemployment rate will rise.*

Firms and workers will eventually adjust their expectations to the new 6 percent rate of inflation and thus newly negotiated wage increases will decline. Profits will be restored, employment will rise, and the unemployment rate will return to its natural rate of 6 percent at point a_2. Because the expected rate of inflation is now 6 percent, the short-run Phillips Curve PC_3 will shift leftward to PC_2.

If aggregate demand falls further, the scenario will continue. Inflation will decline from 6 percent to, say, 3 percent, moving the economy from a_2 to c_2 along PC_2. The reason once again is that the lower-than-expected rate of inflation (lower prices) has squeezed profits and reduced employment. But, in the long run, firms can be expected to respond to the lower profits by reducing their nominal wage increases. Profits will therefore be restored and unemployment will return to its natural rate at a_1 as the short-run Phillips Curve moves from PC_2 to PC_1. Once again, the long-run Phillips Curve is vertical at the natural rate of unemployment.

To repeat: According to the adaptive expectations theory, any particular rate of inflation is compatible in the long run with the natural rate of unemployment.

Rational Expectations Theory

The adaptive expectations theory assumes increases in nominal wages lag behind increases in the price level. This lag gives rise to *temporary* increases in profits which *temporarily* stimulate employment.

The **rational expectations theory**—introduced in Chapter 16—is the second variant of the natural rate hypothesis. This theory contends that businesses, consumers, and workers generally understand how the economy functions and effectively use available information to protect or further their own self-interests. In particular, people understand how government policies will affect the economy and anticipate these impacts in their own decision making.

In this context suppose that, when government invokes expansionary policies, workers anticipate inflation and a subsequent decline in real wages. Therefore, they incorporate this expected inflation into their nominal wage demands. If we assume workers correctly and fully anticipate the amount of price inflation and adjust their current nominal wage demands accordingly to maintain their real wages, then even the temporary increases in profits, output, and employment will *not* occur. Instead of the temporary increase in employment shown by the movement from a_1 to b_1 in Figure 17-5, the movement will be directly from a_1 to a_2. Fully anticipated inflation by labor means there will be no short-run decline in unemployment. Price inflation, fully anticipated in the nominal-wage demands of workers, will generate a vertical line through a_1, a_2 and a_3 in Figure 17-5.

The policy implication is this: Keynesian measures to achieve a misspecified full-employment rate of unemployment will generate an increasing rate of inflation, not a lower rate of unemployment. Note, incidentally, that the adaptive and rational expectations theories are consistent with the conservative philosophy that government's attempts to do good deeds typically fail and at considerable cost to society. In this instance the "cost" is accelerating inflation. Indeed, an activist fiscal policy will be ineffective in achieving its goals.

Changing Interpretations

We therefore see that interpretations of the Phillips Curve have changed dramatically over the past three decades. The original idea of a stable tradeoff between unemployment and inflation gave way to the adaptive expectations view that, while a short-run trade-off existed, no such tradeoff occurred in the long run. The more controversial rational expectations theory stresses that macroeconomic policy is ineffective because it is anticipated by workers. The conclusion is that there does not even exist a short-run tradeoff between unemployment and inflation. Taken together, the natural rate hypotheses (adaptive and rational expectations theories) conclude that demand-management policies cannot influence real output and employment in the long run, but only the price level. This conclusion is clearly contrary to predictions of the original Phillips Curve (Figure 17-2b).

Which view is correct? Does an inverse relationship exist between the unemployment rate and the inflation rate as the original Phillips Curve implied? Or is there no long-run tradeoff as the natural rate theory contends? Perhaps the safest statement is that most economists accept the notion of a short-run tradeoff while recognizing that in the long run such a tradeoff is much less likely. They also believe aggregate supply shocks can cause stagflation. The episodes of rising unemployment and inflation during the 1970s and early 1980s were *not* exclusively the results of misguided stabilization policies.

QUICK REVIEW 17-1

✦ **The original Phillips Curve showed an apparently stable, inverse relationship between annual unemployment rates and inflation rates over a period of years.**

✦ **Stagflation occurred in 1973–1975 and 1978–1980 and produced Phillips Curve data points above and to the right of the Phillips Curve for the 1960s.**

✦ **The following aggregate supply shocks caused stagflation during the 1970s and early 1980s: a OPEC price hikes, b poor agricultural harvests, c rapid dollar depreciation, d the demise of wage-price controls, e a productivity decline, and f inflationary expectations.**

✦ **According to the natural rate hypothesis, the economy automatically gravitates to its natural rate of unemployment; therefore the Phillips Curve is vertical in the long run.**

AGGREGATE SUPPLY REVISTED

The distinction between short-run Phillips Curves and the long-run vertical Phillips Curve has stimulated important new thinking about aggregate supply.

Recall from Figures 17-1 and 17-2a that we derived the Phillips Curve by shifting aggregate demand rightward along a supposedly *stable* aggregate supply curve. Firms responded to the increasing price level by producing more output and increasing their employment. Thus, the unemployment rate fell as the price level increased.

The natural rate theory correctly suggests, however, that the aggregate supply curve in Figure 17-1 is stable only so long as nominal wages do not increase in response to the rise in the price level. Once workers fully recognize that the rise in the price level has occurred, they will demand and receive higher nominal wages to restore their real wages. An increase in nominal wages, other things being equal, will shift the aggregate supply curve leftward. That is, a change in nominal wages is one of the determinants of aggregate supply (Table 9-2).

The simplified aggregate supply curve—with its Keynesian, intermediate, and classical ranges—therefore needs to be refined to account for changes in nominal wages *induced* by changes in the price level. Stated differently, we must distinguish between short-run and long-run aggregate supply.

Definitions: Short Run and Long Run

As used here, *the short run is a period in which input prices—particularly nominal wages—remain fixed in the presence of a change in the price level.* There are two basic reasons why input prices may remain constant for a time even though the price level has changed.
1 Workers may not immediately be aware of the existence of a higher or lower price level. If so, they will not know their real wages have changed and will not adjust their wage demands accordingly.
2 Many employees are hired under conditions of fixed-wage contracts. Unionized employees, for example, receive nominal wages based on the terms of their collective bargaining agreements. Additionally, most managers and many professionals receive set salaries established in annual contracts.

The upshot of the lack of information about the price level and the existence of labor contracts is that changes in the price level normally do not immediately change nominal wages.

The long run is a period in which input prices (wages) are fully responsive to changes in the price level. Given sufficient time, workers can gain full information about price level changes and consequently can ascertain the effects on their real wage. Workers will be aware that a price level increase has reduced their real wage and that a price level decline has increased their real wage. More importantly, workers and employers in the long run are freed from their existing labor contracts and can negotiate changes in nominal wages and salaries.

With these definitions in mind, let's further embellish Chapter 9's discussion of aggregate supply.

Short-Run Aggregate Supply

Consider the **short-run aggregate supply curve** shown as AS_1 in Figure 17-6a. This curve is constructed on the basis of two assumptions: (1) the initial price level is P_1, and (2) nominal wages have been established on the expectation that the price level P_1 will persist. Observe from point a_1 and the vertical white line intersecting it that the economy is operating at its potential level of real output Q_p at price level P_1. This potential real output is the real production forthcoming when the economy is operating at its natural rate of unemployment.

Now let's determine the consequence of changes in the price level by initially examining an *increase* in the price level from P_1 to P_2. Because nominal wages are fixed in the short run, the higher product prices associated with P_2 will enhance profits. In response to the higher profits, producers will increase their output from Q_p to Q_2 as indicated by the move from a_1 to a_2 on AS_1. Observe that at Q_2 the economy is operating beyond its potential output. This is made possible by extending work-hours of part-time and full-time workers, enticing new workers such as homemakers and retirees into the labor force, and hiring and training the structurally unemployed. Thus, the nation's unemployment rate will decline below its natural rate.

How will producers respond when there is a *decrease* in the price level from P_1 to P_3? Firms will discover their profits have diminished or disappeared. After all, product prices have dropped while nominal wages have not. Producers therefore will reduce employment and production and, as revealed by point a_3, real output will fall to Q_3. This decline in real output will be accompanied by an unemployment rate greater than the natural rate.

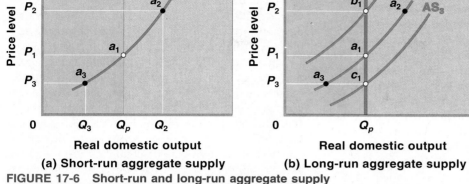

FIGURE 17-6   Short-run and long-run aggregate supply

In the short run (a), input prices such as nominal wages are assumed to be fixed based on price level P_1. An increase in the price level will bolster profits and entice firms to expand real output. Alternatively, a decrease in the price level will reduce profits and real output. The short-run AS curve therefore slopes upward. In the long run (b), a price level rise will increase nominal wages and thus shift the short-run AS curve leftward. Conversely, a decrease in the price level will reduce nominal wages and shift the short-run AS curve rightward. The long-run AS curve therefore may be thought of as being vertical.

Long-Run Aggregate Supply

By definition, nominal wages are assumed to be fully responsive in the long run to changes in the price level. What are the implications of this assumption for aggregate supply?

In Figure 17-6b again assume that the economy initially is at point a_1 (P_1 and Q_p). Our previous discussion indicated that an *increase* in the price level from P_1 to P_2 will move the economy from point a_1 to a_2 along the short-run aggregate supply curve AS_1. In the long run, workers will discover that their real wages have fallen as a result of this increase in the price level. They will therefore presumably demand and receive higher nominal wages to restore their previous level of real wages. The short-run aggregate supply curve will shift leftward from AS_1 to AS_2, and will now reflect the *higher* price level P_2 and the expectation that P_2 will continue. Figure 17-6b shows that the leftward shift in the short-run aggregate supply to curve AS_2 will move the economy from a_2 to b_1. Real output will fall to its potential level and the unemployment rate will return to its natural rate.

Conversely, a *decrease* in the price level from P_1 to P_3 in Figure 17-6b will produce an opposite scenario. As previously noted, the economy will initially move from point a_1 to point a_3, at which profits will be squeezed or eliminated because prices have fallen and nominal

wages have not. But this is simply the short-run response. Given enough time, the lower price level P_3, which has increased the real wage, together with the higher unemployment associated with the reduction in real output, will diminish nominal wages. We know that sufficiently lower nominal wages will shift the short-run aggregate supply curve rightward from AS_1 to AS_3 and real output will return to Q_p at point c_1.

By tracing a line between the long-run equilibrium points b_1, a_1, and c_1, a **long-run aggregate supply curve** appears. Observe that it is vertical at the potential level of output, Q_p.

Keynesian versus New Classical Policy Implications

The conception of aggregate supply presented in Figure 17-6 implies that wage and price flexibility will drive the economy toward full employment. For this reason this model is closely identified with the natural rate hypothesis, or **new classical economics.**

According to new classical thinking, fully *anticipated* price level changes do *not* change the level of real output because nominal wages immediately change in the same direction and by the same percentage as the price level. Only the long-run aggregate supply curve is relevant when price level changes are anticipated. For this reason, government stabilization policies allegedly fail to affect real output. This is simply the rational expectations view.

To be sure, *unanticipated* changes in the price level—so called **price-level surprises**—*do* produce short-term fluctuations in real output. These temporary changes in real output, say the new classical economists, result from unanticipated changes in aggregate demand and supply. In other words, temporary changes in real output arise from aggregate demand or supply shocks.

Example: Suppose an unanticipated increase in foreign demand for American goods increases our price level. As a consequence, the economy will move along its short-run aggregate supply curve to a higher level of real output. But in the long run, nominal wages and other input prices will increase in response to the higher price level and the economy will return to its potential real output.

New classical generalization: *Although price level surprises may create short-run macroeconomic instability, the economy is stable in the long run at the full-employment level of output.*

Modern Keynesians dismiss the assumption of highly competitive markets and instantaneously adjusting prices and wages which underlie the RET aspect of new classical economics. But they do not quarrel with the distinction between short- and long-run aggregate supply. Instead, they contend that experience has shown that the adjustment of nominal wages critical to the vertical long-run aggregate supply curve is painfully slow. Because nominal wages tend to be inflexible downward, years may go by before the economy moves from a point such as a_3 to c_1 in Figure 17-6b. Therefore, the assumption of a fixed aggregate supply curve underlying the analysis in previous chapters is not only useful for simplifying complex theory, but realistic for all but very long periods of time. Moreover, modern Keynesians continue to call for active use of stabilization policies to reduce the high costs of severe unemployment or inflation. New classical economists, on the other hand, view the long run as either instantaneous or relatively short; therefore they favor a hands-off policy by government to permit the economy to adjust *itself* to the full-employment level of real output.

DEMAND-PULL AND COST-PUSH INFLATION

We now can apply our new tools of short-run and long-run aggregate supply to better understand demand-pull and cost-push inflation.

Demand-Pull Inflation

Demand-pull inflation occurs when an increase in aggregate demand pulls up the price level. We earlier depicted this type of inflation by shifting an aggregate demand curve rightward along a stable aggregate supply curve (Figure 9-6b and 9-6c).

In our more detailed version of aggregate supply, however, an increase in the price level will eventually result in an increase in nominal wages and thus a leftward shift of the short-run aggregate supply curve itself. This is shown in Figure 17-7a (Key Graph). Initially suppose the price level is P_1, determined at the intersection of aggregate demand curve AD_1 and aggregate supply curve AS_1. The aggregate supply curve AS_1 is a short-run curve based on the nominal wages associated with the price level P_1. These nominal wages were set on the expectation that P_1 would persist. Observe that at a the economy is achieving its potential real output Q_p.

Now consider the effects of an increase in aggregate demand as shown by the rightward shift from AD_1 to AD_2 in Figure 17-7a. This shift in aggregate demand can result from any one of a number of factors, including an increase in the money supply, an increase in investment spending, and so forth (Table 9-1). Whatever its cause, the increase in aggregate demand increases the price level from P_1 to P_2 and expands output to Q_2 at point b.

So far, nothing new has been said. But now we must ask what will happen to the short-run aggregate supply curve once workers realize their real wages have fallen and once their existing contracts have expired? Our answer is that nominal wages will rise, and as they do, the short-run aggregate supply curve will shift leftward, eventually from AS_1 to AS_2. Consequently, the price level will further increase to P_3 at point c and the equilibrium level of output will return to its potential level Q_p.

Generalization: *In the short run, demand-pull inflation will drive up the price level and increase real output; in the long run, only the price level will rise.* In the long run, the increase in aggregate demand has only moved the economy along its vertical aggregate supply curve AS_{LR}.

Cost-Push Inflation

Cost-push inflation arises from factors which increase the cost of production at each price level—that is, shift the aggregate supply curve leftward—and therefore increase the price level (Figure 9-8). But our previous analysis has, in effect, considered only short-

KEY GRAPH

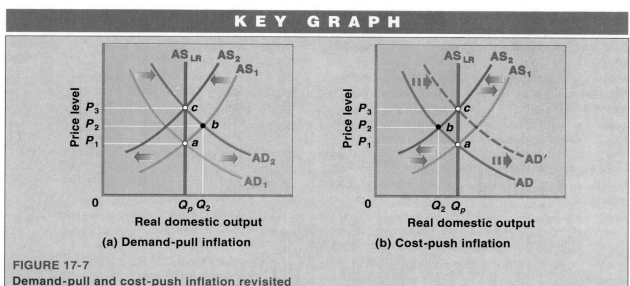

FIGURE 17-7

Demand-pull and cost-push inflation revisited

In (a) an increase in AD will drive up the price level and increase real output in the short run. But, in the long run, nominal wages will rise and AS will shift leftward. Real output will return to its previous level and the price level will rise still further. In (b) cost-push inflation occurs when AS shifts leftward. If government counters the decline in real output by increasing AD to the broken line, the price level will rise even further. On the other hand, if government allows a recession to occur, nominal wages eventually will fall and the AS curve will shift back rightward to it's original location. Observe that the long-run AS curves are vertical in both (a) and (b).

run aggregate supply. We must now examine the cost-push theory in its long-run context.

Analysis Consider Figure 17-7b in which the economy is initially assumed to be operating at the P_1 and Q_p levels of price and output at point *a*. Now suppose that, by exerting monopoly power, labor unions secure nominal wage gains in excess of advances in labor productivity. Moreover, suppose that many nonunion employers, wishing to deter unionism in their own enterprises, respond by increasing the nominal wages they pay to keep them proportionate to union wage scales. As wages rise, the short-run aggregate supply curve shifts leftward, as depicted by the move from AS_1 to AS_2. Consequently, the price level rises from P_1 to P_2, as shown by point *b*. In this case, aggregate supply curve AS_2 has resulted from a wage rate hike and therefore is the *cause* of the price level rise from P_1 to P_2. The shift of the aggregate supply curve from AS_1 to AS_2 is not a *response* to a price level increase as it was in our previous discussions of short versus long-run aggregate supply.

Policy Dilemma Cost-push inflation creates a major dilemma for policy makers. If aggregate demand in Figure 17-7b remains at AD, real output will decline

from Q_p to Q_2. Government can counter this recession and its attendant unemployment by using stabilization policies to increase aggregate demand to AD′. But there is a potential policy trap ready to snare its victim. An increase in aggregate demand to AD′ will further aggravate inflation by increasing the price level from P_2 to P_3 at point *c*.

And the P_2 to P_3 increase in the price level is not likely to be a one-time boost because wage earners will respond to their decline in real wages by seeking and receiving increases in nominal wages. If successful, the higher nominal wages will cause a further increase in production costs. This will shift the short-run aggregate supply curve to a position to the left of AS_2. This (unshown) leftward shift of the short-run aggregate supply curve is in *response* to the higher price level P_3 which was caused by the rightward shift of aggregate demand to AD′. You may wish to draw in this leftward shift of AS to convince yourself that it will regenerate the stagflation problem. In brief, government will have to increase aggregate demand once again to restore the Q_p level of output. But if government does so, the scenario may simply repeat itself.

The point is that leftward shifts in the short-run aggregate supply curve may occur when government applies expansionary demand management policy to alleviate output reductions resulting from cost-push inflation. These shifts in short-run aggregate supply frustrate attainment of full employment and increase the price level.

Alternatively, suppose that government recognizes this policy trap and decides *not* to increase aggregate demand from AD to AD′. Instead, government implicitly decides to allow a cost-push induced recession to run its course. Widespread layoffs, plant shutdowns, and business failures eventually will occur. At some point there will be sufficient slack in labor markets to reduce nominal wages and thus undo the initial leftward shift of short-run aggregate supply. Restated, a severe recession will in time shift the short-run aggregate supply from AS_2 back to AS_1. The price level will therefore return to P_1 at a and the potential level of output will be restored along long-run aggregate supply AS_{LR}.

Two generalizations emerge from our analysis:

1 *If government attempts to maintain full employment under conditions of cost-push inflation, an inflationary spiral is likely to occur.*

2 *If government takes a hands-off approach to cost-push inflation, a recession will probably occur.* Although the recession can be expected eventually to undo the initial rise in production costs, the economy in the meanwhile will experience high unemployment and a loss of real output.

QUICK REVIEW 17-2

♦ *The short-run aggregate supply curve has a positive slope because nominal wages are assumed to be fixed as the price level changes.*

♦ *The long-run aggregate supply curve is vertical because input prices eventually respond fully to changes in the price level.*

♦ *In the short run, demand-pull inflation will increase both the price level and domestic output; in the long run, only the price level will rise.*

♦ *Cost-push inflation creates a policy dilemma for government: If it engages in an expansionary stabilization policy to increase output, an inflationary spiral may ensue; if it does nothing, a recession may occur.*

Other Options Given our experiences with cost-push inflation and the difficulties in using demand-management policies to deal with it (Figure 17-7b), government has sought out additional policy options.

In terms of Figure 17-7b these policies are designed to prevent the aggregate supply curve from shifting leftward as from AS_1 to AS_2. Or, alternatively, if the economy already is experiencing stagflation at the intersection of AD and AS_2, the goal would be to shift the aggregate supply curve rightward toward AS_1. Similarly, in terms of the Phillips Curve (whether conceived of as a downsloping curve or a vertical line) the policy goal is to shift the curve leftward to provide a better inflation rate–unemployment rate tradeoff for society. In particular, economists who interpreted the data points for the 1970s and 1980s in Figure 17-3 as reflecting rightward shifts of the Phillips Curve sought means of shifting the curve back to the more desirable position which seemed relevant for the 1960s.

Generally speaking, three categories of policies have been proposed: (1) market policies; (2) wage-price, or incomes, policies; and (3) the set of policies prescriptions known as "supply-side economics."

MARKET POLICIES

Two kinds of **market policies** can be distinguished. *Employment and training policy* is intended to reduce or eliminate imbalances and bottlenecks in labor markets. A *procompetition policy* attempts to reduce the market power of unions and large corporations. Recall that labor market imbalances and market power constitute the traditional logic underlying the Phillips Curve.

Employment and Training Policy

The goal of employment and training policy is to improve the efficiency of labor markets so that any given level of aggregate demand will be associated with a lower level of unemployment. In other words, the purpose of employment and training policy is to achieve a better matching of workers to jobs, thereby reducing labor market imbalances or bottlenecks. Several different kinds of programs will provide a better matching of workers to jobs. Three of these are vocational training, job information, and antidiscrimination programs.

1 Vocational Training Programs of vocationally oriented education and training will permit marginal and displaced workers to be more quickly reemployed. Various government programs provide for both institutional and on-the-job training for the unemployed, for disadvantaged youth, and for older workers whose skills are meager or obsolete.

2 Job Information A second type of employment and training policy is concerned with improving the flow of job information between unemployed workers and potential employers and with enhancing the geographic mobility of workers. For example, a number of attempts have been made recently to modernize the United States Employment Service to increase its effectiveness in bringing job seekers and employers together.

3 Nondiscrimination Another facet of employment and training policy is concerned with reducing or eliminating artificial obstacles to employment. Discrimination has been an important roadblock in matching workers and jobs; it is a basic factor in explaining why unemployment rates for blacks are roughly twice as high as for whites. The Civil Rights Act of 1964 attempts to improve the use of labor resources by removing discrimination because of race, religion, gender, or ethnic background as an obstacle to employment or union membership.

Procompetition Policy

A second avenue for improving the tradeoff between the unemployment rate and rate of inflation is to reduce the monopoly or market power of unions and businesses. This policy aims at reducing the monopoly power of unions so that they will be less able to push up wage rates ahead of average productivity increases. Similarly, more competition in the product market will reduce the power of large corporations to raise prices.

How can the economy be made more competitive? One recommendation is to apply existing antitrust (antimonopoly) laws much more vigorously to large corporations. Another is to remove remaining legal restrictions on entry to certain regulated industries such as communications, transportation, and power generation and distribution. Similarly, elimination of tariffs and other restrictions on foreign imports will increase competitiveness of American markets.

On the labor front, it is periodically argued that the antimonopoly laws should be applied to unions or that collective bargaining should be less centralized. Also recall that Chapter 10's Last Word outlined a proposal to link a portion of wages to profits in order to make wages more flexible downward. The purpose is to shift the burden of a decline in demand from unemployment to wages.

WAGE-PRICE (INCOMES) POLICIES

A second approach accepts the existence of monopoly power and labor market imbalances as more-or-less inevitable facts of economic life, and seeks to alter the behavior of labor and product-market monopolists to make their wage and price decisions more compatible with the twin goals of full employment and price level stability. Although they differ primarily in degree, it is meaningful to distinguish between **wage-price guideposts** and **wage-price controls.** Guideposts and controls differ in that guideposts rely on the voluntary cooperation of labor and business, whereas controls have the force of law.

Wage-price guideposts and wage-price controls are sometimes called **incomes policies.** The reason for this label is that a person's real income—the amount of goods and services obtained with one's nominal income—depends on the size of that nominal income and the prices of the goods and services bought. Guideposts and controls are designed to constrain both nominal incomes and prices paid, and thus affect real incomes.

There have been five periods in recent history when incomes policies have been applied:
1 Comprehensive controls during World War II
2 Selective controls during the Korean war in the early 1950s
3 Guideposts during the early 1960s under the Kennedy–Johnson administrations
4 The Nixon administration's wage-price controls of 1971–1974
5 The Carter administration's guideposts of 1978

Our discussion will center on the guideposts of the early 1960s and the 1971–1974 controls. These episodes of incomes policies are of more than historical interest; they highlight the basic principles of incomes policies. Governments in several foreign countries experiencing rapid inflation have implemented similar policies within the past decade. Also, invariably there are calls for incomes policies in the United States when inflation begins to approach double-digit levels.

Kennedy–Johnson Guideposts

In the period from 1962 to 1966, the Kennedy and Johnson administrations set forth "guideposts for noninflationary wage and price behavior." These were a set of wage and price rules which, if followed by labor and management, would provide some assurance that the government's plan to stimulate the economy would be translated into increases in real domestic output and employment, rather than dissipated in price increases.

1 Wage Guidepost *The basic wage guidepost was that nominal wage rates in all industries should rise in accordance with the rate of increase in labor productivity for the nation as a whole.* Referring back to equation (1) in our earlier discussion of the productivity decline, we know that nominal wage rate increases equaling the rate of productivity growth will be noninflationary. That is, unit labor costs will be unchanged and there will be no reason for producers to raise prices.

Of course, the productivity increases of some industries will exceed, while those of others will fall short of, the overall or average increase in national productivity. For an industry whose productivity rises by less than national productivity, unit labor costs will rise. For example, if national productivity rose by 3 percent while productivity rose by only 1 percent in industry X, then, with nominal wage rates increasing by 3 percent, that industry would experience approximately a 2 percent *increase* in its unit labor costs. Conversely, if productivity rose by 5 percent in industry Y, then the 3 percent increase in nominal wages would *decrease* its unit labor costs by about 2 percent.

2 Price Guidepost *The basic price guidepost was that prices should change to compensate for changes in unit labor costs.* In industries whose rate of productivity was equal to the national average, prices would be constant because unit labor costs would be unchanged. For industries whose productivity rose by less than the national average, prices could be increased enough to cover the resulting increase in unit labor costs. Industry X, cited earlier, could increase its prices by 2 percent. For industries where productivity increases exceeded the national average, prices would be expected to fall in accordance with the resulting decline in unit labor costs. Industry Y should lower its prices by 2 percent. These price increases and decreases would cancel out and leave the overall price level unchanged.

Nixon Wage-Price Controls

In 1971 controls were put into effect by President Nixon. Faced with stagflation, taxes were cut by some $7 to $8 billion to stimulate aggregate demand and, it was hoped, boost output and employment. The prob-lem, however, was to prevent this expansionary fiscal policy from being translated into additional inflation rather than into increases in employment and real output. The Nixon response was to order a freeze on wages, prices, and rents. The President's executive order made it illegal to (1) increase wages or salaries, (2) charge more for a product than the highest price charged in the 30-day period prior to the freeze, and (3) raise the rents landlords charged tenants. The Nixon freeze was followed by formal wage and price controls which set maximum legal limits on wage and price hikes. These controls were phased out in 1974, which was in time to reinforce the stagflation already being generated by OPEC, agricultural shortfalls, and depreciation of the dollar.

The Wage-Price Policy Debate

There has been heated and prolonged debate in the United States on the desirability and efficacy of incomes policies. The debate centers on two points.

1 Workability and Compliance Critics argue that the voluntary *guideposts* approach will fail because it asks business and labor leaders to abandon their primary functions and forgo the goals of maximum profits and higher wages. A union leader will not gain favor with the rank and file by reducing wage demands; nor does a corporate official become endeared to stockholders by bypassing potentially profitable price increases. For these reasons little voluntary cooperation can be expected from labor and management.

Wage and price *controls* have the force of law and, therefore, labor and management can be forced to obey. Nevertheless, problems of enforcement and compliance can be severe, particularly if wage and price controls are quite comprehensive and maintained for an extended time. *Black markets*—illegal markets in which prices exceed their legal maximums—become commonplace under these circumstances. Furthermore, firms can circumvent price controls by lowering the quality or size of their product. If the price of a candy bar is frozen at 40 cents, its price can be effectively doubled by reducing its size by one-half!

Proponents of incomes policies point out that inflation is frequently fueled by *inflationary expectations*. Workers demand unusually large nominal wage increases because they expect future inflation to diminish their real incomes. Employers acquiesce in these demands because they, too, anticipate an inflationary environment in which higher costs can be easily passed along to consumers. A strong wage-price control program can quell inflationary expectations by convincing labor and management that the government does not intend to allow inflation to continue. Therefore, workers do not need anticipatory wage increases. And firms are put on notice that they may not be able to shift higher costs to consumers via price increases. Expectations of inflation can generate inflation; wage-price controls can undermine those expectations.

2 Allocative Efficiency and Rationing Opponents of incomes policies contend that effective guideposts or controls interfere with the allocative function of the market system. Specifically, effective price controls prohibit the market system from making necessary price adjustments. If an increase in the demand for some product should occur, its price could *not* rise to signal society's wish for more output and therefore more resources in this area of production.

Also, controls strip the market mechanism of its rationing function, that is, of its ability to equate quantity demanded and quantity supplied, and product shortages will result. Which buyers are to obtain the product and which are to do without? The product can be rationed on a first-come-first-served basis or by favoritism. But this is highly arbitrary and inequitable; those first in line or those able to cultivate a friendship with the seller get as much of the product as they want while others get none at all. Government may therefore have to impartially ration the product to all consumers by issuing ration coupons to buyers on an equitable basis. But governmental rationing contributes to the problem of compliance noted earlier.

Defenders of incomes policies respond as follows: If effective guideposts or controls are imposed on a competitive economy, then in time the resulting rigidities will impair allocative efficiency. But it is *not* correct to assume that resource allocation will be efficient in the absence of a wage-price policy. Cost-push inflation allegedly arises *because* big labor and big businesses possess monopoly power and consequently have the capacity to distort the allocation of resources.

Effectiveness

How effective have incomes policies been? The evidence, in a word, is "mixed." The use of direct wage-price controls during World War II did contain—or at least defer—the serious inflation which would other-

wise have occurred. On the other hand, the 1962 wage and price guideposts did little to arrest the growing demand-pull inflation of the mid-1960s. Additionally, the wage and price controls of 1971–1974 not only failed to achieve their purposes, but worsened stagflation by causing inefficiencies in the allocation of resources.

SUPPLY-SIDE ECONOMICS

In the past decade or so, some economists have stressed low growth of productivity and real output as basic causes of stagflation and the overall poor performance of our economy. These **supply-side economists** assert that mainstream economics does not come to grips with stagflation because its focal point is aggregate demand.

Supply-side economists contend that changes in aggregate supply—shifts in the long-run aggregate supply curve—must be recognized as an "active" force in determining both the levels of inflation *and* unemployment. Economic disturbances can be generated on the supply side, as well as on the demand side. Most importantly for present purposes, by emphasizing the demand side, mainstream economists have neglected certain supply-side policies which might alleviate stagflation.

Tax-Transfer Disincentives

Supply-side economists contend that the spectacular growth of our tax-transfer system allegedly has negatively affected incentives to work, invest, innovate, and assume entrepreneurial risks. In short, the tax-transfer system has eroded the economy's productivity and the decline in efficiency has meant higher production costs and stagflation. The argument is that higher taxes will reduce the after-tax rewards of workers and producers, making work, innovations, investing, and risk bearing less financially attractive. Supply-side economists stress the importance of *marginal tax rates* because these rates are most relevant to decisions to undertake *additional* work and *additional* saving and investing.

Incentives to Work Supply-siders argue that how long and how hard individuals work depends on how much additional *after-tax* earnings they derive from this extra work. To induce more work—to increase aggregate inputs of labor—marginal tax rates on earned incomes should be reduced. Lower marginal tax rates increase the attractiveness of work and simultaneously increase the opportunity cost of leisure. Thus, individuals will choose to substitute work for leisure. This increase in productive effort can occur in many ways: by increasing the number of hours worked per day or week; by encouraging workers to postpone retirement; by inducing more people to enter the labor force; by making people willing to work harder; and by discouraging long periods of unemployment.

Transfer Disincentives Supply-side economists also contend that the existence of a wide variety of public transfer programs has eroded incentives to work. Unemployment compensation and welfare programs have made the loss of one's job less of an economic crisis than formerly. The fear of being unemployed and therefore the need to be a disciplined, productive worker is simply less acute than previously. Indeed, most transfer programs are structured to discourage work. Our social security and aid to families with dependent children programs are such that transfers are reduced sharply if recipients earn income. These programs encourage recipients *not* to be productive by imposing a "tax" in the form of a loss of transfer benefits on those who work.

Incentives to Save and Invest The rewards to saving and investing have also been reduced by high marginal tax rates. Assume you save $1000 at 10 percent, so that you earn $100 interest per year. If your marginal tax rate is 40 percent, your after-tax interest earnings will fall to $60 and the after-tax interest rate you receive is only 6 percent. While you might be willing to save (forgo current consumption) for a 10 percent return on your saving, you might prefer to consume when the return is only 6 percent.

Saving, remember, is the prerequisite of investment. Thus supply-side economists recommend lower marginal tax rates on saving. They also call for lower taxes on investment income to ensure there are ready investment outlets for the economy's enhanced pool of saving. We saw in Chapter 10 that one of the determinants of investment spending is the *after-tax* net profitability of that spending.

To summarize, lower marginal tax rates encourage saving and investing to the end that workers will find themselves equipped with more and technologically superior machinery and equipment. Therefore, labor productivity will rise, and as equation (1) reminds us, this will hold down increases in unit labor costs and the price level.

Laffer Curve

According to supply-side economics, reductions of marginal tax rates will shift Figure 17-4's aggregate supply curve from AS_2 toward AS_1, alleviating inflation, increasing real output, and reducing the unemployment rate. Moreover, according to supply-side economists such as Arthur Laffer, lower tax *rates* are compatible with constant or even enlarged tax *revenues*. Supply-side tax cuts need not cause Federal budget deficits.

This position is based on the **Laffer Curve,** which, as shown in Figure 17-8, depicts the relationship between tax rates and tax revenues. The idea is that, as tax rates increase from zero to 100 percent, tax revenue will increase from zero to some maximum level (at *m*) and then decline to zero. Tax revenues decline beyond some point because higher tax rates presumably discourage economic activity and therefore the tax base (domestic output and national income) diminishes. This is easiest to envision at the extreme where tax rates are 100 percent. Tax revenues here are reduced to zero because the 100 percent confiscatory tax rate has brought production to a halt. A 100 percent tax rate applied to a tax base of zero yields no revenue.

In the early 1980s Professor Laffer contended we were at some point such as *n* where tax rates were so high that production had been so discouraged that tax revenues were below the maximum at *m*. If the economy is at *n,* then lower tax *rates* are quite compatible

FIGURE 17-8 The Laffer Curve

The Laffer Curve suggests that up to point *m* higher tax rates will result in larger tax revenues. But still higher rates will adversely affect incentives to produce, reducing the size of the national income tax base to the extent that tax revenues decline. It follows that, if tax rates are above 0*m*, tax reductions will result in increases in tax revenues. The controversial empirical question is to determine at what actual tax rates will tax revenues begin to fall.

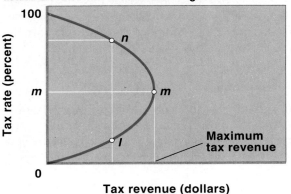

with constant tax *revenues.* In Figure 17-8 we simply lower tax rates, moving from point *n* to point *l,* and government will collect an unaltered amount of tax revenue. Laffer's reasoning is that lower tax rates will stimulate incentives to work, save and invest, innovate, and accept business risks, thus triggering an expansion of domestic output and national income. This enlarged tax base will sustain tax revenues even though tax rates are lower.

According to supply-side economists, a budget deficit can be avoided in two additional ways.

1 Less Tax Evasion   Tax avoidance and evasion will decline. High marginal tax rates prompt taxpayers to avoid taxes through various tax shelters (for example, buying municipal bonds on which interest is tax free) or to conceal income from the Internal Revenue Service. Lower tax rates will reduce the inclination to engage in such activities.

2 Reduced Transfers   The stimulus to production and employment which a tax cut provides will reduce government transfer payments. For example, more job opportunities will reduce unemployment compensation payments and thereby reduce a budget deficit.

Criticisms of the Laffer Curve

The Laffer Curve and its supply-side policy implications have been subject to much criticism.

1 Taxes: Incentives and Time   A fundamental criticism has to do with the sensitivity of economic incentives to changes in tax rates. Skeptics point out that there is ample empirical evidence that the impact of a tax reduction on incentives will be small, of uncertain direction, and relatively slow to emerge. For example, with respect to work incentives, studies indicate that decreases in tax rates lead some people to work more, but others to work less. Those who work more are enticed by the higher after-tax pay; they substitute work for leisure because the opportunity cost of leisure has increased. Those who work less do so because the higher after-tax pay increases their ability to "buy leisure." They can meet their after-tax income goals while working fewer hours.

Furthermore, any positive effects which tax cuts have on real output and therefore tax revenues will be slow to appear:

> In the long run, most tax changes that increase total capital formation and thereby raise the rate of economic growth will eventually raise (tax) revenues. However, the long run is likely to be very long in-

deed since a major proportionate increase in savings and investment will cause only a tiny proportionate increase in the capital stock every year, and it is the latter which is important to economic growth. Consequently, the long run must be measured in terms of decades rather than years.[1]

2 Reinforcing Inflation   Most economists contend that demand-side effects of a tax cut exceed supply-side effects. Hence, tax cuts undertaken when the economy is expanding or at its full-employment output will generate large increases in aggregate demand which will overwhelm any increase in aggregate supply. Large budget deficits and inflation will result.

3 Position on Curve   Skeptics note that the Laffer Curve is merely a logical proposition asserting there must be some level of tax rates between zero and 100 percent at which tax revenues will be maximized. Economists of all persuasions can agree with this statement. But the issue of where a particular economy is located on the Laffer Curve is an empirical question. If we assume—as Laffer did in the early 1980s—that we are at *n* in Figure 17-8, then tax rate cuts will increase tax revenues. But critics contend that the economy's location on the Laffer Curve is undocumented and unknown. If the economy is actually at any point southwest of *m,* then tax reductions will reduce tax revenues and create budget deficits.

Other Supply-Side Tenets

Although removing tax-transfer disincentives is the centerpiece of supply-side economics, there are two additional tenets worth noting.

1 The Tax "Wedge"   Supply-side economists note that the historical growth of the public sector has increased the nation's tax bill both absolutely and as a percentage of the national income. In the Keynesian view, higher taxes represent a withdrawal of purchasing power from the economy and therefore have a contractionary or anti-inflationary effect (Chapter 12). Supply-siders argue to the contrary: They contend that sooner or later most taxes are incorporated into business costs and shifted forward to consumers in the form of higher prices. Taxes, in short, entail a cost-push effect.

Supply-side economists point out that in the 1970s

[1]Testimony of R. G. Penner in Senate Budget Committee, *Leading Economists' Views of Kemp–Roth* (Washington, 1978), p. 139.

and 1980s state and local governments negotiated substantial increases in sales and excise taxes and that the Federal government has boosted dramatically payroll (social security) taxes. These are precisely the kinds of taxes incorporated in business costs and reflected in higher prices. Such taxes constitute a "wedge" between the costs of resources and the price of a product. As government has grown, this **tax wedge** has increased, shifting the aggregate supply curve leftward.

2 Overregulation   Supply-siders also claim that government involvement in the economy in the form of regulation has also had adverse effects on productivity and costs. Two points should be noted in this regard.
1   It is held that "industrial" regulation—government regulation of specific industries such as transportation or communications—frequently has the effect of providing firms in the regulated industry with a kind of legal monopoly or cartel. Governmental regulation protects such firms from competition with the result that these firms are less efficient and incur higher costs of production than they would otherwise.
2   The "social" regulation of industry has increased substantially in the past two decades. New government regulations have been imposed on industry in response to the problems of pollution, product safety, worker health and safety, and equal access to job opportunities. Supply-side economists point out that social regulation has greatly increased costs of doing business. The overall impact of both varieties of regulation is that costs and prices are higher and there is a tendency toward stagflation.

Reaganomics: The Program

The elements of supply-side economics just outlined provided the intellectual underpinnings for the economic policies of the Reagan administration (1981–1988). Specifically, **Reaganomics** consisted of the following four policies:
1   The growth of the Federal government was restrained by freezes and cuts in spending on social and welfare programs. Defense spending, however, was increased significantly.
2   Substantial reductions in government regulation of private businesses occurred.
3   The administration encouraged the Federal Reserve System to hold the growth rate of the money supply to a rate considered to be noninflationary, yet sufficiently expansive to allow for economic growth.
4   Personal and corporate income tax rates were reduced sharply beginning in 1981. The tax system was

reformed in 1986 so that the marginal tax rate on income of wealthy taxpayers fell from 50 percent to 28 percent.

Reaganomics: Did It Work?

The real world is an imperfect laboratory for judging the success of a vast socioeconomic experiment such as Reaganomics. Also, Congress did not accept all the expenditure reductions which the Reagan administration requested in its program. Finally, the Reagan years witnessed significant declines in inflation and interest rates, a record-long peacetime economic expansion, and attainment of full employment. Having acknowledged these points, it is nevertheless fair to say that, *as such*, supply-side economics largely failed to accomplish its goals.

The facts are these:
1   Any immediate output effects of the Reagan tax cuts were overwhelmed by the tight money policy being undertaken by the Federal Reserve to reduce the then-existing rapid inflation. The economy fell into severe back-to-back recessions in 1980–1982.
2   The inflation rate fell sharply from annual rates of 13.5 percent in 1980 to 3.2 percent in 1983. Since 1983 the inflation rate has remained relatively low. But most economists attribute the decline in inflation to the 1980–1982 recessions, caused by the Federal Reserve's tight money policy, and to declines in oil prices. Rightward shifts in aggregate supply predicted by supply-side economists were *not* a major factor in reducing inflation.
3   The Reagan tax cuts contributed to burgeoning Federal budget deficits (Chapter 18). The prediction of the Laffer Curve that tax cuts would enhance tax revenues beyond those associated with normal economic expansions simply did not bear fruit. These large deficits may have increased interest rates, crowding out some unknown amount of private investment and depressing both export-dependent and import-competing industries (Figures 12-6b and 12-6d). A record high U.S. balance of payments deficit resulted. In 1990, the Bush administration and Congress were forced to enact a tax-spending package designed to reduce the deficit by $500 billion over a five-year period.
4   There is little evidence that Reaganomics has had any significant positive impacts on saving and investment rates or incentives to work. The savings rate trended downward throughout the 1980s. Productivity growth surged in 1983 and 1984, as is usual during recovery, but has been disappointingly low since then.
5   Most economists attribute the post-1982 economic

recovery to the demand-side expansionary effects of the Reagan tax cuts and not to the use of tax cuts as an antistagflation, supply-side measure.

In summary, the evidence to date casts considerable doubt on the central supply-side proposition that tax cuts can significantly shift the nation's production possibilities curve and aggregate supply curve rightward more rapidly than their historical pace.

> **QUICK REVIEW 17-3**
>
> *Policy options for stagflation include: market policies (employment and training policies, antitrust); incomes policies (wage-price guideposts and controls); and supply-side economics (tax cuts, deregulation).*
>
> *The Laffer Curve contends that, when tax rates are higher than optimal, tax reductions can stimulate real output and simultaneously increase tax revenue.*

> *The supply-side policies (tax cuts, deregulation) of Reaganomics did not increase aggregate supply more rapidly than otherwise would have been expected.*

RECAP: ALTERNATIVE MACROECONOMIC PERSPECTIVES

We have seen here and in Chapter 16 that a number of theories purport to explain how the national economy operates. In particular, the central ideas and policy implications of Keynesianism, monetarism, rational expectations theory, and supply-side economics have been presented.

Table 17-1 summarizes major aspects of these theories and policy perspectives. In reviewing the table, note there is no direct reference to the terminology

TABLE 17-1 Alternative macroeconomic theories and policies

| Issue | Keynesianism | Natural rate hypothesis | | Supply-side economics |
		Monetarism	Rational expectations	
View of the private economy	Inherently unstable	Stable in long run at natural rate of unemployment	Stable in long run at natural rate of unemployment	May stagnate without proper work, saving, and investment incentives
Cause of the observed instability of the private economy	Investment plans unequal to saving plans (changes in AD); AS shocks	Inappropriate monetary policy	Unanticipated AD and AS shocks in the short run	Changes in AS
Appropriate macro policies	Active fiscal and monetary policy; occasional use of incomes policies	Monetary rule	Monetary rule	Policies to increase AS
How changes in the money supply affect the economy	By changing the interest rate, which changes investments, and real GDP	By directly changing AD which changes GDP.	No effect on output because price-level changes are anticipated	By influencing investment and thus AS
View of the velocity of money	Unstable	Stable	No consensus	No consensus
How fiscal policy affects the economy	Changes AD and GDP via the multiplier process	No effect unless money supply changes	No effect on output because price-level changes are anticipated	Affects GDP and price level via changes in AS
View of cost-push inflation	Possible (wage-push, AS shock)	Impossible in the long run in the absence of excessive money supply growth	Impossible in the long run in the absence of excessive money supply growth	Possible (productivity decline, higher costs due to regulation, etc.)

LAST WORD

"REAL" BUSINESS CYCLE THEORY

A handful of prominent new classical economists stand traditional economic theory on its head by arguing that business cycles are caused by real factors affecting aggregate supply rather than by fluctuations in aggregate demand.

Keynesians and monetarists hold that business cycles result mainly from changes in aggregate demand. But new classical economists tend to rule out demand changes as causes of permanent changes in real output. They contend that flexible nominal wages and changes in other input prices return real output to its potential level through rapid adjustments in short-run aggregate supply (Figures 17-6b and 17-7a). Yet, historical evidence clearly shows that long-lasting business recessions and booms *do* occur. If changes in aggregate demand are not the reason for these observed fluctuations, what are the reasons?

A small, but influential, group of new classical economists has hypothesized that business cycles are caused by factors which disturb the long-run growth

trend of aggregate supply. According to this novel view, recessions begin on the supply side of the economy, not on the demand side as traditionally assumed. In other words, "real" factors—technology, resource availability, and productivity—which affect aggregate supply are the alleged causes of business cycles. In contrast, traditional theory envisions "monetary" factors affecting aggregate demand as the usual source of cyclical instability.

"new classical economics." This viewpoint is simply that associated in a general way with the natural rate hypothesis which asserts that the economy tends automatically to achieve equilibrium at its full potential level

of output—that is, at its natural rate of unemployment. The natural rate hypothesis is supported by economists of the monetarist and rational expectations persuasions.

CHAPTER SUMMARY

1 Using the AD-AS model to compare the impacts of small and large increases in aggregate demand on the price level and real domestic output yields the generalization that high rates of inflation should be associated with low rates of unemployment and vice versa. This inverse relationship is known as the Phillips Curve and empirical data for the 1960s were generally consistent with it. Labor market imbalances and monopoly power are used to explain the Phillips Curve tradeoff.

2 In the 1970s the Phillips Curve apparently shifted rightward, a shift consistent with stagflation. A series of supply shocks in the form of higher energy and food prices, a depreciated dollar, and the demise of the Nixon wage-price freeze were involved in the 1973–1975 stagflation. More subtle factors such as inflationary expectations and a decline in the rate of productivity growth also contributed to stagflationary tendencies. Following the recession of 1981–1982, the Phillips Curve shifted inward toward its original position. By 1989 stagflation had largely subsided.

3 The adaptive expectations variant of the natural rate hypothesis argues that in the long run the traditional Phillips Curve tradeoff does not exist. Expansionary demand-management policies will shift the short-run Phillips Curve upward, resulting in increasing inflation with no permanent decline in unemployment.

4 The rational expectations variant of the natural rate hypothesis contends that the inflationary effects of expansionary policies will be anticipated and reflected in nominal wage demands. As a result, there will be no short-run increase in employment and thus no short-run Phillips Curve.

5 In the short run—where nominal wages are fixed—an increase in the price level increases profits and real output. Conversely, a decrease in the price level reduces profits and real output. Thus, the short-run aggregate supply curve is upward-sloping. In the long run—where nominal wages are variable—price level increases raise nominal wages and shift the short-run aggregate supply curve leftward. Conversely, price level declines shift the short-run aggregate

An example focusing on a recession will clarify the new classical thinking. Suppose that productivity—output per worker—declines because an increase in the world price of oil makes it prohibitively expensive to operate certain types of machinery. This decline in productivity implies a reduction in the economy's ability to produce real output and therefore a leftward shift of its long-run (vertical) aggregate supply curve. As domestic output falls in response to the decline in aggregate supply, less money is needed to exchange the reduced volume of goods and services. That is, the decline in output reduces the demand for money. Moreover, the slowdown in business activity lessens business borrowing from banks, causing a drop in the supply of money. In this scenario, changes in the supply of money respond passively to changes in the demand for money. The decline in the money supply in turn reduces aggregate demand (shifts the AD curve leftward) to the same extent as the initial decline in aggregate supply. The result is that real equilibrium output is lower, while the price level remains unchanged. Like the Keynesian model, then, the real business cycle theory allows for a decline in real output in the presence of a constant price level. (You are urged to test your comprehension of the real business cycle theory by using the AD-AS model to diagram it.)

The policy implications of the real business cycle theory are as unusual and controversial as the theory itself. First, demand-management policies are inappropriate and doomed to fail. Expansionary stabilization policy in this situation will not increase real output; instead, it will cause inflation. Second, deviations of aggregate supply from its long-term growth trend should not be the source of social concern. According to real business cycle theorists, gains from "real" business booms roughly match the output losses arising from "real" downturns. The *net* long-run costs of business cycles therefore are allegedly very modest. The emphasis of public policy should be on stimulating long-term economic growth rather than on trying to stabilize the economy.

Conventional economists vigorously reject the real business cycle theory because it does not square with the facts of past business cycles. But, at a minimum, the theory makes it evident that economics is an exciting, evolving field of study and that conventional macroeconomic theory is not the only analytical game in town.

---

supply curve rightward. The long-run aggregate supply curve therefore is vertical at the potential level of output.

6 In the short run, demand-pull inflation increases the price level *and* real output. Once nominal wages have increased, however, the temporary increase in real output dissipates.

7 In the short run, cost-push inflation increases the price level and reduces real output. Unless government expands aggregate demand, nominal wages eventually will decline under conditions of recession and the short-run aggregate supply curve will shift back to its initial location. Prices and real output will eventually return to their original levels.

8 Market policies, wage-price (incomes) policies, and supply-side policies have been proposed to prevent or alleviate stagflation.

9 Market policies consist of employment and training programs designed to reduce labor market imbalances and procompetition policies which reduce the market power of unions and corporations.

10 Incomes policies take the form of wage-price guideposts or controls. Economists debate the desirability of such policies in terms of their workability and their impact on resource allocation.

11 Supply-side economists trace stagflation to the growth of the public sector and, more specifically, to the adverse effects of the tax-transfer system on incentives. Other factors cited are the growing tax "wedge" between production costs and product prices and government overregulation of businesses. Based on the Laffer Curve, supply-side adherents advocated sizable tax cuts such as those undertaken by the Reagan administration as a remedy for stagflation. Evidence has cast considerable doubt on the validity of the supply-side view.

TERMS AND CONCEPTS

Phillips Curve	natural rate hypothesis	disinflation	wage-price guideposts
stagflation	rational expectations	new classical	wage-price controls
aggregate supply	theory	economics	incomes policies
shocks	short-run aggregate	price-level surprises	supply-side economics
inflationary	supply curve	demand-pull inflation	Laffer Curve
expectations	long-run aggregate	cost-push inflation	tax wedge
theory of adaptive	supply curve	market policies	Reaganomics
expectations			

QUESTIONS AND STUDY SUGGESTIONS

1 Employ the aggregate demand–aggregate supply model to derive the Phillips Curve. What events occurred in the 1970s to cast doubt on the stability and existence of the Phillips Curve?

2 Use an appropriate diagram to explain the adaptive expectations rationale for concluding that in the long run the Phillips Curve is a vertical line.

3 Explain rational expectations theory and its relevance to analysis of the Phillips Curve.

4 Assume the following information is relevant for an industrially advanced economy in the 1993–1995 period:

Year	Price level index	Rate of increase in labor productivity	Index of industrial production	Unemployment rate	Average hourly wage rates
1993	167	4%	212	4.5%	$6.00
1994	174	3	208	5.2	6.50
1995	181	2.5	205	5.8	7.10

Describe in detail the macroeconomic situation faced by this society. Is cost-push inflation evident? What policy proposals would you recommend?

5 Evaluate or explain the following statements:

   a "Taken together, the adaptive expectations and rational expectations theories imply that demand-management policies cannot influence the real level of economic activity in the long run."

   b "The essential difference between the adaptive expectations theory and rational expectations theory is that inflation is unanticipated in the former and anticipated in the latter."

6 Use graphical analysis to show (1) demand-pull inflation in the short run and long run, and (2) cost-push inflation in the short run and long run. Assume in the second case that government does *not* increase aggregate demand to offset the real output effect of the cost-push inflation.

7 Suppose the potential level of real domestic output (*Q*) for a hypothetical economy is $250 and the price level (*P*) initially is 100. Use the short-run aggregate supply schedules below to answer the questions which follow.

AS(P_{100})		AS(P_{125})		AS(P_{75})	
P	Q	P	Q	P	Q
125	280	125	250	125	310
100	250	100	220	100	280
75	220	75	190	75	250

   a What will be the level of real domestic output in the *short run* if the price level unexpectedly rises from 100 to 125 because of an increase in aggregate demand? Falls unexpectedly from 100 to 75 because of a decrease in aggregate demand? Explain each situation.

   b What will be the level of real domestic output in the *long run* when the price level rises from 100 to 125? Falls from 100 to 75? Explain each situation.

   c Show the circumstances described in **a** and **b** on graph paper and derive the long-run aggregate supply curve.

8 Explain the Kennedy–Johnson wage-price guideposts, indicating in detail the relationship between nominal wages, productivity, and unit labor costs. What specific problems are associated with the use of wage-price guideposts and controls? Evaluate these problems and note the arguments in favor of guideposts and controls. Would you favor a special tax on firms which grant wage increases in excess of productivity increases?

9 "Controlling prices to halt inflation is like breaking a thermometer to control the heat. In both instances you are treating symptoms rather than causes." Do you agree? Does the correctness of the statement vary when applied to demand-pull and to cost-push inflation? Explain.

10 What reasons do supply-side economists give to explain leftward shifts of the AS curve? Using the Laffer Curve, explain why they recommend tax cuts to remedy stagflation.

11 Review Table 17-1 and explain to your satisfaction each of the elements contained therein. If an item makes little sense to you, search this and previous chapters to find explicit or implicit explanations of the particular point made in the table.

18

Budget Deficits and the Public Debt

Federal deficits and our rapidly expanding public debt have received much publicity in the past few years. Headlines proclaiming "Exploding Federal Debt" "National Debt Threatens You" and "Runaway Deficits Possible" can hardly escape our attention. Nor can we escape the reality that it took over 200 years for the Federal debt to reach $1 trillion. But, then it required only eight years—1982 to 1990—to pass the $3 trillion mark.

In this chapter we will carefully examine the issues of persistent Federal deficits and the mounting public debt which these deficits have produced. After presenting relevant definitions, we first gain perspective by comparing several different budget philosophies. Next, the quantitative dimensions of the public debt are explored. How large is the debt? How can it be most meaningfully measured? We then consider the problems associated with the public debt and will find that some are essentially false or bogus problems, while others are of substance. Next, we want to assess the great upsurge in the size of deficits and in the public debt occurring in the past decade. We seek to understand why many economists see these deficits as having adverse effects on our domestic investment and international trade. Finally, recent laws and proposals designed to reduce or eliminate budget deficits are examined.

DEFICITS AND DEBT: DEFINITIONS

It is important to understand what we mean by deficits and the public debt. Recall from Chapter 12 that a **budget deficit** is the amount by which government's expenditures exceed its revenues during a particular year. For example, during 1991 the Federal government spent $1323 billion and its receipts were only $1054 billion, giving rise to a $269 billion deficit. The

national or **public debt** is the total accumulation of the Federal government's total deficits and surpluses which have occurred through time. At the end of 1991 the public debt was about $3600 billion.

The term "public debt" as ordinarily used does *not* include the entire public sector; in particular, state and local finance is omitted. In fact, while the Federal government has been incurring large deficits, state and local governments in the aggregate have been realizing surpluses. For example, in 1991 all state and local governments combined had a budgetary surplus in excess of $26 billion.[1]

BUDGET PHILOSOPHIES

Is it desirable to incur deficits and realize a growing public debt? Or should the budget be balanced annually, if necessary by legislation or constitutional amendment? Indeed, we saw in Chapter 12 that the essence of countercyclical fiscal policy is that the Federal budget should move toward a deficit during recession and toward a surplus during inflation. This correctly suggests that an activist fiscal policy is unlikely to result in a balanced budget in any particular year. Is this a matter of concern? Let's approach this question by examining the economic implications of several contrasting budget philosophies.

Annually Balanced Budget

Until the Great Depression of the 1930s, the **annually balanced budget** was generally accepted without question as a desirable goal of public finance. Upon examination, however, it becomes evident that an annually balanced budget largely rules out government fiscal activity as a countercyclical, stabilizing force. Worse yet, an annually balanced budget actually intensifies the business cycle. To illustrate: Suppose that the economy encounters a siege of unemployment and falling incomes. As Figure 12-4 indicates, in such circumstances tax receipts will automatically decline. To balance its budget, government must either (1) increase tax rates, (2) reduce government expenditures, or (3) employ a combination of these two. The problem is that all these policies are contractionary; each one further dampens, rather than stimulates, aggregate demand.

Similarly, an annually balanced budget will intensify inflation. Again, Figure 12-4 tells us that, as money incomes rise during the course of inflation, tax collections will automatically increase. To avoid the impending surplus, government must either (1) cut tax rates, (2) increase government expenditures, or (3) adopt a combination of both. All three of these policies will add to inflationary pressures. *An annually balanced budget is not economically neutral; the pursuit of such a policy is procyclical, not countercyclical.* Despite this and other

problems, there is considerable support for a constitutional amendment requiring an annually balanced budget.

More recently, several prominent economists have advocated an annually balanced budget, not so much because of a fear of deficits and a mounting public debt per se, but rather because they feel an annually balanced budget is essential in constraining an undesirable and uneconomic expansion of the public sector. Budget deficits, they argue, are a manifestation of political irresponsibility. Deficits allow politicians to give the public the benefits of government programs while currently avoiding the associated cost of paying higher taxes.

In other words, these economists believe government has a tendency to grow larger than it should because there is less popular opposition to this growth when it is financed by deficits rather than taxes. Wasteful governmental expenditures are more likely to creep into the Federal budget when deficit financing is readily available. Conservative economists and politicians want legislation or a constitutional amendment to force a balanced budget to slow government growth. They view deficits as a symptom of a more fundamental problem—government encroachment on the private sector.

Cyclically Balanced Budget

The idea of a **cyclically balanced budget** is that government exerts a countercyclical influence and at the same time balances its budget. In this case, however, the budget would not be balanced annually—after all, there is nothing sacred about twelve months as an accounting period—but rather, over the course of the business cycle.

The rationale of this budget philosophy is simple, plausible, and appealing. To offset recession, government should lower taxes and increase spending, thereby purposely incurring a deficit. During the ensuing inflationary upswing, taxes would be raised and government spending slashed. The resulting surplus could then be used to retire the Federal debt incurred in financing the recession. In this way government fiscal operations would exert a positive countercyclical force, and the government could still balance its budget—not annually, but over a period of years.

The problem with this budget philosophy is that the upswings and downswings of the business cycle may not be of equal magnitude and duration (Figure 8-1), and hence the goal of stabilization conflicts with

---

[1]This figure includes the states' pension funds. If these funds are excluded, the states collectively suffered a budgetary deficit in 1991.

balancing the budget over the cycle. A long and severe slump, followed by a modest and short period of prosperity, would mean a large deficit during the slump, little or no surplus during prosperity, and therefore a cyclical deficit in the budget.

Functional Finance

According to **functional finance,** a balanced budget—either annually or cyclically—is secondary. The primary purpose of Federal finance is to provide for noninflationary full employment, that is, to balance the economy, not the budget. If attainment of this objective means either persistent surpluses or a large and growing public debt, so be it. According to this philosophy, the problems involved in government deficits or surpluses are relatively minor compared with the highly undesirable alternatives of prolonged recession or persistent inflation. The Federal budget is first and foremost an instrument for achieving and maintaining macroeconomic stability. Government should not hesitate to incur any deficits and surpluses required to achieve this goal.

In response to those who express concern about the large Federal debt which the pursuit of functional finance might entail, proponents of this budget philosophy offer three arguments.

1 Our tax system is such that tax revenues automatically increase as the economy expands. Hence, given government expenditures, a deficit which is successful in stimulating equilibrium GDP will be partially self-liquidating (Figure 12-4).

2 Given its taxing powers and the ability to create money, the government's capacity to finance deficits is virtually unlimited.

3 Finally, it is contended that the problems of a large Federal debt are less burdensome than most people think.

THE PUBLIC DEBT: FACTS AND FIGURES

Because modern fiscal policy endorses unbalanced budgets for the purpose of stabilizing the economy, its application will possibly lead to a growing public debt. Let's briefly consider the public debt—its causes, characteristics, and size; and the burdens and benefits associated with it.

Growth of the public debt, as Table 18-1 shows, has been substantial since 1929. As noted, the public

debt is the accumulation of all past deficits, minus surpluses, of the Federal budget.

Causes

Why has our public debt increased historically? Or, stated differently, what has caused us to incur large and persistent deficits? The answer is threefold: wars, recessions, and tax cuts.

Wars A considerable portion of the public debt has arisen from the deficit financing of wars. The public debt grew more than fivefold during World War II and it also increased substantially during World War I.

Consider the World War II situation and the options it posed. The task was to reallocate a substantial portion of the economy's resources from civilian to war goods production. Accordingly, government expenditures for armaments and military personnel soared. Financing options were threefold: Increase taxes, print the needed money, or practice deficit financing. Government feared that tax financing would require tax rates so high they would diminish incentives to work. The national interest required attracting more people into the labor force and encouraging those already participating to work longer hours. Very high tax rates were felt to interfere with these goals. Printing and spending additional money was correctly seen as highly inflationary. Thus, much of World War II was financed by selling bonds to the public, thereby draining off spendable income and freeing resources from civilian production so they would be available for defense industries.

Recessions A second source of the public debt is recessions and, more specifically, the built-in stability which characterizes our fiscal system. In periods when the national income declines or fails to grow, tax collections automatically decline and tend to cause deficits. Thus the public debt rose during the Great Depression of the 1930s and, more recently, during the recessions of 1974–1975, 1980–1982, and 1990–1991.

Tax Cuts A third consideration has accounted for much of the large deficits since 1981. The Economic Recovery Tax Act of 1981 provided for substantial cuts in both individual and corporate income taxes. The Reagan administration and Congress did *not* make offsetting reductions in government outlays, thereby building a *structural deficit* into the Federal budget in the sense that the budget would not balance even if the

TABLE 18-1 Quantitative significance of the public debt: the public debt and interest payments in relation to GDP, selected years, 1929–1991*

(1) Year	(2) Public debt, billions	(3) Gross domestic product, billions	(4) Interest payments, billions	(5) Public debt as percentage of GDP, (2) ÷ (3)	(6) Interest payments as percentage of GDP, (4) ÷ (3)	(7) Per capita public debt
1929	$ 16.9	$ 103.2	$ 0.7	16%	0.7%	$ 134
1940	50.7	100.1	1.1	51	1.1	384
1946	271.0	211.6	4.2	128	2.0	1917
1950	256.9	286.7	4.5	90	1.6	1667
1955	274.4	403.3	5.1	68	1.3	1654
1960	290.5	513.4	6.8	57	1.3	1610
1965	322.3	702.7	8.4	46	1.2	1659
1970	380.9	1010.7	14.1	38	1.4	1858
1975	541.9	1585.9	23.0	34	1.5	2507
1980	908.5	2708.0	53.3	34	2.0	3989
1982	1136.8	3149.6	84.6	36	2.7	4889
1984	1564.1	3777.2	115.6	41	3.1	6600
1986	2120.1	4268.6	135.4	50	3.2	8775
1988	2600.8	4900.4	146.0	56	3.0	10611
1990	3206.3	5513.8	177.5	58	3.2	12826
1991	3599.0	5671.8	188.4	63	3.3	14244

*In current dollars.

Source: Economic Report of the President, 1992; U.S. Department of Commerce.

economy were operating at the full-employment level. Unfortunately, the economy was not at full employment during most of the early 1980s. In particular, the 1981 tax cuts combined with the severe 1980–1982 recessions to generate rapidly rising annual deficits which were $128 billion in 1982, accelerating to $221 billion by 1986. Although annual budget deficits declined between 1986 and 1990, they remained historically high even though the economy reached full employment. Due partly to the earlier tax rate cuts, tax revenues simply were not sufficiently high to cover rising Federal spending. Annual deficits, and thus the public debt, rose again in 1991 and 1992 as the economy experienced recession and the Federal government began to incur massive expenses in bailing out failed savings and loan associations.

Without being too cynical one might also assert that deficits and a growing public debt are the result of lack of political will and determination. Spending tends to gain votes; tax increases precipitate political disfavor. While opposition to deficits is widely expressed by both politicians and their constituencies, *specific* pro-posals to raise taxes or cut either domestic or defense programs typically encounter more opposition than support. For example, college students may favor smaller deficits so long as funds for student loans are not eliminated in the process.

In summary, much of the public debt has been caused by wartime finance, recessions, and, more recently, by tax cuts.

Quantitative Aspects

The public debt is estimated to be $3600 billion—that's $3.6 trillion—in 1991. That amount is more than twice what it was a mere seven years ago! How much is $3.6 trillion? Three trillion 600 million $1 bills placed end-to-end would stretch 340 million miles or, in other words, from the earth to the sun and back nearly two times. Or, a stack of $1000 bills 4 inches high would make you a millionaire; it would take a stack 241 miles high to represent our $3.6 trillion public debt.[2]

[2]These illustrations are from *U.S. News & World Report*, September 6, 1985, p. 33. Updated.

But we must not fear large or virtually incomprehensible numbers per se. The reason will become clear when we put the size of the public debt into better perspective.

Debt and GDP   A bald statement of the absolute size of the debt glosses over the fact that the wealth and productive ability of our economy have also increased tremendously over the years. A wealthy nation can more easily incur and carry a large public debt than a poor nation. In other words, it is more realistic to measure changes in the public debt *in relation to* changes in the economy's GDP. Column 5 in Table 18-1 presents such data. Note that instead of the thirteenfold increase in the debt between 1955 and 1991 shown in column 2, we find that the relative size of the debt was less in 1991 than in 1955. However, our data also show that the relative size of the debt has doubled since the early 1980s. Column 7 indicates that on a per capita basis the nominal debt has increased more or less steadily through time.

International Comparisons   Other industrial nations have relative public debts similar to, or greater than, those in the United States. We will see in this chapter's Last Word that, as a percent of GDP, public debt in 1991 was greater in Italy, Canada, and Japan than in the United States.

Interest Charges   Many economists feel that the primary burden of the debt is the annual interest charge that accrues as a result of the debt. The absolute size of these interest payments is shown in column 4 of Table 18-1. Note that interest payments have increased dramatically beginning in the 1970s. This reflects not only increases in the debt, but, more importantly, periods of very high interest rates. Interest on the debt is now the third largest item of expenditures in the Federal budget (Table 6-1). Interest charges as a percentage of the GDP are shown in column 6 of Table 18-1. We find that interest payments as a proportion of GDP have increased significantly in recent years. This ratio reflects the level of taxation (the average tax rate) which is required to service the public debt. In 1991 government had to collect taxes equal to 3.3 percent of the gross domestic product simply to pay interest on its debt.

Ownership   Approximately one-third of the total public debt is held by governmental agencies and our central banks, the remaining two-thirds by state and local governments, private individuals, commercial banks, and insurance companies. Only about 12 percent of the total debt is held by foreigners. This statistic is significant because, as we will see shortly, the implications of internally and externally held debt are quite different.

Accounting and Inflation   While the data on budget deficits and public debt appear to be straightforward and unassailable, this is not the case. Robert Eisner, past president of the American Economic Association, argues that governmental accounting procedures do not reflect government's actual financial position. He points out that private firms have a separate capital budget because, in contrast to current expenses on labor and raw materials, expenditures for capital equipment represent tangible money-making assets. The Federal government treats expenditures for highways, harbors, and public buildings the same as it does welfare payments, while in fact the former outlays are investments in physical assets. According to Eisner, Federal budget deficits of recent years would be greatly reduced if the Federal government employed a capital budget which included depreciation costs.

Eisner also reminds us that inflation works to benefit debtors. A rising price level reduces the real value or purchasing power of the dollars paid back by borrowers. Taking this "inflationary tax" into account further reduces the sizes of budget deficits and public debt.

All of this is quite controversial. But the important point is that there are different ways of measuring the public debt and government's overall financial position. Some of these alternative views differ significantly from the data presented in Table 18-1.

QUICK REVIEW 18-1

♪   *A budget deficit is an excess of government expenditures above tax revenues in a particular year; the public debt is the total accumulation of budget deficits and surpluses through time.*

♪   *The three major budget philosophies are:* a *an annually balanced budget;* b *a budget balanced over the business cycle; and* c *functional finance, which makes balancing the budget secondary to using it to promote macroeconomic goals.*

♪   *The $3.6 trillion public debt has resulted mainly from wartime financing, recessions, and tax cuts.*

♪   *United States public debt as a percentage of GDP is less than what it was in 1955 and lies in the midrange of such debt among major industrial nations.*

ECONOMIC IMPLICATIONS: FALSE ISSUES

How does the public debt and its growth affect the operation of the economy? Can a mounting public debt bankrupt the nation at some point? Does the debt place an unwarranted economic burden on our children and grandchildren?

These are essentially false or bogus issues. The debt is not about to bankrupt the government or the nation. Nor, except under certain specific circumstances, does the debt place a burden on future generations.

Going Bankrupt?

Can a large public debt bankrupt the government, making it unable to meet its financial obligations? The answer to this question is "No" because of the following three points.

1 Refinancing The first point is that there is no reason why the public debt need be reduced, much less eliminated. In practice, as portions of the debt fall due each month, government does not typically cut expenditures or raise taxes to provide funds to *retire* the maturing bonds. (We know that with depressed economic conditions, this would be unwise fiscal policy.) Rather, the government simply *refinances* the debt; it sells new bonds and uses the proceeds to pay off holders of the maturing bonds.

2 Taxation Government has the constitutional authority to levy and collect taxes. If acceptable to voters, a tax increase is a government option for gaining sufficient revenue to pay interest and principal on the public debt. Financially distressed private households and corporations *cannot* raise revenue via taxes; government *can*. Private households and corporations *can* go bankrupt; the Federal government *cannot*.

3 Creating Money A final, important consideration that makes bankruptcy difficult to imagine is that the Federal government has the power to print money to pay both principal and interest on the debt. A government bond simply obligates the government to redeem that bond for some specific amount of money on its maturity date. Government can use the proceeds from the sale of other bonds *or* it can create the needed money to retire the maturing bonds. The creation of new money to pay interest on debt or to retire debt

may be inflationary. But it is difficult to conceive of governmental bankruptcy when government has the power to create new money by running the printing presses.

Shifting Burdens

Does the public debt impose a burden on future generations? Recall that per capita debt in 1991 was $14,244. Does each newborn child in 1991 enter the world to be handed a $14,244 bill from Uncle Sam? Not really!

We first must ask to whom we owe the public debt. The answer is that, for the most part, we owe it to ourselves. About 88 percent of our government bonds are owned and held by citizens and institutions— banks, businesses, insurance companies, governmental agencies, and trust funds—within the United States. Thus *the public debt is also a public credit*. While the public debt is a liability to the American people (as taxpayers), most of the same debt is simultaneously an asset to the American people (as bondholders).

Retirement of the public debt would therefore call for a gigantic transfer payment whereby Americans would pay higher taxes and government would pay out most of those tax revenues to those same taxpaying individuals and institutions in the aggregate in redeeming the bonds they hold. Although a redistribution of income would result from this gigantic financial transfer, it need not entail any immediate decline in the economy's aggregate wealth or standard of living. Repayment of an internally held public debt entails no leakage of purchasing power from the economy of the country as a whole. New babies who on the average inherit the $14,244 per person public debt obligation will also be bequeathed that same amount of government bonds.

We noted earlier that the public debt increased sharply during World War II. Was some of the economic burden of World War II shifted to future generations by the decision to finance military purchases through the sale of government bonds? Again, the answer is "No." Recalling the production possibilities curve, we realize that the economic cost of World War II was the civilian goods society had to forgo in shifting scarce resources to war goods production. Regardless of whether financing of this reallocation was achieved through higher taxes or borrowing, the real economic burden of the war would have been essentially the same. In short, the burden of the war was borne almost entirely by those who lived during the war; they were the ones who did without a multitude of consumer goods to permit the United States to arm itself and its allies.

Also, wartime production may slow the growth of a nation's stock of capital as resources are shifted from production of capital goods to production of war goods. As a result, future generations inherit a smaller stock of capital goods than they otherwise would. This occurred in the United States during World War II (see table on inside covers, line 2). But, again, this shifting of costs is independent of how a war is financed.

QUICK REVIEW 18-2

∮ **There is no danger of the Federal government going bankrupt because it need only refinance (not retire) the public debt and can raise revenues, if needed, through higher taxes or printing money.**

∮ **Usually, the public debt is not a means of shifting economic burdens to future generations.**

ECONOMIC IMPLICATIONS: SUBSTANTIVE ISSUES

We must be careful not to leave the impression that the public debt is of no concern among economists. The large debt *does* pose some real and potential problems, although economists vary in the importance they attach to these problems.

Income Distribution

The distribution of government bond ownership is undoubtedly uneven. Some people own more than their $14,244 per capita share; others less; others none at all. Although our knowledge of the ownership of the public debt by income class is limited, it is presumed that ownership is concentrated among wealthier groups in society. Because the tax system is at best mildly progressive, payment of interest on the public debt probably increases income inequality. If greater income equality is one of our social goals, then this redistributive effect is clearly undesirable.

Incentives

Table 18-1 indicates that the present public debt necessitates annual interest payments well over $185 billion. With no increase in the size of the debt, this annual interest charge must be paid out of tax revenues. These added taxes may dampen incentives to bear risk, to innovate, to invest, and to work. In this indirect way, the existence of a large public debt can impair economic growth. As noted earlier, the ratio of interest payments to GDP indicates the level of taxation needed to pay interest on the debt. Thus, some economists are concerned that this ratio has increased quite sharply in recent years (column 6 of Table 18-1).

External Debt

External debt—our U.S. debt held by citizens and institutions of foreign countries—is a burden. This part of the public debt is *not* "owed to ourselves," and in real terms the payment of interest and principal requires transferring a portion of our real output to other nations. It is worth noting that foreign ownership of the public debt has increased in recent years. In 1960 only about 5 percent of the debt was foreign-owned; currently foreign ownership is about 12 percent. The assertion that "we owe the debt to ourselves" and the implication that the debt should be of little concern is less accurate than it was three decades ago.

Crowding Out and the Stock of Capital

This brings us to a potentially more serious problem. As an exception to our earlier comments, there is one important way the public debt can transfer a real economic burden to future generations. That way is by causing future generations to inherit a smaller stock of capital goods—a smaller "national factory." This possibility involves Chapter 12's **crowding-out effect,** the notion that deficit financing will increase interest rates and reduce investment spending. If this should happen, future generations would inherit an economy with a smaller productive capacity and, other things being equal, the standard of living would be lower than otherwise.

How might this come to pass? Suppose the economy is operating at its full-employment or potential level of output and that the Federal budget is initially in balance. Now for some reason government increases its level of spending. We know from earlier discussion of the economic burden of World War II that the impact of an increase in government spending will fall on those living when it occurs. Think of Chapter 2's production possibilities curve with "government goods" on one axis and "private goods" on the other. In a full-employment economy an increase in government spending will move the economy *along* the curve toward the government-goods axis, meaning that fewer private goods will be available.

But private goods may be either consumer or investment goods. If the increased government goods are provided at the expense of consumer goods, then the present generation bears the entire burden in the form of a lower current standard of living. The current investment level is not affected and therefore neither is the size of the national factory inherited by future generations. But if the increase in government goods means a reduction in production of capital goods, then the present generation's level of consumption (standard of living) will be unimpaired. However, in the future our children and grandchildren will inherit a smaller stock of capital goods and will realize lower income levels than otherwise.

Two Scenarios Let's sketch the two scenarios which yield the two results described.

First Scenario Suppose the presumed increase in government spending is financed by an increase in taxation, say, personal income taxes. We know that most income is consumed and that, therefore, consumer spending will fall by almost as much as the increase in taxes. In this case the burden of the increase in government spending falls primarily on today's generation in the form of fewer consumer goods.

Second Scenario Assume that the increase in government spending is financed by increasing the public debt. In this case the government goes into the money market and competes with private borrowers for funds. Given the supply of money, this increase in money demand will increase the interest rate—the "price" paid for the use of money.

In Figure 18-1 the curve I_{d1} reproduces the investment-demand curve of Figure 10-7. (Ignore curve I_{d2} for now.) The investment-demand curve is downsloping, indicating that investment spending varies inversely with the interest rate. In this instance government deficit financing drives up the interest rate, causing private investment to fall. For example, if government borrowing increases the interest rate from 6 to 10 percent, investment spending would fall from $25 to $15 billion. That is, $10 billion of private investment would be crowded out.

Our conclusion is that the assumed increase in public goods production is much more likely to come at the expense of private investment goods when financed by deficits. In comparison with tax financing the future generation inherits a smaller national factory

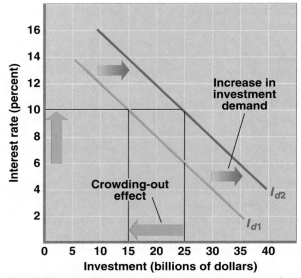

FIGURE 18-1   The investment-demand curve and the crowding-out effect

The crowding-out effect suggests that, given the location of the investment-demand curve (I_{d1}), an increase in the interest rate caused by a government deficit will reduce private investment spending and decrease the size of the "national factory" inherited by future generations. In this case an increase in the interest rate from 6 to 10 percent crowds out $10 billion of private investment. However, if the economy is initially in a recession, the government deficit may improve profit expectations of businesses and shift the investment-demand curve rightward as from I_{d1} to I_{d2}. This shift may offset the crowding-out effect wholly or in part.

and therefore realizes a lower standard of living with deficit financing.

Two Qualifications But there are two important loose ends to our discussion which might mitigate or even eliminate the size of the economic burden shifted to future generations in our second scenario.

1 Public Investment Our discussion has glossed over the character of the increase in government spending. Just as private goods may involve consumption or investment, so it is with public goods. If the increase in government spending is essentially consumption-type outlays—subsidies for school lunches or provision of limousines for government officials—then our second scenario's conclusion that the debt increase has shifted a burden to future generations is correct. But what if the government spending is primarily investment-type outlays, for example, for construction of highways, harbors, and flood-control projects? Similarly, what if they are "human capital" investments in education and health?

Like private expenditures on machinery and equipment, **public investments** increase the economy's future productive capacity. Thus, the capital stock of future generations need not be diminished, but rather its composition is changed so there is more public capital and less private capital.

2 Unemployment The other qualification relates to our assumption that the initial increase in government expenditures occurs when the economy is operating at full employment. Again the production possibilities curve reminds us that, *if* the economy is at less than full employment or, graphically, operating at a point inside the production possibilities frontier, then an increase in government expenditures can move the economy *to* the curve without any sacrifice of either current consumption or capital accumulation. If unemployment exists initially, deficit spending by government need *not* mean a burden for future generations in the form of a smaller national factory.

Consider Figure 18-1 once again. We know that, if deficit financing increases the interest rate from 6 to 10 percent, a crowding-out effect of $10 billion will occur. But now we are saying that the increase in government spending will stimulate a recession economy via the multiplier effect, thereby improving business profit expectations and causing a rightward shift of investment demand to I_{d2}. As a result, in the case shown, investment spending remains at $25 billion despite the higher 10 percent interest rate. Of course, the increase in investment demand might be smaller or larger than that shown in Figure 18-1. In the former case the crowding-out effect would not be fully offset; in the latter case it would be more than offset. The point is that an increase in investment demand counters the crowding-out effect.

RECENT FEDERAL DEFICITS

Federal deficits and the growing public debt have been in the economic spotlight in the last decade. This in part is because of the unusually large size of recent deficits. It also reflects an intertwined group of economic problems which are associated with the deficits.

Growing Concerns

Growing concern over deficits and the public debt spring from several sources.

TABLE 18-2 Recent annual Federal deficits *(selected fiscal years, in billions of dollars)**

Year	Deficit	Year	Deficit
1970	$ 3	1984	$185
1973	15	1985	212
1977	54	1986	221
1979	40	1987	149
1980	74	1988	155
1981	79	1989	154
1982	128	1990	221
1983	208	1991	269

*Fiscal years are twelve-month periods ending September 30 of each year, rather than December 31 as for calendar years. Source: *Economic Report of the President,* 1992.

Enormous Size First, there is the matter of size. As Table 18-2 makes clear, the absolute size of annual Federal deficits increased enormously in the past decade, as did the public debt. The average annual deficit for the 1970s was approximately $35 billion. In the 1980s annual deficits averaged five times that amount. As a consequence, the public debt tripled during the 1980s (Table 18-1).

The Federal deficit increased to $269 billion in 1991, mainly because of the 1990–1991 recession which reduced tax revenues. Government's expensive bailout of failed S&Ls also contributed to this large deficit. The 1992 deficit is expected to exceed the 1991 deficit, perhaps reaching $350 billion.

Understatement? The most recent annual budget deficits shown in Table 18-2 may be severely understated. Over the past few years government has raised more money from social security taxes than it has paid out as benefits to current retirees. The purpose of this surplus is to prepare for the future time when numerous "baby boomers" retire. Some economists argue that these revenues should be excluded when calculating present deficits because they represent future government obligations on a dollar-for-dollar basis. That is, the social security surplus should not be considered as an offset to *current* government spending. When we exclude the social security surplus from the deficit figures, the 1991 budget deficit is $339 billion, not the $269 billion shown in Table 18-2.

Rising Interest Costs Reference to column 4 of Table 18-1 indicates that interest payments on the public debt have increased more than tenfold since 1970. Interest payments were $188 billion in 1991, an amount greater than the entire deficit in many previous years! Because interest payments are part of government expenditures, the debt feeds on itself through interest charges. Interest payments on the debt are the only component of government spending which Congress cannot cut. The spiraling of such payments therefore complicates the problem of controlling government spending and the size of future deficits.

Inappropriate Policy Another concern is that many of our recent large annual deficits occurred in an economy operating close to full employment. Historically, deficits—particularly sizable ones—have been associated with wartime finance and recessions. While the 1980–1982 and 1990–1991 recessions contributed to large deficits, it is clear that the large size of continuing deficits reflects the 1981 tax cuts and rising government spending. In terms of Figure 12-4, the 1981 tax cuts have shifted the tax line downward. Meanwhile, the government spending line in the figure has shifted upward. Thus, even at a full-employment level of output (GDP$_1$) sizable structural deficits can be expected.

Large deficits during times of economic prosperity raise the concern of fueling demand-pull inflation. To counteract potentially rising prices, the Federal Reserve is forced to employ a tighter monetary policy than would otherwise be ideal. Along with the strong demand for money in the private sector, the tight money policy raises real interest rates and reduces investment spending. The point is that the greatest potential for budget deficits to produce a crowding-out effect occurs when the economy is near or at full employment.

Balance of Trade Problems Finally, large budget deficits make it difficult for the nation to achieve a balance in its international trade. As we will see, large annual budget deficits promote imports and stifle exports. Furthermore, budget deficits are thought to be a main cause of two related phenomena much in the news: (1) our recently attained status as the "world's leading debtor nation" and (2) the so-called "selling of America" to foreign investors.

BUDGET DEFICITS AND TRADE DEFICITS

Many, but not all, economists see a direct cause-effect chain between Federal budget deficits and balance of trade deficits. Figure 18-2 is a helpful guide to understanding their thinking.

FIGURE 18-2 Budget deficits and trade deficits
Many economists contend that large deficits have the effects shown below. Deficits increase domestic interest rates, resulting in both crowding out of private investment and an increase in the demand for American securities. The latter increases our externally held debt and the demand for dollars. The strong demand for dollars raises the international value of the dollar, making our exports more expensive to foreigners and imports cheaper to Americans. As our exports fall and our imports rise, a contractionary trade deficit arises.

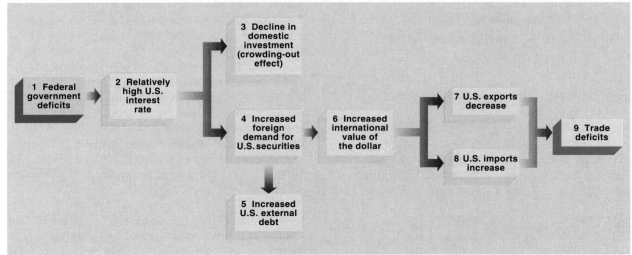

Higher Interest Rates

Beginning with boxes 1 and 2, we note once again that in financing its deficits government must enter the money market to compete with the private sector for funds. We know this drives up interest rates. High interest rates in turn have two important effects. First, as shown in box 3, they discourage private investment spending; this is the crowding-out effect discussed earlier. When the economy is reasonably close to full employment, the crowding-out effect is likely to be large. Therefore, although willing to admit that the short-run impact of deficits is expansionary, some economists express concern that the long-run effect will retard the economy's growth rate. They envision deficits being used to finance defense spending and consumption-type government goods at the expense of investment in modernized factories and equipment. Deficits, it is contended, are forcing the economy onto a slower long-run growth path.

Dollar Appreciation

The second effect, shown by box 4, is that high interest rates on both American government and private securities make financial investment in the United States more attractive for foreigners. While the resulting inflow of foreign funds helps finance both the deficit and private investment, box 5 reminds us that this inflow represents an increase in our external debt. Recall that paying interest on and retiring debts to foreigners means a reduction in future real output available to our domestic economy.

Box 6 indicates that, to purchase high-yielding American securities, foreigners must first buy American dollars with their own currencies. This increases the worldwide demand for dollars and increases the international price or exchange value of the dollar. To illustrate: Suppose that prior to our incurring large deficits, the dollar ($) and the French franc (F) exchanged in the market at a rate of $1 = F10. But now the financing of our large deficits increases interest rates in the United States, increasing the demand for dollars with which to buy American securities. Suppose this raises the price of the dollar to, say, $1 = F11.

Trade Deficits

This appreciation of the dollar will eventually depress our exports (box 7) and increase our imports (box 8), leading to an "unfavorable" balance of trade. Let's see how this comes about. We know that exchange rates link the price levels of the world's nations. When the value of the dollar increases—when dollars become more expensive to foreigners—all American goods become more expensive to foreign buyers.

In our example the increase in the value of the dollar from $1 = F10 to $1 = F11 increases prices of all American goods by 10 percent to the French. The American product that formerly cost 10 francs now costs 11 francs. The French will react to this by buying fewer American goods; American exports will fall. Conversely, at the higher exchange rate Americans now get 11 rather than 10 francs for a dollar, so French goods are cheaper to Americans. We therefore buy more French goods; our imports rise. Or, to bring these two developments together, American net exports (exports *minus* imports) fall and a trade deficit emerges (box 9).

Net exports are a component of aggregate demand. A trade deficit implies negative net exports and has a contractionary effect on the economy. As our exports fall, unemployment will rise in American exporting industries such as agriculture and computers. American import-competing industries such as automobiles and basic steel will also be adversely affected. The increase in the value of the dollar makes Japanese and German imports of these products cheaper and American auto and steel industries find themselves with excess productive capacity and redundant labor.

Note that the foregoing comments reiterate our earlier analysis (Chapter 12) that an expansionary fiscal policy may be less stimulating to the economy than simple analysis suggests. The expansionary impact of a deficit might be softened by both the *crowding-out effect* (box 3) and the negative *net export effect* (box 9) to which it might give rise.

Related Effects

There are three loose ends to this story.

1   The inflow of foreign funds does augment domestic funds and helps keep American interest rates lower than they otherwise would be. Stated differently, the inflow of foreign funds to the United States diminishes the size of the crowding-out effect. From the standpoint of foreign nations transferring funds to the United States, their domestic investment and long-term economic growth will be smaller than otherwise.
2   Deficit-caused high interest rates in America impose an increased burden on heavily indebted underdeveloped countries such as Mexico and Brazil. Their

dollar-denominated debts to American banks and the banks of other industrially advanced nations become more costly to service when American interest rates rise.

Similarly, if declining American net exports lead to protectionism, these nations will have more difficulty selling their products in the United States. This means they will have greater difficulty in earning dollars to pay interest and principal on their debts.

In short, our large budget deficits—particularly through the upward pressure they exert on domestic interest rates—pose something of a threat to the international credit system and to American banks.

3   A trade deficit means we are not exporting enough goods to pay for our imports. The difference can be paid for in two ways. First, we can borrow from people and institutions in foreign lands. In the late 1980s when the American trade deficit was severe, the United States became the world's leading debtor nation. Second, U.S. assets such as factories, shopping centers, and farms can be sold to foreign investors. This, too, happened in the late 1980s and early 1990s. To pay our debts and repurchase these assets, we must in the future export more than we import. In other words, in the future we will need to consume and invest less than we produce.

Contrary View: Ricardian Equivalence Theorem

A few prominent economists disagree with the mainstream analysis we have outlined. They adhere to the **Ricardian equivalence theorem** (Chapter 12) which holds that financing a deficit by borrowing has the same effect on GDP as financing it through a present tax increase. People are allegedly aware that deficits today will require higher future taxes to pay the added interest expense resulting from the increase in the public debt. Households therefore spend less today—saving more—in anticipation of having less future after-tax income available for consumption. Because the increase in private saving perfectly offsets the increase in government borrowing, the interest rate does not change. Thus neither a crowing-out effect nor a trade deficit necessarily emerges from a budget deficit. In Figure 18-2 the Ricardian equivalence theorem breaks the chain between box 1 and box 2, negating all the effects purportedly following (boxes 3 through 9).

But most economists reject this novel perspective. They claim instead that the 1980s and early 1990s pro-

vide ample evidence of negative foreign-sector effects of large budget deficits. A glance at line 4 on the inside back cover of this text shows that high trade deficits (negative net exports) accompanied the large budget deficits of the late 1980s and early 1990s (Table 18-2).

Policy Responses

Concern with large budget deficits and an expanding public debt has spawned several policy responses.

Constitutional Amendment   The most extreme proposal is that a constitutional amendment should be passed which mandates that Congress balance the budget each year. This proposed **balanced budget amendment** is based on the assumption that Congress will continue to act "irresponsibly" because government spending enhances and tax increases diminish a politician's popular support. Political rhetoric notwithstanding, Federal deficits allegedly will continue until a constitutional amendment forces a balanced budget. Critics of this proposal remind us that an annually balanced budget has a procyclical or destabilizing effect on the economy.

Gramm-Rudman-Hollings Act   In December of 1985 Congress passed the **Gramm-Rudman-Hollings Act** (GRH) which was designed to achieve annual reductions in the Federal deficit to ensure that the budget be balanced by 1991. Congress revised the act in 1987 to allow a more gradual reduction in the budget deficits and a balanced budget by 1993.

The idea of GRH was to encourage the President and Congress to agree on an annual budget which achieved the targeted reduction in the deficit. If they could not agree on sufficient spending cuts or tax hikes to achieve the required deficit goals, a series of automatic spending cuts would occur until the deficit goals were realized.

The automatic provisions of GRH were never invoked, and the act probably restrained government spending. But one major problem with the law was that its compliance required only annual submission of a *planned* budget which met the deficit reduction goals. *Actual* budget deficits exceeding those planned did not trigger automatic spending cuts. Also, GRH contained an escape clause exempting the administration from the deficit provisions if the economy experienced recession. Faced with the recession of 1990–1991 and the massive S&L bailout, Congress in effect abandoned the GRH targets as unrealistic.

Budget Legislation of 1990 In November 1990 Congress directly attacked the deficit problem by passing the **Budget Reconciliation Act of 1990,** a package of tax increases and spending cuts designed to reduce budget deficits by $500 billion between 1991 and 1996.

This act sought to enhance tax revenue through (1) an increase in the marginal tax rate for wealthy Americans from 28 to 31 percent; (2) lower allowable deductions and personal exemptions for wealthy individuals; (3) higher payroll taxes for medical care; (4) increased excise taxes on gasoline, tobacco, alcoholic beverages, and airline tickets; and (5) a new luxury tax on expensive jewelry, furs, cars, boats, and personal aircraft. This law also lopped $260 billion from government spending between 1991 and 1996, the brunt of cuts being borne by national defense, farm programs, and Federal pensions.

Tax increases and expenditure cuts in the midst of recession are counter to conventional fiscal policy. But Congress and the Bush administration reasoned that deficit reduction was essential to lower interest rates and increase investment—that is, to achieve a reverse crowding-out effect. They also recognized that without these actions deficits would skyrocket to unprecedented, politically costly heights.

The **Budget Enforcement Act of 1990** accompanied the Budget Reconciliation Act and established a "pay-as-you-go" test for new spending or tax decreases. Between 1991 and 1996 new legislation that increases government spending must be offset by a corresponding decrease in existing spending or an increase in

taxes. Likewise, new tax reductions must be accompanied by offsetting tax increases or spending cuts. Also, this law placed legally binding caps (with exceptions for emergencies) on Federal spending for each of these five years.

The budget legislation of 1990 will keep budget deficits from rising as fast as otherwise, but these laws will *not* reduce budget deficits to zero any time soon. Unless Congress takes further direct action, most observers believe that the "reduced" deficits will remain historically high.

Other Proposals Concern with balancing the budget has prompted a variety of other deficit-reduction proposals. Two significant proposals are the call for greater "privatization" of the economy and for reform which would enable the President to veto spending measures on a line-item basis.

1 Privatization **Privatization** refers to government divesting itself of certain assets and programs through their sale to private firms. This is in keeping with the conservative belief that most economic activities can be performed more efficiently in the private sector than in the public sector. More important for present purposes, the sale of government programs and assets would provide revenue to help reduce budget deficits and public debt. It has been proposed that the Navy's petroleum reserves in California and Wyoming, Amtrak, Washington's Dulles and International airports, the Federal Housing Administration, and the Bonneville Power Administration, among other entities, be sold to private firms. While privatization is very controversial, there are precedents. Margaret Thatcher's conservative government in Great Britain sold more than $25 billion of state-owned enterprises in the 1980s.

2 Line-Item Veto The **line-item veto** would permit the President to veto individual spending items in appropriation bills. A typical appropriations bill merges hundreds of programs and projects into a single piece of legislation. Governors of forty-three states currently possess line-item veto authority for their state budgets, but the President does not have that kind of veto power for the Federal budget. Proponents of this reform argue that it would allow the President to cull from appropriation bills projects for which local or regional benefits are less than the costs to the nation's taxpayers. The line-item veto would tend to reduce government spending and help the Federal government balance its budget. Opponents argue that the line-item

LAST WORD

PUBLIC DEBT: INTERNATIONAL COMPARISONS

Although the United States has the world's largest public debt, several other industrial nations have larger debts as a percentage of their GDPs.

Public debt is not exclusively an American phenomenon. All industrial nations have public debts, and, as shown in the accompanying figure, several have larger relative debts than the United States. Note that in 1991 public debt as a percentage of gross domestic product was larger in Italy, Japan, and Canada than in the United States and that the relative debts of France and Germany were only slightly lower than in the United States.

Whatever the particular combinations of forces giving rise to public debts in various nations, the existence of public debts is universal. More importantly, there is no discernible relationship between a nation's public debt as a percentage of its GDP and the overall health of its economy. Japan, with a high relative debt,

has had an enviable growth record during the past several decades; the United Kingdom, with a small relative debt, has generally struggled. Meanwhile, Germany has had strong economic growth, and its relative debt is below that of Italy, Japan, Canada, the United States, and France.

---

veto would give far too much power to the President—power, they say, which might easily be abused for political purposes.

Positive Role of Debt

Having completed this survey of imagined and real problems associated with deficits and the public debt, we conclude our discussion on a more positive note. Debt—both public and private—plays a positive role in a prosperous and growing economy. As income expands, so does saving. Employment theory and fiscal policy tell us that if aggregate expenditures are to be sustained at the full-employment level, this expanding volume of saving or its equivalent must be obtained and spent by consumers, businesses, or government. The process by which saving is transferred to spenders is *debt creation*. Now, in fact, consumers and businesses *do* borrow and spend a great amount of saving. But if households and businesses are not willing to borrow and thereby increase private debt sufficiently fast to absorb the growing volume of saving, an increase in public debt must absorb the remainder or the economy will falter from full employment and fail to realize its growth potential.

CHAPTER SUMMARY

1 A budget deficit is the excess of government expenditures over its receipts; the public debt is the total accumulation of its deficits and surpluses over time.

2 Budget philosophies include the annually balanced budget, the cyclically balanced budget, and functional finance. The basic problem with an annually balanced budget is that it is procyclical rather than countercyclical. Similarly, it may be difficult to balance the budget over the course of the business cycle if upswings and downswings are not of

roughly comparable magnitude. Functional finance is the view that the primary purpose of Federal finance is to stabilize the economy, and problems associated with consequent deficits or surpluses are of secondary importance.

3 Historically, growth of the public debt has been caused by the deficit financing of wars and by recessions. The large deficits in recent years are primarily the result of earlier tax reductions, accompanied by expenditure increases.

4 The public debt was $3.6 trillion in 1991. Since the

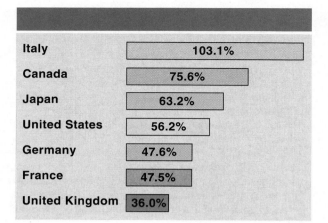

Italy	103.1%
Canada	75.6%
Japan	63.2%
United States	56.2%
Germany	47.6%
France	47.5%
United Kingdom	36.0%

For most economists, the main message from these international comparisons is that Americans need not be overly concerned with the public debt. But other economists warn that the figure demonstrates only that the United States is not alone in making inappropriate fiscal decisions.

1970s the debt and associated interest charges have trended upward as a percentage of the GDP. The debt has also been rising on a per capita basis.

5   The argument that a large public debt may bankrupt the government is false because **a** the debt need only be refinanced rather than refunded and **b** the Federal government has the power to levy taxes and create money.

6   The crowding-out effect aside, the public debt is not a vehicle for shifting economic burdens to future generations.

7   More substantive problems associated with the public debt include the following: **a** Payment of interest on the debt probably increases income inequality. **b** Interest payments on the debt require higher taxes which may impair incentives. **c** Paying interest or principal on the portion of the debt held by foreigners entails a transfer of real output abroad. **d** Government borrowing to refinance or pay interest on the debt may increase interest rates and crowd out private investment spending.

8   Federal budget deficits have been much larger recently than earlier. Many economists think these large deficits have increased interest rates in the United States which in turn have **a** crowded out private investment and **b** increased foreign demand for American securities. Increased demand for American securities has increased the international value of the dollar, causing American exports to fall and American imports to rise. The resulting trade deficits exert a contractionary effect on our domestic economy.

9   Proposed or enacted remedies for deficits and public debt increases include **a** a proposed constitutional amendment mandating an annually balanced budget; **b** the Gramm-Rudman-Hollings Act which required annual deficit reductions; **c** budget legislation of 1990 which raised taxes, cut expenditures, and forced Congress to offset new spending or tax cuts with reductions in existing spending or tax increases; **d** greater privatization of the economy by selling public assets and programs to the private sector; and **e** giving the President line-item veto authority.

TERMS AND CONCEPTS

budget deficit	functional finance	balanced budget	Budget Enforcement
public debt	external debt	amendment	Act of 1990
annually balanced	crowding-out effect	Gramm-Rudman-	privatization
budget	Ricardian equivalence	Hollings Act	line-item veto
cyclically balanced	theorem	Budget Reconciliation	
budget	public investments	Act of 1990	

QUESTIONS AND STUDY SUGGESTIONS

1   Assess the potential for using fiscal policy as a stabilization device under **a** an annually balanced budget, **b** a cyclically balanced budget, and **c** functional finance.

2   What have been the major sources of the public debt historically? Why were deficits so large in the 1980s? Why was the deficit so large in 1991?

3   Discuss the various ways of measuring the size of the public debt. How does an internally held public debt differ from an externally held public debt? What would be the effects of retiring an internally held public debt? An externally held public debt? Distinguish between refinancing and retiring the debt.

4 Explain or evaluate each of the following statements:

a "A national debt is like a debt of the left hand to the right hand."

b "The least likely problem arising from a large public debt is that the Federal government will go bankrupt."

c "The basic cause of our growing public debt is a lack of political courage."

d "The social security reserves are not being reserved. They are being spent, masking the real deficit."

5 Is the crowding-out effect likely to be larger during recession or when the economy is near full employment? Use the aggregate demand–aggregate supply model to substantiate your answer.

6 Some economists argue that the quantitative importance of the public debt can best be measured by interest payments on the debt as a percentage of the GDP. Can you explain why?

7 Explain the essence of the 1990 Budget Reconciliation and Budget Enforcement Acts. Would you favor a constitutional amendment requiring the Federal budget to be balanced annually? Do you favor "privatization," either as a means of reducing budget deficits or as a vehicle for reducing the size of the public sector? Do you favor giving the President the authority to veto line-items of appropriation bills?

8 Is our $3.6 trillion public debt a burden to future generations? If so, in what sense? Why might deficit financing be more likely to reduce the future size of our "national factory" than tax financing of government expenditures?

9 Trace the cause-and-effect chain through which large deficits might affect domestic interest rates, domestic investment, the international value of the dollar, and our international trade. Comment: "There is too little recognition that the deterioration of America's position in world trade is more the result of our own policies than the harm wrought by foreigners." Provide a critique of this position, using the idea of Ricardian equivalence.

10 Explain how a significant decline in the nation's budget deficit would be expected to affect **a** the size of our trade deficit, **b** the total debt Americans owe to foreigners, and **c** foreign purchases of U.S. assets such as factories and farms.

C
H
A
P
T
E
R
19

Economic Growth

Although punctuated by periods of cyclical instability, economic growth in the United States has been impressive during this century. Real output has increased twelvefold and population has tripled, yielding approximately a quadrupling of the goods and services available to the average American. *What explains this expansion of real GDP and real GDP per capita?*

During the 1980s and early 1990s saving as a percentage of GDP in the United States fell to less than half its historical average. Also, according to a recent major study, America's technological edge has ended in a full one-third of ninety-four critical technologies in which we had a lead just a decade ago. *What are the implications of these developments for economic growth in the United States?*

In the 1970s and to a lesser degree in the 1980s and early 1990s productivity growth—increases in output per worker-hour—slowed in the United States relative to earlier periods. *How does productivity growth relate to economic growth? What caused this slowdown?*

The foregoing questions preview part of the subject matter of this chapter. Specifically, our discussion of economic growth is organized as follows. First, we examine how growth is defined and why it is important. Our second goal is to gain analytical perspective on economic growth. Third, we present and assess the long-term growth record of the United States. Fourth, the quantitative importance of various factors contributing to growth are explored. Fifth, we explain the slowdown in the productivity growth of American labor which began in the 1970s. Finally, we briefly examine the controversy surrounding growth and take a fleeting look at policies to promote growth.

GROWTH ECONOMICS

Employment theory and stabilization policy are of a static or short-run character. They assume the economy has fixed amounts of resources or inputs available and therefore is capable of producing some capacity or full-employment level of domestic output. The concern of employment theory is what must be done to use fully the nation's *existing* productive capacity. In contrast, growth economics is concerned with how to *increase*

365

the economy's productive capacity or full-employment GDP.

Two Definitions

Economic growth is defined and measured in two related ways. Specifically, it may be defined as:

1 The increase in real GDP which occurs over a period of time

2 The increase in real GDP *per capita* which occurs over time

Both definitions are useful. For example, in measuring military potential or political preeminence, the first definition is more relevant. But per capita output is clearly superior to compare living standards among nations or regions. While India's GDP is $235 billion as compared to Switzerland's $175 billion, per capita GDP is $29,880 in Switzerland and only $340 in India. In this chapter we deal primarily with the growth of real output and income per capita.

Economic growth by either definition is usually calculated in terms of annual percentage *rates* of growth. For example, if real GDP was $200 billion last year and $210 billion this year, we can calculate the rate of growth by subtracting last year's real GDP from this year's real GDP and comparing the difference to last year's real GDP. Specifically, the growth rate in this case is ($210 − $200)/$200, or 5 percent.

Importance of Growth

Growth is a widely held economic goal. The growth of total output relative to population means a higher standard of living. An expanding real output means greater material abundance and implies a more satisfactory answer to the economizing problem. *A growing economy is in a superior position to meet new needs and resolve socioeconomic problems both domestically and internationally.* A growing economy, by definition, enjoys an increment in its annual real output which it can use to satisfy existing needs more effectively or to undertake new programs.

An expanding real wage or salary income makes new opportunities available to a family—a trip to Europe, a new stereo, a college education for each child—without sacrificing other opportunities and enjoyments. Similarly, a growing economy can undertake new programs to alleviate poverty and clean up the environment *without* impairing existing levels of consumption, investment, and public goods production. *Growth lessens the burden of scarcity.* A growing econ-

omy, unlike a static one, can consume more while simultaneously increasing its capacity to produce more in the future. By easing the burden of scarcity—by relaxing society's production constraints—economic growth allows a nation to attain existing economic goals more fully and to undertake new output-absorbing endeavors.

Arithmetic of Growth

People sometimes wonder why economists get excited about seemingly minuscule changes in the rate of growth. But it really *does* matter whether our economy grows at 4 percent or 3 percent. For the United States, with a current real GDP of about $4848 billion, the difference between a 3 and a 4 percent growth rate is about $48 billion of output per year. For a very poor country, a .5 percent change in the growth rate may mean the difference between starvation and mere hunger.

Furthermore, when viewed over a period of years, an apparently small difference in the rate of growth becomes exceedingly important because of the "miracle" of compound interest. Example: Suppose Alphania and Betania have identical GDPs. But Alphania begins to grow at a 4 percent annual rate, while Betania grows at only 2 percent. Recalling our "rule of 70" of Chapter 8, Alphania would find that its GDP would double in about eighteen years (=70 ÷ 4); Betania would take thirty-five years (=70 ÷ 2) to accomplish the same feat. The importance of the growth rate is undeniable.

One can also argue that the realization of growth is more important than achieving economic stability. The elimination of a recessionary gap might increase the national income by, say, 6 percent on a one-time basis. But a 3 percent annual growth rate will increase the national income by 6 percent in two years and will provide that 6 percent biannual increment indefinitely.

CAUSES: INGREDIENTS OF GROWTH

Basically, there are six strategic ingredients in the growth of any economy.

Supply Factors

Four growth factors relate to the physical ability of an economy to grow. They are (1) the quantity and quality of its natural resources, (2) the quantity and quality of its human resources, (3) the supply or stock of capital goods, and (4) technology. These four items are the **supply factors** in economic growth. These are the physical agents of greater production. The availability of more and better resources, including the stock of technological knowledge, is what permits an economy to produce a greater real output.

Demand and Allocative Factors

But the ability to grow and the actual realization of growth may be quite different things. Specifically, two additional considerations contribute to growth. First, there is a **demand factor** in growth. To realize its growing productive potential, a nation must provide for full employment of its expanding supplies of resources. This requires a growing level of aggregate demand.

Second, there is the **allocative factor** in growth. To achieve its productive potential, a nation must provide not only for full employment of its resources, but also for full production from them. The ability to expand production is not sufficient for the expansion of total output; also required are the actual employment of expanded resource supplies *and* the efficient allocation of those resources to get the maximum amount of useful goods produced.

It is notable that the supply and demand factors in growth are related. Unemployment can retard the rate of capital accumulation and slow expenditures for research. And, conversely, a low rate of innovation and investment can cause unemployment.

ECONOMIC GROWTH: GRAPHICAL ANALYSIS

The factors underlying economic growth can be placed in proper perspective through Chapter 2's production possibilities curves and Chapter 17's aggregate demand and aggregate supply analysis.

Growth and Production Possibilities

Recall that a curve such as *AB* in Figure 19-1 is a best-performance curve. It indicates the various *maximum* combinations of products the economy can produce, given the quantity and quality of its natural, human, and capital resources, and its stock of technological knowledge. An improvement in any of the supply factors will push the production possibilities curve to the

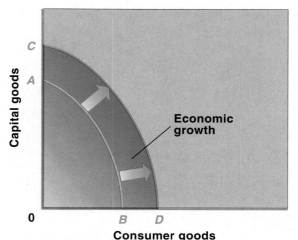

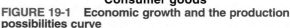

FIGURE 19-1　Economic growth and the production possibilities curve

Economic growth is indicated by an outward shift of the production possibilities curve, as from *AB* to *CD*. Increases in the quantity and quality of resources and technological advance permit this shift; full employment and allocative efficiency are essential to its realization.

right, as shown by the shift from *AB* to *CD* in Figure 19-1. Increases in the quantity or quality of resources and technological progress push the curve to the right. But the demand and allocative factors remind us that the economy need not attain its maximum productive potential; the curve may shift to the right and leave the economy behind at some level of operation *inside* the curve. In particular, the economy's enhanced productive *potential* will not be *realized* unless (1) aggregate demand increases sufficiently to sustain full employment, and (2) the additional resources are employed efficiently so they make the maximum possible contribution to the domestic output.

Example: The net increase in the labor force of the United States is roughly 2 million workers per year. As such, this increment raises the productive capacity, or potential, of the economy. But obtaining the extra output these additional workers are capable of producing presumes they can find jobs and that these jobs are in firms and industries where their talents are fully used. Society doesn't want new labor-force entrants to be unemployed; nor does it want pediatricians working as plumbers.

Although demand and allocative considerations are important, discussions of growth focus primarily on the supply side. Figure 19-2 provides a commonly used framework for discussing the supply factors in growth.

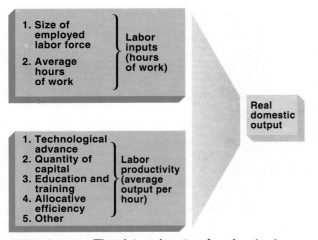

FIGURE 19-2 The determinants of real output

Real GDP can be usefully viewed as the product of the quantity of labor inputs multiplied by labor productivity.

It indicates there are two fundamental ways any society can increase its real output and income: (1) by increasing its inputs of resources, and (2) by increasing the productivity of those inputs. Let's focus on inputs of labor. By so doing we can say that *our real GDP in any year depends on the input of labor (measured in worker-hours) multiplied by* **labor productivity** *(measured as real output per worker per hour)*. That is

Total output = worker-hours × labor productivity

Hypothetical illustration: Assume an economy with 10 workers, each of whom works 2000 hours per year (50 weeks at 40 hours per week) so that total input of worker-hours is 20,000 hours. If productivity—average real output per worker-hour—is $5, then total output or real GDP will be $100,000 (=20,000 × $5).

What determines the number of hours worked each year? And, more importantly, what determines labor productivity? Figure 19-2 provides a framework for answering these questions. The hours of labor input depend on the size of the employed labor force and the length of the average workweek. Labor force size in turn depends on the size of the working age population and the labor force participation rate, that is, the percentage of the working age population actually in the labor force. The average workweek is governed by legal and institutional considerations and by collective bargaining.

Productivity is determined by technological progress, the quantity of capital goods with which workers are equipped, the quality of labor itself, and the efficiency with which inputs are allocated, combined, and managed. Stated differently, productivity increases

when the health, training, education, and motivation of workers are improved; when workers have more and better machinery and natural resources with which to work; when production is better organized and managed; and when labor is reallocated from less efficient industries to more efficient industries.

Note that Figure 19-2 complements Figure 15-4. The latter figure outlines the determinants of the *demand* for domestic output. Figure 19-2 summarizes those factors which determine a nation's capacity to *supply* or produce aggregate output. By locating Figure 19-2 to the left of Figure 15-4, we obtain a more complete model of the economy which sketches the determinants of both the demand for, and the supply of, domestic output.

Aggregate Demand–Aggregate Supply Framework

We can also view economic growth in terms of the long-run aggregate supply and aggregate demand analysis developed in Figures 17-6 and 17-7. Initially, suppose that aggregate demand is AD_1 and long-run and short-run aggregate supply curves are AS_1 and AS_1' as shown in Figure 19-3. Thus, the initial equilibrium price level is P_1 while the level of real output is Q_1.

Recall that the upward slope of short-run aggregate supply curve AS_1' shows that, other things equal, a change in the price level will alter the level of real output. In the long run, however, wages and other input prices will fully adjust to the price level, making the aggregate supply curve vertical at the economy's natural or potential level of real output. As is true of the location of the production possibilities curve, real supply factors—the quantity and quality of resources and technology—determine the long-run level of potential domestic output. Price level changes do not alter the location of the production possibilities curve; neither do price level changes alter the location of the long-run aggregate supply curve.

Aggregate Supply Shifts Now assume that changes in the supply factors listed in Figure 19-2 shift the long-run aggregate supply curve rightward from AS_1 to AS_2. That is, the production possibilities curve in Figure 19-1 has been pushed outward and the long-run aggregate supply curve in Figure 19-3 has shifted to the right. Also, we will soon see that the new relevant short-run aggregate supply curve is AS_2'.

Aggregate Demand Shifts If aggregate demand remains at AD_1, the increase in long-run aggregate

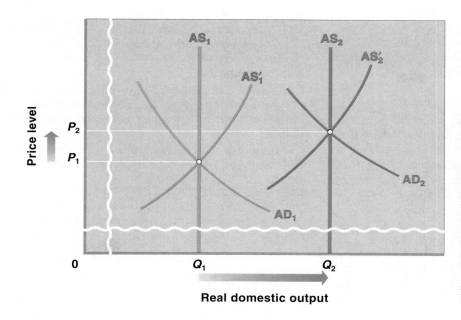

FIGURE 19-3 Economic growth and aggregate demand–aggregate supply analysis

Long-run and short-run aggregate supply curves have shifted rightward over time, as from AS$_1$ and AS$_1'$ to AS$_2$ and AS$_2'$. Meanwhile, aggregate demand has shifted rightward even more rapidly. The outcome of these combined shifts has been economic growth, shown as the increase in real domestic output from Q_1 to Q_2, accompanied by inflation, shown as the rise in the price level from P_1 to P_2.

supply from AS$_1$ to AS$_2$ eventually will overcome any downward price and wage rigidity and reduce the price level. But in recent decades a rising, not a falling, price level has accompanied economic growth. This suggests that aggregate demand has increased more rapidly than long-run aggregate supply. We show this reality in Figure 19-3 by shifting aggregate demand from AD$_1$ to AD$_2$, which results from changes in one or more of the determinants of aggregate demand (Table 9-1).

The combined increases in aggregate supply and aggregate demand shown in Figure 19-3 have produced economic growth of Q_1Q_2 and a rise in the price level from P_1 to P_2. At price level P_2, the economy confronts a new short-run aggregate supply curve AS$_2'$. Also, observe that nominal GDP $(=P \times Q)$ has increased more rapidly than real GDP $(=Q)$ because of inflation. This diagram describes the secular trend of nominal GDP, real GDP, and the price level in the United States, a fact that you can quickly confirm by examining rows 5, 18, and 21 on the inside covers of this book.

GROWTH RECORD OF THE UNITED STATES

Table 19-1 gives us a rough idea of economic growth in the United States over past decades as viewed through our two definitions of growth. Column 2 summarizes

the economy's growth as measured by increases in real GDP. Although not steady, the growth of real GDP has been remarkable. *Real GDP has increased over five-fold since 1940.* But our population has also grown significantly. Thus, using our second definition of growth, we find in column 4 that *real per capita GDP was almost three times larger in 1991 than in 1940.*

TABLE 19-1 Real GDP and per capita GDP, 1929–1991

(1) Year	(2) GDP, billions of 1987 dollars	(3) Population, millions	(4) Per capita GDP, 1987 dollars (2) ÷ (3)
1929	$ 841	122	$ 6,893
1933	592	126	4,698
1940	919	132	6,962
1945	1615	140	11,536
1950	1428	152	9,395
1955	1773	166	10,681
1960	1973	181	10,902
1965	2474	194	12,753
1970	2876	205	14,029
1975	3222	214	15,056
1980	3776	228	16,561
1985	4280	239	17,908
1988	4719	245	19,261
1991	4848	253	19,162

Source: U.S. Department of Commerce.

What about our *rate* of growth? Data presented in Table 19-2 suggest that the post-1948 growth rate of the United States' real GDP has been more than 3 percent per year, while real GDP per capita has grown at almost 2 percent per year.

These bare numbers must be modified in several respects.

1 Improved products The figures of Tables 19-1 and 19-2 do *not* fully take into account improvements in product quality, and thus may understate the growth of economic well-being. Purely quantitative data do not provide an accurate comparison between an era of ice-boxes and one of refrigerators.

2 Added leisure The increases in real GDP and per capita GDP shown in Table 19-1 were accomplished despite sizable increases in leisure. The seventy-hour workweek is a thing of the distant past. The standard workweek is now less than forty hours. The result again is an understatement of economic well-being.

3 Environmental effects On the other hand, these measures of growth do *not* take into account adverse effects which growth may have on the environment and the quality of life itself. To the extent that growth debases the physical environment and creates a stressful work environment our data will overstate the benefits of growth.

4 International comparisons Also, the United States growth record is less impressive than those of several other industrially advanced nations. For example, the growth record of Japan has averaged more than twice that of the United States over the past four decades and there is genuine concern that Japan will overtake America as the world's leading industrial power.

QUICK REVIEW 19-1

◆ *Economic growth can be viewed as either the increase in real GDP or real GDP per capita that occurs over time.*

◆ *Graphically, growth is shown as outward shifts of the production possibilities curve or as combined rightward shifts of aggregate supply and aggregate demand curves.*

◆ *Annual growth of real GDP in the United States has averaged more than 3 percent since World War II.*

ACCOUNTING FOR GROWTH

Edward F. Denison of The Brookings Institution spent most of his professional career trying to quantify the relative importance of the various factors contributing to economic growth. His conceptual framework corresponds closely to the factors in Figure 19-2 and is therefore highly relevant to our discussion. Denison's most recent estimates are shown in Table 19-3. Over the 1929–1982 period he calculates that real national income grew by 2.9 percent per year. He then estimates what percentage of this annual growth was accounted for by each factor shown in the table. We will use Denison's table as a focal point for a series of brief comments on the ingredients in American economic growth.

Inputs versus Productivity

The most evident conclusion from Denison's data is that *productivity growth has been the most important force underlying the growth of our real domestic output*

TABLE 19-2 Growth of real GDP and real GDP per capita in selected countries

	Growth rates of real GDP		Growth rates of real GDP per capita	
	1870–1969	1948–1988	1870–1969	1948–1988
United States	3.7%	3.3%	2.0%	1.9%
Japan	4.2	7.1	—	5.9
Germany	3.0	5.0	1.9	4.2
United Kingdom	1.9	2.6	1.3	2.2
France	2.0	4.1	1.7	3.3
Italy	2.2	4.4	1.5	3.9
Canada	3.6	4.5	1.8	2.7

Source: U.S. Department of Commerce, *Historical Statistics of the United States: Colonial Times to 1970* (Washington, 1975), p. 225; and *Economic Report of the President, 1989*, p. 27.

TABLE 19-3 **The sources of growth in U.S. real national income, 1929–1982**

Sources of growth	Percent of total growth
(1) **Increase in quantity of labor**	**32**
(2) **Increase in labor productivity**	**68**
(3) **Technological advance**	28
(4) **Quantity of capital**	19
(5) **Education and training**	14
(6) **Economies of scale**	9
(7) **Improved resource allocation**	8
(8) **Legal-human environment and other**	−9
	100

Source: Edward F. Denison, *Trends in American Economic Growth, 1929–1982* (Washington: The Brookings Institution, 1985), p. 30. Details may not add to totals because of rounding.

and national income. Increases in the quantity of labor (item 1) account for only about one-third of the increase in real national income over this period; the remaining two-thirds is attributable to rising labor productivity (item 2).

Quantity of Labor

Our population and labor force have both expanded significantly through time. Over the 1929–1982 period considered by Denison, total population grew from 122 to 232 million and the labor force increased from 49 to 110 million workers. Historical reductions in the length of the average workweek have reduced labor inputs, but the workweek has declined very modestly since World War II. Declining birthrates in the past twenty years or so have slowed the rate of population growth. However, largely because of increased participation by women in labor markets, our labor force continues to grow by about 2 million workers per year.

Technological Advance

We note in Table 19-3 that technological advance (item 3) is an important engine of growth, accounting for 28 percent of the increase in real national income realized over the 1929–1982 period. Technological advance is broadly defined to include, not merely new production techniques, but also new managerial techniques and new forms of business organization. More generally, technological advance is linked with the discovery of new knowledge, which permits combining a given amount of resources in new ways to result in a larger output.

In practice, technological advance and capital formation (investment) are closely related processes; technological advance often entails investment in new machinery and equipment. The idea that there is a more efficient way to catch a rabbit than by running it down led to investment in the bow and arrow. And it is clearly necessary to construct new nuclear power plants to apply nuclear power technology. However, modern crop-rotation practices and contour plowing are ideas which contribute greatly to output, although they do not necessarily use new kinds or increased amounts of capital equipment.

Casual observation suggests that, historically, technological advance has been both rapid and profound. Gas and diesel engines, conveyor belts, and assembly lines come to mind as highly significant developments of the past. More recently, the lamp of technology has freed the automation jinni and with it the potential wonders of the push-button factory. Supersonic jets, the transistor and integrated circuitry, computers, xerography, containerized shipping, and nuclear power—not to mention recent breakthroughs in biotechnology and superconductivity—are technological achievements which were in the realm of fantasy only a generation ago. Table 19-3 merely confirms the importance of such developments in the economic growth process.

Quantity of Capital

Some 19 percent—almost one-fifth—of the annual growth of real national income over the indicated period was attributable to increases in the quantity of capital (item 4). It is no surprise that a worker will be more productive when equipped with a larger amount of capital goods. And how does a nation acquire more capital? Capital accumulation results from saving and the investment in plant and equipment which these savings make possible.

The critical consideration in labor productivity is the amount of capital goods *per worker.* The aggregate stock of capital might expand during a specific period, but if the labor force increases more rapidly, then labor productivity will fall because *each worker* will be less well equipped. Something of this sort happened in the 1970s and contributed to a slowing of productivity growth.

To what extent has real capital per worker increased? One long-run estimate concludes that in the

1889 to 1969 period the stock of capital goods increased sixfold and, over this same period, labor-hours doubled. Hence, the quantity of capital goods per labor-hour was roughly three times as large in 1969 than in 1889.[1] While the capital stock is not easy to calculate, data suggest that the amount of capital equipment (machinery and buildings) per worker is currently about $40,000.

Two addenda are in order.

1 We will see shortly that the United States has been saving and investing a smaller percentage of its GDP in recent years than have most other industrially advanced nations. This helps explain our relatively less impressive growth performance (Table 19-2).

2 Investment is not only private, but also public. Our **infrastructure**—our highways and bridges, port facilities, public transit systems, wastewater treatment facilities, municipal water systems, airports, and so on—is encountering growing problems of deterioration, technological obsolescence, and insufficient capacity to serve future growth. Moreover, public capital—the infrastructure—and private capital may be complementary. Investments in new highways promote private investment in new factories and retail establishments along their routes. Some economists view the deterioration of our infrastructure as a significant source of reduced private investment.

Education and Training

Ben Franklin once said, "He that hath a trade hath an estate." This is an archaic way of saying that education and training improve a worker's productivity and result in higher earnings. Like investment in real capital, investment in human capital is an important means of increasing labor productivity. Denison's estimates in Table 19-3 indicate that 14 percent of the growth in our real national income is attributable to such improvements in the quality of labor (item 5).

Perhaps the simplest measure of labor force quality is the level of educational attainment. Figure 19-4 reflects the gains realized in the past several decades. Currently 86 percent of the labor force has received at least a high school education. Of this group more than 26 percent acquired a college education or more. Less than 6 percent of the labor force has received no more than an elementary school education. It is clear that

education has become accessible to more and more people.

But there are persistent concerns about the quality of American education. Scores on Scholastic Aptitude Tests (SATs) have declined relative to scores of a few decades ago. Furthermore, the performance of American students in science and mathematics compares unfavorably to that of students in many other industrialized countries.

Scale Economies and Resource Allocation

Table 19-3 also tells us that labor productivity has increased because of economies of scale (item 6) and improved resource allocation (item 7). Let's consider the latter factor first.

Improved Resource Allocation Improved resource allocation means that workers over time have reallocated themselves from relatively low-productivity employment to relatively high-productivity employment. For example, historically, much labor has been reallocated from agriculture—where labor productivity is relatively low—to manufacturing—where labor productivity is relatively high. As a result, the average productivity of American workers in the aggregate has increased.

Also, labor market discrimination has denied many women and minorities access to those jobs in which they would be most productive. The decline of such discrimination over time has increased labor productivity.

We will find in Chapter 37 that tariffs, import quotas, and other barriers to international trade are conducive to the allocation of labor to relatively unproductive employments. The long-run movement toward freer international trade has therefore improved the allocation of labor and enhanced productivity.

Economies of Scale Economies of scale are production advantages which are derived from market and firm size. A large corporation might be able to select a more efficient production technique than could a small-scale firm. A large manufacturer of automobiles can use elaborate assembly lines, with computerization and robotics, while smaller producers must settle for more primitive technologies. The contribution of economies of scale shown in Table 19-3 means that markets have increased in scope and firms have increased in size so that more efficient production methods are being used. Accordingly, labor productivity has increased.

---

[1] Solomon Fabricant, *A Primer on Productivity* (New York: Random House, Inc., 1969), chap. 5.

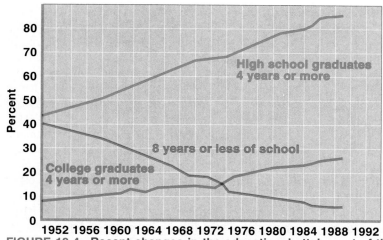

FIGURE 19-4   Recent changes in the educational attainment of the labor force

The percentage of the labor force completing high school and college has been rising steadily in recent years, while the percentage who did not go to high school or complete elementary school has been falling. (*Statistical Abstract of the United States*.)

Detriments to Growth

Unfortunately, some developments detract from labor productivity and growth of real national income. The legal and human environment entry in Table 19-3 (item 8) aggregates these detriments to productivity growth. Over the 1929–1982 period considerable changes were made in the regulation of industry, environmental pollution, and worker health and safety, which have negatively affected growth. The expansion of government regulation of business in such areas as pollution control and worker health and safety diverted investment spending away from productivity-increasing capital goods and toward equipment which provides cleaner air and water and greater worker protection from accident and illness. A firm required to spend $1 million on a new scrubber to meet government standards for air pollution will not have that $1 million to spend on machinery and equipment which would enhance worker productivity. The diversion of resources to deal with dishonesty and crime, the effects of work stoppages because of labor disputes, and the impact of bad weather on agricultural output are also included in item 8.

This point is worth adding. Worker safety, clean air and water, and the overall "quality of life" may come at the expense of productivity. But the reverse is also true. That is, we cannot assume that productivity advances automatically enhance society's welfare. Pro-

ductivity growth may entail opportunity costs of other things (a clean environment) which we value more highly. Productivity measures output per hour of work, not overall "well-being" per hour of work.

Other Factors

There are other difficult-to-quantify considerations which play significant roles in determining an economy's growth rate. For example, the generous and varied supplies of natural resources with which the United States has been blessed have been an important contributor to our economic growth.[2] We enjoy an abundance of fertile soil, desirable climatic and weather conditions, ample quantities of most mineral resources, and generous sources of power. With the possible exception of the former Soviet Union, the United States has a larger variety and greater quantity of natural resources than any other nation.

While an abundant natural resource base is often very helpful to the growth process, a meager resource base does not doom a nation to slow growth. Although Japan's natural resources are severely constrained, its post-World War II growth has been remarkable

[2]Denison omits land (natural resources) from Table 19-3 on the grounds that, unlike inputs of labor and capital, there have been no changes in land inputs to contribute to the growth of real national income. That is, the quantity of land does not change and any qualitative changes are minuscule.

(Table 19-2). On the other hand, some of the less developed countries of Africa and South America have substantial amounts of natural resources.

There are additional unmeasurable factors which affect a nation's growth rate. In particular, the overall social-cultural-political environment of the United States generally has been conducive to economic growth. Several interrelated factors contribute to this favorable environment.

1   As opposed to many other nations, there are virtually no social or moral taboos on production and material progress. Indeed, American social philosophy has embraced material advance as an attainable and desirable economic goal. The inventor, the innovator, and the business executive are generally accorded high degrees of prestige and respect in American society.

2   Americans have traditionally possessed healthy attitudes toward work and risk taking; our society has benefited from a willing labor force and an ample supply of entrepreneurs.

3   Our market system is replete with personal and corporate incentives which encourage growth; our economy rewards actions which increase output.

4   Our economy is founded on a stable political system characterized by internal order, the right of property ownership, the legal status of enterprise, and the enforcement of contracts.

Though not subject to quantification, these characteristics have undoubtedly provided an excellent foundation for American economic growth.

Aggregate Demand, Instability, and Growth

As seen in Table 19-3, Denison's analysis is designed to explain the growth of *actual,* as opposed to *potential* or full-employment, real national income. The 2.9 percent annual growth rate which the table attempts to explain embodies changes in real national income caused by fluctuations in aggregate demand. Denison recognizes that our growth rate would have been higher—3.2 percent per year—if the economy's potential output had been realized year after year. Deviations from full employment due to a deficiency of aggregate demand cause the actual rate of growth to fall short of the potential rate. A glance back at Figure 8-5 reminds us of the extent to which the actual performance of our economy frequently falls short of its potential output. The Great Depression of the 1930s in particular was a serious

blow to the United States' long-run growth record. Between 1929 and 1933 our real GDP (measured in 1987 prices) actually *declined* from $841 to $592 billion. In 1939 the real GDP was approximately at the same level as in 1929 (see line 18 on table inside front cover). More recently it is estimated that the severe 1980–1982 recessions cost the United States more than $600 billion in lost output and income.

But this is only part of the picture. Cyclical unemployment can have certain harmful "carry-over" effects on the growth rate in subsequent years of full employment through the adverse effects it may have on other growth factors. For example, unemployment depresses investment and capital accumulation. Furthermore, the expansion of research budgets may be slowed by recession so that technological progress diminishes; union resistance to technological change may stiffen; and so forth. Though it is difficult to quantify the impact of these considerations on the growth rate, they undoubtedly can be of considerable importance.

QUICK REVIEW 19-2

▪   *Increases in labor productivity account for about two-thirds of increases in real output; the use of more labor inputs accounts for the remaining one-third.*

▪   *Improved technology, more capital, more education and training, economies of scale, and improved resource allocation are the main contributors to growth.*

▪   *Growth rates in the United States have been erratic, particularly because of fluctuations in aggregate demand.*

THE PRODUCTIVITY SLOWDOWN

In the 1970s—and to a lesser degree in the 1980s and early 1990s—the United States experienced a much-publicized productivity slowdown. Table 19-4 portrays the course of United States labor productivity in the post-World War II period. Observe in column 2 that for about two decades following World War II (1948–1966) labor productivity increased at a vigorous average annual rate of 3.2 percent, only to decline rather precipitously in the 1966–1973 period. This was followed by a dismal productivity performance in the 1973–1981 period, and a modest resurgence of productivity growth

TABLE 19-4 Growth of labor productivity and real
per capita GDP, 1948–1990

(1) Period	(2) Productivity growth rate	(3) Real per capita GDP, growth rate
1948–1966	3.2	2.2%
1966–1973	2.0	2.0
1973–1981	0.7	1.1
1981–1990	1.3	1.8

Source: Economic Report of the President, 1988, p. 67. End points of
calculations are cyclical peaks. Updated.

in the 1980s. Although labor productivity growth has
been slowing worldwide, American productivity
growth has been less than that of other major industrialized nations. The United States still enjoys the highest absolute level of output per worker, but its productivity advantage is quickly diminishing.

Significance

The significance of our productivity slowdown is manifold.

I Standard of Living Productivity growth is the
basic source of improvements in real wage rates and
the standard of living. Real income per worker-hour
can only increase at the same rate as real output per
worker-hour. More output per hour means more real
income to distribute for each hour worked. The simplest case is the classic one of Robinson Crusoe on his
deserted island. The number of fish he can catch or
coconuts he can pick per hour *is* his real income or
wage per hour.

We observe in column 3 of Table 19-4 that the
broadest measure of living standards—the growth of
real per capita GDP—followed the path of labor productivity. Living levels thus measured grew by only 1.1
percent per year during the severe 1973–1981 productivity stagnation compared to 2.2 percent in the 1948–
1966 postwar decades.

2 Inflation We saw in Chapter 17 that productivity
increases offset increases in nominal-wage rates and
thereby partly or fully lessen cost-push inflationary
pressures. Other things being equal, a decline in the
rate of productivity growth contributes to rapidly rising
unit labor costs and a higher rate of inflation. Many

economists believe that productivity stagnation contributed to the unusually high inflation rates of the
1970s.

3 World Markets Other things being equal, our
slow rate of productivity growth compared to our major
international trading partners increases relative prices
of American goods in world markets. The result is a
decline in our competitiveness and a loss of international markets for American producers.

Causes of the Slowdown

There is no consensus among experts as to why American productivity growth has slowed and fallen behind
the rates of Japan and western Europe. Indeed, because so many factors affect productivity, there may be
no simple explanation for the slowdown. However, let's
survey some of the possible causes.

Labor Quality One possibility is that slower improvements in labor quality may have dampened productivity growth. Three factors may have been at work.

1 **Decline in Experience Level** The experience
level of the labor force may have declined. The large
number of baby-boom workers who entered the labor
force had little experience and training and were therefore less productive. Similarly, the labor force participation of women increased significantly over the past two
decades. Many were married women with little or no
prior labor force experience and therefore had low productivity.

2 **Less Able Workers** The declining test scores of
students on standardized examinations during the past
few decades perhaps indicates a decline in worker ca-
pabilities. If so, this decline may have contributed to
the productivity slowdown.

3 **Slowing of Increased Educational Attainment**
The average level of educational attainment of the labor
force has been increasing more slowly in recent years.
The median number of years of school completed by
the adult population was 12.3 in 1960 and increased to
only 12.7 by 1989.

Technological Progress Technological advance—
usually reflected in improvements in the quality of capi-

tal goods and the efficiency with which inputs are combined—may also have faltered. Technological progress is fueled by expenditures for formal research and development (R&D) programs. In the United States, R&D spending declined as a percentage of GDP from a peak of 3 percent in the mid-1960s to about 1 percent by the late 1970s, before rising again in the 1980s.

However, some economists discount the R&D decline in explaining the productivity slowdown. They say R&D *spending* alone tells us little about R&D *accomplishments*. There is evidence of continuing technological advance during the past two decades.

Investment There is a high positive correlation between the percentage of a nation's GDP devoted to investment goods and the productivity increases it achieves. A worker using a bulldozer can move more earth per hour than the same worker equipped with a hand shovel. An engineer using a computer can complete a design task more rapidly than with pencil and paper.

As Figure 19-5 shows, the United States has recently been investing a smaller percentage of its GDP than in earlier periods. Note the decline in the 1970s and the even greater decline in the 1980s. Several factors may have contributed to the weak growth of investment.

1 Low Saving Rate The United States has had a relatively low saving rate which, coupled with strong private and public demands for credit, has resulted in high real interest rates relative to historical standards. High interest rates discourage investment spending.

2 Import Competition Growing import competition may have made some American producers reluctant to invest in new capital equipment. Alternatively, they may have shifted more investment overseas toward nations with low-wage workers.

3 Regulation As noted earlier, the expansion of government regulations in the areas of pollution control and worker health and safety diverted some investment spending away from output-increasing capital goods. This investment spending may have increased total utility to society, but did not directly increase output itself. That is, the composition of investment may have shifted toward uses which do not increase productivity.

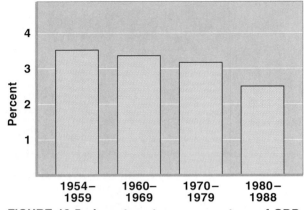

FIGURE 19-5 Investment as a percentage of GDP, selected period averages

Real nonresidential net investment in the United States declined for several reasons in the 1970s and diminished even more significantly in the 1980s. These declines may have been a contributing factor to the slow growth of labor productivity.

4 Reduced Infrastructure Spending Reduced spending on the economy's infrastructure—its highways, bridges, airports, harbors, power plants, and similar installations—may have slowed productivity growth. These public goods are complementary to private capital goods. For example, public investments in new highways and airports increase the productivity of business travelers and the efficiency with which inputs and finished products are transported. Also, public spending on power plants lowers energy costs and therefore the costs of running private manufacturing plants. Data show that in the 1950–1970 period the public capital stock of infrastructure grew at a 4.1 percent annual rate, and labor productivity growth was 2.0 percent per year. In the 1971–1985 era, however, the yearly increase in the infrastructure fell to only 1.6 percent and the annual productivity increase plummeted to 0.8 percent. A slowing of spending on public investment goods may have contributed to diminishing private investments and to declines in productivity growth.

Energy Prices Perhaps the prime suspect in the productivity slowdown was the large increases in oil prices which occurred in 1973–1975 and in 1978–1980. Productivity growth fell off sharply after the quadrupling of oil prices in 1973–1975. Also, the impact of skyrocketing energy prices was worldwide, as was the productivity slowdown.

The direct impact of higher oil prices was to increase the cost of operating capital equipment, in effect raising the "price" of capital relative to labor. Producers were therefore more inclined to use less productive labor-intensive techniques.

The indirect macroeconomic effects of dramatically higher energy prices may have been even more important in reducing productivity growth. The two episodes of soaring energy prices precipitated stagflation—inflationary recessions. Government's use of restrictive macroeconomic policies to control inflation undoubtedly worsened and prolonged the periods of recession and slow economic growth. Recessions diminish productivity—output per worker—in that output tends to decline more rapidly than employment. The prolonged periods of underuse of productive capacity in many industries undoubtedly contributed to the productivity slowdown.

Industrial Relations A different view of the productivity slowdown stresses that forces of an institutional nature—the way work is organized, the attitudes and behavior of workers and managers, communication between labor and management, and the division of authority among managers and workers—account for much of our poor productivity performance compared to Japan and western Europe. The argument is that American industrial relations are characterized by an adversarial relationship between managers and their employees. Feeling alienated from their employers, workers do not participate in the decisions which govern their daily work lives; they do not identify with the objectives of their firms, and therefore are not motivated to work hard and productively. Managers are judged, rewarded, and motivated by short-term profit performance and thus, it is argued, give little attention to long-term plans and strategies critical to attaining high rates of productivity growth.

Japanese industries, in contrast, provide lifetime employment security for a sizable portion of their work force, allow for worker participation in decision making, and use profit-sharing or bonuses to provide a direct link between the economic success of a firm and worker incomes. Furthermore, the direct interest workers have in the competitiveness and profitability of their enterprise reduces the need for supervisory personnel. The result is a commonality of interest and cooperation between management and labor, greater flexibility in job assignment, and enhanced willingness of workers to accept technological change. Lifetime employment is also conducive to heavy investment by employers in training and retraining their workers.

The implication is that an overhaul of our industrial relations system is a key to restoring our productivity growth.

A Resurgence?

The 1981–1990 data in Table 19-4 suggest a modest improvement in productivity growth; the 1.3 percent annual increase for this period compares favorably with the 0.7 percent productivity growth for 1973–1981. Although the recession of 1990–1991 halted this upward trend—productivity growth was only 0.2 percent in 1990—it is evident that some of the factors which may have depressed productivity growth have dissipated or been reversed. Since 1977 R&D spending has generally increased as a percentage of GDP. Important innovations in computerization and robotics may be providing a stimulus to productivity. The inexperienced baby boomers who flooded labor markets in the 1970s are now rapidly becoming mature, experienced, more productive workers.

Also, although American industrial relations remain distinctly different from the cooperative "shared vision" of Japanese managers and workers, the problems imposed by recession and increasing foreign competition are pushing American workers and managers in that direction. Worker involvement and profit-sharing plans are increasingly common in American industry. In fact, employees in the United States collectively now own an estimated $150 billion of stock in the firms for which they work.

Nevertheless, it is unclear at this point whether the recent revival of productivity is transitory or permanent.

IS GROWTH DESIRABLE?

Up to now we have taken for granted that growth is desirable. In fact, growth is an issue of some controversy.

The Case Against Growth

Serious questions have been raised as to the desirability of continued economic growth for already affluent nations. A number of interrelated arguments comprise this antigrowth sentiment.

1 Pollution Concern with environmental deterioration is an important part of the antigrowth position. Industrialization and growth result in serious problems of pollution, industrial noise and stench, ugly cities, traffic jams, and many other disamenities of modern life. These adverse external or spillover costs are held to be the consequence of the hard fact that the production of the GDP changes the form of resources, but does not destroy them. Virtually all inputs in the productive process are eventually returned to the environment in some form of waste.

The more rapid our growth and the higher our standard of living, the more waste there is for the environment to absorb—or attempt to absorb. In an already wealthy society, further growth may mean satisfying increasingly trivial wants at the cost of mounting threats to our ecological system. Antigrowth economists feel that future growth should be purposely constrained.

2 Problem Resolution? There is little compelling evidence that economic growth has solved socioeconomic problems, as its proponents claim. Antigrowth economists assert, for example, that the domestic problem of poverty—income inequality—is essentially a problem of distribution, not production. The requisites for solving the poverty problem are commitment and political courage, not further increases in output. In general, there is no compelling evidence that growth has been, or will be, a palliative for domestic social problems.

3 Human Obsolescence and Insecurity Growth critics contend that rapid growth—and in particular the changing technology at the core of growth—poses new anxieties and new sources of insecurity for workers. Both high-level and low-level workers face the prospect of having their hard-earned skills and experience rendered obsolete by an onrushing technology.

4 Growth and Human Values Critics of growth also offer a group of related arguments which say, in effect, that while growth may permit us to "make a living," it does not give us "the good life." We may, in fact, be producing more, but enjoying it less. More specifically, it is charged that growth means industrialization, uncreative and unsatisfying mass-production jobs, and alienated workers who have little or no control over the decisions affecting their lives.

In Defense of Growth

However, most economists view growth as a high-priority goal. They make the following arguments.

1 Living Standards The primary defense of economic growth is that it is the path to material abundance and rising standards of living for families and individuals (Table 19-1). *Growth makes the unlimited wants–scarce resources dilemma less acute.*

> In a growing economy public choices are less agonizing and divisive. It is possible to modernize the armed forces; keep the nation's infrastructure in repair; provide for the elderly, the sick, and the needy; improve education and other public services; and still have private incomes that rise after taxes.[3]

2 Growth and the Environment Growth proponents feel that the connection between growth, on the one hand, and the environment, on the other, is overdrawn. To a considerable degree these are separable issues. If society should flatly abandon the goal of growth and produce a constant real output every year, it would still have to make choices about the composition of output which would affect the environment and the quality of life. Society would still have to weigh the relative merits of enjoying the natural beauty of a forest or cutting the timber for productive uses. And, if the timber were cut, society would have to decide whether it would be used for housing or fast-food wrappers.

Pollution is not so much a by-product of growth as it is a shortcoming of the market system. Specifically, much of the environment—streams, lakes, oceans, and the air—are treated as "common property" and no charge is made for their use. Thus, our environmental resources are overused and debased. Recalling Chapter 6's terminology, environmental pollution is a case of spillover or external costs, and correcting this problem involves regulatory legislation or specific taxes ("effluent charges") to remedy the market system's flaw and eliminate misuse of the environment. There are, to be sure, serious pollution problems. But limiting growth is the wrong response.

3 Poverty Reduction Economic growth is the only politically feasible way to reduce poverty in our society.

---

[3]Alice M. Rivlin (ed.), *Economic Choices of 1984* (Washington: The Brookings Institution, 1984), p. 2.

Support for highly progressive taxes and major income transfer programs has waned in the United States. In fact, the distribution of income today is more unequal than it was in 1969. It follows that the primary means for improving the economic position of the poor is to move the entire distribution of income upward through economic growth. Similarly, a no-growth policy among industrial nations would most likely end political support for aid to developing nations, perhaps assigning the world's poor to poverty for longer periods.

4 Nonmaterial Considerations Those who defend growth argue that its retardation or cessation will not automatically foster humanistic goals or promote "the good life." Indeed, we should expect the contrary. The ending of growth will not mean elimination of production-line work; historically, growth has been accompanied by a *decline* in the fraction of the labor force so employed. Nor has growth uniformly made labor more unpleasant or hazardous. New machinery is usually less taxing and less hazardous than the machinery it replaces. Air-conditioned workplaces are more pleasant than the sweatshops of old.

Furthermore, why would retardation or prohibition of growth reduce materialism or alienation? Would we not expect results to be the opposite? The loudest protests against materialism are heard in those nations and from those groups who now enjoy the highest levels of material abundance! More positively, it is the high standards of living which growth provides that make it possible for more people "to take the time for education, reflection, and self-fulfillment."[4]

QUICK REVIEW 19-3

✦ *Productivity has slowed down in the past two decades because of declines in labor quality, slowing of technological progress, decreased investment spending as a percentage of GDP, higher energy prices, and deteriorating industrial relations.*

✦ *Although some critics disparage growth because it allegedly increases pollution and fails to solve socioeconomic problems, there are compelling arguments in favor of growth, namely, that it lessens the scarcity problem and increases the standard of living.*

---

[4]Marc J. Roberts, "On Reforming Economic Growth," in Mancur Olson and Hans H. Landsberg (eds.), *The No-Growth Society* (New York: W. W. Norton & Company, Inc., 1973), p. 133.

GROWTH POLICIES

If we accept the view that on balance economic growth is desirable, then the question as to what public policies might best stimulate growth arises. Several types of policy are either in use or have been suggested.

Demand-Side Policies

Low growth is often the consequence of inadequate aggregate demand and resulting GDP gaps. The purpose of demand-side policies is to eliminate or reduce the severity of recessions through active fiscal and monetary policy. The idea is to use government tools to increase aggregate demand at a rapid, noninflationary pace. Strong aggregate demand not only keeps present resources fully employed, it also creates an incentive for firms to expand their operations. In particular, low real interest rates (easy money policy) are conducive to high levels of investment spending. This spending leads to capital accumulation, which expands the economy's capacity to produce.

Supply-Side Policies

These policies emphasize factors which will directly increase the potential or full-capacity output of the economy over time. The goal is to shift Figure 19-3's long-run and short-run aggregate supply curves rightward. Policies which fit this category include tax policies designed to stimulate saving, investment, and entrepreneurship. For example, by lowering or eliminating the tax paid on income placed in saving accounts, the return on saving will increase and therefore so will the amount of saving. Likewise, by lowering or eliminating the deduction of interest expenses on one's personal income tax, consumption will be discouraged and saving encouraged. Some economists favor the introduction of a national consumption tax as a full or partial replacement for the personal income tax. The idea is to penalize consumption and thereby encourage saving.

On the investment side of the picture, some economists propose eliminating the corporate income tax or, more specifically, allowing generous tax credits for business investment spending. If effective, this proposal would simultaneously increase aggregate demand and aggregate supply.

LAST WORD

THE JAPANESE GROWTH MIRACLE

Since World War II Japan has achieved more rapid growth than any other economy (Table 19-2). What factors account for this remarkable progress?

The Japanese economy is showing signs of replacing the United States as the world's leading industrial power. Symbolic of Japan's success is the fact that it surpassed the United States in automobile production in 1980. Similarly, American dominance in the steel and television industries has been usurped by Japan. Japan is also dominant in the production of watches, cameras, electronics equipment, and industrial robots. These economic accomplishments are all the more remarkable because Japan's population is large relative to its land mass and its natural resource base is very limited. For example, Japan is heavily dependent on imported oil and iron ore. Recall, too, that at the end of World War II (1945) the Japanese economy was in ruins. How, then, can we account for the Japanese growth miracle?

1   Saving and investing   Japan has achieved high rates of saving and investment. The cultural thriftiness of the Japanese population has been supplemented by special tax incentives to save. The interest earned on small savings accounts is tax-free. On the investment side of the picture, tax laws embody accelerated depre-

ciation of capital goods for tax purposes when investment involves plant modernization or the introduction of new products and technologies. Japan invests a larger proportion of its GDP than does any other advanced capitalist country and this is reflected in a high rate of productivity growth.

2   Labor-management relations   Many experts contend that a sizable portion of Japan's economic progress is attributable to its quasi-paternalistic system of labor relations. About one-third of the Japanese labor force enjoys the security of guaranteed lifetime employment in large industrial concerns.

Industrial and Other Policies

There are other potential growth-stimulating policies which economists of various persuasions recommend. Some advocate an **industrial policy** whereby government would take a direct, active role in shaping the structure and composition of industry to promote growth. Thus government might take steps to hasten expansion of high-productivity industries and speed the movement of resources out of low-productivity industries. Government might also increase its expenditures on basic research and development to stimulate technological progress. Also, increased expenditures on education may help increase the quality and productivity of labor.

While the litany of potential growth-enhancing policies is long and involved, most economists agree that it is no simple matter to increase a nation's growth rate.

CHAPTER SUMMARY

1   Economic growth may be defined either as   **a** an expanding real output (income) or   **b** an expanding per capita real output (income). Growth lessens the burden of scarcity and provides increases in the domestic output which can be used to resolve domestic and international socioeconomic problems.

2   The supply factors in economic growth are   **a** the quantity and quality of a nation's natural resources,   **b** the

Furthermore, these enterprises have assumed many functions of the welfare state in that they provide medical care, subsidized housing, and a variety of other fringe benefits. As a result, the adversary labor-management relations which are common to the United States are largely supplanted in Japan by a cooperative relationship. Workers realize that their economic futures are intimately linked to the viability and competitiveness of their enterprise.

Given employment security and the fact that a substantial portion of wages is in the form of profit-related bonuses, workers have a strong incentive to accept technological change, learn new skills, and cooperate with management in increasing productivity. More generally, the Japanese labor force is disciplined and well-educated.

3 National purpose and planning A somewhat less tangible factor in Japan's growth performance has to do with a clearer perception of its national interest and the willingness of economic actors to subordinate their self-interests to national goals. This ability of government, business, and labor to achieve a consensus or common perspective on national economic objectives may have cultural roots or it may spring from a recognition that Japan's economic success hinges on its remaining highly competitive in world markets. The net result is a close positive relationship between the government, business, and labor in promoting the national interest, that is, in furthering economic growth.

In fact, the Japanese engage in "indicative" (as opposed to "imperative" or coercive) planning whereby industrial development objectives are determined along with other economic and social goals. Primary responsibility for the overall regulation and guidance of Japanese industries toward these goals rests with the Ministry of International Trade and Industry (MITI). Business and labor are expected to subordinate their private interests to the national goals set forth by MITI. The overall result is that government and business are in a more cooperative posture, as compared to the adversary relationship generally existing in the United States.

Japan, in short, has a more coherent industrial policy and a more clearly defined sense of national purpose than do most of its capitalistic competitors. And economic growth ranks high as a national goal in Japan.

4 Other factors The Japanese growth story has other roots. Since World War II the Japanese have diverted few resources—less than 1 percent of the GDP—to military spending. This has freed high-level personnel and capital goods to improve the productivity of industry. Similarly, the Japanese have been very adept at transferring, applying, and improving on the technological advances of other countries.

While Japan's progress has not been achieved without conflicts and problems, its overall growth record is enviable.

---

quantity and quality of its human resources, **c** its stock of capital facilities, and **d** its technology. Two other factors—a sufficient level of aggregate demand and allocative efficiency—are essential if the economy is to realize its growth potential.

3 Economic growth can be shown graphically as a rightward shift of a nation's production possibilities curve or as a rightward shift of its long-run aggregate supply curve.

4 The post-World War II growth rate of real GDP for the United States has been more than 3 percent; real GDP per capita has grown at about 2 percent.

5 Real GDP in the United States has grown, partly because of increased inputs of labor, and primarily because of increases in the productivity of labor. Technological progress, increases in the quantity of capital per worker, improvements in the quality of labor, economies of scale, and improved allocation of labor are among the more important factors which increase labor productivity.

6 The rate of productivity growth declined sharply in the 1970s, causing a slowdown in the rise of our living standards and contributing to inflation. Although productivity has risen in the 1980s and early 1990s, it remains substantially below the levels attained in the two decades following World War II.

7 Critics of economic growth **a** cite adverse environmental effects; **b** argue that domestic and international problems are matters of distribution, not production; **c** contend that growth is a major source of human obsolescence and insecurity; and **d** argue that growth is frequently in conflict with certain human values.

8 Proponents of growth stress that **a** growth means a better solution to the wants-means dilemma; **b** environmental problems are only loosely linked to growth; **c** growth is the only feasible means by which poverty can be reduced; and **d** growth is more consistent with "the good life" than is stagnation.

TERMS AND CONCEPTS

supply, demand, and
    allocative factors in
    growth

economic growth
labor productivity

infrastructure

industrial policy

QUESTIONS AND STUDY SUGGESTIONS

1 Why is economic growth important? Explain why the difference between a 2.5 percent and a 3.0 percent annual growth rate might be of great importance.

2 What are the major causes of economic growth? "There are both a demand and a supply side to economic growth." Explain. Illustrate the operation of both sets of factors in terms of the production possibilities curve.

3 Suppose an economy's real GDP is $30,000 in year 1 and $31,200 in year 2. What is the growth rate of its GDP? Assume that population was 100 in year 1 and 102 in year 2. What is the growth rate of GDP per capita? Between 1948 and 1991 the nation's price level has risen by over 440 percent while its real output has increased by almost 275 percent. Use the aggregate demand–aggregate supply model to show these outcomes graphically.

4 Briefly describe the growth record of the United States. Compare the rates of growth in real GDP and real GDP per capita, explaining any differences. To what extent might these figures understate or overstate economic well-being?

5 To what extent have increases in our real GDP been the result of more labor inputs? Of increasing labor productivity? Discuss the factors which contribute to productivity growth in order of their quantitative importance.

6 Using examples, explain how changes in the allocation of labor can affect labor productivity.

7 How do you explain the close correlation which exists between changes in the rate of productivity growth and changes in real wage rates? Discuss the relationship between productivity growth and inflation.

8 Account for the recent slowdown in the United States' rate of productivity growth. What are the consequences of this slowdown? "Most of the factors which contributed to poor productivity growth in the 1970s are now behind us and are unlikely to recur in the near future." Do you agree?

9 "If we want economic growth in a free society, we may have to accept a measure of instability." Evaluate. The noted philosopher Alfred North Whitehead once remarked that "the art of progress is to preserve order amid change and to preserve change amid order." What did he mean? Is this contention relevant for economic growth? What implications might this have for public policy? Explain.

10 Comment on the following statements:

    a "Technological advance is destined to play a more important role in economic growth in the future than it has in the past."

    b "Poverty reduction is a matter of redistribution, not of further growth."

    c "The issues of economic growth and environmental pollution are separable and distinct."

11 What specific policies would you recommend to increase the productivity of American workers?

International Economics and the World Economy

International Trade: Comparative Advantage and Protectionism

Backpackers hiking deep into wilderness areas like to think they are "leaving the world behind." Ironically, like Atlas, overnight backpackers often carry the world on their shoulders. Much of their backpacking equipment is imported—knives from Switzerland, rain gear from South Korea, cameras from Japan, pots made in England, miniature stoves from Sweden, sleeping bags containing goosedown from China, instant coffee from Brazil, compasses made in Finland, and chocolate bars with cocoa from Ghana. Some backpackers wear hiking boots from Italy, sunglasses made in France, and watches from Japan or Switzerland. Moreover, they may drive to the trailheads in Toyotas, Volvos, or BMWs, made in Japan, Sweden, and Germany, respectively.

International trade touches all of us daily, whether we are hiking in the wilderness, shopping for groceries, driving our cars, listening to music, or working at our jobs. Thus, this chapter's goals are fundamental.

First, we will look briefly at the volume and unique characteristics of international trade. Second, the principle of comparative advantage, introduced in Chapter 3, is used to explain how international specialization and trade can be mutually beneficial to participating nations. Third, we examine the economic impact of trade barriers such as tariffs and import quotas. Next, we evaluate the arguments for protectionism. The evolution of international trade policies, including the emergence of free-trade areas, is then summarized. Finally, we examine the recent resurgence of protectionism, noting causes, examples, and associated costs.

IMPORTANCE OF WORLD TRADE

The volume of world trade is sufficiently great and its characteristics so unique as to merit special consideration.

Volume and Pattern

Table 20-1 provides a rough index of the importance of world trade for several representative countries. Many nations having restricted resource bases and limited

TABLE 20-1 **Exports of goods and services as a percentage of gross domestic product, selected countries, 1990**

Country	Exports Percentage of GDP
The Netherlands	57
Germany	36
New Zealand	27
Canada	25
United Kingdom	24
France	22
Italy	19
Japan	11

Source: IMF, *International Financial Statistics*, 1992.

domestic markets cannot produce with reasonable efficiency the variety of goods they want to consume. For such countries, exports are the route for obtaining goods they desire and therefore exports may run from 25 to 35 percent or more of their GDPs. Other countries—the United States, for example—have rich and diversified resource bases and vast internal markets and are therefore less dependent on world trade.

I Volume   For the United States and the world the volume of international trade has been increasing both absolutely and relatively. Table 20-2 reflects the substantial growth in the dollar volume of both American exports and imports over the past three decades. Since 1960 United States' exports and imports of goods and services have more than doubled as a percentage of our GDP. Exports and imports currently are each about 10 to 11 percent of GDP. Curiously, however, the United States accounts for a diminishing percentage of total world trade. In 1947 it supplied about one-third of the world's total exports compared to about one-seventh today. World trade has increased more rapidly

for other nations than it has for the United States. *But in terms of absolute volumes of imports and exports the United States is the world's leading trading nation.*

2 Dependence   There can be no question as to the United States' dependence on the world economy. We are almost entirely dependent on other countries for bananas, cocoa, coffee, spices, tea, raw silk, nickel, tin, natural rubber, and diamonds. Casual observation suggests that imported goods compete strongly in many of our domestic markets: Japanese cameras and video recorders, French and Italian wines, English bicycles, and Japanese motorcycles and autos are a few cases in point. Foreign cars have made persistent gains in American markets and now account for about 35 percent of total sales in the United States. Even the great American pastime—baseball—relies heavily on imported gloves.

But world trade is a two-way street, and a host of American industries are highly dependent on foreign markets. Almost all segments of agriculture rely heavily on foreign markets—rice, wheat, cotton, and tobacco exports vary from one-fourth to more than one-half of total output. The chemical, aircraft, automobile, machine tool, coal, and computer industries are only a few of many American industries which sell significant portions of their output in international markets. Table 20-3 shows some of the major commodity exports and imports of the United States.

3 Trade Patterns   An overall picture of the pattern of United States merchandise trade was given in Table 5-6. A quick review of that table provides the basis for several observations.
1   In 1990 our imports of goods from abroad were substantially in excess of our exports of goods.
2   The bulk of our export and import trade is with other developed nations, not with the less developed nations or the countries of eastern Europe.

TABLE 20-2   **Trade in the U.S. economy, 1960–1991*** *(dollars in billions)*

	1960		1975		1991	
	Amount	Percent of GDP	Amount	Percent of GDP	Amount	Percent of GDP
Exports of goods and services	$25.3	4.9	$136.3	8.6	$592.5	10.4
Imports of goods and services	22.8	4.4	122.7	7.7	621.9	11.0
Net exports	2.4	0.5	13.6	0.9	−29.4	0.5

*Data are on a national income accounts basis.
Source: Department of Commerce.

TABLE 20-3 **Principal commodity exports and imports of the United States, 1990 (in billions)**

Exports	Amount	Imports	Amount
Chemicals	$28.4	Petroleum	$62.1
Computers	25.9	Automobiles	45.9
Consumer durables	21.0	Clothing	23.9
Aircraft	18.4	Computers	23.0
Grains	14.9	Household appliances	18.7
Semiconductors	13.3	Chemicals	14.3
Generating equipment	12.7	Semiconductors	12.2
Automobiles	10.9	Iron and steel	11.3
Nonferrous metals	10.9	Toys and sporting goods	9.7
Telecommunications	9.6	Telecommunications	9.4

Source: U.S. Department of Commerce.

3 Canada is our most important trading partner quantitatively. Twenty-two percent of our exports are sold to Canadians, who in turn provide us with 19 percent of our imports.

4 There is a sizable imbalance in our trade with Japan; our imports greatly exceed our exports.

5 Our dependence on foreign oil is reflected in the excess of imports over exports in our trade with the OPEC nations.

4 Level of Output Changes in net exports—the difference between the value of a nation's exports and imports—have multiple effects on the level of domestic output in roughly the same way as do fluctuations in the various types of domestic spending. A small change in the volume of American imports and exports can have magnified repercussions on the domestic levels of output, employment, and prices.

Unique Aspects

Aside from essentially quantitative considerations, world trade has certain unique characteristics.

1 Mobility Differences Though the difference is a matter of degree, the mobility of resources is considerably less among nations than it is within nations. American workers are free to move from Iowa to Idaho or from Maine to Minnesota. Crossing international boundaries is a different story.

Immigration laws, not to mention language and cultural barriers, severely restrict migration of labor between nations. Different tax laws, different governmental regulations, different business practices, and a host of other institutional barriers limit migration of real capital over international boundaries.

International trade is a substitute for the international mobility of resources. If human and property resources do not move readily among nations, the movement of goods and services is an effective substitute.

2 Currency Differences Each nation uses a different currency. An American firm distributing Hondas or BMWs in the United States must buy yen or marks to pay the Japanese or German automobile manufactures. The possible complications which may accompany this exchange of currencies are explored in Chapter 21.

3 Politics As we will note, international trade is subject to political interferences and controls which differ markedly in degree and kind from those applying to domestic trade.

THE ECONOMIC BASIS FOR TRADE

But why do nations trade? What is the basis for trade between nations? *International trade is a way nations can specialize, increase the productivity of their resources, and realize a larger total output than otherwise.* Sovereign nations, like individuals and regions of a nation, can gain by specializing in products they can produce with greatest relative efficiency and by trading for goods they cannot produce efficiently.

While the above rationale for world trade is correct, it in a sense begs the question. A better answer to the question "Why do nations trade?" hinges on two points.

1 The distribution of economic resources—natural, human, and capital goods—among nations is quite uneven; nations are substantially different in their endowments of economic resources.

2 Efficient production of various goods requires different technologies or combinations of resources.

The character and interaction of these two points can be readily illustrated. Japan, for example, has a large, well-educated labor force; skilled labor is abundant and therefore cheap. Hence, Japan can produce efficiently (at low cost) a variety of goods whose design and production require much skilled labor; cameras, transistor radios, and video recorders are examples of such **labor-intensive** commodities.

In contrast, Australia has vast amounts of land in comparison with its human and capital resources and can cheaply produce such **land-intensive** commodities as wheat, wool, and meat. Brazil possesses the soil, tropical climate, rainfall, and ample supplies of unskilled labor needed for efficient low-cost production of coffee.

Industrially advanced nations are in a strategic position to produce cheaply a variety of **capital-intensive** goods, for example, automobiles, agricultural equipment, machinery, and chemicals.

It is important to emphasize that the economic efficiency with which nations produce various goods can and does change over time. Both the distribution of resources and technology can change, altering the relative efficiency with which goods can be produced by various countries. For example, in the past few decades South Korea has upgraded the quality of its labor force and has greatly expanded its stock of capital. Thus, although South Korea was primarily an exporter of agricultural products and raw materials a half-century ago, it now exports large quantities of manufactured goods. Similarly, the new technologies which gave rise to synthetic fibers and synthetic rubber drastically altered the resource-mix needed to produce these goods and thereby changed the relative efficiency of nations in manufacturing them.

In short, as national economies evolve, the size and quality of their labor forces may change, the volume and composition of their capital stocks may shift, new technologies will develop, and even the quality of land and quantity of natural resources may be altered. As these changes occur, the relative efficiency with which a nation can produce various goods will also change.

SPECIALIZATION AND COMPARATIVE ADVANTAGE

Let's now use the concept of comparative advantage to analyze the basis for international specialization and trade.

The Basic Principle

To understand comparative advantage, let's consider the case of a certified public accountant (CPA) who is also a skilled house painter. Suppose the CPA can paint her house in less time than the professional painter she is thinking of hiring. Also suppose the CPA can earn $50 per hour doing her accounting and must pay the painter $15 per hour. Let's say it will take the accountant 30 hours to paint her house; the painter, 40 hours. Finally, assume the CPA receives no special pleasure from painting.

Should the CPA take time off from her accounting to paint her own house or should she hire the painter? The CPA should hire the painter. The CPA's opportunity cost of painting her house is $1500 (=30 hours × $50 per hour of sacrificed income). The cost of hiring the painter is only $600 (=40 hours × $15 per hour paid to the painter). Although the CPA is better at both accounting and painting, her relative or comparative advantage lies in accounting. She will *lower her cost of getting her house painted* by specializing in accounting and using some of the earnings from accounting to hire the house painter.

Similarly, the house painter perhaps can reduce his cost of obtaining accounting services by specializing in painting and using some of his income to hire the CPA. Suppose it would take the painter 10 hours to prepare his income tax, while the CPA could handle this task in 2 hours. The house painter would sacrifice $150 of income (=10 hours × $15 per hour of sacrificed time) to get a task done which he could hire out for $100 (=2 hours × $50 per hour of the CPA's time). By using the CPA to prepare his tax return, the painter *lowers his cost of getting the tax return completed.*

What is true for our CPA and house painter is also true for two nations. Countries can reduce their cost of obtaining desirable goods by specializing where they have comparative advantages.

With this simple example in mind, let's turn to an international trade model to acquire an understanding of the gains from international specialization and trade.

Two Isolated Nations

Suppose the world economy is composed of just two nations, the United States and Brazil. Assume further that each can produce both wheat and coffee, but at differing levels of economic efficiency. Specifically, suppose the United States' and Brazilian domestic production possibilities curves for coffee and wheat are as shown in Figure 20-1a and b. Two characteristics of these production possibilities curves must be stressed.

1 Constant Costs We have purposely drawn the "curves" as straight lines, in contrast to the concave-from-the-origin production possibilities boundaries introduced in Chapter 2. This means the law of increasing costs has been replaced with the assumption of constant costs. This simplification will greatly facilitate our discussion. With increasing costs, the comparative costs of the two nations in producing coffee and wheat would vary with the amounts produced, and comparative advantages might even change. The assumption of constant costs permits us to complete our entire analysis without having to shift to different comparative-cost ratios with every variation in output. The constant-cost assumption will not impair the validity of our analysis and conclusions. We will consider later in our discussion the effect of the more realistic assumption of increasing costs.

2 Different Costs The production possibilities lines of the United States and Brazil are drawn differently, reflecting different resource mixes and differing levels of technological progress. Specifically, the opportunity costs of producing wheat and coffee differ between the two nations.

United States Note in Figure 20-1a that under conditions of full employment, the United States can increase its output of wheat 30 tons by forgoing 30 tons of coffee output. In other words, the slope of the production possibilities curve is -1 $(=-1/1)$, which implies that 1 ton of wheat can be obtained for every 1 ton of coffee sacrificed. That is, in the United States the domestic exchange ratio or **cost ratio** for the two products is 1 ton of wheat for 1 ton of coffee, or $1W = 1C$. The United States, in effect, can "exchange" a ton of wheat for a ton of coffee domestically by shifting resources from wheat to coffee. Our constant-cost assumption means this exchange or cost ratio prevails for all possible moves from one point to another along the United States' production possibilities curve.

Brazil Brazil's production possibilities line in Figure 20-1b reveals a different exchange or cost ratio. In Brazil 20 tons of coffee must be given up to get 10 tons of wheat. Thus, the slope of the production possibilities curve is $-2(=-2/1)$. This means that in Brazil the domestic cost ratio for the two goods is 1 ton of wheat for 2 tons of coffee, or $1W = 2C$.

Self-Sufficiency If the United States and Brazil are isolated and therefore self-sufficient, each must choose some output-mix on its production possibilities line. Assume that point A in Figure 20-1a is the optimal

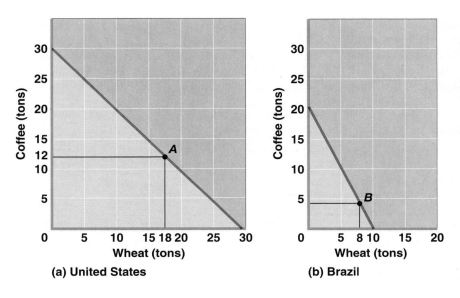

FIGURE 20-1 Production possibilities for the United States and Brazil

The two production possibilities curves show the amounts of coffee and wheat the United States (a) and Brazil (b) can produce domestically. The production possibilities for both countries are straight lines because we are assuming constant costs. The different cost ratios—$I W = I C$ for the United States and $I W = 2C$ for Brazil—are reflected in the different slopes of the two lines.

(a) United States

(b) Brazil

output-mix in the United States. The choice of this combination of 18 tons of wheat and 12 tons of coffee is presumably rendered through the market system. Suppose Brazil's optimal product-mix is 8 tons of wheat and 4 tons of coffee, indicated by point B in Figure 20-1b. These choices are also reflected in column 1 of Table 20-4.

Specializing According to Comparative Advantage

Given these different cost ratios, the guideline for determining the products in which the United States and Brazil should specialize is as follows: The **principle of comparative advantage** says that *total output will be greatest when each good is produced by that nation which has the lower opportunity cost.* For our illustration, the United States' opportunity cost is lower for wheat, that is, the United States need only forgo 1 ton of coffee to produce 1 ton of wheat, whereas Brazil must forgo 2 tons of coffee for 1 ton of wheat. *The United States has a comparative (cost) advantage in wheat, and should specialize in wheat production.* The "world" (the United States and Brazil) clearly is *not* economizing in the use of its resources if a specific product (wheat) is produced by a high-cost producer (Brazil) when it could have been produced by a low-cost producer (the United States). To have Brazil produce wheat would mean that the world economy would have to give up more coffee than is necessary to obtain a ton of wheat.

Conversely, Brazil's opportunity cost is lower for coffee; it must sacrifice only $\frac{1}{2}$ ton of wheat in producing 1 ton of coffee, whereas the United States must forgo 1 ton of wheat in producing a ton of coffee. *Brazil has a comparative advantage in coffee, and should specialize in coffee production.* Again, the world would *not* be employing its resources economically if coffee were produced by a high-cost producer (the United States) rather than a low-cost producer (Brazil). If the United

States produced coffee, the world would be giving up more wheat than necessary to obtain each ton of coffee. *Economizing—using given quantities of scarce resources to obtain the greatest total output—requires that any particular good be produced by that nation which has the lower opportunity cost or, in other words, the comparative advantage.* In our illustration, the United States should produce wheat and Brazil, coffee.

In column 2 of Table 20-4 we can quickly verify that specialized production in accordance with the principle of comparative advantage does, indeed, allow the world to get more output from its fixed amount of resources. By specializing completely in wheat, the United States can produce 30 tons of wheat and no coffee. Similarly, by specializing completely in coffee, Brazil produces 20 tons of coffee and no wheat. The world has more wheat—30 tons compared with 26 (=18 + 8) tons—*and* more coffee—20 tons compared with 16 (=12 + 4) tons—than in the case of self-sufficiency or unspecialized production.

Terms of Trade

But consumers of each nation want *both* wheat and coffee. Specialization implies the need to trade or exchange the two products. What will be the **terms of trade?** At what exchange ratio will the United States and Brazil trade wheat and coffee?

Because $1W = 1C$ in the United States, the United States must get *more than* 1 ton of coffee for each ton of wheat exported or it will not pay the United States to export wheat in exchange for Brazilian coffee. Stated differently, the United States must get a better price (more coffee) for its wheat in the world market than it can get domestically, or else trade will not be advantageous.

Similarly, because $1W = 2C$ in Brazil, it must be able to get 1 ton of wheat by exporting some amount *less than* 2 tons of coffee. Brazil must be able to pay a

TABLE 20-4 International specialization according to comparative advantage and the gains from trade (hypothetical data; in tons)

Country	(1) Outputs before specialization	(2) Outputs after specialization	(3) Amounts exported (−) and imported (+)	(4) Outputs available after trade	(5) = (4) − (1) Gains from specialization and trade
United States	18 wheat	30 wheat	−10 wheat	20 wheat	2 wheat
	12 coffee	0 coffee	+15 coffee	15 coffee	3 coffee
Brazil	8 wheat	0 wheat	+10 wheat	10 wheat	2 wheat
	4 coffee	20 coffee	−15 coffee	5 coffee	1 coffee

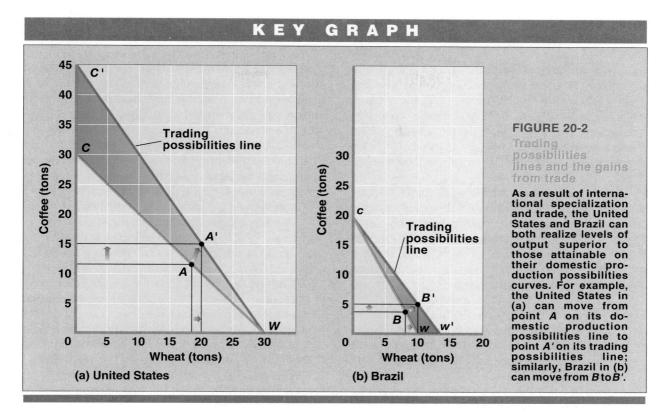

KEY GRAPH

FIGURE 20-2

Trading possibilities lines and the gains from trade

As a result of international specialization and trade, the United States and Brazil can both realize levels of output superior to those attainable on their domestic production possibilities curves. For example, the United States in (a) can move from point *A* on its domestic production possibilities line to point *A'* on its trading possibilities line; similarly, Brazil in (b) can move from *B* to *B'*.

(a) United States

(b) Brazil

---

lower "price" for wheat in the world market than it must pay domestically, or it will not want to engage in international trade. Thus, the international exchange ratio or *terms of trade* must lie somewhere between

$1W = 1C$ (United States' cost conditions)

and

$1W = 2C$ (Brazil's cost conditions)

But where will the actual world exchange ratio fall between the $1W = 1C$ and $1W = 2C$ limits? This question is important, because the exchange ratio or terms of trade determine how the gains from international specialization and trade are divided among the two nations. The United States will prefer a rate close to $1W = 2C$, say, $1W = 1\frac{3}{4}C$. Americans want to get much coffee for each ton of wheat they export. Similarly, Brazil desires a rate near $1W = 1C$, say, $1W = 1\frac{1}{4}C$. Brazil wants to export as little coffee as possible for each ton of wheat it receives in exchange.

The actual exchange ratio materializing between the two limits depends on world supply and demand conditions for the two products. If overall world demand for coffee is weak relative to its supply and the

demand for wheat is strong relative to its supply, the price of coffee will be low and that of wheat high. The exchange ratio will settle near the $1W = 2C$ figure preferred by the United States. Under the opposite world supply and demand conditions, the ratio will settle near the $1W = 1C$ level most favorable to Brazil.

The Gains from Trade

Suppose the international exchange ratio or terms of trade are actually $1W = 1\frac{1}{2}C$. The possibility of trading on these terms permits each nation to supplement its domestic production possibilities line with a **trading possibilities line.** This can be seen in Figure 20-2a and b (Key Graph). Just as a production possibilities line shows the options a full-employment economy has in obtaining one product by shifting resources from the production of another, so a trading possibilities lines shows the options a nation has by specializing in one product and trading (exporting) its speciality to obtain the other product. The trading possibilities lines in Figure 20-2 are drawn on the assumption that both nations specialize in accordance with comparative advantage and therefore that the United States specializes completely in wheat (point W in Figure 20-2a) and Brazil completely in coffee (point c in Figure 20-2b).

Improved Options Now, instead of being constrained by its domestic production possibilities line and having to give up 1 ton of wheat for every ton of coffee it wants as it moves up its domestic production possibilities line from point W, the United States, through trade with Brazil, can get $1\frac{1}{2}$ tons of coffee for every ton of wheat it exports to Brazil as it moves up the trading possibilities line WC'.

Similarly, we can think of Brazil as starting at point c, and instead of having to move down its domestic production possibilities line and having to give up 2 tons of coffee for each ton of wheat it wants, it can now export just $1\frac{1}{2}$ tons of coffee for each ton of wheat it wants by moving down its cw' trading possibilities line.

Specialization and trade give rise to a new exchange ratio between wheat and coffee which is reflected in a nation's trading possibilities line. This new exchange ratio is superior for both nations to the self-sufficiency exchange ratio in the production possibilities line of each. By specializing in wheat and trading for Brazil's coffee, the United States can obtain *more than* 1 ton of coffee for 1 ton of wheat. Similarly, by specializing in coffee and trading for United States' wheat, Brazil can get 1 ton of wheat for *less than* 2 tons of coffee.

Added Output The crucial point is that by specializing according to comparative advantage and trading for those goods produced with the least relative efficiency domestically, both the United States and Brazil can realize combinations of wheat and coffee beyond their production possibilities boundaries. *Specialization according to comparative advantage results in a more efficient allocation of world resources, and larger outputs of both wheat and coffee are therefore available to the United States and Brazil.* To be more specific, suppose that at the $1W = 1\frac{1}{2}C$ terms of trade, the United States exports 10 tons of wheat to Brazil and Brazil in return exports 15 tons of coffee to the United States.

How do the new quantities of wheat and coffee available to the two nations compare with the optimal product-mixes that existed before specialization and trade? Point A in Figure 20-2a reminds us that the United States chose 18 tons of wheat and 12 tons of coffee originally. But, by producing 30 tons of wheat and no coffee, and by trading 10 tons of wheat for 15 tons of coffee, the United States can enjoy 20 tons of wheat and 15 tons of coffee. This new, superior combi-

nation of wheat and coffee is shown by point A' in Figure 20-2a. Compared with the nontrading figures of 18 tons of wheat and 12 tons of coffee, the United States' **gains from trade** are 2 tons of wheat and 3 tons of coffee. Similarly, we assumed Brazil's optimal product-mix was 4 tons of coffee and 8 tons of wheat (point B) before specialization and trade. Now, by specializing in coffee—producing 20 tons of coffee and no wheat— Brazil can realize a combination of 5 tons of coffee and 10 tons of wheat by exporting 15 tons of its coffee in exchange for 10 tons of American wheat. This new position is shown by point B' in Figure 20-2b. Brazil's gains from trade are 1 ton of coffee and 2 tons of wheat.

As a result of specialization and trade, both countries have more of both products. Table 20-4 is a summary statement of these figures and merits your careful study.

The fact that points A' and B' are economic positions superior to A and B is extremely important. Recall from Chapter 2 that a given nation can expand its production possibilities boundary by (1) expanding the quantity and improving the quality of its resources or (2) realizing technological progress. We have now discovered another means—international trade—by which a nation can circumvent the output constraint imposed by its production possibilities curve. The effects of international specialization and trade are tantamount to having more and better resources or discovering improved production techniques.

Increasing Costs

In formulating a straightforward statement of the principles underlying international trade, we have made several simplifications. Our discussion was purposely limited to two products and two nations to minimize verbiage, but multination and multiproduct examples yield similar conclusions. The assumption of constant costs, on the other hand, is a more substantive simplification. Let's therefore consider the significance of increasing costs (concave-from-the-origin production possibility curves) for our analysis.

Suppose, as in our previous constant-cost illustration, that the United States and Brazil are at positions on their production possibilities curves where their cost ratios are initially $1W = 1C$ and $1W = 2C$ respectively. As before, comparative advantage indicates that the United States should specialize in wheat and Brazil in coffee. But now, as the United States begins to expand wheat production, its $1W = 1C$ cost ratio will *fall;* it will have to sacrifice *more than* 1 ton of coffee to get 1 additional ton of wheat. Resources are no longer perfectly shiftable between alternative uses, as the constant-cost assumption implied. Resources less and less suitable to wheat production must be allocated to the American wheat industry in expanding wheat output, and this means increasing costs—the sacrifice of larger and larger amounts of coffee for each additional ton of wheat.

Similarly, Brazil, starting from its $1W = 2C$ cost ratio position, expands coffee production. But as it does, it will find that its $1W = 2C$ cost ratio begins to *rise*. Sacrificing a ton of wheat will free resources which are only capable of producing something *less than* 2 tons of coffee, because these transferred resources are less suitable to coffee production.

As the American cost ratio falls from $1W = 1C$ and Brazil's rises from $1W = 2C$, a point will be reached at which the cost ratios are equal in the two nations, for example, at $1W = 1\frac{1}{2}C$. At this point the underlying basis for further specialization and trade—differing cost ratios—has disappeared, and further specialization is therefore uneconomic. And most important, this point of equal cost ratios may be realized where the United States is still producing some coffee along with its wheat and Brazil is producing some wheat along with its coffee. *The primary effect of increasing costs is to make specialization less than complete.* For this reason we often find domestically produced products competing directly against identical or similar imported products within a particular economy.

The Case for Free Trade Restated

The compelling logic of the case for free trade is hardly new. Indeed, in 1776 Adam Smith asserted:

> It is the maxim of every prudent master of a family, never to attempt to make at home what it will cost him more to make than to buy. The taylor does not attempt to make his own shoes, but buys them of the shoemaker. The shoemaker does not attempt to make his own clothes but employs a taylor. The farmer attempts to make neither the one nor the other, but employs those different artificers. All of them find it for their interest to employ their whole industry in a way in which they have some advantage over their neighbors, and to purchase with a part of its produce, or what is the same thing, with the price of a part of it, whatever else they have occasion for.[1]

[1]Adam Smith, *The Wealth of Nations* (New York: Modern Library, Inc., 1937), p. 424.

In modern jargon, the case for free trade comes down to this one potent argument. *Through free trade based on the principle of comparative advantage, the world economy can achieve a more efficient allocation of resources and a higher level of material well-being.* The resource mixes and technological knowledge of each country are different. Therefore, each nation can produce particular commodities at different real costs. Each nation should produce goods for which its opportunity costs are low relative to those of other nations and exchange these specialties for products for which its opportunity costs are high relative to those of other nations. If each nation does this, the world can realize fully the advantages of geographic and human specialization. That is, the world—and each free-trading nation—can obtain a larger real income from the fixed supplies of resources available to it. Protection—barriers to free trade—lessens or eliminates gains from specialization. If nations cannot freely trade, they must shift resources from efficient (low-cost) to inefficient (high-cost) uses to satisfy their diverse wants.

A side benefit of free trade is that it promotes competition and deters monopoly. The increased competition afforded by foreign firms forces domestic firms to adopt the lowest-cost production techniques. It also compels them to be innovative and progressive with respect to both product quality and production methods, thereby contributing to economic growth. And free trade gives consumers a wider range of products from which to choose. The reasons to favor free trade are essentially the same reasons which endorse competition. Therefore, it is not surprising that most economists embrace the case for free trade as an economically valid position.

QUICK REVIEW 20-1

◆   *World trade is increasingly important to the United States and other nations of the world.*

◆   *International trade enables nations to specialize, enhance the productivity of their resources, and obtain a larger output.*

◆   *The principle of comparative advantage states that total world output will be greatest when each good is produced by that nation having the lowest opportunity cost.*

◆   *Specialization is less than complete among nations because opportunity costs normally rise as more of a particular good is produced.*

TRADE BARRIERS

No matter how compelling the logic of the case for free trade, barriers to free trade do exist.

1 *Tariffs* are excise taxes on imported goods: they may be imposed for purposes of revenue or protection. **Revenue tariffs** are usually applied to products not produced domestically, for example, tin, coffee, and bananas in the case of the United States. Rates on revenue tariffs are typically modest and their purpose is to provide the Federal government with tax revenues.

Protective tariffs, on the other hand, are designed to shield domestic producers from foreign competition. Although protective tariffs are usually not high enough to prohibit importation of foreign goods, they put foreign producers at a competitive disadvantage in selling in domestic markets.

2 **Import quotas** specify the maximum amounts of commodities which may be imported in any period of time. Frequently, import quotas are more effective in retarding international commerce than tariffs. A given product might be imported in relatively large quantities despite high tariffs; low import quotas, on the other hand, completely prohibit imports once quotas are filled.

3 **Nontariff barriers** (NTBs) refer to licensing requirements, unreasonable standards pertaining to product quality and safety, or simply unnecessary bureaucratic red tape in customs procedures. Japan and the European countries frequently require their domestic importers of foreign goods to obtain licenses. By restricting the issuance of licenses, imports can be effectively restricted. Great Britain bars importation of coal in this way.

4 **Voluntary export restrictions** (VERs) are a relatively new trade barrier by which foreign firms "voluntarily" limit the amount of their exports to a particular country. VERs, which have the effect of import quotas, are agreed to by exporters in the hope of avoiding more stringent trade barriers. Thus Japanese auto manufacturers agreed to a VER on exports to the United States under the threat of higher U.S. tariffs or the imposition of low import quotas.

Motivations: Special-Interest Effect

If tariffs and quotas impede free trade and diminish economic efficiency, why do we have them? While nations as a whole gain from free international trade, particular industries and groups of resource suppliers can be hurt. In our comparative advantage example, spe-

cialization and trade adversely affected the American coffee industry and the Brazilian wheat industry. Such groups may seek to preserve or improve their economic positions by persuading the government to impose tariffs or quotas to protect them from the detrimental effects of free trade. The special-interest effect—or concept of rent-seeking activity—is highly relevant.

> The direct beneficiaries of import relief or export subsidy are usually few in number, but each has a large individual stake in the outcome. Thus, their incentive for vigorous political activity is strong.
> But the costs of such policies may far exceed the benefits. It may cost the public $40,000–$50,000 a year to protect a domestic job that might otherwise pay an employee only half that amount in wages and benefits. Furthermore, the costs of protection are widely diffused—in the United States, among 50 States and [254] million citizens. Since the cost borne by any one citizen is likely to be quite small, and may even go unnoticed, resistance at the grass-roots level to protectionist measures often is considerably less than pressures for their adoption.[2]

Also, the costs of protectionism are hidden because tariffs and quotas are embedded in the prices of goods. Thus policy makers face fewer political restraints in responding positively to demands for protectionism.

Later in this chapter we will consider the specific arguments and appeals made to justify protection.

Economic Impact of Tariffs

Simple supply and demand analysis is useful in examining the economic effects of protective tariffs. The D_d and S_d curves in Figure 20-3 show domestic demand and supply for a product in which the United States has a comparative *dis*advantage, for example, cassette recorders. (Disregard $S_d + Q$ for now.) Without world trade, the domestic price and output would be OP_d and Oq, respectively.

Assume now that the domestic economy is opened to world trade, and that the Japanese, who have a comparative advantage in cassette recorders and dominate the world market, begin to sell their recorders in the United States. We assume that with free trade the domestic price cannot differ from the lower world price, which here is OP_w. At OP_w domestic consumption is Od, domestic production is Oa, and the difference between the two, *ad*, reflects imports.

[2]*Economic Report of the President, 1982,* p. 177.

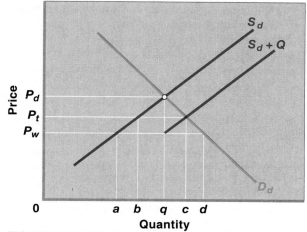

FIGURE 20-3   The economic effects of a protective tariff or an import quota

A tariff of P_wP_t will reduce domestic consumption from Od to Oc. Domestic producers will be able to sell more output (Ob rather than Oa) at a higher price (OP_t rather than OP_w). Foreign exporters are injured because they sell less output (bc rather than ad) in the United States. The orange area indicates the amount of tariffs paid by American consumers. An import quota of bc units will have the same effects as the tariff, with one exception: the [color] area will go to foreign producers rather than to the U.S. Treasury.

Direct Effects   Suppose now that the United States imposes a tariff of P_wP_t per unit on the imported recorders. This will raise the domestic price from OP_w to OP_t and will have several effects.

1 Decline in Consumption   Consumption of recorders in the United States will decline from Od to Oc as the higher price moves buyers up their demand curve. The tariff prompts consumers to buy fewer recorders; that is, to reallocate a portion of their expenditures to less desired substitute products. American consumers are clearly injured by the tariff, since they pay P_wP_t more for each of the Oc units which they now buy at price P_t.

2 Increased Domestic Production   American producers—who are *not* subject to the tariff—will receive a higher price of OP_t per unit. Because this new price is higher than the pretariff or world price of OP_w, the domestic recorder industry will move up its supply curve S_d, increasing domestic output from Oa to Ob. Domestic producers will enjoy both a higher price and expanded sales. These effects explain the interest of domestic producers in lobbying for protective tariffs. From a social point of view, however, the expanded

domestic production of *ab* reflects the fact that the tariff permits domestic producers of recorders to bid resources away from other, more efficient, industries.

3 Decline in Imports   Japanese producers will be hurt. Although the sales price of recorders is higher by P_wP_t, that increase accrues to the United States government and not to Japanese producers. The after-tariff world price, and thus the per unit revenue to Japanese producers, remains at OP_w, while the volume of United States imports (Japanese exports) falls from *ad* to *bc*.

4 Tariff Revenue   Finally, note that the orange rectangle indicates the amount of revenue which the tariff yields. Specifically, total revenue from the tariff is determined by multiplying the tariff of P_wP_t per unit by the number of imported recorders, *bc*. This tariff revenue is essentially a transfer of income from consumers to government and does not represent any net change in the nation's economic well-being. The result is that government gains this portion of what consumers lose.

Indirect Effects   There are more subtle effects of tariffs which go beyond our supply and demand diagram. Because of diminished sales of recorders in the United States, Japan will now earn fewer dollars with which to buy American exports. That is, American export industries—industries in which the United States has a comparative advantage—will cut production and release resources. These are highly efficient industries, as evidenced by their comparative advantage and ability to sell goods in world markets. In short, *tariffs directly promote the expansion of relatively inefficient industries which do not have a comparative advantage and indirectly cause the contraction of relatively efficient industries which do have a comparative advantage.* This means that tariffs cause resources to be shifted in the wrong direction. This is not surprising. We know that specialization and unfettered world trade based on comparative advantage would lead to the efficient use of world resources and an expansion of the world's real output. The purpose and effect of protective tariffs are to reduce world trade. Therefore, aside from their specific effects on consumers and foreign and domestic producers, tariffs diminish the world's real output.

Economic Impact of Quotas

We noted earlier than an import quota is a legal limit placed on the amount of some product which can be imported each year. Quotas have the same economic impact as a tariff with one big difference: While tariffs generate revenue for the United States government, a quota transfers that revenue to foreign producers.

Suppose in Figure 20-3 that, instead of imposing a tariff of P_wP_t per unit, the United States prohibits any Japanese imports of recorders in excess of bc units. In other words, an import quota of bc recorders is imposed on Japan. Note that we have deliberately chosen the size of this quota to be the same amount as imports would be under a P_wP_t tariff, so we are comparing "equivalent" situations. As a consequence of the quota, the supply of recorders is $S_d + Q$ in the United States. This is comprised of the domestic supply plus the constant amount bc ($=Q$) which importers will provide at each domestic price.[3]

Most of the economic results are the same as with a tariff. Recorder prices are higher (P_t instead of P_w) because imports have been reduced from ad to bc. Domestic consumption of recorders is down from Od to Oc. American producers enjoy both a higher price (P_t rather than P_w) and increased sales (Ob rather than Oa).

The critical difference is that the price increase of P_wP_t paid by American consumers on imports of bc—that is, the orange area—no longer goes to the United States Treasury as tariff (tax) revenue, but rather flows to those Japanese firms which have acquired the rights to sell recorders in the United States. For Americans, a tariff produces a better economic outcome than a quota, other things being the same. A tariff generates government revenue which can be used to cut other taxes or to finance public goods and services which benefit Americans. In contrast, the higher price created by quotas results in additional revenue for foreign producers.

It is relevant that in the early 1980s the American automobile industry with the support of its workers successfully lobbied for an import quota on Japanese autos. The Japanese government in turn apportioned this quota among its various auto producers. The restricted supply of Japanese cars in the American market allowed Japanese manufacturers to increase their prices and, hence, their profits. The American import quotas in effect provided Japanese auto manufacturers with a cartel-like arrangement which enhanced their profits. It is significant that when American import quotas were dropped in the mid-1980s, the Japanese government replaced them with its own system of export quotas for Japanese automakers.

THE CASE FOR PROTECTION: A CRITICAL REVIEW

Although free-trade advocates prevail in the classroom, protectionists sometimes dominate the halls of Congress. What arguments do protectionists make to justify trade barriers? How valid are these arguments?

Military Self-Sufficiency Argument

The argument here is not economic but of a political-military nature: Protective tariffs are needed to preserve or strengthen industries producing strategic goods and materials essential for defense or war. It plausibly contends that in an uncertain world, political-military objectives (self-sufficiency) must take precedence over economic goals (efficiency in the allocation of world resources).

Unfortunately, there is no objective criterion for weighing the relative worth of the increase in national security on the one hand, and the decrease in productive efficiency on the other, which accompany reallocation of resources toward strategic industries when such tariffs are imposed. The economist can only point out that certain economic costs are involved when tariffs are levied to enhance military self-sufficiency.

Although we might all agree that it is probably not a good idea to import our missile guidance systems from China, the self-sufficiency argument is nevertheless open to serious abuse. Virtually every industry can directly or indirectly claim a contribution to national security. Can you name an industry which did *not* contribute in some small way to World War II? Aside from abuses, are there not better ways than tariffs to provide for needed strength in strategic industries? When achieved through tariffs, self-sufficiency creates costs in the form of higher domestic prices on the output of the shielded industry. The cost of enhanced military security is apportioned arbitrarily among those consumers who buy the industry's product. A direct subsidy to strategic industries, financed out of general tax revenues, would more equitably distribute these costs.

Increase Domestic Employment

This "save American jobs" argument for tariffs becomes increasingly fashionable as an economy en-

---

[3]The $S_d + Q$ supply curve does not exist below price P_w because Japanese producers would not export recorders to the United States at any price *below* P_w when they can sell them to other countries *at* the world market prices of P_w.

counters a recession. It is rooted in macro analysis. Aggregate expenditures in an open economy are comprised of consumption expenditures (C) plus investment expenditures (I_g) plus government expenditures (G) plus net export expenditures (X_n). Net export expenditures consist of exports (X) minus imports (M). By reducing imports, M, aggregate expenditures will rise, stimulating the domestic economy by boosting income and employment. But there are important shortcomings associated with this policy.

1 Job Creation from Imports While imports may eliminate some American jobs, they create others. Imports may have eliminated jobs of American steel and textile workers in recent years, but others have gained jobs selling Hondas and imported electronics equipment. While import restrictions alter the composition of employment, they may actually have little or no effect on the volume of employment.

2 Fallacy of Composition All nations cannot simultaneously succeed in import restriction; what is true for *one* nation is not true for *all* nations. The exports of one nation must be the imports of another. To the extent that one country is able to stimulate its economy through an excess of exports over imports, another economy's unemployment problem is worsened by the resulting excess of imports over exports. It is no wonder that tariff and import quotas to achieve domestic full employment are termed "beggar my neighbor" policies. They achieve short-run domestic goals by making trading partners poorer.

3 Retaliation Nations adversely affected by tariffs and quotas are likely to retaliate, causing a competitive raising of trade barriers which will choke off trade to the end that all nations are worse off. The **Smoot-Hawley Tariff Act of 1930,** which imposed the highest tariffs ever enacted in the United States, backfired miserably. Rather than stimulate the American economy, this tariff act only induced a series of retaliatory restrictions by adversely affected nations. This caused a further contraction of international trade and lowered the income and employment levels of all nations.

4 Long-Run Feedbacks In the long run an excess of exports over imports is doomed to failure as a device for stimulating domestic employment. It is through American imports that foreign nations earn dollars with which to purchase American exports. In the long run a nation must import in order to export. The long-run impact of tariffs is not to increase domestic employ-

ment but at best to reallocate workers away from export industries and toward protected domestic industries. This shift implies a less efficient allocation of resources.

In summary, the argument that tariffs increase net exports and therefore create jobs is misleading:

> Overall employment in an economy is determined by internal conditions and macroeconomic policies, not by the existence of trade barriers and the level of trade flows. The United States created [more than 18] million payroll jobs over the course of the [1982–1990] economic expansion, a period of U.S. trade deficits and relatively open U.S. markets. During the same period the European Community (EC) created virtually no net new jobs, even though they experienced trade surpluses. The same level of employment can be obtained in the total absence of free trade as when trade is completely free. But without foreign trade a nation will be worse off economically because, in effect, it will throw away part of its productive capability—the ability to convert surplus goods into other goods through foreign trade.[4]

Diversification for Stability

Closely related to the increase-domestic-employment argument for tariff protection is the diversification-for-stability argument. The point here is that highly specialized economies—for example, Saudi Arabia's oil economy or Cuba's sugar economy—are highly dependent on international markets for their incomes. Wars, cyclical fluctuations, and adverse changes in the structure of industry will force large and frequently painful readjustments on such economies. Tariff and quota protection is therefore allegedly needed to promote greater industrial diversification and consequently less dependence on world markets for just one or two products. This will help insulate the domestic economy from international political developments, depressions abroad, and from random fluctuations in world supply and demand for one or two particular commodities, thereby providing greater domestic stability.

There is some truth in this argument. There are also serious qualifications and shortcomings.
1   The argument has little or no relevance to the United States and other advanced economies.
2   The economic costs of diversification may be great; for example, one-crop economies may be highly inefficient in manufacturing.

---

[4]*Economic Report of the President, 1988,* p. 131. Updated

Infant-Industry Argument

The infant-industry argument contends that protective tariffs are needed to allow new domestic industries to establish themselves. Temporarily shielding young domestic firms from the severe competition of more mature and therefore currently more efficient foreign firms will give infant industries a chance to develop and become efficient producers.

This argument for protection rests on an alleged exception to the case for free trade. The exception is that all industries have not had, and in the presence of mature foreign competition, will never have, the chance to make long-run adjustments in the direction of larger scale and greater efficiency in production. Tariff protection for infant industries will therefore correct a current misallocation of world resources now perpetuated by historically different levels of economic development between domestic and foreign industries.

Counterarguments Though the infant-industry argument has logical validity, these qualifying points must be noted.
1   In the less developed nations it is very difficult to determine which industries are the infants capable of achieving economic maturity and therefore deserving of protection.
2   Protective tariffs may persist even after industrial maturity has been realized.
3   Most economists feel that if infant industries are to be subsidized, there are better means than tariffs for doing it. Direct subsidies, for example, have the advantage of making explicit which industries are being aided and to what degree.

Strategic Trade Policy In recent years the infant-industry argument has taken a modified form in advanced economies. The contention is that government should use trade barriers strategically to reduce the risk of product development borne by domestic firms, particularly products involving advanced technology. Firms protected from foreign competition can grow more rapidly and therefore achieve greater economies of scale than unprotected foreign competitors. Thus, the protected firms can eventually dominate world markets because of lower costs. Supposedly, dominance of world markets will enable the domestic firms to return high profits to the home nation. These profits allegedly will exceed the domestic sacrifices caused by trade barriers. Also, specialization in high-technology industries supposedly is beneficial because technology advances achieved in one domestic industry often can be transferred to other domestic industries.

Japan and South Korea, in particular, have been accused of using this form of **strategic trade policy.** The problem with this strategy and therefore this argument for tariffs is that the nations put at a disadvantage by strategic trade policies tend to retaliate with tariffs of their own. The outcome may be higher tariffs worldwide, reductions in world trade, and loss of the gains from specialization and exchange.

Protection Against "Dumping"

The protection-against-dumping argument for tariffs contends that tariffs are needed to protect American firms from foreign producers which "dump" excess goods onto the American market at less than cost. Two reasons have been suggested as to why foreign firms might wish to sell in America at below cost.
1   These firms may use **dumping** to drive out American competitors, obtain monopoly power, and then raise prices. The long-term economic profits resulting from this strategy may more than offset the earlier losses which accompany the dumping.
2   Dumping may be a form of price discrimination—charging different prices to different customers. The foreign seller may find it can maximize its profits by charging a high price in its monopolized domestic market while unloading its surplus output at a lower price in the United States. The surplus output may be needed to obtain the overall per unit cost saving associated with large-scale production.

Because dumping is a legitimate concern, it is prohibited under American trade law. Where dumping occurs and is shown to injure American firms, the Federal government imposes tariffs called "antidumping duties" on the specific goods. But relative to the number of goods exported to the United States, documented cases of dumping are few. Dumping therefore does *not* justify widespread, permanent tariffs. Furthermore, allegations of dumping require careful investigation to determine their validity. Foreign producers often argue that dumping allegations and antidumping duties are an American method of restricting legitimate trade. The fact is that some foreign firms can produce certain goods at substantially less cost than American competitors, and what on the surface may seem to be dumping often is comparative advantage at work. If abused, the antidumping law can increase the price of imports and restrict competition in the American market. This reduced competition allows American firms to raise prices at consumers' expense. And even where true dumping does occur, American consumers gain from the lower-priced product—at least in the short term—much as they gain from a price war among American producers.

Cheap Foreign Labor

The cheap-foreign-labor argument holds that domestic firms and workers must be shielded from the ruinous competition of countries where wages are low. If protection is not provided, cheap imports will flood American markets and the prices of American goods—along with the wages of American workers—will be pulled down and our domestic living standards reduced.

This argument can be rebutted at several levels. The logic of the argument would suggest that it is *not* mutually beneficial for rich and poor persons to trade with one another. However, that is not the case. A low-income farm worker may pick lettuce or tomatoes for a rich landowner and both may benefit from the transaction. And don't American consumers gain when they buy a Taiwanese vest pocket radio for $12 as opposed to a qualitatively similar American-made radio selling for $20?

Also, recall that gains from trade are based on comparative advantage. Looking back at Figure 20-1, suppose the United States and Brazil have labor forces of exactly the same size. Noting the positions of the production possibilities curves, we observe that American labor is absolutely more productive because our labor force can produce more of either good. Because of this greater productivity, we can expect wages and living standards to be higher for American labor. Conversely, Brazil's less-productive labor will receive lower wages.

The cheap-foreign-labor argument would suggest that, to maintain our standard of living, America should not trade with low-wage Brazil. Suppose we follow this suggestion. Will wages and living standards rise in the United States as a result? The answer is "No." To obtain coffee America will now have to reallocate a portion of its labor from its relatively efficient wheat industry to its relatively inefficient coffee industry. As a result, the average productivity of American labor will fall as will real wages and living standards. In fact, the labor forces of *both* countries will have diminished standards of living because without specialization and trade they will have less output available to them. Compare column 4 with column 1 in Table 20-4 or points A' and B' with A and B in Figure 20-2 to confirm this point.

A Summing Up

The arguments for protection are numerous, but they are not weighty. Under proper conditions, the infant-industry argument stands as a valid exception, justifiable on economic grounds. And on political-military grounds, the self-sufficiency argument can be used to validate protection. Both arguments, however, are susceptible to severe abuses, and both neglect alternative means of fostering industrial development and military self-sufficiency. Most other arguments are semi-emotional appeals in the form of half-truths and outright fallacies. These arguments note only the immediate and direct consequences of protective tariffs. They ignore the fact that in the long run a nation must import in order to export.

There is also compelling historical evidence suggesting that free trade has led to prosperity and growth and that protectionism has had the opposite effects. Several examples follow.

1 The United States Constitution forbids individual states from levying tariffs, making America a huge free-trade area. Economic historians acknowledge this is an important positive factor in the economic development of our nation.

2 Great Britain's movement toward freer international trade in the mid-nineteenth century was instrumental in its industrialization and growth in that century.

3 As we will see, the creation of the Common Market in Europe after World War II has eliminated tariffs among member nations. Economists agree that creation of this free-trade area has been an important ingredient in the western European prosperity of recent decades.

4 More generally, the trend toward tariff reduction since the mid-1930s has been a stimulus to post-World War II expansion of the world economy.

5 We have already noted that the high tariffs imposed by our Smoot-Hawley Act of 1930 and the retaliation which it engendered worsened the Great Depression of the 1930s.

6 Studies of less developed countries overwhelmingly suggest that those which have relied on import restrictions to protect their domestic industries have realized slow growth in comparison to those pursuing more open economic policies.[5]

---

[5]Examples are from *Economic Report of the President 1985*, pp. 115–117.

INTERNATIONAL TRADE POLICIES

As Figure 20-4 makes clear, tariffs in the United States have had their ups and downs.[6] Generally, the United States was a high-tariff nation over much of its history. Note that the Smoot-Hawley Tariff Act of 1930 enacted some of the highest tariff rates ever imposed by the United States.

In view of the strong case for free trade, this high-tariff heritage may be a bit surprising. If tariffs are economically undesirable, why has Congress been willing to employ them? As suggested earlier in this chapter, the answer lies in the political realities of tariff making and, more specifically, in the special-interest effect. A small group of domestic producers who will receive large economic gains from tariffs and quotas will press vigorously for protection through well-financed and well-informed political lobbyists. The large number of consumers who individually will have small losses imposed on them will be generally uninformed and indifferent.

Indeed, the public may be won over, not only by the vigor, but also by the apparent plausibility ("Cut imports and prevent domestic unemployment") and the patriotic ring ("Buy American!") of the protectionists. Alleged tariff benefits are immediate and clear-cut to the public. The adverse effects cited by economists are obscure and widely dispersed over the economy. Then, too, the public is likely to stumble on the fallacy

[6]Technical footnote: Average tariff-rate figures understate the importance of tariffs by not accounting for the fact that some goods are *excluded* from American markets because of existing tariffs. Then, too, average figures conceal the high tariffs on particular items: watches, china, hats, textiles, scissors, wine, jewelry, glassware, wood products, and so forth.

of composition: "If a quota on Japanese automobiles will preserve profits and employment in the American automobile industry, how can it be detrimental to the economy as a whole?" When political logrolling is added in —"You back tariffs for the apparel industry in my state and I'll do the same for the auto industry in your state"—the sum can be protective tariffs and import quotas.

Reciprocal Trade Act and GATT

The downward trend of tariffs since Smoot-Hawley was inaugurated with the **Reciprocal Trade Agreements Act of 1934.** Specifically aimed at tariff reduction, the act had two main features:

1 Negotiating Authority It authorized the President to negotiate agreements with foreign nations which would reduce American tariffs up to 50 percent of the existing rates. Tariff reductions were to hinge on the willingness of other nations to reciprocate by lowering tariffs on American exports.

2 Generalized Reductions By incorporating **most-favored-nation clauses** in these agreements, the resulting tariff reductions not only would apply to the specific nation negotiating with the United States, but they would be *generalized* so as to apply to all nations.

But the Reciprocal Trade Act gave rise to only bilateral (two-nation) negotiations. This approach was broadened in 1947 when twenty-three nations, including the United States, signed a **General Agreement on Tariffs and Trade (GATT).** GATT is based on three cardinal principles: (1) equal, nondiscriminatory treatment for all member nations; (2) the reduction of tariffs by *multilateral* negotiations; and (3) the elimination of import quotas. Basically, GATT is a forum for the negotiation of reductions in trade barriers on a multilateral basis. One hundred nations currently belong to GATT, and there is little doubt that it has been an important force in the trend toward liberalized trade. Under its sponsorship, seven "rounds" of negotiations to reduce trade barriers have been completed in the post-World War II period.

In 1986, the eighth "round" of GATT negotiations began in Uruguay. Proposals discussed at the "Uruguay Round" included (1) eliminating trade barriers and domestic subsidies in agriculture, (2) removing barriers to trade in services (which now account for 20 percent of international trade), (3) ending restrictions on foreign economic investments, and (4) establishing and enforcing patent, copyright, and trademark rights

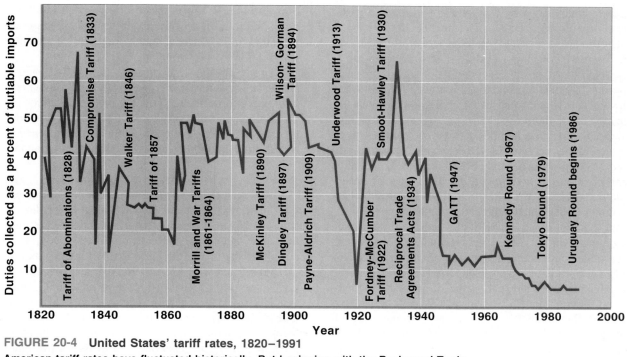

FIGURE 20-4   United States' tariff rates, 1820–1991

American tariff rates have fluctuated historically. But beginning with the Reciprocal Trade Agreements Act of 1934, the trend has been downward. (U.S. Department of Commerce data.)

—so-called *intellectual property rights*—on an international basis.

Reaching agreement on the ambitious Uruguay Round proposals has been difficult. In 1990 the negotiations temporarily collapsed, the main dispute being over European opposition to phasing out export subsidies on agricultural goods and domestic farm subsidies. **Export subsidies** are government payments which reduce the price of a good to buyers abroad; domestic farm subsidies are direct payments to farmers which boost domestic food output. Both types of subsidies artificially reduce export prices and provide unfair advantages to exporting nations. In 1991 the Uruguay Round negotiations were reconvened to try to resolve the remaining trade disagreements.

Economic Integration

Another crucial development in trade liberalization has taken the form of **economic integration**—the joining of the markets of two or more nations into a free-trade zone. Three illustrations of economic integration are the European Economic Community (EC), the U.S.–Canadian Free-Trade Agreement, and the proposed North American free-trade zone.

The Common Market   The most dramatic example of economic integration is the **European Economic Community** (EC), or the **Common Market,** as it is popularly known. Begun in 1958, the EC now comprises twelve western European nations (France, Germany, Italy, Belgium, the Netherlands, Luxemborg, Denmark, Ireland, United Kingdom, Greece, Spain, and Portugal).

Goals   The Common Market called for (1) gradual abolition of tariffs and import quotas on all products traded among the twelve participating nations; (2) establishment of a common system of tariffs applicable to all goods received from nations outside the Common Market; (3) free movement of capital and labor within the Market; and (4) creation of common policies with respect to other economic matters of joint concern, such as agriculture, transportation, and restrictive business practices. By 1992 most of these goals had been achieved.

Results   Motives for creating the Common Market were both political and economic. The primary economic motive was to gain the advantages of freer trade for members. While it is difficult to determine the extent to which EC prosperity and growth has been due to economic integration, it is clear that integration creates the mass markets essential to Common Market industries if economies of large-scale production are to be realized. More efficient production for a large-scale market permits European industries to achieve the lower costs which small, localized markets have historically denied them.

Effects on nonmember nations, such as the United States, are less certain. On the one hand, a peaceful and increasingly prosperous Common Market makes member nations better potential customers for American exports. On the other hand, American firms encounter tariffs which make it difficult to compete in EC markets. For example, *before* the establishment of the Common Market, American, German, and French automobile manufacturers all faced the same tariff in selling their products to, say, Belgium. However, with the establishment of internal free trade among EC members, Belgian tariffs on German Volkswagens and French Renaults fell to zero, but an external tariff still applies to American Chevrolets and Fords. This clearly puts American firms and those of other nonmember nations at a serious competitive disadvantage.

The elimination of this disadvantage has been one of the United States' motivations for promoting freer trade through GATT. And, in fact, the so-called "Kennedy Round" of negotiations completed in 1967 and the "Tokyo Round" which ended in 1979 were quite successful in reducing tariffs.

U.S.–Canadian Free-Trade Agreement A second example of economic integration is the **U.S.–Canadian Free-Trade Agreement** enacted in 1989. Although three-fourths of the trade between the United States and Canada was already duty-free in 1988, the U.S.–Canadian accord is highly significant: It will create the largest free-trade area in the world. Under terms of the agreement, all trade restrictions such as tariffs, quotas, and nontariff barriers will be eliminated within a ten-year period. Canadian producers will gain increased access to a market ten times the size of Canada, while U.S. consumers will gain the advantage of lower-priced Canadian goods. In return, Canada will cut its tariffs by more than the United States because Canadian tariffs are higher than those in the United States. These reduced Canadian tariffs will help American producers and Canadian consumers.

We know from Table 5-3 that Canada is the United States' most significant trade partner quantitatively. Similarly, the United States is the main buyer of Canadian exports. Thus, the potential gain to each country

from the U.S.–Canadian accord is large. It has been estimated that the free-trade agreement will generate $1 billion to $3 billion of annual gains for each nation when it is fully implemented.

The U.S.–Canadian accord has global significance. In particular, it is expected to prod multilateral tariff reductions through GATT negotiations, since nations which are not party to the free-trade agreement do not wish to be disadvantaged in a relative sense in selling their goods in the United States and Canada.

Proposed North American Free-Trade Zone The U.S.–Canadian Free-Trade Agreement has stimulated the United States, Canada, and Mexico to begin discussion of a North American free-trade zone constituting the three nations. This zone would have a combined output similar to the European Economic Community.

Free trade with Mexico is more controversial in the United States than is free trade with Canada. Critics fear a loss of American jobs as firms move to Mexico to take advantage of lower wages and less stringent regulations on pollution and workplace safety. Critics also are concerned that Japan and South Korea will build plants in Mexico to ship goods tariff-free to the United States, further hurting U.S. firms and workers.

Proponents of free trade with Mexico cite the standard free-trade argument: Specialization according to comparative advantage will enable the United States to obtain more total output from its scarce resources. Proponents also note this zone would encourage worldwide investment in Mexico, which would enhance Mexican productivity and national income. Some of this increased income will be used to buy United States' exports. Also, a higher standard of living in Mexico would help stem the flow of illegal immigrants to the United States. Finally, advocates point out that any loss of specific American jobs will occur in any event to other low-wage countries such as South Korea, Taiwan, and Hong Kong. The free-trade zone will enable and encourage American firms to be more efficient, enhancing their competitiveness with firms in Japan and the Common Market countries.

Both critics and defenders of the North American free-trade zone agree on one point: It would constitute a powerful trade bloc to counter the European Common Market. Access to the vast North American market is as important to Common Market nations as is access to the European market by the United States, Canada, and Mexico. Observers believe negotiations between the North American trade bloc and the Common Market would surely follow, eventually resulting in a free-trade agreement between the two blocs. Japan, not wishing to be left out of the world's wealthiest trade markets, would be forced to reduce its tariff and non-tariff trade barriers, as well.

QUICK REVIEW 20-3

✦ *The various "rounds" of the General Agreement on Tariffs and Trade (GATT) have established multinational reductions in tariffs and import quotas among the 100 signatory nations.*

✦ *The European Economic Community (EC) and the U.S.–Canadian Free-Trade Agreement of 1989 have reduced trade barriers by establishing large free-trade zones.*

✦ *Proponents of the proposed North American free-trade zone (United States, Canada, and Mexico) contend it will enable all three nations to increase their standards of living; critics suggest that it will result in large losses of American jobs as firms move to Mexico to take advantage of less costly Mexican labor.*

Protectionism Reborn

Despite marked progress in reducing and eliminating tariffs, much remains to be done. The previously mentioned "Uruguay Round" agenda is a case in point. In the past, GATT negotiations have focused on manufactured goods, with other aspects of international trade and finance receiving little attention. These neglected areas include agriculture, services (for example, transportation, insurance, and banking), international investment, and patents and copyrights. There is also the problem of integrating the many nonmember less developed countries into the GATT framework.

More ominously, there has recently occurred a vigorous resurgence of protectionist pressures. Nontariff barriers continue to be a serious problem; import quotas and voluntary export restrictions have been on the rise.

Causes A number of factors explain the new pressures for protection.

1 Backlash They are in part a backlash to past reductions in trade barriers. Industries and workers whose profits and jobs have been adversely affected by freer trade have sought restoration of protection.

2 Internationalized Economy A closely related point is that the American economy is much more "internationalized" than it was a decade or so ago (Table 20-2); there are simply more firms and workers potentially adversely affected by increased foreign competition.

3 Increased Competition Other nations have in fact become increasingly competitive with American producers. In the late 1970s and 1980s rates of labor productivity growth in Japan and much of western Europe exceeded those of the United States. The result was lower unit labor costs and lower relative prices for imported goods. Competition from a number of the so-called "newly industrialized countries" such as Korea, Taiwan, Hong Kong, and Singapore is also asserting itself.

4 Trade Deficits In the past several years American imports have greatly exceeded American exports. Rising imports have a negative short-run impact on production and employment in those domestic industries which directly compete with imported products. The industries and workers hurt seek government help in the form of trade barriers. Our persistent trade deficit has provided a convenient rationale for the enactment of protectionist measures to help injured industries. Furthermore, the trade deficit has rallied public support for proposals to retaliate against trading partners which restrict the sale of our products in their countries.

Examples While the United States is formally committed to work for reduction of trade barriers through GATT, we have in fact invoked a number of trade-restricting measures during the last decade.

In 1981 a "voluntary" agreement was reached with Japan to limit the number of Japanese automobiles imported to the United States. This agreement expired in 1985 but continues informally today. In 1982 import quotas were imposed on sugar, causing potentially severe problems for Central American and Caribbean nations which are heavily dependent upon sugar exports to the United States. Also in 1982, the United States negotiated a "voluntary" agreement with the Common Market nations which imposed a quota on their steel exports to the United States. Finally, the industrially advanced nations have revised the international textile agreement to tighten restrictions on textile imports from the less developed countries.

Protectionist sentiment is also evidenced in recent trade proposals and laws. The Comprehensive Trade Act of 1988 contains provisions which ease procedures for initiating unfair-trade investigations of countries with consistent patterns of unfair-trade practices (tariffs, quotas, nontariff barriers, dumping).

LAST WORD

PETITION OF THE CANDLEMAKERS, 1845

The French economist Frédéric Bastiat (1801–1850) devastated the proponents of protectionism by satirically extending their reasoning to its logical and absurd conclusions.

Petition of the Manufacturers of Candles, Waxlights, Lamps, Candlesticks, Street Lamps, Snuffers, Extinguishers, and of the Producers of Oil Tallow, Rosin, Alcohol, and, Generally, of Everything Connected with Lighting.

TO MESSIEURS THE MEMBERS
OF THE CHAMBER
OF DEPUTIES.

Gentlemen—You are on the right road. You reject abstract theories, and have little consideration for cheapness and plenty. Your chief care is the interest of the producer. You desire to emancipate him from external competition, and reserve the *national market* for *national industry.*

We are about to offer you an admirable opportunity of applying your—what shall we call it? your theory? No; nothing is more deceptive than theory; your doctrine? your system? your principle? but you dislike doctrines, you abhor systems, and as for principles, you deny that there are any in social economy: we shall say, then, your practice, your practice without theory and without principle.

We are suffering from the intolerable competition

of a foreign rival, placed, it would seem, in a condition so far superior to ours for the production of light, that he absolutely *inundates* our *national market* with it at a price fabulously reduced. The moment he shows himself, our trade leaves us—all consumers apply to him; and a branch of native industry, having countless ramifications, is all at once rendered completely stagnant. This rival . . . is no other than the Sun.

In 1990 both houses of Congress passed protective legislation for the textile industry. The President vetoed this legislation, which would have limited the growth of textile imports to 1 percent a year. Ironically, the U.S. textile industry imports one-half of its machinery.

We should also note that, although overall American tariffs are low, the United States does have very high tariffs on some goods and imposes quantitative restrictions (quotas) on a small but important list of products. Dairy and meat products, tobacco, fruit juices, motorcycles, and cookware are all subject to significant restrictions. In addition, the footwear, machine tool, copper, shipbuilding, wine, costume jewelry, and shrimp and tuna industries, among others, have all sought additional protection during the past decade.

Costs   How costly is existing U.S. trade protection to American consumers? The consumer cost of trade restrictions can be calculated by determining the effect they have on prices of protected goods. Specifically, protection will raise the price of a product in three ways.

1   The price of the imported product goes up (Figure 20-3).

What we pray for is, that it may please you to pass a law ordering the shutting up of all windows, sky-lights, dormerwindows, outside and inside shutters, curtains, blinds, bull's-eyes; in a word, of all openings, holes, chinks, clefts, and fissures, by or through which the light of the sun has been in use to enter houses, to the prejudice of the meritorious manufactures with which we flatter ourselves we have accommodated our country,—a country which, in gratitude, ought not to abandon us now to a strife so unequal.

If you shut up as much as possible all access to natural light, and create a demand for artificial light, which of our French manufactures will not be encouraged by it?

If more tallow is consumed, then there must be more oxen and sheep; and, consequently, we shall behold the multiplication of artificial meadows, meat, wool, hides, and, above all, manure, which is the basis and foundation of all agricultural wealth.

The same remark applies to navigation. Thousands of vessels will proceed to the whale fishery; and, in a short time, we shall possess a navy capable of maintaining the honor of France, and gratifying the patriotic aspirations of your petitioners, the undersigned candlemakers and others.

Only have the goodness to reflect, Gentlemen, and you will be convinced that there is, perhaps, no Frenchman, from the wealthy coalmaster to the humblest vender of lucifer matches, whose lot will not be ameliorated by the success of this our petition.

Source: **Frédéric Bastiat,** *Economic Sophisms* **(Edinburgh: Oliver and Boyd, Tweeddale Court, 1873), pp. 49–53, abridged.**

2 The higher price of imports will cause some consumers to shift their purchases to higher-priced domestically produced goods.

3 The prices of domestically produced goods may rise because import competition has declined.

Several research studies indicate the costs to consumers of protected products is strikingly high. One study examined thirty-one classes of protected products and found that total annual consumer losses from protection on these goods was about $82.6 billion.[7]

Annual consumer losses from trade restrictions were particularly large for clothing ($27 billion), petroleum products ($6.9 billion), carbon steel ($6.8 billion), automobiles ($5.8 billion), and dairy products ($5.5 billion). These large costs indicate that trade barriers are an expensive means of saving jobs. Specifically, the estimated cost of trade restrictions per job saved is $750,000 in the carbon steel industry; $550,000 in the bolt, nuts, and large screws industry; $220,000 in the dairy industry; $240,000 in the orange juice industry; and $200,000 in the glassware industry. Because wages per job in these industries are only a fraction of these amounts, protectionism can hardly be called a bargain.

Other studies show that import restrictions affect low-income families proportionately more than high-income families.[8] Given that tariffs and quotas are much like sales taxes, it is no surprise that these trade restrictions are highly regressive. For example, the cost of protection was found to be seven times as large for the lowest-income group (incomes under $10,000 per year) as for the highest-income group (incomes over $60,000 per year).

But might not the gains to American producers together with the tariff revenues received by the U.S. government outweigh the high consumer costs of trade protection? The answer is a definite "No." Research studies indicate that gains from trade restrictions are substantially less than costs imposed on consumers.[9] Furthermore, net losses from trade barriers are greater than the losses estimated by the statistical studies. Tariffs and quotas produce myriad costly, difficult-to-quantify secondary effects. For example, import restraints on foreign steel drive up the price of steel to all American buyers of steel—such as American automakers. Therefore American automakers have higher costs and are less competitive in world markets.

Also, industries employ large amounts of economic resources for the purpose of influencing Congress to pass and retain protectionist laws. To the extent that these rent-seeking efforts divert resources away from more socially desirable purposes, society bears an added cost of trade restrictions.

To repeat: *The gains which trade barriers create for protected industries come at the expense of much greater losses for the economy as a whole.*

---

[7]Cletus C. Coughlin et al., "Protectionist Trade Policies: A Survey of Theory, Evidence and Rationale," *Review* (Federal Reserve Bank of St. Louis), January/February 1988), pp. 17–18.

[8]"The Consumer Cost of U.S. Trade Restraints," *Quarterly Review* (Federal Reserve Bank of New York), Summer 1985, pp. 1–12.

[9]Coughlin et al., op. cit., p. 19.

CHAPTER SUMMARY

1 International trade is important, quantitatively and otherwise, to most nations. World trade is vital to the United States in several respects. **a** The absolute volumes of American imports and exports exceed those of any other single nation. **b** The United States is completely dependent on trade for certain commodities and materials which cannot be obtained domestically. **c** Changes in the volume of net exports can have magnified effects on domestic levels of output and income.

2 International and domestic trade differ in that **a** resources are less mobile internationally than domestically: **b** each nation uses a different currency; and **c** international trade is subject to more political controls.

3 World trade is based on two considerations: the uneven distribution of economic resources among nations, and the fact that efficient production of various goods requires particular techniques or combinations of resources.

4 Mutually advantageous specialization and trade are possible between any two nations so long as the domestic cost ratios for any two products differ. By specializing according to comparative advantage, nations can realize larger real incomes with fixed amounts of resources. The terms of trade determine how this increase in world output is shared by the trading nations. Increasing costs impose limits on gains from specialization and trade.

5 Trade barriers take the form of protective tariffs, quotas, nontariff barriers, and "voluntary" export restrictions. Supply and demand analysis reveals that protective tariffs and quotas increase the prices and reduce the quantities demanded of affected goods. Foreign exporters find their sales diminish. Domestic producers, however, enjoy higher prices and enlarged sales. Tariffs and quotas promote a less efficient allocation of domestic and world resources.

6 When applicable, the strongest arguments for protection are the infant-industry and military self-sufficiency arguments. Most of the other arguments for protection are half-truths, emotional appeals, or fallacies which typically emphasize the immediate effects of trade barriers while ignoring long-run consequences. Numerous historical examples suggest that free trade promotes economic growth and protectionism does not.

7 The Reciprocal Trade Agreements Act of 1934 was the beginning of a trend toward lower American tariffs. In 1947 the General Agreement on Tariffs and Trade (GATT) was formed **a** to encourage nondiscriminatory treatment for all trading nations, **b** to achieve tariff reduction, and **c** to eliminate import quotas.

8 Economic integration is an important means of liberalizing trade. The outstanding illustration is the European Common Market in which internal trade barriers are abolished, a common system of tariffs is applied to nonmembers, and free internal movement of labor and capital occurs. The 1989 U.S.–Canadian Free-Trade Agreement is another example of economic integration, as is the proposed United States–Canadian–Mexican free-trade zone.

9 In recent years there has been a resurgence of protectionist pressures, but empirical evidence indicates that costs of protectionist policies outweigh benefits.

TERMS AND CONCEPTS

labor- (land-, capital-) intensive commodity	**gains from trade**	**strategic trade policy**	**General Agreement on Tariffs and Trade (GATT)**
cost ratio	**revenue and protective tariffs**	**dumping**	
principle of comparative advantage	**import quotas**	**Reciprocal Trade Agreements Act of 1934**	**European Economic Community (Common Market)**
	nontariff barriers		
terms of trade	**voluntary export restrictions**	**most-favored-nation clauses**	**U.S.–Canadian Free-Trade Agreement**
trading possibilities line	**Smoot-Hawley Tariff Act of 1930**	**export subsidies**	
		economic integration	

QUESTIONS AND STUDY SUGGESTIONS

1 In what ways are domestic and foreign trade similar? In what ways do they differ?

2 Assume that by using all its resources to produce X, nation A can produce 80 units of X; by devoting all its resources to Y, it can produce 40 Y. Comparable figures for nation B are 60 X and 60 Y. Assuming constant costs, in which product should each nation specialize? Why? Indicate the limits of the terms of trade.

3 "The United States can produce product X more efficiently than can Great Britain. Yet we import X from Great Britain." Explain.

4 State the economist's case for free trade. Given this

case, how do you explain the existence of artificial barriers to international trade?

5 Draw a domestic supply and demand diagram for a product in which the United States does not have a comparative advantage. Indicate the impact of foreign imports on domestic price and quantity. Now show a protective tariff which eliminates approximately one-half the assumed imports. Indicate the price-quantity effects of this tariff to **a** domestic consumers, **b** domestic producers, and **c** foreign exporters. How would the effects of a quota which gave rise to the same amount of imports differ?

6 "The most valid arguments for tariff protection are also the most easily abused." What are these arguments? Why are they susceptible to abuse? Carefully evaluate the use of artificial trade barriers, such as tariffs and import quotas, as a means of achieving and maintaining full employment.

7 The following are production possibilities tables for Japan and Hawaii. Assume that prior to specialization and trade, the optimal product-mix for Japan is alternative B and for Hawaii alternative D.

Product	Japan's production alternatives					
	A	B	C	D	E	F
Radios (in thousands)	30	24	18	12	6	0
Pineapples (in tons)	0	6	12	18	24	30

Product	Hawaii's production alternatives					
	A	B	C	D	E	F
Radios (in thousands)	10	8	6	4	2	0
Pineapples (in tons)	0	4	8	12	16	20

a Are comparative-cost conditions such that the two areas should specialize? If so, what product should each produce?

b What is the total gain in radio and pineapple output which results from this specialization?

c What are the limits of the terms of trade? Suppose actual terms of trade are 1 unit of radios for 1½ units of pineapples and that 4 units of radios are exchanged for 6 units of pineapples. What are the gains from specialization and trade for each area?

d Can you conclude from this illustration that specialization according to comparative advantage results in more efficient use of world resources? Explain.

8 Carefully evaluate the following statements:

a "Protective tariffs limit both the imports and the exports of the nation levying tariffs."

b "The extensive application of protective tariffs destroys the ability of the international market system to allocate resources efficiently."

c "Apparent unemployment can often be reduced through tariff protection, but by the same token disguised unemployment typically increases."

d "Foreign firms which 'dump' their products onto the American market are in effect presenting the American people with gifts."

e "Given the rapidity with which technological advance is dispersed around the world, free trade will inevitably yield structural maladjustments, unemployment, and balance of payments problems for industrially advanced nations."

f "Free trade can improve the composition and efficiency of domestic output. Only the Volkswagen forced Detroit to make a compact car, and only foreign success with the oxygen process forced American steel firms to modernize."

g "In the long run foreign trade is neutral with respect to total employment."

9 In the 1981–1985 period the Japanese agreed to a voluntary export restriction which reduced American imports of Japanese automobiles by about 10 percent. What would you expect the short-run effects to have been on the American and Japanese automobile industries? If this restriction were permanent, what would be its long-run effects on **a** the allocation of resources, **b** the volume of employment, **c** the price level, and **d** the standard of living in the two nations?

10 Use "economies of scale" analysis to explain why the Common Market has enabled many European industries to compete more effectively in international markets. Explain: "Economic integration leads a double life: It can promote free trade among members, but pose serious trade obstacles for nonmembers."

11 What are the benefits and the costs of protectionist policies? Compare the two.

12 Explain the following findings from a study on the effects of the 1984 imports restraints which limited the level of steel imports to the United States: increased employment in the steel industry, 14,000; increased employment in the industries producing inputs for steel, 2,800; job losses by American steel-using firms, 52,400.[10]

---

[10]Arthur T. Denzau, "How Import Restraints Reduce Employment" (Washington University Center for the Study of American Business, Formal Publication #80, June 1987), as reported in Coughlin, op. cit., p. 6.

CHAPTER 21

Exchange Rates, the Balance of Payments, and Trade Deficits

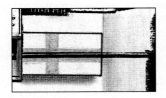

If you take an American dollar to the bank and ask to exchange it for United States currency, you will get a puzzled look. If you persist, you may get in exchange another dollar. One American dollar can buy exactly one American dollar. But, as of January 24, 1992, one United States dollar could buy 5340 Turkish lira, 1.34 Australian dollars, .56 British pounds, 1.16 Canadian dollars, 5.48 French francs, 1.61 German marks, 123.93 Japanese yen, or 5.84 Swedish krona. What explains this seemingly haphazard array of exchange rates?

In Chapter 20 we examined comparative advantage as the underlying economic basis of world trade and discussed the effects of barriers to free trade. In this chapter we first introduce the monetary or financial aspects of international trade. How are currencies of different nations exchanged when import and export transactions occur? Second, we analyze and interpret a nation's international balance of payments. What is meant by a "favorable" or "unfavorable" balance of trade? Third, the kinds of exchange rate systems which trading nations have used are explained and evaluated. In this discussion we examine the polar extremes of freely flexible and fixed exchange rates and then survey actual systems which have existed historically. Finally, we explore the balance of trade deficits the United States has encountered over the past decade.

FINANCING INTERNATIONAL TRADE

A basic feature distinguishing international from domestic payments is that two different national currencies are exchanged. When American firms export goods to British firms, the American exporter wants to be paid in dollars. But British importers have pounds sterling. The problem, then, is to exchange pounds for dollars to permit the American export transaction to occur.

This problem is resolved in *foreign exchange markets* where dollars can be used to purchase British pounds, Japanese yen, German marks, Italian lira, and so forth, and vice versa. Sponsored by major banks in New York, London, Zurich, Tokyo, and elsewhere, foreign exchange markets facilitate American exports and imports.

American Export Transaction

Suppose an American exporter agrees to sell $30,000 worth of computers to a British firm. Assume that the *rate of exchange*—the rate or price at which pounds can be exchanged for, or converted into, dollars, and vice versa—is $2 for £1. This means that the British importer must pay £15,000 to the American exporter. Let's summarize what occurs in terms of simple bank balance sheets (Figure 21-1).

a To pay for the American computers, the British buyer draws a check on its demand deposit in a London bank for £15,000. This is shown by the −£15,000 demand deposit entry in the righthand side of the balance sheet of the London bank.

b The British firm then sends this £15,000 check to the American exporter. But the American exporting firm must pay its employees and materials suppliers, as well as its taxes, in dollars, not pounds. So the exporter sells the £15,000 check or draft on the London bank to a large American bank, probably in New York City, which is a dealer in foreign exchange. The American firm is given a $30,000 demand deposit in the New York bank in exchange for the £15,000 check. Note the new demand deposit entry of +$30,000 in the New York bank.

c What does the New York bank do with the £15,000? It deposits it in a correspondent London bank for future sale. Thus, +£15,000 of demand deposits appear in the liabilities column of the balance sheet of the London bank. This +£15,000 ($30,000) is an asset as viewed by the New York bank. To simplify, we assume that the correspondent bank in London is the same bank from which the British importer obtained the £15,000 draft.

Note these salient points.

1 *American exports create a foreign demand for dollars, and the satisfaction of this demand generates a supply of foreign monies—pounds, in this case—held by American banks and available to American buyers.*

2 The financing of an American export (British import) reduces the supply of money (demand deposits) in Britain and increases the supply of money in the United States by the amount of the purchase.

American Import Transaction

But why would the New York bank be willing to give up dollars for pounds sterling? As just indicated, the New York bank is a dealer in foreign exchange; it is in the business of buying—for a fee—and, conversely, in selling—also for a fee—pounds for dollars.

Having just explained that the New York bank would buy pounds with dollars in connection with an American export transaction, we will now examine how it would sell pounds for dollars in financing an American import (British export) transaction. Suppose that an American retail concern wants to import £15,000 worth of woolens from a British mill. Again, simple commercial bank balance sheets summarize our discussion (Figure 21-2).

a Because the British exporting firm must pay its obligations in pounds rather than dollars, the American importer must exchange dollars for pounds. It does this by going to the New York bank and purchasing £15,000 for $30,000—perhaps the American importer

FIGURE 21-1   Financing a U.S. export transaction

American export transactions create a foreign demand for dollars. The satisfaction of this demand increases the supplies of foreign monies held by American banks.

LONDON BANK			
Assets			**Liabilities and net worth**
			Demand deposit of British importer −£15,000(a)
			Deposit of New York bank +£15,000(c)

NEW YORK BANK			
Assets			**Liabilities and net worth**
Deposit in London bank +£15,000(c) ($30,000)			Demand deposit of American exporter +$30,000(b)

LONDON BANK		NEW YORK BANK	
Assets	Liabilities and net worth	Assets	Liabilities and net worth
	Demand deposit of British exporter +£15,000(b)	Deposit in London bank −£15,000(a) ($30,000)	Demand deposit of American importer −$30,000(a)
	Deposit of New York bank −£15,000(a)		

FIGURE 21-2 Financing a U.S. import transaction
American import transactions create an American demand for foreign monies. The satisfaction of that demand reduces the supplies of foreign monies held by American banks.

purchases the same £15,000 which the New York bank acquired in the previous American export transaction. In Figure 21-2, this purchase reduces the American importer's demand deposit in the New York bank by $30,000 and the New York bank gives up its £15,000 deposit in the London bank.

b The American importer sends its newly purchased check for £15,000 to the British firm, which deposits it in the London bank. Note the +£15,000 deposit in the liabilities and net worth column of Figure 21-2.

We find that:

1 *American imports create a domestic demand for foreign monies (pounds sterling, in this case) and that fulfillment of this demand reduces the supplies of foreign monies held by American banks.*

2 An American import transaction increases the money supply in Britain and reduces the money supply in the United States.

By combining these two transactions, a further point comes into focus. American exports (computers) make available, or "earn," a supply of foreign monies for American banks, and American imports (British woolens) create a demand for these monies. In a broad sense, *any nation's exports finance or "pay for" its imports.* Exports provide the foreign currencies needed to pay for imports. From Britain's point of view, its exports of woolens earn a supply of dollars, which are then used to meet the demand for dollars associated with Britain's imports of computers.

Postscript: Although our examples are confined to the exporting and importing of goods, we will find that demands for and supplies of pounds also arise from transactions involving services and the payment of in-

terest and dividends on foreign investments. Thus Americans demand pounds not only to finance imports, but also to purchase insurance and transportation services from the British, to vacation in London, to pay dividends and interest on British investments in the United States, and to make new financial and real investments in Britain.

THE INTERNATIONAL BALANCE OF PAYMENTS

We now explore the wide variety of international transactions which create a demand for and generate a supply of a given currency. This spectrum of international trade and financial transactions is reflected in the United States' international **balance of payments.** A nation's balance of payments statement records *all* transactions which take place between its residents (including individuals, businesses, and governmental units) and the residents of all foreign nations. These transactions include merchandise exports and imports, tourist expenditures, purchases and sales of shipping and insurance services, interest and dividends received or paid abroad, purchases and sales of financial or real assets abroad, and so forth. The United States' balance of payments shows the balance between all the payments the United States receives from foreign countries and all the payments which we make to them. A simplified balance of payments for the United States in 1990 is shown in Table 21-1. Let's analyze this accounting statement to see what it reveals about our international trade and finance.

TABLE 21-1   The United States' balance of payments, 1990 *(in billions)*

Current account			
(1) U.S. merchandise exports		$+390	
(2) U.S. merchandise imports		−498	
(3) Balance of trade			$−108
(4) U.S. exports of services		+133	
(5) U.S. imports of services		−107	
(6) Balance on goods and services			−82
(7) Net investment income		+12	
(8) Net transfers		−22	
(9) Balance on current account			−92
Capital account			
(10) Capital inflows to the U.S.		+117*	
(11) Capital outflows from the U.S.		−59	
(12) Balance on capital account			+58
(13) Current and capital account balance			−34
(14) Official reserves			+34
			$ 0

*Includes a $64 billion statistical discrepancy which is believed to be comprised primarily of unaccounted capital inflows.

Source: Survey of Current Business, December 1991.

Current Account

The top portion of Table 21-1 summarizes the United States' trade in currently produced goods and services and is called the **current account.** Items 1 and 2 show American exports and imports of merchandise (goods) respectively in 1990. We have designated American exports with a *plus* sign and our imports with a *minus* sign because American merchandise exports (and other export-type transactions) are **credits** in that they create or earn supplies of foreign exchange. As we saw in our discussion of how international trade is financed, any export-type transaction obligating foreigners to make "inpayments" to the United States generates supplies of foreign monies in American banks.

Conversely, American imports (and other import-type transactions) are **debits;** they use up foreign exchange. Again, our earlier discussion of trade financing indicated that American imports obligate Americans to make "outpayments" to the rest of the world which draw down available supplies of foreign currencies held by American banks.

Trade balance   Items 1 and 2 in Table 21-1 tell us that in 1990 our merchandise exports of $390 billion did *not* earn enough foreign monies to finance our merchandise imports of $498 billion. Specifically, the merchan-

dise balance of trade or, more simply, the **trade balance** refers to the difference between a country's merchandise exports and merchandise imports. If exports exceed imports, then a *trade surplus* or "favorable balance of trade" is being realized. If imports exceed exports, then a *trade deficit* or "unfavorable balance of trade" is occurring. We note in item 3 that in 1990 the United States incurred a trade deficit of $108 billion.

Balance on Goods and Services   Item 4 reveals that the United States not only exports autos and computers, but also sells transportation services, insurance, and tourist and brokerage services to residents of foreign countries. These service sales or "exports" totaled $133 billion in 1990. Item 5 indicates that Americans buy or "import" similar services from foreigners. These service imports were $107 billion in 1990.

The **balance on goods and services,** shown in Table 21-1 as item 6, is the difference between our exports of goods and services (items 1 and 4) and our imports of goods and services (items 2 and 5). In 1990 our exports of goods and services fell short of our imports of goods and services by $82 billion.

Balance on Current Account   Item 7 reflects that historically the United States has been a net international lender. Over time we have invested more abroad than foreigners have invested in the United States. Thus net investment income represents the excess of interest and dividend payments which foreigners have paid us for the services of our exported capital over what we paid in 1990 in interest and dividends for their capital invested in the United States. Table 21-1 shows that, on balance, our net investment income earned us $12 billion worth of foreign currencies for "exporting" the services of American money capital invested abroad.

Item 8 reflects net transfers, both public and private, from the United States to the rest of the world. Included here is American foreign aid, pensions paid to Americans living abroad, and remittances of immigrants to relatives abroad. These $22 billion of transfers are "outpayments" and exhaust available supplies of foreign exchange. As it has been facetiously put, net transfers entail the importing of "goodwill" or "thank-you notes."

By taking all transactions in the current account into consideration we obtain the **balance on current account** shown by item 9 in Table 21-1. In 1990 the United States realized a current account deficit of $92 billion. This means that our current account import transactions (items 2, 5, and 8) created a demand for a larger dollar amount of foreign currencies than our export transactions (items 1, 4, and 7) supplied.

Capital Account

The **capital account** reflects capital flows in the purchase or sale of real and financial assets which occurred in 1990. For example, Honda or Nissan might acquire an automobile assembly plant in the United States. Or, alternatively, the investments may be of a financial nature, for example, an Arabian oil sheik might purchase GM stock or Treasury bonds. In either event such transactions generate supplies of foreign currencies for the United States. They are therefore credit or inpayment items, designated with a plus sign. The United States is exporting stocks and bonds and thereby earning foreign exchange. Item 10 in Table 21-1 shows that such transactions amounted to $117 billion in 1990.

Conversely, Americans invest abroad. General Electric might purchase a plant in Hong Kong or Singapore to assemble pocket radios or telephones. Or an American might buy stock in an Italian shoe factory. Or an American bank might finance construction of a meat processing plant in Argentina. These transactions have a common feature; they all use up or exhaust supplies

of foreign currencies. We therefore attach a minus sign to remind us that these are debit or outpayment transactions. The United States is importing stocks, bonds, and IOUs from abroad. Item 11 in Table 21-1 reveals that $59 billion of these transactions occurred in 1990. When items 10 and 11 are combined, the **balance on the capital account** was a *plus* $58 billion—the United States enjoyed a capital account surplus of $58 billion in 1990.

Interrelationships

The current and capital accounts are interrelated; they are essentially reflections of one another. The current account *deficit* means that American exports of goods and services were not sufficient to pay for our imports of goods and services.[1] How did we finance the difference? The answer is that the United States must either borrow from abroad or give up ownership of some of its assets to foreigners as reflected in the capital account.

A simple analogy is useful here. Suppose in a given year your expenditures exceed your earnings. How will you finance your "deficit"? You might sell some of your assets or borrow. You might sell some real assets (your car or stereo) or perhaps some financial assets (stocks or bonds) which you own. Or you might obtain a loan from your family or a bank.

Similarly, when a nation incurs a deficit in its current account, its expenditures for foreign goods and services (its imports) exceed the income received from the international sales of its own goods and services (its exports). It must somehow finance that current account deficit by selling assets and by borrowing, that is, by going into debt. And that is what is reflected in the capital account surplus. Our capital account surplus of $58 billion (item 12) indicates that in 1990 the United States "sold off" real assets (buildings, farmland) and received loans from the rest of the world in that amount to help finance our current account deficit of $92 billion.

Recap: A nation's current account deficit will be financed essentially by a net capital inflow in its capital account. Conversely, a nation's current account *surplus* would be accompanied by a net capital *outflow* in its capital account. The excess earnings from its current account surplus will be used to purchase real assets of, and make loans to, other nations.

---

[1]We ignore transfer payments (item 8) in making this statement.

Official Reserves

The central banks of nations hold quantities of foreign currencies called **official reserves** which are added to or drawn on to settle any *net* differences in current and capital account balances. In 1990 the surplus in our capital account was considerably less than the deficit in our current account so we had a $34 billion net deficit on the combined accounts (item 13). That is, the United States earned less foreign monies in all international trade and financial transactions than it used. This deficiency of earnings of foreign currencies was subtracted from the existing balances of foreign monies held by our central banks. The *plus* $34 billion of official reserves shown by item 14 in Table 21-1 represents this reduction of our stocks of foreign currencies. The plus sign indicates this is a credit or "export-type" transaction which represents a supply of foreign exchange.

Frequently the relationship between the current and capital account is just the opposite of that shown in Table 21-1. That is, the current account deficit is less than the capital account surplus. Hence, our central reserves shown by item 14 in Table 21-1 represents this reduction of our stocks of foreign currencies. The plus sign indicates this is a credit or "export-type" transaction which represents a supply of foreign exchange.

Frequently the relationship between the current and capital account is just the opposite of that shown in Table 21-1. That is, the current account deficit is less serves account—must sum to zero. Every unit of foreign exchange used (as reflected in our "minus" outpayment or debit transactions) in our international transactions must have a source (our "plus" inpayment or credit transactions).

Payments Deficits and Surpluses

Although the balance of payments must always sum to zero, economists and political officials frequently speak of **balance of payments deficits and surpluses.** In doing so they are referring to the "current and capital account balance" shown as item 13 in Table 21-1. If this is a negative item, a balance of payments deficit is being realized as was the case for the United States in 1990. In 1990 the United States earned less foreign monies from all its trade and financial transactions than it used. The United States did not "pay its way" in world trade and finance and therefore depleted its official reserves of foreign monies. If the current and capital account balance were positive, then the United States would be faced with a balance of payments surplus. The United States would have earned sufficient foreign exchange from its export-type transactions to pay for its import-type transactions. As we have just seen, it would add to its stocks of foreign monies—that is, increase its official reserve holdings.

A decrease in official reserves (shown by a positive official reserves item in Table 21-1) measures a nation's balance of payments deficit; an increase in official reserves (shown by a negative official reserves item) measures its balance of payments surplus.

Deficits and Surpluses: Bad or Good?

Having defined a variety of deficits and surpluses, we must now inquire as to their desirability. Are deficits bad, as the term implies? Is a surplus desirable, as that word suggests? The answer to both questions is "not necessarily." A large merchandise trade deficit such as the United States has been incurring in recent years is regarded by many as "unfavorable" or "adverse," as it suggests American producers are losing their competitiveness in world markets. Our industries seem to be having trouble selling their goods abroad and are simultaneously facing strong competition from imported goods. On the other hand, a trade deficit is *favorable* from the vantage point of American consumers who are currently receiving more goods as imports than they are forgoing as exports.

Similarly, the desirability of a balance of payments deficit or surplus depends on (1) the events causing them and (2) their persistence through time. For example, the large payments deficits imposed on the United States and other oil-importing nations by OPEC's dramatic runup of oil prices in 1973–1974 and 1979–1980 were very disruptive in that they forced the United States to invoke policies to curtail oil imports.

Also, any nation's official reserves are limited. Persistent or long-term payments deficits, which must be financed by drawing down those reserves, would ultimately deplete reserves. In this case that nation would have to undertake policies to correct its balance of payments. These policies might require painful macroeconomic adjustments, trade barriers and similar restrictions, or changing the international value of its currency.

KEY GRAPH

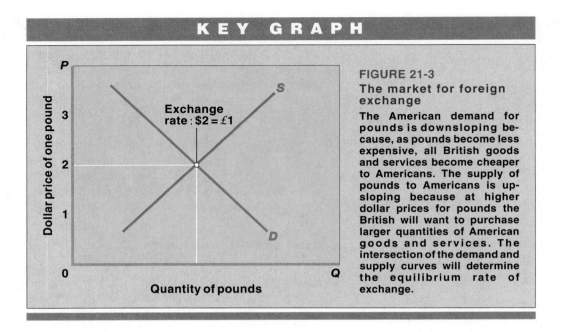

FIGURE 21-3
The market for foreign exchange

The American demand for pounds is downsloping because, as pounds become less expensive, all British goods and services become cheaper to Americans. The supply of pounds to Americans is upsloping because at higher dollar prices for pounds the British will want to purchase larger quantities of American goods and services. The intersection of the demand and supply curves will determine the equilibrium rate of exchange.

QUICK REVIEW 21-1

✦   *American* exports *create a demand for dollars and a supply of foreign currencies; American* imports *create a demand for foreign currencies and a supply of American dollars.*

✦   *The current account balance is a nation's exports of goods and services less its imports of goods and services plus its net investment income and net transfers.*

✦   *The capital account balance is a nation's capital inflows less its capital outflows.*

✦   *A balance of payments deficit occurs when the sum of the balances on current and capital accounts is negative; a balance of payments surplus arises when the sum of the balances on current and capital accounts is positive.*

EXCHANGE RATE SYSTEMS AND BALANCE OF PAYMENTS ADJUSTMENTS

Both the size and persistence of a nation's balance of payments deficits and surpluses and the kind of adjustments it must make to correct these imbalances depend on the system of exchange rates being used. There are two polar options: (1) a system of **flexible** or **floating exchange rates** where the rates at which national currencies exchange for one another are deter-

mined by demand and supply, and (2) a system of rigidly **fixed exchange rates** by which governmental intervention in foreign exchange markets or some other mechanism offsets the changes in exchange rates which fluctuations in demand and supply would otherwise cause.

Freely Floating Exchange Rates

Freely floating exchange rates are determined by the unimpeded forces of demand and supply. Let's examine the rate, or price, at which American dollars might be exchanged for, say, British pounds sterling. As indicated in Figure 21-3 (Key Graph), the demand for pounds will be downsloping; the supply of pounds, upsloping.

The downsloping *demand for pounds* shown by *D* indicates that, if pounds become less expensive to Americans, British goods will become cheaper to Americans. Americans will demand larger quantities of British goods and therefore larger amounts of pounds to buy those goods.

The *supply of pounds* is upsloping, as *S,* because, as the dollar price of pounds *rises* (that is, the pound price of dollars *falls*), the British will purchase more American goods. At higher and higher dollar prices for pounds, the British can get more American dollars and therefore more American goods per pound. Thus, American goods become cheaper to the British, inducing them to buy more of these goods. When the British buy American goods, they supply pounds to the foreign exchange market because they must exchange pounds for dollars to purchase our goods.

The intersection of the supply and demand for pounds will determine the dollar price of pounds. In this instance the equilibrium rate of exchange is $2 to £1.

Depreciation and Appreciation An exchange rate determined by free-market forces can and does change frequently. When the dollar price of pounds increases, for example, from $2 for £1 to $3 for £1, the value of the dollar has **depreciated** relative to the pound. Currency depreciation means that it takes more units of a country's currency (dollars) to buy a single unit of some foreign currency (pounds).

Conversely, when the dollar price of pounds decreases—from $2 for £1 to $1 for £1—the value of the dollar has **appreciated** relative to the pound. Currency appreciation means that it takes fewer units of a country's currency (dollars) to buy a single unit of some foreign currency (pounds).

In our American-British illustrations, when the dollar depreciates the pound necessarily appreciates and vice versa. When the exchange rate between dollars and pounds changes from $2 = £1 to $3 = £1, it now takes *more* dollars to buy £1 and the dollar has depreciated. But it now takes *fewer* pounds to buy a dollar. At the initial rate it took £$\frac{1}{2}$ to buy $1; at the new rate it only takes £$\frac{1}{3}$ to buy $1. The pound has appreciated relative to the dollar. *If the dollar depreciates vis-à-vis the pound, the pound appreciates vis-à-vis the dollar. Conversely, if the dollar appreciates vis-à-vis the pound, the pound depreciates vis-à-vis the dollar.* These relationships are summarized in Figure 21-4.

Determinants of Exchange Rates Why are the demand for and the supply of pounds located as they are in Figure 21-3? What forces will cause the demand and supply curves for pounds to change, thereby causing the dollar to appreciate or depreciate?

Changes in Tastes Any change in consumer tastes or preferences for the products of a foreign country will alter the demand for, or supply of, that nation's currency and change its exchange rate. If American technological advances in computers make them more attractive to British consumers and businesses, then they will supply more pounds in exchange markets in purchasing more American computers and the dollar

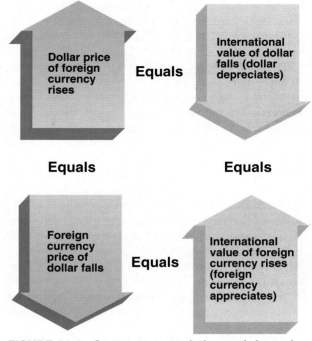

FIGURE 21-4 Currency appreciation and depreciation

An increase in the dollar price of foreign currency is equivalent to a decline in the international value of the dollar (dollar depreciates). An increase in the dollar price of foreign currency also implies a decline in the foreign currency price of dollars. That is, the international value of foreign currency rises relative to the dollar (foreign currency appreciates).

will appreciate. Conversely, if British tweeds become more fashionable in the United States, our demand for pounds will increase and the dollar will depreciate.

Relative Income Changes If the growth of a nation's national income is more rapid than other countries', its currency is likely to depreciate. A country's imports vary directly with its level of income. As incomes rise in the United States, American consumers buy more domestically produced goods *and* also more foreign goods. If the United States' economy is expanding rapidly and the British economy is stagnant, American imports of British goods—and therefore U.S. demand for pounds—will increase. The dollar price of pounds will rise, meaning the dollar has depreciated.

Relative Price Changes If the domestic price level rises rapidly in the United States and remains constant in Britain, American consumers will seek out relatively low-priced British goods, increasing the demand for pounds. Conversely, the British will purchase fewer American goods, reducing the supply of pounds. This combination of an increase in the demand for, and a reduction in the supply of, pounds will cause the dollar to depreciate.

In fact, differences in relative price levels among nations—which reflect changes in price levels over time—help explain persistent differences in exchange rates. In 1992 an American dollar could buy .56 British pounds, 124 Japanese yen, or 5340 Turkish lira. One reason for these differences is that the prices of British goods and services in pounds were far lower than the prices of Japanese goods and services in yen and the prices of Turkish goods and services in lira. For example, the same market basket of products costing $500 in the United States might cost 250 pounds in England, 67,500 yen in Japan, and 2,500,000 lira in Turkey. *Generally, the higher the prices of a nation's goods and services in terms of its own currency, the greater the amount of that currency which can be obtained with an American dollar.*

Taken to its extreme, this **purchasing power parity theory** holds that differences in exchange rates *equate* the purchasing power of various currencies. That is, the exchange rates among national currencies perfectly adjust in such a way as to equal the ratios of the nations' price levels. For example, if a market basket of goods costs $100 in the United States and £50 in Great Britain, the exchange rate should be $2 = £1. Thus, a dollar spent on goods sold in Britain, Japan, Turkey, and other nations supposedly will have equal purchasing power. In practice, however, exchange rates depart significantly from purchasing power parity, even over long periods. Nevertheless, relative price levels are clearly a major determinant of exchange rates.

Relative Real Interest Rates Suppose the United States restricts the growth of its money supply (tight money policy), as it did in the late 1970s and early 1980s, to control inflation. As a result, *real* interest rates—nominal interest rates adjusted for the rate of inflation—were high in the United States compared to most other nations. Consequently, British individuals and firms found the United States an attractive place to make financial investments. This increase in the demand for American financial assets meant an increase in the supply of British pounds and the dollar therefore appreciated in value.

Speculation Suppose it is widely anticipated that the American economy will *(a)* grow faster than the Brit-

ish economy, *(b)* experience more rapid inflation than the British economy, and *(c)* have lower future real interest rates than Britain. All these expectations would lead one to believe that in the future the dollar will depreciate and, conversely, the pound will appreciate. Holders of dollars will thus attempt to convert them into pounds, increasing the demand for pounds. This conversion causes the dollar to depreciate and the pound to appreciate. A self-fulfilling prophecy arises: The dollar depreciates and the pound appreciates because speculators act on the supposition that these changes in currency values will in fact happen.

Flexible Rates and the Balance of Payments
Proponents of flexible exchange rates argue that such rates have a compelling virtue: *They automatically adjust so as eventually to eliminate balance of payments deficits or surpluses.* We can explain this by looking at S and D in Figure 21-5 which restate the demand for, and supply of, pounds curves from Figure 21-3. The equilibrium exchange rate of $2 = £1 correctly suggests there is no balance of payments deficit or surplus. At the $2 = £1 exchange rate the quantity of pounds demanded by Americans to import British goods, buy

FIGURE 21-5 Adjustments under flexible exchange rates, fixed exchange rates, and the gold standard

Under flexible rates an American trade deficit at the $2-for-£1 rate would be corrected by an increase in the rate to $3 for £1. Under fixed rates the *ab* shortage of pounds would be met out of international monetary reserves. Under the gold standard the deficit would cause changes in domestic price and income levels which would shift the demand for pounds (*D'*) to the left and the supply (*S*) to the right, sustaining equilibrium at the $2-for-£1 rate.

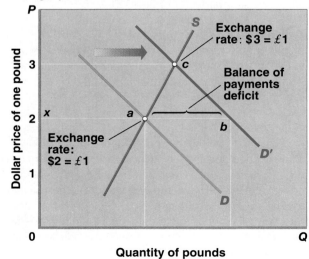

British transportation and insurance services, and pay interest and dividends on British investments in the United States equals the amount of pounds supplied by the British in buying American exports, purchasing services from Americans, and making interest and dividend payments on American investments in Britain. In brief, there would be no change in official reserves in Table 21-1.

Now suppose tastes change and Americans decide to buy more British automobiles. Or assume that the American price level has increased relative to Britain, or that interest rates have fallen in the United States compared to Britain. Any or all of these changes will cause the American demand for British pounds to increase from D to, say, D' in Figure 21-5.

We observe that *at the initial \$2 = £1 exchange rate* an American balance of payments deficit has been created in the amount ab. That is, at the $2 = £1$ rate there is a shortage of pounds in the amount ab to Americans. American export-type transactions will earn xa pounds, but Americans will want xb pounds to finance import-type transactions. Because this is a free competitive market, the shortage will change the exchange rate (the dollar price of pounds) from $2 = £1$ to, say, $3 = £1$; that is, the dollar has *depreciated*.

At this point it must be emphasized that *the exchange rate is a very special price which links all domestic (United States') prices with all foreign (British) prices.* Specifically, the dollar price of a foreign good is found by multiplying the foreign product price by the exchange rate in dollars per unit of the foreign currency. At an exchange rate of $2 = £1$, a British Triumph automobile priced at 9000 will cost an American \$18,000 (= 9000 × \$2).

A change in the exchange rate therefore alters the prices of all British goods to Americans and all American goods to potential British buyers. Specifically, the change in the exchange rate from $2 = £1$ to $3 = £1$ will alter the relative attractiveness of American imports and exports in such a way as to restore equilibrium in the balance of payments of the United States. From the American point of view, as the dollar price of pounds changes from \$2 to \$3, the Triumph priced at £9000, which formerly cost an American \$18,000, now costs \$27,000 (= 9000 × \$3). Other British goods will also cost more to Americans, and American imports of British goods and services will decline. Graphically, this is shown as a move from point b toward point c in Figure 21-5.

Conversely, from Britain's standpoint the exchange rate, that is, the pound price of dollars, has fallen (from £$\frac{1}{2}$ to £$\frac{1}{3}$ for \$1). The international value of

the pound has *appreciated*. The British previously got only \$2 for £1; now they get \$3 for £1. American goods are therefore cheaper to the British, and American exports to Great Britain will rise. In Figure 21-5 this is shown by the move from point a toward point c.

The two adjustments described—a decrease in American imports from Great Britain and an increase in American exports to Great Britain—are precisely those needed to correct the American balance of payments deficit. (You should reason through the operation of freely fluctuating exchange rates in correcting an initial American balance of payments *surplus* in its trade with Great Britain.)

In summary, the free fluctuation of exchange rates in response to shifts in the supply of, and demand for, foreign monies automatically corrects balance of payments deficits and surpluses.

Disadvantages   Even though freely fluctuating exchange rates automatically work eventually to eliminate payments imbalances, they may involve several significant problems:

1 Uncertainty and Diminished Trade   The risks and uncertainties associated with flexible exchange rates may discourage the flow of trade. Suppose an American automobile dealer contracts to purchase ten Triumph cars for £90,000. At the current exchange rate of, say \$2 for £1, the American importer expects to pay \$180,000 for these automobiles. But if in the three-month delivery period the rate of exchange shifts to \$3 for £1, the £90,000 payment contracted by the American importer will now be \$270,000.

This unheralded increase in the dollar price of pounds may easily turn the potential American importer's anticipated profits into substantial losses. Aware of the possibility of an adverse change in the exchange rate, the American importer may not be willing to assume the risks involved. The American firm therefore may confine its operations to domestic automobiles, with the result that international trade does not occur in this item.

The same rationale applies to investment. Assume that, when the exchange rate is \$3 to £1, an American firm invests \$30,000 (or £10,000) in a British enterprise. It estimates a return of 10 percent, that is, it anticipates earnings of \$3000 or £1000. Suppose these expectations prove correct in that the British firm earns £1000 the first year on the £10,000 investment. But suppose that during the year, the value of the dollar *appreciates* to $2 = £1$. The absolute return is now only \$2000 (rather than \$3000) and the rate of return falls from the anticipated 10 percent to only 6⅔ percent (= $2000/ $30,000). Investment is inherently risky. The added risk posed by adverse changes in exchange rates may persuade the potential American investor to avoid overseas ventures.[2]

2 Terms of Trade A nation's terms of trade will be worsened by a decline in the international value of its currency. For example, an increase in the dollar price of pounds will mean that the United States must export more goods and services to finance a given level of imports from Britain.

3 Instability Freely fluctuating exchange rates may also have destabilizing effects on the domestic economy as wide fluctuations stimulate and then depress those industries producing internationally traded goods. If the American economy is operating at full employment and the international value of its currency depreciates as in our illustration, the results will be inflationary for two reasons. Foreign demand for American goods will increase, that is, the net exports component of aggregate expenditures will increase and cause demand-pull inflation. Also, prices of all American imports will increase. Conversely, appreciation of the dollar would lower exports and increase imports, causing unemployment.

From the vantage point of policy, acceptance of floating exchange rates may complicate the use of domestic fiscal and monetary policies in seeking full employment and price stability. This is especially so for nations whose exports and imports are large relative to their GDPs (Table 20-1).

Fixed Exchange Rates

At the other extreme nations have often fixed or "pegged" their exchange rates to circumvent the disadvantages associated with floating rates. To analyze the implications and problems associated with fixed rates,

assume that the United States and Britain agree to maintain a $2 = £1 exchange rate.

The basic problem is that a governmental proclamation that a dollar will be worth so many pounds does *not* mandate stability of the demand for, and supply of, pounds. As demand and supply shift over time, government must intervene directly or indirectly in the foreign exchange market if the exchange rate is to be stabilized.

In Figure 21-5 suppose the American demand for pounds increases from D to D' and an American payments deficit of ab arises. This means that the American government is committed to an exchange rate ($2 = £1) which is below the equilibrium rate ($3 = £1). How can the United States prevent the shortage of pounds—reflecting an American balance of payments deficit—from driving the exchange rate up to the equilibrium level? The answer is to alter market demand or supply or both so that they continue to intersect at the $2 = £1 rate of exchange. There are several means for achieving this.

1 Use of Reserves The most desirable means of pegging an exchange rate is to manipulate the market through the use of official reserves. International monetary *reserves* are stocks of foreign monies owned by a particular government. How do reserves originate? Let's assume that in the past the opposite market condition prevailed in which there was a surplus, rather than a shortage, of pounds, and the United States government had acquired that surplus. That is, at some earlier time the United States government spent dollars to buy surplus pounds which were threatening to reduce the $2 = £1 exchange rate to, say, $1 = £1. By now selling part of its reserve of pounds, the United States government could shift the supply of pounds curve to the right so that it intersects D' at b in Figure 21-5, thereby maintaining the exchange rate at $2 = £1.

Historically nations have used gold as "international money" or, in other words, as reserves. Thus, in our example the United States government might sell some of the gold it owns to Britain for pounds. The pounds thus acquired could be used to augment the supply earned through American trade and financial transactions to shift the supply of pounds to the right to maintain the $2 = £1 exchange rate.

It is critical that the amount of reserves be enough to accomplish the required increase in the supply of pounds. This is *not* a problem if deficits and surpluses occur more or less randomly and are of approximately

---

[2]At some cost and inconvenience a *trader* can circumvent part of the risk of unfavorable exchange rate fluctuations by "hedging" in the "futures market" for foreign exchange. For example, our American auto importer can purchase the needed pounds at the current $2 for £1 exchange rates to be made available three months in the future when the British cars are delivered. Unfortunately, this does not eliminate entirely exchange rate risks. Suppose the dollar price of pounds *falls* (the dollar appreciates) in the three-month delivery period and a competing importing firm did not hedge its foreign exchange purchase. This means the competitor will obtain its shipment of Triumphs at a lower price and will be able to undersell our original importer.

equivalent size. That is, last year's balance of payments surplus with Britain will increase the United States' reserve of pounds and this reserve can be used to "finance" this year's deficit. But if the United States encounters persistent and sizable deficits for an extended period, the reserves problem can become critical and force the abandonment of a system of fixed exchange rates. Or, at least, a nation whose reserves are inadequate must resort to less appealing options to maintain exchange rate stability. Let's consider these other options.

2 Trade Policies One set of policy options includes measures designed to control the flows of trade and finance directly. The United States might try to maintain the $2 = £1 exchange rate in the face of a shortage of pounds by discouraging imports (thereby reducing the demand for pounds) and by encouraging exports (thereby increasing the supply of pounds). Imports can be reduced by imposing tariffs or import quotas. Similarly, special taxes may be levied on the interest and dividends Americans receive for foreign investments. Also, the United States government might subsidize certain American exports and thus increase the supply of pounds.

The fundamental problem with these policies is that they reduce the volume of world trade and distort its composition or pattern away from that which is economically desirable. Tariffs, quotas, and the like can be imposed only at the sacrifice of some portion of the economic gains or benefits attainable from a free flow of world trade based on comparative advantage. These effects should not be underestimated; the imposition of trade barriers can elicit retaliatory responses from other nations which are adversely affected.

3 Exchange Controls: Rationing Another option is exchange controls or rationing. Under exchange controls the United States government would handle the problem of a pound shortage by requiring that all pounds obtained by American exporters be sold to it. Then, in turn, the government allocates or rations this short supply of pounds (*xa* in Figure 21-5) among various American importers who demand the quantity *xb*. In this way the American government would restrict American imports to the amount of foreign exchange earned by American exports. American demand for British pounds in the amount *ab* would be unfulfilled. Government eliminates a balance of payments deficit by restricting imports to the value of exports.

There are many objections to exchange controls.

1 Like trade controls—tariffs, quotas, and export subsidies—exchange controls distort the pattern of international trade away from that based on comparative advantage.

2 The process of rationing scarce foreign exchange necessarily involves discrimination among importers. Serious problems of equity and favoritism are implicit in the rationing process.

3 Controls impinge on freedom of consumer choice. Americans who prefer Mazdas may be forced to buy Mercuries. The business opportunities of some American importers will necessarily be impaired because imports are being constrained by government.

4 There are likely to be enforcement problems. The market forces of demand and supply indicate there are American importers who want foreign exchange badly enough to pay *more* than the $2 = £1 official rate; this sets the stage for extralegal or "black market" foreign exchange dealings.

4 Domestic Macro Adjustments A final means of maintaining a stable exchange rate is to use domestic fiscal and monetary policies to eliminate the shortage of pounds. In particular, restrictive fiscal and monetary measures will reduce the United States' national income relative to Britain's. Because American imports vary directly with our national income, our demand for British goods, and therefore for pounds, will be restrained.

To the extent that these contractionary policies reduce our price level relative to Britain's, American buyers of consumption and investment goods will divert their demands from British to American goods, also restricting the demand for pounds. Finally, a restrictive (tight) money policy will increase United States' interest rates compared to Britain and reduce American demand for pounds to make financial investments in Britain.

From Britain's standpoint lower prices on American goods and higher American interest rates will increase British imports of American goods and stimulate British financial investment in the United States. Both developments will increase the supply of pounds. The combination of a decrease in the demand for and an increase in the supply of pounds will eliminate the initial American payments deficit. In Figure 21-5 the new supply and demand curves will intersect at some new equilibrium point on the *ab* line where the exchange rate persists at $2 = £1.

This means of maintaining pegged exchange rates is hardly appealing. The "price" of exchange rate stability for the United States is falling output, employment, and price levels—in other words, a recession. Achieving a balance of payments equilibrium and realizing domestic stability are both important national economic objectives; but to sacrifice the latter for the former is to let the tail wag the dog.

INTERNATIONAL EXCHANGE RATE SYSTEMS

There have been three different exchange rate systems which nations have employed in recent history.

The Gold Standard: Fixed Exchange Rates

Over the 1879–1934 period—except for the World War I years—an international monetary system known as the gold standard prevailed. The **gold standard** provided for fixed exchange rates. A look at its operation and ultimate downfall is instructive as to the functioning and some of the advantages and problems associated with fixed-rate systems. Currently a number of economists advocate fixed exchange rates and a few even call for a return to the international gold standard.

Conditions   A nation is on the gold standard when it fulfills three conditions:
1   It must define its monetary unit in terms of a certain quantity of gold.
2   It must maintain a fixed relationship between its stock of gold and its domestic money supply.
3   It must allow gold to be freely exported and imported.

If each nation defines its monetary unit in terms of gold, the various national currencies will have a fixed relationship to one another. For example, suppose the United States defines a dollar as being worth 25 grains of gold and Britain defines its pound sterling as being worth 50 grains of gold. This means that a British pound is worth $50/25$ dollars or, simply, £1 equals $2.

Gold flows   Now, ignoring costs of packing, insuring, and shipping gold between countries, under the gold standard the rate of exchange would not vary from this $2-for-£1 rate. No one in the United States would pay more than $2 for £1, because you could always buy 50 grains of gold for $2 in the United States, ship it to Britain, and sell it for £1. Nor would the English pay more than £1 for $2. Why should they, when they could buy 50 grains of gold in England for £1, send it to the United States, and sell it for $2?

In practice the costs of packing, insuring, and shipping gold must be taken into account. But these costs would only amount to a few cents per 50 grains of gold. If these costs were 3 cents for 50 grains of gold, Americans wanting pounds would pay up to $2.03 for a pound rather than buy and export 50 grains of gold to get the pound. Why? Because it would cost them $2 for the 50 grains of gold plus 3 cents to send it to England to be exchanged for £1. This $2.03 exchange rate, above which gold would begin to flow out of the United States, is called the **gold export point.**

Conversely, the exchange rate would fall to $1.97 before gold would flow into the United States. The English, wanting dollars, would accept as little as $1.97 in exchange for £1, because from the $2 which they could get by buying 50 grains of gold in England and reselling it in the United States, 3 cents must be subtracted to pay shipping and related costs. This $1.97 exchange rate, below which gold would flow into the United States, is called the **gold import point.**

Our conclusion is that *under the gold standard the flow of gold between nations would result in exchange rates which for all practical purposes are fixed.*

Domestic Macro Adjustments   Figure 21-5 helps explain the kinds of adjustments the gold standard would entail. Here, initially the demand for and the supply of pounds are D and S respectively and the resulting intersection point at a coincides with the fixed exchange rate of $2 = £1 which results from the "in gold" definitions of the pound and the dollar. Now suppose for some reason American preferences for British goods increase, shifting the demand for pounds curve to D'. In Figure 21-5 there is now a shortage of pounds equal to *ab,* implying an American balance of payments deficit.

What will happen? Remember that the rules of the gold standard prohibit the exchange rate from moving from the fixed $2 = £1 relationship; the rate can *not* move up to a new equilibrium of $3 = £1 at point *c* as it would under freely floating rates. Instead, the exchange rate would rise by a few cents to the American gold export point at which gold would flow from the United States to Britain.

Recall that the gold standard requires participants to maintain a fixed relationship between their domestic money supplies and their quantities of gold. Therefore, the flow of gold from the United States to Britain would bring about a contraction of the money supply in America and an expansion of the money supply in Britain. Other things being equal, this will reduce aggregate demand and, therefore, lower real domestic output, employment, and the price level in the United States. Also, the reduced money supply will boost American interest rates.

The opposite occurs in Britain. The inflow of gold increases the money supply, causing aggregate demand, national income, employment, and the price level to all increase. The increased money supply will also lower interest rates in Britain.

In Figure 21-5 declining American incomes and prices will reduce our demand for British goods and services and therefore reduce the American demand for pounds. Lower relative interest rates in Britain will make it less attractive for Americans to invest there, also reducing the demand for pounds. For all these reasons the D' curve will shift to the left.

Similarly, higher incomes and prices in Britain will increase British demand for American goods and services and higher American interest rates will encourage the British to invest more in the United States. These developments all increase the supply of pounds available to Americans, shifting the S curve of Figure 21-5 to the right.

In short, domestic macroeconomic adjustments in America and Britain, triggered by the international flow of gold, will produce new demand and supply for pound curves which intersect at some point on the horizontal line between points *a* and *b*.

Note the critical difference in the adjustment mechanisms associated with freely floating exchange rates and the fixed rates of the gold standard. With floating rates the burden of the adjustment is on the exchange rate itself. In contrast, the gold standard in-

volves changes in the domestic money supplies of participating nations which in turn precipitate changes in price levels, real domestic output and employment, and interest rates.

Although the gold standard boasts the advantages of stable exchange rates and the automatic correction of balance of payments deficits and surpluses, its basic drawback is that nations must accept domestic adjustments in such distasteful forms as unemployment and falling incomes, on the one hand, or inflation, on the other. In using the gold standard nations must be willing to submit their domestic economies to painful macroeconomic adjustments. Under this system a nation's monetary policy would be determined largely by changes in the demand for and supply of foreign exchange. If the United States, for example, was already moving toward recession, the loss of gold under the gold standard would reduce its money supply and intensify the problem. Under the international gold standard nations would have to forgo independent monetary policies.

Demise The worldwide Great Depression of the 1930s signaled the end of the gold standard. As domestic outputs and employment plummeted worldwide, the restoration of prosperity became the primary goal of afflicted nations. Protectionist measures such as the United States' Smoot-Hawley Tariff were enacted as nations sought to increase net exports and stimulate their domestic economies. And each nation was fearful that its economic recovery would be aborted by a balance of payments deficit which would lead to an outflow of gold and consequent contractionary effects. Indeed, nations attempted to devalue their currencies in term of gold to make their exports more attractive and imports less attractive. These devaluations undermined a basic condition of the gold standard and the system broke down.

The Bretton Woods System

Not only did the Great Depression of the 1930s lead to the downfall of the gold standard, it also prompted erection of trade barriers which greatly impaired international trade. World War II was similarly disruptive to world trade and finance. Thus, as World War II drew to a close the world trading and monetary systems were in shambles.

To lay the groundwork for a new international monetary system, an international conference of Allied nations was held at Bretton Woods, New Hampshire, in

1944. Out of this conference evolved a commitment to an *adjustable-peg system* of exchange rates, sometimes called the **Bretton Woods system.** The new system sought to capture the advantages of the old gold standard (fixed exchange rates), while avoiding its disadvantages (painful domestic macroeconomic adjustments).

Furthermore, the conference created the **International Monetary Fund** (IMF) to make the new exchange rate system feasible and workable. This international monetary system, emphasizing relatively fixed exchange rates and managed through the IMF, prevailed with modifications until 1971. The IMF continues to play a basic role in international finance and in recent years has performed a major role in ameliorating debt problems of the less developed countries.

IMF and Pegged Exchange Rates Why did the Bretton Woods adjustable-peg system evolve? We have noted that during the depressed 1930s, various countries resorted to the practice of **devaluation**—devaluing[3] their currencies to try to stimulate domestic employment. For example, if the United States was faced with growing unemployment, it might devalue the dollar by *increasing* the dollar price of pounds from $2.50 for £1 to, say, $3 for £1. This action would make American goods cheaper to the British and British goods dearer to Americans, increasing American exports and reducing American imports. The resulting increase in net exports, abetted by the multiplier effect, would stimulate output and employment in the United States.

But the problem is that every nation can play the devaluation game, and most gave it a whirl. The resulting rounds of competitive devaluations benefited no one; on the contrary, they actually contributed to further demoralization of world trade. Nations at Bretton Woods therefore agreed that the postwar monetary system must provide for overall exchange rate stability whereby disruptive currency devaluations could be avoided.

What was the adjustable-peg system of exchange rates like? First, as with the gold standard, each IMF member was obligated to define its monetary unit in terms of gold (or dollars), thereby establishing par

rates of exchange between its currency and the currencies of all other members. Each nation was further obligated to keep its exchange rate stable vis-à-vis any other currency.

But how was this obligation to be fulfilled? The answer, as we saw in our discussion of fixed exchange rates, is that governments must use international monetary reserves to intervene in foreign exchange markets. Assume, for example, that under the Bretton Woods system the dollar was "pegged" to the British pound at $2 = £1. Now suppose in Figure 21-5 that the American demand for pounds temporarily increases from *D* to *D'* so that a shortage of pounds of *ab* arises at the pegged rate. How can the United States keep its pledge to maintain a $2 = £1 rate when the new market or equilibrium rate would be at $3 = £1? The United States could supply additional pounds in the exchange market, shifting the supply of pounds curve to the right so that it intersects *D'* at *b* and thereby maintains the $2 = £1 rate of exchange.

Where would the United States obtain the needed pounds? Under the Bretton Woods system there were three main sources.

1 Reserves The United States might currently possess pounds in a "stabilization fund" as the result of the opposite exchange market condition existing in the past. That is, at some earlier time the United States government may have spent dollars to purchase surplus pounds which were threatening to reduce the $2 = £1 exchange rate to, say, $1 = £1.

2 Gold Sales The United States government might sell some of the gold it holds to Britain for pounds. The proceeds would then be offered in the exchange market to augment the supply of pounds.

3 IMF Borrowing The needed pounds might be borrowed from the IMF. Nations participating in the Bretton Woods system were required to make contributions to the IMF on the basis of the size of their national income, population, and volume of trade. Thus, if necessary, the United States could borrow pounds on a short-term basis from the IMF by supplying its own currency as collateral.

Fundamental Imbalances: Adjusting the Peg A fixed-rate system such as Bretton Woods functions well so long as a nation's payments deficits and surpluses occur more or less randomly and are approximately equal in size. If a nation's payments surplus last year

[3]A note on terminology is in order. We noted earlier in this chapter that the dollar has *appreciated (depreciated)* when its international value has increased (decreased) as the result of changes in the demand for, or supply of, dollars in foreign exchange markets. The terms *revalue* and *devalue* are used to describe an increase or decrease, respectively, in the international value of a currency which occurs as the result of governmental action.

allows it to add a sufficient amount to its international monetary reserves to finance this year's payments deficit, no problems will arise. But what if the United States, for example, encountered a "fundamental imbalance" in its international trade and finance and was confronted with persistent and sizable payments deficits? In this case it is evident that the United States would eventually run out of reserves and be unable to maintain its fixed exchange rate.

Under the Bretton Woods system, a fundamental payments deficit was corrected by devaluation, that is, by an "orderly" reduction in the nation's pegged exchange rate. Also, the IMF allowed each member nation to alter the value of its currency by 10 percent without explicit permission from the Fund to correct a deeply rooted or "fundamental" balance of payments deficit. Larger exchange rate changes required the sanction of the Fund's board of directors. By requiring approval of significant rate changes, the Fund guarded against arbitrary and competitive currency devaluation prompted by nations seeking a temporary stimulus to their domestic economies. In our illustration, devaluing the dollar would increase American exports and lower American imports, correcting its persistent payments deficits.

The objective of the adjustable-peg system was to realize a world monetary system which embraced the best features of both a fixed exchange rate system (such as the old international gold standard) and a system of freely fluctuating exchange rates. By reducing risk and uncertainty, short-term exchange rate stability—pegged exchange rates—would presumably stimulate trade and lead to the efficient use of world resources. Periodic exchange rate adjustments—adjustments of the pegs—made in an orderly fashion through the IMF, and on the basis of permanent or long-run changes in a country's payments position, provided a mechanism by which persistent international payments imbalances could be resolved by means other than painful changes in domestic levels of output and prices.

Demise of the Bretton Woods System Under the Bretton Woods system gold and the dollar came to be accepted as international reserves. The acceptability of gold as an international medium of exchange was derived from its role under the international gold standard of an earlier era. The dollar became acceptable as international money for two reasons.

1 The United States emerged from World War II as the free world's strongest economy.

2 The United States had accumulated large quantities of gold and between 1934 and 1971 maintained a policy of buying gold from, and selling gold to, foreign monetary authorities at a fixed price of $35 per ounce. Thus the dollar was convertible into gold on demand; the dollar came to be regarded as a substitute for gold and therefore "as good as gold."

But the role of the dollar as a component of international monetary reserves contained the seeds of a dilemma. Consider the situation as it developed in the 1950s and 1960s. The problem with gold as international money was a quantitative one. The growth of the world's money stock depends on the amount of newly mined gold, less any amounts hoarded for speculative purposes or used for industrial and artistic purposes. Unfortunately, the growth of the gold stock lagged behind the rapidly expanding volume of international trade and finance. Thus the dollar came to occupy an increasingly important role as an international monetary reserve.

Economies of the world acquire dollars as reserves as the result of United States' balance of payments deficits. With the exception of some three or four years, the United States incurred persistent payments deficits throughout the 1950s and 1960s. These deficits were financed in part by drawing down American gold reserves. But for the most part United States' deficits were financed by growing foreign holdings of American dollars which were "as good as gold" until 1971.

As the amount of dollars held by foreigners soared and as our gold reserves dwindled, other nations inevitably began to question whether the dollar was really "as good as gold." The ability of the United States to maintain the convertibility of the dollar into gold became increasingly doubtful, and, therefore, so did the role of the dollar as generally accepted international monetary reserves. Hence, the dilemma: ". . . to preserve the status of the dollar as a reserve medium, the payments deficit of the United States had to be eliminated; but elimination of the deficit would mean a drying up of the source of additional dollar reserves for the system."[4] The United States had to reduce or eliminate its payments deficits to preserve the dollar's status as an international medium of exchange. But success in this endeavor would limit the expansion of international reserves or liquidity and restrict the growth of international trade and finance.

[4]Delbert A. Snider, *Introduction to International Economics,* 7th ed. (Homewood, Ill.: Richard D. Irwin, Inc., 1979), p. 352.

This problem came to a head in the early 1970s. Faced with persistent and growing United States' payments deficits, President Nixon suspended the dollar's convertibility into gold on August 15, 1971. This suspension abrogated the policy to exchange gold for dollars at $35 per ounce, which had existed for thirty-seven years. This new policy severed the link between gold and the international value of the dollar, thereby "floating" the dollar and allowing its value to be determined by market forces. The floating of the dollar withdrew American support from the old Bretton Woods system of fixed exchange rates and sounded the death knell for that system.

The Managed Float

The system of exchange rates which has since evolved is not easily described; it can probably best be labeled a system of **managed floating exchange rates.** It is recognized that changing economic conditions among nations require continuing changes in exchange rates to avoid persistent payments deficits or surpluses; exchange rates must be allowed to float. But short-term changes in exchange rates—perhaps accentuated by purchases and sales by speculators—disrupt and discourage the flow of trade and finance. Thus, it is generally agreed that the central banks of the various nations should buy and sell foreign exchange to smooth out such fluctuations in rates. That is, central banks should "manage" or stabilize short-term speculative variations in their exchange rates.

These characteristics were formalized by a leading group of IMF nations in 1976. Thus, ideally, the managed floating system will have not only the needed long-term exchange rate flexibility to correct fundamental payments imbalances, but also sufficient short-term stability of rates to sustain and encourage international trade and finance.

Actually, the current exchange rate system is more complicated than the previous paragraphs suggest. While the major currencies—German marks, American and Canadian dollars, Japanese yen, and the British pound—fluctuate or float in response to changing demand and supply conditions, most of the European Common Market nations are attempting to peg their currencies to one another. Furthermore, many less developed nations peg their currencies to the dollar and allow their currencies to fluctuate with it. Finally, some nations peg the value of their currencies to a "basket" or group of other currencies.

How well has the managed floating system worked? It has both proponents and critics.

Pros Proponents argue that the system has functioned well—far better than anticipated—during its relatively brief existence.

1 Trade Growth In the first place, fluctuating exchange rates did not lead to the diminution of world trade and finance that skeptics had predicted. In real terms world trade has grown at approximately the same rate under the managed float as it did during the decade of the 1960s under the fixed exchange rates of the Bretton Woods system.

2 Managing Turbulence Proponents argue that the managed float has weathered severe economic turbulence which might well have caused a fixed exchange regime to have broken down. Such dramatic events as worldwide agricultural shortfalls in 1972–1974, extraordinary oil-price increases in 1973–1974 and again in 1979–1980, worldwide stagflation in 1974–1976 and 1981–1983, and large U.S. budget deficits in the 1980s, all generated substantial international trade and financial imbalances. Flexible rates facilitated international adjustments to these developments, whereas the same events would have put unbearable pressures on a fixed-rate system.

Cons But there is still considerable sentiment in favor of a system characterized by greater exchange rate stability. Those favoring stable rates see problems with the current system.

1 Volatility and Adjustment Critics argue that exchange rates have been excessively volatile under the managed float. This volatility, it is argued, has occurred even when underlying economic and financial conditions of particular nations have been stable. Perhaps more importantly, the managed float has not readily resolved balance of payments imbalances as flexible rates are presumably capable of doing. Thus the United States has run persistent trade deficits in recent years, while Germany and Japan have had persistent surpluses. Changes in the international values of the dollar, mark, and yen have not yet corrected these imbalances.

2 A "Nonsystem"? Skeptics feel that the managed float is basically a "nonsystem"; the rules and guidelines circumscribing the behavior of each nation as to its exchange rate are not sufficiently clear or constraining to make the system viable in the long run. Nations will inevitably be tempted to intervene in foreign exchange markets, not merely to smooth out short-term or speculative fluctuations in the value of their currencies, but to prop up their currency if it is chronically weak or to manipulate the value of their currency to achieve domestic stabilization goals. In brief, there is fear that in time there may be more "managing" and less "floating" of exchange rates, and this may be fatal to the present loosely defined system.

An example of more "managing" and less "floating" of exchange rates occurred in February 1987 when the "Group of Seven" industrial nations **(G-7 nations)**—the United States, West Germany, Japan, Britain, France, Italy, and Canada—agreed to take actions to stabilize the value of the dollar. In the previous two years the dollar had declined rapidly because of a sizable U.S. trade deficit. Although the U.S. trade deficit remained large, it was felt that a further depreciation of the dollar might be disruptive to economic growth in several G-7 economies. The G-7 nations thus bought large quantities of dollars to prop up the dollar's value. Since 1987 the G-7 nations have periodically intervened in foreign exchange markets to help stabilize the value of the dollar. Do these actions represent an admission by the industrial economies that the system of flexible exchange rates is seriously flawed?

The jury is still out on the managed float and no clear assessment has been reached: "Flexible rates have neither attained their proponents' wildest hopes nor confirmed their opponents' worst fears. But they have seen the major industrial economies through [two decades] mined with major disturbances to the international economy."[5]

QUICK REVIEW 21-3

◆ *Under the gold standard (1789–1934), nations fixed exchange rates by valuing their currencies in terms of gold, by tying their stocks of money to gold, and by allowing gold to flow between nations when balance of payment deficits and surpluses occurred.*

◆ *The Bretton Woods, or adjustable-peg, system of exchange rates (1944–1971) fixed or pegged short-run exchange rates, but permitted orderly long-run adjustments of the pegs.*

◆ *The managed floating system of exchange rate (1971–present) relies on foreign exchange markets to establish equilibrium exchange rates, but permits central banks to buy and sell foreign currencies to manage or stabilize short-term speculative changes in exchange rates.*

---

[5]Richard E. Caves and Ronald W. Jones, *World Trade and Payments,* 3d ed. (Boston: Little, Brown and Company, 1981), p. 471.

RECENT UNITED STATES' TRADE DEFICITS

As shown in Figure 21-6, the United States had large trade deficits in the 1980s and early 1990s. Specifically, our merchandise trade deficit jumped from $25 billion in 1980 to $160 billion in 1987, then fell to $74 billion in 1991. In 1980 the United States had a current account surplus of $2 billion; by 1987 this had changed to a $160 billion deficit. By 1991 the current account deficit had narrowed to $92 billion.

What caused these large trade deficits? What were their effects? Why have they recently diminished?

Causes of the Trade Deficits

It is generally agreed that three major factors contributed to the large trade deficits of the 1980s and early 1990s.

The Rise of the Dollar   As Figure 21-7 indicates, there was a pronounced rise in the international value of the dollar between 1980 and 1985. Here the value of the dollar is compared to ten other major currencies (weighted by the amount of trade we carry on with each country). By the end of 1984 the dollar was about 65 percent above its 1980 average value and at the highest level since floating exchange rates were adopted in the early 1970s. A strong or appreciated dollar means that foreign monies are cheaper to Americans and, conversely, dollars are more expensive to foreigners. As a result, foreign goods are cheap to Americans and our imports rise. Conversely, American goods are expensive to foreigners and our exports fall.

But why did the value of the dollar surge between 1980 and 1985? The basic answer is that real interest rates in the United States—nominal interest rates less the rate of inflation—rose in the United States compared to foreign countries. High real interest rates made the United States a very attractive place for foreigners to invest. As a result, the demand for dollars to make such investments increased, causing the dollar to appreciate in value.

Real interest rates were relatively high in America for two reasons.

1   The large Federal budget deficits of the 1980s are cited by many economists as a basic cause of high interest rates. Simply put, government borrowing to finance its deficits increased the domestic demand for money and boosted interest rates.

2   In 1979 the United States shifted to a tighter money policy in its efforts to control inflation. This

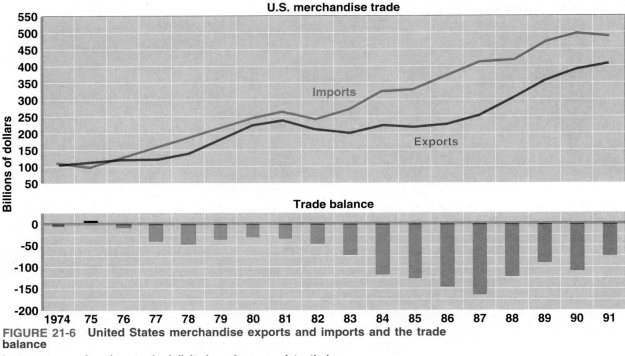

FIGURE 21-6 United States merchandise exports and imports and the trade balance

In recent years American trade deficits have been persistently large.

action increased interest rates directly by reducing the supply of money relative to its demand. Indirectly the lower rate of inflation kept the demand of foreign investors for dollars high because lower inflation means a higher *real* rate of return on investments in the United States.

By 1985 the value of the dollar had reached record heights relative to other currencies. Two factors then began to interact to reduce the dollar's value sharply over the next two years.

1 Five industrial nations—the United States, West Germany, Great Britain, France, and Japan—collectively decided to nudge the dollar downward to help correct the massive U.S. trade deficit and the trade surpluses in Japan and other nations. These five nations agreed to increase the supply of dollars in foreign exchange markets to reduce the dollar's value.

2 The demand for foreign currency in the United States rose sharply because more foreign money was needed to pay for the expanding volume of imports. This increase in the demand for yen, francs, and other foreign currencies increased the value of these currencies relative to the dollar. As shown in Figure 21-7, the value of the dollar declined sharply relative to other currencies over the 1985–1987 period.

Despite the sharp decline in the dollar between 1985 and 1987, the American trade imbalance stubbornly persisted. The major reason was that Japanese and other foreign importers did not immediately increase their dollar prices of products by as much as the decline in the international value of the dollar. Instead of increasing their prices, major importers accepted lower per unit profits on their goods. Therefore, imports to the United States for a time continued to rise, offsetting increases in American exports. Also, recall that in 1987 the G-7 nations agreed to halt the decline in the value of the dollar. Only in the second half of 1988 did the American trade deficit finally begin to shrink.

Rapid American Growth A second cause of the large trade deficits of the 1980s and 1990s is that the United States experienced a more rapid recovery from the 1980–1982 world recession than did its major trading partners. For example, American growth was about double that of Europe in 1983 and nearly triple the European rate in 1984. Although the gap in growth rates narrowed, the American growth rate continued to outpace the European rate between 1985 and 1990. This is significant because, like domestic consumption, a nation's purchases of foreign goods (its imports) vary di-

Index, March 1973 = 1.0

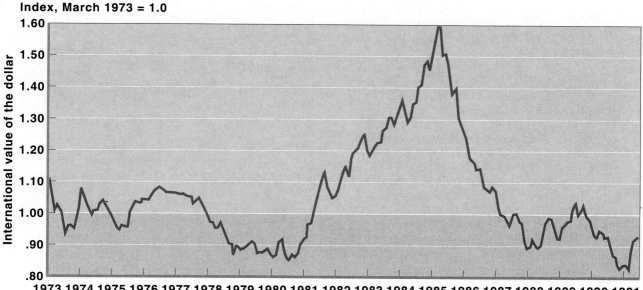

FIGURE 21-7 The international value of the dollar

Between 1980 and 1985 the value of the dollar increased greatly relative to other major currencies, tending to increase our imports and decrease our exports. The dollar fell sharply from 1985 through 1987 but trade deficits continued into the 1990s.

rectly with the level of domestic income. Because our national income expanded relatively rapidly, our imports also expanded rapidly. The slower growth of foreign national incomes meant their imports (our exports) grew slowly.

Exports to Less Developed Countries A third factor contributing to the large trade deficits was a falloff in our exports to the less developed countries (LDCs). An important source of the LDCs' external debt problem was their need to finance large international trade deficits by borrowing from the industrially advanced nations. As part of rescheduling and restructuring their debts in the 1980s, the less developed countries agreed to lessen their trade deficits. Thus they reduced their imports by using more restrictive monetary and fiscal policies to restrain the growth of their national incomes. In so doing their demands for imported goods declined. Part of those import reductions involved American goods, that is, United States exports. Many LDCs also *devalued* their currencies or, in other words, lowered the exchange rate value of their currencies by governmental decree. Devaluation restricted their imports and stimulated their exports. Thus the LDCs bought less from, and sold more to, the United States.

Effects of U.S. Trade Deficits

What have been the effects or consequences of our foreign trade deficits?

Dampened Aggregate Demand A trade deficit—more specifically, negative net exports—reduces aggregate demand and therefore, unless offset by other spending, diminishes the levels of real domestic output and employment via the multiplier effect. While this was a factor in keeping our level of employment below the full-employment rate for much of the 1980s, it also helped restrain inflation. A strong, appreciated dollar lowers the prices of all imported goods. Furthermore, a surging volume of imports exerts downward pressure on the prices of domestic goods that compete with those imports.

The constraining effect of a trade deficit is concentrated on industries which are highly dependent on export markets or are most competitive with imports. Some of the problems faced by American farmers, automobile manufacturers, and steel producers in the 1980s, for example, were related to the strong dollar and the associated trade deficits. These difficulties contributed greatly to the upsurge in political pressure for protectionist policies discussed in Chapter 20. They

LAST WORD

BUY AMERICAN: THE GLOBAL REFRIGERATOR

Humorist Art Buchwald pokes fun at those who suggest we could end our trade deficits by buying American consumer products.

"There is only one way the country is going to get on its feet," said Baleful.

"How's that?" I asked, as we drank coffee in his office at the Baleful Refrigerator Company.

"The consumer has to start buying American," he said, slamming his fist down on the desk. "Every time an American buys a foreign refrigerator it costs one of my people his job. And every time one of my people is out of work it means he or she can't buy refrigerators."

"It's a vicious circle," I said.

Baleful's secretary came in. "Mr. Thompson, the steel broker is on the phone."

My friend grabbed the receiver. "Thompson, where is that steel shipment from Japan that was supposed to be in last weekend? . . . I don't care about weather. We're almost out of steel, and I'll have to close down the refrigerator assembly line next week. If you can't deliver when you promise, I'll find myself another broker."

"You get your steel from Japan?" I asked Baleful.

"Even with shipping costs, their price is still lower than steel made in Europe. We used to get all our sheets from Belgium, but the Japanese are now giving them a run for their money."

The buzzer on the phone alerted Baleful. He listened for a few moments and then said, "Excuse me, I have a call from Taiwan. Mark Four? Look, R&D designed a new push-button door handle and we're going to send the specs to you. Tell Mr. Chow if his people send us a sample of one and can make it for us at the

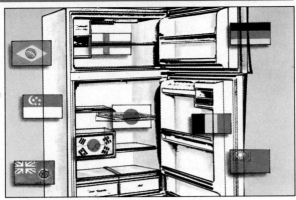

same price as the old handle, we'll give his company the order."

A man came in with a plastic container and said, "Mr. Baleful, you said you wanted to see one of these before we ordered them. They are the containers for the ice maker in the refrigerator."

Baleful inspected it carefully and banged it on the floor a couple of times. "What's the price on it?"

"Hong Kong can deliver it at $2 a tray, and Dong-Fu Plastics in South Korea said they can make it for $1.70."

"It's just a plastic tray. Take the South Korea bid. We'll let Hong Kong supply us with the shelves for the freezer. Any word on the motors?"

"There's a German company in Brazil that just came out with a new motor, and it's passed all our tests, so Johnson has ordered 50,000."

"Call Cleveland Motors and tell them we're sorry, but the price they quoted us was just too high."

"Yes, sir," the man said and departed.

---

also generated interest in industrial policies designed to provide special help for allegedly "key" industries deemed critical to American industrial preeminence.

Increased American Indebtedness A trade deficit is also considered "unfavorable" because it must be financed by increased American indebtedness to foreigners. A trade deficit means we must borrow from the rest of the world to finance that deficit. This failure to "pay our way" in international trade is usually interpreted as a sign of domestic economic weakness and, hence, undesirable. However, economists point out that, at the time a trade or current account deficit is

occurring, it is clearly beneficial to American consumers. After all, a trade deficit means that Americans are currently receiving more goods and services as imports from the rest of the world than we are sending to the rest of the world as exports. Trade deficits augment our domestic living standards during the period in which they occur.

A related consequence of our recent trade deficits is that in 1985 the United States' status changed from that of a net creditor to that of a *net debtor* for the first time since 1914. That is, the United States now owes foreigners more than they owe this country. Recall that current account deficits are financed primarily by net

The secretary came in again and said, "Harry telephoned and wanted to let you know the defroster just arrived from Finland. They're unloading the box cars now."

"Good. Any word on the wooden crates from Singapore?"

"They're at the dock in Hoboken."

"Thank heaven. Cancel the order from Boise Cascade."

"What excuse should I give them?"

"Tell them we made a mistake in our inventory, or we're switching to plastic. I don't care what you tell them."

Baleful turned to me. "Where were we?"

"You were saying that if the consumer doesn't start buying American, this country is going to be in a lot of trouble."

"Right. It's not only his patriotic duty, but his livelihood that's at stake. I'm going to Washington next week to tell the Senate Commerce Committee that if they don't get off the stick, there isn't going to be a domestic refrigerator left in this country. We're not going to stay in business for our health."

"Pour it to them," I urged him.

Baleful said, "Come out with me into the showroom."

I followed him. He went to his latest model, and opened the door. "This is an American refrigerator made by the American worker, for the American consumer. What do you have to say to that?"

"It's beautiful," I said. "It puts foreign imports to shame."

Source: Art Buchwald, "Being Bullish on Buying American." Reprinted by permission. We discovered this article in *Master Curriculum Guide in Economics: Teaching Strategies for International Trade* (New York: Joint Council on Economic Education, 1988).

capital inflows to the United States. When our exports are insufficient to pay for our imports, we finance the difference by borrowing from foreigners or, in other words, by going into debt. The financing of our recent large trade deficits has caused foreigners to accumulate a larger volume of claims against American assets than we have accumulated against foreign assets. The U.S. foreign debt burden climbed to $721 billion in 1990, making us the largest debtor nation in the world.

One implication of net debtor status is that we can no longer look forward to a net inflow of dividend and interest payments (see item 7 in Table 21-1's balance of payments) to help cover deficits in our merchandise

and services trade. A second implication is that more of our corporations are foreign-owned.

The above comments on the economic effects of our trade deficit for the United States economy can be reversed as far as our industrialized trading partners are concerned. The current accounts of Japan and Germany, for example, tended to move toward surplus. These countries experienced an expansionary-inflationary stimulus and unusual growth in their export-dependent industries. They also increased their holdings of American debt.

QUICK REVIEW 21-4

♦   In the 1980s and early 1990s the United States experienced large trade deficits, caused by a strong dollar, relatively rapid American growth prior to the 1990–1991 recession, and reduced purchases of our exports by less developed nations.

♦   These large deficits had a contractionary, anti-inflationary impact, hurt export-dependent industries, and resulted in the United States becoming a debtor nation; they also temporarily enhanced America's standard of living.

Reducing the Trade Deficit

Two kinds of policies for reducing large trade deficits are most often cited: reduction of the Federal budget deficit and measures to accelerate economic growth abroad.

Reduction of the Budget Deficit   Many economists agree that the most critical cause of our continuing trade deficits has been our large annual Federal budget deficits. It is argued that a reduction in the size of our Federal budget deficit will lower the real interest rate in the United States compared to other nations. In other words, a reduction in the government's demand for funds to finance its deficits will lower domestic interest rates and thus make financial investments in the United States less attractive to foreigners. The demand for dollars by foreigners will decline and the dollar will depreciate. Given a depreciated dollar, our exports will increase and imports will fall, correcting our trade deficit. This scenario is exactly opposite to the one shown earlier in Figure 18-2.

Would not a "managed" depreciation of the dollar by the G-7 nations produce a decline in the U.S. trade deficit, even without a reduction in our budget deficit? Perhaps so, but this point may be moot. Our trading partners have not been interested in allowing the dollar to fall appreciably below its 1988 level, unless we reduce our budget deficit. In effect, these nations contend that the United States must "get its fiscal house in order" to achieve a better balance of international trade.

Economic Growth Abroad   The American trade deficit can also be reduced if nations abroad speed up their rates of economic growth. Higher levels of foreign national income increase the demand for American exports. The G-7 group of industrial nations has recognized the importance of economic growth in the nations which have trade surpluses as a way to reduce these surpluses and lower the American trade deficit. In the late 1980s, the governments of Japan and Germany established expansionary fiscal and monetary policies to bolster national income and increase the demand for goods produced in America.

Other "Remedies"   There are several other possible "remedies" to the persistent United States' trade deficits.

Easy Money Policy   Under appropriate circumstances, an easy money policy lowers real interest rates and reduces a trade deficit. The process works as follows. The decline in interest rates reduces the international demand for dollars, which results in a depreciation of the dollar. Dollar depreciation raises our exports and lowers our imports (Table 15-4).

Protective Tariffs   Protective tariffs can be used to reduce imports, but this strategy results in the loss of the gains from specialization and international trade. Furthermore, it may not be successful: Tariffs which reduce our *imports* foster retaliatory tariffs abroad which reduce our *exports*. Trade deficits do not disappear in this circumstance; instead, all trading partners suffer declines in their living standards.

Recession   Recessions in the United States reduce disposable income and thus spending on all goods, including imports. Because exports are largely unaffected, the decline in imports trims the trade deficit. This is precisely what happened in the United States during the recession of 1990–1991. But recession is an undesirable way to reduce trade deficits; it imposes higher economic costs (lost output) on society than the costs associated with the trade deficit itself. Also, unless the fundamental causes of the deficits have in the meanwhile been remedied, imports and thus trade deficits again rise when the economy begins to recover from recession.

Increased American Competitiveness   The American trade deficits can be reduced by lowering the costs of, and improving the quality of, American goods and services relative to foreign goods. Cost-saving production technologies, development of improved products, and more efficient management techniques each can contribute to a decline in the trade deficit by lowering United States demand for imported goods and increasing foreign demand for American goods.

Direct Foreign Investment   Ironically, our persistent trade deficit has set off a chain of events which has begun to feed back to reduce the trade deficit itself. The vast accumulation of American dollars in foreign hands has enabled foreign individuals and firms to buy American factories or to build new plants in the United States. Furthermore, the fall in the value of the dollar has provided an incentive for foreign firms to produce in the United States rather than in their own nations.

In short, the trade deficit has given rise to an increase in *direct foreign investment* in the form of plant and equipment. Foreign-owned factories are beginning to turn out increasing volumes of goods that otherwise would have been imported. Hondas and Mazdas, produced in American factories, have replaced Hondas and Mazdas formerly imported from Japan. Other examples abound. The upshot is that the American trade deficit may shrink as imports are replaced with goods produced in foreign-owned factories in the United States.

CHAPTER SUMMARY

1   American exports create a foreign demand for dollars and make a supply of foreign exchange available to Americans. Conversely, American exports simultaneously create a demand for foreign exchange and make a supply of dollars available to foreigners. Generally, a nation's exports earn the foreign currencies needed to pay for its imports.

2   The balance of payments records all international trade and financial transactions taking place between a given nation and the rest of the world. The trade balance compares merchandise exports and imports. The balance on goods and services compares exports and imports of both goods and services. The current account balance considers not

only goods and services transactions, but also net investment income and net transfers.

3 A deficit on the current account will be largely offset by a surplus on the capital account. Conversely, a surplus on the current account will be largely offset by a deficit on the capital account. A balance of payments deficit occurs when the sum of the current and capital accounts is in deficit. A payments deficit is financed by drawing down official reserves. A balance of payments surplus occurs when the sum of the current and capital accounts is in surplus. A payments surplus results in an increase in official reserves. The desirability of a balance of payments deficit or surplus depends on its causes and its persistence over time.

4 Flexible or floating exchange rates are determined by the demand for and supply of foreign currencies. Under floating rates a currency will depreciate or appreciate as a result of changes in tastes, relative income changes, relative price changes, relative changes in real interest rates, and speculation.

5 Maintenance of fixed exchange rates requires adequate reserves to accommodate periodic payments deficits. If reserves are inadequate, nations must invoke protectionist trade policies, engage in exchange controls, or endure undesirable domestic macroeconomic adjustments.

6 Historically, the gold standard provided exchange rate stability until its disintegration during the 1930s. Under this system, gold flows between nations precipitated sometimes painful changes in price, income, and employment levels in bringing about international equilibrium.

7 Under the Bretton Woods system exchange rates were pegged to one another and were stable. Participating nations were obligated to maintain these rates by using stabilization funds, gold, or borrowings from the IMF. Persistent or "fundamental" payments deficits could be resolved by IMF-sanctioned currency devaluations.

8 Since 1971 a system of managed floating exchange rates has been in use. Rates are generally set by market forces, although governments intervene with varying frequency to alter their exchange rates.

9 Between 1980 and 1991 the United States experienced large international trade deficits. Causes include **a** a rapidly appreciating dollar between 1980 and 1985; **b** relatively rapid expansion of the American economy prior to the recession of 1990–1991; and **c** curtailed purchases of our exports by the less developed countries.

10 The effects of large trade deficits have been manifold. They have had a contractionary, anti-inflationary effect on our domestic economy. American export-dependent industries have experienced declines in output, employment, and profits, thereby generating political pressures for protection. The United States has become the world's largest debtor nation. However, the trade deficit has meant a current increase in the living standards of American consumers.

11 Two solutions to the trade deficit are **a** reduction of the budget deficit and **b** faster economic growth abroad. Other "remedies" are an easy money policy, protective tariffs, recession, improved U.S. competitiveness, and direct foreign investment.

TERMS AND CONCEPTS

balance of payments	capital account	flexible or floating	points
current account	balance on the capital	exchange rates	Bretton Woods system
credits	account	depreciation and	International Monetary
debits	official reserves	appreciation	Fund
trade balance	balance of payments	purchasing power	devaluation
balance on goods and	deficits and	parity	managed floating
services	surpluses	gold standard	exchange rates
balance on current	fixed exchange rates	gold import and export	G-7 nations
account			

QUESTIONS AND STUDY SUGGESTIONS

1 Explain how an American automobile importer might finance a shipment of Toyotas from Japan. Demonstrate how an American export of machinery to Italy might be financed. Explain: "American exports earn supplies of foreign monies which Americans can use to finance imports."

2 "A rise in the dollar price of yen necessarily means a fall in the yen price of dollars." Do you agree? Illustrate and elaborate: "The critical thing about exchange rates is that they provide a direct link between the prices of goods and services produced in all trading nations of the world." Explain the purchasing power parity theory of exchange rates.

3 The Swedish auto company Saab imports car components from Germany and exports autos to the United States. In 1990 the dollar depreciated, and the German mark appreciated, relative to the Swedish krona. Speculate as to how this hurt Saab—twice.

4 Indicate whether each of the following creates a demand for, or a supply of, French francs in foreign exchange markets:

a An American importer purchases a shipload of Bordeaux wine

b A French automobile firm decides to build an assembly plant in Los Angeles

c An American college student decides to spend a year studying at the Sorbonne

d A French manufacturer exports machinery to Morocco on an American freighter

e The United States incurs a balance of payments deficit in its transactions with France

f A United States government bond held by a French citizen matures

g It is widely believed that the international value of the franc will fall in the near future

5 Explain why the American demand for Mexican pesos is downsloping and the supply of pesos to Americans is upsloping. Assuming a system of floating exchange rates between Mexico and the United States, indicate whether each of the following would cause the Mexican peso to appreciate or depreciate:

a The United States unilaterally reduces tariffs on Mexican products

b Mexico encounters severe inflation

c Deteriorating political relations reduce American tourism in Mexico

d The United States' economy moves into a severe recession

e The Board of Governors embarks on a tight money policy

f Mexican products become more fashionable to Americans

g The Mexican government invites American firms to invest in Mexican oil fields

h The rate of productivity growth in the United States diminishes sharply

6 Explain whether or not you agree with the following statements:

a "A country which grows faster than its major trading partners can expect the international value of its currency to depreciate."

b "A nation whose interest rate is rising more rapidly than in other nations can expect the international value of its currency to appreciate."

c "A country's currency will appreciate if its inflation rate is less than that of the rest of the world."

7 "Exports pay for imports. Yet in 1990 the rest of the world exported about $108 billion more worth of goods and services to the United States than were imported from the United States." Resolve the apparent inconsistency of these two statements.

8 Answer the following questions on the basis of Scorpio's balance of payments for 1993 as shown below. All figures are in billions of dollars. What is the balance of trade? The balance on goods and services? The balance on current account? The balance on capital account? Does Scorpio have a balance of payments deficit or surplus? Would you surmise that Scorpio is participating in a system of fixed or flexible exchange rates? Are Scorpio's international transactions having a contractionary or expansionary effect on its domestic economy?

Merchandise exports	+$40	**Net transfers**	+$10
Merchandise imports	− 30	**Capital inflows**	+ 10
Service exports	+ 15	**Capital outflows**	− 40
Service imports	− 10	**Official reserves**	+ 10
Net investment income	− 5		

9 Explain in detail how a balance of payments deficit would be resolved under **a** the gold standard, **b** the Bretton Woods system, and **c** freely floating exchange rates. What are the advantages and shortcomings of each system?

10 Outline the major costs and benefits associated with a large trade or current account deficit. Explain: "A current account deficit means we are receiving more goods and services from abroad than we are sending abroad. How can that be called 'unfavorable'?"

11 Some people assert that the United States is facing a foreign trade crisis. What do you think they mean? What are the major causes of this "crisis"?

12 Cite and explain two reasons for the decline in the international value of the dollar between 1985 and 1987. Why did the U.S. trade deficit remain high, even though the dollar fell in value?

13 Explain how a eduction in the Federal budget deficit could contribute to a decline in the U.S. trade deficit. Why do trade deficits fall during recessions? Is recession a desirable remedy to trade deficits?

A
P
T
E
R

22

Growth and the Less Developed Countries

It is exceedingly difficult for the typical American family, whose 1990 average income was $35,353, to grasp the hard fact that some two-thirds of the world's population persistently lives at, or perilously close to, the subsistence level. In fact, hunger, squalor, and disease are commonplace in many nations of the world. The World Bank estimates that over 1 billion people—approximately 20 percent of the world's population—lives on less than $1 per day!

In this chapter we first identify the poor or less developed nations of the world. Second, we seek to determine why they are poor. What are the obstacles to growth? Third, the potential role of government in the process of economic development is considered. Fourth, international trade, private capital flows, and foreign aid are examined as vehicles of growth. Fifth, the external debt problems faced by many of the poor nations are analyzed. Finally, we present the demands of poor nations to establish a "new international economic order."

THE RICH AND THE POOR

Just as there is considerable income disparity among individual families within a nation, so there also is great economic inequality among the family of nations. Table 22-1 identifies the following groups of nations.

1 Industrially Advanced Countries The **industrially advanced countries (IACs)** include the United States, Canada, Australia, New Zealand, Japan, and most of the nations of western Europe. These nations have developed market economies based on large stocks of capital goods, advanced production technologies, and well-educated labor forces. As column 1 of

Table 22-1 indicates, the salient feature of these nineteen economies is a high per capita (per person) GNP.

2 Less Developed Countries Most of the remaining nations of the world[1]—located in Africa, Asia, and Latin America—are underdeveloped or **less developed countries (LDCs).** These ninety-seven nations are unindustrialized with their labor forces heavily committed to agriculture. Literacy rates are low, unem-

---

[1]We omit here the former Soviet Union and the eastern European nations which currently do not report their economic data.

TABLE 22-1 **GNP per capita, population, and growth rates**

	GNP per capita		Population	
	(1) Dollars, 1989	(2) Annual growth rate, 1965–1989	(3) Millions, 1989	(4) Annual growth rate, 1980–1989
Industrially advanced countries: **IACs (19 nations)**	$18,330	2.4%	830	0.7%
Less developed countries: **LDCs (97 nations)**				
Middle-income LDCs (56 nations)	2,040	3.3	1,105	2.1
Low-income LDCs (41 nations)	330	2.9	2,948	2.0

Source: World Bank, *World Development Report, 1991* (New York: Oxford University Press).

ployment is high, population growth is rapid, and exports consist largely of agricultural commodities (cocoa, bananas, sugar, raw cotton) and raw materials (copper, iron ore, natural rubber). Capital equipment is scarce, production technologies are typically primitive, and labor force productivity is low. About three-fourths of the world's population lives in these nations, which share the characteristic of widespread poverty.

In Table 22-1 we have divided the poor nations into two groups.

The first group comprises fifty-six "middle-income" LDCs with an average annual per capita GNP of $2040. The range of per capita GNPs of this rather diverse group is from $610 to $5,350. The other group is made up of forty-one "low-income" LDCs with per capita GNPs ranging from $120 to $450 and averaging only $330. This unfortunate group is dominated by India, China, and the sub-Saharan nations of Africa.

Several simple comparisons may bring global income disparities into even sharper focus. Example: The United States' 1989 GNP was approximately $5.2 trillion; the combined GNPs of the ninety-seven LDCs in that year were only $3.1 trillion. Example: The United States with only about 5 percent of the world's population produces approximately one-fourth of the world's output. Example: The annual sales of many large U.S. corporations exceed the GNPs of many of the LDCs. General Motors—America's largest corporation in 1990—had sales of $126 billion in that year. This volume of sales was greater than the GNP of all but 20 or so nations of the world. Example: Per capita GNP in the United States is 261 times greater than in Mozambique, the world's poorest nation.

Not shown in Table 22-1 is a handful of rich oil-exporting nations. For example, Kuwait and the United Arab Emirates have per capita GNPs of $16,150 and $18,430 respectively. However, these nations are not highly industrialized.

Growth, Decline, and Income Gaps

We need to append two other points to our discussion of Table 22-1.

1 There have been considerable differences in the ability of the various LDCs to improve their circumstances over time. On the one hand, a group of so-called newly industrialized economies—Singapore, Hong Kong, Taiwan, and South Korea—have achieved very high annual growth rates of real GNP of 6 to 7 percent over the 1960–1989 period. As a consequence, real per capita GNPs rose fivefold in these nations. In vivid contrast, many of the highly indebted LDCs and the very poor sub-Saharan nations of Africa have experienced *declining* real per capita GNPs during the past decade.

2 We observe in column 2 of Table 22-1 that the average annual growth rates of per capita GNP were quite similar for the LDCs and the IACs over the 1965–1989 period. Despite this similarity, the income gap between rich and poor nations has been widening. Let's simplify and assume that the per capita GNPs of the advanced and less developed countries have both been growing at about 2 percent per year. The fact that the income base in the advanced countries is initially much higher causes the income gap to increase. If per capita income is $400 a year, a 2 percent growth rate means an $8 increase in income. Where per capita income is $4000 per year, the same 2 percent growth rate translates into an $80 increase in income. Thus, the absolute income gap will have increased from $3600 (=$4000 − $400) to $3672 (=$4080 − $408). The LDCs must grow faster than the IACs to catch up.

TABLE 22-2 Selected socioeconomic indicators of development

Country	(1) Per capita GNP, 1989	(2) Life expectancy at birth, 1989	(3) Infant mortality per 1000 live births, 1989	(4) Adult literacy rate, 1985	(5) Daily per capita calorie supply, 1988	(6) Per capita energy consumption, 1989*
Japan	$23,810	79 years	4	99%	2,848	3,484
United States	20,910	76	10	99	3,666	7,794
Brazil	2,540	66	59	78	2,709	897
Mauritania	500	46	123	17	2,528	114
Haiti	360	55	94	5	1,911	51
India	340	59	95	43	2,104	226
Bangladesh	180	51	106	33	1,925	51
Ethiopia	120	48	133	5	1,658	20
Mozambique	80	49	137	28	1,632	84

*Kilograms of oil equivalent.

Source: World Development Report, 1991, and Statistical Abstract of the United States, 1991.

Implications

Mere statistics conceal the human implications of the extreme poverty characterizing so much of our planet:

Let us examine a typical "extended" family in rural Asia. The Asian household is likely to comprise ten or more people, including parents, five to seven children, two grandparents, and some aunts and uncles. They have a combined annual income, both in money and in "kind" (i.e., they consume a share of the food they grow), of from $150 to $200. Together they live in a one-room poorly constructed house as tenant farmers on a large agricultural estate owned by an absentee landlord who lives in the nearby city. The father, mother, uncle, and the older children must work all day on the land. None of the adults can read or write, and of the five school-age children only one attends school regularly; and he cannot expect to proceed beyond three or four years of primary education. There is only one meal a day; it rarely changes and it is rarely sufficient to alleviate the constant hunger pains experienced by the children. The house has no electricity, sanitation, or fresh water supply. There is much sickness, but qualified doctors and medical practitioners are far away in the cities attending to the needs of wealthier families. The work is hard, the sun is hot and aspirations for a better life are constantly being snuffed out. In this part of the world the only relief from the daily struggle for physical survival lies in the spiritual traditions of the people.[2]

[2]Michael P. Todaro, Economic Development in the Third World, 3d ed. (New York: Longman, 1985), p. 4.

In Table 22-2 various socioeconomic indicators for selected LDCs are contrasted with those for the United States and Japan. These data confirm the major points stressed in the above quotation.

BREAKING THE POVERTY BARRIER

The avenues of economic growth are essentially the same for both industrially advanced and less developed nations:

1   Existing supplies of resources must be used more efficiently. This means not only elimination of unemployment but also achievement of greater efficiency in the allocation of resources.

2   Supplies of productive resources must be altered— typically, increased. By expanding supplies of raw materials, capital equipment, effective labor, and technological knowledge, a nation can push its production possibilities curve to the right (Chapter 19).

Why have some nations been successful in pursuing these avenues of growth while others lag far behind? The answer lies largely in differences in the physical and sociocultural environments of the various nations. We will examine the obstacles in the LDCs to altering the quantities and improving efficiency in the use of (1) natural resources, (2) human resources, (3) capital goods, and (4) technological knowledge. Emphasis here will be on the private sector of the economy. In addition, social, institutional, and cultural impediments to growth will be illustrated. Finally, we will analyze the roles of government and foreign aid in the development process.

Natural Resources

There is no simple generalization as to the role of natural resources in the economic development of LDCs. This is true mainly because the distribution of natural resources among these nations is very uneven. Some less developed nations have valuable deposits of bauxite, tin, copper, tungsten, nitrates, and petroleum. Some LDCs have been able to use their natural resource endowments to achieve rapid growth and a significant redistribution of income from the rich to the poor nations. The Organization of Petroleum Exporting Countries (OPEC) is the outstanding example. On the other hand, in many cases natural resources are owned or controlled by the multinational corporations of industrially advanced countries, with the economic benefits from these resources largely diverted abroad. Furthermore, world markets for many of the farm products and raw materials which the LDCs export are subject to great price fluctuations which contribute to instability in their economies.

Other LDCs simply lack mineral deposits, have little arable land, and have few sources of power. Also, the vast majority of the poor countries are in Central and South America, Africa, the Indian subcontinent, and Southeast Asia where tropical climates prevail. The hot, humid climate is not conducive to productive labor; human, crop, and livestock diseases are widespread; and weed and insect infestations plague agriculture.

In a very real sense a weak resource base can pose a particularly serious obstacle to growth. Real capital can be accumulated and the quality of the labor force improved through education and training. But the natural resource base is largely unaugmentable. Thus, it may be unrealistic for many of the LDCs to envision an economic destiny comparable with that of, say, the United States and Canada. But, again, we must be careful in generalizing: Switzerland, Israel, and Japan, for example, have achieved high levels of living *despite* restrictive natural resource bases.

Human Resources

Three statements describe many of the LDCs' circumstances with respect to human resources:

1   They are overpopulated.

2   Unemployment and underemployment are widespread.

3   Labor force productivity is low.

Overpopulation   As column 3 of Table 22-1 makes clear, many of the LDCs with the most meager natural and capital resources have the largest populations to support. Table 22-3 compares population densities and population growth rates of a few selected nations with those of the United States and the world as a whole. Most important for the long run is the vivid contrast of population growth rates: The middle- and low-income LDCs of Table 22-1 are now experiencing approximately a 2 percent annual increase in population compared with a 0.7 percent annual rate for advanced countries. Recalling the "rule of 70," the current rate suggests that the total population of the LDCs will double in about 35 years.

These simple statistics are a significant reason why the per capita income gap between the LDCs and the IACs has widened. In some of the less developed countries rapid population growth actually presses on the food supply to the extent that per capita food consumption is pulled down perilously close to the subsistence level. In the worst instances, only the despicable team of malnutrition and disease and the high death rate they engender keep incomes near subsistence.

It would seem at first glance that, since

$$\frac{\text{Per capita}}{\text{standard}} = \frac{\text{consumer goods (food) production}}{\text{population}}$$
$$\text{of living}$$

TABLE 22-3   Population statistics for selected countries

Country	Population per square mile, 1990	Annual rate of population increase, 1980–1990
United States	69	0.9%
Pakistan	369	3.0
Bangladesh	2,130	3.0
Venezuela	56	2.7
India	669	2.1
Haiti	573	1.2
Kenya	110	3.9
Philippines	570	2.6
World	101	1.7

Source: Statistical Abstract of the United States, 1991.

the standard of living could be raised merely by boosting consumer goods—particularly food—production. But in reality the problem is much more complex than this, because any increase in consumer goods production which initially raises the standard of living is likely to induce a population increase. This increase, if sufficient in size, will dissipate the improvement in living standards, and subsistence living levels will again prevail.

But why does population growth in LDCs accompany increases in output? First, the nation's *death* or *mortality rate* will decline with initial increases in production. This decline is the result of (1) a higher level of per capita food consumption, and (2) the basic medical and sanitation programs which almost invariably accompany the initial phases of economic development.

Second, the *birthrate* will remain high or may even increase, particularly as medical and sanitation programs cut infant mortality. The cliché that "the rich get richer and the poor get children" is uncomfortably accurate for many LDCs. In short, an increase in the per capita standard of living may lead to a population upsurge which will cease only when the standard of living has again been reduced to the level of bare subsistence.

In addition to the fact that rapid population growth can convert an expanding GDP into a stagnant or slow-growing GDP per capita, there are less obvious reasons why population expansion is an obstacle to development.

1 Large families reduce the capacity of households to save, and this inability restricts the economy's capacity to accumulate capital.

2 As population grows, more investment is required simply to maintain the amount of real capital per person. If investment fails to keep pace, each worker will have fewer tools and equipment, reducing worker productivity (output per worker). Declining productivity implies stagnating or declining per capita incomes.

3 Because most less developed countries are heavily dependent on agriculture, rapid population growth may result in overuse of limited natural resources such as land. The much-publicized African famines are partially the result of past overgrazing and overplanting of land caused by the pressing need to feed a growing population.

4 Finally, rapid population growth in the cities of the LDCs, accompanied by unprecedented flows of rural migrants, are generating massive urban problems.

Substandard housing in impoverished slums, deteriorating public services, congestion, pollution, and crime are all problems seriously exacerbated by rapid population growth. The resolution or amelioration of these difficulties necessitates a diversion of resources from growth-oriented uses.

Most authorities advocate birth control as the obvious and most effective means for breaking out of this dilemma. And breakthroughs in contraceptive technology in the past three or four decades have made this solution increasingly relevant. But the obstacles to population control are great. Low literacy rates make it difficult to disseminate information on contraceptive devices. In peasant agriculture, large families are a major source of labor. Furthermore, adults may look upon having many children as a kind of informal social security system; the more children one has, the greater the probability of having a relative to care for one during old age. Finally, many nations which stand to gain the most through birth control are often the least willing, for religious and sociocultural reasons, to embrace contraception programs. Population growth in Latin America, for example, is among the most rapid in the world.

China—with about one-fifth of the world's population—adopted a harsh "one-child" program in 1980. Under this program the government advocated late marriages and one child per family. Couples having more than one child are fined or lose various social benefits. Even though the rate of population growth has diminished under this program, China's population continues to expand at about 100 million per decade and its political leaders have publicly expressed doubt about the nation's ability to feed and house itself. India, the world's second most populous nation, experienced a 161 million or 23 percent population increase in the decade of the 1980s. With a total population of 850 million, India has 16 percent of the world's population but less than 2.5 percent of its land mass.

But not all less developed nations suffer from overpopulation, nor does a large population necessarily mean underdevelopment. The points to note are: (1) A large and rapidly growing population may pose a special obstacle to economic development; and (2) many of the LDCs are so burdened.

Unemployment and Underemployment Reliable unemployment statistics for the LDCs are not readily available. But observation suggests that unemployment and underemployment are both quite high in most LDCs. **Unemployment** occurs when someone who is willing and able to work cannot find a job. In contrast, **underemployment** occurs when workers are employed fewer hours or days per week than they desire, or work at jobs that do not fully use their skills.

Many economists contend that unemployment is high—perhaps as much as 15 to 20 percent—in the rapidly growing urban areas of the LDCs. Most less developed countries have experienced substantial migration of population from rural to urban areas. This migration is motivated by the *expectation* of finding jobs with higher wage rates than are available in agricultural and other rural employments. But this huge migration makes it unlikely that a migrant will in fact obtain a job. Migration to the cities has greatly exceeded the growth of urban job opportunities, resulting in very high urban unemployment rates. Thus, rapid rural-urban migration has given rise to urban unemployment rates which are two or three times as great as rural rates.

Underemployment is widespread and endemic to most LDCs. In many LDCs rural agricultural labor may be so abundant relative to capital and natural resources that a significant percentage of this labor contributes little or nothing to agricultural output. Similarly, many LDC workers are self-employed as proprietors of small shops, in handicrafts, or as street vendors. A lack of demand means that small shop owners or vendors spend more time in idleness in the shop or on the street. While they are not without jobs, they are underemployed.

Low Labor Productivity   Labor productivity tends to be very low in most LDCs. As we will see, the LDCs have found it difficult to invest in *physical capital*. As a result, their workers are underequipped with machinery and tools and are relatively unproductive.

In addition, most poor countries have not been able to invest sufficiently in their *human capital* (Table 22-2, columns 4 and 5); that is, expenditures on health and education have been meager. Low levels of literacy, malnutrition, absence of proper medical care, and insufficient educational facilities all contribute to populations ill equipped for economic development and industrialization.

Particularly vital is the absence of a vigorous entrepreneurial class willing to bear risks, accumulate capital, and provide the organizational requisites essential to economic growth. Closely related is the dearth of labor prepared to handle the routine supervisory functions basic to any program of development. Ironically, the higher education systems of many LDCs are oriented heavily toward the humanities and offer little work in business, engineering, and the sciences.

An additional irony is that, while migration from the LDCs has modestly offset rapid population growth, it has also deprived some LDCs of highly productive workers. Often the best-trained and most highly motivated workers—physicians, engineers, teachers, and nurses—leave the LDCs to seek their fortunes in the IACs. This so-called **brain drain** contributes to the deterioration in the overall skill level and productivity of the labor force.

Capital Accumulation

An important focal point of economic development is the accumulation of capital goods. There are several reasons for this emphasis on capital formation:

1   All LDCs suffer from a critical shortage of capital goods—factories, machinery and equipment, public utilities, and so forth. Better-equipped labor forces would greatly enhance their productivity and help boost the per capita standard of living. As we found in Chapter 19, there is a close relationship between output per worker (labor productivity) and real income per worker. A nation must produce more goods and services per worker to enjoy more goods and services per worker as income. One basic means of increasing labor productivity is to provide each worker with more tools and equipment. Indeed, empirical studies for the LDCs confirm a significant positive relationship between investment and the growth of GDP. On the average a 1 percentage point increase in the ratio of investment to GDP raises the overall growth rate by about one-tenth of 1 percentage point. Thus an increase in the investment-to-GDP ratio from 10 to 15 percent would increase the growth of real GDP by one-half of 1 percentage point.[3]

2   Increasing the stock of capital goods is crucial because of the very limited possibility of increasing the supply of arable land. If there is little likelihood of increasing agricultural output by increasing the supply of land, an alternative is to use more and better capital equipment with the available agricultural work force.

3   Once initiated, the process of capital accumulation *may* be cumulative. If capital accumulation can increase output ahead of population growth, a margin of saving may arise which permits further capital formation. In a sense, capital accumulation can feed on itself.

Let's first consider the prospects for less developed nations to accumulate capital domestically. Then

[3]International Monetary Fund, *World Economic Outlook* (Washington, D.C., 1988), p. 76.

we will examine the possibility of foreign capital flowing into them.

Domestic Capital Formation A less developed nation—or any nation for that matter—accumulates capital through the processes of saving and investing. A nation must save or, in other words, refrain from consumption, to release resources from consumer goods production. Investment spending must then occur to absorb these released resources in the production of capital goods. But impediments to saving and investing are much greater in a low-income nation that in an advanced economy.

Savings Potential Consider first the savings side of the picture. The situation here is mixed and varies greatly between countries. Some of the very poor countries such as Ethiopia, Bangladesh, Uganda, Haiti, and Madagascar save only from 2 to 5 percent of their domestic outputs. They simply are too poor to save a significant portion of their incomes. Interestingly, however, other less developed countries save as large a percentage of their domestic outputs as do advanced industrial countries. In 1989 India and China saved 21 and 36 percent of their domestic outputs, respectively, compared to 33 percent for Japan, 27 percent for West Germany, and 13 percent for the United States. The problem is that the domestic outputs of the LDCs are so low that even when saving rates are comparable to advanced nations, the total absolute volume of saving is not large. As we will see, foreign capital inflows and foreign aid are means of supplementing domestic saving.

Capital Flight Many of the LDCs have experienced a substantial **capital flight.** Citizens of the LDCs have transferred their savings to, or invested their savings in, the IACs. The primary reason is that citizens of many LDCs regard the risks of investing at home to be high compared to the industrially advanced nations. These risks include loss of savings or real capital due to government expropriation, taxation, higher rates of inflation, or changes in exchange rates. If an LDC's political climate is volatile, savers may shift their funds overseas to a "save haven" in fear that a new government might confiscate their wealth. Likewise, rapid or galloping inflation in an LDC would have similar confiscatory effects (Chapter 8). The transfer of savings overseas may also be a means of evading domestic taxes on interest income or capital gains. Finally, financial capital may flow to the IACs because of higher interest rates or simply because of the greater variety of investment opportunities available in the industrialized countries.

Whatever the motivation, research studies suggest that capital flight from the LDCs is quantitatively significant. One estimate suggested that the five largest Latin American debtors had capital outflows of $101 billion of private assets between 1979 and 1984. At the end of 1987 Mexicans are estimated to have held some $84 billion in assets abroad. Foreign asset holdings for Venezuelans, Argentinians, and Brazilians were $58, $46, and $31 billion respectively. The critical point is that a significant portion of capital lending by the IACs to the LDCs is offset by LDC capital flights to the industrially advanced nations. The World Bank estimates that the inflows of foreign aid and loans to Latin America were essentially negated by corresponding capital flight in the 1980s.

Investment Obstacles The investment side of the capital formation process abounds with equally serious obstacles. These obstacles undermine the rate of capital formation even when a sufficient volume of saving is available to finance the needed investment. Major obstacles to investment fall into two categories: lack of investors and lack of incentives to invest.

Oddly enough, in some less developed countries the major obstacle to investment is basically the lack of business executives willing to assume the risks associated with investment. This, of course, is a special case of qualitative deficiencies of the labor force previously discussed.

But even if substantial savings and a vigorous entrepeneurial class are present, an essential ingredient in capital formation—the incentive to invest—may be weak. A host of factors may combine in an LDC to cripple investment incentives. Indeed, we have just mentioned such factors as political instability and higher rates of inflation in our discussion of capital flight. Similarly, very low incomes mean a limited domestic market—a lack of demand—for most nonagricultural goods. This factor is especially crucial when one recognizes that the chances of successfully competing with mature industries of advanced nations in international markets are meager. Then, too, the previously cited lack of trained administrative and operating personnel may be a vital factor in retarding investment. Finally, many LDCs simply do not have an adequate **infrastructure,** that is, the public capital goods, which are prerequisite to private investment of a productive nature. Poor roads and bridges, inadequate railways, little gas and electricity production, antiquated communications, unsatisfactory housing, and meager educational and public health facilities scarcely provide an inviting environment for investment spending.

The absence of an adequate infrastructure presents more of a problem than one might first surmise. The dearth of public capital goods means that a great deal of investment spending which does not *directly* result in the production of goods and which may not be capable of bearing profits must take place before, and simultaneously with, productive investment in manufacturing machinery and equipment. Statistics for advanced nations indicate that about 60 percent of gross investment goes for housing, public works, and public utilities, leaving about 40 percent for directly productive investment in manufacturing, agriculture, and commerce.[4] These figures probably understate the percentage of total investment which must be devoted to infrastructure in emerging nations. The volume of investment required to initiate economic development may be much greater than it first appears.

One potential bright spot in this picture is the possibility of accumulating capital through *in-kind* or **nonfinancial investment.** Given leadership and willingness to cooperate, capital can be accumulated by transferring surplus agricultural labor to improvement of agricultural facilities or the infrastructure. If each agricultural village allocated its surplus labor to the construction of irrigation canals, wells, schools, sanitary facilities, and roads, significant amounts of capital might be accumulated at no significant sacrifice of consumer goods production. Nonfinancial investment simply bypasses the problems inherent in the financial aspects of the capital accumulation process. Such investment does not require consumers to save portions of their money income, nor does it presume the presence of an entrepreneurial class anxious to invest. In short, when leadership and cooperative spirit are present, nonfinancial investment is a promising avenue for accumulation of basic capital goods.

Technological Advance

Technological advance and capital formation are frequently part of the same process. Yet, there are advantages in treating technological advance—the discovery and application of new methods of producing—and capital formation, or the accumulating of capital goods, as separate processes.

[4]W. Arthur Lewis, *The Theory of Economic Growth* (Homewood, Ill.: Richard D. Irwin, Inc., 1955), p. 210.

The rudimentary state of technology in the LDCs puts these nations far from the frontiers of technological advance. There already exists an enormous body of technological knowledge accumulated by advanced nations which less developed countries *might* adopt and apply without undertaking expensive research. Adopting modern crop-rotation practices and contour plowing require no additional capital equipment, and may contribute significantly to productivity. By raising grain storage bins a few inches above ground, a large amount of grain spoilage can be avoided. Such changes may sound trivial to people of advanced nations. However, resulting gains in productivity can mean the difference between subsistence and starvation in some poverty-ridden nations.

In most instances application of either existing or new technological knowledge involves use of new and different capital goods. But, within limits, this capital can be obtained without an increase in the rate of capital formation. If the annual flow of replacement investment is rechanneled from technologically inferior to technologically superior capital equipment, productivity can be increased out of a constant level of investment spending. Actually, some technological advances may be **capital-saving** rather than **capital-using.** A new fertilizer, better adapted to a nation's topography and climate, might be cheaper than that currently employed. A seemingly high-priced metal plow which will last ten years may be cheaper in the long run than an inexpensive but technologically inferior wooden plow which requires annual replacement.

To what extent have LDCs transferred and effectively used available IAC technological knowledge? The picture is mixed. There can be no doubt that such technological borrowing has been instrumental in the rapid growth of such Pacific Rim countries as Japan, South Korea, Taiwan, and Singapore. Similarly, the OPEC nations benefited greatly from IAC knowledge of oil exploration, production, and refining. Recently the former Soviet Union and other eastern European nations are seeking western technology to revitalize their faltering economies.

At the same time, we must be realistic about the transferability of advanced technologies to less developed countries. In industrially advanced nations technologies are usually predicated on relatively scarce, highly skilled labor and relatively abundant capital. Such technologies tend to be capital-using or, alternatively stated, labor-saving. In contrast, less developed economies require technologies appropriate to *their* resource endowments or, in other words, to large quantities of abundant, unskilled labor and very limited quantities of capital goods. Labor-using and capital-saving technologies are typically appropriate to LDCs. Much of the highly advanced technology of advanced nations is therefore inappropriate in the less developed countries; they must develop their own technologies. Recall, too, that many less developed nations have "traditional economies" (Chapter 2) and are not highly receptive to change. This is particularly true in peasant agriculture which dominates the economies of most LDCs. A potential technological advance which fails can mean hunger and malnutrition; therefore, there is a strong propensity to retain traditional production techniques.

Sociocultural and Institutional Factors

Purely economic considerations are not sufficient to explain the occurrence or absence of economic growth. Substantial social and institutional readjustments are usually an integral part of the growth process. Economic development means not only changes in a nation's physical environment (new transportation and communications facilities, new schools, new housing, new plants and equipment), but also drastic changes in the ways people think, behave, and associate with one another. Emancipation from custom and tradition is frequently a fundamental prerequisite of economic development. A potentially critical but intangible ingredient in economic development is **the will to develop.** Economic growth may hinge on "what individuals and social groups *want,* and *whether they want it badly enough to change their old ways of doing things* and to work hard at installing the new."[5]

Sociocultural Obstacles Sociocultural impediments to growth are numerous and varied.
1   Some of the least developed countries have failed to achieve the preconditions for a national economic unit. Tribal allegiances take precedence over national identity. Warring tribes confine all economic activity within the tribe, eliminating any possibility for production-increasing specialization and trade.
2   Religious beliefs and observances may seriously restrict the length of the workday and divert resources which might have been used for investment to ceremonial uses. In rural India total ceremonial expenditures

are estimated at about 7 percent of per capita income.[6] Generally, religious and philosophical beliefs may be dominated by the **capricious universe view,** that is, the notion that there is little or no correlation between an individual's activities and endeavors, on the one hand, and the outcomes or experiences which that person encounters, on the other.

> If the universe is deemed capricious, the individual will learn to expect little or no correlation between actions and results. This will result in a fatalistic attitude. . . .
>   These attitudes impinge on all activities including saving, investment, long-range perspective, supply of effort, and family planning. If a higher standard of living and amassing of wealth is treated as the result of providence rather than springing from hard work and saving, there is little rationale for saving, hard work, innovations, and enterprise.[7]

3   The existence of a caste system—formal or informal—causes labor to be allocated to occupations on the basis of caste or tradition rather than on the basis of skill or merit. The result is clearly a misallocation of human resources.

Institutional Obstacles Political corruption and bribery are commonplace in many LDCs. School systems and public service agencies are often ineptly administered and their functioning impaired by petty politics. Tax systems are frequently arbitrary, unjust, cumbersome, and detrimental to incentives to work and invest. Political decisions are often motivated by a desire to enhance the nation's international prestige, rather than to foster development. For example, India's explosion of a nuclear bomb in 1974 created a substantial controversy over societal priorities.
    Because of the predominance of farming in LDCs, the problem of achieving that institutional environment in agriculture most conducive to increasing production must be a vital consideration in any growth program. Specifically, the institutional problem of **land reform** demands attention in virtually all LDCs. But needed reform may vary tremendously between specific nations. In some LDCs the problem is excessive concentration of land ownership in the hands of a few wealthy families. This situation is demoralizing for tenants,

[5]Eugene Staley, *The Future of Underdeveloped Countries,* rev. ed. (New York: Frederick A. Praeger, 1961), p. 218.

[6]Inder P. Nijhawan, "Socio-Political Institutions, Cultural Values, and Attitudes: Their Impact on Indian Economic Development," in J. S. Uppal (ed.), *India's Economic Problems* (New Delhi: Tata McGraw-Hill Publishing Company, Ltd., 1975), p. 31.
[7]Ibid., p. 33.

weakening their incentive to produce, and is typically not conducive to capital improvements. At the other extreme is the absurd arrangement whereby each family owns and farms a minute fragment of land far too small for the application of modern agricultural technology. An important complication to the problem of land reform lies in the fact that political considerations sometimes push reform in that direction which is least defensible on economic grounds. For many nations, land reform may well be the most acute institutional problem to be resolved in initiating the process of economic development.

Examples: Land reform in South Korea undermined the political control of the landed aristocracy and made way for the development of strong commercial and industrial middle classes, all to the benefit of the country's economic development. In contrast, the prolonged dominance of the landed aristocracy in the Philippines has helped stifle the development of that economy.[8]

QUICK REVIEW 22-1

♦ *About three-fourths of the world's population lives in the LDCs of Africa, Asia, and Latin America.*

♦ *Natural resource scarcities and inhospitable climates restrict growth in many LDCs.*

♦ *The LDCs are characterized by overpopulation, high unemployment rates, underemployment, and low labor productivity.*

♦ *Low saving rates, capital flight, weak infrastructures, and lack of investors impair capital accumulation.*

♦ *Sociocultural and institutional factors are often serious impediments to growth.*

THE VICIOUS CIRCLE: A SUMMING UP

Many of the characteristics of LDCs just described are simultaneously causes and consequences of their poverty. These countries are caught in a **vicious circle of poverty.** They *stay* poor because they *are* poor! Consider Figure 22-1. The fundamental feature of an LDC is low per capita income. Being poor, a family has little ability or incentive to save. Furthermore, low incomes mean low levels of demand. Thus, there are few avail-

[8]Mrinal Datta-Chaudhuri, "Market Failure and Government Failure," *Journal of Economic Perspectives,* Summer, 1990, p. 36

able resources, on the one hand, and no strong incentives, on the other, for investment in physical or human capital. This means labor productivity is low. And, since output per person is real income per person, it follows that per capita income is low.

Many experts feel that the key to breaking out of this vicious circle is to increase the rate of capital accumulation, to achieve a level of investment of, say, 10 percent of the national income. But Figure 22-1 reminds us that the real villain for many LDCs—rapid population growth—may be waiting in the wings to undo the potentially beneficial effects of this higher rate of capital accumulation. For example, using hypothetical figures, suppose that initially an LDC is realizing no growth in its real GDP. But now it somehow manages to increase its saving and investment to 10 percent of its GDP. As a result, its real GDP begins to grow at, say, 2.5 percent per year. Given a stable population, real GDP per capita will also grow at 2.5 percent per year. If this persists, the standard of living will *double* in about 28 years. But what if population grows at the Latin American rate of 2.5 percent per year? Then real income per person is unchanged and the vicious circle persists.

More optimistically, *if* population can be kept constant or constrained to some growth rate significantly below 2.5 percent, then real income per person will rise. This implies the possibility of still further enlargement in the flows of saving and investment, continued advances in productivity, and the continued growth of per capita real income. In short, if a process of self-sustaining expansion of income, saving, investment, and productivity can be achieved, the self-perpetuating vicious circle of poverty can be transformed into a self-regenerating, beneficent circle of economic progress. The trick is to make effective those policies and strategies which will accomplish this transition.

ROLE OF GOVERNMENT

Economists do not agree on the appropriate role of government in seeking economic growth.

A Positive Role

One view is that, at least during initial stages of development, government should play a major role. The reasons for this stem in large part from the character of the obstacles facing LDCs.

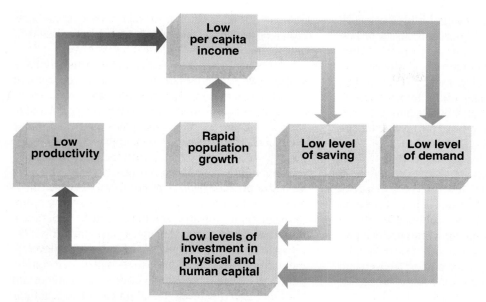

FIGURE 22-1   The vicious circle of poverty

Low per capita incomes make it extremely difficult for poor nations to save and invest, a condition that perpetuates low productivity and low incomes. Furthermore, rapid population growth may quickly absorb increases in per capita real income and thereby may negate the possibility of breaking out of the poverty circle.

1 Law and Order Some of the poorest countries are plagued by widespread banditry and intertribal warfare which divert both attention and resources from the task of development. A strong and stable national government is needed to establish domestic law and order and to achieve peace and unity.

2 Lack of Entrepreneurship The absence of a sizable and vigorous entrepreneurial class, ready and willing to accumulate capital and initiate production, indicates than in many cases private enterprise is intrinsically not capable of spearheading the growth process.

3 Infrastructure Many obstacles to economic growth center on deficiencies of public goods and services, or, in other words, an inadequate infrastructure. Sanitation and basic medical programs, education, irrigation and soil conservation projects, and construction of highways and transportation-communication facilities are all essentially nonmarketable goods and services yielding widespread spillover benefits. Government is the sole institution in a position to provide these goods and services in required quantities.

4 Forced Saving and Investment Government action may also be required to break through the saving-investment dilemma which impedes capital formation in LDCs.

It may well be that only governmental fiscal action can provide a solution by forcing the economy to accumulate capital. There are two alternatives. One is to force the economy to save by increasing taxes. These tax revenues can then be channeled into priority investment projects. The problems of honestly and efficiently administering the tax system and achieving a relatively high degree of compliance with tax laws are frequently very great.

The other alternative is to force the economy to save through inflation. Government can finance capital accumulation by creating and spending new money or by selling bonds to banks and spending the proceeds. The resulting inflation is the equivalent of an arbitrary tax on the economy.

There are serious arguments against the advisability of saving through inflation. In the first place, inflation tends to distort the composition of investment away from productive facilities to such items as luxury housing, precious metals and jewels, or foreign securities, which provide a better hedge against rising prices. Furthermore, significant inflation may reduce voluntary private saving as potential savers become less willing to accumulate depreciating money or securities payable in money of declining value. Internationally, inflation may boost the nation's imports and retard its flow of exports, creating balance of payments difficulties.

5 Social-Institutional Problems Government is in the key position to deal effectively with the social-institutional obstacles to growth. Controlling population growth and land reform are basic problems which call for the broad approach that only government can provide. And government is in a position to stimulate the will to develop, to change a philosophy of "Heaven and faith will determine the course of events" to one of "God helps those who help themselves."

Public Sector Problems

But serious problems and disadvantages may exist with a governmentally directed development program. If entrepreneurial talent is lacking in the private sector, can we expect leaders of quality to be present in the ranks of government? Is there not a real danger that government bureaucracy will impede, not stimulate, much-needed social and economic change? And what of the tendency of centralized economic planning to favor spectacular "showpiece" projects at the expense of less showy but more productive programs? Might not political objectives take precedence over the economic goals of a governmentally directed development program?

Development experts are significantly less enthusiastic about the potential role of government in the growth process than they were twenty-five or thirty years ago. Government maladministration and corruption are commonplace in many LDCs. Government officials often line their own pockets with foreign aid funds. Similarly, political leaders frequently confer monopoly privileges on relatives, friends, and political supporters. A political leader may grant exclusive rights to relatives or friends to produce, import, or export certain products. These monopoly privileges lead to higher domestic prices for the relevant products and diminish the LDC's ability to compete in world markets. Similarly, managers of state-owned enterprises are often appointed on the basis of cronyism rather than competence. In recent years the perception of

government has shifted from that of catalyst and promoter of growth to that of a potential impediment to development.

Once again it is possible to muster casual evidence on both sides of this question. Positive government contributions to development are evident in the cases of Japan, South Korea, and Taiwan. In comparison, Mobutu's Zaire, Marcos' Philippines, and Haiti under the Duvaliers are recognized examples of corrupt and inept governments which functioned as substantial impediments to economic progress. Certainly the revolutionary transformations of the former Soviet Union and other eastern European nations away from communism and toward market-oriented economies make it clear that central planning is no longer widely recognized as an effective mechanism for development. Most LDCs have come to recognize that competition and individual economic incentives are important ingredients in the development process, and that their citizens need to see direct personal gains from their efforts to motivate them to take actions which will expand production.

ROLE OF THE ADVANCED NATIONS

What are the ways by which industrially advanced nations can help less developed countries in their quest for growth? To what degree have these avenues of assistance been pursued?

Generally, less developed nations can benefit from (1) an expanding volume of trade with advanced nations; (2) foreign aid in the form of grants and loans from governments of advanced nations; and (3) flows of private capital from more affluent nations. Let's consider these possibilities in the order stated.

Expanding Trade

Some authorities maintain that the simplest and most effective means by which the United States and other industrially advanced nations can aid less developed nations is by lowering international trade barriers, enabling LDCs to expand their national incomes through increased trade.

Though there is some truth in this view, lowered trade barriers are not a panacea. It is true that some poor nations need only large foreign markets for their raw materials to achieve growth. But the problem for many is not that of obtaining markets for utilizing existing productive capacity or the sale of relatively abundant raw materials, but the more fundamental one of getting the capital and technical assistance needed to produce something for export.

Furthermore, close trade ties with advanced nations are not without disadvantages. The old quip, "When Uncle Sam gets his feet wet, the rest of the world gets pneumonia," contains considerable truth for many less developed nations. A recession among the IACs can have disastrous consequences for the prices of raw materials and the export earnings of the LDCs. For example, in mid-1974 copper was $1.52 per pound; by the end of 1975 it had fallen to $.53 per pound! Stability and growth in industrially advanced nations are clearly important to progress in less developed countries.

Foreign Aid: Public Loans and Grants

Our vicious circle of poverty emphasizes the importance of capital accumulation in achieving economic growth. Foreign capital—both public and private—can be used to supplement an emerging country's saving and investment efforts and play a crucial role in breaking the circle of poverty.

As noted earlier, most LDCs have inadequate infrastructures. They are sadly lacking in basic public goods—irrigation and public health programs and educational, transportation, and communications systems—prerequisites to attracting either domestic or foreign private capital. Foreign public aid is needed to tear down this major roadblock to the flow of private capital to the LDCs.

Direct Aid The United States and other IACs have assisted LDCs directly through a variety of programs and through participating in international institutions designed to stimulate economic development. Over the 1976–1989 period. American aid to the LDCs—including both loans and grants—averaged $10 billion per year. In 1992 American aid was almost $15 billion. The bulk of this aid is administered by our Agency for International Development (AID). Some, however, takes the form of grants of surplus food under the Food for Peace program. Other advanced nations have also embarked on substantial foreign aid programs. In 1989 foreign aid from all industrially advanced nations was about $47 billion. In addition, the OPEC nations donated almost $2.5 billion.

The aid programs of the IACs merit several additional comments. First, aid is typically distributed on the basis of political and military, rather than economic,

considerations. Israel, Turkey, and Greece are major recipients of American aid at the potential expense of Asian, Latin American, and African nations with much lower standards of living. Second, aid from the IACs only amounts to about one-third of 1 percent of the IACs' collective GDPs. Finally, LDCs are increasingly concerned that the shift of the former Soviet Union and eastern Europe toward more democratic, market-oriented systems will make these nations "new players" in the foreign aid field. The LDCs worry that IAC aid which formerly flowed to Latin America, Asia, and Africa may be partially redirected to, say, Poland, Hungary, and Russia.

The World Bank Group The United States is a major participant in the **World Bank,** whose major objective is assisting LDCs in achieving growth. Supported by some 159 member nations, the World Bank not only lends out of its capital funds, but also (1) sells bonds and lends the proceeds, and (2) guarantees and insures private loans.

Several characteristics of the World Bank merit comment.

1 The World Bank is a "last resort" lending agency; its loans are limited to productive projects for which private funds are not readily available.

2 Because many World Bank loans have been for basic development projects—multipurpose dams, irrigation projects, health and sanitation programs, communications and transportation facilities—it has been hoped that the Bank's activities will provide the infrastructure prerequisite to substantial flows of private capital.

3 The Bank has played a significant role in providing technical assistance to the LDCs by helping them discover what avenues of growth seem most appropriate for their economic development.

Two World Bank affiliates function in areas where the World Bank has been weak. The *International Finance Corporation (IFC)* has the primary function of investing in *private* enterprises in the LDCs. The *International Development Association (IDA)* makes "soft loans"—loans which may not be self-liquidating—to the poorest of the LDCs on more liberal terms than does the World Bank.

Private Capital Flows

The LDCs have also received substantial flows of private capital from the IACs. These private investors for the most part are large corporations and commercial banks. General Motors or Chrysler might finance construction of a plant in Mexico or Brazil to assemble autos or produce auto parts. Or Citicorp or Bank of America may make loans to the governments of Argentina or the Philippines.

Although these private capital flows were relatively modest in the 1950s and 1960s—ranging from $2 to $4 billion per year—they grew dramatically in the 1970s. Specifically, average annual private flows of capital to the LDCs in the decade of the 1970s was $28 billion. Then in the early 1980s an LDC debt crisis developed and since then private capital flows to the poor nations have fallen precipitously.

THE LDC DEBT CRISIS

What is the magnitude of LDC debt? What are its causes? And effects? What, if anything, might be done to resolve the debt problem?

The Debt and Its Growth

The external debt (that is, debts owed to foreign governments and foreign financial institutions) of the LDCs has grown tremendously in the past two decades. Figure 22-2 portrays the external debt growth of those LDCs which have had debt-servicing difficulties. Debt owed to foreign governments is shown in green and debt owed to foreign private lenders is in orange. The total debts exceeds $800 billion. If the debts of other LDCs not experiencing repayment difficulties were added, aggregate LDC debt in 1992 would be $1,530 billion. This latter figure is equal to about 26 percent of the aggregated gross national products of the LDCs. Table 22-4 lists some of the heavily indebted LDCs and indicates both the absolute amount of their external debts and the size of these debts in comparison to their GNPs.

Causes of the Crisis

We have noted that private capital flows—particularly from large IAC commercial banks—increased greatly in the 1970s. But in the 1970s and early 1980s a series of converging world economic events had serious adverse effects on the LDCs and precipitated a debt crisis.
1 The dramatic runup of oil prices by OPEC in 1973–1974 and again in 1979–1980 (raising the price of a

FIGURE 22-2 **The external debt of LDCs with debt-servicing difficulties, 1970–1992**

The external debt of LDCs to both foreign governments (in green) and foreign private financial institutions (in orange) has grown significantly over the past two decades. [Source: International Monetary Fund, *World Economic Outlook: October 1991* (Washington, D.C., 1991), p. 24. Data for 1991 and 1992 are IMF estimates.]

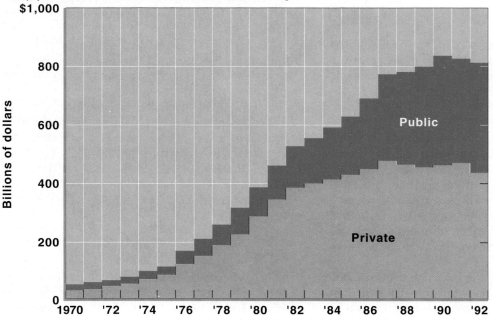

TABLE 22-4 Selected heavily indebted LDCs, 1989

Country	Total external debt (billions of dollars)	External debt as a percentage of GNP
Brazil	$111	35%
Mexico	96	48
Argentina	65	123
India	63	27
Indonesia	53	56
Venezuela	33	75
Nigeria	33	114
Philippines	29	66
Thailand	23	32
Chile	18	72
Colombia	17	44

Source: The World Bank, *World Development Report, 1991* (New York: Oxford University Press, 1991), pp. 244–245 and 250–251.

barrel of oil from about $2.50 to $35) greatly increased the energy bills of the oil-importing LDCs. Oil-importing LDCs were faced with growing current account deficits in their balance of payments which were financed largely by increased borrowing. Hence, the external debt of oil-importing LDCs grew from $130 billion in 1973 to $700 billion by 1982. Borrowed funds which could have been used for development were instead used to pay higher energy costs.

2   In the early 1980s the IACs—and the United States in particular—invoked strong anti-inflationary monetary policies. These tight money policies triggered two adverse effects for the LDCs. On the one hand, growth of IAC national incomes slowed; indeed, in 1980–1982 the United States suffered its most serious postwar recession. As a result, IAC demands for the raw material and farm product exports of LDCs declined. This meant sharp reductions in the export earnings which the LDCs needed to pay interest and principal on their debts. On the other hand, tight money policies in the IACs resulted in substantially higher interest rates. This greatly increased the cost to the LDCs in servicing their debts.

3   The burden of LDC debt rose for still another reason. Over the 1981–1984 period the international value of the dollar appreciated. This meant that LDCs now had to pay more for their imports of American manufactured goods. And, because much LDC debt is denominated in dollars, it also meant that LDCs would have to export a larger amount of goods to acquire each dollar needed to pay interest and principal on their debts.

4   Finally, in 1982 Mexico was on the verge of defaulting on its debt. Creditors were forced to reschedule that debt and make further loans to Mexico. This Mexican debt crisis precipitated an abrupt loss of confidence in the creditworthiness of many highly indebted LDCs. As a result, private voluntary lending to LDCs declined sharply. This was complicated by the fact that the United States was incurring very large Federal budget deficits during the 1980s (Chapter 18). The sale of United States government bonds to finance these deficits absorbed a significant portion of the world's financial capital which might otherwise have been available to LDCs.

In short, higher prices on imported oil, declines in LDC export earnings, higher interest rates, appreciation of the dollar, and declines in recent private lending to the LDCs all combined to create a debt crisis. By 1982 and 1983 many LDCs were unable to make scheduled payments on their external debts.

Economic Consequences

There followed a period of "muddling through" during which creditor nations in cooperation with the International Monetary Fund attempted to deal with the LDC debt crisis on a nation-by-nation basis. The debts of many LDCs were rescheduled (stretched out over a longer period of time) to reduce the burden of annual interest and principal payments. In return for these concessions the LDCs had to agree to domestic austerity programs to improve their prospects for debt repayment. This typically meant that LDCs had to reduce their imports and increase their exports to realize more international trade earnings for debt repayment. But increased exports and reduced imports clearly imply a further impairment of living standards in the LDCs. Similarly, with net export earnings being used primarily for debt retirement little or nothing is left to invest in development projects. It is not by chance that, while the growth of real GDP for the LDCs as a group was 3.8 percent per year over the 1980–1989 period, the rate for highly indebted LDCs was only 1.9 percent.

The debt crisis has also had adverse repercussions in the IACs. IAC commercial banks have been forced to write off some LDC debt as uncollectible. For example, in mid-1987 Citicorp increased its bad-debt reserves by $3 billion in recognition that as much as 25 percent of its loans to LDCs would not be repaid. Some experts fear that LDC debt is a potential threat to the banking and financial systems of the IACs.

Solutions?

What, if anything, can be done to alleviate or correct the lingering LDC debt crisis? There seem to be two general routes to follow in seeking a solution.

One is to continue the piecemeal, country-by-country approach followed since 1982. The problem with this approach is that it may go on for decades, and, as it does, continue to thwart the possibilities that the highly indebted LDCs will achieve significant growth.

The other option is debt relief. The IACs might simply forgive a significant portion of outstanding LDC debt. There are several problems with this solution. First and most obviously, the forgiving of private debt imposes costs upon the lending commercial banks and their stockholders. The forgiving of public debt imposes costs on American and other IAC taxpayers. Second, any significant "write-down" of the debt will undoubtedly have a highly adverse effect on new private lending to LDCs. It is unrealistic to expect creditors to take large losses and then turn around and extend new loans. On the borrowing side, the problem is that debt forgiveness may be an invitation for LDCs to default on debts incurred in the future. Obviously, no easy solution to the debt issue presents itself.

QUICK REVIEW 22-2

∮ **LDC governments may encourage growth by a providing law and order; b engaging in entrepreneurial activities; c improving the infrastructure; d forcing higher levels of saving and investing; and e resolving social-institutional problems.**

∮ **The IACs can assist the LDCs through expanded trade, foreign aid, and private capital flows.**

∮ **Many LDCs have huge external debts which have become an additional obstacle to growth.**

TOWARD A "NEW INTERNATIONAL ECONOMIC ORDER"?[9]

Despite flows of private investment and foreign aid, the LDCs are far from content with their relationships with industrially advanced nations. As noted earlier, the ab-

solute income gap between IACs and LDCs has widened over time. Furthermore, despite achieving political independence, LDCs feel that an economic-based **neocolonialism** persists. Both private investment and public aid, it is contended, have tended to exploit LDCs and keep them dependent upon, and subservient to, rich nations. In the past decade or so the LDCs have pressed more aggressively for basic changes in the international economic order which would accelerate their growth and redistribute world income to their benefit. In arguing for the creation of a **New International Economic Order (NIEO),** spokesmen for the LDCs make the following arguments and proposals.

1 Rules of the Game Although they represent the vast majority of the world's population, LDCs have less than one-third of the total votes in the key international institutions which formulate the overall character of the world economy. Indeed, LDCs were simply not involved in the creation of the post-World War II institutions and programs which establish the rules and regulations by which international trade, finance, and investment are conducted. For example, the industrially advanced nations control the International Monetary Fund which provides monetary reserves for the financing of international trade. The LDCs question the equity and legitimacy of these rules and argue that the institutions and programs of the existing economic order are stacked against them.

2 Trade Barriers Poor nations contend that, rhetoric to the contrary, advanced nations have retarded their development by using a variety of trade barriers—for example, tariffs and import quotas—to deprive them of export markets. The LDCs feel they are in a "Catch-22" situation. If they effectively use the financial and technical aid provided by advanced nations to create efficient low-cost manufacturing industries, the LDCs then become competitive with industries in the advanced nations. The IACs respond to this situation by using trade barriers to protect their domestic industries from the new competition. The LDCs have argued for **preferential tariff treatment**—that is, lower tariffs than those paid by developed countries—to stimulate their industrial growth.

---

[9]This section draws on Edwin P. Reubens, ed., *The Challenge of the New International Economic Order* (Boulder, Colo.: Westview Press, 1981), chap. 1; and Todaro, op. cit., pp. 559–565. For a detailed statement on the NIEO, see Mahbub ul Haq, *The Third World and the*

International Economic Order (Washington: Overseas Development Council, 1976). The term "New International Economic Order" arose from a 1974 United Nations declaration on the problem of economic development.

3 Exploitation and Dependence The LDCs also contend that most of the contracts, leases, and concessions which multinational corporations of advanced countries have negotiated with them have benefited the multinationals at the expense of the host countries. The poor countries argue that the major portion of benefits from the exploitation of their natural resources accrues to others. Furthermore, LDCs seek to achieve greater diversification and therefore greater stability in their economies. Foreign private capital, however, seeks out those industries which are currently the most profitable, that is, the ones now producing for the export market. In brief, while LDCs strive for less dependence on world markets, flows of foreign private capital often enhance that dependence. Exxon, Alcoa, United Fruit, and the rest are after profits and allegedly have no particular interest in either the economic independence, diversification, or overall progress of the LDCs.

4 Terms of Trade As exporters of raw materials (bauxite, tin, copper, manganese) and basic farm products (cocoa, coffee, cotton, rubber, tea, timber), the LDCs are greatly affected by the extreme price fluctuations which characterize these highly competitive markets. In particular, the high variability of their import earnings makes it very difficult for LDCs to plan and finance development programs. Worse yet, the long-run price trend of LDC commodity exports has been downward. On the other hand, the LDCs import manufactured goods produced by the corporate giants of the advanced nations which have the market power to charge high prices. Thus the LDCs argue that over time the **terms of trade** have shifted against them; the prices of their exports tend to be depressed while the prices of their imports tend to rise. Hence, it takes more of the LDCs' exports to purchase a given quantity of imports.

The poor countries have pushed two proposals designed to relieve this alleged inequality. First, they seek establishment of a **stabilization fund** for some twenty basic food and raw material exports of major importance to them. The fund would be used to buy each of these various products when its world price fell and, conversely, to sell those products when world prices rose. Thus, prices would tend to be stabilized. The second proposal involves *indexing*. That is, LDCs want to tie the prices of their commodity exports to the prices they must pay for their imports from the IACs to maintain the purchasing power of their exports.

5 Debt Relief The LDCs have also sought debt relief. Their view is that the present debt is so large that it constitutes a severe obstacle to LDC growth. Arguing that the prosperity of the IACs depends on the prosperity of the LDCs, LDCs feel that forgiving some portion of the debt would be mutually beneficial. Thus, in the fall of 1987 some twenty-four LDC governments sought both debt relief and additional loans at the annual joint meeting of the World Bank and the International Monetary Fund.

6 Aid and Redistribution The LDCs take the position that past foreign aid has been insufficient and ineffective. It has been insufficient in that, as a group, the advanced nations have only made annual aid contributions equal to about one-third of 1 percent of their GDPs. Aid has been relatively ineffective for several reasons. First, much of it is "tied" to the donor country; for example, American aid must be spent on American goods and services. This means that the LDCs cannot "shop around" in world markets for potentially better buys on capital goods and technological assistance. Second, inflation has greatly eroded the real value of aid dollars to recipient nations. Third, as already noted, a large portion of aid must be used to pay interest on the external debts of the LDCs and, hence, is not available for development.

One of the objectives of the NIEO is to have each of the IACs progressively increase its aid to 0.7 percent of its GDP as recommended by the United Nations over a decade ago. This aid should have "no strings attached" and should be provided on a long-term and automatic basis. The influential Brandt Commission[10] has endorsed this 0.7 percent goal. This implies a doubling of the current level of developmental aid.

The NIEO agenda is very controversial. While the poor countries feel the NIEO proposals are egalitarian and just, many advanced nations envision them as a demand for a massive redistribution of world income and wealth which is simply not in the cards. Many industrialized nations feel that there is no "quick fix" for underdevelopment and that the LDCs must undergo the same process of patient hard work and gradual capital formation as did the advanced nations over the past two centuries.

[10]*North-South: A Program for Survival* (Cambridge, Mass.: MIT Press, 1980). This commission, which studied a far-ranging agenda of international economic issues, was chaired by Willy Brandt, former Chancellor of West Germany.

L A S T   W O R D

FAMINE IN AFRICA

The roots of Africa's persistent famines include both natural and human causes.

Famine in Africa is not uncommon. The world was shocked during the 1984–1985 Ethiopian famine by pictures of fly-tormented, emaciated children with bloated bellies. Despite an outpouring of aid from the rich nations, that famine caused 1 million deaths. A number of African nations—including Ethiopia, Sudan, Angola, Liberia, Mozambique, and Malawi—are persistently threatened by famine. Various estimates put from 5 to 20 million Africans at risk. This tragic situation is especially ironic because most African countries were self-sufficient in food at the time they became independent nations; they are now heavily dependent on imported foodstuffs for survival.

The immediate and much-publicized cause of this catastrophe is drought. But the ultimate causes of Africa's declining ability to feed itself are more complex and multifaceted, an interplay of natural and human conditions. In addition to a lack of rainfall, these include chronic civil strife, rapid population growth, widespread soil erosion, and counterproductive public policies.

1   Civil Strife   Regional rebellions and prolonged civil wars have devastated some African nations. Both Ethiopia and the Sudan, for example, have been plagued by decades of civil strife. Not only do these conflicts divert precious resources from civilian uses, but they greatly complicate the ability of wealthy nations to provide famine and developmental aid. Ethiopia's government has often denied food aid to areas occupied by antigovernment forces. Donated food is

frequently diverted to the army and denied to starving civilians.

2   Population Growth   The hard fact is that in Africa population is growing more rapidly than is food production. Specifically, population is increasing at about 3 percent per year while food output is growing at only 2 percent per year. This grim arithmetic suggests de-

CHAPTER SUMMARY

1   Most of the nations of the world are less developed (low per capita income) nations. While some LDCs have been achieving quite rapid growth rates in recent years, others have realized little or no growth at all.

2   Initial scarcities of natural resources and the limited possibility of augmenting existing supplies may impose a serious limitation on a nation's capacity to develop.

3   The presence of large and rapidly growing populations in most LDCs contributes to low per capita incomes. In particular, increases in per capita incomes frequently induce

rapid population growth, to the end that per capita incomes again deteriorate to near subsistence levels.

4   Most LDCs suffer from both unemployment and underemployment. Labor productivity is low because of insufficient investment in physical and human capital.

5   In many LDCs both the saving and investment aspects of capital formation are impeded by formidable obstacles. In some of the poorest LDCs the savings potential is very low. Many LDC savers have chosen to transfer their funds to the IACs rather than invest domestically. The absence of a vig-

clining living standards, hunger, and malnutrition. The World Bank reports that during the 1980s the per capita incomes of the sub-Saharan nations fell to about three-quarters of the level reached by the end of the 1970s.

3 Ecological Degradation But apart from the simple numbers involved, population growth has apparently contributed to the ecological degradation of Africa. Given population pressures and the increasing need for food, marginal land has been deforested and put into crop production. In many cases trees which have served as a barrier to the encroachment of the desert have been cut for fuel, allowing the fragile topsoil to be blown away by desert winds. The ultimate scarcity of wood which has accompanied deforestation has forced the use of animal dung for fuel, thereby denying its traditional use as fertilizer. Furthermore, traditional fallow periods have been shortened, resulting in overplanting and overgrazing and, in simple terms, a wearing out of the soil. Deforestation and land overuse have reduced the capacity of the land to absorb moisture, diminishing its productivity and its ability to resist drought. Some authorities feel that the diminished ability of the land to absorb water reduces the amount of moisture which evaporates into the clouds to return ultimately as rainfall. All of this is complicated by the fact that there are few facilities for crop storage. Thus, even when crops are good, it is difficult to accumulate a surplus for future lean years. A large percentage of domestic farm output in some parts of Africa is lost to rats, insects, and spoilage.

4 Public Policies and Debt Ill-advised public policies have contributed to Africa's famines. In the first place, African governments have generally neglected investment in agriculture in favor of industrial develop-

ment and military strength. It is estimated that African governments on the average spend four times as much on armaments as they do on agriculture. Over 40 percent of Ethiopia's budget is for the support of an oppressive military. Second, many African governments have followed the policy of establishing the prices of agricultural commodities at low levels to provide cheap food for growing urban populations. This low-price policy has diminished the incentives of farmers to increase productivity. While foreign aid has helped to ease the effects of Africa's food-population problems, most experts reject aid as a long-term solution. Indeed, experience suggests that aid in the form of foodstuffs can only provide temporary relief and may undermine the realization of long-run local self-sufficiency. Foreign food aid, it is contended, merely treats symptoms and not causes.

All of this is made more complex by the fact that the sub-Saharan nations are burdened with relatively large and growing external debts. The IMF reports that the aggregate debt of these nations rose from $21 billion in 1976 to $127 billion in 1990. As a condition of further aid, these nations have had to invoke austerity programs which have contributed to declines in their per capita incomes. One tragic consequence is that many of these nations have cut back on social service programs for children. A UNICEF spokesman has indicated that 3 million children died in 1987 worldwide "because they didn't have 50 cents worth of vaccine in them."

To summarize: the famine confronting much of Africa is partly a phenomenon of nature and in part self-inflicted. Drought, overpopulation, ecological deterioration, and errant public policies have all been contributing factors. This complex of causes implies that hunger and malnutrition in Africa may persist long after the rains return.

---

orous entrepreneurial class and the weakness of investment incentives are also serious impediments to capital accumulation.

6 Appropriate social and institutional changes and, in particular, the presence of "the will to develop" are essential ingredients in economic development.

7 The vicious circle of poverty brings together many of the obstacles to growth, saying in effect that "poor countries stay poor because of their poverty." Low incomes inhibit saving and accumulation of physical and human capital, making it difficult to increase productivity and incomes. Rapid population growth can offset otherwise promising attempts to break the vicious circle.

8 The nature of the obstacles to growth—the absence of an entrepreneurial class, the dearth of infrastructure, the saving-investment dilemma, and the presence of social-institutional obstacles to growth—suggests the need for government action in initiating the growth process. However, the corruption and maladministration which are quite common to the public sectors of the LDCs suggest that government may be relatively ineffective as an instigator of growth.

9 Advanced nations can assist in development by reducing trade barriers and by providing both public and private capital.

10 Rising energy prices, declining export prices, depreciation of the dollar, and concern about LDCs' creditworthiness combined to create an LDC debt crisis in the early 1980s. External debt problems of LDCs remain serious and inhibit their growth.

11 The LDCs are calling for a New International Economic Order (NIEO) which will give them **a** a greater voice in the policies of international financial institutions, **b** preferential tariff treatment, **c** a greater share of the income derived from contracts and leases negotiated with multinational corporations, **d** improved terms of trade, **e** cancellation or rescheduling of their external debts, and **f** a larger and automatic inflow of foreign aid.

TERMS AND CONCEPTS

industrially advanced
   countries (IACs)
less developed
   countries (LDCs)
unemployment and
   underemployment
brain drain
capital flight

infrastructure
nonfinancial
   investment
capital-saving and
   capital-using
   technological
   advance

the will to develop
capricious universe
   view
land reform
vicious circle of poverty
World Bank
neocolonialism

New International
   Economic Order
   (NIEO)
preferential tariff
   treatment
terms of trade
stabilization fund

QUESTIONS AND STUDY SUGGESTIONS

1 What are the major characteristics of an LDC? List the major avenues of economic development available to such a nation. State and explain obstacles which face LDCs in breaking the poverty barrier. Use the "vicious circle of poverty" to outline in detail steps an LDC might take to initiate economic development.

2 Explain how the absolute per capita income gap between rich and poor nations might increase, even though per capita GDP is growing faster in LDCs than it is in IACs.

3 Discuss and evaluate:

   a "The path to economic development has been clearly blazed by American capitalism. It is only for the LDCs to follow this trail."

   b "Economic inequality is conducive to saving, and saving is the prerequisite of investment. Therefore, greater inequality in the income distribution of the LDCs would be a spur to capital accumulation and growth."

   c "The IACs fear the complications which stem from oversaving; the LDCs bear the yoke of undersaving."

   d "The core of the development process involves changing human beings more than it does altering a nation's physical environment."

   e "America's 'foreign aid' program is a sham. In reality it represents neocolonialism—a means by which the LDCs can be nominally free in a political sense but remain totally subservient in an economic sense."

   f "Poverty and freedom cannot persist side by side; one must triumph over the other."

   g "The biggest obstacle facing poor nations in their quest for development is the lack of capital goods."

   h "A high per capita GDP does not necessarily identify an industrially advanced nation."

4 Explain how population growth might be an impediment to economic growth. How would you define the optimal population of a country? Some experts argue that children are "net assets" in poor countries, but "net liabilities" in rich countries. Can you provide a rationale for this assertion? If the statement is true, does it imply that a rising per capita income is the prerequisite for population control?

5 Much of the initial investment in an LDC must be devoted to infrastructure which does not directly or immediately lead to a greater production of goods and services. What bearing might this have on the degree of inflation which results as government finances capital accumulation through the creating and spending of new money?

6 "The nature of the problems faced by the LDCs creates a bias in favor of a governmentally directed as opposed to a decentralized development process." Do you agree? Substantiate your position.

7 What is the LDC debt crisis? How did it come about? What solutions can you offer?

8 What types of products do the LDCs export? Can you use Chapter 20's law of comparative advantage to explain the character of these exports?

9 Outline the main components of the New International Economic Order proposed by the LDCs. Which of these demands do you feel are most justified?

10 What would be the implications of a worldwide policy of unrestricted immigration between nations for economic efficiency and the global distribution of income?

11 Use Figure 22-1 (changing box labels as necessary) to explain rapid economic growth in a country such as Japan or South Korea. What factors other than those contained in the figure might contribute to growth?

23

The Soviet Economy in Transition

In 1957 Communist Party Chairman Nikita Khrushchev bluntly asserted that the centrally planned Soviet economy would prove itself superior to the United States economy:

> We declare war upon you—excuse me for using such an expression—in the peaceful field of trade. We declare war. We will win over the United States. The threat to the United States is not the ICBM, but in the field of peaceful production. We are relentless in this and it will prove the superiority of our system.

But in October of 1990 Soviet President Mikhail Gorbachev announced to the world that the Soviet economy was unraveling:

> The position of the economy continues to deteriorate. The volume of production is declining. Economic links are being broken. Separatism is on the increase. The consumer market is in dire straits. The budget deficit and the solvency of the government are now at critical levels. Antisocial behavior and crime are increasing. People are finding life more and more difficult and are losing their interest in work and their belief in the future. The economy is in very great danger. The old administrative system of management has been destroyed but the impetus to work under a market system is lacking. Energetic measures must be taken, with the consent of the public, to stabilize the situation and to accelerate progress towards a market economy.

In the early 1990s there was compelling evidence that the economy of the former Soviet Union was in severe disarray. Consumers were queuing up for hours to buy food and shoddy consumer goods, frequently to find only empty store shelves. One-fifth of 1991's grain production was either unharvested or left to rot because of inadequate storage and transportation. Government rationing of consumer staples was common and black markets were flourishing. Confidence in the monetary unit—the ruble—was rapidly waning and exchange by the use of such "hard" foreign currencies as dollars, yen, and marks and by barter was becoming commonplace. Both government budget deficits and trade deficits were substantial and rising. Official government statistics chronicled a falling real domestic output, increasing unemployment, and a rapidly rising price level.

Economic disarray has been accompanied by political turmoil. An abortive August 1991 coup pushed Soviet President Mikhail Gorbachev into the background and brought Russian Republic President Boris Yeltsin to the fore. The Baltic states—Estonia, Latvia, and Lithuania—have declared their independence. The remaining twelve republics—with the possible exception of Georgia—are attempting to align themselves in some sort of confederation. Thus, the media refers to the remaining republics as the "Commonwealth of Independent States" or the "former Soviet Union," a practice we shall adopt in this chapter. The political situation remains highly volatile. Given the ethnic conflict between Christian Armenia and Muslim Azerbaijan, civil war is not unthinkable. Nor is the resurrection of an authoritarian system similar to the fallen communist regime.

In this final chapter we will examine the economy of the former Soviet Union and the problems it now faces. Specific questions addressed are: What were the main characteristics and goals of the Soviet planned economy? Why did it fail? What must be done to achieve the transition to the market economy envisioned in Gorbachev's remarks? What are the major obstacles in implementing the transition from central planning to a market economy? What role might the United States and other western nations play in this transition?

There are important by-products of examining an economy which has been at the opposite end of the ideological and institutional spectrum. By understanding the problems and ultimate failure of Soviet communism, we cannot help but more fully understand and appreciate the functioning of our own system. It also helps us grasp the transition problems of other eastern European nations such as Poland, Hungary, and Czechoslovakia which also seek to change from central planning to market-oriented systems. Finally, there are lessons for the less developed countries, many of which sought forced economic development by emulating the Soviet system of central planning.

IDEOLOGY AND INSTITUTIONS

To understand the Soviet planned economy we must understand its ideology and institutions.

Marxian Ideology

The Communist Party, until recently the dominant force in Soviet political and economic life, viewed itself as a dictatorship of the proletariat or working class. Based on Marxism–Leninism, the Communists envisioned their system as the inevitable successor to capitalism, the latter being plagued by internal contradictions stemming from the exploitation, injustice, and insecurity which it allegedly generates.

Especially important for our purposes is the Marxian concept of a **labor theory of value**—the idea that the economic or exchange value of any commodity is determined solely by the amount of labor time required for its production. Thanks to the capitalistic institution of private property, capitalists own the machinery and equipment necessary for production in an industrial society. The propertyless working class is therefore dependent on the capitalists for employment and for its livelihood. Given the worker's inferior bargaining position and the capitalist's pursuit of profits, the capitalist will exploit labor by paying a daily wage which is much less than the value of the worker's daily production. The capitalist can and will pay workers a subsistence wage and expropriate the remaining fruits of their labor as profits, or what Marx termed **surplus value.** In the Soviet system, surplus value was to be extracted by the state as an agency of the working class and distributed in large part through subsidies to what we would call public or quasi-public goods, for example, education, transportation, health care, and housing.

The function of communism was to overthrow capitalism and replace it with a classless society within which human exploitation is absent. The Communist Party viewed itself as the vanguard of the working class, and its actions were held to be in keeping with the goals of the proletariat. In fact, it was a strong dictatorship. Many westerners characterized the Soviet government as a dictatorship *over* the proletariat, rather than *of* the proletariat.

Institutions

The two outstanding institutional characteristics of the Soviet economy were: (1) state ownership of property resources, and (2) authoritarian central economic planning.

State Ownership **State ownership** meant the Soviet state owned all land, natural resources, transportation and communication facilities, the banking system, and virtually all industry. Most retail and wholesale enterprises and most urban housing were governmentally owned. In agriculture many farms were state-owned; most, however, were government-organized collective farms, that is, essentially cooperatives to which the state assigned land "for free use for an unlimited time." An exception to state ownership was the small plot of land which each state collective farm family had set aside for its personal use. Workers in factories also had the use of small plots of land.

Central Economic Planning **Central economic planning,** in contrast with the decentralized market economy of the United States, meant that the Soviet Union had a centralized "command" economy functioning in terms of a detailed economic plan. The Soviet economy was government-directed rather than market-directed. Choices made primarily through the market in our United States' economy were made by bureaucratic decision in the U.S.S.R. The overall character of the Soviet Five-year Plans has been succinctly described in these words:

> The Soviet economic plan is a gigantic, comprehensive blueprint that attempts to govern the economic activities and interrelations of all persons and institutions in the U.S.S.R., as well as the economic relations of the U.S.S.R. with other countries. To the extent that the plan actually controls the development

of events, all the manifold activities of the Soviet economy are coordinated as if they were parts of one incredibly enormous enterprise directed from the central headquarters in Moscow.[1]

CENTRAL PLANNING AND ITS PROBLEMS

The Soviet system of central planning was put in place in the late 1920s and early 1930s. Although occasional reforms were experimented with in the 1950s and 1960s, the system remained fundamentally unchanged for almost seven decades.

Ends and Means

The following generalizations describe how Soviet planning has functioned historically.

1 Industrialization and Military Strength The economy of the former Soviet Union has been described as "totalitarianism harnessed to the task of rapid industrialization and economic growth."[2] Planning goals put heavy emphasis on rapid industrialization and military strength. This was achieved through extensive investment in heavy industries—steel, chemicals, and machine tools—and the allocation of a large percentage of domestic output to the military. As a consequence, development of consumer goods industries, the distribution and service sectors, and the infrastructure were neglected.

2 Resource Overcommitment Production increases sought in the various Soviet Five-year Plans were very ambitious, tending to overcommit the economy's available resources. As a result, not all planning targets could be achieved. And, as already suggested, Soviet planning priorities were to achieve those goals associated with heavy industry and the military at the expense of consumption.

3 Resource Mobilization Industrialization and rapid economic growth were initially achieved through mobilization of labor, capital, and raw materials. In the

[1]Harry Schwartz, *Russia's Soviet Economy,* 2d ed. (Englewood Cliffs, N.J.: Prentice-Hall, Inc., 1954), p. 146.
[2]Robert W. Campbell, *The Soviet-type Economies,* 3d ed. (Boston: Houghton Mifflin Company, 1974), p. 3. Also see Campbell's *The Socialist Economies in Transition: A Primer on Semi-Reformed Systems* (Bloomington: Indiana University Press, 1991).

early years of planning there was substantial surplus labor in agriculture which the plans reallocated to industrial production. Similarly, a larger proportion of the population was induced or coerced into the labor force. Early Soviet growth was achieved through the use of more inputs rather than using given inputs more productively. In the 1930s and again in the early post-World War II era, this strategy produced growth rates greater than the United States and other industrialized nations.

4 Allocation by Directives   Soviet central planners directed the allocation of inputs among industries and firms, thereby determining the composition of output. Planning directives were substituted for the market or price system as an allocational mechanism.

5 Government Price Fixing   In the former Soviet Union prices were set by government direction rather than by the forces of demand and supply. Consumer good prices were changed infrequently and, as a matter of social policy, the prices of "necessities"—for example, housing and many foodstuffs—were established at low levels. Rents on Soviet housing averaged only about 3 percent of income and did not change between 1928 and 1992! Input prices and the price of an enterprise's output were also governmentally determined and were used primarily as accounting devices to gauge a firm's progress in meeting its production target.

6 Self-Sufficiency   The Soviet Union viewed itself as a single socialist nation surrounded by hostile capitalistic countries. Therefore, the central plans stressed economic self-sufficiency. Trade with western nations was greatly restricted because the ruble was not convertible into other currencies. Soviet trade was largely with the other communist bloc nations of eastern Europe.

7 Passive Macroeconomic Policies   The Soviet economy has been a quantity-directed system with money and prices playing only a limited role in resource allocation. Unlike most market economies, monetary and fiscal policies were passive rather than active in the Soviet Union. In the United States and other market systems, monetary and fiscal policies are used to manipulate the aggregate levels of output, employment, and prices. Historically, unemployment in the Soviet Union has been kept very low, perhaps only 1 or 2 percent of the labor force. This is partly the result of ambitious planning targets and various admonitions to work. Low unemployment has also been due to over-staffing (managers cannot fire redundant workers), a

disinterest in cost-minimization (gross output being the overriding objective), and a population whose growth rate has been steadily diminishing.

Similarly, government price determination was the primary device used to control the price level. The state banking system, *Gosbank,* issued credit or working capital to enterprises, based on what was needed to fulfill their planned production targets. But it did not use, and did not have the control mechanisms, to manipulate the money supply to achieve macroeconomic stability.

The Coordination Problem

The market system is a powerful organizing force which coordinates millions of individual decisions by consumers, resources suppliers, and businesses, and fosters a reasonably efficient allocation of scarce resources. It is not an easy matter to substitute central planning as a coordinating mechanism.

A simple example illustrates this problem. Suppose a Soviet enterprise in Minsk is producing men's shoes. Planners must establish a realistic production target for that enterprise and then see that all the necessary inputs—labor, electric power, leather, rubber, thread, nails, appropriate machinery, transportation—for production and delivery of that product are made available. When we move from a simple product such as shoes to more complex products such as television sets and farm tractors, planners' allocational problems are greatly compounded.

Because the outputs of many industries are inputs to other industries, the failure of any single industry to fulfill its output target is likely to cause a whole chain of adverse repercussions. If iron mines—for want of machinery or labor or transportation inputs—fail to supply the steel industry with the required inputs of iron ore, the steel industry in turn will be unable to fulfill the input needs of the myriad industries dependent on steel. All these steel-using industries—for example, automobiles, tractors, and transportation—will therefore be unable to fulfill their planned production goals. And so the bottleneck chain reaction goes on to all those firms which use steel parts or components as inputs.

There were some 47,000 industrial enterprises producing goods in the former Soviet Union. The central planners had to see that all the resources needed by these enterprises to fulfill their assigned production targets were somehow allocated to them.

The literally billions of planning decisions that must be made to achieve consistency result in a complex and complete interlocking of macro- and micro- management . . . . The number of planned interconnections increases more rapidly than the size of the economy . . . . Even with the most sophisticated mathematical techniques and electronic computers, the task of interrelating demands and factor inputs for every possible item by every possible subcategory becomes impossible for the central planners alone.[3]

There is much evidence from Soviet sources indicating that bottlenecks occurred with alarming regularity in the 1980s and early 1990s. Moreover, bottlenecks were nothing new to the Soviet economy.

> The Byelorussian Tractor Factory, which has 227 suppliers, had its production line stopped 19 times in 1962 because of the lack of rubber parts, 18 times because of ball bearings, and 8 times because of transmission components. The pattern of breakdowns continued in 1963. During the first quarter of 1963 only about one-half of the plant's ball bearing and rubber needs were satisfied, and only half of the required batteries were available. One supplier shipped 19,000 less wheels than called for in the contract. In total, they were short of 27 different items. . . .

> It is not surprising that 90 enterprises out of 100 surveyed in the Chelyabinsk region blamed their underfulfillment of production plans in 1962 on supply deficiencies.[4]

QUICK REVIEW 23-1

✦ *Marxian ideology is based on the labor theory of value and views capitalism as a system for expropriating profits or surplus value from workers.*

✦ *The primary institutional features of the former Soviet economy were state ownership of property resources and central economic planning.*

✦ *Soviet plans were characterized by a an emphasis on rapid industrialization and military power, b resource overcommitment; c growth through the use of more inputs rather than greater efficiency; d resource allocation by government directives rather than markets; e government price determination; f an emphasis on economic self-sufficiency; and g passive monetary and fiscal policies.*

✦ *The basic planning problem is to direct needed resources to each enterprise so that production targets can be achieved.*

---

[3]Barry M. Richman, *Soviet Management* (Englewood Cliffs, N.J.: Prentice-Hall, Inc., 1965), p. 17.
[4]Ibid., p. 123.

THE FAILURE OF SOVIET COMMUNISM

Soviet economic growth in the 1950s and 1960s was impressive. In the 1950s Soviet real domestic output expanded at roughly 6 percent per year compared to about 3 percent for the United States. The Soviet economy continued to grow at about 5 percent per year in the 1960s. But growth fell to an annual rate of about $2\frac{1}{2}$ or 3 percent in the 1970s and further declined to 2 percent by the mid-1980s. More recent data indicate that growth has halted and in the last few years real domestic output has declined. Official Soviet estimates indicate that real domestic output fell by 4 percent in 1990 and 14 percent in 1991.

Further evidence of economic failure is reflected in the quality of goods. In such vital manufacturing sectors as computers and machine tools it is estimated that Soviet technology lags some seven to twelve years behind that of the United States. Overall, the quality of most Soviet manufactured goods is far short of international standards. Consumer goods are of notoriously poor quality and product assortment is greatly limited. Durable goods— automobiles, refrigerators, and consumer electronics products—are primitive by world standards. Furthermore, widespread shortages of basic goods, interminable shopper queues, black markets, and corruption in the distribution of products are all characteristic of the consumer sector.

The major contributing factor to the downfall of Soviet communism has been its inability to efficiently supply the goods and services which consumers want to buy. In the early decades of Soviet communism the government established a "social contract" with its citizenry to the effect that, by enduring the consumer sacrifices associated with the high rates of saving and investment necessary for rapid industrialization and growth, the population would be rewarded with consumer abundance in the future (Figure 2-4). The failure of the system to meet consumer expectations has contributed to frustration and deteriorating morale among consumers and workers. "All future and no present, certainly as in the USSR after six decades, begins to appear after a while more like a long term confidence game than a meaningful program of economic development."[5]

Comparisons with the United States are revealing. While the United States has 565 cars and 789 tele-

[5]Marshall I. Goldman, *USSR in Crisis: The Failure of an Economic System* (New York: W. W. Norton & Company, 1983), p. 175.

phones per 1000 people, the former Soviet Union has only 46 cars and 124 phones for each 1000 citizens. Overall, Soviet per capita consumption is less than 30 percent of that achieved in the United States. When qualitative deficiencies in Soviet goods and services and the cost of time spent searching for goods and waiting in queues are taken into account, this figure may overstate Soviet consumption levels.

Causes of the Collapse

Having chronicled the deteriorating performance of the economy of the former Soviet Union, we now consider causes. The following interrelated factors have contributed to the collapse of the Soviet system.

1 Military Burden Large Soviet military expenditures of 15 to 20 percent of domestic output—compared to 6 percent for the United States—absorbed great quantities of resources which would otherwise have been available for the production of consumer and investment goods. During the extended cold war era it was the government's policy to channel superior management and the best scientists and engineers to defense and space research, which undoubtedly adversely affected technological progress and the quality (productivity) of investment in the civilian sector.

2 Agricultural Drag By western standards agriculture in the former Soviet Union is something of a monument to inefficiency and is a drag on economic growth, engulfing some 30 percent of the labor force and roughly one-fourth of annual investment. Furthermore, output per worker is only 10 to 25 percent of the United States' level. The low productivity of Soviet agriculture is attributable to many factors: relative scarcity of good land; vagaries in rainfall and length of growing season; serious errors in planning and administration; and, perhaps most important, the failure to construct an effective incentive system.

Once a major exporter of grain and other agricultural products, the former Soviet Union has recently become one of the world's largest importers of agricultural commodities. Indeed, agricultural imports have been a serious drain on foreign currency reserves which its leadership would prefer to use in financing imports of western capital goods and technology.

3 More Inputs versus Increased Efficiency Much of the former Soviet Union's rapid growth in the early

decades of central planning was the result of simply using more labor, capital, and land in the production process. But in recent years this means of increasing real domestic output has been virtually exhausted. Soviet labor force participation rates are among the highest in the world so there is little or no opportunity to recruit more workers. Furthermore, population and labor force growth have slowed significantly. While the annual average increase in the labor force was about 1.5 percent in the 1970s, it slowed to about 0.6 percent in the 1980s, and no growth is forecast for the 1990s. Similarly, the percentage of domestic output devoted to investment is comparatively high and could only be increased by reducing the proportion of output devoted to consumption. Given the comparatively low standard of living in the former Soviet Union, it would be extremely unpopular and politically difficult to further increase the input of capital goods at the expense of consumption. Also, natural conditions limit the availability of additional farmland. Indeed, occasional attempts to bring more land of marginal quality into crop production has been counterproductive in that yields have been minimal and the land has been lost to grazing.

The alternative to growth through the use of more inputs is to increase the productivity or efficiency of available inputs. But this is universally recognized as a much more complex and difficult means of achieving economic growth. Productivity growth requires, among other things, modern capital equipment, innovation and technological progress, and strong material incentives for workers and managers—none of which have been characteristic of the traditional Soviet planning system. Indeed, labor productivity in the former Soviet Union is estimated to be only 35 to 40 percent that of American workers.

4 Planning Problems The problem of centrally coordinating economic activity becomes much more complex as an economy grows and develops. Early planning under Stalin in the 1930s and 1940s resembled the simple World War II planning of western capitalist nations. A few key production goals were established and resources were centrally directed toward fulfillment of those goals regardless of costs or consumer welfare. But the past success of such "campaign planning" has resulted in a more complex, industrially advanced economy. Products are now more sophisticated and complex and there are more industries for which to plan. The planning techniques which were workable in the Stalinist era were inadequate and inefficient in the more advanced Soviet economy of the past two decades. In a sense, the Soviet economy had outgrown its planning mechanisms.

> Over time the inherent inefficiency of a command-administered economic system has come to dominate its effectiveness in achieving the priority objectives of the central authorities. Methods and institutions that were effective at an earlier, simpler stage of development no longer generate the desired outcomes. The mobilization of resources and effort that produced collectivization, industrialization, and a sizable chemical industry failed to develop modern computer technology, or to modernize consumer goods industries. The administrative superstructure, methods of planning, and plans themselves have become ever less adequate to the needs and flow of economic activity. The natural consequence is an increase in dysfunctional behavior by subordinates, increasingly obvious microeconomic waste and inefficiency, slowing (or declining) economic growth and productivity, and ever more frequent failures to achieve proclaimed priorities.[6]

5 Inadequate Success Indicators Market economies have a single, comprehensive success indicator—profits. Each firm's success or failure is measured by its profits or losses. As we know, profits depend on consumer demand, production efficiency, and product quality.

In contrast, the major success indicator of a Soviet enterprise was its fulfillment of a quantitative production target assigned by the central planners. This generated inefficient practices because production costs, product quality, and product-mix became secondary considerations at best. Achieving least-cost production is nearly impossible without a system of genuine market prices accurately reflecting the relative scarcity of various resources. Product quality was frequently sacrificed by managers and workers who were awarded bonuses for fulfilling quantitative, not qualitative, targets. If meeting production goals of a television or automobile manufacturing plan meant sloppy assembly work, so be it.

Finally, it is difficult for planners to assign quantitative production targets without unintentionally producing ridiculous distortions in output. If an enterprise manufacturing nails specifies its production target in weight (tons of nails), it will tend to produce all large nails. But if its target is a quantity (thousands of nails), it will be motivated to use available inputs to produce all

small nails. The obvious problem is that the economy needs *both* large and small nails.

6 Incentive Problems Perhaps the main deficiency of central planning has been the lack of economic incentives. The market systems of western economies have built-in signals resulting in the efficient use of resources. Profits and losses generate incentives for firms and industries to increase or decrease production. If a product is in short supply, its price and profitability will increase and producers will be motivated to expand production. Conversely, surplus supply means falling prices and profits and a reduction in output. Successful innovations in the form of either product quality or production techniques are sought because of their profitability. Greater work effort by labor means higher money incomes which can be translated into a higher real standard of living.

These actions and adjustments do not occur under central planning. The output-mix of the former Soviet economy was determined by the central planners. If their judgments as to the quantities of automobiles, razor blades, underwear, and vodka wanted by the populace at governmentally determined prices were incorrect, there would be persistent shortages and surpluses of products. But the managers who oversaw the production of these goods were rewarded for fulfilling their assigned production goals; they had no incentive to adjust production in response to product shortages or surpluses. And they did not have changes in prices and profitability to signal that more or less of each product was desired. Thus in the former Soviet Union many products were in short supply, while other unwanted goods languished in warehouses.

Incentives to innovate were almost entirely absent; indeed, innovation was often resisted. Soviet enterprises were essentially governmentally owned monopolies. As a result, there was no private gain to managers or workers for improving product quality or developing more efficient production techniques. Historically, government-imposed innovations were resisted by enterprise managers and workers. The reason was that new production processes were usually accompanied by higher and unrealistic production targets, underfulfillment, and loss of bonuses.

Innovation also lagged because there was no competition. New firms could not come into being to introduce better products, superior managerial techniques, or more efficient productive methods. Similarly, the Soviet goal of economic self-sufficiency isolated its enterprises from the competitive pressures of interna-

[6]Richard E. Ericson, "The Classical Soviet-Type Economy: Nature of the System and Implications for Reform," *Journal of Economic Perspectives,* Fall 1991, p. 23.

tional markets. In general, over an extended period Soviet enterprises produced the same products with the same techniques, with both goods and techniques becoming increasingly obsolete by world standards.

Nor were individual workers motivated to work hard, because of a lack of material incentives. Because of the low priority assigned to consumer goods in the Five-year Plans, there was only a limited array of relatively low-quality goods and services available to Soviet workers–consumers. (The price of an automobile is far beyond the means of average factory workers, and for those able to buy, the waiting period may be one to five years.) While hard work might result in promotions and bonuses, the increase in *money* income did not translate into a proportionate increase in *real* income. As we will note later, there was a substantial amount of involuntary saving—a "ruble overhang"—in the Soviet Union because of a lack of consumer goods. Why work hard for additional income if there is nothing to buy with the money you earn? As a Soviet worker once lamented to a western journalist: "The government pretends to pay us and we pretend to work."

THE GORBACHEV REFORMS

The deteriorating Soviet economy of the 1970s and early 1980s prompted President Mikhail Gorbachev to introduce in 1986 a reform program described as **perestroika,** a restructuring of the economy. This economic restructuring was accompanied by **glasnost,** a campaign for greater openness and democratization in both political and economic affairs. Under *glasnost,* workers, consumers, enterprise managers, political leaders, and others were provided greater opportunity to voice complaints and make suggestions for improving the functioning of the economy.

Basically, the **Gorbachev reforms** involved six interrelated elements: (1) the modernization of industry; (2) greater decentralization of decision making; (3) provision for a limited private enterprise sector; (4) improved worker discipline and incentives; (5) a more rational price system; (6) an enlarged role in the international economy.

Modernization was sought through reallocation of investment toward research and development and toward high-tech industries. Decentralization of decision making was intended to keep the planning bureaucracy from interfering in the day-to-day internal operations of individual enterprises. In exchange for greater enterprise autonomy, enterprise success indicators were reoriented from output targets to profitability, thus obligating enterprises to be more conscious of the salability (quality) of their products.

Small-scale private production of some consumer goods and services—such as clothing, furniture, rugs, taxi transport, hairdressing, and appliance repair—was also permitted. But those engaged in such activities also had to hold full-time state jobs or be housewives or retirees. The size of these private enterprises was limited by the Marxist prohibition on hiring someone else's labor.

The Gorbachev reforms also attempted to improve the human factors in production. Actions were taken to dismiss incompetent planners and enterprise managers, trim the size of the planning bureaucracies, and improve worker attitudes and behavior. Campaigns against corruption and alcoholism would reduce inefficiency resulting from theft, absenteeism, industrial accidents, and high worker turnover.

Price reforms would reduce over time the number of prices fixed by central planning with such prices ultimately applying only to what was regarded as the most essential consumer and producer goods. Enterprises were to be able to negotiate sales contracts in much the same manner as capitalist firms.

The reforms also hinted at closer economic relationships with the industrialized nations of the west. A related effort was to encourage joint ventures in the Soviet Union with western firms in a wide variety of activities ranging from fast-food restaurants to construction and operation of petrochemical plants. Such ventures were undoubtedly viewed by the Soviets as an inexpensive means of acquiring western technologies and management skills.

While *perestroika* met with some initial success, it did not comprehensively address the systemic economic problems facing the Soviet Union. In retrospect, *perestroika* was more in the nature of traditional Soviet "campaigns" to elicit better performance within the general framework of the planned economy. It was *not* an overall program of institutional change such as those adopted by Poland and Hungary. Thus, in 1986–1987 the Soviet economy was stagnating; some estimates put its growth rate at only 2 percent per year, while others indicated it did not grow at all. Sharply declining world oil prices also were damaging because the Soviet Union is a major oil exporter. In any event, by 1990 *perestroika* had given way to a greater emphasis on sweeping reforms designed to create a western-style market economy.

● *The failure of central planning in the former Soviet Union was evidenced by diminished growth rates, low-quality goods, and the failure to provide a rising standard of living.*

● *The recent collapse of the Soviet economy is attributable to a a large military burden; b chronic inefficiencies in agriculture; c the need to expand real output by increasing input productivity rather than increasing the quantity of inputs; d the inability of traditional planning techniques to deal with the growing complexity of the Soviet economy; e inadequate success indicators; and f ineffectual incentives to produce, innovate, and work.*

● *The Gorbachev reforms of the late 1980s centered on* perestroika *("restructuring") and* glasnost *("openness") but failed to provide major systemic change.*

TRANSITION TO A MARKET SYSTEM

The former Soviet republics—particularly Russia—have committed themselves to making the transition to a market economy. What are the components of such a dramatic reform program?

Privatization

If entrepreneurship is to come into existence, private property rights must be established and protected by law. This means that existing government property—farmland, housing, factories, machinery and equipment, stores—must be transferred to private owners. It also means that new private firms must be allowed to form and develop.

It is not yet clear how this can be effectively and equitably accomplished, but there are a number of options. Small enterprises and retail outlets might be sold directly to private individuals or cooperatives through public auctions. Another possibility is employee stock ownership plans where workers, aided by government loans, buy an enterprise and then retire their debt from future earnings. The privatization of large state enterprises may be more difficult. One proposal is for the government to distribute vouchers, each having a designated monetary value, to all citizens. Owners of these vouchers can then pool them in the purchase of enterprises. An interim option is the "commercialization" of

Soviet enterprises, meaning that the firm is made financially and managerially independent but remains publicly owned. Privatization is made more complex because it is difficult to determine the economic value of an enterprise in the absence of genuine product and resource prices.

Promotion of Competition

The industrial sector of the former Soviet Union consisted of some 47,000 large state-owned enterprises in which average employment exceeded 800 workers. An estimated 30 to 40 percent of total industrial production comprised products for which there was only one producer. When several enterprises produce a given product, their actions were usually coordinated by the planning process to create a cartel. In short, much Commonwealth production took place under monopoly or near-monopoly conditions.

Realization of a reasonably efficient market economy requires the dismantling of these public monopolies and the creation of antitrust laws to sustain competition. Privatization without "demonopolization" will be of limited benefit to the economy. Existing monopolies must be restructured or split apart as separate, competing firms. For example, a tractor manufacturing enterprise with four plants could be separated into four independent and competing firms. The establishment and guarantee of property rights are prerequisite to the creation and entry of new firms into previously monopolized industries. Joint ventures between Commonwealth and foreign companies provide a further avenue for increasing competition, as does opening the economy to international trade. Recent legislation has opened the door for foreign firms to invest directly in the new Commonwealth.

Limited and Reoriented Role for Government

The transition to a market economy will sharply curtail government's economic role. The government must reduce its involvement to those tasks associated with a market economy: providing an appropriate legal framework; maintaining competition; reducing excessive inequality in the distribution of income and wealth; making market adjustments where spillover costs or benefits are large; providing public goods and services; and stabilizing the economy (Chapter 6).

Many of these functions will be new to the governments within the Commonwealth, at least in the environment of a market system. Unemployment and overt inflation were not evident to Soviet citizens under central planning. Historically, ambitious production plans and overstaffing of enterprises have made for very low unemployment rates while government price-setting has been a direct means of controlling the price level. The task will be to develop monetary and fiscal policies—and institutional arrangements appropriate to their implementation—to indirectly provide macroeconomic stability. Restructuring will likely result in substantial short-run unemployment as inefficient public enterprises are closed or fail to be viable under private ownership. Thus, a priority goal will be to establish a social safety net for Soviet citizens. In particular, a program of unemployment insurance must be established, not only on equity grounds but also to reduce worker resistance to the transition. Similarly, antitrust legislation of some sort will be needed to maintain reasonably competitive markets.

Price Reform: Removing Controls

Unlike competitive market prices, the prices established by the government bear no relationship to the economic value of either products or resources. In an effectively functioning competitive market system the price of a product equates, at the margin, the value consumers place on that good and the value of the resources used in its production. When free markets achieve this equality for all goods and services, the economy's scarce resources are being used efficiently to satisfy consumer wants.

But, as noted, in the former Soviet Union both input and output prices were fixed by government and in many instances were not changed for extended periods of time. Because input prices did not measure the relative scarcities of various resources, it was impossible for a firm to minimize real production costs. That is, with fixed prices it is impossible to produce a unit of X in such a way as to minimize sacrifice of alternative goods. Example: Relatively high energy prices have caused firms in market economies to curtail its use. But energy has been underpriced in the former Soviet Union (the world's largest producer of energy) and its industries use two to three times as much energy per unit of output as do leading industrial countries.

A difficult problem arises in making the transition from government- to market-determined prices because historically the prices of many basic consumer goods have been fixed at low levels. The Soviet rationale for this was that low prices would ensure everyone

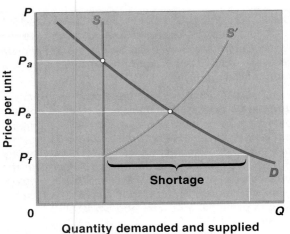

FIGURE 23-1 The effects of government price fixing

Central planners establish below-equilibrium prices such as P_f on many basic consumer goods to make them widely available to everyone. But in fact at such low prices quantity demanded exceeds quantity supplied and this shortage means that many consumers cannot obtain such goods. Assuming no privatization, abandonment of government price fixing would raise price from P_f to P_a. With privatization and an accompanying increase in output as price rises, price would increase from P_f to P_e. In either event, the decontrol of prices can be expected to be inflationary.

ready access to such goods. As Figure 23-1 shows, this pricing policy helps explain the chronic product shortages and long queues which frustrate consumers in the former Soviet Union. The perfectly inelastic supply curve S reflects the fixed output of, say, shoes for which the plan provides. (Disregard supply curve S' for the moment.) The demand curve slopes downward as it would in a market economy. Given S, the equilibrium price would be P_a. But in an effort to make shoes accessible to those with lower incomes, the government fixes the price at P_f.

However, Figure 23-1 makes clear that not everyone who wants shoes at price P_f will be able to obtain them. At P_f quantity demanded is substantially greater than quantity supplied, so there is excess demand or, in other words, a shortage. This explains the long, impatient lines of consumers and the empty shelves we saw in television news clips of Soviet shoppers. It is no surprise that black markets—illegal markets where goods are sold at much higher prices than those fixed by the government—were widespread in the former Soviet Union.

Given that Figure 23-1 was characteristic of most Soviet markets, it is obvious that the transition to free markets poses a serious inflationary problem. Without privatization, shoe prices will rise from P_f to P_a when the market for shoes is decontrolled. Similarly, prices will rise for butter, soap, meat, housing, vodka, and a host of other goods. With privatization, this runup of prices will be dampened somewhat by the extra output induced by the rising prices. As shown by supply curve S' in Figure 23-1, private producers will respond to higher prices by increasing quantity supplied. Nevertheless, prices will rise substantially, as from P_f to P_e. An important need during the transition period will be to control inflationary pressures through appropriate macroeconomic policies. The prospect of rampant inflation is an important reason why many Soviet citizens are apprehensive about the transition to a market economy.

In January of 1992 Boris Yeltsin unilaterally decontrolled prices in the Russian Republic. Prices on many products tripled or quadrupled overnight. His strategy is based on the expectation that higher prices will induce farms to supply in the market foodstuffs they are now hoarding and thereby ease growing food shortages. But if inflation continues, the needed food may be withheld in the anticipation of still higher prices.

Joining the World Economy

The Soviet Union was largely isolated from the world economy for almost three-quarters of a century. A key aspect of transition is to open the economy to international trade and finance.

One basic task is to make the ruble a convertible currency, meaning that it must be exchangeable for other foreign currencies. Convertibility is necessary for the former Soviet Union to achieve an enlarged role in international trade and finance. Firms cannot buy from or sell to the former Soviet Union unless a realistic exchange rate is established for the ruble (Chapter 21). Nor can western firms be expected to invest in the former Soviet Union unless they are certain that rubles can be exchanged for dollars. American and other western firms want their profits in dollars, yen, pounds, and marks, not rubles.

Opening the Soviet economy to world trade will be beneficial because world markets are important sources of competition and a means of acquiring much-needed superior technologies from industrially advanced capitalist nations. Liberalized international trade will put pressure on privatized Soviet firms to produce efficiently products which meet world quality standards. Furthermore, free world trade will allow the former Soviet Union to realize the benefits from production based on comparative advantage—income gains which its isolation has long denied it.

Macroeconomic Stability

Unfortunately, the transition to free markets can be accompanied by high rates of inflation. There are several reasons for this.

1 Decontrolling Prices As just discussed (Figure 23-1), the government has kept consumer prices artificially low for decades. Decontrol of these prices will result in a substantially higher price level. If workers respond by demanding and receiving higher nominal wages, a serious and prolonged price-wage spiral could result.

2 Ruble Overhang In what is called the **ruble overhang,** Soviet households have stored massive amounts of currency and deposits at savings banks during years of waiting for scarce consumer goods to become more abundant. Historically, consumer prices fixed at low levels and restricted supplies of consumer goods gave consumers no other choice but to save. This ruble overhang—estimated to be 250 billion rubles—could generate an inflationary surge when prices are decontrolled and more goods begin to appear in consumer markets.

3 Inflationary Finance The most important potential source of inflation is the recent financing of government deficits by printing additional currency. The Soviet government incurred large deficits in the late 1980s and early 1990s, the result of two considerations. First, the main source of government revenue is the *turnover tax,* which is essentially an excise tax of varying amounts on consumer goods. Because of the stagnation and decline of economic activity, revenues from the turnover tax have declined. Second, given the uncertainty as to the future of the Soviet Union as a political entity, the various republics have withheld their tax collections from the central government.

The consequence is that the central government has incurred substantial deficits which it has financed by the expedient of printing and distributing additional rubles. This is the most inflationary form of government finance and a potential cause of hyperinflation. More money chasing a diminishing amount of goods is a classic inflationary scenario. In fact, in late 1991 Soviet economists estimated that inflation was occurring at almost a 100 percent annual rate and accelerating.

The problem is that an environment of high and volatile inflation greatly complicates achieving other components of transition. The purchase of formerly public enterprises by private buyers, the establishing of a convertible ruble, and the encouragement of both domestic and foreign investment to modernize the economy are all more difficult with the uncertainties posed by a rapidly rising price level.

CAN THE TRANSITION BE IMPLEMENTED?

What are the prospects for transforming the former Soviet economy from central planning to a market system? It is not difficult to list obstacles to such a transformation.

Technical Problems

Our discussion of the components of the transition to a market economy has touched on many of the technical economic problems involved. How can the state efficiently and equitably divest itself of public enterprises? How is an effective degree of competition to be achieved and maintained in an economy which has been dominated by public monopolies for some seven decades? Can government create an effective unemployment insurance program, a workable system of antitrust laws, consumer protection legislation, and the legal framework to protect private property and enterprise? Will it be possible to create the institutions and mechanisms needed to implement monetary and fiscal policies? How can the potential inflationary effects of the ruble overhang be offset?

Public Support: Attitudes and Values

The reforms comprising the transition from central planning to a market system must have wide public support. Consider some of the potential difficulties.

1 Bureaucratic Resistance   The reforms threaten the jobs and status of many former party members and bureaucrats. These individuals continue in many instances to have positions of power and prestige and therefore have a strong interest in maintaining the status quo. Ironically, there is fear that those most likely to have access to Soviet enterprises and other assets will be those very same bureaucrats who formerly administered the failed system of central planning.

2 Worker Incentives   Under a system of capitalist incentives most workers and managers will be required to be more disciplined and to work harder and more productively. This may be difficult to accept in an economy which historically has served consumers–workers poorly. Money wage increases do not provide incentives without corresponding improvements in the quantity and quality of housing, food, and other consumer goods and services.

Some observers say that many citizens in the former Soviet Union and other communist nations have acquired work habits and personality traits which will only change slowly. These include working at a leisurely pace, avoiding responsibility, resistance to innovation and change, stressing output quantity over quality, and promotion based on connections and party affiliation rather than productive efficiency. It may be wishful thinking to assume that the Soviet populace is imbued with a strong work ethic and a latent entrepreneurial spirit, and that these attributes will emerge when the heavy hand of central planning is removed. The Soviet citizenry has been indoctrinated for some seventy years regarding the evils of private property, profits, and capitalist enterprise. The "mental residue" of communism may not be easily removed.

The Political Problem: National Disintegration

At this time (early 1992), the political status of the former Soviet republics is unclear. The Baltic states have declared themselves independent nations and the Georgian Republic may follow suit. It is uncertain at this point as to the nature of the future political alignment, if any, which may evolve among the remaining republics.

What is vital to the success of the transition process is that the republics *not* become separate and distinct *economic* entities. The worst scenario would be that each republic establish its own currency, its own external tariffs and import quotas, its own banking and tax systems and its own economic laws and policies. By becoming distinct economic units the advantages of specialization based on comparative advantage would be partially sacrificed and each political unit would suffer diminished domestic output.

In fact, diminishing trade between the republics in 1991 contributed to the former Soviet Union's economic and political deterioration. Given impending food shortages, the Ukraine (the main agricultural producer among the republics) stopped food shipments to other republics to conserve stocks for its own citizens. Other republics adopted similar policies. Azerbaijan curtailed its shipments of oil-drilling equipment to the Russian Republic and the latter responded by stopping oil shipments to Azerbaijan. An "every republic for itself" policy could be especially devastating because an estimated 40 percent of Soviet industrial production comes from state monopolies. For example, if for some curious reason Ford should decide not to sell its autos in Illinois, there is no doubt that General Motors and Chrysler, along with foreign producers, would be more than pleased to serve the market. But when Azerbaijan cuts off shipments of oil-drilling equipment to Russia, no alternative domestic source of that equipment is available.

A related point is that the transition process will be greatly facilitated by the influx of foreign investment. This will not occur until the former Soviet Union demonstrates political stability and continuity.

The Simultaneity Problem

A more subtle problem is that the components of reform must be pursued, not piecemeal, but more or less simultaneously. Reform components are interlinked; not to move forward on all fronts is to enhance the prospects for failure. Examples: Private ownership will do little to increase productive efficiency unless prices are reformed to accurately measure relative scarcities. Privatization—the selling off of state enterprises—may be helpful in reducing budget deficits. When market prices for inputs and output are unknown, it is extremely difficult to determine the value of an enterprise when it is being privatized. The creation of a more competitive environment depends significantly on the economy being opened to world trade and foreign investment.

Positive Factors

There are also several positive factors which may facilitate the plan-to-market economy transition.

1 Natural Resource Base The former Soviet Union has a generous and varied natural resource base. Although differing significantly in composition, the natural resources of the Commonwealth are roughly comparable with those of the United States. The Commonwealth comprises about one-sixth of the earth's land mass and its resources include gold, diamonds, timber, oil, and natural gas. Its population is 288 million, compared to 252 million for the United States.

2 Peace Dividend The end of the cold war will allow Russia, the Ukraine, and other former Soviet republics to reduce their heavy commitment of resources to the military and to reallocate freed resources to the civilian sector. Westerners estimate that a 50 percent reduction in military spending could save $90 billion per year. Recent arms agreements with the United States and its allies, the withdrawal of Soviet troops from Afghanistan, and reductions in the size of the Red army have been motivated by the desire to revitalize the lagging economy.

3 The "Second Economy" For years the former Soviet Union has had a thriving underground or "second" economy. Black markets where scarce goods sell at two or three times government-fixed prices were widespread. Peasants "borrowed" government fertilizer to use on their "private" plots of ground. Physicians stole medicines for their unofficial private practices. Plant managers hired "expediters" to illegally obtain needed inputs which the planning system failed to supply. The point is that all of these second economy activities reflected a degree of initiative and entrepreneurship which could be legal and useful in a market economy.

4 Democratization Democratization and, more specifically, freedom from the ideological baggage of the Communist Party, is a prerequisite for the transition to capitalism. The Communist Party was created to abolish private property, free enterprise, and genuine markets. It would be unrealistic to expect the Party to reverse these accomplishments. The Soviet Union under *glasnost* has made great strides toward democratization in the past several years. The dissolution of the Communist Party in 1991 was as significant economically as it was politically.

ROLE OF ADVANCED CAPITALIST NATIONS

What might the world's industrialized capitalist nations do to facilitate the Soviet plan-to-market economy metamorphosis?

LAST WORD

OBITUARY: THE SOVIET UNION

Contradictions of the world's first communist state killed Marx's vision of a free and prosperous society.

The Soviet Union is dead. It was 74.

Marketed as utopia, run by slogan and fear, it blended genuine achievement with elaborate facade. It created a system whose top priority seemed to be concealing its own failings.

Foreigners, intimidated by its military prowess and obsessive secrecy, frequently overestimated its strength. Its own citizens, bombarded by buoyant propaganda as they went about their harsh existence, sometimes had no idea if their lives were really growing better or worse.

Irony and artifice were everywhere. The Soviet Union led the world in production of steel, oil, tractors and locomotives, all as it moved inexorably to economic ruin.

Construction crews competed to build whole apartment buildings in a month, a week, a day. Yet the Soviet dream of abolishing "communal apartments," where three or four families had to share a tiny kitchen and toilet, was never achieved.

The Soviets were a nuclear super-power that projected military and diplomatic strength around the world. Yet at home, medical care was poor, citizens' diets poorer, and shoddy goods were the norm.

And a nation that claimed to publish more books and newspapers than any other had a ruthless system of censorship, political control and suppression of free ideas.

What went wrong? Why did a nation rich in natural resources—with a literate, educated work force and one-sixth of the world's land mass to stretch out in— fail to build the vibrant, prosperous, free society that was supposed to be a beacon to the world?

Most Soviets blame, first of all, "scientific socialism," the shaky and untested economic model that Lenin's Communists forced on backward Russia.

It was imposed from above and preserved through brute force. There were huge economic advances at first, but accomplished through intimidation as much as economic logic. After World War II, the "planned economy" operated as a continent-wide shell game, with resources wastefully rushed here and there to maintain an illusion of economic progress.

Since the economy essentially did not work, the leaders who depended on it had to find other ways to preserve their strength and build national pride.

They created a genuine center of accomplishment in the Soviet military, which was denied no human or financial resource. The Soviets also excelled in areas of high technology, mathematics and space; brought electricity, communications and industry to backward zones of their nation; and provided an example of quick, forced economic development that many in the Third World admired and attempted to emulate.

For anyone who was unimpressed by these accomplishments, the Soviets also created a system of terror that silenced political dissidents, religious activists, nationalist agitators and anyone else whose cause might be more appealing than communism.

But perhaps most important of all, the leaders built their strength on a suffocating cradle-to-grave so-

Foreign Aid

In 1991 President Gorbachev appealed to the industrialized countries for $20 to $30 billion in aid. The argument for granting this aid was that it would ease the painful transition process when central planning was being dismantled and free enterprise had not yet taken

hold. During this critical period the Soviet economy may further deteriorate. In addition, the abortive August 1991 coup indicates clearly that economic collapse can threaten to reverse the Soviet Union's substantial progress toward political democracy and the apparent demise of the cold war.

cial structure that made citizens totally beholden to the state—and then demanded practically nothing of them.

The state provided food, apartments, medicine, education, jobs and old-age pensions. It ran factories, department stores, farms, film studios and excellent orchestras and ballet companies. It may not have provided the weather, but it certainly controlled the news and sports.

This benevolence, such as it was, was practically free of charge. Citizens were judged mainly by political reliability—or political indifference, which also was acceptable.

During Leonid Brezhnev's reign, the situation steadily worsened and hypocrisy was elevated to the level of state policy. Bluster covered the increasing weakness.

Incompetence, sloppiness and corruption at work were widely overlooked. Citizens quickly learned that an effective way to get along was to do the minimum and challenge nothing—neither politics, nor the efficiency of their workplace.

Under such conditions, many believed the Soviet economy—and the country's whole spirit—was heading for a crash long before Mikhail Gorbachev came to power in 1985. He accelerated the slide by public openness about the country's troubles, a tactic that invigorated a few reformers but threw millions into despair and inactivity when facades came down and they realized how far their country had already crumbled.

Gorbachev's attempts at restructuring the economy were too tentative and too late. They could not make up for seven decades of an economic system that did not work, and the intricate structure established to maintain it at all cost.

That cost included stamping out personal initiative and putting political order ahead of everything else—including the welfare of the Soviet people.

Source: **Thomas Kent, "Soviets Mixed Achievement, Facade as Dreams Failed,"** *The Lincoln Star,* **Lincoln, Nebraska, December 26, 1991. Reprinted by permission.**

The United States and the other market democracies have a great economic stake in the former Soviet Union's transition to democracy and capitalism. If the transition fails, the peace dividend associated with the end of the cold war will not be realized and the possibility of accelerated economic growth through expanded international trade with a free-market Commonwealth will also be sacrificed. The political benefit is that a democratic Commonwealth will isolate the last strongholds of communism—China, Cuba, North Korea, and Vietnam—and perhaps force their leaders toward political and economic reform.

But there are serious reservations concerning aid to the Soviet Union. One argument is that aid is likely to be ineffectual and wasteful until the transition to market capitalism has been accomplished. Aside from humanitarian aid in the form of foodstuffs and medicine, economic aid is not likely to be of much help under existing institutional arrangements.

A second contention is that the Soviet Union has not yet exploited the opportunity it now has to divert vast amounts of resources from the military to the civilian sector. Cutting military spending in half would release resources three or four times as large as the amount of aid Gorbachev requested.

Third, it is pointed out that the Soviet Union is in fact a gigantic $2 trillion economy. Even granting the $30 billion in aid would only amount to about $100 per year per Soviet citizen.

Finally, there is the hard political fact that foreign aid for a long-time cold war foe may not be popular among the voters of industrialized nations who see their own countries troubled with problems of unemployment, poor education, poverty, and drug abuse.

The United States' position has been that at this time it is appropriate to provide food and other humanitarian aid along with technical and educational assistance to Soviet enterprises and political officials, but to withhold unrestricted aid until substantial reform of the economy has been achieved.

In fact, in the spring of 1992 the United States and its G-7 partners (Germany, Japan, France, Britain, Canada, and Italy) have promised Russia a $24 billion aid package. This includes $11 billion in direct aid; $6 billion to provide a fund for stabilizing the ruble; $4.5 billion of IMF and World Bank loans; and $2.5 billion in debt rescheduling (on an estimated $89 billion debt). The United States' share is approximately $5 billion.

Private Investment

As the former Soviet Union attempts to move toward a capitalistic system, will it be able to attract foreign investment to shore up its economy? Given the vast potential market provided by some 288 million citizens, we would expect the answer to be "Yes." Furthermore, it is undoubtedly true that flows of private investment could be extremely helpful to the Soviet economy, perhaps more so than public aid. The reason is that, in addition to providing real capital, profit-seeking private investors will bring in managerial skills, entrepreneurial behavior, and marketing connections.

But in fact there are serious obstacles to foreign firms in doing business in the former Soviet Union. One is determining who is in charge. As the country moves toward decentralization politically, companies must discover whether they should deal with a Commonwealth trade minister in Minsk, officials at the republic level, or both. To whom does a foreign firm pay taxes, and with whom does one sign contracts? Who issues the necessary permits and licenses?

A second problem is that neither suppliers of inputs nor a dependable infrastructure are available. Enterprises manufacturing inputs are still generally committed to selling most of their supplies to the state. How do new "outsiders" acquire necessary resources? Furthermore, Soviet communication and transportation systems are grossly inadequate by world standards. McDonald's spent fourteen years establishing its Moscow fast-food restaurant and its earnings are in rubles rather than dollars.

A third difficulty is the inconvertibility of the ruble. How does an American firm which establishes a successful company in Kiev or St. Petersburg withdraw its profits? The attractive feature of *joint ventures*—businesses in which American firms and Soviet enterprises cooperate in a productive endeavor—is that the convertibility problem may be circumvented. Firms such as Chevron and Amoco which intend to help the former Soviet Union exploit its vast oil reserves can take their earnings in oil rather than currency.

Membership in International Institutions

Historically the Soviet Union has distanced itself from the major international trade and financial institutions such as the International Monetary Fund (IMF), the World Bank, and the General Agreement on Tariffs and Trade (GATT). There is no doubt that membership in these institutions could benefit the Soviet Union. For example, membership in the IMF and World Bank could provide additional sources of economic aid. Membership in GATT would result in lower tariff barriers for Soviet exports. In the spring of 1992 Russia was admitted to the IMF and other republics are expected to follow. IMF and World Bank officials have indicated they would provide $45 to $50 billion in aid to the Commonwealth over the next four years.

QUICK REVIEW 23-3

◆ *The former Soviet Union has made the commitment to become a capitalistic system. Ingredients in the transition from planning to markets include: a creating private property and property rights; b promoting competition; c limiting and reformulating government's role; d removing domestic price controls; e opening the economy to international market forces; and f establishing monetary and fiscal policies to stabilize the economy.*

◆ *In addition to the technical economic problems associated with the transition, reforms require widespread public support, the maintenance of economic unity among the republics, and more-or-less simultaneous realization of the reform components.*

◆ *Factors helpful to the transition include a generous natural resource base, the potential release of large amounts of resources from the military sector, the entrepreneurship implicit in the underground economy, and substantial strides toward political democracy.*

◆ *The reform effort in the former Soviet Union may also be assisted by foreign technical and economic aid, private investment by foreign firms, and membership in international trade and lending institutions.*

PROSPECTS

What are the prospects for a successful transition from central planning to markets? At this time there is no definitive answer. The failed August 1991 coup suggests that anarchy and civil war are not beyond imagination. And there is some consensus that the damage done to the Soviet economy by seven decades of communism will not be easily nor quickly undone. The immediate future may bring considerable pain and suffering to citizens in Russia and the other Commonwealth republics. Yet we must keep in mind that the political and economic changes which have occurred in the former Soviet Union in the past several years have been remarkable and justify some measure of optimism.

CHAPTER SUMMARY

1 The labor theory of value is a central principle of Marxian ideology. Capitalists, as property owners, allegedly expropriate most of labor's value as profits or surplus value.

2 Virtually complete state ownership of property resources and central planning historically were the major institutional features of the Soviet economy.

3 Characteristics of Soviet planning included **a** emphasis on industrialization and military strength; **b** overcommitment of resources; **c** economic growth based on additional inputs rather than increased productivity; **d** allocation of resources by bureaucratic rather than market decisions; **e** economic self-sufficiency; and **f** passive macroeconomic policies.

4 The basic problem facing central planners is achieving coordination or internal consistency in their plans to avoid bottlenecks and the chain reaction of production failures which they cause.

5 Diminishing growth rates, shoddy consumer goods, and the inability to provide a promised high standard of living are all evidence of the failure of Soviet central planning.

6 Stagnation of the agricultural sector, a growing labor shortage, and the burden of a large military establishment contributed to the failure of the Soviet economy. However, the primary causes of failure were the inability of central planning to coordinate a more complex economy, the absence of rational success indicators, and the lack of adequate economic incentives.

7 The recent Gorbachev reforms attempted to restructure the economy and introduce greater political "openness," but did not address fundamental systemic deficiencies.

8 To change from central planning to a market economy, the former Soviet Union must move from public to private ownership of property; establish a competitive environment for businesses; restructure government's role to activities appropriate to capitalism; abandon state-determined prices in favor of market-determined prices; bring its economy into nomic policies and institutions to provide employment and price level stability.

9 In addition to resolving the technical economic problems inherent in the transformation of the Soviet economy to a market system, it is also necessary to achieve the support of bureaucrats and workers, preserve economic unity among the republics, and put reforms into effect simultaneously.

10 Reform efforts by the former Soviet republics may be furthered by the Commonwealth's abundant natural resources; the freeing of resources from the military; entrepreneurial talent evident in the underground economy; the democratization of the political system; and the assistance provided by foreign governments, foreign private investment, and international lending and trade institutions.

TERMS AND CONCEPTS

labor theory of value	central economic	Gorbachev reforms	*glasnost*
surplus value	planning	*perestroika*	ruble overhang
state ownership			

QUESTIONS AND STUDY SUGGESTIONS

1 Compare the ideology and institutional framework of the former Soviet economy with that of American capitalism. Contrast the manner in which production is motivated in these two systems.

2 Discuss the problem of coordination which faces central planners. Explain how a planning failure can cause a chain reaction of additional failures.

3 How was the number of automobiles to be produced determined in the former Soviet Union? In the United States? How are the decisions implemented in the two different types of economies?

4 What have been the major characteristics and goals of Soviet central planning?

5 What is the evidence of the failure of Soviet planning? Explain why Soviet economic growth diminished after 1970.

6 Explain why the use of quantitative output targets as the major success indicator for Soviet enterprises contributed to economic inefficiency.

7 Use a supply and demand diagram to explain the persistent shortages of many Soviet consumer goods. Why might the transformation to a market economy be accompanied by inflation? Why were black markets so common in the Soviet Union?

8 What specific changes must be made to transform the Soviet economy to a market system? Why is it important that these changes be introduced simultaneously?

9 Citing both specific obstacles and facilitating factors, do you think that the former Soviet Union will be successful in becoming a capitalistic system?

10 "It has become increasingly difficult for thoughtful men to find meaningful alternatives posed in the traditional choices between socialism and capitalism, planning and the free market, regulation and laissez faire, for they find their actual choices neither simple nor so grand."[7] Explain and evaluate.

[7]Robert A. Dahl and Charles E. Lindblom, *Politics, Economics and Welfare* (New York: Harper & Row, Publishers, Inc., 1953), p. 1.

GLOSSARY

Abstraction Elimination of irrelevant and noneconomic facts to obtain an economic principle.

Actual budget The amount spent by the Federal government (to purchase goods and services and for transfer payments) less the amount of tax revenue collected by it in any (fiscal) year; and which can *not* reliably be used to determine whether it is pursuing an expansionary or contractionary fiscal policy. Compare (*see*) the Full-employment budget.

Actual deficit The size of the Federal government's Budget deficit (*see*) or surplus actually measured or recorded in any given year.

Actual investment The amount which business Firms do invest; equal to Planned investment plus Unplanned investment.

Actual reserves The amount of funds which a Member bank has on deposit at the Federal Reserve Bank of its district (plus its Vault cash).

Adaptive expectations theory The idea that people determine their expectations about future events (for example, inflation) on the basis of past and present events (rates of inflation) and only change their expectations as events unfold.

Adjustable pegs The device used in the Bretton Woods system (*see*) to change Exchange rates in an orderly way to eliminate persistent Payments deficits and surpluses: each nation defined its monetary unit in terms of (pegged it to) gold or the dollar, kept the Rate of exchange for its money stable in the short run, and changed (adjusted) it in the long run when faced with international disequilibrium.

Aggregate demand A schedule or curve which shows the total quantity of goods and services that will be demanded (purchased) at different price levels.

Aggregate demand–aggregate supply model The macroeconomic model which uses Aggregate demand and Aggregate supply (*see* both) to determine and explain the Price level and the real Domestic output.

Aggregate expenditures The total amount spent for final goods and services in the economy.

Aggregate expenditures–domestic output approach Determination of the Equilibrium gross domestic product (*see*) by finding the real GDP at which Aggregate expenditures are equal to the Domestic output.

Aggregate expenditures schedule A schedule or curve which shows the total amount spent for final goods and services at different levels of real GDP.

Aggregate supply A schedule or curve which shows the total quantity of goods and services that will be supplied (produced) at different price levels.

Aggregation Combining individual units or data into one unit or number. For example, all prices of individual goods and services are combined into a Price level, or all units of output are aggregated into Real gross domestic product.

Allocative efficiency The apportionment of resources among firms and industries to obtain the production of the products most wanted by society (consumers); the output of each product at which its Marginal cost and Price are equal.

Allocative factor The ability of an economy to reallocate resources to achieve the Economic growth which the Supply factors (*see*) make possible.

Annually balanced budget The equality of government expenditures and tax collections during a year.

Anticipated inflation Inflation (*see*) at a rate which was equal to the rate expected in that period of time.

Applied economics (*See* Policy economics.)

Appreciation of the dollar An increase in the value of the dollar relative to the currency of another nation; a dollar now buys a larger amount of the foreign currency. For example, if the dollar price of a British pound changes from $3 to $2, the dollar has appreciated.

Asset Anything of monetary value owned by a firm or individual.

Asset demand for money The amount of money people want to hold as a Store of value (the amount of their financial assets they wish to have in the form of Money); and which varies inversely with the Rate of interest.

Authoritarian capitalism An economic system (method of organization) in which property resources are privately owned and government extensively directs and controls the economy.

Average product The total output produced per unit of a resource employed (total product divided by the quantity of a resource employed).

Average propensity to consume Fraction of Disposable income which households spend for consumer goods and services; consumption divided by Disposable income.

Average propensity to save Fraction of Disposable income which households save; Saving divided by Disposable income.

Average tax rate Total tax paid divided by total (taxable) income; the tax rate on total (taxable) income.

Balanced-budget amendment Proposed constitutional amendment which would require Congress to balance the Federal budget annually.

Balanced budget multiplier The effect of equal increases (decreases) in government spending for goods and services and in taxes is to increase (decrease) the Equilibrium gross domestic product by the amount of the equal increases (decreases).

Balance of payments deficit The sum of the Balance on current account (*see*) and the Balance on the capital account (*see*) is negative.

Balance of payments surplus The sum of the Balance on current account (*see*) and the Balance on the capital account (*see*) is positive.

Balance on current account The exports of goods (merchandise) and services of a nation less its imports of goods (merchandise) and services plus its Net investment income and Net transfers.

Balance on goods and services The exports of goods (merchandise) and services of a nation less its imports of goods (merchandise) and services.

Balance on the capital account The Capital inflows (*see*) of a nation less its Capital outflows (*see*).

Balance sheet A statement of the Assets (*see*), Liabilities (*see*), and Net worth (*see*) of a firm or individual at some given time.

Bank deposits The deposits which banks have at the Federal Reserve Banks (*see*).

Bankers' bank A bank which accepts the deposits of and makes loans to Depository institutions; a Federal Reserve Bank.

Bank reserves Bank reserves held at the Federal Reserve Banks (*see*) plus bank Vault cash (*see*).

Barrier to entry Anything that artificially prevents the entry of Firms into an industry.

Barter The exchange of one good or service for another good or service.

Base year The year with which prices in other years are compared when a Price index (*see*) is constructed.

Benefit-cost analysis Deciding whether to employ resources and the quantity of resources to employ for a project or program (for the production of a good or service) by comparing the marginal benefits with the marginal costs.

Big business A business Firm which either produces a large percentage of the total output of an industry, is large (in terms of number of employees or stockholders, sales, assets, or profits) compared with other Firms in the economy, or both.

Board of Governors The seven-member group that supervises and controls the money and banking system of the United States; formally, the Board of Governors of the Federal Reserve System; the Federal Reserve Board.

Brain drain The emigration of highly educated, highly skilled workers from a country.

Break-even income The level of Disposable income at which Households plan to consume (spend) all of their income (for consumer goods and services) and to save none of it; also denotes that level of earned income at which subsidy payments become zero in an income maintenance program.

Bretton Woods system The international monetary system developed after World War II in which Adjustable pegs (*see*) were employed, the International Monetary Fund (*see*) helped to stabilize Foreign exchange rates, and gold and the dollar (*see*) were used as International monetary reserves (*see*).

Budget deficit The amount by which the expenditures of the Federal government exceed its revenues in any year.

Built-in stability The effect of Nondiscretionary fiscal policy (*see*) on the economy; when Net taxes vary directly with the Gross domestic product, the fall (rise) in Net taxes during a recession (inflation) helps to eliminate unemployment (inflationary pressures).

Business cycle Recurrent ups and downs over a period of years in the level of economic activity.

Capital Human-made resources used to produce goods and services; goods which do not directly satisfy human wants; capital goods.

Capital account The section in a nation's International balance of payments (*see*) in which are recorded the Capital inflows (*see*) and the Capital outflows (*see*) of that nation.

Capital account deficit A negative Balance on the capital account (*see*).

Capital account surplus A positive Balance on the capital account (*see*).

Capital flight The transfer of savings from less developed to industrially advanced countries to avoid government expropriation, taxation, and high rates of inflation or to realize better investment opportunities.

Capital gain The gain realized when securities or properties are sold for a price greater than the price paid for them.

Capital goods (*See* Capital.)

Capital inflow The expenditures made by the residents of foreign nations to purchase real and financial capital from the residents of a nation.

Capital-intensive commodity A product which requires a relatively large amount of Capital to produce.

Capital outflow The expenditures made by the residents of a nation to purchase real and financial capital from the residents of foreign nations.

Capital-saving technological advance An improvement in technology that permits a greater quantity of a product to be produced with a given amount of Capital (or the same amount of the product to be produced with a smaller amount of Capital).

Capital-using technological advance An improvement in technology that requires the use of a greater amount of Capital to produce a given quantity of a product.

Causation A cause-and-effect relationship; one or several events bring about or result in another event.

CEA (*See* Council of Economic Advisers.)

Central bank A bank whose chief function is the control of the nation's money supply.

Central economic planning Government determination of the objectives of the economy and the direction of its resources to the attainment of these objectives.

***Ceteris paribus* assumption** (*See* "Other things being equal" assumption.)

Change in amount consumed Increase or decrease in consumption spending that results from an increase or decrease in Disposable income, the Consumption schedule (curve) remaining unchanged; movement from one row (point) to another on the same Consumption schedule (curve).

Change in amount saved Increase or decrease in Saving that results from an increase or decrease in Disposable income, the Saving schedule (curve) remaining unchanged; movement from one row (point) to another on the same Saving schedule (curve).

Change in the consumption schedule An increase or decrease in consumption at each level of Disposable income caused by changes in the Nonincome determinants of consumption and saving (*see*); an upward or downward movement of the Consumption schedule.

Change in the saving schedule An increase or decrease in Saving at each level of Disposable income caused by changes in the Nonincome determinants of consumption

and saving (*see*); an upward or downward movement of the Saving schedule.

Checkable deposit Any deposit in a commercial bank or Thrift institution against which a check may be written; includes Demand deposits and NOW, ATS, and share draft accounts.

Checking account A Checkable deposit (*see*) in a Commercial bank or Thrift institution.

Circuit velocity of money (*See* Velocity of money.)

Circular flow of income The flow of resources from Households to Firms and of products from Firms to Households accompanied in an economy using money by flows of money from Households to Firms and from Firms to Households.

Classical range The vertical segment of the Aggregate supply curve along which the economy is at Full employment.

Classical theory The Classical theory of employment (*see*).

Classical theory of employment The Macroeconomic generalizations accepted by most economists before the 1930s which led to the conclusion that a capitalistic economy would employ its resources fully.

Closed economy An economy which neither exports nor imports goods and services.

Coincidence of wants The item (good or service) which one trader wishes to obtain is the same item which another trader desires to give up and the item which the second trader wishes to acquire is the same item the first trader desires to surrender.

COLA (*See* Cost-of-living adjustment.)

Collection of checks The process by which funds are transferred from the checking accounts of the writers of checks to the checking accounts of the recipients of the checks; also called the "clearing" of checks.

Collusive oligopoly Occurs when the few firms composing an oligopolistic industry reach an explicit or unspoken agreement to fix prices, divide a market, or otherwise restrict competition; may take the form of a Cartel (*see*), Gentleman's agreement (*see*), or Price leadership (*see*).

Command economy An economic system (method of organization) in which property resources are publicly owned and Central economic planning (*see*) is used to direct and coordinate economic activities.

Commercial bank Firm which has a charter from either a state government or the Federal government to engage in the business of banking.

Commercial banking system All Commercial banks and Thrift institutions as a group.

Communism (*See* Command economy.)

Comparative advantage A lower relative or Comparative cost (*see*) than another producer.

Comparative cost The amount the production of one product must be reduced to increase the production of another product; Opportunity cost (*see*).

Compensation to employees Wages and salaries paid by employers to workers plus Wage and salary supplements (*see*).

Competing goods (*See* Substitute goods.)

Competition The presence in a market of a large number of independent buyers and sellers and the freedom of buyers and sellers to enter and leave the market.

Complementary goods Goods or services for which there is an inverse relationship between the price of one and the demand for the other; when the price of one falls (rises) the demand for the other increases (decreases).

Complex multiplier The Multiplier (*see*) when changes in the Gross domestic product change Net taxes and Imports, as well as Saving.

Conglomerate combination A group of Plants (*see*) owned by a single Firm and engaged at one or more stages in the production of different products (of products which do not compete with each other).

Consumer goods Goods and services which satisfy human wants directly.

Consumer sovereignty Determination by consumers of the types and quantities of goods and services that are produced from the scarce resources of the economy.

Consumption of fixed capital Estimate of the amount of Capital worn out or used up (consumed) in producing the Gross domestic product; depreciation.

Consumption schedule Schedule which shows the amounts Households plan to spend for Consumer goods at different levels of Disposable income.

Contractionary fiscal policy A decrease in Aggregate demand brought about by a decrease in Government expenditures for goods and services, an increase in Net taxes, or some combination of the two.

Corporate income tax A tax levied on the net income (profit) of Corporations.

Corporation A legal entity ("person") chartered by a state or the Federal government, and distinct and separate from the individuals who own it.

Correlation Systematic and dependable association between two sets of data (two kinds of events).

Cost-of-living adjustment An increase in the incomes (wages) of workers which is automatically received by them when there is inflation in the economy and guaranteed by a clause in their labor contracts with their employer.

Cost-push inflation Inflation that results from a decrease in Aggregate supply (from higher wage rates and raw material prices) and which is accompanied by decreases in real output and employment (by increases in the Unemployment rate).

Cost ratio The ratio of the decrease in the production of the product to the increase in the production of another product when resources are shifted from the production of the first to the production of the second product; the amount the production of one product decreases when the production of a second product increases by one unit.

Council of Economic Advisers A group of three persons which advises and assists the President of the United States on economic matters (including the preparation of the economic report of the President to Congress).

Credit An accounting notation that the value of an asset (such as the foreign money owned by the residents of a nation) has increased.

Credit union An association of persons who have a common tie (such as being employees of the same Firm or members of the same Labor union) which sells shares to (accepts deposits from) its members and makes loans to them.

Crowding-out effect The rise in interest rates and the resulting decrease in planned investment spending in the economy caused by increased borrowing in the money market by the Federal government.

Currency Coins and Paper money.

Currency appreciation (*See* Exchange rate appreciation.)

Currency depreciation (*See* Exchange rate depreciation.)

Current account The section in a nation's International balance of payments (*see*) in which are recorded its exports and imports of goods (merchandise) and services, its net investment income, and its net transfers.

Current account deficit A negative Balance on current account (*see*).

Current account surplus A positive Balance on current account (*see*).

Customary economy (*See* Traditional economy.)

Cyclical deficit A Federal Budget deficit which is caused by a recession and the consequent decline in tax revenues.

Cyclical unemployment Unemployment caused by insufficient Aggregate expenditures.

Cyclically balanced budget The equality of Government expenditures and Net tax collections over the course of a Business cycle; deficits incurred during periods of recession are offset by surpluses obtained during periods of prosperity (inflation).

Debit An accounting notation that the value of an asset (such as the foreign money owned by the residents of a nation) has decreased.

Declining economy An economy in which Net private domestic investment (*see*) is less than zero (Gross private domestic investment is less than Depreciation).

Declining industry An industry in which Economic profits are negative (losses are incurred) and which will, therefore, decrease its output as Firms leave the industry.

Decrease in demand A decrease in the Quantity demanded of a good or service at every price; a shift of the Demand curve to the left.

Decrease in supply A decrease in the Quantity supplied of a good or service at every price; a shift of the Supply curve to the left.

Deduction Reasoning from assumptions to conclusions; a method of reasoning that tests a hypothesis (an assumption) by comparing the conclusions to which it leads with economic facts.

Deflating Finding the Real gross domestic product (*see*) by decreasing the dollar value of the Gross domestic product produced in a year in which prices were higher than in the Base year (*see*).

Deflation A fall in the general (average) level of prices in the economy.

Demand A Demand schedule or a Demand curve (*see* both).

Demand curve A curve which shows the amounts of a good or service buyers wish to purchase at various prices during some period of time.

Demand deposit A deposit in a Commercial bank against which checks may be written; a Checking account or checking-account money.

Demand-deposit multiplier (*See* Monetary multiplier.)

Demand factor The increase in the level of Aggregate demand which brings about the Economic growth made possible by an increase in the productive potential of the economy.

Demand management The use of Fiscal policy (*see*) and Monetary policy (*see*) to increase or decrease Aggregate demand.

Demand-pull inflation Inflation which is the result of an increase in Aggregate demand.

Demand schedule A schedule which shows the amounts of a good or service buyers wish to purchase at various prices during some period of time.

Dependent variable A variable which changes as a consequence of a change in some other (independent) variable; the "effect" or outcome.

Depository institution A Firm that accepts the deposits of Money of the public (businesses and persons); Commercial banks, Savings and loan associations, Mutual savings banks, and Credit unions.

Depository Institutions Deregulation and Monetary Control Act Federal legislation of 1980 which, among other things, allowed Thrift institutions to accept Checkable deposits and to use the check-clearing facilities of the Federal Reserve and to borrow from the Federal Reserve Banks; subjected the Thrifts to the reserve requirements of the Fed; and provided for the gradual elimination of the maximum interest rates that could be paid by Depository institutions on Savings and Time deposits.

Depreciation (*See* Consumption of fixed capital.)

Depreciation of the dollar A decrease in the value of the dollar relative to another currency; a dollar now buys a smaller amount of the foreign currency. For example, if the dollar price of a British pound changes from $2 to $3, the dollar has depreciated.

Derived demand The demand for a good or service which is dependent on or related to the demand for some other good or service; the demand for a resource which depends on the demand for the products it can be used to produce.

Descriptive economics The gathering or collection of relevant economic facts (data).

Determinants of aggregate demand Factors such as consumption, investment, government, and net export spending which, if they change, will shift the aggregate demand curve.

Determinants of aggregate supply Factors such as input prices, productivity, and the legal-institutional environment which, if they change, will shift the aggregate supply curve.

Determinants of demand Factors other than its price which determine the quantities demanded of a good or service.

Determinants of supply Factors other than its price which determine the quantities supplied of a good or service.

Devaluation A decrease in the defined value of a currency.

DI (*See* Disposable income.)

DIDMCA (*See* Depository Institutions Deregulation and Monetary Control Act.)

Directing function of prices (*See* Guiding function of prices.)

Directly related Two sets of economic data that change in the same direction; when one variable increases (decreases) the other increases (decreases).

Direct relationship The relationship between two variables which change in the same direction, for example, product price and quantity supplied.

Discount rate The interest rate which the Federal Reserve Banks charge on the loans they make to Depository institutions.

Discouraged workers Workers who have left the Labor force (*see*) because they have not been able to find employment.

Discretionary fiscal policy Deliberate changes in taxes (tax rates) and government spending (spending for goods and services and transfer payment programs) by Congress to achieve a full-employment noninflationary Gross domestic product and economic growth.

Disinflation A reduction in the rate of Inflation (*see*).

Disposable income Personal income (*see*) less personal taxes; income available for Personal consumption expenditures (*see*) and Personal saving (*see*).

Dissaving Spending for consumer goods and services in excess of Disposable income; the amount by which Personal consumption expenditures (*see*) exceed Disposable income.

Division of labor Dividing the work required to produce a product into a number of different tasks which are performed by different workers; Specialization (*see*) of workers.

Dollar votes The "votes" which consumers and entrepreneurs in effect cast for the production of the different kinds of consumer and capital goods, respectively, when they purchase them in the markets of the economy.

Domestic capital formation Adding to a nation's stock of Capital by saving part of its own domestic output.

Domestic economic goal Assumed to be full employment with little or no inflation.

Domestic output Gross (or net) domestic product; the total output of final goods and services produced in the economy.

Double counting Including the value of Intermediate goods (*see*) in the Gross domestic product; counting the same good or service more than once.

Double taxation Taxation of both corporate net income (profits) and the dividends paid from this net income when they become the Personal income of households.

Dumping The sale of products below cost in a foreign country.

Durable good A consumer good with an expected life (use) of one year or more.

Dynamic progress The development over time of more efficient (less costly) techniques of producing existing products and of improved products; technological progress.

Earnings The money income received by a worker; equal to the Wage (rate) multiplied by the quantity of labor supplied (the amount of time worked) by the worker.

Easy money policy Expanding the Money supply.

EC European Economic Community (*See* European Common Market).

Economic analysis Deriving Economic principles (*see*) from relevant economic facts.

Economic cost A payment that must be made to obtain and retain the services of a resource; the income a Firm must provide to a resource supplier to attract the resource away from an alternative use; equal to the quantity of other products that cannot be produced when resources are employed to produce a particular product.

Economic efficiency The relationship between the input of scarce resources and the resulting output of a good or service; production of an output with a given dollar-and-cents value with the smallest total expenditure for resources; obtaining the largest total production of a good or service with resources of a given dollar-and-cents value.

Economic growth (1) An increase in the Production possibilities schedule or curve that results from an increase in resource supplies or an improvement in Technology; (2) an increase either in real output (Gross domestic product) or in real output per capita.

Economic integration Cooperation among and the complete or partial unification of the economies of different nations; the elimination of the barriers to trade among these nations; the bringing together of the markets in each of the separate economies to form one large (a common) market.

Economic law (*See* Economic principle.)

Economic model A simplified picture of reality; an abstract generalization.

Economic perspective A viewpoint which envisions individuals and institutions making rational or purposeful decisions based on a consideration of the benefits and costs associated with their actions.

Economic policy Course of action intended to correct or avoid a problem.

Economic principle Generalization of the economic behavior of individuals and institutions.

Economic profit The Total revenue of a firm less all its Economic costs; also called "pure profit" and "above normal profit."

Economic rent The price paid for the use of land and other natural resources, the supply of which is fixed (perfectly inelastic).

Economics Social science concerned with using scarce resources to obtain the maximum satisfaction of the unlimited material wants of society.

Economic theory Deriving economic principles (*see*) from relevant economic facts; an Economic principle (*see*).

Economizing problem Society's material wants are unlimited but the resources available to produce the goods and services that satisfy wants are limited (scarce); the inability of any economy to produce unlimited quantities of goods and services.

Efficiency wage A wage which minimizes wage costs per unit of output.

Efficient allocation of resources That allocation of the resources of an economy among the production of different products which leads to the maximum satisfaction of the wants of consumers.

Employment Act of 1946 Federal legislation which committed the Federal government to the maintenance of economic stability (Full employment, stable prices, and Economic growth); established the Council of Economic Advisers (*see*); and the Joint Economic Committee (*see*); and provided for the annual economic report of the President to Congress.

Employment rate The percentage of the Labor force (*see*) employed at any time.

Entrepreneurial ability The human resource which combines the other resources to produce a product, makes nonroutine decisions, innovates, and bears risks.

Equation of exchange $MV = PQ$; in which M is the Money supply (*see*), V is the Income velocity of money (*see*), P is the Price level, and Q is the physical volume of final goods and services produced.

Equilibrium domestic output The real Domestic output at which the Aggregate demand curve intersects the Aggregate supply curve.

Equilibrium gross domestic product The Gross domestic product at which the total quantity of final goods and services produced (the Domestic output) is equal to the total quantity of final goods and services purchased (Aggregate expenditures).

Equilibrium price The price in a competitive market at which the Quantity demanded (*see*) and the Quantity supplied (*see*) are equal; at which there is neither a shortage nor a surplus; and at which there is no tendency for price to rise or fall.

Equilibrium price level The price level at which the Aggregate demand curve intersects the Aggregate supply curve.

Equilibrium quantity The Quantity demanded (*see*) and Quantity supplied (*see*) at the Equilibrium price (*see*) in a competitive market.

Equilibrium real domestic output The real domestic output which is determined by the equality (intersection) of Aggregate demand and Aggregate supply.

European Common Market The association of twelve European nations initiated in 1958 to abolish gradually the Tariffs and Import quotas that exist among them, to establish common Tariffs for goods imported from outside the member nations, to allow the eventual free movement of labor and capital among them, and to create other common economic policies.

European Economic Community (EC) (*See* European Common Market.)

Excess reserves The amount by which a member bank's Actual reserves (*see*) exceed its Required reserves (*see*); Actual reserves minus Required reserves.

Exchange control (*See* Foreign exchange control.)

Exchange rate The Rate of exchange (*see*).

Exchange rate appreciation An increase in the value of a nation's money in foreign exchange markets; an increase in the Rates of exchange for foreign monies.

Exchange rate depreciation A decrease in the value of a nation's money in foreign exchange markets; a decrease in the Rates of exchange for foreign monies.

Exchange rate determinant Any factor other than the Rate of exchange (*see*) that determines the demand for and the supply of a currency in the Foreign exchange market (*see*).

Excise tax A tax levied on the expenditure for a specific product or on the quantity of the product purchased.

Exclusion principle The exclusion of those who do not pay for a product from the benefits of the product.

Exhaustive expenditure An expenditure by government that results directly in the employment of economic resources and in the absorption by government of the goods and services these resources produce; a Government purchase (*see*).

Expanding economy An economy in which Net private domestic investment (*see*) is greater than zero (Gross private domestic investment is greater than Depreciation).

Expansionary fiscal policy An increase in Aggregate demand brought about by an increase in Government expenditures for goods and services, a decrease in Net taxes, or some combination of the two.

Expectations What consumers, business Firms, and others believe will happen or what conditions will be in the future.

Expected rate of net profits Annual profits which a firm anticipates it will obtain by purchasing Capital (by investing) expressed as a percentage of the price (cost) of the Capital.

Expenditures approach The method which adds all the expenditures made for Final goods and services to measure the Gross domestic product.

Expenditures-output approach (*See* Aggregate expenditures–domestic output approach.)

Explicit cost The monetary payment a Firm must make to an outsider to obtain a resource.

Exports Goods and services produced in a given nation and sold to customers in other nations.

Export subsidies Government payments which reduce the price of a product to foreign buyers.

Export transactions A sale of a good or service which increases the amount of foreign money held by the citizens, firms, and governments of a nation.

External benefit (*See* Spillover benefit.)

External cost (*See* Spillover cost.)

External debt Public debt (*see*) owed to foreign citizens, firms, and institutions.

External economic goal (*See* International economic goal.)

Externality (*See* Spillover.)

Face value The dollar or cents value stamped on a coin.

Factors of production Economic resources: Land, Capital, Labor, and Entrepreneurial ability.

Fallacy of composition Incorrectly reasoning that what is true for the individual (or part) is therefore necessarily true for the group (or whole).

FDIC (*See* Federal Deposit Insurance Corporation.)

Federal Advisory Committee The group of twelve commercial bankers which advises the Board of Governors (*see*) on banking policy.

Federal Deposit Insurance Corporation (FDIC) The Federally chartered corporation which insures the deposit liabilities of Commercial banks and Thrift Institutions.

Federal funds rate The interest rate that lending depository institutions charge borrowing institutions for the use of excess reserves.

Federal Open Market Committee (*See* Open Market Committee.)

Federal Reserve Bank Any one of the twelve banks chartered by the United States government to control the Money supply and perform other functions; (*See* Central bank, Quasi-public bank, *and* Banker's bank.)

Federal Reserve Note Paper money issued by the Federal Reserve Banks.

Feedback effects The effects which a change in the money supply will have (because it affects the interest rate, planned investment, and the equilibrium GDP) on the demand for money which is itself directly related to the GDP.

Fiat money Anything that is Money because government has decreed it to be Money.

Final goods Goods which have been purchased for final use and not for resale or further processing or manufacturing (during the year).

Financial capital (*See* Money capital.)

Financing exports and imports The use of Foreign exchange markets by exporters and importers to receive and make payments for goods and services they sell and buy in foreign nations.

Firm An organization that employs resources to produce a good or service for profit and owns and operates one or more Plants (*see*).

Fiscal federalism The system of transfers (grants) by which the Federal government shares its revenues with state and local governments.

Fiscal policy Changes in government spending and tax collections for the purpose of achieving a full-employment and noninflationary domestic output.

Five fundamental economic questions The five questions which every economy must answer: what to produce, how to produce, how to divide the total output, how to maintain Full employment, and how to assure economic flexibility.

Fixed exchange rate A Rate of exchange that is prevented from rising or falling.

Flexible exchange rate A rate of exchange that is determined by the demand for and supply of the foreign money and is free to rise or fall.

Floating exchange rate (*See* Flexible exchange rate.)

Foreign competition (*See* Import competition.)

Foreign exchange control The control a government may exercise over the quantity of foreign money demanded by its citizens and business firms and over the Rates of exchange in order to limit its outpayments to its inpayments (to eliminate a Payments deficit, *see*).

Foreign exchange market A market in which the money (currency) used by one nation is used to purchase (is exchanged for) the money used by another nation.

Foreign exchange rate (*See* Rate of exchange.)

Foreign purchases effect The inverse relationship between the Net exports (*see*) of an economy and its Price level (*see*) relative to foreign Price levels.

45-degree line A line along which the value of the GDP (measured horizontally) is equal to the value of Aggregate expenditures (measured vertically).

Fractional reserve A Reserve ratio (*see*) that is less than 100 percent of the deposit liabilities of a Commercial bank.

Freedom of choice Freedom of owners of property resources and money to employ or dispose of these resources as they see fit, of workers to enter any line of work for which they are qualified, and of consumers to spend their incomes in a manner which they deem to be appropriate (best for them).

Freedom of enterprise Freedom of business Firms to employ economic resources, to use these resources to produce products of the firm's own choosing, and to sell these products in markets of their choice.

Freely floating exchange rates   Rates of exchange (*see*) which are not controlled and which may, therefore, rise and fall; and which are determined by the demand for and the supply of foreign monies.

Free-rider problem   The inability of those who might provide the economy with an economically desirable and indivisible good or service to obtain payment from those who benefit from the good or service because the Exclusion principle (*see*) cannot be applied to it.

Free trade   The absence of artificial (government imposed) barriers to trade among individuals and firms in different nations.

Frictional unemployment   Unemployment caused by workers voluntarily changing jobs and by temporary layoffs; unemployed workers between jobs.

Full employment   (1) Using all available resources to produce goods and services; (2) when the Unemployment rate is equal to the Full-employment unemployment rate and there is Frictional and Structural but no Cyclical unemployment (and the Real output of the economy is equal to its Potential real output).

Full-employment budget   What government expenditures and revenues and its surplus or deficit would be if the economy were to operate at Full employment throughout the year.

Full-employment unemployment rate   The Unemployment rate (*see*) at which there is no Cyclical unemployment (*see*) of the Labor force (*see*); and because some Frictional and Structural unemployment is unavoidable, equal to about 5 or 6 percent.

Full production   The maximum amount of goods and services that can be produced from the employed resources of an economy; the absence of Underemployment (*see*).

Functional distribution of income   The manner in which the economy's (the national) income is divided among those who perform different functions (provide the economy with different kinds of resources); the division of National income (*see*) into wages and salaries, proprietors' income, corporate profits, interest, and rent.

Functional finance   Use of Fiscal policy to achieve a full-employment noninflationary Gross domestic product without regard to the effect on the Public debt (*see*).

GATT   (*See* General Agreement on Tariffs and Trade.)

GDP   (*See* Gross domestic product.)

GDP deflator   The Price index (*see*) for all final goods and services used to adjust the money (or nominal) GDP to measure the real GDP.

GDP gap   Potential Real gross domestic product less actual Real gross domestic product.

General Agreement on Tariffs and Trade   The international agreement reached in 1947 by twenty-three nations (including the United States) in which each nation agreed to give equal and nondiscriminatory treatment to the other nations, to reduce tariff rates by multinational negotiations, and to eliminate Import quotas.

Generalization   Statistical or probability statement; statement of the nature of the relation between two or more sets of facts.

Glasnost   A Soviet campaign of the mid-1980s for greater "openness" and democratization in political and economic activities.

GNP   (*See* Gross national product.)

Gold export point   The rate of exchange for a foreign money above which—when nations participate in the International gold standard (*see*)—the foreign money will not be purchased and gold will be sent (exported) to the foreign country to make payments there.

Gold flow   The movement of gold into or out of a nation.

Gold import point   The Rate of exchange for a foreign money below which—when nations participate in the International gold standard (*see*)—a nation's own money will not be purchased and gold will be sent (imported) into that country by foreigners to make payments there.

Gorbachev's reforms   A mid-1980s series of reforms designed to revitalize the Soviet economy. The reforms stressed the modernization of productive facilities, less centralized control, improved worker discipline and productivity, more emphasis on market prices, and an expansion of private economic activity.

Gosbank   The state-owned and operated bank in the former U.S.S.R.

Government purchases   Disbursements of money by government for which government receives a currently produced good or service in return; the expenditures of all governments in the economy for Final goods (*see*) and services.

Government transfer payment   The disbursement of money (or goods and services) by government for which government receives no currently produced good or service in return.

Gramm-Rudman-Hollings Act   Legislation enacted in 1985 by the Federal government requiring annual reductions in Federal budget deficits and, as amended, a balanced budget by 1993; and mandating an automatic decrease in expenditures when Congress and the President cannot agree on how to meet the targeted reductions in the budget deficit.

Gross domestic product (GDP)   The total market value of all Final goods (*see*) and services produced annually within the boundaries of the United States, whether by American or foreign-supplied resources.

Gross national product (GNP) The total market value of all Final goods **(see)** and services produced annually by land, labor, and capital, and entrepreneurial talent supplied by American residents, whether these resources are located in the United States or abroad.

Gross private domestic investment Expenditures for newly produced Capital goods **(see)**—machinery, equipment, tools, and buildings—and for additions to inventories.

Guiding function of prices The ability of price changes to bring about changes in the quantities of products and resources demanded and supplied (See Incentive function of price.)

Horizontal axis The "left–right" or "west–east" axis on a graph or grid.

Horizontal combination A group of Plants **(see)** in the same stage of production which are owned by a single Firm **(see)**.

Household An economic unit (of one or more persons) which provides the economy with resources and uses the money paid to it for these resources to purchase goods and services that satisfy material wants.

Hyperinflation A very rapid rise in the price level.

IMF (See International Monetary Fund.)

Import competition Competition which domestic firms encounter from the products and services of foreign suppliers.

Import quota A limit imposed by a nation on the quantity of a good that may be imported during some period of time.

Imports Spending by individuals, Firms, and governments of an economy for goods and services produced in foreign nations.

Import transaction The purchase of a good or service which decreases the amount of foreign money held by citizens, firms, and governments of a nation.

Income approach The method which adds all the incomes generated by the production of Final goods and services to measure the Gross domestic product.

Income effect The effect which a change in the price of a product has on the Real income (purchasing power) of a consumer and the resulting effect on the quantity of that product the consumer would purchase after the consequences of the Substitution effect **(see)** have been taken into account (eliminated).

Income inequality The unequal distribution of an economy's total income among persons or families in the economy.

Incomes policy Government policy that affects the Nominal incomes of individuals (the wages workers receive) and the prices they pay for goods and services and thereby affects their Real incomes; (see Wage-price policy).

Income velocity of money (See Velocity of money.)

Increase in demand An increase in the Quantity demanded of a good or service at every price; a shift in the Demand curve to the right.

Increase in supply An increase in the Quantity supplied of a good or service at every price; a shift in the Supply curve to the right.

Independent goods Goods or services such that there is no relationship between the price of one and the demand for the other; when the price of one rises or falls the demand for the other remains constant.

Independent variable The variable which causes a change in some other (dependent) variable.

Indirect business taxes Such taxes as Sales, Excise, and business Property taxes **(see all)**, license fees, and Tariffs **(see)** which Firms treat as costs of producing a product and pass on (in whole or in part) to buyers of the product by charging them higher prices.

Individual demand The Demand schedule **(see)** or Demand curve **(see)** of a single buyer of a good or service.

Individual supply The Supply schedule **(see)** or Supply curve **(see)** of a single seller of a good or service.

Induction A method of reasoning that proceeds from facts to Generalization **(see)**.

Industrially advanced countries (IACs) Countries such as the United States, Canada, Japan, and the nations of western Europe which have developed Market economies based on large stocks of technologically advanced capital goods and skilled labor forces.

Industry The group of (one or more) Firms that produce identical or similar products.

Inferior good A good or service of which consumers purchase less (more) at every price when their incomes increase (decrease).

Inflating Finding the Real gross domestic product **(see)** by increasing the dollar value of the Gross domestic product produced in a year in which prices are lower than they were in the Base year **(see)**.

Inflation A rise in the general (average) level of prices in the economy.

Inflationary expectations The belief of workers, business Firms, and consumers that there will be substantial inflation in the future.

Inflationary gap The amount by which the Aggregate-expenditures schedule (curve) must decrease (shift downward) to decrease the nominal GDP to the full-employment noninflationary level.

Inflationary recession (*See* Stagflation.)

Infrastructure For the economy, the capital goods usually provided by the Public sector for the use of its citizens and Firms (e.g., highways, bridges, transit systems, wastewater treatment facilities, municipal water systems, and airports). For the Firm, the services and facilities which it must have to produce its products, which would be too costly for it to provide for itself, and which are provided by governments or other Firms (e.g., water, electricity, waste treatment, transportation, research, engineering, finance, and banking).

Injection An addition of spending to the income-expenditure stream: Investment, Government purchases, and Exports.

In-kind investment Nonfinancial investment (*see*).

Innovation The introduction of a new product, the use of a new method of production, or the employment of a new form of business organization.

Inpayments The receipts of (its own or foreign) money which the individuals, Firms, and governments of one nation obtain from the sale of goods and services, investment income, Remittances, and Capital inflows from abroad.

Interest The payment made for the use of money (of borrowed funds).

Interest income Income of those who supply the economy with Capital (*see*).

Interest rate The Rate of interest (*see*).

Interest-rate effect The tendency for increases (decreases) in the Price level to increase (decrease) the demand for money; raise (lower) interest rates; and, as a result, to reduce (expand) total spending in the economy.

Intermediate goods Goods which are purchased for resale or further processing or manufacturing during the year.

Intermediate range The upsloping segment of the Aggregate supply curve that lies between the Keynesian range and the Classical range (*see both*).

Internal economic goal (*See* Domestic economic goal.)

Internally held public debt Public debt (*see*) owed to (United States government securities owned by) American citizens, Firms, and institutions.

International balance of payments Summary statement of the transactions which took place between the individuals, Firms, and governments of one nation and those in all other nations during the year.

International balance of payments deficit (*See* Balance of payments deficit.)

International balance of payments surplus (*See* Balance of payments surplus.)

International Bank for Reconstruction and Development (*See* World Bank.)

International economic goal Assumed to be a current-account balance of zero.

International gold standard An international monetary system employed in the nineteenth and early twentieth centuries in which each nation defined its money in terms of a quantity of gold, maintained a fixed relationship between its gold stock and money supply, and allowed the free importation and exportation of gold.

International Monetary Fund The international association of nations which was formed after World War II to make loans of foreign monies to nations with temporary Payments deficits (*see*) and to administer the Adjustable pegs (*see*).

International monetary reserves The foreign monies and such assets as gold a nation may use to settle a Payments deficit (*see*).

International value of the dollar The price that must be paid in foreign currency (money) to obtain one American dollar.

Intrinsic value The market value of the metal in a coin.

Inverse relationship The relationship between two variables which change in opposite directions, for example, product price and quantity demanded.

Investment Spending for (the production and accumulation of) Capital goods (*see*) and additions to inventories.

Investment curve A curve which shows the amounts firms plan to invest (along the vertical axis) at different income (Gross domestic product) levels (along the horizontal axis).

Investment-demand curve A curve which shows Rates of interest (along the vertical axis) and the amount of Investment (along the horizontal axis) at each Rate of interest.

Investment-demand schedule Schedule which shows Rates of interest and the amount of Investment at each Rate of interest.

Investment schedule A schedule which shows the amounts Firms plan to invest at different income (Gross domestic product) levels.

Invisible hand The tendency of Firms and resource suppliers seeking to further their self-interests in competitive markets to further the best interest of society as a whole (the maximum satisfaction of wants).

JEC (*See* Joint Economic Committee.)

Joint Economic Committee Committee of Senators and members of Congress which investigates economic problems of national interest.

Keynesian economics The macroeconomic generalizations which are today accepted by most (but not all) economists and which lead to the conclusion that a capitalistic economy does not always employ its resources fully and that Fiscal policy (*see*) and Monetary policy (*see*) can be used to promote Full employment (*see*).

Keynesianism The philosophical, ideological, and analytical views of the prevailing majority of economists; and their employment theory and stabilization policies.

Keynesian range The horizontal segment of the Aggregate-supply curve along which the price level is constant as real domestic output changes.

Labor The physical and mental talents (efforts) of people which can be used to produce goods and services.

Labor force Persons sixteen years of age and older who are not in institutions and who are employed or are unemployed and seeking work.

Labor-intensive commodity A product which requires a relatively large amount of Labor to produce.

Labor productivity Total output divided by the quantity of labor employed to produce the output; the Average product (*see*) of labor or output per worker per hour.

Labor theory of value The Marxian notion that the economic value of any commodity is determined solely by the amount of labor required to produce it.

Laffer curve A curve which shows the relationship between tax rates and the tax revenues of government and on which there is a tax rate (between zero and 100 percent) at which tax revenues are a maximum.

Laissez faire capitalism (*See* Pure capitalism.)

Land Natural resources ("free gifts of nature") which can be used to produce goods and services.

Land-intensive commodity A product which requires a relatively large amount of Land to produce.

Law of demand The inverse relationship between the price and the Quantity demanded (*see*) of a good or service during some period of time.

Law of diminishing returns When successive equal increments of a Variable resource (*see*) are added to the Fixed resources (*see*), beyond some level of employment, the Marginal product (*see*) of the Variable resource will decrease.

Law of increasing opportunity cost As the amount of a product produced is increased, the Opportunity cost (*see*)—Marginal cost (*see*)—of producing an additional unit of the product increases.

Law of supply The direct relationship between the price and the Quantity supplied (*see*) of a good or service during some period of time.

Leakage (1) A withdrawal of potential spending from the income-expenditures stream: Saving (*see*), tax payments, and Imports (*see*); (2) a withdrawal which reduces the lending potential of the Commercial banking system.

Leakages-injections approach Determination of the Equilibrium gross domestic product (*see*) by finding the Gross domestic product at which Leakages (*see*) are equal to Injections (*see*).

Least-cost combination rule (of resources) The quantity of each resource a Firm must employ if it is to produce any output at the lowest total cost; the combination on which the ratio of the Marginal product (*see*) of a resource to its Marginal resource cost (*see*) (to its price if the resource is employed in a competitive market) is the same for all resources employed.

Legal reserves (deposit) The minimum amount which a Depository institution (*see*) must keep on deposit with the Federal Reserve Bank in its district, or in Vault cash (*see*).

Legal tender Anything that government has decreed must be accepted in payment of a debt.

Lending potential of an individual commercial bank The amount by which a single Commercial bank can safely increase the Money supply by making new loans to (or buying securities from) the public; equal to the Commercial bank's Excess reserves (*see*).

Lending potential of the banking system The amount by which the Commercial banking system (*see*) can increase the Money supply by making new loans to (or buying securities from) the public; equal to the Excess reserves (*see*) of the Commercial banking system multiplied by the Monetary multiplier (*see*).

Less developed countries (LDCs) Most countries of Africa, Asia, and Latin America which are characterized by a lack of capital goods, primitive production technologies, low literacy rates, high unemployment, rapid population growth, and labor forces heavily committed to agriculture.

Liability A debt with a monetary value; an amount owed by a Firm or an individual.

Limited liability Restriction of the maximum that may be lost to a predetermined amount; the maximum amount that may be lost by the owners (stockholders) of a Corporation is the amount they paid for their shares of stock.

Line-item veto A proposal to give the President the power to delete specific expenditure items from spending legislation passed by Congress.

Liquidity Money or things which can be quickly and easily converted into Money with little or no loss of purchasing power.

Loaded terminology Terms which arouse emotions and elicit approval or disapproval.

Long-run aggregate supply curve The aggregate supply curve associated with a time period in which input prices (especially nominal wages) are fully responsive to changes in the price level.

M1 The narrowly defined Money supply; the Currency and Checkable deposits (*see*) not owned by the Federal government, Federal Reserve Banks, or Depository institutions.

M2 A more broadly defined Money supply; equal to M1 (*see*) plus Noncheckable savings deposits, small Time deposits (deposits of less than $100,000), Money market deposit accounts, and individual Money market mutual fund balances.

M3 A still more broadly defined Money supply; equal to M2 (*see*) plus large Time deposits (deposits of $100,000 or more).

Macroeconomics The part of economics concerned with the economy as a whole; with such major aggregates as the household, business, and governmental sectors and with totals for the economy.

Managed floating exchange rate An Exchange rate that is allowed to change (float) to eliminate persistent Payments deficits and surpluses and is controlled (managed) to reduce day-to-day fluctuations.

Marginal propensity to consume Fraction of any change in Disposable income which is spent for Consumer goods; equal to the change in consumption divided by the change in Disposable income.

Marginal propensity to save Fraction of any change in Disposable income which households save; equal to change in Saving (*see*) divided by the change in Disposable income.

Marginal tax rate The fraction of additional (taxable) income that must be paid in taxes.

Market Any institution or mechanism that brings together the buyers (demanders) and sellers (suppliers) of a particular good or service.

Market demand (*See* Total demand.)

Market economy An economy in which only the private decisions of consumers, resource suppliers, and business Firms determine how resources are allocated; the Market system.

Market failure The failure of a market to bring about the allocation of resources that best satisfies the wants of society (that maximizes the satisfaction of wants). In particular, the over- or underallocation of resources to the production of a particular good or service (because of Spillovers or informational problems) and no allocation of resources to the production of Public goods (*see*).

Market policies Government policies designed to reduce the market power of labor unions and large business firms and to reduce or eliminate imbalances and bottlenecks in labor markets.

Market socialism An economic system (method of organization) in which property resources are publicly owned and markets and prices are used to direct and coordinate economic activities.

Market system All the product and resource markets of the economy and the relationships among them; a method which allows the prices determined in these markets to allocate the economy's scarce resources and to communicate and coordinate the decisions made by consumers, business firms, and resource suppliers.

Medium of exchange Money (*see*); a convenient means of exchanging goods and services without engaging in Barter (*see*); what sellers generally accept and buyers generally use to pay for a good or service.

Microeconomics The part of economics concerned with such individual units within the economy as Industries, Firms, and Households; and with individual markets, particular prices, and specific goods and services.

Mixed capitalism An economy in which both government and private decisions determine how resources are allocated.

Monetarism An alternative to Keynesianism (*see*); the philosophical, ideological, and analytical view of a minority of American economists; and their employment theory and stabilization policy which stress the role of money.

Monetary multiplier The multiple of its Excess reserves (*see*) by which the Commercial banking system (*see*) can expand the Money supply and Demand deposits by making new loans (or buying securities); and equal to one divided by the Required reserve ratio (*see*).

Monetary policy Changing the Money supply (*see*) to assist the economy to achieve a full-employment, noninflationary level of total output.

Monetary rule The rule suggested by Monetarism (*see*); the Money supply should be expanded each year at the same annual rate as the potential rate of growth of the Real gross domestic product; the supply of money should be increased steadily at from 3 to 5 percent.

Money Any item which is generally acceptable to sellers in exchange for goods and services.

Money capital Money available to purchase Capital goods (*see*).

Money income (*See* Nominal income.)

Money interest rate The Nominal interest rate (*see*).

Money market The market in which the demand for and the supply of money determine the Interest rate (or the level of interest rates) in the economy.

Money market deposit account (MMDA) Interest-earning accounts at banks and thrift institutions which pool the funds of depositors to buy various short-term securities.

Money market mutual funds (MMMF) Interest-bearing accounts offered by brokers which pool depositors' funds for the purchase of short-term securities; depositors may write checks in minimum amounts or more against their accounts.

Money supply Narrowly defined (*see*) *M*1, more broadly defined (*see*) *M*2 and *M*3.

Money wage The amount of money received by a worker per unit of time (hour, day, etc.); nominal wage.

Money wage rate (*See* Money wage.)

Monopoly A market in which the number of sellers is so small that each seller is able to influence the total supply and the price of the good or service.

Moral hazard problem The possibility that individuals or institutions will change their behavior in unanticipated ways as the result of a contract or agreement. Example: A bank whose deposits are insured against loss may make riskier loans and investments.

Most-favored-nation clause A clause in a trade agreement between the United States and another nation which provides that the other nation's Imports into the United States will be subjected to the lowest tariff levied then or later on any other nation's Imports into the United States.

Multiplier The ratio of the change in the Equilibrium GDP to the change in Investment (*see*), or to the change in any other component of the Aggregate expenditures schedule or to the change in Net taxes; the number by which a change in any component in the Aggregate expenditures schedule or in Net taxes must be multiplied to find the resulting change in the Equilibrium GDP.

Multiplier effect The effect on Equilibrium gross domestic product of a change in the Aggregate expenditures schedule (caused by a change in the Consumption schedule, Investment, Net taxes, Government expenditures for goods and services, or Net exports).

Mutually exclusive goals Goals which conflict and cannot be achieved simultaneously.

Mutual savings bank A Firm without stockholders which accepts deposits primarily from small individual savers and which lends primarily to individuals to finance the purchases of residences.

National bank A Commercial bank (*see*) chartered by the United States government.

National income Total income earned by resource suppliers for their contributions to the production of the Gross domestic product (*see*); equal to the Gross domestic product minus the Nonincome charges (*see*) plus net American income earned abroad (*see*).

National income accounting The techniques employed to measure (estimate) the overall production of the economy and other related totals for the nation as a whole.

Natural monopoly An industry in which the Economies of scale (*see*) are so great that the product can be produced by one Firm at an average cost which is lower than it would be if it were produced by more than one Firm.

Natural rate hypothesis The idea that the economy is stable in the long run at the natural rate of unemployment; views the long-run Phillips Curve (*see*) as being vertical at the natural rate of unemployment.

Natural rate of unemployment (*See* Full-employment unemployment rate.)

NDP (*See* Net domestic product.)

Near-money Financial assets, the most important of which are Noncheckable savings accounts, Time deposits, and U.S. short-term securities and savings bonds, that are not a medium of exchange but can be readily converted into Money.

Negative relationship (*See* Inverse relationship.)

Net American income earned abroad Receipts of resource income from the rest of the world minus payments of resource income to the rest of the world; the difference between GDP (*see*) and GNP (*see*).

Net capital movement The difference between the real and financial investments and loans made by individuals and Firms of one nation in the other nations of the world and the investments and loans made by individuals and Firms from other nations in a nation; Capital inflows less Capital outflows.

Net domestic product Gross domestic product (*see*) less that part of the output needed to replace the Capital goods worn out in producing the output (Consumption of fixed capital, *see*).

Net export effect The notion that the impact of a change in Monetary policy (Fiscal policy) will be strengthened (weakened) by the consequent change in Net exports (*see*). For example, a tight (easy) money policy will increase (decrease) domestic interest rates, thereby increasing (decreasing) the foreign demand for dollars. As a result, the dollar appreciates (depreciates) and causes American net exports to decrease (increase).

Net exports Exports (*see*) minus Imports (*see*).

Net investment income The interest and dividend income received by the residents of a nation from residents of other nations less the interest and dividend payments made by the residents of that nation to the residents of other nations.

Net private domestic investment Gross private domestic investment (*see*) less Consumption of fixed capital (*see*); the addition to the nation's stock of Capital during a year.

Net taxes   The taxes collected by government less Government transfer payments (*see*).

Net transfers   The personal and government transfer payments made to residents of foreign nations less the personal and government transfer payments received from residents of foreign nations.

Net worth   The total Assets (*see*) less the total Liabilities (*see*) of a Firm or an individual; the claims of the owners of a firm against its total Assets.

New classical economics   The theory that, although unanticipated price level changes may create macroeconomic instability in the short run, the economy is stable at the full-employment level of domestic output in the long run because of price and wage flexibility.

New International Economic Order   A series of proposals made by the Less developed countries (LDCs) (*see*) for basic changes in their relationships with the advanced industrialized nations that would accelerate the growth of and redistribute world income to the LDCs.

NIEO   New International Economic Order (*see*).

Nominal gross domestic output (GDP)   The GDP (*see*) measured in terms of the price level at the time of measurement (unadjusted for changes on the price level).

Nominal income   The number of dollars received by an individual or group during some period of time.

Nominal interest rate   The rate of interest expressed in dollars of current value (not adjusted for inflation).

Nominal wage   The Money wage (*see*).

Noncheckable savings account   A Savings account (*see*) against which a check can not be written.

Nondiscretionary fiscal policy   The increases (decreases) in Net taxes (*see*) which occur without Congressional action when the gross domestic product rises (falls) and which tend to stabilize the economy.

Nondurable good   A Consumer good (*see*) with an expected life (use) of less than one year.

Nonexhaustive expenditure   An expenditure by government that does not result directly in the employment of economic resources or the production of goods and services; *see* Government transfer payment.

Nonfinancial investment   An investment which does not require households to save a part of their money incomes; but which uses surplus (unproductive) labor to build Capital goods.

Nonincome charges   Consumption of fixed capital (*see*) and Indirect business taxes (*see*).

Nonincome determinants of consumption and saving   All influences on consumption spending and saving other than the level of Disposable income.

Noninterest determinants of investment   All influences on the level of investment spending other than the rate of interest.

Noninvestment transaction   An expenditure for stocks, bonds, or second-hand Capital goods.

Nonmarket transactions   The production of goods and services not included in the measurement of the Gross domestic product because the goods and services are not bought and sold.

Nonproductive transaction   The purchase and sale of any item that is not a currently produced good or service.

Nontariff barriers   All barriers other than Tariffs (*see*) which nations erect to impede trade among nations: Import quotas (*see*), licensing requirements, unreasonable product-quality standards, unnecessary red tape in customs procedures, etc.

Normal good   A good or service of which consumers will purchase more (less) at every price when their incomes increase (decrease).

Normal profit   Payment that must be made by a Firm to obtain and retain Entrepreneurial ability (*see*); the minimum payment (income) Entrepreneurial ability must (expect to) receive to induce it to perform the entrepreneurial functions for a Firm; an Implicit cost (*see*).

Normative economics   That part of economics which pertains to value judgments about what the economy should be like; concerned with economic goals and policies.

NTBs   (*See* Nontariff barriers.)

Official reserves   The foreign monies (currencies) owned by the central bank of a nation.

Okun's law   The generalization that any one percentage point rise in the Unemployment rate above the Full-employment unemployment rate will increase the GDP gap by 2.5 percent of the Potential output (GDP) of the economy.

OPEC   An acronym for the Organization of Petroleum Exporting Countries (*see*).

Open economy   An economy which both exports and imports goods and services.

Open Market Committee   The twelve-member group that determines the purchase-and-sale policies of the Federal Reserve Banks in the market for United States government securities.

Open-market operations   The buying and selling of United States government securities by the Federal Reserve Banks.

Opportunity cost   The amount of other products that must be forgone or sacrificed to produce a unit of a product.

Organization of Petroleum Exporting Countries   The cartel formed in 1970 by thirteen oil-producing countries to control the price at which they sell crude oil to foreign importers and the quantity of oil exported by its members and which accounts for a large proportion of the world's export of oil.

"Other things being equal" assumption Assuming that factors other than those being considered are constant.

Outpayments The expenditures of (its own or foreign) money which the individuals, Firms, and governments of one nation make to purchase goods and services, for Remittances, as investment income, and Capital outflows abroad.

Paper money Pieces of paper used as a Medium of exchange (*see*); in the United States, Federal Reserve Notes (*see*).

Paradox of thrift The attempt of society to save more results in the same amount of, or less, Saving.

Partnership An unincorporated business Firm owned and operated by two or more persons.

Payments deficit (*See* Balance of payments deficit.)

Payments surplus (*See* Balance of payments surplus.)

Payroll tax A tax levied on employers of Labor equal to a percentage of all or part of the wages and salaries paid by them; and on employees equal to a percentage of all or part of the wages and salaries received by them.

Perestroika The essential feature of Mikhail Gorbachev's reform program to "restructure" the Soviet economy; includes modernization, decentralization, some privatization, and improved worker incentives.

Personal consumption expenditures The expenditures of Households for Durable and Nondurable consumer goods and services.

Personal distribution of income The manner in which the economy's Personal or Disposable income is divided among different income classes or different households.

Personal income The income, part of which is earned and the remainder of which is unearned, available to resource suppliers and others before the payment of Personal taxes (*see*).

Personal income tax A tax levied on the taxable income of individuals (households and unincorporated firms).

Personal saving The Personal income of households less Personal taxes (*see*) and Personal consumption expenditures (*see*); Disposable income not spent for Consumer goods (*see*).

Phillips Curve A curve which shows the relationship between the Unemployment rate (*see*) (on the horizontal axis) and the annual rate of increase in the Price level (on the vertical axis).

Planned economy An economy in which only government determines how resources are allocated.

Planned investment The amount which business firms plan or intend to invest.

Plant A physical establishment (Land and Capital) which performs one or more of the functions in the production (fabrication and distribution) of goods and services.

Policy economics The formulation of courses of action to bring about desired results or to prevent undesired occurrences (to control economic events).

Political business cycle The tendency of Congress to destabilize the economy by reducing taxes and increasing government expenditures before elections and to raise taxes and lower expenditures after elections.

Positive economics The analysis of facts or data to establish scientific generalizations about economic behavior; compare Normative economics.

Positive relationship The relationship between two variables which change in the same direction, for example, product price and quantity supplied.

Post hoc, ergo propter hoc fallacy Incorrectly reasoning that when one event precedes another the first event is the cause of the second.

Potential output The real output (GDP) an economy is able to produce when it fully employs its available resources.

Preferential tariff treatment Setting Tariffs lower for one nation (or group of nations) than for others.

Premature inflation Inflation (*see*) which occurs before the economy has reached Full employment (*see*).

Price The quantity of money (or of other goods and services) paid and received for a unit of a good or service.

Price-decreasing effect The effect in a competitive market of a decrease in Demand or an increase in Supply upon the Equilibrium price (*see*).

Price guidepost The price charged by an industry for its product should increase by no more than the increase in the Unit labor cost (*see*) of producing the product.

Price increasing effect The effect in a competitive market of an increase in Demand or a decrease in Supply on the equilibrium price.

Price index An index number which shows how the average price of a "market basket" of goods changes through time. A price index is used to change nominal output (income) into real output (income).

Price level The weighted average of the Prices paid for the final goods and services produced in the economy.

Price level surprises Unanticipated changes in the price level.

Price-wage flexibility Changes in the prices of products and in the Wages paid to workers; the ability of prices and Wages to rise or to fall.

Prime interest rate The interest rate banks charge their most credit-worthy borrowers, for example, large corporations with impeccable financing credentials.

Private good A good or service to which the Exclusion principle (*see*) is applicable and which is provided by privately owned firms to those who are willing to pay for it.

Private property The right of private persons and Firms to obtain, own, control, employ, dispose of, and bequeath Land, Capital, and other Assets.

Private sector The Households and business firms of the economy.

Production possibilities curve A curve which shows the different combinations of two goods or services that can be produced in a Full-employment (*see*), Full-production (*see*) economy in which the available supplies of resources and technology are constant.

Production possibilities table A table which shows the different combinations of two goods or services that can be produced in a Full-employment (*see*), Full-production (*see*) economy in which the available supplies of resources and technology are constant.

Productive efficiency The production of a good in the least costly way; occurs when production takes place at the output where Average total cost is at a minimum and where Marginal product per dollar's worth of each input is the same.

Productivity A measure of average output or real output per unit of input. For example, the productivity of labor may be determined by dividing hours of work into real output.

Productivity slowdown The recent decline in the rate at which Labor productivity (*see*) in the United States has increased.

Product market A market in which Households buy and Firms sell the products they have produced.

Profit (*See*) Economic profit and Normal profit; without an adjective preceding it, the income of those who supply the economy with Entrepreneurial ability (*see*) or Normal profit.

Progressive tax A tax such that the Average tax rate increases as the taxpayer's income increases and decreases as income decreases.

Property tax A tax on the value of property (Capital, Land, stocks and bonds, and other Assets) owned by Firms and Households.

Proprietors' income The net income of the owners of unincorporated Firms (proprietorships and partnerships).

Prosperous industry (*See* Expanding industry.)

Protective tariff A Tariff (*see*) designed to protect domestic producers of a good from the competition of foreign producers.

Public debt The total amount owed by the Federal government (to the owners of government securities) and equal to the sum of its past Budget deficits (less its budget surpluses).

Public finance The branch of economics which analyzes government revenues and expenditures.

Public good A good or service to which the Exclusion principle (*see*) is not applicable; and which is provided by government if it yields substantial benefits to society.

Public sector The part of the economy that contains all its governments; government.

Purchasing power parity The idea that exchange rates between nations equate the purchasing power of various currencies; exchange rates between any two nations adjust to reflect the price level differences between the countries.

Pure capitalism An economic system (method of organization) in which property resources are privately owned and markets and prices are used to direct and coordinate economic activities.

Pure competition (1) A market in which a very large number of Firms sells a Standardized product (*see*), into which entry is very easy, in which the individual seller has no control over the price at which the product sells, and in which there is no Nonprice competition (*see*); (2) a market in which there is a very large number of buyers.

Pure profit (*See* Economic profit.)

Quantity-decreasing effect The effect in a competitive market of a decrease in Demand or a decrease in Supply on the Equilibrium quantity (*see*).

Quantity demanded The amount of a good or service buyers wish (or a buyer wishes) to purchase at a particular price during some period of time.

Quantity-increasing effect The effect in a competitive market of an increase in Demand or an increase in Supply on the Equilibrium quantity (*see*).

Quantity supplied The amount of a good or service sellers offer (or a seller offers) to sell at a particular price during some period of time.

Quasi-public bank A bank which is privately owned but governmentally (publicly) controlled; each of the Federal Reserve Banks.

Quasi-public good A good or service to which the Exclusion principle (*see*) could be applied, but which has such a large Spillover benefit (*see*) that government sponsors its production to prevent an underallocation of resources.

R&D Research and development; activities undertaken to bring about Technological progress.

Ratchet effect The tendency for the Price level to rise when Aggregate demand increases, but not fall when Aggregate demand declines.

Rate of exchange The price paid in one's own money to acquire one unit of a foreign money; the rate at which the money of one nation is exchanged for the money of another nation.

Rate of interest Price paid for the use of Money or for the use of Capital; interest rate.

Rational An adjective that describes the behavior of any individual who consistently does those things that will enable him or her to achieve the declared objective of the individual; and that describes the behavior of a consumer who uses money income to buy the collection of goods and services that yields the maximum amount of Utility (*see*).

Rational expectations theory The hypothesis that business firms and households expect monetary and fiscal policies to have certain effects on the economy and take, in pursuit of their own self-interests, actions which make these policies ineffective.

Rationing function of price The ability of a price in a competitive market to equalize Quantity demanded and Quantity supplied and to eliminate shortages and surpluses by rising or falling.

Reaganomics The policies of the Reagan administration based on Supply-side economics (*see*) and intended to reduce inflation and the Unemployment rate (Stagflation).

Real-balances effect The tendency for increases (decreases) in the price level to lower (raise) the real value (or purchasing power) of financial assets with fixed money values; and, as a result, to reduce (expand) total spending in the economy.

Real capital (*See* Capital.)

Real gross domestic product Gross domestic product (*see*) adjusted for changes in the price level; Gross domestic product in a year divided by the GDP deflator (*see*) for that year expressed as a decimal.

Real income The amount of goods and services an individual or group can purchase with his, her, or its Nominal income during some period of time. Nominal income adjusted for changes in the Price level.

Real interest rate The rate of interest expressed in dollars of constant value (adjusted for inflation); and equal to the Nominal interest rate (*see*) less the rate of inflation.

Real rate of interest The Real interest rate (*see*).

Real wage The amount of goods and services a worker can purchase with his or her Nominal wage (*see*); the purchasing power of the Nominal wage; the Nominal wage adjusted for changes in the Price level.

Real wage rate (*See* Real wage.)

Recessionary gap The amount by which the Aggregate expenditures schedule (curve) must increase (shift upward) to increase the real GDP to the full-employment noninflationary level.

Reciprocal Trade Agreements Act of 1934 The Federal act which gave the President the authority to negoti-

ate agreements with foreign nations and lower American tariff rates by up to 50 percent if the foreign nations would reduce tariff rates on American goods and which incorporated Most-favored-nation clauses (*see*) in the agreements reached with these nations.

Refinancing the public debt Paying owners of maturing United States government securities with money obtained by selling new securities or with new securities.

Remittance A gift or grant; a payment for which no good or service is received in return; the funds sent by workers who have legally or illegally entered a foreign nation to their families in the nations from which they have migrated.

Rental income Income received by those who supply the economy with Land (*see*).

Required reserve ratio (*See* Reserve ratio.)

Required reserves (*See* Legal reserves.)

Reserve ratio The specified minimum percentage of its deposit liabilities which a Member bank (*see*) must keep on deposit at the Federal Reserve Bank in its district, or in Vault cash (*see*).

Resolution Trust Corporation (RTC) A Federal institution created in 1989 to oversee the closing and sale of failed savings and loan institutions.

Resource market A market in which Households sell and Firms buy the services of resources.

Retiring the public debt Reducing the size of the Public debt by paying money to owners of maturing United States government securities.

Revaluation An increase in the defined value of a currency.

Revenue tariff A Tariff (*see*) designed to produce income for the (Federal) government.

Ricardian equivalence theorem The idea that an increase in the public debt will have little or no effect on real output and employment because taxpayers will save more in anticipation of future higher taxes to pay the higher interest expense on the debt.

Roundabout production The construction and use of Capital (*see*) to aid in the production of Consumer goods (*see*).

Ruble overhang The large amount of forced savings held by Russian households due to the scarcity of consumer goods; these savings could fuel inflation when Russian prices are decontrolled.

Rule of 70 A method by which the number of years it will take for the Price level to double can be calculated; divide 70 by the annual rate of inflation.

Sales tax A tax levied on expenditures for a broad group of products.

Saving   Disposable income not spent for Consumer goods (*see*); not spending for consumption; equal to Disposal income minus Personal consumption expenditures (*see*).

Savings account   A deposit in a Depository institution (*see*) which is interest-earning and which can normally be withdrawn by the depositor at any time.

Savings and loan association   A Firm which accepts deposits primarily from small individual savers, and lends primarily to individuals to finance purchases of residences.

Saving schedule   Schedule which shows the amounts Households plan to save (plan not to spend for Consumer goods, *see*) at different levels of Disposable income.

Savings institution   A Thrift institution (*see*).

Say's law   The (discredited) macroeconomic generalization that the production of goods and services (supply) creates an equal Aggregate demand for these goods and services.

Scarce resources   The fixed (limited) quantities of Land, Capital, Labor, and Entrepreneurial ability (*see all*) which are never sufficient to satisfy the material wants of humans because their wants are unlimited.

Seasonal variation   An increase or decrease during a single year in the level of economic activity caused by a change in the season.

"Second economy"   The semilegal and illegal markets and activities which existed side by side with the legal and official markets and activities in the former U.S.S.R.

Secular trend   The expansion or contraction in the level of economic activity over a long period of years.

Selective controls   The techniques the Federal Reserve Banks employ to change the availability of certain specific types of credit.

Self-interest   What each Firm, property owner, worker, and consumer believes is best for itself and seeks to obtain.

Separation of ownership and control   Difference between the group that owns the Corporation (the stockholders) and the group that manages it (the directors and officers) and between the interests (goals) of the two groups.

Service   That which is intangible (invisible) and for which a consumer, firm, or government is willing to exchange something of value.

Shortage   The amount by which the Quantity demanded of a product exceeds the Quantity supplied at a given (below-equilibrium) price.

Short-run aggregate supply curve   The aggregate supply curve relevant to a time period in which input prices (particularly nominal wages) remain constant when the price level changes.

Simple multiplier   The Multiplier (*see*) in an economy in which government collects no Net taxes (*see*), there are no Imports (*see*), and Investment (*see*) is independent of the level of income (Gross domestic product); equal to one divided by the Marginal propensity to save (*see*).

Slope of a line   The ratio of the vertical change (the rise or fall) to the horizontal change (the run) in moving between two points on a line. The slope of an upward sloping line is positive, reflecting a direct relationship between two variables; the slope of a downward sloping line is negative, reflecting an inverse relationship between two variables.

Smoot-Hawley Tariff Act   Passed in 1930, this legislation established some of the highest tariffs in United States history. Its objective was to reduce imports and stimulate the domestic economy.

Social accounting   (*See* National income accounting.)

Socially optimal price   The price of a product which results in the most efficient allocation of an economy's resources and which is equal to the Marginal cost (*see*) of the last unit of the product produced.

Sole proprietorship   An unincorporated business firm owned and operated by a single person.

Specialization   The use of the resources of an individual, a Firm, a region, or a nation to produce one or a few goods and services.

Spillover   A benefit or cost associated with the consumption or production of a good or service which is obtained by or inflicted without compensation on a party other than the buyer or seller of the good or service (*see* Spillover benefit and Spillover cost).

Spillover benefit   The benefit obtained neither by producers nor by consumers of a product but without compensation by a third party (society as a whole).

Spillover cost   The cost of producing a product borne neither by producers nor by consumers of the product but without compensation by a third party (society as a whole).

Stabilization fund   A stock of money or of a commodity that is used to prevent the price of the commodity from changing by buying (selling) the commodity when its price decreases (increases).

Stabilization policy dilemma   The use of monetary and fiscal policy to decrease the Unemployment rate increases the rate of inflation, and the use of monetary and fiscal policy to decrease the rate of inflation increases the Unemployment rate.

Stagflation   Inflation accompanied by stagnation in the rate of growth of output and a high unemployment rate in the economy; simultaneous increases in both the Price level and the Unemployment rate.

State bank   A Commercial bank chartered to engage in the business of banking by a state government.

State ownership The ownership of property (Land and Capital) by government (the state); in the former U.S.S.R by the central government (the nation).

Static economy (1) An economy in which Net private domestic investment (*see*) is equal to zero—Gross private domestic investment (*see*) is equal to the Consumption of fixed capital (*see*); (2) an economy in which the supplies of resources, technology, and the tastes of consumers do not change and in which, therefore, the economic future is perfectly predictable and there is no uncertainty.

Store of value Any Asset (*see*) or wealth set aside for future use.

Strategic trade policy The use of trade barriers to reduce the risk of product development by domestic firms, particularly products involving advanced technology.

Structural deficit The difference between Federal tax revenues and expenditures when the economy is at full employment.

Structural unemployment Unemployment caused by changes in the structure of demand for Consumer goods and in technology; workers who are unemployed either because their skills are not demanded by employers or because they lack sufficient skills to obtain employment.

Subsidy A payment of funds (or goods and services) by a government, business firm, or household for which it receives no good or service in return. When made by a government, it is a Government transfer payment (*see*).

Substitute goods Goods or services such that there is a direct relationship between the price of one and the Demand for the other; when the price of one falls (rises) the Demand for the other decreases (increases).

Substitution effect (1) The effect which a change in the price of a Consumer good would have on the relative expensiveness of that good and the resulting effect on the quantity of the good a consumer would purchase if the consumer's Real income (*see*) remained constant; (2) the effect which a change in the price of a resource would have on the quantity of the resource employed by a firm if the firm did not change its output.

Superior good (*See* Normal good.)

Supply A Supply schedule or a Supply curve (*see both*).

Supply curve A curve which shows the amounts of a good or service sellers (a seller) will offer to sell at various prices during some period of time.

Supply factor An increase in the available quantity of a resource, an improvement in its quality, or an expansion of technological knowledge which makes it possible for an economy to produce a greater output of goods and services.

Supply schedule A schedule which shows the amounts of a good or service sellers (or seller) will offer at various prices during some period of time.

Supply shock One of several events of the 1970s and early 1980s which increased production costs, decreased Aggregate supply, and generated Stagflation in the United States.

Supply-side economics The part of modern macroeconomics that emphasizes the role of costs and Aggregate supply in its explanation of Inflation, unemployed labor, and Economic growth.

Supply-side view The view of fiscal policy held by the advocates of Supply-side economics which emphasizes increasing Aggregate supply (*see*) as a means of reducing the Unemployment rate and Inflation and encouraging Economic Growth.

Support price (*See* Price support.)

Surplus The amount by which the Quantity supplied of a product exceeds the Quantity demanded at a given (above-equilibrium) price.

Surplus value A Marxian term; the amount by which the value of a worker's daily output exceeds his daily wage; the output of workers appropriated by capitalists as profit.

Tangent The point at which a line touches, but does not intersect, a curve.

Target dilemma A problem which arises because monetary authorities cannot simultaneously stabilize both the money supply and the level of interest rates.

Tariff A tax imposed (only by the Federal government in the United States) on an imported good.

Tax A nonvoluntary payment of money (or goods and services) to a government by a Household or Firm for which the Household or Firm receives no good or service directly in return and which is not a fine imposed by a court for an illegal act.

Tax incidence The income or purchasing power which different persons and groups lose as a result of the imposition of a tax after Tax shifting (*see*) has occurred.

Tax shifting The transfer to others of all or part of a tax by charging them a higher price or by paying them a lower price for a good or service.

Tax "wedge" Such taxes as Indirect business taxes (*see*) and Payroll taxes (*see*) which are treated as a cost by business firms and reflected in the prices of the products produced by them; equal to the price of the product less the cost of the resources required to produce it.

Technology The body of knowledge that can be used to produce goods and services from Economic resources.

Terms of trade The rate at which units of one product can be exchanged for units of another product; the Price (*see*) of a good or service; the amount of one good or service that must be given up to obtain one unit of another good or service.

Thrift institution   A Savings and loan association, Mutual savings bank, or Credit union (*see all*).

Tight money policy   Contracting, or restricting the growth of, the nation's Money supply (*see*).

Till money   (*See* Vault cash.)

Time deposit   An interest-earning deposit in a Depository institution (*see*) which may be withdrawn by the depositor without a loss of interest on or after a specific date or at the end of a specific period of time.

Token money   Coins which have a Face value (*see*) greater than their Intrinsic value (*see*).

Total demand   The Demand schedule (*see*) or the Demand curve (*see*) of all buyers of a good or service.

Total demand for money   The sum of the Transactions demand for money (*see*) and Asset demand for money (*see*); the relationship between the total amount of money demanded, nominal GDP, and the Rate of Interest.

Total product   The total output of a particular good or service produced by a firm (a group of firms or the entire economy).

Total revenue   The total number of dollars received by a Firm (or Firms) from the sale of a product; equal to the total expenditures for the product produced by the Firm (or firms); equal to the quantity sold (demanded) multiplied by the price at which it is sold—by the Average revenue (*see*) from its sale.

Total spending   The total amount buyers of goods and services spend or plan to spend.

Total supply   The Supply schedule (*see*) or the Supply curve (*see*) of all sellers of a good or service.

Trade balance   The export of merchandise (goods) of a nation less its imports of merchandise (goods).

Trade controls   Tariffs (*see*), export subsidies, Import quotas (*see*), and other means a nation may employ to reduce Imports (*see*) and expand Exports (*see*).

Trade deficit   The amount by which a nation's imports of merchandise (goods) exceed its exports of merchandise (goods).

Trade surplus   The amount by which a nation's exports of merchandise (goods) exceed its imports of merchandise (goods).

Trading possibilities line   A line which shows the different combinations of two products an economy is able to obtain (consume) when it specializes in the production of one product and trades (exports) this product to obtain the other product.

Traditional economy   An economic system (method of organization) in which traditions and customs determine how the economy will use its scarce resources.

Transactions demand for money   The amount of money people want to hold to use as a Medium of exchange (to make payments); and which varies directly with the nominal GDP.

Transfer payment   A payment of money (or goods and services) by a government or a Firm to a Household or Firm for which the payer receives no good or service directly in return.

Unanticipated inflation   Inflation (*see*) at a rate which was greater than the rate expected in that period of time.

Underemployment   Failure to produce the maximum amount of goods and services that can be produced from the resources employed; failure to achieve Full production (*see*).

Undistributed corporate profits   The after-tax profits of corporations not distributed as dividends to stockholders; corporate or business saving.

Unemployment   Failure to use all available Economic resources to produce goods and services; failure of the economy to employ fully its Labor force (*see*).

Unemployment compensation   (*See* Unemployment insurance).

Unemployment insurance   The insurance program which in the United States is financed by state Payroll taxes (*see*) on employers and makes income available to workers who are unable to find jobs.

Unemployment rate   The percentage of the Labor force (*see*) that is unemployed at any time.

United States–Canadian Free-Trade Agreement   An accord signed in 1988 to eliminate all trade barriers between the two nations over a ten-year period.

Unit labor cost   Labor costs per unit of output; equal to the Nominal wage rate (*see*) divided by the Average product (*see*) of labor.

Unlimited liability   Absence of any limit on the maximum amount that may be lost by an individual and that the individual may become legally required to pay; the amount that may be lost and that a sole proprietor or partner may be required to pay.

Unlimited wants   The insatiable desire of consumers (people) for goods and services that will give them pleasure or satisfaction.

Unplanned investment   Actual investment less Planned investment; increases or decreases in the inventories of business firms that result from production greater than sales.

Unprosperous industry   (*See* Declining industry.)

Utility   The want-satisfying power of a good or service; the satisfaction or pleasure a consumer obtains from the consumption of a good or service (or from the consumption of a collection of goods and services).

Value added The value of the product sold by a Firm less the value of the goods (materials) purchased and used by the Firm to produce the product; and equal to the revenue which can be used for Wages, rent, interest, and profits.

Value judgment Opinion of what is desirable or undesirable; belief regarding what ought or ought not to be (regarding what is right or just and wrong or unjust).

Value of money The quantity of goods and services for which a unit of money (a dollar) can be exchanged; the purchasing power of a unit of money; the reciprocal of the Price level.

Vault cash The Currency (*see*) a bank has in its safe (vault) and cash drawers.

Velocity of money The number of times per year the average dollar in the Money supply (*see*) is spent for Final goods (*see*).

VERs (*See* Voluntary export restrictions.)

Vertical axis The "up–down" or "north–south" axis on a graph or grid.

Vertical combination A group of Plants (*see*) engaged in different stages of the production of a final product and owned by a single Firm (*see*).

Vertical intercept The point at which a line meets the vertical axis of a graph.

Vicious circle of poverty A problem common to the less developed countries where their low per capita incomes are an obstacle to realizing the levels of saving and investment requisite to acceptable rates of economic growth.

Voluntary export restrictions The limitations by firms of their exports to particular foreign nations to avoid the erection of other trade barriers by the foreign nations.

Wage The price paid for Labor (for the use or services of Labor, *see*) per unit of time (per hour, per day, etc.).

Wage and salary supplements Payments made by employers of Labor into social insurance and private pension, health, and welfare funds for workers; and a part of the employer's cost of obtaining Labor.

Wage guidepost Wages (*see*) in all industries in the economy should increase at an annual rate equal to the rate of increase in the Average product (*see*) of Labor in the economy.

Wage-price controls A Wage-price policy (*see*) that legally fixes the maximum amounts by which Wages (*see*) and prices may be increased in any period of time.

Wage-price guideposts A Wage-price policy (*see*) that depends on the voluntary cooperation of Labor unions and business firms.

Wage-price inflationary spiral Increases in wage rates which bring about increases in prices which in turn result in further increases in wage rates and in prices.

Wage-price policy Government policy that attempts to alter the behavior of Labor unions and business firms in order to make their Wage and price decisions more nearly compatible with the goals of Full employment and a stable Price level.

Wage rate (*See* Wage.)

Wages The income of those who supply the economy with Labor (*see*).

Wealth effect (*See* Real balances effect.)

Welfare programs (*See* Public assistance programs.)

(The) "will to develop" Wanting economic growth strongly enough to change from old to new ways of doing things.

World Bank A bank which lends (and guarantees loans) to less developed nations to assist them to grow; formally, the International Bank for Reconstruction and Development.

INDEX